EU ENFORCEMENT AUTHORITIES

EU enforcement authorities are on the rise, entrusted with investigating breaches of EU law by individuals and economic actors. What are the implications for legal practice of their increasing prominence? This books explores this pertinent question from a constitutional and comparative perspective. It sets out the perimeters for composite enforcement and explores the pertinent issues such as the interface between criminal and administrative law enforcement, the protection of fundamental rights and legal protection, as well as the admissibility of evidence, including unlawfully obtained evidence. Given the very real implications of the authorities' investigations, this book will appeal to practitioners and scholars, in fields from criminal law to competition and banking law.

Volume 19 in the series Hart Studies in European Criminal Law

Hart Studies in European Criminal Law

Since the Lisbon Treaty, European criminal law has become an increasingly important field of research and debate. Working with the European Criminal Law Academic Network (ECLAN), the series will publish works of the highest intellectual rigour and cutting edge scholarship which will be required reading for all European criminal lawyers.

The series is happy to consider both edited and single authored titles. The series defines 'European' and 'criminal law' in the broadest sense, so books on European criminal law, justice and policy will be considered. The series also welcomes books which offer different methodological approaches.

Volume 1: *EU Criminal Law after Lisbon: Rights, Trust and the Transformation of Justice in Europe*
Valsamis Mitsilegas

Volume 2: *Challenges in the Field of Economic and Financial Crime in Europe and the US*
Edited by Vanessa Franssen and Katalin Ligeti

Volume 3: *Chasing Criminal Money: Challenges and Perspectives On Asset Recovery in the EU*
Edited by Katalin Ligeti and Michele Simonato

Volume 4: *Limits to EU Powers: A Case Study of EU Regulatory Criminal Law*
Jacob Öberg

Volume 5: *The Needed Balances in EU Criminal Law: Past, Present and Future*
Edited by Chloé Brière and Anne Weyembergh

Volume 6: *Redefining Organised Crime: A Challenge for the European Union?*
Edited by Stefania Carnevale, Serena Forlati and Orsetta Giolo

Volume 7: *White Collar Crime: A Comparative Perspective*
Edited by Katalin Ligeti and Stanislaw Tosza

Volume 8: *Criminal Liability of Managers in Europe: Punishing Excessive Risk*
Stanisław Tosza

Volume 9: *The European Union and Deprivation of Liberty: A Legislative and Judicial Analysis from the Perspective of the Individual*
Leandro Mancano

Volume 10: *The Legitimacy of EU Criminal Law*
Irene Wieczorek

Volume 11: *The Fight Against Impunity in EU Law*
Edited by Luisa Marin and Stefano Montaldo

Volume 12: *Controlling Immigration Through Criminal Law: European and Comparative Perspectives on 'Crimmigration'*
Edited by Gian Luigi Gatta, Valsamis Mitsilegas, and Stefano Zirulia

Volume 13: *The Principle of Mutual Trust in EU Criminal Law*
Auke Willems

Volume 14: *Surveillance and Privacy in the Digital Age: European, Transatlantic and Global Perspectives*
Edited by Valsamis Mitsilegas and Niovi Vavoula

Volume 15: *The External Dimension of the EU's Policy against Trafficking in Human Beings*
Chloé Brière

Volume 16: *Criminal and Quasi-criminal Enforcement Mechanisms in Europe: Origins, Concepts, Future*
Edited by Vanessa Franssen and Christopher Harding

Volume 17: *Data protection, Migration and Border Control: The GDPR, the Law Enforcement Directive and Beyond*
Teresa Quintel

Volume 18: *Corporations and the Privilege against Self-Incrimination*
Stijn Lamberigts

Volume 19: *EU Enforcement Authorities: Punitive Law Enforcement in a Composite Legal Order*
Edited by Michiel Luchtman, Katalin Ligeti and John Vervaele

EU Enforcement Authorities

Punitive Law Enforcement in a Composite Legal Order

Edited by
Michiel Luchtman
Katalin Ligeti
and
John Vervaele

•HART•
OXFORD • LONDON • NEW YORK • NEW DELHI • SYDNEY

HART PUBLISHING

Bloomsbury Publishing Plc

Kemp House, Chawley Park, Cumnor Hill, Oxford, OX2 9PH, UK

1385 Broadway, New York, NY 10018, USA

29 Earlsfort Terrace, Dublin 2, Ireland

HART PUBLISHING, the Hart/Stag logo, BLOOMSBURY and the Diana logo are trademarks of Bloomsbury Publishing Plc

First published in Great Britain 2023

A catalogue record for this book is available from the British Library.

A catalogue record for this book is available from the Library of Congress.

Library of Congress Control Number: 2022947750

ISBN: HB: 978-1-50994-646-4
ePDF: 978-1-50994-648-8
ePub: 978-1-50994-647-1

Typeset by Compuscript Ltd, Shannon

ACKNOWLEDGEMENTS

We, as editors, wish to extend our sincere gratitude to our publisher and to the authors who were willing to contribute to this volume. Without their expertise and insights, this project would not have been possible. A word of thanks also goes to the European Commission, for supporting three consecutive academic studies under the Hercule III programme, and to the Dutch Research Council (NWO), for funding the multiannual project of one of the editors on 'The rise of EU law enforcement authorities – Protecting fundamental rights and liberties in a transnational law enforcement area'. And, lastly, we thank Julian Koenders and Liv Bennink, both student-assistants at Utrecht Law School, for their invaluable help with the editing of this volume, as well as Catherine Minahan for her meticulous copy-editing.

CONTENTS

PART III
CAPITA SELECTA: TOPICAL ISSUES OF EU ENFORCEMENT AUTHORITIES AND THEIR RELATIONS WITH THE NATIONAL LEGAL ORDERS

PART IV
OUTLOOK AND PERSPECTIVES

LIST OF CONTRIBUTORS

Prof Dr S Allegrezza is associate professor in Criminal Law, University of Luxembourg, Luxembourg.

Prof Dr M Böse is professor in Criminal Law, Criminal Procedure and European and International Criminal Law, University of Bonn, Germany.

KHP Bovend'Eerdt LLM, is lecturer and PhD candidate at the Willem Pompe Institute for Criminal Law and Criminology, Utrecht University, the Netherlands.

Dr F Giuffrida is a Policy Officer at the European Commission, Brussels, Belgium, and obtained his PhD in European Criminal Law at Queen Mary University of London.

Dr AM Karagianni is assistant professor at the department of International and European Law, Utrecht University, the Netherlands.

Prof Dr K Ligeti is professor in European and International Criminal Law, University of Luxembourg, Luxembourg. She is also Vice-President of the International Association of Criminal Law (AIDP) in charge of scientific coordination.

Prof Dr MJJP Luchtman is professor in Transnational Law Enforcement and Fundamental Rights, Utrecht University, the Netherlands.

A Moraiti LLM is a PhD candidate in criminal law at the University of Luxembourg, Luxembourg.

Dr GL Robinson is assistant professor at the Willem Pompe Institute for Criminal Law and Criminology, Utrecht University, the Netherlands.

L Romanò LLM is a PhD candidate in criminal law at the University of Luxembourg, Luxembourg.

A Salemi LLM is associate legal counsel at Grimaldi Studio Legale, Brussels, Belgium.

Prof Dr A Schneider is professor in German, European and International Criminal Law, University of Düsseldorf, Germany.

G Theodorakakou LLM is a research assistant at the European Criminal Law Academic Network, Brussels, Belgium.

Prof Dr JAE Vervaele is professor in Economic and European Criminal Law, Utrecht University, Utrecht, the Netherlands, and professor in European Criminal Law, College of Europe, Bruges, Belgium. He is also President of the International Association of Criminal Law (AIDP).

AJ de Vries LLM is lecturer and PhD candidate at the Willem Pompe Institute for Criminal Law and Criminology, Utrecht University, the Netherlands.

Prof Dr RJGM Widdershoven is professor in European Administrative Law, Utrecht University, the Netherlands.

Introduction

MICHIEL LUCHTMAN, KATALIN LIGETI AND JOHN VERVAELE

Law enforcement and European Union (EU) law have always been in a somewhat uneasy relationship. The enforcement of EU rules and policies, by which we mean in this book the monitoring, investigation, prosecution and punishment breaches of rules of law by private individuals, has for a long time been left to the discretion of the EU Member States. That goes particularly for punitive law enforcement,[1] which is traditionally linked closely to the competences of the nation state and which has given rise to institutional battles between the EU and national legal orders in the past.

Numerous recent crises, scattered around as many areas of EU law, show an ever increasing interest in and attention to a coherent enforcement policy at the EU level and the legal instruments to implement that policy. In addition to the efforts to increase the enforcement of EU laws and policies by national authorities under the supervision of the European institutions (so-called 'indirect enforcement') came the trend towards what has been called 'direct enforcement', that is, the enforcement of those laws and policies by EU authorities (institutions, bodies, agencies or otherwise). The development has by no means come to an end yet, as is demonstrated by the recent proposal to establish a European anti-money laundering agency and by perhaps the most ambitious project of them all, the European Public Prosecutor's Office, which launched its the operations in June 2021. More policy areas are expected to follow.

The concept of direct enforcement, however, is also somewhat misleading. It suggests that EU authorities are fully autonomous actors, responsible for and equipped to deal with all the enforcement stages, from the first investigations into alleged breaches of the law by individuals, to the decision on punitive follow-up, to the actual commencement of punitive sanctioning procedures, including review and appeal. Direct enforcement suggests that the EU is, like the United States of America, an entity based on the concept of dual jurisdictions, wherein the EU level and the national level are two autonomous, distinct areas of competence. Indeed, the concept of direct enforcement is closely linked to the enforcement of EU competition law, which was – at the least until early 2003 – a predominantly European affair.

[1] As defined by the Court of Justice of the European Union in Case C-489/10 *Bonda* ECLI:EU:C:2012:319 and by the European Court of Human Rights (ECtHR) in *Engel and Others v Netherlands* App nos 5100/71, 5101/71, 5102/71, 5354/72 and 5370/72 (ECtHR, 8 June 1976).

However, legal reality has developed in a different direction. In the EU, competition law is now decentralised. National law and national authorities are also not far away in other policy areas, not even in areas of exclusive EU competence where EU authorities are now entrusted with enforcement tasks. That is why the relevant enforcement procedures are better characterised as composite procedures, being a mixture of national and European elements that comprise not only the vertical relationships between the EU and the national levels, but also the horizontal, transnational relationships between different Member States and their enforcement authorities.

This development is a highly pertinent issue, both in academic terms and with respect to its implications for legal practice. It forces all stakeholders – the relevant authorities and their national partners, the legislature, the judiciary, lawyers – to reflect upon how to deal with these new bodies. It requires the development of new prosecutorial policies, of good working relationships between the national and EU levels, of new arrangements for legal protection, etc. All of these issues have been the topic of longstanding debates within the confines of the nation-state, but now need readjustment and adaptation to a completely different setting, that of the European legal order.

This book is the result of three consecutive studies, funded by the European Commission under the Hercule III Programme.[2] In these three studies, the editors of this book, together with academic experts from a great number of EU states, analysed the strengths and weaknesses of the legal framework of the European Anti-Fraud Office (OLAF) in term of its capabilities to effectively execute its tasks and mission. The approach of the three projects was a comparative one, in a double sense. They included a comparison of OLAF's legal framework with those of other EU authorities with mandates in the area of punitive administrative law, that is, the European Central Bank (ECB), the European Securities and Markets Authority (ESMA) and the Directorate-General for Competition (DG Competition). Moreover, they analysed how the respective EU legal frameworks incorporate the national laws of different Member States and how they facilitate cooperation with national partners, which is so important for their proper functioning.

In this book, we build on the materials that we have gathered, yet we also have broadened our focus. This book discusses the constitutional implications of the process towards composite punitive enforcement and its relationships with criminal justice at the national level. Par excellence, this is a process that merits a cross-sectoral approach. The focus is consequently no longer primarily on OLAF but on the concept of composite punitive enforcement procedures as such, as well as on its relationships to national criminal justice. This book discusses the pertinent issues, questions and benchmarks for law enforcement in a composite legal order. What models for composite enforcement do currently exist? What constitutional parameters define and guide the interactions between the many authorities from the legal orders involved? What powers do these

[2] In chronological order: MJJP Luchtman et al, *Investigatory Powers and Procedural Safeguards: Improving OLAF's legislative framework through a comparison with other EU law enforcement authorities (ECN/ESMA/ECB)* (Utrecht University 2017); M Simonato, M Luchtman and J Vervaele (eds), *Exchange of Information with EU and National Enforcement Authorities: Improving OLAF legislative framework through a comparison with other EU authorities (ECN/ESMA/ECB)* (Utrecht University 2018); F Giuffrida and K Ligeti (eds), *Admissibility of OLAF Final Reports as Evidence in Criminal Proceedings* (Luxembourg University 2019).

authorities need for the fulfilment of their punitive tasks? And what can individuals expect from these authorities in turn; are their rights, safeguards and remedies guaranteed? How does EU administrative enforcement relate to (national) criminal justice? Are there lessons to be learned by one policy area from another? These are the questions that have structured our debates, as well as the outline of this book.

As in the Hercule studies, this book does not include all enforcement stages. Our focus is on the preliminary stages of punitive enforcement, particularly the gathering of the relevant information from private actors and the transfer of that information to partners in other jurisdictions under the framework of composite procedures, with a view to later use in punitive procedures. Obviously, we could not completely cut the ties with the subsequent stages in the procedures. For one thing, this is because the punitive finality of procedures will cast its shadow forward over the investigatory stage in many ways, even when no formal charges have yet been brought. The potential use as evidence for punitive purposes may, for instance, affect the exercise of defence rights of individuals or undertakings later on. Moreover, as the investigative stage obviously raises important questions with respect to the right to effective judicial protection, as guaranteed by the EU Charter of Fundamental Rights, we cannot entirely exclude the trial stages; questions with respect to the admissibility of evidence and the use of unlawfully gathered or transferred evidence are closely related to the pre-trial stage.

Studying composite enforcement processes and their relations with national criminal justice cannot focus only on the effectiveness of their operations. As the principle of effectiveness includes not only the effective enforcement of substantive norms of EU law, but also the enforcement of rights, as guaranteed by EU law, these questions have been taken on board too. The focus is on those rights that have particular relevance for the investigative stage, that is, the privilege against self-incrimination, the right of access to a lawyer, legal professional privilege, the right to privacy and the principle of *ne bis in idem*. The processing of personal data within the framework of composite procedures is not as such included in this project.

This book is divided into four parts. Part I, 'Punitive Enforcement in Composite Procedures: The Constitutional Setting', contains three chapters. Chapter 1 (Luchtman) delves into definitional issues, including a further elaboration of the concept of composite procedures and its distinctive institutional trademarks. The subsequent chapters then discuss the most important constitutional principles that guide composite enforcement (chapter 2: De Vries and Widdershoven) and the legal arrangements that offer legal protection in a composite setting (chapter 3: Ligeti and Robinson).

Part II of the book, 'Models for Punitive Enforcement in Composite Procedures', presents the main findings of our previous studies, on the basis of the comparative approach in the double sense of the word. They include both a comparison of different EU authorities, and also the most relevant findings of the comparison of their integration into the national orders. The chapters have been organised around the stage of the gathering of information (chapter 4: Böse and Schneider), the transfer of information (chapter 5: Bovend'Eerdt and Karagianni) and the use as evidence in punitive procedures (chapter 6: Giuffrida and Theodorakakou).

Part III, '*Capita Selecta*: Topical Issues of EU Enforcement Authorities and Their Relations with the National Legal Orders', then provides a selection of topical issues, including the determination of the applicable law, forum choices and *ne bis in idem* (chapter 7: Robinson), administrative enforcement at EU level and its relationship with national criminal justice (chapter 8: Allegrezza, Moraiti, Romanò and Salemi) and how to deal with unlawfully obtained evidence from other jurisdictions (chapter 9: Vervaele).

Part IV, 'Outlook and Perspectives', offers a helicopter view of the foregoing chapters and discusses the issues that have been identified, both from the perspective of effective enforcement of EU laws and from the perspective of effective legal protection. It concludes with a series of normative benchmarks that have thus far not been included in the legal debates on composite punitive enforcement (chapter 10: Luchtman). The book's final chapter (chapter 11: Vervaele) offers an outlook on the lessons to be learned from our work for the European Public Prosecutor's Office.

PART I

Punitive Enforcement in Composite Procedures: The Constitutional Setting

1

Setting the Scene: The Rise of EU Law Enforcement Authorities

MICHIEL LUCHTMAN

I. Introduction

Direct enforcement by European Union (EU) authorities is one of the major developments in the European enforcement landscape.[1] June 2021 saw the start of operations of the European Public Prosecutor's Office (EPPO), without a doubt one of the most ambitious projects in the area of criminal justice. New plans for an European anti-money laundering agency have recently been launched.[2] The trend, however, undoubtedly has its roots in administrative law. An increasing number of EU policy areas are now enforced by EU authorities. Unlike in previous decades, where the role of EU institutions was to monitor the enforcement activities of national authorities, EU authorities have now themselves become entrusted with the monitoring of compliance with EU rules and regulations by individuals and other private actors, with investigations into alleged breaches of these norms and with the sanctioning of established breaches, including sanctioning through punitive (pecuniary) sanctions.[3] This inherently means that the EU's operational mandates and powers have entered further into the domain of national enforcement competences and the administration of criminal justice.

This development was not the result of an overarching 'grand design'. One can safely assume that these developments have been largely sector-specific or path-dependent.[4] Punitive enforcement is often put in the hands of EU authorities that

[1] M Scholten and MJJP Luchtman (eds), *Law Enforcement by EU Authorities: Implications for Political and Judicial Accountability* (Edward Elgar Publishing 2017).

[2] Commission, 'Proposal for a Regulation establishing the Authority for Anti-Money Laundering and Countering the Financing of Terrorism and amending Regulations (EU) No 1093/2010, (EU) 1094/2010, (EU) 1095/2010' COM (2021) 421 final.

[3] This definition of enforcement was introduced by JAE Vervaele, 'Shared Governance and Enforcement of European Law: From Comitology to a Multi-level Agency Structure?' in C Joerges and E Vos (eds), *EU Committees: Social Regulation, Law and Politics* (Hart Publishing 1999) 131.

[4] Cf ch 5 of this volume (Bovend'Eerdt and Karagianni).

were already entrusted with regulatory, supervisory and/or indirect enforcement tasks. Direct enforcement then presents a next, logical step in cases where law enforcement by national authorities proves inadequate. These largely sectoral developments also explain why there are significant differences in the institutional frameworks of the authorities involved. These differences relate to, for instance, whether or not the enforcement activities take place in an 'open environment', where no supervisory EU enforcement regimes exist (such as in competition law or the area of the protection of the EU's financial interests (PIF)), or whether they are preceded by highly harmonised supervisory regimes, such as in the financial sector. There are also significant differences in the persons that are the object of investigations. Banking supervision is mainly exercised over legal persons, often multinational financial institutions with significant economic weight. That is different in the PIF area, where investigations by the European Anti-Fraud Office (OLAF) also cover natural persons. All of these and other differences have an impact on the institutional choices that have been made, as well as on the threats and opportunities with which the EU authorities, citizens and undertakings are confronted.

However, the path-dependent logic of these developments does not mean that one should close one's eyes to the general, cross-sectoral trend towards direct enforcement and the commonalities and questions faced by all of the EU authorities involved. To the best of my knowledge, there has not been a broader debate on the institutional and constitutional implications of this shift towards direct enforcement for legal protection in cases of EU enforcement action, for the protection of fundamental rights in this transnational and supranational setting, nor, more generally, for its relationship with the domain of national criminal justice. The logic and speed by which existing authorities with regulatory or supervisory tasks now become entrusted with operational enforcement tasks conceal an important doctrinal shift in legal thinking on law enforcement and its traditional focus on the nation-state context. One of the common features of all EU enforcement authorities is their European-wide operational mandate. These authorities are no longer dependent on traditional, international law rules for mutual administrative or legal assistance in cross-border cases. Instead, part of the efficiency gains for which their institutional frameworks strive is precisely the removal of these elements of international law from their legal frameworks for the benefit of shared operational goals, policies and informal types of enforcement cooperation. In and of itself, these are major legal innovations.[5]

In this chapter, I intend to connect the notion of law enforcement to the notion of the EU and its Member States as a composite institutional, or perhaps even constitutional, entity. Within this composite legal order, the tasks and competences of the EU authorities are capable of, on the one hand, connecting and integrating the legal orders of the participating Member States and their authorities into an enforcement design that cannot build, on the other hand, on the narrative of the nation-state with respect to arrangements for fundamental rights, legal protection or political accountability.[6]

[5] MJJP Luchtman, 'Transnational Law Enforcement Cooperation: Fundamental Rights in European Cooperation in Criminal Matters' (2020) 28 *European Journal of Crime, Criminal Law and Criminal Justice* 14.

[6] Though the latter concept is not a part of this volume, it certainly merits future studies, for instance with respect to the EPPO.

A new narrative is needed for that, yet it remains under-studied, and this in an area of law where interferences with the legal position of individuals are particularly intrusive. Existing studies on EU regulatory governance provide valuable input[7] yet do not take full account of the specifics of law enforcement as such. Vice versa, national debates on law enforcement still remain focused predominantly on the setting of the nation-state. The role and position of national enforcement actors, including courts, as part of the larger European project remain under-studied and do not appear to have a prominent place on the political and legislative agendas in the EU's Member State capitals.

To study law enforcement as a composite affair does justice to empirical reality. It illustrates how the significance of national borders and, consequently, the principles and vocabulary of international law in cross-border cases have been deliberately mitigated or even removed from the institutional frameworks of the EU authorities and their national partners. The notion of composite enforcement consequently also has normative implications. It sheds light on a number of blind spots in the current enforcement designs of the competent authorities that need attention in light of the effective enforcement of EU law, as well as effective legal protection. Composite enforcement stresses that law enforcement by EU authorities is not a derivative of national enforcement, nor can it be regarded as an exclusively European affair. Composite enforcement includes and connects – and should connect – all three traditional branches of government, at the EU as well as at the national levels.

In the subsequent sections of this chapter, I will first briefly introduce three of the administrative actors of our previous studies (section II) and will then elaborate further on the notion of the EU and its Member States as a composite legal order (section III). As a more specific form of compositeness, section IV will subsequently explain what is meant by composite administrative enforcement procedures, as well as why the relationship with national criminal justice is so important for them. I will conclude with the consequences of all this for the approach and subsequent chapters in this book (section V).

Though the EPPO was never a part of our previous studies, we have included a separate chapter on this important new actor as well, in which we highlight the relevance of the main findings of our previous work to this new actor in the domain of criminal justice.[8] That is also why some introductory remarks on the EPPO have been made in the next section of this chapter.

II. Punitive Enforcement by EU Authorities: Four Case Studies

As said in the Introduction to this volume, this book's methodology builds upon a comparison of four EU authorities and their integration into a number of national legal orders. These authorities were OLAF, the Directorate-General for Competition

[7] See, for instance, M Busuioc, *The Accountability of European Agencies: Legal Provisions and Ongoing Practices* (Utrecht University 2010).

[8] Ch 11 of this volume (Vervaele).

(DG Competition), the European Securities and Markets Authority (ESMA)[9] and the European Central Bank (ECB) in relation to the Single Supervisory Structure (SSM). As noted, another EU enforcement authority has meanwhile entered the scene. The EPPO will be responsible for the investigation, prosecution and bringing to judgment by national courts of criminal offences against the EU's financial interests. It goes without saying that all of these authorities operate in different areas of EU policy and have different mandates and powers. Before answering the question of why a comparison is nonetheless necessary and fruitful, it is good to introduce these actors in brief, as the following chapters will also build upon this comparison.

A. OLAF

In the area of the protection of the financial interests of the EU, OLAF and the EPPO are key players. OLAF is a Commission directorate with a dual task.[10] It has a policy function, but it is also an operational body, entrusted with carrying out external administrative investigations in the Member States or internal administrative investigations within the European institutions. It is independent when it comes to its investigative tasks. Its mandate covers both the expenditure side of the EU and the income side. Value added tax, though part of the EU's budget, is not, however, within its operational competences, or at least that is still disputed.[11]

OLAF is an administrative office, with administrative powers, that combats fraud and related activities.[12] The Office operates at the brink of administrative law and criminal law. OLAF itself is an investigative body. It is not competent to commence procedures for fraud or recovery. Those procedures are the responsibility of other actors, at the EU level (including the EPPO) or at the national level. The follow-up may be of a punitive nature (including criminal procedures), but that is not necessarily the case. In fact, many OLAF cases end in disciplinary or recovery procedures. This highlights the Office's complicated institutional position. It is highly dependent on partner institutions at the national and the European levels to realise an effective fight against EU fraud. That means OLAF needs to cooperate with a wide variety of partners, as national legal orders are organised in very different ways. In some cases, it is not even clear precisely which national authority is OLAF's partner. This is why a network of Anti-Fraud Coordination Services (AFCOS) was introduced, to enable OLAF to do

[9] I will not discuss ESMA and its tasks in relation to credit-rating agencies in this chapter.

[10] Decision 1999/352/EC of 28 April 1999 establishing the European Anti-Fraud Office (OLAF) [1999] OJ L136/20.

[11] J Inghelram, *Legal and Institutional Aspects of the European Anti-Fraud Office (OLAF)* (Europa Law Publishers 2011) 77–78; M Luchtman and M Wasmeier, 'The Political and Judicial Accountability of OLAF' in M Scholten and M Luchtman (eds), *Law Enforcement by EU Authorities: Implications for Political and Judicial Accountability* (Edward Elgar Publishing 2017) 221.

[12] See Regulation No 883/2013 of 11 September 2013 concerning investigations conducted by the European Anti-Fraud Office (OLAF) [2013] OJ L248/1, as recently amended by Regulation 2020/2223 of 23 December 2020, as regards cooperation with the European Public Prosecutor's Office and the effectiveness of the European Anti-Fraud Office investigations [2020] OJ L437/49.

its work more effectively. Yet, as it has turned out, these AFCOS also show great differences in their design and powers.[13]

OLAF's legal position is complicated further by its fragmented legal framework and instruments. It can conduct external investigations autonomously, or coordinate procedures between competent national authorities.[14] Under the former heading, it may conduct on-the-spot checks.[15] Though OLAF's framework has been strengthened recently, to the extent that it will be less dependent on national law in cases of cooperation by the economic actor under investigation, it remains dependent on national law and its national partners in cases of non-cooperation by those actors.[16] OLAF is not allowed to use physical force or to impose fines in cases of non-cooperation. Moreover, when it conducts its investigations, it needs to take account of a number of safeguards that are reminiscent of criminal procedures, though OLAF itself has no powers to initiate criminal charges.

A particular problem for OLAF is, as said, the follow-up of its work at the national level. The OLAF Regulation requires the competent authorities of the Member State concerned to take 'such action as the results of the external investigation warrant' and to report back to the Office.[17] Of course, the question is to what extent a provision like this is now capable of binding national authorities to specific further action. That finding is relevant for future actions for annulment, which may be launched by persons that are affected by OLAF investigations. As is well known, the Court of Justice has thus far rejected most OLAF cases under Article 263 of the Treaty on the Functioning of the European Union (TFEU).[18] Recent case law seems to suggest, impliedly, that this will not change with the entry into force of the new Regulation.[19]

The rules on the admissibility of evidence in national proceedings were also recently changed.[20] OLAF reports shall constitute admissible evidence in judicial proceedings of a non-criminal nature before national courts and in administrative proceedings in the Member States. For criminal procedures, the rules remain complicated, as they do under the new Regulation.[21] Reports are admissible when their use proves necessary in the same way and under the same conditions as administrative reports drawn up by national administrative inspectors, and shall be subject to the same evaluation rules as those applicable to administrative reports drawn up by national administrative inspectors and shall have the same evidentiary value as such reports. In effect, this rule bridges two gaps at once, that is, a transfer of the report from the EU jurisdiction to the national one and from an administrative to a criminal procedure.

[13] See ch 4 (Böse and Schneider) and ch 5 (Bovend'Eerdt and Karagianni) of this volume; and also, *in extenso*, Bovend'Eerdt in his forthcoming dissertation.

[14] See Art 12ter Regulation 2020/2223.

[15] Regulation No 2185/96 of 11 November 1996 concerning on-the-spot checks and inspections carried out by the Commission in order to protect the European Communities' financial interests against fraud and other irregularities [1996] OJ L292/2.

[16] Art 3 Regulation 883/2013, as revised by Regulation 2020/2223.

[17] Art 11(3) Regulation 883/2013, as revised by Regulation 2020/2223.

[18] Ch 3 of this volume (Ligeti and Robinson), with further references.

[19] Case C-591/19 P *De Esteban Alonso v Commission* ECLI:EU:C:2021:468, para 70.

[20] Art 11(2) Regulation 883/2013, as revised by Regulation 2020/2223.

[21] Ch 6 of this volume (Giuffrida and Theodorakakou).

B. DG Competition

Another enforcement directorate of the European Commission is DG Competition.[22] Like OLAF, it operates in what one could call an open context. It is entrusted with market surveillance in light of Articles 101 and 102 TFEU. Consequently, like OLAF, it has no specific legal relationships with private undertakings when it commences its investigations. Its task is to seek and find, together with national competition authorities, infringements of the said articles and to ensure that undertakings terminate those infringements. The Commission may also impose punitive fines for violations of Articles 101 and 102 TFEU.[23]

The operation of the system of enforcement of EU competition law is based on a decentralised model. Whereas competition law was previously enforced by the Commission itself, the large reforms of 2003 saw the introduction of a decentralised model within which the Commission and national competition authorities (NCAs) enforce EU competition rules in close cooperation.[24] Infringements of EU competition rules will therefore certainly not always be investigated by the Commission, though the Commission has the right to intervene in pending national procedures.[25] That explains the need for continuous mutual consultation and coordination via the European Competition Network in which DG Competition and NCAs participate. In those situations, NCAs apply EU competition rules, as well as the standards of the EU Charter of Fundamental Rights.[26] In addition to this, NCAs enforce national competition rules.

The relationship between national and European competition law is complicated. Though both types of competition law are considered to protect different legal values, there will be overlap and, hence, potential for conflict in specific cases. It was for this reason that the rules on the national enforcement of Articles 101 and 102 TFEU and those on the parallel application of national competition laws were recently harmonised by a Directive having both Article 103 TFEU and Article 114 TFEU as its legal basis.[27] The ECN+ Directive aligns the institutional position of the NCAs and their powers with those of DG Competition.

The investigative powers of DG Competition are laid down in Articles 17–22 of Regulation 1/2003. They include the powers to request (voluntary) statements and to obtain information, but also to conduct on-site inspections ('dawn raids'). The inspection powers cover not only business premises, but also, under certain extra conditions, private homes.[28] As an alternative, DG Competition may also request the national

[22] Regulation No 1/2003 of 16 December 2002 on the implementation of the rules on competition laid down in Articles 81 and 82 of the Treaty [2002] OJ L1/1.

[23] Art 23 Regulation 1/2003.

[24] Art 11 Regulation 1/2003; and Commission, 'Commission Notice on cooperation within the Network of Competition Authorities' [2004] OJ C101/43.

[25] Art 11(6) Regulation 1/2003.

[26] Cf Art 3 Regulation 1/2003.

[27] Directive 2019/1 of 11 December 2018 to empower the competition authorities of the Member States to be more effective enforcers and to ensure the proper functioning of the internal market [2018] OJ L11/3 (the so-called 'ECN+ Directive').

[28] See Arts 20 and 21 Regulation 1/2003 respectively.

authorities to perform investigative measures on its behalf.[29] It cannot exercise physical coercion itself in case of non-cooperation. For that, it needs the assistance of national authorities. It does have the power, however, to impose administrative sanctions, including punitive sanctions, for non-cooperation. Coercion, therefore, is not a Commission power, but compulsion is.

The EU competition rules do not pay much attention to procedural safeguards and the rights of the defence. These have been elaborated mainly by case law and were, occasionally, subsequently implemented in the legislative framework. Nonetheless, Regulation 1/2003 does provide for rules on the admissibility of evidence in competition procedures. Article 12 stipulates, for the purposes of applying Articles 81 and 82 TFEU, a rule of mutual admissibility of evidence. Additional conditions apply, however, when information is used for the application of national competition law or when used against natural persons. In the latter case, the information exchanged can be used in evidence to impose sanctions only where

- the law of the transmitting authority foresees sanctions of a similar kind in relation to an infringement of Article 81 or Article 82 of the Treaty or, in the absence thereof,
- the information has been collected in a way which respects the same level of protection of the rights of defence of natural persons as provided for under the national rules of the receiving authority. However, in this case, the information exchanged cannot be used by the receiving authority to impose custodial sanctions.[30]

It goes without saying that this provision can have significant repercussions for criminal law enforcement of competition law and related offences.

C. The ECB and the SSM Framework

In the wake of the financial crisis of 2007–08, the enforcement tasks of the ECB (and other EU authorities on the financial markets) have been widened considerably. Banking supervision, and the punitive enforcement thereof, is of a different nature than the open context within which OLAF and DG Competition operate. Banks and other financial institutions are subject to a largely harmonised set of EU rules that generally require prior authorisation by financial supervisors, before those institutions are allowed to enter the markets and offer financial services to customers. Once allowed to be active, EU and national implementing rules provide for a detailed set of prudential and 'conduct-of-business' rules to be monitored by the supervisory authority (the so-called 'single rule book'). This is a continuous process in which banks and their supervisors constantly exchange information. Most supervisors consequently emphasise a relationship of trust with the financial institutions as being essential for their effective operation. At times, this position may be at odds with the power of that same supervisor to impose punitive sanctions or refer cases for criminal investigation and prosecution. Nonetheless, these powers exist and have on occasion also been used.

[29] Art 22 Regulation 1/2003. In those instances, national law – recently harmonised by the ECN+ Directive – is applied.

[30] Art 12(3) Regulation 1/2003.

As an essential pillar of the EU's banking union, the Single Supervisory Mechanism (SSM) appoints the ECB as the central prudential supervisor of financial institutions in the euro area and in non-euro EU countries that chose to join the SSM.[31] Under this framework, the ECB directly supervises the largest banks (so-called 'significant entities'), while the national supervisory authorities monitor the so-called 'less significant entities'. In the execution of their tasks, the ECB and the national supervisors work closely together to ensure that banks comply with the EU banking rules.

The structure of the SSM system is such that there are no parallel competences within the system, unlike in the competition network. The supervisory competences of the ECB and national banks are, under the oversight of the ECB, mutually exclusive. This structure, with the ECB clearly in the lead, does not mean that the national authorities have been removed from the ECB's operations. In practice, national banks and their officials still play a significant role as part of the ECB's supervision and enforcement structures. For instance, national officials are part of the ECB's joint supervisory teams, acting as functional agents of the ECB, applying the ECB's legal regime. A specific innovation of the SSM regime is that the ECB is also called upon to apply national implementing laws, that is, the material banking laws of that state.[32]

The supervisory and investigatory powers of the ECB have been laid down in SSM Regulation 1024/2013. These very much resemble the powers of DG Competition, and include the power to request information and to conduct investigations on site. However, unlike DG Competition, the ECB has no powers to enter private homes. Non-cooperation is often punishable with a fine or penalty payment. The powers are available to the ECB during all stages of the procedures, from the stage of monitoring, to the investigation of violations of EU law, to the stage of punitive sanctioning. Moreover, the ECB can call in the assistance of the national competent authorities (NCAs) and instruct them to use any additional investigatory powers they may have under national law.[33] National authorities may also be called upon to offer assistance in cases where physical coercion is needed.

The ECB has direct sanctioning powers on the basis of Article 18(1) and (7) of the SSM Regulation.[34] These powers entail the imposition of punitive sanctions (particularly fines) in cases where norm violations are based on directly applicable EU law, that is Regulation No 575/2013[35] and other technical standards. Moreover, the ECB can require the NCAs to commence proceedings in other cases.[36] National competent authorities are competent, at least under the prevailing opinion, for the sanctioning

[31] Regulation No 1024/2013 of 15 October 2013 conferring specific tasks on the European Central Bank concerning policies relating to the prudential supervision of credit institutions [2013] OJ L287/63, and Regulation No 468/2014 of the European Central Bank of 16 April 2014 establishing the framework for cooperation within the Single Supervisory Mechanism between the European Central Bank and national competent authorities and with national designated authorities (SSM Framework Regulation) [2014] OJ L141/1.

[32] Art 4(3) Regulation 1024/2013.

[33] Art 9(1) Regulation 1024/2013.

[34] Art 18(1) and (7) Regulation 1024/2013.

[35] Regulation No 575/2013 of 26 June 2013 on prudential requirements for credit institutions and investment firms [2013] OJ L176/1.

[36] See, specifically, Art 18(5) Regulation 1024/2013.

of violations of norms contained in Directive 2013/36/EU,[37] which consequently must be implemented in national law. This indirect sanctioning power of the ECB does not mean, however, that the ECB can also require NCAs to achieve a certain result in this respect.[38]

As is also the case for DG Competition, procedural safeguards and defence rights have only been dealt with in passing in the SSM framework.[39] The obvious conflict between the ECB's powers of investigation and the rights of the defence in punitive procedures is, for instance, left untouched. The general assumption is that for banking supervision, where legal persons are the supervised entities, the Court's case law in competition law procedures is to be applied *mutatis mutandis*. The ECB framework contains no rule on the admissibility of evidence gathered in one jurisdiction (including the EU's) and subsequently introduced in another.

The relationship with actors in the area of criminal justice is a particularly sensitive one in banking supervision. Criminal proceedings against banks, if possible at all, may indeed have very negative consequences for the reputation and operations of the particular bank. The fact remains, however, that criminal prosecution for violations of banking supervision rules or related offences, such as anti-money laundering offences, is possible in a number of Member States. The coordination of procedures and mutual exchange of information with national criminal justice authorities is therefore an issue that cannot be overlooked in the punitive enforcement of banking regulations. The topic is dealt with in passing in the ECB's legal framework[40] and in more detail in Decision 2016/1162 on the disclosure of confidential information for criminal investigations.[41] The latter Decision reveals that information exchanges between the ECB's national partners and criminal justice bodies are possible, subject to the ECB's oversight of the NCAs. Yet clearly, this Decision leaves open a great number of issues, such as the coordination of punitive procedures and the nature and degree of the ECB's oversight. Moreover, the conflict that may occur between criminal powers of investigation and a supervisor's duty of secrecy, and which is dealt with differently in the participating Member States, is not touched upon.[42]

[37] Directive 2013/36/EU of 26 June 2013 on access to the activity of credit institutions and the prudential supervision of credit institutions and investment firms [2013] OJ L176/338.

[38] See *in extenso* S Allegrezza, 'The Single Supervisory Mechanism' in S Allegrezza (ed), *The Enforcement Dimension of the Single Supervisory Mechanism* (CEDAM/Wolters Kluwer 2021) 21; G Lasagni, 'Investigatory, Supervisory and Sanctioning Powers within the SSM' in S Allegrezza (ed), *The Enforcement Dimension of the Single Supervisory Mechanism* (CEDAM/Wolters Kluwer 2021) 63; O Voordeckers, 'Administrative and Judicial Review of Supervisory Acts and Decisions under the SSM System' in S Allegrezza (ed), *The Enforcement Dimension of the Single Supervisory Mechanism* (CEDAM/Wolters Kluwer 2021) 117; A Karagianni, *The Protection of Fundamental Rights in Composite Banking Supervision Proceedings* (Europa Law Publishing 2022).

[39] For an overview of the defence rights that have been included in the framework, see Lasagni (n 38) 74; and G Lasagni, *Banking Supervision and Criminal Investigation: Comparing the EU and US Experiences* (Springer 2019).

[40] Particularly Art 136 Regulation 468/2014.

[41] Commission Implementing Regulation (EU) 2016/1157 of 11 July 2016 amending Implementing Regulation (EU) No 964/2014 as regards standard terms and conditions for financial instruments for a co-investment facility and for an urban development fund [2016] OJ L192/7, discussed by Allegrezza et al in ch 8 of this volume.

[42] See Allegrezza et al, ch 8 of this volume; Allegrezza, 'The Single Supervisory Mechanism' (n 38) 40; G Lasagni and I Rodopoulos, 'Comparative Overview' in Allegrezza (ed) (n 37) 607; and Karagianni (n 38).

D. A Brief Outlook: The EPPO

Though the EPPO was not part of our previous studies, it does present a development that is too important to be left undiscussed. The position of the EPPO is unique to the extent that, as an EU organ, it is empowered to prosecute criminal cases before national criminal courts. Under the framework of the EPPO Regulation,[43] the EPPO shall be responsible for investigating, prosecuting and bringing to judgment the perpetrators of, and accomplices to, criminal offences affecting the financial interests of the Union that are provided for in the so-called PIF Directive.[44] It undertakes acts of criminal prosecution and exercises the functions of prosecutor in the competent courts of the Member States. Within the scope of its mandate *ratione materiae*, the EPPO shares its competences with national prosecutors, though it has a certain priority competence within the limits of the Regulation.

The EPPO is an indivisible Union body, operating as a single office. However, the organisational structure of this EU organ is complicated. The EPPO is composed of two levels – a central level in Luxembourg and a decentralised level, consisting of the European Delegated Prosecutors (EDPs) within the 22 participating Member States. The central level consists of a European Chief Prosecutor, who is the head of the EPPO as a whole and the head of the College of European Prosecutors, the Permanent Chambers and the European Prosecutors. The general strategic and policy issues are for the central level; the operational work is done by the delegated prosecutors, whose operational competence is limited to the territory of their jurisdiction of origin. The EDPs act on behalf of the EPPO in their respective Member States and have the same powers as national prosecutors in respect of investigations, prosecutions and bringing cases to judgment.[45] Their limited territorial mandate also means that for cross-border cases, cooperation with delegated prosecutors from other Member States remains a necessity.[46] In other words, there is no concept of European territoriality.

The EDPs wear a double hat; though they are functionally a part of the EPPO for their EPPO work, they are also national prosecutors and allowed to act in that capacity, as long as this does not interfere with their work for the EPPO.[47] They work under the supervision of so-called permanent chambers that supervise and coordinate the investigations. Once the decision has been taken to seize a criminal court, it is the delegated prosecutor who acts before the national court as prosecutor in the case.

As the work of the EPPO will usually involve multiple participating states,[48] the Regulation has designed a system of case allocation. A case shall as a rule be initiated and handled by a European delegated prosecutor from the Member State where the

[43] Regulation 2017/1939 of 12 October 2017 implementing enhanced cooperation on the establishment of the European Public Prosecutor's Office ('the EPPO') [2017] OJ L283/1.

[44] Directive 2017/1371 of 5 July 2017 on the fight against fraud to the Union's financial interests by means of criminal law [2017] OJ L198/29.

[45] Art 13(1) Regulation 2017/1939.

[46] See Arts 31–33 Regulation 2017/1939.

[47] Art 13(3) Regulation 2017/1939.

[48] Not to mention third states and non-participating EU states; see N Franssen, 'The Future Judicial Cooperation Between the EPPO and Non-Participating Member States' [2018] *New Journal of European Criminal Law* 291; and N Franssen, 'Judicial Cooperation Between the EPPO and Third Countries: Chances and Challenges' [2019] *Eucrim* 198.

focus of the criminal activity is, or, if several connected offences within the competences of the EPPO have been committed, the Member State where most of the offences have been committed.[49] The applicable law is found in the EPPO Regulation itself. However, the national law of the handling delegated prosecutor applies to the extent that a matter is not regulated by this Regulation. Where a matter is governed by both national law and this Regulation, the latter shall prevail.[50]

Regarding the powers of the European delegated prosecutor handling a case, he or she may either undertake the investigation measures and other measures on his or her own, or may instruct the competent authorities in his or her Member State. Those authorities shall, in accordance with national law, ensure that all instructions are followed and undertake the measures assigned to them. The EPPO Regulation does not define operational powers, nor does it define the applicable safeguards and defence rights. This is left to national law, including laws implementing the relevant EU Directives. The Regulation does, however, prescribe which investigative methods should be available for its work.[51] That means that, in cross-border cases, there will be a number of (diverging) national legal systems relevant for the case work of the EPPO.

The system of legal protection in the EPPO Regulation is unique. Unlike any other area of law, the Regulation dictates that procedural acts of the EPPO that are intended to produce legal effects vis-à-vis third parties shall be subject to review by the competent national courts (and not the EU judicature), in accordance with the requirements and procedures laid down by national law. The competences of the Court of Justice have been reconfirmed in the Regulation only for a limited number of specific situations.[52]

Article 37 of the Regulation is also a particularly relevant provision for legal protection. It deals with the admissibility of evidence in criminal procedures. This article stipulates that evidence presented by the prosecutors of the EPPO or the defendant shall not be denied admission on 'the mere ground that the evidence was gathered in another Member State or in accordance with the law of another Member State'. This rule bridges the diverging national standards that will continue to exist in cases of cross-border evidence gathering. Arguably, it may also introduce a rule of non-inquiry, as the materials must be accepted without further investigation, even though this does not affect the freedom of judge to freely assess the evidence presented. It is unclear whether such a rule would also apply in cases where issues are raised as regards the lawfulness of the investigative work.[53] Because of its indivisible structure, it is highly uncertain to what extent the existing national case law on unlawfully obtained foreign evidence still holds in the specific, integrative setting of the EPPO. That case law, after all, often builds upon the formal separations between the national legal orders involved. Materials that may have been unlawfully obtained in or transferred by another jurisdiction may as a rule be used as evidence, as long as this does not affect the fairness of the

[49] Art 26(4) Regulation 2017/1939.
[50] Art 5(3) Regulation 2017/1939.
[51] Art 30 Regulation 2017/1939.
[52] Art 42 Regulation 2017/1939.
[53] See in more detail ch 11 of this volume (Vervaele); see also M Luchtman, 'Het Europees Openbaar Ministerie in Nederland: Over Zijn Ondeelbaarheid en Verhouding tot de Nederlandse Strafrechter' (2021) *Delikt en Delinkwent*, 806.

trial (the so-called *Trennungsprinzip*). Such an approach is not easily reconcilable with the EPPO's status as an indivisible organ of EU law.

Finally, the EPPO clearly has a structure that is meant to promote the vertical and horizontal integration of national legal systems. These integrative effects will become visible in the horizontal (cross-border) investigations, but also in the vertical relationships between the EPPO and its national partners. As is the case for OLAF, those partners are very diverse and manifold. They include the national organs responsible for both the expenditure side of the EU budget and the income side. That means that presumably, similar issues will arise for the EPPO as have been noted for OLAF in our studies. The question is to what extent its national partners – who are not defined in the Regulation but are referred to in general as the 'competent national authorities' – will be aware of the European dimension of their tasks and will be given sufficiently wide powers to cooperate and share information with the Office.[54]

III. Law Enforcement in a Composite Legal Order

The authorities that were discussed in section II are indicative of a trend in which EU authorities are made responsible for direct, punitive enforcement of violations of EU law by natural persons or other economic actors. It is also clear, however, that this trend is not the result of a top-down strategy or 'grand design'. Rather, one notices a strong sectoral focus for each of the authorities, where developments towards punitive enforcement by EU authorities have been largely path-dependent and responsive to the specifics of the policy area in play.

Yet, as said, that there are considerable differences between the EU authorities involved should not obfuscate what they have in common, in terms of common features, problems and challenges. In all of their legal frameworks, the relationships between the relevant EU authorities and their national partners are a decisive, institutional characteristic. A system of distinct, dual enforcement jurisdictions, like in the United States (federal level–State level), is non-existent in the EU. The institutional design of the EU authorities is of such a nature that they function as vehicles that connect and integrate the different legal orders of the Member States involved. All of the authorities combine vertical (EU-Member State) and horizontal (inter-state) dimensions in a single institutional framework that has EU-wide operational competence. The EU authorities may be competent to perform acts of investigation themselves, but we have also seen many examples in which national authorities perform such acts on behalf of those authorities. Information that is transferred from national jurisdictions to the EU authorities may end up in their case files, or in case files before courts in another national jurisdiction, after having been transferred by the relevant EU authority. All of this illustrates that the legal frameworks of these authorities are designed for the bundling and pooling

[54] M Luchtman, 'Het Europees Openbaar Ministerie in Nederland: Over Zijn Prioritaire Bevoegdheid, Verhouding tot het OM en de Bestuursrechtelijke Handhavingskolom' (2021) *Delikt en Delinkwent*, 694.

of information, staff and resources, with the aim of fulfilling that authority's mandate. In many cases, it will be impossible to clearly differentiate between the horizontal and vertical dimensions of an investigation.

The integrationist models fit well with the qualification of the European legal order as a composite one. That legal order is characterised, first of all, by the way in which it incorporates natural and legal persons in the transnational polity of the EU.[55] Like the national enforcement authorities, individuals have acquired a dual capacity in this legal order. They are no longer only nationals of a certain state. Citizens and other actors that are economically active in the territory of the EU have been awarded, inter alia, enforceable rights vis-à-vis states in transnational affairs and, for EU citizens, rights to participate in the political process at EU level or the local level of the state of residence. The EU is, in the words of the Court of Justice, 'a new legal order, possessing its own institutions, for the benefit of which the Member States thereof have limited their sovereign rights, in ever wider fields, and the subjects of which comprise not only those States but also their nationals'.[56]

The notion of the European legal order of the EU and its Member States as a 'composite' one also emphasises the vertical and horizontal, transnational relationships between the branches of the *trias politica*. National state branches – whether they are part of the executive, judiciary or the legislature – also have EU tasks to fulfil, such as to ensure that EU rules and policies are effectively enforced and that they cooperate loyally with EU authorities and partners in other states. Vice versa, those branches may expect that their partners in other jurisdictions (including the EU) do the same. These relationships were established for the purpose of achieving a series of common goals and policies, as defined in the Treaty on European Union. To achieve these goals and policies, the European composite legal order deliberately pierces the veil of the participating nation-states and of the national enforcement structures, by regrouping those national structures under a single (yet often complicated) legal framework with EU-wide competences. The same goes, in essence, for the judiciary, which is encouraged to engage in dialogues with the Court of Justice and courts from other states. Their role as *juges de droit commun* has been emphasised many times in the internal market, and is increasingly becoming clear in the Area of Freedom, Security and Justice.[57]

In this composite institutional setting, it is vital to stress and recognise the importance and relevance of the EU institutions themselves. Even in cases where autonomous investigative powers have been withheld from the EU level, as is the case for OLAF, the coordinative activities that take place within the confines of these EU authorities demonstrate their autonomous value. The EU authorities are not derivates from national enforcement powers but have an independent, autonomous role to fulfil. Though self-evident for many, there are still many authoritative sources that explicitly question this capacity, certainly in the area of enforcement integration and

[55] Cf H van Eijken, *European Citizenship and the Constitutionalisation of the European Union* (Utrecht University 2014).

[56] *Opinion of the Court of 18 December 2014 [on the accession of the European Union to the European Convention for the Protection of Human Rights and Fundamental Freedoms] pursuant to Article 218(11) TFEU* ECLI:EU:C:2014:2454, para 157.

[57] Cf Joined Cases C-562/21 PPU and C-563/21 PPU *X and Y* ECLI:EU:C:2022:100, paras 40–49.

criminal justice. As has already been noted elsewhere,[58] the added value of the EU in the enforcement landscape rests upon three distinct capacities:

1. The EU offers its Member States the opportunity to regain control over crime-related problems that have become too big for individual states. Those problems require swift and effective cooperation, tackling concerns both of crime control as well as of due process.
2. The EU possesses the instruments to open up national legal systems, if necessary in the area of criminal justice too. Those who strive to regain control over crime can promote not only their own interests and perspectives; they also need to be open to the interests of other legal orders. Common goals, procedures, institutions and narratives are – or rather should be – offered by the EU.
3. Membership of the EU and the constitutional principles on which it is based also imposes what has been called 'external constitutional discipline' on the Member States, and one that is particularly important in law enforcement these days.

It matters a great deal how one views the institutional design of the EU authorities and their national partners. A perspective from which EU actors are presented as mere coordinative bodies, facilitating national authorities in the realisation of their tasks and duties, will inevitably conceal a number of pertinent questions and issues of real concern to individuals and enforcement authorities. Yet, as said, this perspective is still omnipresent in the area of criminal law enforcement, where institutions such as the EPPO or OLAF have been qualified by some as bodies of enforcement *coordination*, ultimately supporting the national legal orders. From that perspective, the main focus remains on what is needed – in terms of effective enforcement, as well as legal protection – in the legal orders of the individual Member States. Accordingly, there is less need to grant these bodies full operational autonomy or to revise national enforcement structures in light of their existence, nor is there a real need to rethink fundamental rights in light of their composite setting.

State sovereignty in the area of criminal justice can also be maintained via another technique. The limited punitive competences of a small number of distinct, highly specialised administrative EU authorities, such as in banking law or competition law, means that the domain of national enforcement, and particularly that of criminal justice, remains largely unaffected. Also from this perspective, criminal enforcement remains a national affair, largely unaffected by the development of direct enforcement.

The empirical lens of a composite legal order, by contrast, leads to questions of a different evaluative and normative nature. Composite enforcement starts from the viewpoint that though nation-states remain distinct, autonomous entities, their interactions with the EU and other states are guided by a series of rules and principles that serve

[58] See MJJP Luchtman, 'Transnational Law Enforcement Cooperation: Fundamental Rights in European Cooperation in Criminal Matters' (2020) 28 *European Journal of Crime, Criminal Law and Criminal Justice* 14, referring to M Poiares Maduro, 'Three Claims of Constitutional Pluralism' in M Avbelj and J Komárek (eds), *Constitutional Pluralism in the European Union and Beyond* (Hart 2012) 67, and, in response, J Komárek, 'European Constitutionalism and the European Arrest Warrant: In Search of the Limits of "Contrapunctual Principles"' (2007) 44 *CML Rev* 9. On the EU as a sovereign, also N Walker, 'Late Sovereignty in the European Union' in N Walker (ed), *Sovereignty in Transition* (Hart 2003) 3.

common goals and are inevitably geared towards further (enforcement) integration.[59] Enforcement by EU authorities is consequently not only the responsibility of those authorities, but also that of the Member States and the three branches of the *trias*. Not only do EU Member States need to open up, but they are also in need of a common narrative regarding what effective law enforcement is and what constitutes effective legal protection in a transnational setting. Yet before we delve further into the implications of our composite lens for the central questions of this book, it is necessary to clarify one more concept – that of EU enforcement authorities and their relationships to national criminal justice.

IV. Composite Enforcement Procedures

While the notion of the European legal order as 'a composite' refers to the European legal order of the EU and its Member States, the notion of composite enforcement is a species of it, presented in this volume as the conceptual lens for a study into punitive law enforcement by EU authorities. Composite enforcement procedures reconcile the seemingly contradictory notions of EU-wide territorial competences on the one hand, and decentralisation and subsidiarity on the other. These EU-wide competences are achieved by removing traditional mutual administrative assistance arrangements from the operational frameworks of the authorities. Decentralisation and subsidiarity bring to the fore that, one way or another, national legal orders remain a significant factor in the applicable legal instruments. The EU authorities continue to rely on the input of national legal orders, either because national enforcement are part of and act under the responsibility of those EU authorities, and/or because national law must be applied during their enforcement activities, in addition to or implementing EU rules.

The consequence of this structure is that it is not always easy to differentiate between those elements of the tasks of national authorities that are part and parcel of the legal frameworks of the EU authorities and tasks that remain in the national domain. The European competition network, for instance, combines the composite procedures of the Commission itself and simultaneously coordinates the enforcement procedures by national competition authorities. A more precise conceptual delineation of composite enforcement procedures is therefore necessary, also because it may have normative implications for the applicable frameworks.

Respect for national procedural autonomy, subsidiarity and the consequent fragmentation of the applicable legal rules cannot do away with the fact that composite enforcement is meant to establish a certain degree of coherence. There can be no 'composite' without it. There are two elements that distinguish composite procedures from being merely a set of related yet distinct enforcement procedures. To start with, coherence shows itself by taking account of the connections between the different stages of the enforcement procedure, starting from the stage when investigations are initiated, to the stage when decisions on the follow-up are made, to the stage when punitive

[59] *Opinion of the Court of 18 December 2014* (n 56) para 172.

procedures are ultimately conducted and concluded, at either the EU or the national level. To be part of a composite enforcement procedure means that each of these different stages is without meaning in and of itself, and that those stages are connected through legal arrangements. The procedures are capable of leading to punitive sanctions, although this need not necessarily be the goal from the start of the proceedings.

Second, for a procedure to be a composite within the scope of this project, the gathering of the relevant information or the subsequent imposition of the sanction must be the responsibility either of the EU authority itself, or a national authority subsuming its place by legal arrangements or a national authority that operates under the auspices of that EU authority. The last element – that of acting 'under the auspices of' – does not imply that there is a legal obligation of the national authority to achieve a specific, prescribed result.[60] Rather, for national authorities to be acting 'under the auspices of', they must be under the legal obligation to continue the procedures or execute specific measures if 'requested', 'instructed' or even 'ordered' to do so by the EU authority. Whether or not such an obligation exists depends on the degree of discretion that is left to national authorities to formally decline such a request or instruction. For such discretion to be absent, the request, order or instruction should fall within the scope of the applicable legal instruments and leave the national authorities no formal possibilities (refusal grounds) to decline it. The required absence of discretion, therefore, relates to what is called in international criminal law the *granting decision* of the national authorities, that is, to the decision to provide assistance to the EU authority.[61] The principle of loyal cooperation then takes precedence and such requests are to be executed, though it follows from that same principle that the EU authority, in turn, pays due attention to legitimate objections that may exist on the national side and seeks to accommodate those objections. That the subsequent *execution* of the request may remain within the hands of the national authority does not change its qualification as being part of a composite structure. National authorities are under a duty to deliver a reasonable degree of effort to achieve the result, in accordance with their national laws and obviously without interfering with such rights as the presumption of innocence.

To show the different ways in which procedures can be composite by nature, it is helpful to re-introduce the model that the present author and John Vervaele used in the first Hercule study on the stage of information gathering, yet with some slight adjustments.[62] Three factors are key in it:

1. The issue of which authority is the acting authority, that is, the authority that ultimately performs the investigative acts. Is this the EU authority itself or its national partner (on behalf of the EU authority or in its own name)?

[60] That, in turn, also has consequences for the remedies available, see ch 3 of this volume (Ligeti and Robinson).

[61] On that concept, see M Böse, M Bröcker and A Schneider (eds), *Judicial Protection in Transnational Criminal Proceedings* (Springer 2021); A Eser, O Lagodny and L Blakesley (eds), *The Individual as Subject of International Cooperation in Criminal Matters: A Comparative Study* (Nomos 2002).

[62] The following models are derived from that report, M Luchtman and J Vervaele, 'Comparison of the Legal Frameworks' in MJJP Luchtman et al, *Investigatory Powers and Procedural Safeguards: Improving OLAF's Legislative Framework through a Comparison with Other EU Law Enforcement Authorities (ECN/ESMA/ECB)* (Utrecht University 2017) 248.

2. The issue of whether the national partner functionally becomes a part of the EU organisation, or whether assistance is provided to the EU authority by the national partner as a representative of its national administration.
3. The issue of who instructs the national partners: are instructions provided by the EU authority, or through the national chains of command?

On the basis of these factors, we distinguished a number of models for composite enforcement:

1. **Autonomous investigative acts (*Vor-Ort-Kontrolle*).**[63] In this model, EU authorities perform the investigative acts themselves. This means that the laws to be applied are mostly EU regulations and that the remedies are, in principle, to be found at the EU level. Although national authorities are usually allowed to be present, their assistance is not related to the performance of their own tasks. It is seen as administrative assistance, *Amtshilfe*,[64] and mostly comprises the use of coercive power in cases of non-cooperation or assistance of a practical nature. Physical force remains, after all, a power that is only available to the national authorities. National authorities are under the obligation to provide that assistance, and apply their own national laws in that process.

   We can find examples of acts of *Amtshilfe* in all legal frameworks, for instance in Regulation 2185/96 for OLAF (on-the-spot checks), Articles 20 and 21 of Regulation 1/2003 (DG Competition), and on-site inspections within the framework of the ECB and ESMA. Here, we can already note major differences between the OLAF framework and those of other authorities. Whereas OLAF does have the power to perform on-the-spot checks, it is highly dependent in law and practice on its national partners. The applicable Regulations do not provide for autonomous powers or means to deal with a lack of cooperation by economic actors. This is different for DG Competion and the ECB.
2. **Mandated investigations, or even *Organleihe*.** In this constellation too, EU authorities lead the investigations but national authorities also have a clear role, which certainly exceeds the mere 'opening of doors'. Both models (mandates and *Organleihe*) have in common that the investigative acts of the national partners are ascribed to the EU authorities; national authorities perform tasks on behalf of the EU authorities (not in their own name).[65] The law to be applied is usually (directly applicable) EU law. Where EU authorities give such orders and retain the power of oversight and to act themselves, we speak of mandated delegations.[66] The (gradual) difference between a mandate and *Organleihe* is that, in the latter case, the (national) authority also becomes a part of the EU structure in legal terms; participating states lose control over their authorities, which act as a functional part of the EU authority. They operate within the framework of EU laws.[67]

[63] See *in extenso* also A Althaus, *Amtshilfe und Vor-Ort-Kontrolle* (Stämpfli 2001); A David, *Inspektionen im Europäischen Verwaltungsrecht* (Dunckler & Humblot 2003).

[64] F Wettner, *Die Amtshilfe im Europäischen Verwaltungsrecht* (Mohr Siebeck 2005) 154; David (n 63) 309.

[65] Wettner (n 64) 147.

[66] ibid 148–49.

[67] ibid 152–53; AAH van Hoek and MJJP Luchtman, 'Transnational Cooperation in Criminal Matters and the Safeguarding of Human Rights' (2005) 1 *Utrecht Law Review* 28.

It is submitted that the two models can be found in the ESMA (delegation) and ECB frameworks (joint supervisory teams, possibly also on-site inspection teams). Article 30 CRAR deals with delegation.[68] That article holds that ESMA may also require competent authorities to carry out specific investigatory tasks and on-site inspections as provided for in the Regulation. National partners then have the same powers as ESMA.[69]

Organleihe appears to be the most accurate form to qualify the cooperation between the ECB and NCAs for significant entities in the framework of joint supervisory teams (responsible for the monitoring of significant entities), as defined in the SMM Framework Regulation. Also the position of European (Delegated) Prosecutors in the EPPO framework resembles the features of an *Organleihe*.[70]

3. **Assistance (*Amtshilfe*), including instructions**. This is the oldest and most well-known form of interaction. Administrative assistance means that, upon the request of the EU authorities, national authorities perform specific acts of investigation in their own name, but for the fulfilment of the tasks of the EU authorities (not for their own tasks therefore). In principle, they apply national laws (which may have been harmonised). *Amtshilfe* as such creates no changes in the legislative framework of the requested party (in terms of its powers, for instance).[71] Hierarchically, the assisting national authorities do not take instructions from their EU partners but via their national chains of command in the execution of such acts. However, though *Amthshilfe* constructions originate from international law,[72] the legal regimes of the EU authorities that we have studied often no longer show a degree of discretion for national authorities to kindly refuse such 'requests' for assistance. Though such 'requests' may not (and often cannot) entail a duty to achieve a specific result, they do contain an obligation of effort. That is why I consider them as a part of composite procedures.

   Examples of *Amtshilfe* are found in the legal frameworks of ESMA and the ECB, where they mostly refer to providing assistance to the relevant authorities in cases of opposition. A similar provision is found in Article 4 of OLAF Regulation 2185/96. Within the setting of competition law, DG Competition has the power to 'ask' national partners to collect evidence on its behalf, applying their own law (Article 22(2) Regulation 1/2003). The latter power is somewhat different from the other types of mutual assistance within the framework of EU authorities, as the national competition authority then performs acts of

[68] Regulation 1060/2009 of 16 September 2009 on credit rating agencies ('CRAR') [2009] OJ L302/1, as revised.

[69] The question, incidentally, is to what extent Art 30 truly concerns a delegation, ie a transfer, of powers. The legal construction of the provision rather resembles a mandated power. The construction, after all, does not affect the responsibility of ESMA and does not limit ESMA's ability to conduct and oversee the delegated activity (Art 30(4) CRAR). A different opinion can be found in ch 4 of this volume (Böse and Schneider).

[70] Luchtman (n 53).

[71] Of course, those powers and safeguards may have been harmonised by EU law (case law and legislation).

[72] The term 'mutual administrative assistance' is used in the setting of international law, the word 'mutual' illustrating the element of reciprocity. That element is usually absent in the top-down types of assistance in composite procedures.

investigation individually, but on behalf of DG Competition and applying EU law.[73] This provision appears to be rarely used.[74]

A category related to 'mutual assistance' is the *instructions*, available in the SSM framework.[75] Instructions allow the ECB to oblige the national partner/NCA to use powers or take further procedural steps that are not available to the ECB itself. The applicable legal regime is the regime of the agent, not the principal EU authority. Likewise, the consequences of the acts are, in principle, not imputed to the EU authority.[76]

Table 1.1 Different models for interaction between EU authorities and national partners; the role of national partners

	Autonomous	***Organleihe***	**Mandate**	**Assistance**
Acting authority is …	EU authority	national	national	national
Act is part of …	EU organisation	EU	national	national
Instructions via …	EU hierarchy	EU	EU	national

The models illustrate the different modalities of how national authorities can assist their EU partners in composite procedures and how their actions are imputed to the respective national or EU legal orders. As a rule of thumb, the differences between the specific legal regimes will have consequences, for instance for the applicable law (on powers, safeguards, evidence,[77] etc), the legal remedies available and for questions of political accountability.[78] Yet these differences are not decisive for their qualification as being a part of administrative composite procedures.

Composite administrative procedures not only cover the vertical or 'multilevel' relationships between the authority and its partners in a specific legal order, they also relate to the more horizontal relationships between the many national legal orders in

[73] This is why one may doubt whether this is really mutual assistance or rather a different type of assistance. Most academic writings qualify it as mutual administrative assistance; see M Böse, 'The System of Vertical and Horizontal Cooperation in Administrative Investigations in EU Competition Cases' in K Ligeti (ed), *Toward a Prosecutor for the European Union*, vol 1: *A Comparative Analysis* (Hart Publishing 2012) 840.

[74] Ch 4 of this volume (Böse and Schneider).

[75] Arguably, instructions may also be regarded as a separate category, particularly where they are so specific that national partners are left without discretion. In that situation, national lines of hierarchy are less relevant. The difference between instructions and mandated investigations is that, under the latter regime, one cannot transfer more powers than one has oneself. In that respect, instructions come closer to mutual administrative assistance. In fact, some mutual assistance regimes are so specific in their terms and conditions that the differences between the two forms have become small. That is why the two forms have been placed in a single category.

[76] See L Wissink et al, 'Shifts in Competences between Member States and the EU in the New Supervisory System for Credit Institutions and their Consequences for Judicial Protection' (2014) 10 *Utrecht Law Review* 110. This may be different where discretion for national authorities is fully absent; see A Witte, 'The Application of National Banking Supervision Law by the ECB: Three Parallel Modes of Executing EU Law?' [2014] *Maastricht Journal of European and Comparative Law* 89.

[77] See also Vervaele in ch 9 of this volume, section V.

[78] There are some tricky areas, particularly when national authorities are left with no discretion by the EU authorities but their actions do affect the position of individuals and undertakings; cf Witte (n 75) 97–103; P Schammo, 'EU Day-to-Day Supervision or Intervention-based Supervision: Which Way Forward for the European System of Financial Supervision' (2012) 32 *OJLS* 771, 785–86. This particularly holds true for mandated investigations and instructions.

the context of composite procedures. It is certainly thinkable, for instance, that materials collected in the Netherlands end up in a punitive enforcement procedure in, say, Greece. The legal arrangements that aim to achieve the necessary degree of 'horizontal' coherence often remain implicit in the legal frameworks. That does not mean that they are not there. The dominant model within the scope of this project is the hierarchical (or 'star-pattern') model, in which the interactions between legal orders essentially run through the EU authority (cf OLAF, DG Competition, the ECB). The resulting focus of these models on the vertical axis of coherence conceals that important decisions on case allocation, the applicable law, etc are made within the confines of the EU authorities, but often without a clear framework.[79]

There are also collegial (or 'web pattern') models, based on joint decision-making structures, such as within the EPPO. It is not coincidental that the latter type of models usually include rules for case allocation or forum choices. It is also not without reason that in the EPPO structure, its 'indivisibility' has been explicitly confirmed in its founding Regulation.[80] There is no reason to do this in star-pattern models. For web patterns, however, it is absolutely vital.

V. The Lens of Compositeness: Implications and Research Questions

As composite procedures are intended to achieve a certain degree of coherence, legal questions follow from them, relating to the (foreseeability of the) applicable law, judicial protection and the scope of fundamental rights. The lens of punitive enforcement by EU authorities through composite processes certainly has analytical and normative implications. I will highlight two of those in the remainder of this chapter. Using such a lens implies, first of all, that even though decentralisation and diversity are an intrinsic part of their legal design, these procedures also require coherence in terms of the foreseeability of the applicable legal rules. It makes a difference for questions of legal protection or the foreseeability of legal rules whether or not individuals and legal persons are confronted with these questions in the framework of enforcement procedures that are conducted in parallel by different authorities or within a composite framework, under the responsibility of an EU authority. The latter framework should offer those individuals, and also the involved authorities, sufficient clarity on the applicable legal rules, at the relevant stages in the procedure.[81]

The second implication touches upon the relationships with national criminal justice. Composite enforcement procedures allocate the responsibilities between and within the different enforcement stages to actors from different legal orders. They are characterised by a high degree of organisational or decisional interdependence and coherence. It is clear that criminal justice as such is not, save for the EPPO, a part of the composite

[79] See further ch 7 (Robinson) and ch 10 (Luchtman) of this volume.
[80] Art 8(1) Regulation 1939/2017.
[81] See further ch 7 (Robinson) and ch 10 (Luchtman) of this volume.

enforcement structures that we have studied. There are good reasons, however, not to exclude criminal justice from this book's scope. By their very definition, the ties between administrative enforcement and criminal enforcement are tight. First of all, punitive administrative enforcement regimes serve as alternatives to criminal justice, for various reasons. Administrative enforcement regimes may, for instance, have been introduced to decriminalise certain behaviour or because of the advantages that administrative enforcement structures bring, including the presence of highly specialised administrative agencies. Moreover, administrative and criminal investigations often run in parallel and have complementary functions. This shows itself in the complementary goals that both types of enforcement may have and in the temporal connections between them, as socio-economic crime often will remain undisclosed – and criminal justice mechanisms therefore ineffective – without administrative enforcement.

In a composite setting, the interactions between the many legal orders that are involved add to the legal challenges. For instance, one of the most pressing issues in the area of EU fraud is why the composite enforcement procedures by OLAF still do not connect to the final stages of those procedures, that is, the stage when administrative investigations lead to punitive or non-punitive follow-up, particularly at national level.[82] Composite enforcement procedures by OLAF have been confined to the stages of investigation and do not regulate the stages of prosecution and sanctioning at national level. Yet with OLAF procedures regarded as distinct, separate procedures, the connection to national follow-up, criminal or administrative, remains loose. Follow-up is still a predominantly national affair, even after the recent revision of the OLAF framework. Clearly, this can have implications, both for the effective enforcement of EU law, for the legal protection of persons concerned, as well as for the overall legitimacy of OLAF's – and the EU's – operations. This issue also has a flip side: OLAF investigations of course do influence the work of national authorities – administrative and criminal alike – in a way that is not always in line with their own priorities, policies or standards. Though the OLAF framework remains puzzling and rather loose, it does require national authorities to respond.[83] Under the recently revised framework, the EU legislator focused mainly on the relationships between OLAF and the EPPO, and left this part of the puzzle largely untouched.

Also in other areas of EU law and policy, the relationships between composite administrative enforcement and criminal justice are underregulated or even deliberately disconnected. Authorities such as the ECB and DG Competition have the power to impose administrative sanctions themselves, or can entrust their national partners to do so, yet their institutional frameworks do not regulate the relationships with criminal justice actors. In fact, in competition law, the provision of information for purposes other than those for which it was originally obtained is said to be at odds with the rights

[82] As will be analysed in detail by Bovend'Eerdt in his forthcoming dissertation.

[83] Art 11(3) of the revised OLAF Regulation reads, inter alia, 'The competent authorities of the Member State concerned … shall take such action as the results of the external investigation warrant and shall report thereon to the Office within a time limit laid down in the recommendations … and, in addition, at the request of the Office.' See also, however, Recital 30 of Regulation 2020/2223: 'In accordance with the settled case-law of the CJEU, the Office recommendations included in its reports have no binding legal effects on such authorities of Member States or on institutions, bodies, offices and agencies.'

of the defence.[84] However, because such information may be taken into account to justify the initiation of a national procedure, the overlap in scope of composite administrative and national criminal investigations cannot be disregarded and causes many other complications, in terms both of the effective enforcement of EU laws and policies, as well as the protection of the individual.[85]

Therefore, as is the case in purely national cases of enforcement, composite enforcement procedures under the auspices of EU authorities inevitably will have links with criminal justice. There are temporal links, in which criminal justice is the necessary follow-up to administrative investigations or in which both set of procedures run in parallel. There are also substantive and personal links, because the facts and persons under investigation in administrative and criminal procedures will be the same or be closely related to one another. In a large number of these cases, national judicial authorities are also in the process of implementing EU law and, hence, acting within the scope of EU law. This also occurs in cases where ordinary criminal offences, such as forgery, are used as the basis for prosecution for violations of substantive norms of EU law.[86] That, in turn, means that the provisions of the EU Charter of Fundamental Rights are applicable, and that the mechanisms for cooperation between EU authorities and national criminal justice authorities should be an integral part of the scope of this study, from the perspective both of the effective enforcement of EU law, as well as that of the legal protection of individuals. Criminal justice is not a distinct, separate domain but is part and parcel of the same policy that EU administrative authorities serve to implement. Consequently, both sets of procedures should be aligned to prevent problems with, for instance, the *ne bis in idem* principle or the privilege against self-incrimination.

The lens of composite punitive enforcement thus pushes to the fore two different perspectives and related questions. There is an internal perspective, focusing on the legal architecture of the relevant models and on the legal position of the many authorities involved therein, as well as the position of the individuals concerned. Furthermore, there is the external perspective in which the relationships of composite punitive enforcement with national criminal justice are taken on-board. As indicated in the Introduction, our research questions are:

- What models for composite enforcement do currently exist?
- What constitutional parameters define and guide the interactions between the many authorities from the involved legal orders?
- What powers do these authorities need for the effective fulfilment of their punitive tasks, during the consecutive stages of the enforcement process? And what may individuals expect from these authorities in turn; are their rights, safeguards and remedies guaranteed?

[84] MJJP Luchtman, AM Karagianni and KHP Bovend'Eerdt, 'EU Administrative Investigations and the Use of Their Results as Evidence in National Punitive Proceedings' in F Giuffrida and K Ligeti (eds), *Admissibility of OLAF Final Reports as Evidence in Criminal Proceedings* (Luxembourg University 2019) 7, 17 and 33, with further references.

[85] See also Karagianni (n 38).

[86] As was the situation in Case C-617/10 *Åkerberg Fransson* ECLI:EU:C:2013:105.

- How does EU administrative enforcement relate to (national) criminal justice?

All of these questions are linked both to the EU and to the national levels. They relate not only to the executive branches, but also to the other two branches of government. Moreover, they involve cross-policy considerations in relation to the domain of criminal justice and vice versa.

The following chapters of this book focus on the main constitutional parameters for composite enforcement (chapters 2 and 3), on the exemplary models for composite enforcement (chapters 4–6), on a number of topical issues regarding EU enforcement authorities and their relations with the national legal orders (chapters 7–9). The book concludes with a series of overarching observations and an outlook towards the EPPO (chapters 10 and 11).

2

Constitutional Principles and Composite Punitive Enforcement in the EU

AART DE VRIES AND ROB WIDDERSHOVEN

I. Introduction – A Changing Landscape of Punitive Enforcement in the EU

Effective and fundamental rights-compliant enforcement of substantive rules is essential in a legal order based on the rule of law. Guaranteeing such enforcement has always been challenging in the legal order of the European Union (EU), characterised by shared administration or executive federalism, where in its most common form EU law sets out the general rules – Treaty provisions, regulations and directives – while their application and enforcement is in the hands of national authorities of 27 Member States ('indirect enforcement'). During the past 35 years the EU has made serious efforts, both legislative and judge-made, to achieve within this system a level of enforcement in the Member States that is more or less equivalent as regards instrumental and protective requirements.[1] As a result, enforcement of EU law has indeed improved, although it is certainly not perfect.

In recent years it has been possible to witness a shift in the enforcement of EU law, according to which complex composite or mixed forms of enforcement of EU law are applied, in addition to the traditional form of shared administration mentioned above.[2]

[1] J Jans, S Prechal and R Widdershoven (eds), *Europeanisation of Public Law* (Europa Law Publishing 2015) 268.

[2] In this context, see eg M Scholten and M Luchtman (eds), *Law Enforcement by EU Authorities: Implications for Political and Judicial Accountability* (Edward Elgar Publishing 2017); M Scholten and A Brenninkmeijer (eds), *Controlling EU Agencies: The Rule of Law in a Multi-jurisdictional Legal Order* (Edward Elgar Publishing 2020); K Ligeti (ed), *Toward a Prosecutor for the European Union* (Hart Publishing 2012); L Bachmaier Winter (ed), *The European Public Prosecutor's Office: The Challenges Ahead* (Springer 2018). See also the Hercule Programme studies in M Luchtman and J Vervaele (eds), *Investigatory Powers and Procedural Safeguards: Improving OLAF's Legislative Framework through a Comparison with Other EU Law Enforcement Authorities (ECN/ESMA/ECB)* (Utrecht University 2017); M Simonato, M Luchtman and J Vervaele (eds), *Exchange of Information with EU and National Enforcement Authorities: Improving OLAF Legislative Framework through a Comparison with Other EU Authorities (ECN/ESMA/ECB)* (Utrecht University 2018); F Giuffrida and K Ligeti (eds), *Admissibility of OLAF Final Reports as Evidence in Criminal Proceedings* (University of Luxembourg 2019).

Within these new composite forms, enforcement action does not take place in the legal order of one Member State but by means of interdependent action exercised at the EU level and/or at the level of one or more Member States. At the end of composite punitive proceedings, a sanctioning decision is taken by an EU authority, or by an authority or court of a Member State.[3] The sanction is, however, based on evidence gathered at another level, at either the Union level or the level of one or more Member States. The investigation and monitoring means by which this gathering by EU and national authorities has taken place may be rather different, as regards both powers and the procedural safeguards that apply when exercising them. Moreover, it may be possible that evidence gathered by means of administrative law competences at the EU level or in one of the Member States is used for imposing a criminal law sanction in (another) Member State.

II. Models of Composite Enforcement and Constitutional Principles

It seems clear that these new forms of composite or mixed enforcement raise new and difficult questions. For example, can national or EU authorities base their decision to impose a sanction upon evidence gathered in another legal order, most notably in another Member State or at EU level respectively? Which standards apply to the gathering in that Member State or at the EU level if the evidence is subsequently used at another level? Should the judicial assessment of the lawfulness of the evidence gathering take place in the legal order where the evidence was gathered, or rather in the legal order where it is used? In accordance with which fundamental rights standards will that review be performed? And how intense will judicial scrutiny be? To answer these questions in respect of composite vertical (bottom-up and top-down) and horizontal enforcement action, this chapter will examine (i) *which* court is competent to assess the gathering of evidence, (ii) *what* fundamental rights standards apply, and (iii) *how intense* the assessment of the competent court of review can and should be. The aforementioned topics will be examined in a conceptual manner in two ways.

First and foremost, we will examine models of composite enforcement action and, consequently, will not focus on concrete, composite actions in specific areas of law. In this respect three models will be distinguished.[4] First, the *bottom-up vertical model*, where the evidence is gathered at the national level while the punitive sanctioning on the basis of it takes place at the Union level by an EU institution or European enforcement agency (EEA). This model may be applied in the areas of banking supervision or European competition enforcement, where sanctions, imposed by the European Central Bank (ECB) or the European Commission respectively, can partly be based

[3] See eg Scholten and Luchtman (eds) (n 2).

[4] These models are partly based on L Wissink, *Effective Legal Protection in Banking Supervision* (Europa Law Publishing 2021) 11–13. It must be observed that these enforcement models are not necessarily mutually exclusive within a given substantive policy field. For example, EU customs rules are often enforced by the Member States according to the horizontal model, but enforcement of these rules may be top-down vertical as well, if it requires the involvement of the EPPO or OLAF.

on the evidence gathered in the Member States.[5] Second, the *top-down vertical model*, where the gathering of evidence takes place at the EU level by an EU institution, agency or office, while the imposition of punitive sanctions based on it may be situated at the national level. This model is applied in the area of banking supervision and competition law enforcement as well, but also, for instance, in the areas of the financial interests of the Union and pharmaceutical and fisheries enforcement. In all areas, the sanctions imposed by Member States authorities may be based on evidence gathered by an EEA such as the European Anti-Fraud Office (OLAF) and the European Public Prosecutor's Office (EPPO) – which are both tasked with the protection of the financial interests of the Union – or the European Medicine Authority (EMA) and the European Fisheries Control Agency (EFCA).[6] Lastly, there is the *horizontal model*, where the gathering of evidence takes place in one Member State, while the sanction based on it is imposed in another Member State. This model is used in various substantive policy fields, for instance market abuse and customs matters.

Second, the approach of this chapter is conceptual as it will stay away from the detailed rules governing composite enforcement action in specific sectors and instead focus on the constitutional principles guiding such actions. In this respect we discuss in depth three principles connected to the three main research questions of our contribution. First, the principle of effective judicial protection (PEJP), which is the guiding principle as regards the court(s) competent to review composite enforcement action (see section III). In this respect the main research question is which court will review the gathering of evidence? Will that be the court of the legal order where the punitive sanction is imposed, or (partially) the court of the legal order where the gathering of evidence took place? Second, the principle of compliance with fundamental rights, which determines the applicable legal standards for gathering evidence in composite enforcement actions (see section IV). In this regard the main research questions are what are the most important fundamental rights related to evidence gathering and which legal order determines the content of these rights? Will that be the legal order where the gathering took place, the legal order where the sanctions are imposed, or is their content harmonised or unified by EU law? Lastly, we address the principles of mutual trust and mutual recognition, which, together with the PEJP, answers the question how intensely the gathering of evidence in a certain legal order can and should be judicially tested in another legal order where that evidence is subsequently used to impose punitive sanctions (see section V).

[5] See, in respect of supervision by the Single Supervisory Mechanism (SSM), eg, ibid 180; T Duijkersloot, A Karagianni and R Kraayeveld, 'Political and judicial accountability in the EU shared system of banking supervision and enforcement' in Scholten and Luchtman (eds) (n 2) 28. See, in respect of competition enforcement, eg, K Cseres and A Outhuijse, 'Parallel Enforcement and Accountability: The Case of EU Competition Law' in Scholten and Luchtman (eds) (n 2) 82.

[6] See in this context, eg, M Luchtman and M Wasmeier, 'The Political and Judicial Accountability of OLAF' in Scholten and Luchtman (eds) (n 2) 221, and J Vervaele, 'Judicial and Political Accountability for Criminal Investigation and Prosecutions by a European Public Prosecutor's Office in the EU: The Dissymmetry of Shared Enforcement' in Scholten and Luchtman (eds) (n 2) 272; M Chamon and S Wirtz, 'Complex Procedures as Hurdle to Accountability: Verticalisation of Pharmaceutical Enforcement' in Scholten and Luchtman (eds) (n 2) 146, and F Cacciatore and M Eliantonio, 'Fishing in Troubled Waters? Shared Enforcement of the Common Fisheries Policy and Accountability Gaps' in Scholten and Luchtman (eds) (n 2) 168.

III. The Principle of Effective Judicial Protection – Competent Court in Composite Enforcement Proceedings

A. Evolution and Content

The PEJP implies that individuals should be able to enforce all rights conferred on them by Union law before a court of law.[7] The principle was recognised as a general principle of EU law in the seminal cases of *Johnston* and *Heylens*,[8] as it underlies the constitutional traditions common to the Member States and is also laid down in Articles 6 and 13 of the European Convention on Human Rights (ECHR). With the entry into force of the Lisbon Treaty, the principle acquired written primary law status in two respects. First, it has been codified as a fundamental right in Article 47 of the EU Charter of Fundamental Rights ('the Charter'), stating that everyone whose rights and freedoms guaranteed by Union law are violated has the right to an effective remedy before a tribunal previously established by law and meeting the well-known requirements of independence, impartiality, fair trial and so forth. Article 47 of the Charter applies to judicial protection offered by the EU courts, but also to national judicial protection in cases 'within the scope of Union law' (see section IV). A second written legal base for the PEJP is provided by Article 19(1) of the Treaty on European Union (TEU), which requires the Member States to establish a system of legal remedies and procedures ensuring effective judicial protection in the fields covered by EU law. Article 19(1) TEU has a wider scope than Article 47 of the Charter, because – according to the Court of Justice of the European Union (Court of Justice) – it does not require the particular case to be within the scope of Union law but applies if national courts may be potentially called upon to apply or interpret Union law.[9] As all national courts may potentially be confronted with cases with an EU dimension, Article 19(1) of the Charter seems to apply to the national judiciary as such.

In the case law of the Court of Justice, the PEJP has been linked to the rule of law since 1986.[10] This link has been reinforced by Article 19(1) TEU, which, according to the Court of Justice, gives a concrete expression to the rule of law, stated in Article 2 TEU as one of the values on which the EU is founded.[11] Respect for the rule of law means

[7] S Prechal and R Widdershoven, 'Principle of Effective Judicial Protection' in M Scholten and A Brenninkmeijer (eds), *Controlling EU Agencies: The Rule of Law in a Multi-jurisdictional Legal Order* (Edward Elgar Publishing 2020) 80; S Prechal, 'Effective Judicial Protection: Some Recent Developments – Moving to the Essence' [2020] *Review of European Administrative Law* 175.

[8] Case 222/84 *Johnston* ECLI:EU:C:1986:206; Case 222/86 *Heylens* ECLI:EU:C:1987:442.

[9] Case C-64/16 *Associação Sindical dos Juízes Portugueses* ECLI:EU:C:2018:117, paras 29 and 40.

[10] Case 294/83 *Les Verts v European Parliament* ECLI:EU:C:1986:166; Case C-50/00P *Unión de Pequeños Agricultores v Council of the European Union* ECLI:EU:C:2002:462. See K Lenaerts, 'The Rule of Law and the Coherence of the Judicial System of the European Union' (2007) 44(6) *CML Rev* 1625. Important more recent examples are found in Case C-824/18 *AB and Others (Nomination of Judges to the Supreme Court)* ECLI:EU:C:2021:153 and Case C-619/18 *Commission v Poland* ECLI:EU:C:2019:531.

[11] *Associação Sindical dos Juízes Portugueses* (n 9) paras 31–33; Case C-284/16 *Achmea* ECLI:EU:C:2018:158, para 36.

that neither the EU institutions nor the Member States can avoid judicial review of the question whether the measures adopted by them are in conformity with EU law. The responsibility for ensuring this review in the EU legal order is with the Court of Justice and the national courts. Therefore the PEJP applies both to the judicial protection offered by the national courts acting as *juge du droit commun* in EU cases, and to the judicial protection before the Union courts. Moreover, the PEJP may have a composite nature, meaning that in cases of composite or shared administration of EU law, observance of it is partly (within the limits of Article 263(4) of the Treaty on the Functioning of the European Union (TFEU)) a matter for the Union courts and should, for the other part, be guaranteed by the national courts who are allowed, and in the last instance in principle obliged, to refer questions of interpretation and validity of Union law to the Court of Justice (Article 267 TFEU).[12] As a whole, both judicial venues (should) offer – in the words of the Court – 'a complete system of legal remedies in EU cases, necessary to respect the rule of law'.[13]

As stated above, the PEJP comprises various elements or sub-principles. Most important for the purpose of this chapter is that in EU law cases the PEJP requires a right of access to a court that must be able to review both the facts and law of the case, applying an intensity of review meeting certain standards.[14] The PEJP, however, does not require one single standard of scrutiny in all cases – the precise level of intensity of review is discussed in section V – as it depends on the applicable EU rules. From the case of *Berlioz*, it appears that in composite procedures the principle of mutual trust may seriously limit the level of scrutiny by national courts required by the PEJP. In *Berlioz*, in the area of tax cooperation – which is based on mutual trust – the Court of Justice prescribed very restrained scrutiny by national courts of an information request that originated in other Member States.[15]

In this section we further concentrate on the right of access to the court as such. The PEJP, as codified in Article 47 of the Charter, does not constitute an absolute right of access that cannot be limited or regulated in any way. Within the limitation clause of Article 52(1) of the Charter, restriction of the PEJP may be justified, as may restrictions concerned with access to the court as such. Important to note in the context of review of composite enforcement action is that under Article 52(1) of the Charter, it may be allowed that individual steps in composite procedures are not directly appealable before a court but can only be incidentally reviewed in the judicial procedure against the final

[12] Case C-97/91 *Oleificio Borelli v Commission* ECLI:EU:C:1992:491; Case C-562/12 *Liivimaa Lihaveis* ECLI:EU:C:2014:2229.

[13] See also ch 3 of this volume (Ligeti and Robinson). See further in this context, eg, *Les Verts* (n 10) para 23; Case C-50/00P *Unión de Pequeños Agricultores* (n 10); Case C-583/11P *Inuit Tapiriit Kanatami and Others v Parliament and Council* ECLI:EU:C:2013:625. See also K Lenaerts, I Maselis and K Gutman (eds), *EU Procedural Law* (Oxford University Press 2014) paras 1.03–1.04; Jans, Prechal and Widdershoven (eds) (n 1) 336–39.

[14] See, regarding the general factors determining the intensity of judicial scrutiny of decisions, Case C-579/19 *Association of Independent Meat Suppliers* ECLI:EU:C:2021:665, paras 78–80. For further details, see R Widdershoven, 'National Procedural Autonomy and General EU Law Limits' [2019] *Review of European Administrative Law* 5, 21–24.

[15] Case C-682/15 *Berlioz Investment Fund* ECLI:EU:C:2017:373, para 86, limiting judicial scrutiny of information requests to whether the information sought by the other Member State 'is not devoid of any foreseeable relevance'. See, for an application of the criterion, Case C-437/19 *État luxembourgeois v L* ECLI:EU:C:2021:953.

decision taken on the basis of evidence gathered in those steps.[16] We will come back to this point when we discuss the access issue related to the three models of composite enforcement action (see sections III.C and III.D).

B. Top-Down Vertical Composite Procedures

In vertical top-down composite procedures, the gathering of evidence takes place at the EU level by an EU institution, agency or office – in other words, an EEA – while the use of evidence and the imposition of punitive sanctions based upon it occur at the national level. In such procedures, the EEA opens an investigation, which may include the use of specific investigative powers, such as information requests and on-site inspections, leading to a report that is communicated to the national authorities with a view to the possible imposition of sanctions by the national authorities or courts. In general these EEA investigatory actions are not directly appealable before the EU Courts under Article 263(4) TFEU, as they are considered to be preparatory only, and are not intended to have binding legal effects vis-à-vis individuals.[17] After all, although the national authorities are, on the basis of Article 4(3) TEU, obliged to examine the EEA information carefully and to draw the appropriate consequences from it in order to comply with EU law, it is – save for the specific context of the EPPO – the national authorities and courts who decide on the imposition of a sanction and are fully responsible for its lawfulness.[18]

The question to what extent national courts, when deciding on the imposition of the sanction, are allowed to review the gathering of evidence at the EU level, and on the basis of which (national or EU) standards, is discussed in sections IV and V. If the EEA input raises with the national court questions of interpretation of EU law or of validity of the EEA input-gathering process, a preliminary question should be referred to the Court of Justice (Article 267 TFEU). It must be observed that the option to refer preliminary questions is restricted in the specific context of the EPPO: the applicable regulation clarifies that national courts may not refer preliminary questions on the validity of the procedural acts of the EPPO with regard to national procedural law or to national measures transposing directives.[19] In addition, when considering the referral of a validity question, the national court is entitled to approach the EEA in order to obtain specific information and evidence from it, which the court considers essential

[16] Case C-432/05 *Unibet* ECLI:EU:C:2007:163; *Inuit Tapiriit Kanatami and Others v Parliament and Council* (n 13); Joined Cases C-245/19 and C-246/19 *État Luxembourgeois v B and Others* ECLI:EU:C:2020:795.

[17] Case 60/81 *IBM* ECLI:EU:C:1981:264.

[18] See eg, Case T-193/04 *Tillack* ECLI:EU:T:2006:292, para 70. See also M de Bellis, 'Multi-level Administration, Inspections and Fundamental Rights: Is Judicial Protection Full and Effective?' (2021) 22 *German Law Journal* 416, 424 and 435–36. As mentioned, a notable exception to this rule concerns the EPPO. The EPPO brings cases before national courts itself, see Regulation (EU) 2017/1939 implementing enhanced cooperation on the establishment of the European Public Prosecutor's Office ('the EPPO') [2017] OJ L283/1, Art 36.

[19] See Regulation (EU) 2017/1939 (n 18) Art 42. In turn, preliminary references concerning the interpretation of EU primary law, including the Treaties and the Charter, or the interpretation and validity of any provision of Union secondary law, including the Regulation concerning the EPPO and applicable directives, can be made by national courts.

to dispel or, as the case may be, confirm its doubts.[20] On the basis of the principle of sincere cooperation of Article 4(3) TEU, the authority must in principle provide the national court with the evidence and documents requested. Moreover, also on the basis of Article 4(3) TEU, national courts may request the EEA inspectors who conducted certain investigations to appear as witnesses before the court.[21]

Finally, as regards investigations or inspections conducted by EEAs, it may sometimes be possible that specific inspection acts are contestable separately before the EU Courts under Article 263(4) TFEU, because they 'are binding on, and capable of affecting the interests of, the applicant by bringing about a distinct change in his legal position'.[22] In competition cases this may be so if such an act of the Commission in the preparatory phase would irremediably impair the rights of defence of the individual, in particular the right to legal professional privilege and the right not to self-incriminate.[23] Moreover, it seems necessary for such an inspection act to be separately appealable, that it constitutes a final act in a special procedure distinct from the one that is intended to permit the Commission to take a decision on the substance of the case.[24] In order for the special procedure to be opened, the inspected entity must oppose the inspection act before it takes place, raising the fact that it would directly affect the right to respect for private life or rights of defence of the party.[25] The Commission's response to this claim may amount to a reviewable act.

It is not completely clear whether this right of appeal to the EU Courts against some EEA inspection acts limits the possibility for the entity to raise questions of lawfulness of the inspection act before the national court if the evidence gathered during the inspection is used for imposition of a sanction. The main rule in this respect is that if the entity would be undoubtedly directly and individually affected by such an EEA inspection decision, it should make use of this right of appeal. If this possibility is not used by the entity concerned, the national court, ruling on the sanction that was imposed on that entity based on the relevant information, must act on the assumption that the inspection decision is lawful.[26] Therefore it cannot even refer a preliminary question regarding the validity of the decision anymore. However, such a strict approach does not seem to be very reasonable in the situation described, as the conditions for an admissible separate appeal against inspection acts are very restrictive. To make use of it, the entity should formally object during the inspection, identifying which specific documents can infringe its own rights or the rights of its employees.[27] Especially if an unannounced inspection is performed, these conditions would seem hard to meet. Therefore, we presume that questions of validity of the inspection can still

[20] Case C-644/17 *Eurobolt* ECLI:EU:C:2019:555.

[21] Case C-2/88 *JJ Zwartveld and Others* ECLI:EU:C:1990:440. See also ch 3 of this volume (Ligeti and Robinson).

[22] *IBM v Commission* (n 17).

[23] Case T-125/03 *Akzo Nobel Chemicals v Commission* ECLI:EU:T:2007:287 and Case C-550/07 P *Akzo Nobel and Akcros v Commission* ECLI:EU:C:2010:512 (legal professional privilege); Case 374/87 *Orkem* ECLI:EU:C:1989:387 (right not to incriminate oneself). See also Wissink (n 4) 119–20; de Bellis (n 18) 434.

[24] Case C-255/17 *Mousquetaires and ITM Entreprises* ECLI:EU:C:2020:460.

[25] de Bellis (n 18) 434.

[26] Case C-188/92 *Textilwerke Deggendorf* ECLI:EU:C:1994:90.

[27] de Bellis (n 18) 435.

be raised in the national procedure and can be referred as preliminary questions to the Court of Justice.

C. Bottom-Up Vertical Composite Procedures

In bottom-up vertical composite procedures, the evidence is gathered at the national level using national monitoring or investigative powers, while punitive sanctioning on the basis of it takes place at the Union level by an EU institution or agency. This situation was at stake in the case of *Berlusconi and Fininvest*,[28] in which an ECB decision to oppose to the acquisition by Berlusconi and Fininvest of a qualifying holding in a banking institution was based on a proposal to oppose adopted, after certain inquiries, by the national competent authority (NCA), the Bank of Italy. In a preliminary question the issue was raised before the Court of Justice whether it is for the national courts or the EU Courts to review the legality of national decisions to initiate procedures, national measures of inquiry or proposals adopted by an NCA in such an authorisation procedure. According to the Court of Justice, on the basis of Article 263 TFEU, the EU Courts enjoy exclusive jurisdiction to review the legality of acts adopted by an EU institution, such as the ECB, following a decision-making process in which acts of an NCA constitute intermediate stages. Whether the national court may also be competent to assess the lawfulness of the national intermediate act depends on whether the national act is binding on the EU institution or not. If the national act is binding, it is for the national courts to rule on any irregularities that may vitiate such a national act;[29] where appropriate, the national court can make a reference for a preliminary ruling. If the national act is not binding on the EU institution, it is a matter for the EU Courts to rule on the legality of the final decision adopted by the EU institution and to examine, as an incidental matter, whether 'any defects vitiating the preparatory acts or proposals of the national authorities that would be such to affect the validity of that final decision'.[30] The legality of those acts cannot be reviewed by national courts. The Court bases the principle of 'single judicial review' by the EU Courts on the principle of sincere cooperation of Article 4(3) TEU. It avoids risks of diverging assessments of the legality of the final decision, in particular where that decision follows the NCA's analysis and proposal, and is necessary for the effectiveness of the composite procedure.

From the previous, it is clear that in vertical bottom-up composite procedures, which end up with a sanction imposed by an EU authority, the EU Courts are exclusively competent to review the lawfulness of the EU sanction, and that this exclusive competence extends to the lawfulness of national inquiries and other means of evidence gathering on which the EU sanction is based, if these inquiries and other forms

[28] Case C-219/17 *Berlusconi and Fininvest* ECLI:EU:C:2018:1023. For a similar approach, see Case C-414/18 *Iccrea Banca* ECLI:EU:C:2019:1036. See also Prechal and R Widdershoven (n 7) 86–89.

[29] *Oleificio Borelli SpA v Commission* (n 12); Case C-758/18 *GAEC Jeanninggros* ECLI:EU:C:2020:46. See also F Brito Bastos, 'Judicial Annulment of National Preparatory Acts and the Effects on Final Union Administrative Decisions: Comments on the Judgment of 29 January 2020, Case C-785/*18 GEAC Jeanningros*, EU:C:2020:46' [2021] *Review of European Administrative Law* 109 (note).

[30] *Berlusconi and Fininvest* (n 28) para 44.

are not binding on the EU institution imposing the sanction. How far the exclusion of the national courts goes, is, however, less clear, in particular if the evidence is gathered by means of coercive investigatory powers. In this respect, EU law *allows*, for instance, the *ex ante* authorisation by a national court of on-site inspections, conducted in the course of the enforcement of EU law by an EEA, although the evidence gathered may be used for the imposition of an EU sanction by the EEA.[31] Similarly, it seems obvious that national judicial authorisations in respect of other coercive investigatory powers, such as the interception of telecommunication or the conduct of search and seizure, can be maintained in composite procedures that end up in an EU sanction as well. However, if national law does not provide for judicial authorisation of a coercive investigation measure, such as on-site inspection, the Court of Justice does not *require* the Member State to create such a remedy. According to the Court, the lawfulness of the investigation can, incidentally, be reviewed *ex post* by the EU Courts when assessing the sanction based on the evidence gathered.[32] Apparently they are considered to be able to test an investigation measure, conducted in a Member State, for excessiveness and arbitrariness as well.[33]

A question that has not yet been answered explicitly by the Court of Justice is on the basis of which – EU or national – standards, the EU Courts should examine the gathering of evidence in the national intermediate phase through non-binding measures of inquiry, including coercive investigatory means that could not be tested by a national court in a certain Member State. In most literature – and we tend to agree – it is presumed that these national preparatory measures are tested by the EU Court on grounds of EU law only.[34] First, to ensure that the legality of a final EU decision is exclusively based on rules and principles of EU law and does not depend on different standards for evidence gathering in the Member States. This would hamper both the autonomy and unity of EU law.[35] Second, to preserve the limits of the jurisdiction of the EU Courts, which are only competent to interpret and apply EU law. Finally, this point of view seems to

[31] Case C-94/00 *Roquette Frères SA* ECLI:EU:C:2002:603. The judicial assessment of the inspection by the national court is limited, however, to the question whether the coercive measure envisaged is neither arbitrary nor excessive having regard to the subject matter of the inspection. The necessity of the inspection decision should be contested before the EU Courts. See Regulation 2003/1 on the implementation of the rules on competition [2003] OJ L1/1, Arts 20(6) and 20(7) (EU competition law) and Regulation (EU) 1024/2013 conferring specific tasks on the European Central Bank concerning policies relating to the prudential supervision of credit institutions [2013] OJ 287/63, Arts 12 and 13 (ECB supervision).

[32] R Widdershoven and P Craig, 'Pertinent Issues of Judicial Accountability in EU Shared Enforcement' in M Scholten and M Luchtman (eds), *Law Enforcement by EU Authorities* (Edward Elgar Publishing 2017) 343, on the basis of Case C-583/13 P *Deutsche Bahn* ECLI:EU:C:2015:404.

[33] In our view, it remains to be seen whether national courts are able to perform an effective judicial review of investigative measures that have been performed in another Member State (see section V.C). In this context, see eg, Widdershoven and Craig (n 32) 343 and 347–48; L Wissink, T Duijkersloot and R Widdershoven, 'Shifts in Competences between Member States and EU in the New Supervisory System for Credit Institutions and their Consequences for Judicial Protection' (2014) 10 *Utrecht Law Review* 92, 109–10.

[34] F Brito Bastos, 'Derivative Illegality in European Composite Administrative Procedures' (2018) 55 *CML Rev* 101, 126; Prechal and Widdershoven (n 7) 88–89; Wissink (n 4) 286–87.

[35] See also *Akzo Nobel and Akcros v Commission* (n 23), where the Court ruled, for reasons of 'unity of EU law', that the (more limited) EU principle of legal professional privilege was applicable to an on-site inspection ordered by the Commission, conducted in the United Kingdom, although the investigation concerned correspondence between the general manager of the company and an in-house lawyer, who was a member of the Dutch Bar and therefore protected by the Dutch legal professional privilege, offering more protection than the EU principle (see section IV).

be supported by the consideration of the Court of Justice in *Berlusconi and Fininvest*, according to which the examination by the EU Courts is limited to the question whether 'any defects vitiating the preparatory acts' of national authorities 'would be such to affect the validity of the final [ECB] decision'.[36] From this consideration, we deduce that flaws in the national stage seem to be disastrous for the final EU decision only if they affect the validity – which concerns legality as well as compliance with the relevant standards of the right to a fair trial – of the latter from the viewpoint of EU law.

D. Horizontal Composite Procedures

In horizontal composite procedures, the gathering of evidence takes place in one Member State, while the sanction based on it is imposed in another. Obviously, it is the court of the latter Member State – which can be referred to as the forum State – that has the jurisdiction to impose the sanction or assess one on appeal, and conduct a judicial review of the evidence in that context. The gathering of evidence itself may also be judicially controlled in the Member State of gathering, in particular if the evidence is gathered by means of coercive investigatory powers such as on-site inspections or the interception of telecommunication.[37] Unless EU law requires the existence of legal remedies, the national law of the Member State in which the evidence is gathered decides whether and, if so, which legal remedies are available.[38] In this context, specific regard can be had to the Directive on the European Investigation Order (EIO), which expressly requires that the executing Member State must provide legal remedies equivalent to those available in a similar domestic case to challenge the investigative measure indicated in the incoming EIO.[39] Nevertheless, the substantive reasons for issuing an EIO cannot be challenged in the executing Member State but only in the issuing Member State.

Nevertheless, Member States may, in domestic procedures, have chosen a system in which the evidence gathering is only, indirectly and incidentally, judicially assessed in the appeal procedure against the sanction based on the evidence.[40] In that situation, the question can be raised whether this system ensures effective judicial protection of

[36] *Berlusconi and Fininvest* (n 28) para 58.

[37] Such direct judicial control of the investigatory instruments employed may be *ex ante* or *ex post*, and may be contradictory or not. If the procedure is not contradictory, the lawfulness of the investigation is, on the basis of Art 47 of the Charter, contestable in the Member State where the sanction based on the information gathered is imposed; see Case C-419/14 *WebMindLicences* ECLI:EU:C:2015:832.

[38] Case C-852/19 *Gavanozov II* ECLI:EU:C:2021:902; *Berlioz Investment Fund* (n 15).

[39] See Directive 2014/41/EU of the European Parliament and of the Council regarding the European Investigation Order in criminal matters [2014] OJ L130/1, Art 14 ('EIO Directive'). The EIO Directive has, in principle, replaced the 'classic' instruments of mutual legal assistance in criminal matters between the EU Member States in the Area of Freedom, Security and Justice (AFSJ). See, for more detail on the EIO, section V.B.i.

[40] In this context, see *Gavanozov II* (n 38) paras 26–27; Case C-852/19 *Gavanozov II* ECLI:EU:C:2021:902, Opinion of AG Bobek, paras 41 and 52. The EIO Directive does not require Member States to introduce new legal remedies if those are *not* available under national law, but only prescribes that equivalent legal remedies to those that *are* available in domestic proceedings can be called upon in the context of an incoming EIO. If Member States have opted not to include specific remedies during the investigation, remedies will only be available during the criminal trial. In composite proceedings, this trial will be held in another Member State; see M Böse, M Bröcker and A Schneider (eds), *Judicial Protection in Transnational Criminal Proceedings* (Springer 2021) 361–65.

the evidence-gathering process in horizontal composite procedures as well, and if not, whether it should be adjusted on the basis of EU law? This issue has played out in the context of the exchange of information in tax matters on the basis of Directive 2011/16/EU on administrative cooperation in the field of taxation (the Directive on tax cooperation).[41] The question was referred to the Court of Justice whether a penalty enforcing an information order of the Luxembourg tax authorities, in response to a request for exchange of information from the authorities of another Member State, based on the Directive on tax cooperation, should be appealable before the Luxembourg courts and, if so, by whom.[42]

In its answer the Court of Justice distinguished between the person holding the information in Luxembourg to whom the information order was addressed, and other individuals concerned, more particularly the taxpayer who was affected by the order, as his information would be exchanged but to whom the order as such was not directed. As regards the first person holding the information ordered to be provided by a decision of the Luxembourg tax authorities, and who was or would be sanctioned in the event of non-compliance, Article 47 of the Charter required a direct right of access to the Luxembourg court in order to challenge the information order itself.[43] Otherwise this person would be unable to access a court without first infringing that decision and raising its unlawfulness indirectly in a procedure against the penalty imposed for non-compliance. This would – according to the Court – not respect the essence of the right to an effective remedy guaranteed by Article 47 of the Charter.[44]

However, such a direct right of access to the court in Luxembourg was not granted to the taxpayer whose information would be exchanged, because this person, not being the addressee of the information order, was neither subject to any legal obligation by that decision nor exposed to the risk of receiving a penalty in the event of non-compliance with it. The lack of (direct) access was not in breach of the essence of the right to an effective remedy under Article 47 of the Charter, because the taxpayer would, according to the Court, have an effective remedy against the correction or adjustment decision, taken in the other Member State on the basis of the information exchanged. In this procedure the competent court of that forum State could, incidentally, verify whether the way the evidence on which that act was based had been obtained (ie, in Luxembourg) or used (ie, in the forum State) was in breach of the rights and freedoms guaranteed to the person concerned by EU law, more specifically Article 7 of the Charter.[45] According to the Court of Justice, this indirect right of appeal was a justified limitation of Article 47 of the Charter, because it favoured speed and efficiency of tax cooperation and was therefore suitable and necessary to achieve the objective of combating international tax fraud and evasion of Directive on tax cooperation.[46]

[41] Council Directive 2011/16/EU of 15 February 2011 on administrative cooperation in the field of taxation [2011] OJ L 64/1. In this context, see Case C-682/15 *Berlioz Investment Fund* (n 15); *État Luxembourgeois v B and Others* (n 16).

[42] P Mazzotti and M Eliantonio, 'Transnational Judicial Review in Horizontal Composite Procedures: *Berlioz, Donnellan*, and the Constitutional Law of the Union' (2020) 5 *European Papers* 41.

[43] Case C-682/15 *Berlioz Investment Fund* (n 15); *État Luxembourgeois v B and Others* (n 16) para 69.

[44] *État Luxembourgeois v B and Others* (n 16) para 68.

[45] ibid para 82.

[46] ibid paras 90–91.

The question can also be raised whether the foregoing is relevant outside the area of tax cooperation. The rule that an information order that is enforceable by means of a penalty should, on the basis of Article 47 of the Charter, be directly appealable by the addressee in the Member State where it is issued, seems also to apply to other areas where EU law requires the authorities of a Member State to gather information with a view to exchanging the information with another Member State.[47] After all, in such other areas too, the only way to have the order judicially tested would be to violate it, taking the risk of being (criminally) penalised. This would, according to the Court of Justice, violate the essence of Article 47 of the Charter. If, on the basis of the foregoing, an individual is not entitled to have the evidence gathering itself judicially tested in the State of gathering – for example because the investigation order is not directed to him or her, or is not enforceable by means of a penalty – the possible unlawfulness of it can and should be raised in the forum State where the sanctioning decision is taken on the basis of the evidence. How intensively the (un)lawfulness is tested and whether the competent court of the forum State has sufficient means to obtain the information necessary to assess the lawfulness of the gathering of evidence in another Member State will be discussed in more detail in section V.

IV. Principle of Compliance with EU Fundamental Rights and the Standard of Protection in Composite Punitive Proceedings

In EU enforcement proceedings, fundamental rights must be upheld. Indeed, compliance with fundamental rights constitutes one of the constitutional values upon which the Union is based (Article 2 TEU) and it is strongly connected to the rule of law.[48] Although it is clear that Member States and EU authorities must ensure that fundamental rights are upheld, the question can be raised which standard must be taken into account in the setting of composite horizontal and vertical enforcement proceedings. For example, Member State A has obtained evidence within its national legal order and Member State B wants to use that evidence to impose penalties of a criminal nature. Which standard will then determine the *gathering* of the evidence and its subsequent *use*? These questions also rise in the vertical setting: which standard applies to evidence that is obtained by national authorities and then used at the EU level by an EEA (bottom-up), or which standard applies to evidence that is gathered by EU authorities and then subsequently used in a Member State (top-down)?

[47] As an example, regard can be had to Regulation (EU) 596/2014 of the European Parliament and of the Council of 16 April 2014 on market abuse (market abuse regulation) [2014] OJ L173. In the Market Abuse Regulation – often abbreviated to MAR – several competences are found that must be available to national financial supervisory authorities, including the power to demand information from anyone (Art 23(2)(b) MAR). These powers can be relied upon to implement incoming requests for administrative assistance from financial supervisory authorities in other EU Member States (Art 30 MAR).

[48] See eg *AB and Others (Nomination of Judges to the Supreme Court)* (n 10) paras 108 et seq; Case C-216/18 PPU *LM* ECLI:EU:C:2018:586, paras 48 et seq; *Opinion 2/13* ECLI:EU:C:2014:2454, paras 168–169.

In short, the standard rule in the horizontal setting is that the applicable standard during gathering is determined by the national law of the Member State where the evidence is gathered (*locus regit actum*), whereas the applicable standard during use is governed by the national law of the Member State where the evidence is used (*forum regit actum*). For our example, this would mean that the evidence is obtained in accordance with the standard of Member State A, while its use is determined by the standard of Member State B. In the vertical context, authorities in Member States will, in principle, gather and use evidence in accordance with national law, while EU authorities must adhere to the standard under Union law. Nevertheless, these rules are mere starting points and can be significantly altered in accordance with EU law.[49]

Despite the undeniable relevance of national law, we will focus on the principle of compliance with EU fundamental rights in this section. In that regard, the Charter will be especially relevant to determine the standard of fundamental rights protection that is guaranteed on the Union level. The standard under national law must always be compatible with the EU fundamental rights standard. In that regard, the principle of compliance with EU fundamental rights establishes the *minimum* level of fundamental rights protection that must always be observed within the scope of Union law, but may also set requirements as to the *maximum* level of protection that national law may guarantee. In this light, several questions warrant attention. When does the Charter apply? Which fundamental rights standards does it establish on the EU level? And how do the Union standards relate to the standards that may apply on the basis of national (constitutional) law of the Member States?

A. Fundamental Rights and the Charter

In the early days of European integration, the protection of fundamental rights was not amongst the policy aims of the EU's predecessors; the goal was economic cooperation and integration between the nations of Europe.[50] This changed due to pressure from national constitutional courts, and as a means to ensure the acceptance of the new European legal order and its characteristics.[51] Fundamental rights were gradually but steadily elevated to the rank of general principles of Union law by the Court of Justice: they were part of the constitutional principles of the Member States and, therefore, amongst the basic principles of the Union. Consequently, the protection of those rights also had to be provided within the structure and goals of the

[49] For example, in the context of horizontal cooperation, an important exception to the so-called 'locus rule' is found in the EIO Directive. The Directive prescribes that the executing authority 'shall comply with the formalities and procedures expressly indicated by the *issuing authority* unless otherwise provided in this Directive and provided that such formalities and procedures are not contrary to the fundamental principles of law of the executing State' (emphasis added). This is referred to as the rule of '*forum regit actum*'. See Art 9(2) EIO Directive.

[50] See Jans, Prechal and Widdershoven (eds) (n 1) 142 ff.

[51] P de Hert, 'EU Criminal Law and Fundamental Rights' in V Mitsilegas, M Bergström and T Konstadinides (eds), *Research Handbook on EU Criminal Law* (Edward Elgar Publishing 2016) 106. See also Case 1/58 *Stork* ECLI:EU:C:1959:4; Joined Cases 36/59, 37/59, 38/59 and 40/59 *Nold KG* ECLI:EU:C:1960:36; Case 29/69 *Stauder v City of Ulm* ECLI:EU:C:1969:57.

Union itself.[52] This case law of the Court of Justice has been codified in the Treaties: fundamental rights as guaranteed by the ECHR and as they result from the constitutional traditions of the Member States still constitute general principles of Union law (Article 6(3) TEU).

Since the entry into force of the Lisbon Treaty in 2009, the Charter constitutes the primary source of fundamental rights in the EU. The Charter has the same legal value as the Treaties and enshrines the fundamental rights that should be taken into account under Union law. The Charter clarifies that its provisions are addressed to the institutions, bodies, offices and agencies of the Union, as well as to the Member States when they are implementing Union law (Article 51(1) of the Charter). It follows from this wording that the institutions and bodies of the EU are always subject to compliance with the Charter, whereas Member States are only bound by the instrument when they implement Union law.

When do Member States implement Union law? At first glance, the scope of application of the Charter seems to be restricted to implementation in the strict sense – which can be referred to as the 'agent situation' – where a Member State implements into its national law specific Union obligations that are derived from, inter alia, a directive or regulation.[53] However, the Court of Justice adopted a broad interpretation concerning the scope of application of the Charter in the case of *Åkerberg Fransson*.[54] In reference to the *Explanations in relation to the Charter of Fundamental Rights*, the Court ruled that the Charter should be complied with by Member States when they act 'within the scope of Union law'.[55] In *Åkerberg Fransson*, the suspect was subjected to national tax penalties and criminal proceedings for value added tax (VAT) fraud. The rules on VAT were harmonised within the Union, and Member States were required to take all legislative and administrative measures appropriate for ensuring collection of VAT within their territory. This also required them to combat VAT fraud through, inter alia, sanctions in accordance with Article 325 TFEU, which codifies the obligation to impose effective and dissuasive penalties for fraud that affects the financial interests of the Union. In this light the Court concluded that the authorities were implementing Union law through the fiscal fines and criminal proceedings.[56]

The importance of the judgment in *Åkerberg Fransson* should not be underestimated. In essence, it ensures that national enforcement proceedings of Union policies are brought within the scope of the Charter even if primary or secondary Union law does not impose specific obligations concerning enforcement upon Member States but does contain a provision that establishes the so-called *Greek Maize*-criteria, which

[52] Case 11/70 *Internationale Handelsgesellschaft* ECLI:EU:C:1970:114. See also Case 136/79 *National Panasonic* ECLI:EU:C:1980:169. In *National Panasonic*, the Court of Justice specifically established that measures that were adopted by the Community would not be valid if they were contrary to the provisions of the ECHR; although the ECHR was strictly not a part of the legal order of the Community, its provisions still had to be complied with.

[53] Jans, Prechal and Widdershoven (eds) (n 1) 148. See also M Luchtman and R Widdershoven, 'Het Nederlandse Strafrecht in de Ban van het Unierecht' (2018) 11 *Ars Aequi* 873, 877.

[54] Case C-617/10 *Åkerberg Fransson* ECLI:EU:C:2013:280. See also de Hert (n 51) 109–10.

[55] *Åkerberg Fransson* (n 54) paras 20–21. See also *Explanations relating to the Charter of Fundamental Rights* [2007] OJ C303/02.

[56] *Åkerberg Fransson* (n 54) paras 26–28.

prescribe that 'effective, dissuasive and proportionate' penalties must be established under national law to enforce substantive EU policies.[57]

B. The Substance of Fundamental Rights under the Charter

The Charter guarantees various fundamental rights that might be relevant during composite enforcement proceedings, but what is their substance? For vertical and horizontal composite enforcement proceedings, the right to silence and privilege against self-incrimination, professional legal privilege, and the right to respect for private life and inviolability of the home are most important. Therefore, we will focus on these fundamental rights below. The right to an effective judicial remedy before an independent and impartial tribunal has been addressed previously (see section III).

It must be observed that most fundamental rights enshrined in the Charter are also codified in the ECHR. Although the Treaties provide that the EU shall accede to the ECHR, the Union is, at present, not directly bound by the Convention or the case law of the European Court of Human Rights (ECtHR).[58] Nevertheless, the Charter clarifies that in so far as it contains rights that correspond to rights guaranteed by the ECHR, their meaning and scope shall at least be the same as those laid down by the Convention; but Union law can offer more extensive protection (Article 52(3) of the Charter).[59] Thus, the level of protection offered by the ECHR constitutes the minimum level of protection in the EU; and while the Charter cannot provide less protection, it can give Convention rights additional substance under Union law. The minimum level of protection offered by the Charter must always be complied with by Member States and EU authorities alike. As mentioned before, it must also be noted that most fundamental rights enshrined in the Charter can be limited in accordance with Article 52(1) of the Charter (see section III.A).

i. Right to Silence and Privilege against Self-Incrimination

The Charter provides that anyone who is charged should be presumed innocent until proved guilty according to law, and the rights of the defence of persons who are charged shall be guaranteed (Article 48 of the Charter). The right to silence and privilege against

[57] Luchtman and Widdershoven (n 53) 879. See also Case 68/88 *Commission v Greece* ECLI:EU:C:1989:339. Since the mid-1990s, virtually all secondary Union legislation features the requirement that substantive rules must be enforced through 'effective, dissuasive and proportionate' penalties, see eg Regulation (EU) 596/2014 of the European Parliament and of the Council of 16 April 2014 on market abuse (market abuse regulation) [2014] OJ L173, Art 30; Regulation (EC) 1013/2006 of the European Parliament and of the Council of 14 June 2006 on shipments of waste [2006] OJ L190, Art 50.

[58] See Art 6(2) TEU. The negative recommendation of the Court of Justice in *Opinion 2/13* renders it unlikely that the EU will accede to the ECHR in the near future, but negotiations were re-opened in 2019, see 'Legislative Train Schedule Area of Justice and Fundamental Rights: Completion of EU Accession to the European Convention on Human Rights' at www.europarl.europa.eu/legislative-train/theme-area-of-justice-and-fundamental-rights/file-completion-of-eu-accession-to-the-echr (accessed 31 August 2021).

[59] de Hert (n 51) 111. Although only the Convention itself is mentioned, the case law of the ECtHR should also be taken into account to assess the substance of fundamental rights. This has been recognised in *Explanations relating to the Charter of Fundamental Rights* (n 55).

self-incrimination constitute important defence rights; but before we elaborate upon them, it is prudent to determine by whom and when the rights can be called upon.

The Charter does not establish when a person is 'charged' under Union law, but in the case of *Bonda* the Court of Justice defined the concept of 'penalties of a criminal nature' under the Charter and adopted the same approach as the ECtHR.[60] The ECtHR elaborated the concept of 'criminal charge' from Article 6 ECHR as an autonomous one, and established three criteria that are relevant to assess the existence of a criminal charge: the legal classification under national law constitutes an authoritative starting point, but even if the offence does not belong to the sphere of criminal law *sensu stricto*, it can still amount to a criminal charge on the basis of the very nature of the offence, and the degree of severity of the penalty should be taken into account.[61] In that regard, the Court of Justice has – albeit under verification by national courts – recognised in its case law that administrative fines constitute 'penalties of a criminal nature'.[62]

Can the person who is charged be forced to make a statement if he or she is at risk of incriminating himself or herself? And can he or she be required to surrender incriminating documents? In regard to these questions, the right to silence and privilege against self-incrimination are pivotal defence rights. What is their substance under the Charter? For quite some time, the leading case of the Court of Justice concerning the right to silence and privilege against self-incrimination was *Orkem v Commission*.[63] In its judgment, the Court adopted a 'limited' approach to the right to silence for undertakings in competition matters: the right to remain silent applied only in so far as the statement concerned the admission of guilt to an infringement, and factual questions still had to be answered. No absolute right to remain silent was accepted. This narrow understanding was subsequently reiterated by the Court in its case law and was long perceived as the applicable standard under Union law.[64]

However, the Court of Justice has recently substantiated the right to silence and privilege against self-incrimination under Article 48 of the Charter for *natural* persons under reference to well-established case law of the ECtHR.[65] In short, the ECtHR has repeatedly held that while the right to silence and the privilege against self-incrimination are not explicitly mentioned in Article 6 ECHR, they constitute generally recognised international standards that lie at the heart of the notion of a fair trial.[66]

[60] Case C-489/10 *Bonda* ECLI:EU:C:2012:319, para 37. See also *Åkerberg Fransson* (n 54) paras 34–35.

[61] *Engel and Others v Netherlands* App nos 5100/71; 5101/71; 5102/71; 5354/72; and 5370/72 (ECtHR, 8 June 1976); *Öztürk v Germany* App no 8544/79 (ECtHR, 21 February 1984). Unsurprisingly, penalties are not always 'punitive' and can pursue reparatory aims as well, see Case C-439/19 *Latvijas Republikas Saeima* ECLI:EU:C:2021:504, paras 85 et seq; *Bonda* (n 60) para 39.

[62] See eg Case C-524/15 *Menci* ECLI:EU:C:2018:197, para 33; Case C-596/16 *Di Puma* ECLI:EU:C:2018:192, para 38; Case C-537/16 *Garlsson Real Estate and Others* ECLI:EU:C:2018:193, para 35. See also *Grande Stevens and Others v Italy* App nos 18640/10; 18647/10; 18663/10; 18668/10; and 18698/10 (ECtHR, 4 March 2014) paras 94–101.

[63] *Orkem v Commission* (n 23). See also Jans, Prechal and Widdershoven (eds) (n 1) 310; Widdershoven and Craig (n 32). See further ch 4 of this volume (Böse and Schneider).

[64] Case C-238/99 *Limburgse Vinyl Maatschappij* ECLI:EU:C:2002:582, para 35. See also Case C-466/19 P *Qualcomm v Commission* ECLI:EU:C:2021:76.

[65] Case C-481/19 *DB v Consob* ECLI:EU:C:2021:84, para 37. See Case C-481/19 *DB v Consob* ECLI:EU:C:2020:861, Opinion of AG Pikamäe, paras 97–106.

[66] *DB v Consob* (n 65) para 38. See also *Ibrahim and Others v UK* App nos 50541/08; 50571/08; 50573/08; and 40351/09 (ECtHR, 13 September 2016) para 266; *Saunders v UK* App no 19187/91 (ECtHR, 17 December 1996) para 68.

The privilege against self-incrimination specifically protects against 'improper' compulsion that destroys the very essence of the notion that a person cannot be forced to contribute to his or her own conviction; consequently, the privilege does not constitute an absolute right and the accused cannot refuse *all* cooperation with the authorities.[67] To assess whether compulsion has been 'improper', regard must be had to the nature and degree of compulsion, the availability of procedural safeguards and the use to which the evidence obtained is put.[68] The ECtHR has identified several circumstances in which the nature and degree of compulsion raise concerns that it has been improper. Most notably, such concerns arise if a person is obliged to make a statement under threat of a sanction, and either makes an incriminating statement or refuses to testify and is sanctioned as a result.[69]

An important rule established by the ECtHR is that the privilege against self-incrimination is, in principle, not concerned with evidence that has an existence independent of the will of the accused, such as documents acquired pursuant to a warrant, or blood and urine samples.[70] While this distinction is not elaborated upon by the Court of Justice, we would argue that it applies mutatis mutandis under Union law.[71]

[67] *DB v Consob* (n 65) para 39. See also *DB v Consob* Opinion of AG Pikamäe (n 65) para 100; *Ibrahim and Others v UK* (n 66) para 267; *Jalloh v Germany* App no 54810/00 (ECtHR, 11 July 2006) para 100; *Saunders v UK* (n 66) para 68.

[68] The aforementioned factors should be assessed together to establish whether the very essence of the privilege against self-incrimination has been destroyed. See *DB v Consob* Opinion of AG Pikamäe (n 65) para 101. See also *Ibrahim and Others v UK* (n 66) paras 267–269; *Jalloh v Germany* (n 67) para 101; *Saunders v UK* (n 66) para 69.

[69] *DB v Consob* (n 65) para 39. See also *Saunders v UK* (n 66) para 70.

[70] *Saunders v UK* (n 66) para 69. It should be noted that the ECtHR has occasionally extended the protection of the privilege against self-incrimination to include evidence that has an existence independent of the will of the accused. In short, this is the case if a measure that violates Art 3 ECHR (prohibition of torture) is used to retrieve rather than to obtain evidence. If the authorities are not certain that evidence exists or are unaware of its substance, and require the active participation of the suspect to obtain the evidence, the privilege against self-incrimination can also be applicable even if the material has an existence independent of the will of the accused. Still, whether compulsion has been 'improper' must be assessed on the basis of the nature and degree of compulsion, the availability of procedural safeguards and the use to which the evidence that has been obtained is put. In this context, see *Jalloh v Germany* (n 67); *Funke v France* App no 10828/84 (ECtHR, 25 February 1993); *JB v Switzerland* App no 31827/96 (ECtHR, 3 May 2001); *Chambaz v Switzerland* App no 11663/04 (ECtHR, 5 April 2012).

[71] The explicit reference to Art 52(3) of the Charter in the judgment in *DB v Consob* suggests that the Court of Justice is fully committed to following the case law of the ECtHR on the right to silence and privilege against self-incrimination, and hence the distinction between statements and 'evidence which has an existence independent of the will of the accused'. Additionally, we would point to the fact that relevant secondary Union legislation also provides that 'the right not to incriminate oneself should not prevent the competent authorities from gathering evidence which may be lawfully obtained from the suspect or accused person through the use of legal powers of compulsion and which has an existence independent of the will of the suspect or accused person such as material acquired pursuant to a warrant, material in respect of which there is a legal obligation of retention and production upon request, breath, blood or urine samples and bodily tissue for the purpose of DNA testing', see Directive (EU) 2016/343 on the strengthening of certain aspects of the presumption of innocence and of the right to be present at the trial in criminal proceedings [2016] OJ L65/1, Recital 29. Moreover, the privilege against self-incrimination is implemented through the right to remain silent in most EU Member States as well, see eg ABRvS 30 May 2018, ECLI:NL:RVS:2018:1729 and HR 9 February 2021, ECLI:NL:HR:2021:202; Conseil constitutionnel 2 March 2004, nº 2004-492 DC and Crim 6 January 2015, nº 13-87.652 – Cassation. In Germany, the privilege against self-incrimination is sometimes extended to documentary evidence on the basis of statutory provisions – eg, § 393 AO and § 95 StPO – but the *Bundesverfassungsgericht* has still ruled that the primary implementation of the privilege constitutes the right to remain silent in its so-called *Gemeinschuldnerbeschluß*, see 'BVerfG Decision of 13 January 1981' [1981] *Neue Juristische Wochenschrift* 1431.

The exclusion of 'evidence which has an existence independent of the will of the accused' from the scope of the right to silence and privilege against self-incrimination means that an accused can, in principle, be required to cooperate with the authorities and surrender documentary evidence under coercion.

ii. Legal Professional Privilege

Legal professional privilege (LPP) guarantees secrecy between lawyer and client; it constitutes an important defence right that applies to all measures and sanctions – both punitive *and* non-punitive – on the basis of Articles 41, 47 and 48 of the Charter.[72] The Court of First Instance and the Court of Justice have elaborated on LPP in competition matters, most notably in the case of *Akzo and Akros v Commission*.[73] In short, LPP seeks to safeguard the public interest in the proper administration of justice, ensuring that a client is free to consult his or her lawyer without fear that any confidences the client imparts may subsequently be disclosed, and aims to avoid the harm that might be caused to the rights of the defence of the undertaking if the Commission were to read the content of a confidential file and improperly add it to the case file.[74]

Legal professional privilege is not absolute and several limitations to its substance can be discerned from case law.[75] First, the documents that are required by the Commission should concern confidential written communication between lawyer and client. An undertaking that invokes LPP and refuses to produce written communications between itself and its lawyer should provide the Commission with relevant material demonstrating that the communications fall under LPP.[76] Second, LPP does not extend to in-house lawyers. According to the Court of First Instance and the Court of Justice, only communications between clients and independent lawyers who are not bound to clients through an employment relationship fall within the scope of the privilege.[77]

iii. Right to Respect for Private Life and Inviolability of the Home

Under Union law, the right to respect for private life is guaranteed for everyone (Article 7 of the Charter). The right corresponds to Article 8 ECHR, and the case law

[72] See Widdershoven and Craig (n 32) 338. See also *Campbell v UK* App No 13590/88 (ECtHR, 25 March 1992).

[73] Joined Cases T-125/03 and T-253/03 *Akzo and Akcros* ECLI:EU:T:2007:58; *Akzo and Akcros v Commission* (n 23).

[74] *Akzo and Akros* (n 73) paras 77 and 87.

[75] See Widdershoven and Craig (n 32) 338.

[76] *Akzo and Akros* (n 73) paras 79–80. Consequently, the mere fact that an undertaking states that a document is protected does not suffice.

[77] ibid para 168; *Akzo and Akcros v Commission* (n 23) para 49. See also Case 155/79 *AM and S v Commission* ECLI:EU:C:1982:157, para 24. This distinction follows from the distinct role of an independent lawyer: he or she collaborates in the administration of justice by courts and is required to provide, in full independence and in the interest of the administration of justice, the assistance the client needs. The Court of Justice has explicitly stated that an in-house lawyer does not enjoy a same degree of independence and has much closer ties with the undertaking by which he or she is employed.

of the ECtHR should be taken into account to establish the meaning and scope of the right.[78] We focus specifically on the right to respect for private life with regard to inviolability of the home.[79] It should be acknowledged that the ECtHR has long attributed an autonomous meaning to the notion of 'home', which does not depend on a statutory classification under national law. Consequently, the locations that can fall under the protection of the right to inviolability of the home are quite diverse, and the ECtHR famously ruled that business premises are also included.[80] Although the Court of Justice had long restricted the right to inviolability of the home to private persons, it followed the broad approach of the ECtHR and accepted that businesses could also rely upon the right.[81]

The right to respect for private life is not absolute and can be limited in accordance with the Charter. The search of private or business premises and the seizure of documents constitute examples of interferences with the right to respect for private life and inviolability of the home.[82] In short, the requirement that an interference should be prescribed by law not only entails that there is legal basis in domestic law, but also relates to the quality of the law. The law should be compatible with the rule of law, which supposes that it is formulated in clear terms, but also that it is foreseeable and accessible.[83] The legal basis in domestic law should provide protection against arbitrary interferences by the authorities. In that regard, the availability of safeguards that protect against abuse and arbitrariness should be taken into account.[84]

The Court of Justice has recognised that prior judicial authorisation constitutes an important safeguard in the light of Article 7 of the Charter, but the lack of a prior warrant does not amount to a violation of the right. An ex-post judicial review can also satisfy the requirements, as long as the national court can assess the legality and the necessity of the measure.[85] For the context of vertical cooperation, the Court of Justice has ruled that the judicial review that is performed during judicial authorisation cannot concern an autonomous assessment of the need for the measure, which

[78] *Explanations relating to the Charter of Fundamental Rights* [2007] OJ C303/02. See also *Deutsche Bahn AG v Commission* (n 32) para 19.

[79] Evidently, the right to respect for private life is also highly relevant with regard to other investigative measures, such as the interception of telecommunications. In that regard, see *WebMindLicences* (n 37). Although the general approach of the Court of Justice and ECtHR is similar for all investigative measures that constitute infringements of the right to respect for private life, the relevance and assessment of specific criteria can diverge. In that regard, it can also depend on whether the case concerns the right of a natural or legal person.

[80] *Niemietz v Germany* App no 13710/88 (ECtHR, 16 December 1992) paras 30–33; *Colas Est v France* App no 37971/97 (ECtHR 16 April 2002) paras 41–42.

[81] Joined Cases 46/87 and 227/88 *Hoechst AG v Commission* ECLI:EU:C:1989:337, paras 17–18; Case 85/87 *Dow Benelux v Commission* ECLI:EU:C:1989:379, paras 28–29; *Roquette Frères SA* (n 31) para 52.

[82] *Deutsche Bahn AG v Commission* (n 32) para 19. See also *Murray v UK* App no 14310/88 (ECtHR, 28 October 1994) para 86; *Funke v France* (n 70) para 48.

[83] *Bykov v Russia* App no 4378/02 (ECtHR 10 March 2009) para 76.

[84] *Roman Zakharov v Russia* App no 47143/06 (ECtHR, 4 December 2015) para 232.

[85] *Deutsche Bahn AG v Commission* (n 32) paras 25–26. See Jans, Prechal and Widdershoven (eds) (n 1) 316–17.

is reserved to the Community judicature. The assessment by the national court must only allow it to establish that the coercive measures applied for are not arbitrary and that they are proportionate to the subject matter of the investigation.[86]

C. Non-Regression and More Protection – The Role of National Standards

As mentioned in section IV.B, the standards under the Charter should be complied with *at minimum* during all proceedings that fall within the scope of Union law. But what about the role of national standards in the Member States? Member States often have their own constitutional or statutory standards that determine domestic enforcement proceedings. What role do such national standards have in light of the primary role of the Charter? Is it permissible for Member States to adopt higher national standards compared to Union law? For example, can Member States extend the protection of the privilege against self-incrimination to documents that exist independently of the will of the accused, or can they decide that LPP covers in-house lawyers as well, in accordance with national law? In composite proceedings, the pressing question is not only whether national fundamental rights standards can be taken into account during enforcement actions – for example the gathering of evidence – but also whether those standards can be relied upon to perform judicial review in the forum State of evidence obtained at another EU level or in another EU Member State, and, potentially, to exclude such evidence from the punitive proceedings if it does not comply with the national standard.

Article 53 of the Charter establishes that it should not be interpreted as restricting or adversely affecting human rights and fundamental freedoms as recognised, in their respective fields of application, by Union law and international law and by international agreements to which the Union, the Community or all the Member States are party, including the ECHR, and by the Member States' constitutions. In short, this 'non-regression clause' guarantees that the level of protection offered within the scope of EU law cannot be lowered on the basis of the Charter, and consequently ensures that the maximum level of fundamental rights protection shall apply.[87] Nevertheless, Member States are not always allowed to invoke (higher) national standards within the scope of Union law.

In *Melloni*, the Court of Justice ruled that Article 53 neither established the general authorisation for the Member States to apply a higher standard of protection of fundamental rights on the basis of the national constitution, nor entailed that a higher national standard had automatic primacy over Union law.[88] Such an interpretation of the Charter would undermine the effectiveness of EU law and the principles of mutual trust and mutual recognition. Instead, the Court of Justice held that Article 53 provides

[86] See *Hoechst AG v Commission* (n 81) para 45; Case C-94/00 *Roquette Frères SA* (n 31) paras 39–40.

[87] de Hert (n 51) 111.

[88] Case C-399/11 *Melloni* ECLI:EU:C:2013:107, para 57. See also Jans, Prechal and Widdershoven (eds) (n 1) 160.

that, where an EU legal act calls for national implementing measures, national authorities and courts remain free to apply national standards of protection of fundamental rights, as long as the level of protection offered by the Charter and the primacy, unity and effectiveness of EU law are not compromised as a result.[89]

But how must the requirements from *Melloni* be interpreted and understood? The fact that the minimum level of protection offered by the Charter must be upheld does not raise many questions. But what do the notions of 'primacy', 'unity' and 'effectiveness' entail, and how do they limit the application of national fundamental rights standards by Member States? The Court of Justice has never specifically elaborated the aforementioned notions, but we would submit the following interpretation: if the Union legislator has *not* fully harmonised the applicable standard, a Member State *may* apply national fundamental rights standards, *unless* (i) the standard under national law conflicts with the regulated EU standard; (ii) divergence between non-harmonised national fundamental rights standards jeopardises the uniform application of harmonised substantive norms in a distinctly 'European' policy area; and/or (iii) the national standard precludes 'effective and dissuasive' enforcement of substantive Union policies in the Member State and its disapplication does not infringe fundamental rights.

First, *primacy* can limit the application of national standards. This will be the case if the national standard conflicts with the fundamental rights standard that has been regulated at the EU level. In case of conflict, the regulated EU standard takes precedence and there will be no room for the national standard.[90] In turn, *unity* can restrict the application of national standards if divergence between non-harmonised national fundamental rights standards jeopardises the uniform application of harmonised substantive norms in the EU. In that regard, we would submit the basic rule of thumb that there will be *less* room for national standards if substantive policy fields are *more* 'European' and, conversely, *more* room for such standards in substantive policy fields that are *less* 'European'. In our view, EU competition law and the Single Supervisory Mechanism (SSM) are excellent examples of substantive policy fields where unity can limit the room for national standards in the vertical context. In addition, we would suggest that unity might play a similar role in horizontal composite enforcement proceedings in the context of the General Data Protection Regulation (GDPR), as the rules in that field are highly uniform.[91]

The way in which unity can restrict the room for national standards may be illustrated by the ruling of the Court of Justice in the competition case of *Akzo Nobel and Akros*.[92] The case concerned, inter alia, the application of the national standard of LLP. While the substantive rules in EU competition law have been harmonised at the Union level, their enforcement fell to the Commission and national competition authorities together. The standard of LLP differed between the national laws of Member States, as well as between national laws and Union law. In this light, it was questioned which standard of LLP applied: the national standard or the – less protective – EU

[89] *Melloni* (n 88) para 60.

[90] See Jans, Prechal and Widdershoven (eds) (n 1) 39–40.

[91] Regulation (EU) 2016/679 on the protection of natural persons with regard to the processing of personal data and on the free movement of such data [2016] OJ L119/1.

[92] *Akzo and Akros v Commission* (n 23).

standard? Although the Union legislator had not elaborated a harmonised standard for LLP – which would prohibit national competition authorities from applying their national fundamental rights standards on the basis of primacy – and in spite of the principle of national autonomy, the Court of Justice ruled that the uniform interpretation and application of the principle of LLP at the EU level was essential to ensure that inspections by the Commission in competition law proceedings could be carried out under equal conditions, including equal standards of fundamental rights protection. The Court acknowledged that if this were not the case, 'the use of rules or legal concepts in national law and deriving from the legislation of a Member State would adversely affect *the unity* of European Union law'.[93] In other words, if national law were to determine the standard of protection, the application and enforcement of substantive competition rules would inevitably differ between the Member States while those rules should necessarily apply identically across the Member States. In this light, the Court of Justice ruled that it was not allowed to apply the national standard of LLP.[94] While the relevant investigations in *Akzo Nobel and Akros* were carried out by the Commission, we would argue that the outcome would have been similar if national authorities had assisted the Commission and/or acted on its behalf; after all, if they were allowed to invoke their national standards, this would similarly result in a normative patchwork, which the Court seeks to prevent in competition matters.

Third, the restriction on the application of national standards by 'effectiveness' has been assessed by the Court of Justice in light of the Union obligation of Member States to establish and impose 'effective and dissuasive' penalties to enforce substantive Union policies.[95] In several cases, the Court of Justice was required to decide whether national fundamental rights standards should be disapplied to ensure such 'effective and dissuasive' penalties. Most importantly, in *Taricco*, the Court of Justice assessed the Italian statute of limitation in light of the Union obligation to impose penalties for VAT fraud. In short, the national limitation rule for VAT fraud was over-protective: it rendered it practically impossible to impose penalties, and had the effect that, in a considerable number of cases, the commission of serious VAT fraud would escape criminal prosecution due to time-bars.[96] The Union legislator had not harmonised the statute of limitation for VAT offences.

In its judgment, the Court of Justice ruled that the Italian statute of limitation should be disapplied to ensure the 'effectiveness and dissuasiveness' of penalties for VAT fraud, but it also acknowledged that the fundamental rights of the person concerned – for example the principle of legality of criminal sanctions – needed to be upheld.[97] The Court of Justice subsequently elaborated and conditioned its ruling from *Taricco*, most notably in the case of *MAS and MB*.[98] In essence, it recognised that Italy was

[93] ibid para 115.

[94] ibid para 119.

[95] See *Commission v Greece* (n 57).

[96] Case C-105/14 *Taricco* ECLI:EU:C:2015:555. See also Case C-612/15 *Kolev and Others* ECLI:EU:C:2018:392. In *Kolev and Others*, the offences themselves did not become time-barred, but Bulgarian law dictated that the *prosecution* should be terminated after a specific period had elapsed and the public prosecutor had not completed his investigation.

[97] *Taricco* (n 96) para 53.

[98] Case C-42/17 *MAS and MB* ECLI:EU:C:2017:936.

allowed to apply its national standard of fundamental rights protection as long as the applicable standard had not been set at the Union level: the principle of legality precluded the disapplication of the Italian statute of limitation in proceedings concerning persons who were suspected of VAT fraud committed *before* the ruling in *Taricco*.[99]

V. The Principles of Mutual Trust and Mutual Recognition and the Intensity of Judicial Review in Composite Proceedings

In vertical and horizontal enforcement proceedings, the competent (Union or national) court must review the proceedings, including the way in which relevant evidence has been gathered and used, to guarantee compliance with the minimum standards from the Charter (see section IV). But how intense can or should judicial scrutiny be? Is the national court of a Member State allowed to review whether authorities in another Member State or Union authorities have complied with the applicable standard?

In this context, we touch upon the principles of mutual trust and mutual recognition in the EU. Although mutual trust is not expressly mentioned in the Treaties or the Charter, it constitutes an overarching principle that underlies the whole EU integration process.[100] In recent years, the Court of Justice has primarily elaborated upon mutual trust in the context of the AFSJ, but the principle also extends to the internal market; in fact, it was introduced in the internal market in the 1970s and has proved to be a pivotal driver for integration ever since.[101] What are the foundations of the principle of mutual trust under Union law? What does the principle entail, and how does it determine the relationships between Member States or between national and EU authorities in the enforcement context? And what does mutual trust mean in practice? For instance, does mutual trust amount to a quasi-absolute rule of non-inquiry, precluding review of decisions, measures or actions from other Member States, or can its implementation also be more nuanced?

A. Foundations of Mutual Trust in the EU

Before we elaborate on what mutual trust entails and how the principle functions in practice, its foundation in EU law merits attention. In short, the principle of mutual

[99] ibid paras 59–60. In this regard, the wording of the Court of Justice suggests that the outcome will be different for proceedings concerning VAT fraud committed *after* the judgment in *Taricco*. After all, the disapplication of the Italian statute of limitation was foreseeable after the ruling of the Court of Justice, which, in turn, means that disapplying the limitation rule in 'post-*Taricco*' cases would not infringe the principle of legality.

[100] See C Rizcallah, 'The Challenges to Trust Based Governance in the European Union: Assessing the Use of Mutual Trust as a Driver of EU Integration' (2019) 25 *European Law Journal* 37.

[101] In this context, see N Cambien, 'Mutual Recognition and Mutual Trust in the Internal Market' (2017) 2 *European Papers* 93, 9596. See also Case C-420/19 *Maksu-ja Tolliamet vs Heavyinstall OÜ* ECLI:EU:C:2021:33, paras 40 et seq.

trust is based upon the premise that Member States share and recognise that they share common values, which, in turn, justifies trust that these values are acknowledged and upheld despite the undeniable differences between their legal orders.[102] As mentioned before, the Treaties and the Charter do not feature an explicit legal base for the principle of mutual trust, but we would submit that mutual trust rests upon several interconnected pillars.

First and foremost, the EU is founded on the values of respect for human dignity, freedom, democracy, equality, the rule of law and respect for human rights (Article 2 TEU). These values are shared by the Member States, and upholding them constitutes an essential requirement for membership of the Union.[103] The protection of fundamental rights and adherence to the rule of law are especially relevant for the existence of mutual trust: the Court of Justice has acknowledged that the principle of mutual trust requires that Member States consider each other to be complying with fundamental rights in particular, and consequently such rights are at the 'heart of the structure' of EU law.[104] Second, the principle of equality under the Treaties (Article 4(2) TEU) guarantees that all EU Member States are equal, despite their differences. Consequently, Member States should trust that they abide by the aforementioned values in equal though not necessarily identical ways.[105] Third, the principle of sincere cooperation has a role, as it ensures that Member States must endeavour to uphold the values from the Treaties. This means that they should take all appropriate measures to ensure fulfilment of the obligations arising out of the Treaties and facilitate the achievement of the Union's tasks, but must also refrain from any measure that could jeopardise the attainment of those objectives.[106] In this light, the principle of sincere cooperation reinforces the duty to uphold fundamental rights and the rule of law, and determines the relationship between Member States: they should, inter alia, trust each other to be loyal to their Union obligations.[107]

Although the principle of mutual trust is often assessed in the context of horizontal cooperation between the national authorities of different Member States, we would argue that it also determines – *cum grano salis* – the vertical relationship between Member States and EU institutions.[108] After all, EU institutions should uphold the common values – most notably, the rule of law – as well, and are bound by the Charter too. Moreover, it has been recognised that the principle of sincere cooperation also determines the relationship between Member States and EU institutions.[109]

[102] S Prechal, 'Mutual Trust Before the Court of Justice of the European Union' (2017) 2 *European Papers* 75, 81. See also *LM* (n 48) para 35; *Commission v Poland* (n 10) paras 42–43.

[103] *Opinion 2/13* (n 48) para 168; *LM* (n 48) para 35; *Commission v Poland* (n 10) paras 42–43. See also P Craig and G de Búrca, *EU Law: Text, Cases, and Materials* (Oxford University Press 2020) 44 ff.

[104] *Opinion 2/13* (n 48) para 169.

[105] K Lenaerts, 'La vie après l'avis: Exploring the Principle of Mutual (Yet Not Blind) Trust' (2017) 54 *CML Rev* 805, 808–09.

[106] *Opinion 2/13* (n 48) para 173.

[107] A Klip, *European Criminal Law* (Intersentia 2016) 72.

[108] M Luchtman, A Karagianni and K Bovend'Eerdt, 'EU Administrative Investigations and the Use of Their Results as Evidence in National Punitive Proceedings' in Giuffrida and Ligeti (eds) (n 2) 15.

[109] *JJ Zwartveld and Others* (n 21).

B. Implementation of Mutual Trust – Rule of Non-Inquiry or Marginal Review?

In its case law, the Court of Justice has held that the principle of mutual trust is of fundamental importance in EU law, because it allows an area without internal borders to be created and maintained.[110] But what does mutual trust mean? According to the Court, mutual trust requires that Member States consider each other to be complying with EU law and fundamental rights in particular, save for in exceptional circumstances.[111] This is especially – but not *exclusively* – required for the functioning of the AFSJ.[112] Member States cannot impose their higher national standard of fundamental rights protection upon another Member State, but also cannot check whether the fundamental rights guaranteed by Union law have actually been observed in the other Member State.[113] But what if there are indications to the contrary? What if it is argued that fundamental rights have been or will be violated in another Member State? Does mutual trust amount to a rule of non-inquiry; and if so, how hard will that rule be?

To answer these complex questions, we would distinguish between what can be referred to as the 'regulated' and 'unregulated' implementation of mutual trust. Regulated mutual trust refers to the context where the Union legislator has exhaustively prescribed which facts and circumstances can be reviewed by the competent court and, consequently, has implemented mutual trust as a rule of non-inquiry concerning all facts and circumstances that *cannot* be brought under the harmonised grounds of review. In turn, unregulated mutual trust relates to the context where the principle is not effectuated through specific legal rules that determine what can and cannot be reviewed. Although the Union principle of mutual trust still governs the relationship between the competent authorities, the rule of non-inquiry is, at the minimum, less strict, and seems to allow marginal review of foreign measures and decisions.[114]

i. 'Regulated Mutual Trust' – Mutual Recognition and the Rule of Non-Inquiry

The Union instruments that are based upon the EU principle of mutual recognition constitute excellent paradigms of regulated mutual trust. Mutual recognition has been introduced and further developed in the internal market, and has long constituted a driving force for European integration. More recently, it has also obtained a central role in the AFSJ, where it has been fittingly characterised as the 'cornerstone' of horizontal cooperation between judicial authorities across the Member States.[115] Although a legislative definition does not exist, mutual recognition essentially entails the quasi-automatic recognition and execution of, among other things, judicial decisions and investigative measures from other Member States, which obtain the same legal value as their national

[110] *Opinion 2/13* (n 48) para 191.
[111] ibid.
[112] ibid. See also Luchtman, Karagianni and Bovend'Eerdt (n 108).
[113] *Opinion 2/13* (n 48) para 192.
[114] See Luchtman, Karagianni and Bovend'Eerdt (n 108).
[115] V Mitsilegas, *EU Criminal Law after Lisbon* (Hart Publishing 2018) 125.

equivalents.[116] Unsurprisingly, the system of mutual recognition is firmly based upon the Union principle of mutual trust: Member States can be required to recognise each other's decisions or measures, because it should be assumed they all comply with Union law and adhere to common values, albeit not necessarily in an identical manner.[117]

Mutual recognition encompasses an obligation to recognise and execute decisions from another Member State, and execution may or must only be refused if one of the exhaustively listed grounds for refusal applies. In its case law, the Court of Justice has recognised that refusal to execute constitutes an exception to the rule of execution, and that refusal grounds must be interpreted strictly.[118] Consequently, the review of foreign decisions or measures should be strictly limited to the refusal grounds that have been regulated by the Union legislator; facts and circumstances that cannot trigger a ground for refusal can, in principle, not be assessed and are covered by a quasi-absolute rule of non-inquiry.

The aforementioned characteristics can be illustrated through a brief assessment of the EIO Directive.[119] In short, an EIO entails a decision that has been issued or validated by a judicial authority of a Member State to have one or more specific investigative measures carried out in another Member State to gather evidence, or to obtain evidence that is already held by the authorities in another Member State.[120] In accordance with the principle of mutual recognition, an incoming EIO shall be executed, unless one of the exhaustively listed grounds for refusal applies.[121] For example, execution may be refused if it would be contrary to the principle of *ne bis in idem*, or if it would be at odds with the obligation to protect fundamental rights in accordance with the Treaties and the Charter. The review in the executing Member State should be limited to the applicable grounds for refusal; arguments concerning facts and circumstances that do not fall within the scope of those grounds should be addressed in the issuing Member State instead. The EIO Directive also explicitly states that while the national remedies of the executing Member State apply mutatis mutandis, the substantive reasons to issue

[116] Commission, 'Mutual Recognition of Final Decisions in Criminal Matters' (Communication) COM (2000) 0495 final. See also L Klimek, *Mutual Recognition of Judicial Decisions in European Criminal Law* (Springer 2017) 6.

[117] *LM* (n 48) para 36; Case C-270/17 *Tupikas* ECLI:EU:C:2017:628, para 49. See also Klip (n 107) 101; Prechal (n 102) 76; Lenaerts (n 105) 812.

[118] See eg Case C-66/08 *Kozłowski* ECLI:EU:C:2008:437, para 43; Case C-123/08 *Wolzenburg* ECLI:EU:C:2009:616, para 57; Case C-261/09 *Mantello* ECLI:EU:C:2010:683, para 37; *Tupikas* (n 117) paras 49–50; Case C-854/19 *Staatsanwaltschaft Wien* ECLI:EU:C:2020:1002, para 64.

[119] In this context, see also M Böse, M Bröcker and A Schneider (eds), *Judicial Protection in Transnational Criminal Proceedings* (Springer 2021) 2.

[120] Although most mutual recognition instruments exclusively concern criminal law *sensu stricto*, the EIO can also extend to punitive administrative proceedings, provided they can give rise to proceedings before 'a court having jurisdiction in particular in criminal matters'. The Court of Justice has held that this concept constitutes an autonomous concept of Union law and must be interpreted as covering any court or tribunal that applies a procedure satisfying the essential characteristics of criminal procedure; see Case C-60/12 *Baláž* ECLI:EU:C:2013:733, para 42. Moreover, in addition to judicial authorities – eg, a judge, a court, an investigative judge or a public prosecutor – national law can also award the competence to any other authority that, in the specific case, is acting as an investigative authority with the competence to order the gathering of evidence in criminal proceedings or punitive administrative proceedings. Consequently, administrative authorities can also issue an EIO, although it should always be validated by a judicial authority prior to its transmission to the authorities in another Member State; see Klimek (n 116) 440.

[121] Klimek (n 116) 445 and 451.

an EIO – for example the reasonable suspicion or similar requirements – can *only* be challenged in the issuing Member State. Hence, the authorities in the executing Member States are precluded from assessing or verifying the substantive reasons and, as a result, are held to trust their foreign counterparts when national remedies are launched against the execution of the EIO or its implementation.[122]

It should be observed that the Court of Justice has acknowledged circumstances that are so exceptional that they warrant limits to the principles of mutual trust and mutual recognition even if no ground for refusal applies in the context of the European Arrest Warrant (EAW) mechanism. In *Aranyosi and Căldăraru*, the Court had to decide if a real risk of violation of the prohibition of inhuman and degrading treatment – which constitutes an absolute right under the Charter – in the issuing Member State could justify the refusal to execute an EAW; while the Court had to rule in *LM* whether an EAW could be refused in light of recent reforms of the Polish judiciary that affected the independence of courts and, therefore, compromised the essence of the right to a fair trial.[123] In both cases the Court ruled that mutual trust and mutual recognition had fundamental importance under EU law, but that they did not have an absolute character and could be set aside.[124] The real risk of inhuman and degrading treatment or violation of the essence of the right to a fair trial amounted to 'exceptional circumstances', which could preclude the execution of an EAW, but it should be established that such risks applied to the person concerned himself.

ii. 'Unregulated Mutual Trust' – The Intensity of Judicial Review of the Use of Evidence

Earlier we stated that the principle of mutual trust defines the relationship between the Member States, as well as between Member States and EU authorities, even if there are no specific legal rules that implement the principle (see section V.A). However, it can be questioned whether mutual trust will still amount to a strict rule of non-inquiry that precludes national and EU authorities from performing *any* review. No definitive answer can be provided, but we submit that it *will* be permissible – and, in fact, that it may even be required under Union law – to perform a review of foreign decisions or measures, but that this review should be marginal and limited to safeguarding the overall fairness of the proceedings.

To illustrate this, we draw attention to judicial review of the use of evidence in punitive proceedings in the (i) bottom-up vertical and (ii) top-down vertical context, as well as in (iii) the horizontal context. In principle, the rules of evidence have not been harmonised within the EU. This means that there are no specific legal rules that implement the

[122] Art 14(2) EIO Directive. See also *Gavanozov II* Opinion of AG Bobek (n 40) paras 35–36.

[123] Joined Cases C-404/15 and C-659/15 PPU *Aranyosi and Căldăraru* ECLI:EU:C:2016:198; *LM* (n 48). Despite the fact that the cases of *Aranyosi and Căldăraru* and *LM* both concern the implementation of EAWs, the discussion of the equilibrium between mutual trust and fundamental rights protection is not unique to the context of surrender. For example, the relationship between both principles has also been hotly debated in asylum matters, see Joined Cases C-411/10 and C-493/10 *NS and Others* ECLI:EU:C:2011:865. See also Prechal (n 102) 77.

[124] *Aranyosi and Căldăraru* (n 123); *LM* (n 48). In this context, see also Klip (n 107) 434; Prechal (n 102) 85; Lenaerts (n 105) 834 ff.

principle of mutual trust for evidence matters. Are EU and national courts precluded from reviewing evidence that was obtained in another legal order in light of the fact that the principle of mutual trust requires Member States to consider each other to be complying with EU law and fundamental rights in particular?

a. The Bottom-Up Vertical Context – *FSL Holdings* and Required Marginal Review

In the vertical context, the competition case of *FSL Holdings* and the Opinion of Advocate General Kokott in particular are highly relevant.[125] In short, the case concerned the use as evidence by the Commission during punitive proceedings of incriminating private notes obtained by the Italian Finance Police (bottom-up). It was argued by the defence that the evidence had been gathered in 'complete disregard of the fundamental rights of the person concerned' and could therefore not be relied upon by the Commission. In essence, the argument was whether the Commission could rely upon the evidence, and whether its use could be subjected to a review by the EU courts to ascertain its (un)lawfulness.

In her Opinion, Advocate General Kokott clarified that competition offences can be demonstrated by any appropriate evidence: unfettered evaluation of evidence constitutes the prevailing principle, and the only relevant criterion for the purpose of assessing the evidence is its credibility.[126] The use of evidence by the Commission is exceptionally precluded if it is subject to a prohibition that is based on the fact that evidence was obtained in breach of essential procedural requirements intended to protect the individual concerned, or that evidence is used for an unlawful purpose.[127] The Advocate General subsequently acknowledged that the gathering and transfer of evidence was governed by national law and that EU courts did not have jurisdiction to rule on the lawfulness, but that this did not mean that the Commission or EU courts may 'knowingly rely upon evidence which was quite clearly obtained in breach of essential procedural requirements'.[128] In this light, the Advocate General stated that fundamental principles of EU law, such as the right to a fair trial and the right to good administration, *require* at least a summary examination of all circumstances of the case that are known to them.[129]

Compared to the Opinion, the judgment of the Court of Justice is quite concise and does not specifically elaborate on the possibility of review and its intensity; but the approach proposed by the Advocate General is not rejected and the Court – albeit

[125] See Case C-469/15 P *FSL Holdings* ECLI:EU:C:2017:308; Case C-469/15 P *FSL Holdings* ECLI:EU:C:2016:884, Opinion of AG Kokott.

[126] *FSL Holdings* Opinion of AG Kokott (n 125) paras 31–33.

[127] ibid para 34.

[128] ibid para 37. See J Vervaele, 'Lawful and Fair Use of Evidence from a European Human Rights Perspective' in Giuffrida and Ligeti (eds) (n 2) 78–79.

[129] *FSL Holdings* Opinion of AG Kokott (n 125) para 37. In the case at hand, there were indications that the evidence had been gathered lawfully: the Italian courts had not opposed the transmission of evidence even though the appellants had, according to their own statements, exercised their rights on the national level. Therefore, AG Kokott concluded that the evidence could be used by the Commission.

impliedly – accepts that the Commission and General Court have performed a review on the gathering and use of the evidence.[130] Although it is difficult to draw definitive conclusions from *FSL Holdings*, it is clear that no strict rule of non-inquiry was upheld. In this light, we deduce from the case that the principle of mutual trust did not, in the view of the Advocate General and the Court of Justice, preclude EU Courts from performing *any* review of evidence obtained by national authorities in Member States (bottom-up); in fact, according to Advocate General Kokott – and we tend to agree – they can even be required to conduct a *marginal* review to ensure that the evidence is not unlawful.[131]

b. The Top-Down Vertical Context – *Foto-Frost* and Preliminary Ruling

While we would argue that the principle of mutual trust also determines the relationship between EU and national authorities in top-down vertical proceedings, the review of evidence also raises additional questions. What if a national court were to find that an EEA has (possibly) violated the applicable standard? Can it then perform a review of the evidence and exclude it from the proceedings?

The Court of Justice famously ruled in *Foto-Frost* that national courts cannot invalidate EU actions as that competence is reserved to EU Courts.[132] Although the review of evidence that has been obtained by EU authorities and, possibly, its exclusion from the proceedings in the Member State do not strictly concern an *invalidation* of EU action, the unity and coherence of Union law – which formed the rationale of the ruling in *Foto-Frost* – could still be compromised; after all, the central matter is not whether evidence is accurate, reliable and sufficient to form the basis of a *national* sanctioning decision, but rather whether an EU authority has acted contrary to the applicable *Union* standard or – provided that it is allowed under the *Melloni* requirements (see section IV.C) – national law.[133] If the applicable standard is set by national law, the competent court in the Member State is required to assess compliance with that standard. However, if the applicable standard is decided by Union law, the national court cannot perform a review if it would find that the EEA has violated the standard. Instead, the court should refer the case to the Court of Justice for a preliminary ruling (see section III).

[130] *FSL Holdings* (n 124) paras 33–34. See also Luchtman, Karagianni and Bovend'Eerdt (n 108) 20.

[131] In this context, see Luchtman, Karagianni and Bovend'Eerdt (n 108) 20. Luchtman, Karagianni and Bovend'Eerdt raise an interesting question: would the outcome in *FSL Holdings* have been different if the transfer of evidence had taken place within the context of the European Competition Network (ECN) between the Italian competition authority and the Commission? Within the ECN, specific rules govern the transfer and admissibility of evidence. Evidence that is transferred can only be used to impose sanctions if the law of the transmitting authority foresees sanctions of a similar kind for competition offences or, in the absence thereof, the information has been collected in a way that respects the same level of protection of the rights of defence of natural persons as provided for under the national rules of the receiving authority. In this light, it is certainly possible that the Court of Justice would accept a rule of non-inquiry, but it is not certain.

[132] Case 314/85 *Foto-Frost* ECLI:EU:C:1987:452. See Luchtman, Karagianni and Bovend'Eerdt (n 108) 22–23.

[133] Luchtman, Karagianni and Bovend'Eerdt (n 108) 23.

c. The Horizontal Context – Review of Evidence Obtained in Another Member State

Because the rules of evidence have not been harmonised at the EU level, it is primarily left to national law to determine the applicable standard of proof, but also whether and, if so, under which conditions national as well as foreign evidence can be used for punitive purposes. National law decides when the available evidence suffices to impose a punitive sanction, and national authorities and courts are free in their assessment of the probative value of evidence. In this light, there is no obligation to use evidence, and it is permissible to discard national and foreign evidence that has been gathered unlawfully or in violation of fundamental rights, provided that the Union principles of equivalence and effectiveness are complied with.[134] But what if national authorities do want to use foreign evidence, for example if an offence can *only* be proved through such evidence?

Although the rules of evidence are found in national law, the Court of Justice has touched upon evidence matters in several judgments and has established broad EU parameters concerning the use of evidence. First and foremost, the gathering, sharing and use of evidence within the scope of Union law should be in accordance with the Charter, and national courts must be able to assess whether the Charter has been complied with.[135] If evidence is gathered, shared or used in violation of the Charter, it is – in the absence of EU rules – left to national law to decide the consequences of the breach; and while Member States may opt for a 'strict' approach, where unlawfully obtained evidence is excluded, in principle Union law does not impose an obligation upon Member States to discard unlawful evidence.[136] In fact, the Court of Justice has acknowledged that other solutions to address violations of fundamental rights are also acceptable, for example national rules and practices governing the assessment and weighting of evidence ('balancing'), or by factoring in whether that material is unlawful when determining the sentence.[137] It seems that Union law only requires the exclusion of evidence if its use would violate the right to a fair trial.[138]

In its case law the Court of Justice has had the opportunity to assess evidence matters through the lens of 'domestic' proceedings only, and it has not yet been required to elaborate the rules of evidence for a composite setting involving several Member States. Therefore, it remains unclear whether the Court of Justice will adopt a more limited approach in composite proceedings, especially in light of the EU principle of mutual

[134] In this context, see also Widdershoven and Craig (n 32) 349.

[135] *WebMindLicences* (n 37) para 87.

[136] See eg, Case C-310/16 *Dzivev and Others* ECLI:EU:C:2019:30, paras 38–39; Joined Cases C-511/18, C-512/18 and C-520/18 *La Quadrature du Net and Others* ECLI:EU:C:2020:791, paras 221 et seq; Case C-746/18 *HK v Prokuratuur* ECLI:EU:C:2021:152, paras 41 et seq.

[137] *La Quadrature du Net and Others* (n 136) para 225; *HK v Prokuratuur* (n 136) para 43.

[138] Vervaele (n 128) 79. In its recent considerations concerning evidence, the Court of Justice seems to align its case law with that of the ECtHR, see *Ibrahim and Others v UK* (n 66) para 254; *Bykov v Russia* (n 83) 89. Breaches of fundamental rights during the gathering and sharing of evidence can prejudice the fairness of the trial beyond repair and, thus, require the exclusion of evidence; but it is also possible that the use of evidence would itself render the procedure unfair. For instance, if evidence is lawfully obtained and subsequently transferred from a non-punitive procedure to proceedings of a criminal nature, the rights of the defence (Art 48 of the Charter) could be compromised, and if a court is altogether unable to perform a review concerning the (lawfulness of) evidence this negates the 'effectiveness' of judicial protection required for a fair trial (Article 47 of the Charter). In this context, see *DB v Consob* (n 65) para 44; *WebMindLicences* (n 37) paras 87–88. See also ch 1 (Luchtman) and ch 9 (Vervaele) of this volume.

trust. We would argue that the Court must, at a minimum, allow a marginal review by competent national courts if fundamental rights are at stake.[139] While the principle of mutual trust entails that Member States must presume compliance with fundamental rights and cannot check whether the fundamental rights guaranteed by Union law have actually been observed in other Member States, the principle can – in our view – not preclude competent courts from verifying that the proceedings remain compatible with the Charter.

First and foremost, it should be permissible for courts to conduct a marginal review of transnational proceedings when it is argued that the use of evidence from another Member State would violate the right to a fair trial.[140] Articles 47 and 48 of the Charter constitute the standard that must be complied with instead of national procedural safeguards or defence rights; in other words, the fact that specific procedural safeguards or defence rights under national law have not been complied with does not necessarily mean that evidence will be excluded, because the focus is on the 'proceedings as a whole', which leaves ample room for compensation. The judicial review of violations of other fundamental rights from the Charter – most notably, the right to respect for private life – in another Member State is also required, but violations need not lead to the exclusion of evidence, as in principle they do not jeopardise the fairness of the proceedings.[141]

Indeed, the focus on the fairness of the proceedings as a whole can already be discerned in national case law on the review of foreign evidence in Member States such as the Netherlands, Germany and France.[142] Although the EU principle of mutual trust is not always specifically mentioned by national courts, a study of their case law shows that the review of evidence that was obtained in another Member State is primarily concerned with an assessment of the fairness of the proceedings as a whole. In this regard, it must be recognised that the assessment of foreign proceedings that national courts must perform will often be quite challenging. Most notably, the competent court in the forum State may not always have all the required information to allow it to determine whether the proceedings – including the investigative measures that were performed in another Member State to obtain the evidence – were fair; the assessment of compliance with other fundamental rights from the Charter is similarly challenging.[143]

[139] In this context, see Case C-682/15 *Berlioz Investment Fund* (n 15); *État Luxembourgeois v B and Others* (n 16). In these cases, the Court of Justice recognised that the requested authorities and the competent court of review in the requested Member State may assess the legality of an incoming request for information on the basis of the Directive on tax cooperation (n 41), but do not have an unlimited jurisdiction to assess the legality. Due to the principle of mutual trust, they can only perform a limited review. Although the cases of *Berlioz Investment Fund* and *État Luxembourgeois v B and Others* do not concern the review of evidence in the forum Member State – but rather the review of foreign measures in the *requested* Member State – the approach of the Court of Justice still shows that mutual trust allows a marginal review in transnational cases.

[140] Luchtman, Karagianni and Bovend'Eerdt (n 108) 21.

[141] See *Khan v UK* App no 35394/97 (ECtHR, 12 May 2000); *Bykov v Russia* (n 83).

[142] See HR 1 December 2020, ECLI:NL:HR:2020:1889 and HR 5 October 2010, ECLI:NL:HR:2010:BL5629; BGH Decision of 21 November 2012 [2013] *Neue Zeitschrift für Strafrecht* 596; Crim 4 November 1997, n° 97-83.463 – Cassation and Crim. 12 June 2012, n° 12-81.024 – Cassation.

[143] See also ch 1 (Luchtman) and ch 3 (Ligeti and Robinson) of this volume.

C. Strengthening Vertical and Horizontal Cooperation between the Courts

In composite enforcement cases it will, in principle, be the court in the forum Member State that decides on (an appeal against) the imposition of a sanction. This court should sometimes exercise a legality assessment – albeit a marginal one – of the gathering of evidence in another Member State or, in vertical relations, at another (EU or national) level. In order to perform such an assessment, the court of review must have information about the course of events during an investigation or inspection; it may also be necessary for it to be informed in some way about the law concerning investigations of another Member State or at another level. The question is whether such cooperation between the courts is already possible or should be facilitated more extensively.

In respect of *top-down* vertical composite procedures, national courts are often empowered to refer preliminary questions of interpretation or validity of the EEA input-gathering process (Article 267 TFEU) (see section III.B).[144] Moreover, in validity cases the national court can request information from the EEA; this request should, in principle, be answered by the EEA.[145] Because this power is based on Article 4(3) TEU, it may arguably be used by national courts for gathering factual information from the EU level in general. Finally, national courts can request the EEA inspectors who conducted an investigation to appear as a witnesses before the court.[146] Similar cooperation mechanisms do not exist during *bottom-up* vertical procedures yet. In legal literature, it has been argued that the Court of Justice could rely upon Article 24 of the Statute of the Court of Justice – which allows the Court to 'require the Member States and institutions, bodies, offices and agencies, not being party to the case' to supply all information it considers necessary for the proceedings – to ask national courts for information about national laws.[147] In addition, several authors have proposed a so-called 'reverse preliminary ruling procedure', which could be used by the Court of Justice to request a ruling or an opinion of the highest national court on the interpretation of national law.[148] Similarly, it could be used for obtaining an impartial and authoritative description of the course of events during an investigation. This procedure could possibly find its legal basis in Article 4(3) TEU.

[144] As mentioned, the option for national courts to refer preliminary questions to the Court of Justice is restricted in the context of the EPPO (see section III.B). The EPPO Regulation expressly states that national courts may not refer to the Court of Justice preliminary questions on the validity of the procedural acts of the EPPO with regard to national procedural law or to national measures transposing directives, even if the Regulation refers to them. Preliminary references concerning the interpretation of EU primary law, including the Treaties and the Charter, or the interpretation and validity of any provision of Union secondary law, including the EPPO Regulation and applicable directives, can be made by national courts.

[145] *Eurobolt* (n 20).

[146] *JJ Zwartveld and Others* (n 21).

[147] Wissink (n 4) 297.

[148] H Hofmann, 'Composite Decision Making Procedures in EU Administrative Law' in H Hofmann and A Türk (eds), *Legal Challenges in EU Administrative Law: Towards an Integrated Administration* (Edward Elgar Publishing 2009) 159; SA de León, *Composite Administrative Procedures in the European Union* (Iustel 2017) 357–60; M Eliantonio 'Judicial Review in an Integrated Administration: The Case of "Composite Procedures"' (2014) 7 *Review of European Administrative Law* 65.

In *horizontal* composite procedures, it would also be desirable if the court of review in the forum Member State were allowed to ask a court in the Member State where the evidence was gathered for information on an investigation or an authoritative interpretation of the relevant law. The best-known example of the competence to request information and the corresponding duty to respond to such questions in horizontal procedures is found within the framework of the EAW.[149] Despite the fact that the EAW Framework Decision is based upon the principles of mutual recognition and mutual trust, the instrument establishes an explicit legal basis for a 'judicial dialogue' between the executing and issuing judicial authorities: if the former finds the information in the incoming EAW to be insufficient to allow it to decide on the surrender of a person, it can request additional information from the issuing judicial authority.[150] It must be recognised that the EIO Directive also establishes several options for consultation and information between the executing and issuing judicial authorities. However, those options only exist during the implementation of the EIO, and cannot be relied upon by the court of review in the forum Member State to obtain an impartial and authoritative description from the national court of the Member State where evidence was gathered pursuant to an EIO of the course of events during an investigation or an interpretation of the national law that determined the gathering of evidence.[151]

Even though options to request additional information are – especially in the context of mutual recognition instruments – rather scarce at present, we submit that their existence must not be regarded as an exception to the strict rules of non-inquiry and mutual trust, but rather as promising new paradigms that could enable more judicial dialogue between national courts in the future. Despite the fact that no specific legal basis allows the court of review in the forum State to engage in a 'judicial dialogue' with counterparts in other Member States, we would argue that, in so far as such judicial cooperation is necessary to guarantee effective judicial protection in composite procedures, such an obligation could be based provisionally on Article 4(3) TEU. Of course, it remains to be seen whether the Court of Justice would also opt for such an approach.

VI. Conclusions

It must be ensured that the enforcement of substantive Union policies is effective as well as compatible with the rule of law, including fundamental rights. In light of these requirements, composite vertical or horizontal punitive enforcement of Union law can raise many complicated questions. For example, which court is competent to

[149] Framework Decision 2002/584/JBZ on the European arrest warrant and the surrender procedures between Member States [2002] OJ L190/1.

[150] In this context, see eg *Aranyosi and Căldăraru* (n 123) paras 95–97; *LM* (n 48) paras 76–77.

[151] In the context of the EIO, the options of consultation and information allow the executing judicial authority to obtain information from the issuing judicial authority concerning, inter alia, the fulfilment of the conditions for issuing a decision, or inform that authority on the unavailability of specific investigative measures; see Arts 6(3) and 10(5) EIO Directive.

review enforcement action in the context of composite proceedings? Which fundamental rights standard must be taken into account during that judicial review? And how intense should that review be? In this contribution, we have examined these core questions in a conceptual manner. We have focused on models of composite enforcement instead of specific composite actions in designated areas of Union law. Moreover, we have assessed the most important constitutional principles that determine composite enforcement – effective judicial protection, compliance with fundamental rights, and mutual trust – instead of the detailed rules in the substantive policy field. What main conclusions can be drawn from our analysis?

First, the principle of effective judicial protection entails that individuals must be able to enforce all rights conferred on them by Union law before a court and, in that regard, obtain judicial review of enforcement actions. In composite proceedings, the competent court can be an EU or a national court, depending on the specific context. The number of competent courts may be limited to what is necessary to guarantee effective judicial protection. It is neither required nor feasible that the person concerned can challenge every individual step in composite enforcement procedures wherever or whenever. What should be guaranteed, however, is that the lawfulness of all these steps can be incidentally reviewed in the judicial procedure against the final decision taken on the basis of evidence gathered in those steps. Second, the principle of compliance with fundamental rights requires that enforcement action – implemented by either national or EU authorities – must always be compatible with the minimum standard of fundamental rights protection as guaranteed by the Charter. Although there may often be room for more protective national fundamental rights standards, Union law can set limits as to the maximum level of protection that may be offered by national law as well, in particular in highly Europeanised areas of law. Lastly, the principles of mutual trust and mutual recognition may significantly limit the intensity of review in composite punitive enforcement proceedings. The competent Union or national court does not have unlimited jurisdiction to review enforcement action that has taken place at another EU level or in another Member State, but a marginal review must be performed at a minimum. With regard to the judicial review of evidence, we have argued that courts should primarily assess whether the right to a fair trial within the meaning of Articles 47 and 48 of the Charter has been guaranteed, because EU law requires the exclusion of evidence if its use would violate the fairness of the proceedings as a whole under the Charter. In our view, compliance with other fundamental rights – most notably, the right to respect for private life – should be reviewed as well, but EU law does not require the exclusion of evidence obtained in violation of such other fundamental rights; other consequences – for example national rules and practices governing the assessment and weighting of evidence, or factoring in whether that material is unlawful when determining the sentence – will then suffice to address the violation.

3

Composite Enforcement and Comprehensive Judicial Protection

KATALIN LIGETI AND GAVIN ROBINSON*

I. Introduction

A. The Concept of Judicial Review and the Definition of 'Full Jurisdiction' According to the ECtHR

Judicial review is the means by which courts exercise their supervisory control over the administrative measures or penalties applied by a state enforcement agency.[1] The right to effective judicial protection, now enshrined in Article 47 of the Charter of Fundamental Rights of the European Union ('the Charter'), is an essential component of the rule of law within any legal system. Within the legal system of the European Union (EU), Article 47 provides that everyone whose rights and freedoms guaranteed by EU law are violated has the right to a fair and public hearing and an effective remedy within a reasonable time by an independent and impartial tribunal previously established by law.

The Union legal order, marked by the shared administration of EU institutions and national authorities, requires the principle of effective judicial protection to be realised at both national and Union level.[2] Article 19(1) of the Treaty on European Union (TEU) thus provides that Member States shall ensure that remedies sufficient to ensure effective legal protection in the fields covered by Union law are available. At Union level, the Treaty on the Functioning ot the European Union (TFEU) provides several routes for the review of the legality of legislative acts, of acts of the Council, of the Commission and of the European Central Bank (ECB), of the European Parliament and of the European

* The authors are greatly indebted to Dr Hannah Brodensen (Post-doctoral Researcher at the University of Neuchâtel) for her contributions and comments toward the making of this chapter.

[1] R Wilson QC, 'Judicial review. An introduction to the Key Principles' in P von Berg (ed), *Criminal Judicial Review: A Practitioner's Guide to Judicial Review in the Criminal Justice System and Related Areas* (Hart Publishing 2014) 3.

[2] See P Craig, *EU Administrative Law*, 2nd edn (Oxford University Press 2012) chs 22 and 23.

Council, and of bodies, offices or agencies of the Union intended to produce legal effects vis-à-vis third parties. The most important of these routes are actions for annulment launched against such acts,[3] and references for a preliminary ruling[4] concerning the interpretation and validity of such acts under EU law.

The completeness of judicial review takes on great importance in the context of investigations carried out either in part or entirely by EU institutions or agencies, and which may lead to the imposition of administrative and/or criminal penalties by that same institution or agency. In EU competition law, for instance, absent an adequate review mechanism, the Commission would in practice act as a *de facto* 'tribunal' without meeting the basic criteria of judicial independence.[5] There is thus a long-standing debate on whether the General Court exercises 'full jurisdiction' as defined by the Strasbourg jurisprudence – a debate that has recently been revived by the elevation of the Charter to Treaty status, the process of EU accession to the European Convention for the Protection of Human Rights and Fundamental Freedoms (ECHR), and the intensification of the Commission's fining policy over the course of the past decade.[6] Meanwhile, the newer 'composite administration' scenarios presented by the ECB and the European Securities and Markets Authority (ESMA) (wherein coercive measures and administrative sanctions may be actioned either autonomously or in cooperation with national authorities) and the 'composite inspections' carried out by national authorities along with the European Anti-Fraud Office (OLAF) all entail an interplay between (at least) two legal systems, which is liable to create uncertainty as to both the formal and substantive aspects of judicial review: respectively, which acts may be subject to judicial review before which court(s), and what the content of such a review ought to be.[7] This confusion risks substantially weakening the judicial review of investigative acts, to the direct (and often irreparable) detriment of the fundamental rights of those under scrutiny.[8]

The jurisprudence of the European Court of Human Rights (ECtHR) is clear that

> where an adjudicatory body determining disputes over civil rights and obligations does not comply with Article 6(1) in some respect, no violation of the Convention can be found if the proceedings before that body are subject to subsequent control by a judicial body that has full jurisdiction and does provide the guarantees of Article 6(1).[9]

[3] Art 263(1) TFEU.

[4] Art 267(1)(b) TFEU.

[5] A Scordamaglia-Tousis, *EU Cartel Enforcement: Reconciling Effective Public Enforcement with Fundamental Rights* (Wolters Kluwer 2013) §3.4[A].

[6] WPJ Wils, 'The Compatibility with Fundamental Rights of the EU Antitrust Enforcement System in Which the European Commission Acts Both as Investigator and as First-Instance Decision Maker' (2014) 37(1) *World Competition* 5, 7–8.

[7] S Allegrezza and O Voordeckers, 'Investigative and Sanctioning Powers of the ECB in the Framework of the Single Supervisory Mechanism', *eucrim* 4/2015, 151, 158.

[8] On this topic see ch 2 of this volume (De Vries and Widdershoven). See, eg, in relation to OLAF, J Wakefield, 'Good Governance and the European Anti-Fraud Office' (2006) 12 *European Public Law* 549; X Groussot and Z Popov, 'What's Wrong with OLAF? Accountability, Due Process and Criminal Justice in European Anti-Fraud Policy' (2010) 47 *CML Rev* 605, 607.

[9] *Fazia Ali v UK* App no 40378/10 (ECtHR, 20 October 2015) para 75 and cited case law; *Tsfayo v UK* App no 60860/00, (ECtHR, 14 November 2006) para 42, citing *Albert and Le Compte v Belgium* App nos 7299/75; 7496/76 (ECtHR, 24 October 1983) para 29.

The defining characteristics of full jurisdiction include 'the power to quash in all respects, on questions of fact and law, the decision of the body below'.[10] The Court reaffirmed these principles in *Ramos Nunes de Carvalho*[11] and more recently in *Miroslava Todorova v Bulgaria*,[12] recalling that where an authority responsible for examining disputes concerning rights and obligations in a suit at law does not meet all the requirements of Article 6(1) ECHR, there is no violation of the Convention if the proceedings before that body can be subject to 'subsequent review by a judicial body of full jurisdiction which has the guarantees of that article', that is, if structural or procedural defects identified in the proceedings are corrected as part of the subsequent review by a judicial body with full jurisdiction.[13] Notwithstanding this, the jurisprudence is clear that the requirement of full jurisdiction may be flexibly applied depending on the nature of the case, in particular in 'specialised areas of law' such as antitrust enforcement. In these areas, the ECtHR does not demand a *de novo* or *ex proprio* review of the facts, especially in cases where the facts have previously been established in a quasi-judicial procedure governed by many Article 6(1) safeguards. This was confirmed, for example, in *Menarini*, where the ECtHR deemed that the Italian administrative courts had in fact been able to apply a thorough proportionality check in reviewing the correct exercise of discretion by the independent administrative authority.[14] In the recent *Miroslava Todorova v Bulgaria* case, the ECtHR reaffirmed its settled case law and emphasised that the 'the Supreme Administrative Court had sufficient jurisdiction in this case and that the defects in the proceedings before the [administrative authority] alleged by the applicant could be corrected, if necessary, in the judicial proceedings'.[15]

B. Scope of this Chapter and Outline

This chapter deals with *ex post* judicial review in relation to the investigative acts and penalty decisions of the Directorate-General (DG) Competition, the ECB, ESMA and OLAF, or their domestic counterparts. This implies a two-fold limitation of the scope: on the one hand, aspects of *ex ante* authorisation are excluded,[16] and on the other hand

[10] *Produkcija Plus Storitveno Podjetje DOO v Slovenia* App no 47072/15 (ECtHR, 23 October 2018) para 51; *A Menarini Diagnostics SRL v Italy* App no 43509/08 (ECtHR, 27 September 2011) para 59; *Schmautzer v Austria* App no 15523/89 (ECtHR, 23 October 1995) para 36.

[11] *Ramos Nunes de Carvalho e Sá c Portugal* App no 55391/13 (ECtHR GC, 6 November 2018) paras 176–184.

[12] *Miroslava Todorova v Bulgaria* App no 40072/13 (ECtHR, 19 October 2021) para 109.

[13] ibid.

[14] In *Menarini* (n 11), the Court recognised that the administrative review performed by the Italian *Consiglio di Stato* satisfied the full jurisdiction requirement since it went beyond a mere 'external' control of the motivation of the decision of the national competition authority (see paras 63–66). The Court reaffirmed this position in *Produkcija Plus Storitveno Podjetje DOO* (n 11) at para 2 of the Concurring Opinion of Judge Bosnjak, stating that 'according to our Court's well-established case-law under Article 6 § 1 of the Convention, the decisions taken by administrative authorities in cases involving the determination of an individual's civil rights and obligations or of criminal charges against him or her must be subject to subsequent control by a judicial body that has full jurisdiction over the case, which means jurisdiction to examine all questions of fact and law relevant to the dispute before it'.

[15] *Miroslava Todorova* (n 14) para 112; *Peleki v Greece* App no 69291/12 (ECtHR, 5 March 2020) para 59; *Ramos Nunes de Carvalho* (n 12) paras 201 and 212; *Tsanova-Gecheva v Bulgaria* App no 43800/12 (ECtHR, 15 September 2015) paras 93–94; and *Albert and Le Compte v. Belgium* (n 10) para 36.

[16] On this topic see ch 2 of this volume (De Vries and Widdershoven).

only *investigative acts* carried out and/or *sanctions* imposed by the four authorities (or their domestic counterparts) are addressed. Judicial review in relation to supervisory tasks or measures of the ECB and ESMA are thus not dealt with. For the sake of completeness, the chapter also addresses *ex post* non-judicial (or *quasi-judicial*) review in all four cases, touching on the relationship between those internal review mechanisms and *ex post* judicial review by the EU Courts.

As for the parts on review at national level, this chapter is based on research conducted on the EU's composite law enforcement area.[17] The research assessed the national rules of France, Germany, Hungary, Italy, Luxembourg, the Netherlands and Poland.[18]

Section II sketches the human rights framework applicable to investigations by the four EU actors studied (referred to collectively as 'authorities') and explains the jurisdiction of the Court of Justice of the European Union (CJEU) in relation to alleged breaches of the human rights framework in the context of those EU authorities' investigative acts. Section III then addresses judicial remedies at the EU level, while section IV is dedicated to judicial protection at national level. Section V concludes this chapter.

II. Applicable Human Rights Framework and Court Organisation

A. Applicable Human Rights Framework

Investigations and sanctions carried out or issued by all four authorities have the potential to interfere with and/or violate the fundamental rights, enshrined in the Charter and the ECHR, of those subject to investigation or sanction. Since the Lisbon Treaty reforms, the Charter is legally binding.[19] Although EU accession to the ECHR, as required by Article 6(2) TEU, is still pending, the content of ECHR rights may be read across to Charter rights – but the latter may provide more protection than the former.[20] Furthermore, it is now well established in the jurisprudence of the CJEU that the protection of fundamental rights, 'including the review by the Community judicature of the lawfulness of Community measures as regards their consistency with those fundamental rights', is a principle forming 'part of the very foundations of the Community legal order'.[21]

[17] The research was conducted within the Hercule III programme, financed by the European Commission and OLAF. The first study, published in April 2017, was on 'Investigatory powers and procedural safeguards: Improving OLAF's legislative framework through a comparison with other EU law enforcement authorities (ECN/ESMA/ECB)'; the second, published in March 2018, carried the title 'Exchange of information with EU and national enforcement authorities: Improving OLAF legislative framework through a comparison with other EU authorities (ECN/ESMA/ECB)'; and the third, 'Admissibility of OLAF Final Reports as Evidence in Criminal Proceedings' was published in June 2019.

[18] As the United Kingdom (UK) is no longer a member of the EU, it will be excluded from the analysis of this chapter.

[19] Art 6(1) TEU.

[20] Art 52 of the Charter.

[21] Joined Cases C-402/05 P and C-415/05 P *Yassin Abdullah Kadi and Al Barakaat International* ECLI:EU:C:2008:461, para 304.

The key fundamental rights in the context of this chapter[22] are the rights to an effective remedy[23] and to a fair trial,[24] the rights to respect for private and family life, home and communications,[25] the presumption of innocence and the rights of the defence,[26] including the right to be heard, the right to access the case file, the right to information and interpretation, legal professional privilege, the right not to incriminate oneself, the right to access a lawyer, and the right to examine and present witnesses.[27] The EU legislator responded to the elevation of the Charter to Treaty status with the Lisbon reforms: in 2009, the EU Council adopted a Roadmap for strengthening procedural rights of suspected or accused persons in criminal proceedings.[28] To date, the Roadmap has inspired the promulgation of six directives: Directive 2010/64/EU on the right to interpretation and translation in criminal proceedings; Directive 2012/13/EU on the right to information in criminal proceedings; Directive 2013/48/EU on the right to access a lawyer; Directive 2016/343/EU on the presumption of innocence and the right to be present at trial; Directive 2016/800/EU on procedural safeguards for children who are suspects or accused persons in criminal proceedings; and Directive 2016/1919/EU on legal aid.

Specifically relevant to this chapter, the fundamental rights of investigated persons or entities are further protected by Article 41 of the Charter, which sets out the right to good administration entailing the right to have one's affairs handled impartially, fairly and within a reasonable time by the institutions, bodies, offices and agencies of the Union. Article 41(2) also partially codifies the proclaimed protection of defence rights in the Union actor context, by enshrining the right to be heard, to have access to one's file and the obligation on the administration to give reasons for its decisions.

B. Court Organisation

At EU level, Article 263 TFEU provides that the CJEU shall review the legality of legislative acts, of acts of the Council, of the Commission and of the ECB (other than recommendations and opinions), of acts of the European Parliament and of the

[22] For an overview of the content of several of these rights, see ch 2 of this volume (De Vries and Widdershoven), section IV.B.

[23] Inherently bound up with the principle of effective judicial protection, a general principle of EU law stemming from the constitutional traditions common to the Member States and enshrined in Arts 6 and 13 ECHR: see Case 222/84 *Johnston* ECLI:EU:C:1986:206, paras 18 and 19; Case 222/86 *Heylens and Others* ECLI:EU:C:1987:442, para 14; Case C-424/99 *Commission v Austria* ECLI:EU:C:2001:642, para 45; Case C-50/00 P *Unión de Pequeños Agricultores v Council* ECLI:EU:C:2002:462, para 39; Case C-467/01 *Eribrand* ECLI:EU:C:2003:364, para 61; Case C-432/05 *Unibet* ECLI:EU:C:2007:163, para 37; Case C-279/09 DEB ECLI:EU:C:2010:811, para 29.

[24] Entailing 'a fair and public hearing within a reasonable time by an independent and impartial tribunal previously established by law. Everyone shall have the possibility of being advised, defended and represented': Art 47 of the Charter; Arts 6 and 13 ECHR.

[25] Art 7 of the Charter; Art 8 ECHR.

[26] Art 48(2) of the Charter.

[27] In accordance with Art 52(3) of the Charter, Art 48 has the same meaning and scope as the rights guaranteed in Art 6(2) and (3) ECHR; see *Explanations relating to the Charter of Fundamental Rights* '[2007] OJ C303/17, 30.

[28] Council Resolution of 30 November 2009, Roadmap for strengthening procedural rights of suspected or accused persons in criminal proceedings [2009] OJ C295/1.

European Council, and of bodies, offices or agencies of the Union intended to produce legal effects vis-à-vis third parties. Any natural or legal person may institute proceedings against such an act addressed to that person or that is of direct and individual concern to them, and against a regulatory act that is of direct concern to them and does not entail implementing measures.[29]

A review may be brought on grounds of lack of competence, infringement of an essential procedural requirement, infringement of the Treaties or of any rule of law relating to their application, or misuse of powers.[30] Plaintiffs have two months from publication of the measure, or of its notification to the plaintiff, or, in the absence thereof, of the day on which it came to the knowledge of the latter, to institute proceedings.[31] Significantly for the remit of this chapter, Article 263(5) TFEU provides that acts setting up bodies, offices and agencies of the Union may lay down specific conditions and arrangements concerning actions brought by natural or legal persons against acts of these bodies, offices or agencies intended to produce legal effects in relation to them.

Article 267 TFEU sets out the jurisdiction of the CJEU to give preliminary rulings, at the request of a court or tribunal of a Member State, concerning the interpretation of the Treaties and the validity and interpretation of acts of the institutions, bodies, offices or agencies of the Union. Where any such question is raised in a case pending before a national court or tribunal against whose decisions there is no judicial remedy under national law, that court or tribunal must make a request to the CJEU for a preliminary ruling.[32]

Finally, Article 340 TFEU provides that in the case of non-contractual liability, the Union shall, in accordance with the general principles common to the laws of the Member States, make good any damage caused by its institutions or by its servants in the performance of their duties. Actions for damages in relation to investigative acts and/or sanctions carried out or imposed by the four authorities are therefore also addressed in the following sections.

C. Effective Judicial Protection: Overarching Issues

The relationship between *ex ante* and *ex post* review is the first issue common to all four sub-chapters.[33] For instance, in relation to inspection of private premises, the lack of prior judicial authorisation is not incompatible as such with Article 8 ECHR; it can be counterbalanced by the availability of an *ex post* judicial review. In order to comply with the Convention, however, there must be effective access to the remedy, a review of both the legality of the measure and the factual circumstances justifying its adoption, and appropriate redress in the event of unlawfulness of the inspection

[29] Art 263(4) TFEU.
[30] Art 263(2) TFEU.
[31] Art 263(6) TFEU.
[32] Art 267(3) TFEU.
[33] For an overview of the evolution and content of the principle of effective judicial protection, see ch 2 of this volume (De Vries and Widdershoven), section III.

performed.[34] This last qualification is a persistent source of concern in the context of investigative acts carried out by the four authorities: to what extent can a remedy consisting of purely financial compensation be either 'effective' or 'appropriate' where (in the case of OLAF) the material or information gleaned from the contravening inspection is forwarded to national authorities regardless?[35] In what follows, reference will be made where instructive to *ex ante* judicial authorisation.[36]

A second common feature is the at times foggy relationship between *ex post* non-judicial review and judicial review by the EU Courts. Depending on the authority, the form of *ex post* non-judicial review possible ranges from the (voluntary) public issuing of non-binding opinions or recommendations by internal yet independent departments (eg the OLAF Supervisory Committee), to a formalised, quasi-judicial process seized by aggrieved parties as a mandatory first step on the path to eventual review by the CJEU (eg ESMA decisions challenged before the Board of Appeal of the European Supervisory Authorities). Several aspects of such review mechanisms remain unclear or as yet undecided due to their ambit and/or novelty; those most significant to this contribution are the overall stringency of the controls operated, the proportion of potential objections filtered through to court level (or filtered out beforehand) and the exact procedural safeguards used in practice in order to ensure that Charter standards are upheld.

Finally, since justice delayed is justice denied, the issue of timeliness is another key concern for effective judicial protection in the ensuing analysis. The Charter provides that everyone whose rights and freedoms guaranteed by EU law are violated is entitled to 'a fair and public hearing within a reasonable time'.[37] As noted in section II.B, Article 263(6) TFEU establishes a two-month rule for challenging acts of bodies, offices or agencies of the Union. Once that period has elapsed, their legality is unchallengeable – only the manner in which investigative acts are carried out may be challenged.[38] Although proceedings must therefore be lodged fairly swiftly, unless and until the impugned act is declared invalid, it remains enforceable unless the Court declares otherwise[39] – in other words, the decision stands until it is quashed (and will most often be acted upon long before). The applicant's interest in a timely resolution of the main proceedings is thus clear – and all the more so given the immense difficulty of proving to the requisite level the risk of irreparable damage in order to qualify for interim relief (discussed in sections III.A.iii, III.B.iii, III.C.iii and III.D.iv).[40]

[34] *Smirnov v Russia* App no 71362/01 (ECtHR, 7 June 2007) para 45; *Heino v Finland* App no 56720/09 (ECtHR, 15 February 2011) para 45; *Harju v Finland* App no 56716/09 (ECtHR, 15 February 2011) para 44; *Delta Pekárny v Czech Republic* App no 97/11 (ECtHR, 2 October 2014) paras 82, 87, 92.

[35] Potentially causing extensive reputational and professional damage; in the OLAF context, see Case T-308/03 *Camós Grau v Commission* ECLI:EU:T:2006:110.

[36] On this topic see, M Scholten and M Simonato, 'EU Report' in M Luchtman and J Vervaele (eds), *Investigatory powers and procedural safeguards: Improving OLAF's legislative framework through a comparison with other EU law enforcement authorities (ECN/ESMA/ECB)* (Utrecht University 2017).

[37] Art 47 of the Charter.

[38] 'Such a rule is based in particular on the consideration that the periods within which legal proceedings must be brought are intended to ensure legal certainty by preventing Community measures which produce legal effects from being called into question indefinitely': Joined Cases T-305/94 et al *Limburgse Vinyl Maatschappij and Others v Commission* [the 'PVC cases'] ECLI:EU:T:1999:80, paras 408–414.

[39] Art 278 TFEU; Joined Cases 46/87 and 227/88 *Hoechst AG v Commission* ECLI:EU:C:1989:337, para 64.

[40] K Lenaerts, I Maselis and K Gutman, *EU Procedural Law* (Oxford European Union Library 2014) 277.

III. Judicial Remedies at the EU Level

This section discusses judicial remedies at EU level in relation to the investigative acts of DG Competition, the ECB, ESMA and OLAF. It addresses direct review by the EU Courts (actions for annulment; actions for damages), *ex post* (internal) non-judicial or *quasi-judicial* review and – in the case of OLAF – indirect review by the EU Courts (references for a preliminary ruling).

A. DG Competition

Article 263 TFEU gives the EU Courts exclusive jurisdiction to review the legality and necessity of Commission decisions in the competition enforcement field. This means that the EU Courts may annul such decisions on points of fact and law in the first instance (before the General Court) and on points of law in the final instance (before the Court of Justice), but in neither instance may they carry out a complete *de novo* review of the facts and evidence or substitute an *ex proprio* decision at EU level for that of the relevant national jurisdiction. It is for the General Court to evaluate the evidence presented to it; the Court of Justice can check for possible 'manifest errors'.

Article 261 TFEU also hands the EU Courts broader jurisdiction with regard to the penalties provided for in regulations. The General Court and the Court of Justice may therefore quash a fine, reduce or increase it, taking into account all factual evidence presented.

i. Direct Review: Actions for Annulment

a. Requests for Information

Article 18(3) of Regulation 1/2003[41] enables the Commission to require by decision undertakings and associations of undertakings to supply information. Fines and periodic penalty payments are applicable in case of non-compliance.[42] The Commission must state the legal basis and the purpose of the request, specify what information is required and fix the time limit within which it is to be provided. Addressees of such a decision are entitled to have it reviewed before the EU Courts. However, if the action for annulment has not been launched autonomously within the two-month time limit, the review of the legality of the request for information is, according to the jurisprudence of the General Court, foreclosed in the action for annulment brought against the final decision finding an infringement.[43]

[41] Council Regulation (EC) No 1/2003 of 16 December 2002 on the implementation of the rules on competition laid down in Articles 81 and 82 of the Treaty [2003] OJ L1/1 ('Regulation 1/2003').

[42] Arts 23 and 24 respectively, Regulation 1/2003.

[43] See the 'PVC cases' (n 38) paras 441 and 442. The same applies for inspection decisions: see Lenaerts, Maselis and Gutman (n 40) 275 and 277. It is, however, important to distinguish between the lawfulness of the decision itself and the lawfulness of the manner in which the inspection is carried out; in the latter case, the PVC foreclosure does not apply (see paras 413 and 414 of the PVC judgment). See C Kerse and N Khan, *EU Antitrust Procedure* (Sweet & Maxwell 2012) 175 and 176.

In the CJEU judgment in *HeidelbergCement*,[44] the applicant challenged the legality of a Commission decision issued under Article 18 of Regulation 1/2003 requesting that the applicant and its EU subsidiaries answer a questionnaire comprising 94 pages and 11 sets of questions. The Commission had earlier inspected the premises of the applicant and of other companies active in the cement industry, before sending the applicant a draft questionnaire, which it had completed and returned to the Commission.

Following the General Court's dismissal of the applicant's action for annulment of the latest decision to request information, HeidelbergCement lodged an appeal before the Court of Justice relying on seven grounds attacking various aspects of the Commission decision, all related to its alleged imprecision: the purpose of the request for information; the reasons stated for the choice of the investigating measure and for the time limit imposed for responding; the 'necessity' of the information requested; the format of the information requested; the proportionality of the time limits imposed; the vagueness of the questions; and that the General Court had interpreted excessively restrictively the appellant's right to avoid self-incrimination.

Of the seven grounds of appeal, five were upheld by Advocate General Wahl in his Opinion;[45] those focusing on the choice of the investigating measure and time limits were dismissed. In its judgment, the Court of Justice concluded that the General Court had erred in law in finding that the decision at issue contained an adequate statement of reasons; there was no need to examine the appellant's other pleas.[46] In so doing, the Court of Justice referred by analogy to its own jurisprudence on inspection decisions in order to emphasise the importance of the 'fundamental requirement' to state *specific* reasons, not only in order to demonstrate that a request for information is justified but also in order to enable the undertakings concerned to assess the scope of their duty to cooperate whilst at the same time safeguarding their rights of defence.[47]

The Court of Justice thereby rejected the Commission's contentions, which insisted on the one hand that it generally lacks information at such a preliminary investigation stage and should not therefore be required to describe in detail the nature, geographical scope and duration of, or type of products specifically concerned by the alleged infringement;[48] and, on the other hand, that its decision *did* contain sufficient details of the nature of the alleged infringement.[49] The Court's judgment was unequivocal: the statement of reasons was 'excessively succinct, vague and generic – and in some respects ambiguous', especially given that the decision at issue was taken more than two years

[44] Case C-247/14 P *HeidelbergCement AG v European Commission* ECLI:EU:C:2016:149.

[45] Case C-247/14 P *HeidelbergCement AG v European Commission* Opinion of AG Wahl [2015] ECLI:EU:C:2015:694.

[46] *HeidelbergCement* (n 44) paras 26, 39–41.

[47] ibid para 19, referring to Case C-179/12 P *Dow Chemical Ibérica and Others v Commission* ECLI:EU:C:2013:605 and Joined Cases 97/87-99/87 *Dow Chemical Ibérica and Others v Commission* ECLI:EU:C:1989:380, para 26; Case C-94/00 *Roquette Frères* ECLI:EU:C:2002:603, para 47; Case C-37/13 P *Nexans and Nexans France v Commission* ECLI:EU:C:2014:2030, para 34; and Case C-583/13 P *Deutsche Bahn and Others v Commission* ECLI:EU:C:2015:404, para 56; since then, see also Case T-249/17 *Casino, Guichard-Perrachon and Achats Marchandises Casino SAS (AMC) v Commission* ECLI:EU:T:2020:458, para 111.

[48] *HeidelbergCement* (n 44) para 13.

[49] ibid para 14.

after the initial inspections of the cement companies.[50] As such, the Court of Justice's stance in *HeidelbergCement* represents a forceful prohibition of Commission 'fishing expeditions'[51] in questionnaire form.[52]

b. Inspections

Article 20 of Regulation 1/2003 sets out the Commission's powers to carry out inspections of the premises of undertakings and associations of undertakings, whilst Article 21 sets out slightly different powers in relation to inspections of any other premises where a reasonable suspicion of a serious violation of the competition rules exists. One key distinction is that inspections of 'any other premises' require *ex ante* judicial authorisation, whereas inspections of the premises of undertakings and associations of undertakings do not – unless national rules provide otherwise.[53] This underlines the pressing need for effective judicial review at EU level of the Commission's decisions to inspect and the manner in which its inspections are carried out.

Most significantly, the Commission is obliged to specify the subject matter and purpose of its inspections.[54] This is considered a fundamental requirement in order both to show that the investigation to be carried out at the premises of the undertakings concerned is justified, enabling those undertakings to assess the scope of their duty to cooperate, and to safeguard the rights of the defence guaranteed primarily by Article 47 of the Charter.[55] In particular, the need for protection against arbitrary or disproportionate intervention by public authorities in the sphere of the private activities of any person, whether natural or legal, constitutes a general principle of EU law,[56] which now finds expression at Treaty level via Article 7 of the Charter. In ensuring that a Commission decision to inspect is in no way arbitrary, the EU courts do not demand that the Commission communicate to the recipient of such a decision all of the information at its disposal concerning the presumed infringements, or make a precise legal analysis of those infringements, but it must nonetheless clearly indicate the presumed facts it intends to investigate.[57]

For example, in *Nexans*, the applicants challenged the Commission inspection decision on two grounds. On the one hand, the product scope ('the supply of electric cables and material associated with such supply') was challenged as overly broad and vague, making it impossible for the applicants to exercise their right of defence or to distinguish the documents the Commission was able to consult and copy from other documents in the possession of the applicant that could be withheld. On the other hand, it was relatedly contended that it was only in the *high-voltage underwater* cable sector that the Commission had detailed information leading it to suspect an

[50] ibid para 39.
[51] See discussion of *Deutsche Bahn*, below.
[52] See also the judgment of the General Court in Joined Cases T-458/09 and T-171/10 *Slovak Telekom as v European Commission* ECLI:EU:T:2012:145 and the case law referred to.
[53] Art 20(7) Regulation 1/2003.
[54] Art 20(3)–(4) Regulation 1/2003.
[55] *Dow Chemical Ibérica* (n 47) para 26; cited in *Nexans* (n 47) para 39.
[56] *Roquette Frères* (n 47) para 27.
[57] *Dow Chemical Ibéria* (n 47) para 45.

infringement of competition rules. A technical analysis thus led the General Court to allow the action for annulment in so far as it concerned electric cables *other* than high-voltage underwater and underground cables and the material associated with those cables.[58] More recently, in its judgment in *Deutsche Bahn*,[59] the Court of Justice also recalled that the specification of the subject matter and scope in the inspection decision, and the prohibition on the use of information obtained during investigations for purposes other than those indicated in the inspection decision, 'is aimed at preserving, in addition to business secrecy ... , [an] undertaking's rights of defence'[60] and that 'those rights would be seriously endangered if the Commission were able to rely on evidence against undertakings which was obtained during an investigation but was not related to the subject matter or purpose thereof'. In other words, 'fishing expeditions' are not permitted.

Finally, it ought to be noted that in addition to applying for annulment of the Commission's inspection decision, the applicants in *Nexans* specifically challenged two acts adopted by the inspectors during the inspection: the decision to make copies of a number of computer files and of the hard drive of an employee's computer for the purposes of examining them later in the Commission's offices; and the decision to interview that employee on the spot. In this regard, the General Court recalled that the review of the lawfulness of acts performed during an inspection falls within the scope of an action for the annulment of the final decision of the Commission and cannot be the object of an action for annulment of the inspection decision itself.[61]

c. Review of Fines

'Unlimited jurisdiction' in relation to fines signifies that the EU Courts may quash, reduce or increase a fine on the basis of all factual evidence presented before them.[62] The 'unlimited' nature of the jurisdiction does not, however, entail a review of the Court's own motion; it is for the applicant to adduce evidence in support of his pleas.[63] It may be contrasted, however, with the EU Courts' jurisdiction in relation to decisions taken by the Commission in the enforcement of EU competition law, which in principle amounts to a comprehensive legality test, albeit one that is 'limited' in two senses. First, the EU Courts are not entitled to carry out a complete *de novo* review of the facts and evidence or substitute an *ex proprio* decision at EU level for that of the relevant national jurisdiction. Should an action for annulment be successful, therefore, the contested act is merely voided. Second, the EU judges' review is 'limited' in order to accommodate

[58] *Nexans* (n 47).

[59] *Deutsche Bahn* (n 47) paras 57 and 58. This line of case law dates back to Case C-85/87 *Dow Benelux NV v European Commission* ECLI: EU:C.1989:379; ibid, para 17.

[60] Reiterated in Case C-601/18 P *Prysmian SpA and Prysmian Cavi e Sistemi Srl v Commission* ECLI. EU:C:2020:751, para 58, although the action for annulment was dismissed in this case.

[61] *Nexans* (n 47) para 132; see, in this regard, the 'PVC cases' (n 38) paras 413 and 414.

[62] Pursuant to Art 261 TFEU.

[63] JC Laguna da Paz, 'Understanding the limits of judicial review in European competition law' (2014) 2(1) *Journal of Antitrust Enforcement* 203, 210–11.

the Commission's margin of discretion to assess the complex economic and technical issues bound up with antitrust matters.[64] This has often been criticised for potentially failing to meet the ECtHR standard of 'full jurisdictional control' as evoked in *Menarini*. However, in *Tetra Laval*[65] and the more recent cases *KME*[66] and *Chalkor*,[67] the Court insisted that the fact that the Commission has a margin of discretion 'does not mean that the [EU Courts] must decline to review the Commission's interpretation of economic or technical data'.[68] The Court even adopted a more specific approach by exercising a more intensive assessment of the facts according to the *MasterCard Inc* case, where it argued that

> it is apparent from EU case-law that where the General Court is seised, in accordance with Article 263 TFEU, of an action for annulment of a decision applying Article 81(1) EC, the General Court must as a general rule undertake, … a full review of the question whether or not the conditions for the application of that provision are met.[69]

ii. Direct Review: Actions for Damages

Should an act carried out by the Commission cause the targeted entity to suffer harm such as to cause the EU to incur liability, an action may be brought against the Commission for non-contractual liability.[70] A remedy of this kind is not part of the system of the legality of acts of the EU that have legal effects binding on, and are capable of affecting the interests of, the applicant, but it is available where a party has suffered harm on account of unlawful conduct on the part of an institution.[71]

Settled CJEU jurisprudence presents a high hurdle to any such action against a DG Competition investigative act: the rule of law infringed must be intended to confer

[64] Complex technical appraisals are in principle subject to limited review; the Court of Justice has stated in several cases that the Commission 'has a certain discretion, especially with respect to assessments of an economic nature, and that consequently, review by the Community Courts of the exercise of that discretion … must take account of the margin of discretion implicit in the provision of an economic nature' (Case C-12/03 *Tetra Laval* ECLI:EU:C:2005:87, para 38); the case law of the General Court has been more explicit – see Case T-201/04 *Microsoft Corp v Commission* ECLI:EU:T:2007:289, para 87: 'The Court observes that it follows from consistent case-law that, although as a general rule the Community Courts undertake a comprehensive review of the question as to whether or not the conditions for the application of the competition rules are met, their review of complex economic appraisals made by the Commission is necessarily limited to checking whether the relevant rules on procedure and on stating reasons have been complied with, whether the facts have been accurately stated and whether there has been any manifest error of assessment or a misuse of powers (Case T-65/96 *Kish Glass v Commission* [2000] ECLI:EU:T:2000:93, paragraph 64, upheld on appeal by order of the Court of Justice in Case C-241/00 P *Kish Glass v Commission* [2001] ECLI:EU:C:2001:556; see also, to that effect, with respect to Article 81 EC, Case 42/84 *Remia and Others v Commission* [1985] ECLI:EU:C:1985:327, paragraph 34, and Joined Cases 142/84 and 156/84 *BAT and Reynolds v Commission* [1987] ECLI:EU:C:1987:490, paragraph 62)'.

[65] *Tetra Laval* (n 64) para 39.

[66] Case C-272/09 *KME and Others v Commission* ECLI:EU:C:2011:816.

[67] Case C-386/10 P *Chalkor v Commission* ECLI:EU:C:2011:815.

[68] *KME* (n 66) para 94; *Chalkor* (n 67) para 54.

[69] Case C-382/12 P *MasterCard Inc* ECLI:EU:C:2014:2201, para 155.

[70] Under Arts 268 and 340 TFEU.

[71] See judgment of the General Court in Case T-135/09 *Nexans and Nexans v Commission* ECLI:EU:T:2012:596 para 133; Case C-131/03 P *Reynolds Tobacco and Others v Commission* ECLI:EU:C:2006:541, paras 82 and 83.

rights on individuals, the breach must be sufficiently serious, and a direct causal link between such a breach and the damage allegedly sustained must be established.[72]

iii. Direct Review: Interim Relief in Actions for Annulment and Actions for Damages

Article 278 TFEU provides that 'actions brought before the Court of Justice of the European Union shall not have suspensory effect. The Court may, however, if it considers that circumstances so require, order that application of the contested act be suspended.' According to Article 160(3) of the Rules of Procedure of the Court of Justice and Article 104(2) of the Rules of Procedure of the General Court, an application for interim relief must establish a prima facie case and must be urgent. In addition, the case law developed a third substantive condition of admissibility, namely, that the applicant's interest in the interim measure must outweigh the other interests at stake in the main proceedings.[73]

With regard to competition proceedings and the urgency requirement, it is important to highlight that purely financial losses are not regarded as an 'irreparable form of harm', unless their magnitude would be such as to imperil the applicant's existence before the final judgment in the main action.[74] In competition proceedings, interim relief has been granted against decisions ordering undertakings to alter their conduct (cease and desist orders; United Brands,[75] Magill,[76] Net Book Agreements[77]), while a much stricter approach has been adopted with regard to the suspension of investigative measures and decisions ordering the payment of fines.[78]

iv. Ex Post *Non-Judicial (or Quasi-Judicial) Review*

Internal (non-judicial) review of the respect for certain procedural safeguards during the Commission's investigations is exercised by the hearing officer.[79] In particular, the hearing officer is competent to resolve disputes relating to respect for legal professional privilege and the privilege against self-incrimination in the context of requests for information and inspections, and to certain disclosure and information issues. The hearing officers are not part of DG Competition but are directly attached to the office of the Commissioner, to whom they must report on the lawfulness of the conduct of the procedure before a final decision on an infringement is taken.

[72] Case C-352/98 P *Bergaderm and Goupil v Commission* ECLI:EU:C:2000:361, para 42.

[73] See Lenaerts, Maselis and Gutman (n 40) 591.

[74] In this regard, see the orders of the President in Case T-181/02 *Neue Erba Lautex v Commission* ECLI:EU:T:2002:294, para 84 and Case T-53/01 *Poste Italiane v European Commission* ECLI:EU:T:2001:143, para 120.

[75] Case C-27/76 *United Brands v Commission* ECLI:EU:C:1976:51.

[76] Joined Cases C-76/89, 77/89 and 91/89 *Radio Telefis Eireann v European Commission* ECLI:EU:C:1989:192.

[77] Case C-56/89 *Publishers Association v Commission* ECLI:EU:C:1989:238.

[78] See Kerse and Khan (n 43) 178–79 et seq.

[79] For the mandate of the hearing officer, see the Decision of the President of the European Commission of 13 October 2011 on the function and terms of reference of the hearing officer in certain competition proceedings, 2011/695/EU, [2011] OJ L275/29.

B. The ECB

The SSM Regulation[80] grants the ECB the following investigatory powers: to require supervised entities to provide information (Article 10); to carry out 'general investigations' (Article 11); and to conduct on-site inspections (Article 12).[81] Cooperation between the ECB and NCAs as regards these powers is fleshed out in Part XI of the SSM Framework Regulation;[82] notably, Article 144 provides for the establishment and composition by the ECB of separate on-site inspection teams, with the head of the team designated from among ECB and NCA staff members.

The mixed composition of on-site inspection teams reflects the mixed administration inherent to the day-to-day monitoring of significant financial institutions by Joint Supervisory Teams (JSTs), composed of ECB and NCA staff members, with the possibility to include National Central Bank staff members,[83] headed by an ECB staff member (the 'JST coordinator') and one or more NCA sub-coordinators.[84] As for judicial review, although there is no requirement to do so, the ECB always indicates the right to challenge a decision in its interaction with the monitored entities.[85]

i. Direct Review: Actions for Annulment

a. Requests for Information

Unlike Regulation 1/2003 in the competition law field, the SSM Regulation makes no distinction between simple requests for information (no obligation to reply; no penalty attached to non-compliance) and requests for information taken by decision (obligation to reply; penalty attached to non-compliance), merely providing that recipients shall provide all necessary information.[86] Cross-reading from competition law jurisprudence allows us to posit that the reviewability of an ECB request for information will hinge on its obligatory nature: in particular, where such a request is taken by decision and the threat of a fine in case of non-compliance exists, this changes the recipient's legal position, and the request is open to review by the EU Courts.[87]

[80] Council Regulation (EU) No 1024/2013 of 15 October 2013 conferring specific tasks on the European Central Bank concerning policies relating to the prudential supervision of credit institutions [2014] OJ L287/63 ('SSM Regulation').

[81] In order to carry out its tasks, the ECB also has the power to instruct national competent authorities (NCAs) 'to make use of their powers, under and in accordance with the conditions set out in national law', where the SSM Regulation does not confer such powers on the ECB. Art 9(1) SSM Regulation.

[82] Regulation (EU) No 468/2014 of the European Central Bank of 16 April 2014 establishing the framework for cooperation within the Single Supervisory Mechanism between the European Central Bank and national competent authorities and with national designated authorities (SSM Framework Regulation) (ECB/2014/17) [2014] OJ L141/1 ('SSM Framework Regulation').

[83] Art 5 SSM Framework Regulation.

[84] See Arts 3 et seq SSM Framework Regulation.

[85] Source: informal discussions with ECB representative, November 2016.

[86] Art 10(2) SSM Regulation.

[87] L Wissink, T Duijkersloot and R Widdershoven, 'Shifts in Competence between Member States and the EU in the New Supervisory System for Credit Institutions and their Consequences for Judicial Protection' (2014) 10(5) *Utrecht Law Review* 92, 105.

The SSM Framework Regulation does not include any obligations on the ECB to formulate its requests for information in a precise way, along the lines of the CJEU jurisprudence in competition law. The information position of the ECB is very strong due to the information supplied by the supervisors in the course of regular supervision. Consequently, external requests (for information not already available through supervision) are used rarely, where there exist indications that SSM rules have been breached, potentially leading to sanctions.[88] Moreover, as it is very difficult to secure a formal decision (under the SSM, a hearing is required), if a request is issued it usually takes the form of a 'soft letter' or 'operational request'. Although the privilege against self-incrimination applies both to decisions and 'soft letters', the latter cannot lead to a fine. In practice, the same criteria apply as for a formal decision, in so far as the recipient must be informed of the purpose of the request, the suspected breach and so on.

The ECB, differently from the comparable situation with OLAF, may require NCAs 'to open proceedings with a view to taking action in order to ensure that appropriate penalties are imposed'.[89] It remains an open question whether or not an instruction from the ECB to a national authority may change the legal position of the person involved, although this would appear unlikely.[90] Although NCAs may in theory challenge such a request, the fact that one representative of each NCA is on the ECB's internal Supervisory Board[91] would seem to limit this possibility in practice.

b. General Investigations and On-Site Inspections

Under Article 11 of the SSM Regulation, the ECB may by decision[92] require the submission of documents, examine books and records, and take copies or extracts, obtain written or oral explanations from the targeted legal or natural persons, and interview any other person who consents to be interviewed for the purpose of collecting information relating to the subject matter of an investigation. Article 12 sets out the framework for inspections at the business premises and on the land of the relevant persons carried out by (potentially mixed) on-site inspection teams, also on the basis of an ECB decision.

Where any person obstructs the conduct of general investigations, the local NCA shall afford the necessary assistance in accordance with national law,[93] and that person will be considered in breach of an ECB decision within the meaning of Article 18(7) of the SSM Regulation, potentially leading to sanctions.[94] These consequences are liable to change the legal position of the addressee, suggesting that review of 'general investigations' by the EU Courts is possible.[95] Any such review will take into account the legal basis for the decision and its purpose, as set out in the ECB decision.[96] Analogous

[88] Source: informal discussions with ECB representative, November 2016.

[89] Art 18(5) SSM Regulation.

[90] See discussion in section III.B.i.c.

[91] Art 26(1) SSM Regulation.

[92] Art 11(2) SSM Regulation.

[93] ibid. It is unclear how the obstruction of a general investigation may be resolved where no judicial authorisation is forthcoming at the national level.

[94] This is to be communicated in the terms of the decision request to its addressee. See Art 142(c), SSM Framework Regulation.

[95] Wissink, Duijkersloot and Widdershoven (n 88) 105.

[96] Art 142(a) SSM Framework Regulation.

provisions apply to on-site inspections: obstruction is considered a breach of an ECB decision liable to trigger penalties,[97] whilst the ECB decision must at a minimum specify the subject matter and the purpose of the on-site inspection.[98]

Targeted persons shall be informed of an impending on-site inspection at least five working days before it begins, except where the proper conduct and efficiency of the inspection require the inspection to take place unannounced.[99] The lawfulness of an ECB decision ordering an on-site inspection may only be challenged before the CJEU through an action for annulment *ex* Article 263 TFEU.[100] Meanwhile, the SSM Regulation leaves judicial authorisation prior to the carrying out of on-site inspections, clearly of heightened importance in such cases, to national law.[101] As pointed out by Wissink et al, across the national systems different fields feature different rules on judicial authorisation: it may be optional but not required (and, eg in competition law in the Netherlands, in practice rarely applied for) or simply unavailable (eg in the Netherlands, in the area of banking supervision).[102] Where there is no *ex ante* check and sanctions are imposed by the ECB or the national authority of another Member State based partly on information obtained during that (unlicensed) inspection, the same authors submit that it is highly unlikely that either the EU or national courts will seriously assess the effectiveness of the inspection. In this way, the rule of non-inquiry and the principle of mutual trust are respected, but a gap in substantive legal protection is opened.[103]

c. Review of Fines

Under the SSM Regulation, measures and penalties are in general imposed by the ECB and are thus open to review before the EU Courts. The CJEU has unlimited jurisdiction based on Article 261 TFEU and Article 5 of Regulation 2532/98[104] to review administrative penalties imposed pursuant to Article 18 of the SSM Regulation. Other administrative measures adopted pursuant to Article 16 of the SSM Regulation are subject to annulment actions before the CJEU according to Article 263 TFEU. The case law on the review of 'complex economic and technical assessments' may also be relevant in the context of the review of ECB decisions (with the same caveats laid down by case law of the CJEU in *KME* and *Chalkor* – see section III.A.i.c). In that sense, the CJEU recently reaffirmed its jurisdiction to review decisions and measures as well as penalties imposed by the ECB in two cases. Accordingly, the General Court declared its full and unlimited jurisdiction to review decisions and measures of the ECB under the principle of sound administration, 'which entails the duty of the

[97] Art 143(2)(b) SSM Framework Regulation.

[98] Art 143(2)(a) SSM Framework Regulation.

[99] Art 12(1) SSM Regulation in conjunction with Art 145 SSM Framework Regulation.

[100] Art 13(2) of the SSM Regulation, similar to Art 20(8) and Art 21(3) of Regulation 1/2003, provides that the review of the lawfulness of the inspection decision can be performed only by the Court of Justice (reaffirming the *Roquette Frères* (n 47) and *Foto-Frost* rules; Case 314/85 *Foto-Frost* ECLI:EU:C:1987:452).

[101] Art 13(1) SSM Regulation.

[102] Wissink, Duijkersloot and Widdershoven (n 87) 110.

[103] ibid 110–11. On the rule of non-inquiry and mutual trust, see ch 2 of this volume (De Vries and Widdershoven), section V.B.

[104] Council Regulation (EC) No 2532/98 of 23 November 1998 concerning the powers of the European Central Bank to impose sanctions [1998] OJ L318/4.

competent institution to examine carefully and impartially all the relevant aspects of the individual case'.[105] At the same time, while the Court restated its powers of unlimited jurisdiction for the review of legality under Article 263 TFEU, it specified that 'in respect of penalties imposed by the ECB, by virtue of Article 18(1) of Regulation No 1024/2013, the scope of those powers of unlimited jurisdiction would be strictly limited … to the determination of the amount of the penalty',[106] as the 'judicial review that the Court must carry out … must not lead to it to substitute its own assessment for that of the ECB'.[107]

In addition, Article 18(5) of the SSM Regulation provides that the ECB may require NCAs to open proceedings with a view to taking action in order to ensure that appropriate penalties are imposed in cases not covered by Article 18(1). The latter provision covers breaches of requirements under relevant directly-applicable acts of Union law in relation to which administrative pecuniary penalties shall be made available to competent authorities under the relevant Union law; in such cases, the ECB may levy fines.

Article 18(5) provides that ECB requests for NCAs to open proceedings with a view to applying appropriate penalties shall be applicable in particular

> to pecuniary penalties to be imposed on credit institutions, financial holding companies or mixed financial holding companies for breaches of national law transposing relevant Directives, and to any administrative penalties or measures to be imposed on members of the management board of a credit institution, financial holding company or mixed financial holding company or any other individuals who under national law are responsible for a breach by a credit institution, financial holding company or mixed financial holding company.

Since such requests from the ECB aim at the opening of proceedings by national authorities, following the *Tillack* precedent set in the context of the judicial review of OLAF final reports,[108] ECB requests will thus not be open to review before national courts,[109] even if the ECB is empowered to *require* national authorities to open proceedings – there is, after all, no obligation to levy a fine.

ii. Direct Review: Actions for Damages

The SSM Regulation does not expressly provide for non-contractual liability, but in its Preamble the Regulation recalls that in accordance with Article 340 TFEU, the ECB should make good any damage caused by it or by its servants in the performance of their duties.[110] As mentioned above, the three-step test in CJEU jurisprudence presents a high hurdle to any such action against an ECB act: the rule of law infringed must be intended to confer rights on individuals, the breach must be sufficiently serious, and a direct causal link between such a breach and the allegedly sustained damage must be established. In particular here, the second criterion may be difficult to establish

[105] See Case T-733/16 *La Banque postale v ECB* ECLI:EU:T:2018:477, para 70.
[106] See Case T-203/18 *VQ v ECB* ECLI:EU:T:2020:313, para 94.
[107] *La Banque postale v ECB* (n 105) para 7069.
[108] See discussion in section II.D.
[109] See Wissink, Duijkersloot and Widdershoven (n 87) 103.
[110] This should be without prejudice to the liability of NCAs to make good any damage caused by them or by their servants in the performance of their duties in accordance with national legislation; see Recital 61, SSM Regulation.

given the discretionary nature of the decision-making powers handed to the ECB.[111] Moreover, the ECB's reliance on national authorities in the day-to-day assessment of a credit institution's situation and on-site verifications may create difficulties in attributing responsibility for a specific act or decision to the ECB or to the national level.[112]

iii. Direct Review: Interim Relief in Actions for Annulment and Actions for Damages

In respect of ECB supervisory decisions, Article 34 of the SSM Framework Regulation provides that the ECB may suspend the decision at the request of the addressee. This is, however, without prejudice to actions for interim relief under Article 278 TFEU.

iv. Ex Post *Non-Judicial (or Quasi-Judicial) Review*

Decisions of the ECB adopted under Regulation 1024/2013 finding an infringement and applying sanctions[113] may be reviewed by the Administrative Board of Review of the ECB.[114] The scope of review of the Administrative Board pertains to the 'procedural and substantive conformity' of the decision with the SSM Regulation. The Administrative Board cannot directly annul or declare void the decision; it can only express an opinion and remit the case to the Supervisory Board. The opinion of the Administrative Board has to be taken into account when adopting a new decision.

The request for review before the Administrative Board of Review of the ECB is, in any case, without prejudice to the right to launch an annulment action before the CJEU in accordance with Article 263 TFEU.[115] Every formal decision can be challenged before the Board of Review, whereas 'soft letters' cannot be. It ought to be underlined that no cases have so far arisen, and such discussions remain theoretical.[116]

C. ESMA

When the ESMA[117] supervisory teams find indications of possible infringements listed in the Annex to Regulation 648/2012[118] and Regulation 513/2011[119] with regard,

[111] TMC Arons, 'Judicial Protection of Supervised Credit Institutions in the European Banking Union' in D Busch and G Ferrarini (eds), *European Banking Union* (Oxford University Press 2015) 433, 471.

[112] ibid.

[113] Pursuant to Art 4b(5) Regulation 2532/98, as amended by Council Regulation (EU) 2015/159 of 27 January 2015 amending Regulation (EC) No 2532/98 concerning the powers of the European Central Bank to impose sanctions [2015] OJ L27/1.

[114] Art 24 SSM Regulation.

[115] See Art 24(11) SSM Regulation.

[116] Source: informal discussions with ECB representative, November 2016.

[117] Established by Regulation (EU) No 1095/2010 of the European Parliament and of the Council of 24 November 2010 establishing a European Supervisory Authority (European Securities and Markets Authority), amending Decision No 716/2009/EC and repealing Commission Decision 2009/77/EC, [2010] OJ L331/84 ('ESMA Regulation').

[118] Regulation (EU) No 648/2012 of the European Parliament and of the Council of 4 July 2012 on OTC derivatives, central counterparties and trade repositories [2012] OJ L201/1 ('EMIR').

[119] Regulation (EU) No 513/2011 of the European Parliament and of the Council of 11 May 2011 amending Regulation (EC) No 1060/2009 on credit ratings agencies [2011] OJ L145/30 ('CRA Regulation').

respectively, to trade repositories and credit-rating agencies, the Executive Director is informed and may appoint an independent investigation officer from within ESMA to follow up on the matter. Such indications will mostly arise from prior investigative acts, but may also emerge from a supervised entity's response(s) to requests for information sent out in the context of regular supervisory contact. The entity under investigation is informed of the appointment of an independent investigation officer, and in practice the latter in turn then informs the entity of the purpose of the investigation and of the indication(s) that there may have been a breach.

This is the formal opening of an investigation. The investigation officer shall take into account any comments submitted by the persons subject to the investigations, and has powers to request information[120] and to conduct investigations[121] and on-site inspections.[122] The officer's independence implies that he or she must seek out both incriminating and exculpatory evidence. The officer's complete file is submitted to the Board of Supervisors, which, should it find an infringement, decides on measures and sanctions. For instance, in 2022, ESMA imposed a fine of €186,000 on the trade repository REGIS-TR, ranked second among the EU-based trade repositories in terms of clientele and revenue, for breaches related to negligent failures to ensure data integrity and to provide direct and immediate access to regulators.[123]

The joint Board of Appeal[124] provides a first opportunity to challenge the finding of an infringement, before potential subsequent review by the EU Courts via actions for annulment under Article 263 TFEU or actions for failure to act under Article 265 TFEU.[125] The EU Courts alone are entitled to review the legality or 'lawfulness' of the relevant ESMA act.[126] The relevant provisions of EMIR and the CRA Regulation confirm that *ex ante* judicial authorisation at the national level, where required,[127] shall entail verification of the authenticity of the ESMA decision, but also a proportionality test: the national judicial authority is to check that the coercive measures envisaged are neither arbitrary nor excessive in relation to the subject matter of the investigation.[128] The national judicial authority may ask ESMA for detailed explanations as to, inter alia, the grounds for suspicion, the seriousness of suspected infringements and the nature of the involvement of the person targeted by the coercive investigative measures,

[120] Art 61 EMIR; Art 23b CRA Regulation.

[121] Art 62 EMIR; Art 23c CRA Regulation.

[122] Art 63 EMIR; Art 23d CRA Regulation.

[123] ESMA, Decision of the Board of Supervisions to adopt supervisory measures and impose fines in respect of infringments committed by REGIS-TR, S.A., Decision 2022/1, 22 March 2022, ESMA41-356-271.

[124] Arts 58–60 ESMA Regulation. The competent body of ESMA shall be bound by the decision of the Board of Appeal and adopt an amended decision regarding the case concerned; see Art 60(5).

[125] Art 61 ESMA Regulation.

[126] Arts 61(3)(g), 62(6) and 63(9) EMIR; and Arts 23b(3)(g), 23c(6) and 23d(8) CRA Regulation.

[127] Neither EMIR nor the CRA Regulation mentions *ex ante* judicial authorisation in the context of (the non-coercive) requests for information – whether simple requests or requests made by decision. In contrast, in relation to on-site inspections (Art 63(8) EMIR; Art 23d(8) CRA Regulation) and, in the context of general investigations, a request for records of telephone or data traffic (Art 62(5) EMIR; Art 23c(5) CRA Regulation), where prior judicial authorisation is required by national law such authorisation shall be applied for. *Ex ante* authorisation of all other general investigative acts (listed in Art 62 EMIR; Art 23c CRA Regulation.) is thus left to the national level.

[128] Arts 62(6) and 63(9) EMIR; and Arts 23c(6) and 23d(9) CRA Regulation.

but cannot demand access to ESMA's file.[129] As such, national-level *ex ante* judicial control of ESMA investigative acts represents a 'meantime accountability check'[130] before possible internal and external appeals to the Board of Appeal and CJEU respectively.

i. Direct Review: Actions for Annulment

a. Requests for Information

As with DG Competition,[131] ESMA may issue simple requests[132] for information or requests pursuant to a decision.[133] In the former case, since no obligation to provide the requested information exists, it may be assumed that a simple request for information does not alter its recipient's legal position, and thus cannot be challenged under Article 263 TFEU, notwithstanding the fact that where a 'voluntary' reply is incorrect or misleading[134] a fine is foreseen.[135] In practice, in such cases there has been no formal decision to request information – and thus no threat as yet of fines in case of non-cooperation.

On the other hand, as requests for information that emanate from an ESMA decision carry the threat of monetary penalties in case of non-compliance,[136] that decision may ultimately be subject to an action for annulment before the CJEU[137] should the matter not be resolved at the Board of Appeal stage. When requiring information by decision, ESMA must state the legal basis and purpose of the request, specify what information is required, set a time limit and so on.[138] As such, the framework for ESMA's request powers closely resembles that of DG Competition, and the the case law cited in section III.A may prove instructive in evaluating the legality of their application.[139] That being said, it would seem unlikely that much jurisprudence

[129] Arts 62(6) and 63(9) EMIR; and Arts 23c(6) and 23d(9) CRA Regulation.

[130] M van Rijsbergen and M Scholten, 'ESMA inspecting: the implications for judicial enforcement under shared enforcement' (2016) 7(3) *European Journal of Risk Regulation* 569, 576.

[131] During the CRA Regulation legislative process under the Belgian EU Presidency, a number of powers available to ESMA were, in fact, copy-pasted from Regulation 1/2003 (source: meeting with ESMA, November 2016).

[132] Art 61(1) EMIR; Art 23b(1) CRA Regulation.

[133] Art 61(3) EMIR; Art 23b(3) CRA Regulation.

[134] Art 61(2)(e) EMIR; Art.23b(2)(e) CRA Regulation.

[135] Art 65 and Point IV(a), Annex I to EMIR; Art 36a and Point II(7), Annex III to the CRA Regulation.

[136] Where information provided is incomplete (Art 23b(e) EMIR; Art 61(3)(e) CRA Regulation), or where answers are incorrect or misleading (Art 23b(f) EMIR; Art 61(3)(f) CRA Regulation).

[137] Art 61(5) EMIR; Art 23b(3)(g) CRA Regulation.

[138] Art 61(3)(a)–(d) EMIR; Art 23b(3)(a)–(d) CRA Regulation.

[139] Although ESMA has not yet published any request for information based on the enforcement of a decision, the Consolidated version of the CRA Regulation in Art 23e(1) provides for the power to appoint an independent investigation officer (IIO) where, 'in carrying out its duties under this Regulation, ESMA finds that there are serious indications of the possible existence of facts liable to constitute one or more of the infringements listed in Annex III'. It also stipulates that the IIO 'shall not be involved or have been involved in the direct or indirect supervision or registration process of the credit rating agency concerned and shall perform his functions independently from ESMA's Board of Supervisors'. Moreover, under Art 23b, CRA Regulation, ESMA may issue requests for information, as can be seen in specific sectors, such as the cooperation with the International Accounting Standards Board ('IASB'), according to the ESMA32-63-1101 Report on enforcement and regulatory activities of European enforcers of 6 April 2021, para 202. In that framework, 'while not an official observer to the IFRS IC [International Financial Reporting Standards Interpretations Committee], ESMA contributed to the IFRS IC work by identifying and submitting agenda

will be generated in the near future; notably, since November 2016 ESMA had not yet issued a request for information based on a decision in the enforcement context (as opposed to the supervision side of ESMA's remit), indicating a cooperative relationship between the Authority and supervised entities.[140]

b. General Investigations and Inspections

ESMA is empowered to examine records, data and procedures, take or obtain copies of such material, summon relevant representatives or staff for oral or written explanations, interview any other natural or legal person that consents to being interviewed, and request records of telephone and data traffic.[141] These 'general investigation' measures may be taken upon production of a written authorisation specifying the subject matter and purpose of the investigation along with the periodic penalty payments attached to non-compliance;[142] where measures are taken on the basis of a decision, this may be reviewed by the Court of Justice.[143]

Very similar conditions (written authorisation, specification of purpose, and penalties in case of non-compliance) apply to on-site inspections – which may be carried out without prior announcement, where the proper conduct and efficiency of the inspection so require – in order to seal any business premises and books or records for the period of, and to the extent necessary for, the inspection.[144] An ESMA decision to carry out an on-site inspection shall be subject to review only by the CJEU.[145]

Van Rijsbergen and Scholten reported in February 2016 that ESMA had completed two enforcement investigations, neither of which featured on-site inspections.[146] By November 2016, there had still not been an on-site inspection (ESMA investigations are almost entirely paper-based) but the number of completed investigations had risen to four. This may appear prima facie to be a small return, but it must be kept in mind that ESMA only supervises a total of 40 entities – 10 per cent of which have thus been investigated.

c. Review of Fines

The CJEU has unlimited jurisdiction based on Article 261 TFEU and the ESMA legal framework to review ESMA decisions imposing a fine or a periodic penalty payment.[147] The case law on the review of 'complex economic and technical assessments' in

item requests in relation to two issues where ESMA identified diversity in application of the accounting standards, because the requirements were not considered sufficiently clear'. To that effect, see ESMA32-63-1051 Letter to the IFRS IC – *Agenda Item Request: Costs necessary to make the sale (IAS 2)*, 12 October 2020; and ESMA32-63-1052 Letter to the IFRS IC – *Agenda Item Request: Derecognition of a warrant (IAS 32)*, 12 October 2020.

[140] Source: meeting with ESMA, November 2016.

[141] Art 62(1) EMIR; Art 23c(1) CRA Regulation.

[142] Art 62(2) EMIR; Art 23c(3) CRA Regulation.

[143] Art 62(3) EMIR; Art 23c(6) CRA Regulation.

[144] Art 63(1)–(2) EMIR; Art 23d(1)–(2) CRA Regulation.

[145] Art 63(9) EMIR; Art 23d(9) CRA Regulation.

[146] See Van Rijsbergen and Scholten (n 130).

[147] Art 69 EMIR; Art 36e CRA Regulation.

competition law may also be relevant in the context of the review of ESMA decisions (with the same caveats laid down by the case law of the CJEU in *KME* and *Chalkor* (see section III.A.i.c), and in the most recent judgment *VQ v ECB*[148]).

ii. Direct Review: Actions for Damages

Article 69 of the ESMA Regulation provides that ESMA shall make good any damage caused by it or by its staff in the performance of their duties, and confirms that the CJEU has jurisdiction in any dispute over the remedying of such damage.

iii. Direct Review: Interim Relief in Actions for Annulment and Actions for Damages

Article 278 TFEU provides that actions brought before the CJEU shall not have suspensory effect. The Court may, however, if it considers that circumstances so require,[149] order that application of the contested act be suspended as well as prescribe any necessary interim measures.[150] Since, as noted in several other parts of this chapter, suspensory effect is difficult to obtain, one possible solution might be to suspend not the levying of a sanction against an entity supervised by ESMA, but its publication, preserving to a considerable extent the reputation of the entity involved until all appeal routes have been exhausted. This is, however, precluded by the current legal framework, which provides that ESMA shall publicly disclose any such decision to levy a sanction on its website within 10 working days of adopting it.[151]

At the temporally prior non-judicial stage, the ESMA Regulation also establishes that an appeal to the joint Board of Appeal shall not have suspensive effect; the Board may, however, decide to suspend the application of the contested decision (see section III.C.iv).[152]

iv. Ex Post *Non-Judicial (or Quasi-Judicial) Review*

Members of the joint Board of Appeal shall be independent in making their decisions; they shall not perform any other duties in relation to ESMA.[153] Proceedings before the Board of Appeal are organised in a quasi-judicial manner: a Notice of Appeal is first filed by the appellant, before the respondent files its Response,[154] and parties are invited to file observations and are entitled to make oral representations.[155] If the review is of a decision (to sanction or to carry out investigative acts), the Board of Appeal may

[148] Case T-203/18 *VQ v ECB* ECLI:EU:T:2020:313.
[149] See discussion of interim relief in relation to OLAF in section III.D.iii.
[150] Art 279 TFEU.
[151] Art 73(3) EMIR; Art 24(5) CRA Regulation.
[152] Art 60(3) ESMA Regulation; see further Art 10, Rules of Procedure, Board of Appeal of the European Supervisory Authorities, BOA 2012 002.
[153] Art 59(1) ESMA Regulation.
[154] See Arts 5 and 6, Rules of Procedure (n 152).
[155] Art 60(4) ESMA Regulation.

establish a standard of review that is different from that of the General Court. The Board of Appeal is not bound by the case law of the CJEU and can examine the facts.

Only recently has the Board of Appeal delivered decisions in relation to ESMA investigative acts or sanctions as, up to now, those that have been handed down in relation to ESMA have concerned other matters: for example, the challenging of a decision to refuse to register a credit-rating agency.[156] This is unsurprising given that (as noted in section III.C.i.a) no investigative measures in the enforcement context have yet been carried out on the basis of an ESMA decision – only through simple requests for information.[157] In the most recent decision,[158] an appeal brought by Scope Ratings GmbH (a credit-rating agency) against ESMA regarding the interpretation of the CRA Regulation[159] was dismissed by the joint Board of Appeal of the European Supervisory Authorities, finding that ESMA rightfully interpreted the applicable legal provisions of the regulation in question. Similarly, in 2019, a joint appeal was brought by four Swedish credit institutions against sanctioning measures imposed upon them by the ESMA Board of Supervisors[160] for failure to register according to the aforementioned CRA Regulation. In this situation, the appeal was only partly successful, as the cases were sent back to the Board of Supervisors, the Board of Appeal having confirmed the finding of negligence.[161]

From a procedural rights perspective, the issue of access to a lawyer is of lesser importance than in the OLAF or DG Competition contexts, since the Board of Appeal procedure is largely paper-based. One possible future issue, however, concerns the right to interpretation: whilst a large share of ESMA's interaction is currently with supervised entities based in London[162] or entirely comfortable using English, translation and interpretation will need to be ensured should the number of supervised entities based further afield continue to grow.

Finally, depending on how its future body of decisions takes shape, the timeliness of the Board of Appeal procedure – as a necessary first step to judicial review by the CJEU – may arguably raise concerns in relation to effective judicial protection. Although the appeals so far made to the Board have not been overly complicated, when an enforcement

[156] Decision of the Board of Appeal of the European Supervisory Authorities, *Global Private Rating Company 'Standard Rating' Ltd v. ESMA*, 10 January 2014. Looking beyond ESMA, a decision of the Board of Appeal in relation to a decision of the European Banking Authority was annulled by the General Court in Case T-660/14 *SV Capital OÜ v EBA*, ECLI:EU:T:2015:608, but this case hinged on grounds of lack of competence, rather than any procedural irregularity at the Board of Appeal stage.

[157] Supervisory measures, on the other hand, have been taken on the basis of a decision. However, none has yet to found an appeal to the Board of Appeal (source: discussion with ESMA representatives, March 2017).

[158] ESMA Board of Appeal Decision in Case 2020-D-03 of 28 December 2020.

[159] Regulation (EU) No 462/2013 of the European Parliament and of the Council of 21 May 2013 amending Regulation (EC) No 1060/2009 on credit rating agencies [2013] OJ L146/1.

[160] ESMA Board of Appeal Decision in Cases BoA-D-2019-01, BoA-D-2019-02, BoA-D-2019-03, BoA-D-2019-04 of 27 February 2019.

[161] ibid 325.

[162] Post-Brexit, 3 Central Counterparties ('CCPs') are recognised as third-country CCPs (ICE Clear Europe Limited, LCH Limited and LME Clear Limited): they are eligible to provide their services in the EU as of the official withdrawal of the UK on 1 January 2021. Otherwise, other UK companies will have to undergo registration with ESMA and proceed to meet the compliance requirements as established in the MiFIR equivalence regime; Regulation (EU) No 600/2014 of the European Parliament and of the Council of 15 May 2014 on markets in financial instruments and amending Regulation (EU) No 648/2012 [2014] OJ L173/84 ('MiFIR').

appeal does eventually arise, the time limits set out in the Rules of Procedure may be greatly tested, due in part to the fact that members of the Board of Appeal are spread across multiple Member States, making swift correspondence more difficult. Moreover, Article 20(1) of the Rules of Procedure allows the President of the Board of Appeal to deem that the appeal is lodged – thereby triggering the two-month period in which it must decide an appeal[163] – when he or she considers that the evidence is complete. As such, should the exchange of evidence, making of oral representations and so on drag on for months, the effectiveness of (quasi-)judicial protection may be jeopardised. In such circumstances, recourse to suspensive effect[164] might provide welcome succour, although it remains to be seen whether the Board of Appeal would apply the (exacting) established CJEU criteria.

D. OLAF

Since OLAF has no legal personality of its own, actions for annulment[165] and actions for damages[166] brought before the EU Courts against the legality of its investigative acts are lodged against the Commission.[167] In relation to both types of action the EU Courts may, upon request of the applicant, grant interim relief provisionally suspending the effects of the contested act(s).[168] Furthermore, an indirect[169] review of such acts is available before the EU Courts where an act or decision taken by an authority other than OLAF is based – entirely or partly – on an OLAF investigative act.

i. Direct Review: Actions for Annulment

a. Transfer of Final OLAF Report to National Authorities

Since the creation of OLAF, the EU Courts have systematically construed the wording in Article 263 TFEU to the effect that any natural or legal person may 'institute proceedings against an act addressed to that person or which is of direct and individual concern to them' in order to reject as inadmissible actions for annulment in relation to the Office's investigative procedures that are deemed not to bring about a distinct change in the applicant's legal position.[170] The reasoning at the core of this consistent[171] interpretation is that the forwarding of OLAF's findings, in the shape of a final report, to NCAs does not lead automatically to the opening of judicial or disciplinary proceedings:

[163] Under Art 60(2) ESMA Regulation.

[164] Under Art 60(3) ESMA Regulation and Art 10, Board of Appeal Rules of Procedure.

[165] On the basis of Art 263(4) TFEU and, for EU staff, Art 270 TFEU in combination with Art 91 of the Staff Regulations.

[166] Arts 268 and 340 TFEU.

[167] See JFH Inghelram, 'Judicial review of investigative acts of the European anti-fraud Office (OLAF): A search for balance' (2012) 49 *CML Rev* 601, 603–05.

[168] Arts 278 and 279 TFEU.

[169] JFH Inghelram, *Legal and Institutional Aspects of the European Anti-Fraud Office (OLAF): An Analysis with a Look Forward to a European Public Prosecutor's Office* (Europa Law Publishing 2011) 203 and 225 et seq.

[170] ibid 204.

[171] Only one action for annulment against an OLAF investigative act has been considered admissible by the EU Courts, in Case T-48/05 *Franchet and Byk v Commission* ECLI:EU:T:2008:257.

the recipient competent authorities remain entirely free to decide whether or not to act upon the report – and thus whether or not to alter the legal position of the person(s) concerned by OLAF's investigations.[172] As such, investigations carried out by OLAF represent a preliminary stage of proceedings that may or may not lead to a decision establishing the liability of the person concerned.[173]

In *Tillack*, the CJEU thus held that the possible initiation of legal proceedings subsequent to the forwarding of information by OLAF, and the possible legal acts capable of affecting the legal position of the applicant, belonged to the sole and entire responsibility of the national authorities.[174] The action for annulment in *Tillack* against OLAF's forwarding of information on internal investigations to the Belgian prosecuting authorities was therefore deemed inadmissible. According to the reasoning in *Tillack*, should the adverse conclusion be drawn to the effect that NCAs are *not* free to assess the content and significance of the information they receive from OLAF – in other words, should national authorities be considered bound to initiate proceedings in relation to the person(s) concerned – this would 'alter the division of tasks and responsibilities as prescribed' in the (then-applicable) OLAF Regulation.[175] This does not seem to have changed subsequent to the amendments of the (now-applicable) OLAF Regulation,[176] which inter alia strengthened the evidentiary value of OLAF reports by declaring them admissible in all procedures before the CJEU, in proeedings of a non-criminal nature before national courts and in national administrative proceedings.[177] In an order rendered in 2020, the General Court confirmed that 'OLAF's reports and recommendations drawn up following an external or internal investigation and sent to the competent authorities of the Member States are only recommendations or opinions which have no binding legal effects'.[178]

b. OLAF Investigative Acts

Actions for annulment against investigative acts carried out by OLAF prior to the delivery of any final report have not met with success before the EU Courts either.

[172] Case T-29/03 *Comunidad Autónoma de Andalucía v Commission* ECLI:EU:T:2004:235, para 37; *Camós Grau* (n 36) para 51; Case T-193/04 *Tillack v Commission* ECLI:EU:T:2006:292, paras 69 and 70.

[173] See Case 60/81 *IBM v Commission* ECLI:EU:C:1981:264, para 10 (emphasis added): '[I]n principle an act is open to review only if it is a measure definitively laying down the position of the Commission or the Council on the conclusion of that procedure, and not a *provisional measure intended to pave the way for the final decision*.'

[174] *Tillack* (n 172) para 70.

[175] ibid para 72; Regulation (EC) No 1073/1999 of the European Parliament and of the Council of 25 May 1999 concerning investigations conducted by the European Anti-Fraud Office (OLAF) [1999] OJ L136/1.

[176] Regulation (EU, Euratom) No 883/2013 of the European Parliament and of the Council of 11 September 2013 concerning investigations conducted by the European Anti-Fraud Office (OLAF) and repealing Regulation (EC) No 1073/1999 of the European Parliament and of the Council and Council Regulation (Euratom) No 1074/1999 [2013] OJ L248/1 ('OLAF Regulation'), as amended by Regulation (EU, Euratom) 2020/2223 of the European Parliament and of the Council of 23 December 2020 amending Regulation (EU, Euratom) No 883/2013, as regards cooperation with the European Public Prosecutor's Office and the effectiveness of the European Anti-Fraud Office investigations [2020] OJ L437/49.

[177] New Art 11(2) OLAF Regulation; in criminal proceedings, the current rule remains, ie OLAF reports are admissible in the same way as the reports of national administrative inspectors; T Wahl, 'OLAF's New Amended Legal Framework' *eucrim* 20 January 2021, available at https://eucrim.eu/news/olafs-new-amended-legal-framework/ (accessed 11 September 2021).

[178] Case T-738/18 *Dragnea v Commission* ECLI:EU:T:2020:208, para 40.

Settled case law provides that acts or decisions adopted in the course of preparatory proceedings would be open to review only if they 'were themselves the culmination of a special procedure distinct'[179] from the final decision on liability – meaning, in the OLAF context, that taken at national level. This reasoning has been applied in rejecting as inadmissible actions for annulment brought against an OLAF decision to open an investigation,[180] acts performed by OLAF in the course of an investigation,[181] the drawing up by the Office of a final report,[182] decisions by OLAF to close an investigation[183] and not to annul investigative acts allegedly compromised by a conflict of interest,[184] OLAF's refusal to inform an investigated person of certain acts taken against that person in order to allow for a defence in the context of the investigation,[185] and OLAF's forwarding of a report concluding an internal investigation to an EU institution.[186]

Crucial to this line of reasoning are the direct consequences – at the supranational level – of an economic actor's refusal to cooperate with OLAF. Where an undertaking subject to investigation refuses to cooperate by, for example, denying the Office access to its premises, OLAF's only option is to request the aid of the NCAs to perform the operation.[187] Although those authorities are in principle bound by the duty of sincere cooperation,[188] this in no way diminishes their freedom to adopt the action they deem to be appropriate in accordance with national law: they may very well decline to offer assistance. Here, a useful contrast[189] can be drawn between OLAF and the enforcement of EU competition law, where the Commission may, unlike OLAF, order undertakings to submit to inspections,[190] bolstered by the threat of fines in the event of non-compliance.[191] As such, an order to submit to inspection clearly affects the legal position of the relevant undertakings or associations of undertakings – and is hence open to review by the EU Courts.[192]

[179] *IBM* (n 173) para 11.
[180] Case C-471/02 P(R) *Gómez-Reino v Commission* ECLI:EU:C:2003:210.
[181] ibid.
[182] *Comunidad Autónoma de Andalucía* (n 172).
[183] Case C-127/13 P *Strack v Commission* ECLI:EU:C:2014:2250.
[184] *Camós Grau* (n 35).
[185] *Gómez-Reino* (n 180).
[186] ibid.
[187] See V Covolo, *L'émergence d'un droit pénal en réseau: Analyse critique du système européen de lutte antifraude* (Nomos 2015) 567 et seq; this is still the case after the amendment of Regulation 883/2013; see new Arts 3(6) and 7(3). The amendments to Art 3 are in conformity with the interpretation given by the General Court in its ruling in Case T-48/16 *Sigma Orionis SA v European Commission* ECLI:EU:T:2018:245, paras 81-82. However, when operators submit to a check by OLAF, the amendment clarifies, inspections are subject to Union law alone. This includes the procedural guarantees provided for in the OLAF legal framework, the application of which is clarified in the context of on-the-spot checks and inspections in the new Art 3(8). This provision holds that the economic operator concerned has the right not to incriminate himself or herself and to be assisted by a person of his or her choice. Furthermore, when making statements during on-the-spot checks, the economic operator has the possibility to use any of the official languages of the Member State in which he or she is located.
[188] Art 4(3) TEU.
[189] See Inghelram (n 169) 208–10.
[190] Art 20(4) Regulation 1/2003.
[191] Art 23(1)(c) Regulation 1/2003.
[192] Art 20(4) Regulation 1/2003.

A 'tentative exception'[193] to the EU Courts' refusal to admit actions for annulment against OLAF investigative acts appeared in *Violetti*,[194] where the Civil Service Tribunal found, pursuant to an OLAF investigation into high rates of invalidity pensions granted to personnel at the Commission's site in Ispra (Italy), in favour of the plaintiffs, who argued, inter alia, that they had had no opportunity to be heard before the transmission of the Office's final report on the matter to the Italian judicial authorities. In contrast to the judgment of the Court of Justice in *Tillack*, the Civil Service Tribunal first accepted that the decision to forward the information contained in that report met the criterion of an 'act adversely affecting'[195] the officials.[196] It went on to insist that the fundamental principle of the rights of the defence (in this case, the right to be heard) would not be effectively protected 'in sufficient time' were it not to carry out a review of legality in relation to that decision. This was because the national court would retain before it information received from OLAF upon which it ought to be barred from acting.[197]

The decision in *Violetti* was later reversed[198] by the General Court in a return to the established case law, albeit in a decision that insisted it is not impossible for an action for annulment to succeed against OLAF investigative acts, depending on the specific (and likely exceptional) context.[199] The General Court added, as had the Court of Justice in *Tillack*,[200] that effective judicial protection is secured by other EU-level remedies: actions for damages and preliminary ruling procedures.[201]

Finally, since the legality of an OLAF investigative act may in turn affect the legality of another decision taken by an EU institution partly or entirely on the basis of that act, there have also been attempts to seek the review of the prior OLAF act indirectly via a review of the later decision. In *CPEM*,[202] the applicant challenged a Commission decision to cancel European Social Fund (ESF) assistance that was partially based on an OLAF report. The applicant argued, unsuccessfully, that the preceding OLAF investigation had violated his defence rights. All analogous instances of this version of indirect judicial review by the EU courts of OLAF investigative acts have also been dismissed.[203]

[193] Inghelram (n 169) 206.

[194] Joined Cases F-5/05 and F-7/05 *Violetti and Others v Commission* ECLI:EU:F:2009:39, esp paras 56–58.

[195] Art 90a, Staff Regulations.

[196] *Violetti* (CST) (n 194) para 77. The Tribunal also stressed at para 75 that such a decision 'is liable to have significant consequences for the career of the persons concerned'.

[197] ibid para 78.

[198] Case T-261/09 P *Commission v Violetti and Others* ECLI:EU:T:2010:215; see also Case T-289/16 *Inox Mare Srl v Commission* ECLI:EU:T:2017:414, para 16.

[199] *Commission v Violetti* (n 198) para 71: '[I]l convient de rappeler que le fait qu'un acte intervienne au cours d'une procédure complexe n'implique pas nécessairement qu'il sera dépourvu d'effets juridiques … et que la conclusion selon laquelle une décision de transmission d'informations ne constitue pas un acte faisant grief ne préjuge pas de la position du juge à l'égard de la qualification d'autres actes de l'OLAF.'

[200] ibid para. 80.

[201] ibid paras 65 et seq.

[202] Case T-444/07 *Centre de promotion de l'emploi par la micro-entreprise (CPEM) v Commission* ECLI:EU:T:2009:227.

[203] Case T-259/05 *Spain v Commission* ECLI:EU:2009:232; Case C-432/04 *Commission v Cresson* ECLI:EU:C:2006:455.

c. OLAF's Refusal to Open an Investigation into the Conduct of Previous Investigations and to Grant Access to Documents Contained in the Files Relating to those Investigations

In a judgment rendered in 2022, the Court held:

> OLAF's refusal to open an investigation into the conduct of previous investigations could not be regarded as a measure producing binding legal effects capable of affecting the interests of the appellant by bringing about a distinct change in his legal position. The refusal therefore did not constitute a decision against which an action for annulment may be brought under Article 263 TFEU.[204]

In doing so, the Court rejected the appellant's arguments that OLAF's refusal to open an investigation into the conduct of its previous investigations had infringed his right to an effective remedy under Article 47 of the Charter, because Regulation 883/2013 does not confer on natural or legal persons the right to request OLAF to open an investigation into its own previous investigations.[205]

Nevertheless, the Court held that OLAF's refusal to grant access to documents is subject to judicial review. By failing to inform the appellant of his right to make a confirmatory application under Article 7(2) of Regulation 1049/2001 regarding public access to European Parliament, Council and Commission documents, OLAF had definitively established its position of refusing his request for access to documents, and therefore its letter of refusal could be the subject to an action for annulment.[206] According to the Court's reasoning, it did not matter that the appellant had not mentioned Regulation 1049/2001 in his letter by which he requested access to the documents, because Regulation 1049/2001 did not impose any obligation to specify the legal basis of the request and, furthermore, provides 'a very extensive right of access to the documents of the institutions concerned'.[207] Therefore, OLAF should have examined his request under Regulation 1049/2001 and should have informed him of his right to a confirmatory application.[208] The Court concluded that the General Court had erred in law by holding that 'the refusal of access to the documents requested … could not be regarded as a definitive act against which an action for annulment may be brought'.[209]

ii. Direct Review: Actions for Damages

Articles 268 and 340(2) TFEU provide that where non-contractual liability is proved, the EU is to make good any damage caused by its institutions or servants in performance of their duties. Three conditions must be met for reparation to be awarded: the

[204] Case C-351/20 P *Dragnea v Commission* ECLI:EU:C:2022:8, para 43.
[205] ibid para 45.
[206] ibid para 76; Regulation (EC) No 1049/2001 of the European Parliament and of the Council of 30 May 2001 regarding public Access to European Parliament, Council and Commission documents [2001] OJ L145/43.
[207] ibid paras 69–72.
[208] ibid para 73.
[209] ibid para 77.

rule of law infringed must be intended to confer rights on persons; the breach must be sufficiently serious; and there must be a direct causal link between the breach of the obligation and the damage sustained by the injured parties.[210]

To date, damages have been awarded in only a handful of cases – all concerning internal investigations.[211] In all cases of an alleged violation of individual rights in external investigations, on the other hand, application of the *Tillack* rationale distancing action taken in respect of information forwarded by OLAF from the Office's preceding contested act(s) has precluded fulfilment of the 'direct causal link' condition.

From a defence rights perspective, the progress represented by successful actions for damages[212] is tapered by the fact that damages awarded have no effect on the validity of the legal effect giving rise to reparation. So it was in *Camós Grau*, where a final report deemed 'one-sided and biased'[213] by the General Court was nonetheless forwarded to prosecuting authorities. This is further compounded by the fact that actions for damages, similarly to actions for annulment, take a considerable length of time before judgment is passed.[214]

iii. Direct Review: Interim Relief in Actions for Annulment and Actions for Damages

Although actions brought before them have no suspensory effect, where the EU Courts consider that the circumstances so require – in essence, in order to avoid the situation in which the time needed to establish the existence of a right does not have the effect of depriving that right of substance by eliminating any possibility of exercising it[215] – they may order that application of the contested act(s) be suspended.[216] Interim relief is necessarily provisional in nature, and is an ancillary mechanism in the sense that an application for interim relief is admissible only if the applicant is challenging the measure per se in the relevant proceedings. As such, where the primary claim is thrown out, any application for interim relief falls with it.

This package effect poses particular difficulty in actions for annulment, the admissibility of which is construed narrowly by the EU Courts. Where the admissibility threshold *is* met in such an action, Inghelram sees no obstacles to the granting of interim relief suspending OLAF operations pending the outcome of the court proceedings, provided that the order is justified prima facie in law and fact, that there

[210] *Bergaderm and Goupil* (n 72) para 42.

[211] *Camós Grau* (n 35); *Franchet and Byk* (n 171); Case C-220/13 P *Nikolaou v Court of Auditors* ECLI:EU:C:2014:2057. The action for damages by Fernando De Esteban Alonso (also concerning internal investigations) was first granted by the General Court (Case T-138/18 *Fernando De Esteban Alonso v Commission* ECLI:EU:T:2019:398) but later dismissed by the Court of Justice (Case C-591/19 P *Fernando De Esteban Alonso v Commission* ECLI:EU:C:2021:468).

[212] For a violation of the obligation of impartiality (*Camós Grau*), unauthorised leaks of confidential information (*Nikolaou; Franchet and Byk*) and for infringement of the right to be heard (also *Franchet and Byk*).

[213] *Camós Grau* (n 35) para 129.

[214] Inghelram (n 169) 220.

[215] ibid 220.

[216] Art 278 TFEU.

is an urgent need for interim relief in order to avoid serious and irreparable damage to the applicants' interests, and that those interests outweigh others at stake in the proceedings.[217] The same author sees the immediacy of interim relief as a potentially very effective form of legal protection for suspects in OLAF investigations.[218] The jurisprudence remains unclear on whether interim relief is a realistic proposition in the context of actions for damages targeting OLAF investigative acts.[219]

iv. Indirect Review: Preliminary Rulings

Where a national measure amenable to judicial review is taken on the basis of OLAF findings delivered to national authorities or information or evidence brought to light following a request for assistance issued by OLAF to national authorities, individuals subject to such a measure may request that the CJEU rule on the validity of the relevant OLAF act under EU law.[220] In this regard it is irrelevant that an OLAF investigative act is not legally binding: primary EU law confers on the Court jurisdiction to give a preliminary ruling on the validity and interpretation of all acts of the EU institutions without exception.[221]

To date, two requests[222] for a preliminary ruling on the validity of OLAF investigative acts have been made, with one producing answers to the questions asked by the national court. In *Afasia Knits Deutschland*, the Court of Justice found that an on-the-spot check carried out by OLAF in Jamaica was consistent with the international agreement on Office investigations in third countries, underlining that the local authorities took part in the inspections and endorsed the results of the investigation.[223]

The continued paucity of requests for a preliminary ruling on the validity of OLAF investigative acts may be explained by two facets of Article 263 TFEU: such a ruling must be deemed essential by the national jurisdiction in order to reach judgment, and is mandatory only in cases pending before a court or tribunal against whose decisions there is no judicial remedy under national law.[224] In practice, in the vast majority of cases national law enforcement authorities' assistance provided to OLAF may not be demonstrably (exclusively) based on the information provided to them by OLAF: separate, further investigation will often take place on the national level before a prosecution is brought on the strength of all available evidence. In this scenario, the applicant challenging a national measure – in their eyes, based on OLAF's activity – will have difficulty establishing that the validity of that national measure depends on the validity of a

[217] Inghelram (n 169) 221.

[218] ibid 225.

[219] See the President of the Court of Justice in Case C-51/90 *Comos-Tank and Others* ECLI:EU:C:1990:228, para 33: '[I]t can also be left open whether an application for the suspension of the operation of a measure is admissible where it is made by a party which has brought an action solely for compensation for the damage which it claims to be suffering as a result of the application of the measure in question …' See also Case T-203/95 *Connolly v Commission* ECLI:EU:T:1999:101, paras 23–25; and Inghelram (n 169) 222 et seq.

[220] Art 267 TFEU.

[221] Case C-322/88 *Grimaldi* ECLI:EU:C:1989:646, para 8.

[222] Case C-409/10 *Afasia Knits Deutschland* ECLI:EU:C:2011:843; and Case C-348/11 *Thomson Sales Europe* ECLI:EU:C:2012:169.

[223] *Afasia Knits Deutschland* (n 222) para 34.

[224] Respectively Art 267(3) and (4) TFEU.

prior OLAF investigative act, and hence in turn that a request for a preliminary ruling on the OLAF act is required in order to resolve the national proceedings.[225]

v. Ex Post *Non-Judicial (or Quasi-Judicial) Review*

The Supervisory Committee (SC) monitors OLAF's implementation of its investigative function, in particular the application of procedural guarantees and the duration of investigations, in order to reinforce its independence.[226] The SC addresses opinions and recommendations to the Director-General (and may submit reports to the European Parliament, the Council, the Commission and the Court of Auditors), but must not interfere with the conduct of investigations in progress.[227] In practice, the division is not always clear between systemic supervision and review of individual cases, where the SC has levelled severe criticism at OLAF and its Director-General.[228] However, the SC was not designed as a complaints body and its opinions and recommendations are not legally binding on OLAF.

Regulation 2020/2223 on cooperation with the European Public Prosecutor's Office and the effectiveness of the European Anti-Fraud Office investigations, which amended OLAF Regulation 883/2013, established a 'Controller of procedural guarantees',[229] who is administratively attached to the SC.[230] While the initial proposal of the Commission envisaged that the tasks of the Controller should include both an *ex post* review of OLAF investigative acts in relation to any person concerned by such acts[231] and an *ex ante* authorisation mechanism in relation to certain investigative measures taken against members of EU institutions,[232] only the *ex post* review was eventually adopted.[233]

The Controller exercises his functions 'in complete independence and shall neither seek nor take instructions from anyone in the performance of [his] duties'.[234] Nevertheless, the Controller's *ex post* review is non-binding; where the Director-General decides not to follow a recommendation, he is bound only to provide reasons for doing so to the Controller and (where this would not affect an ongoing investigation) the complainant.[235] Those reasons shall also be stated by the Director-General in a motivated note attached to the final investigation report.[236] The *ex post* complaints mechanism is limited to a review by the Controller of the 'Office's compliance with the procedural guarantees referred to in Article 9, as well as on the grounds of an infringement of the rules applicable to investigations by the Office, in particular

[225] Covolo (n 187) 18.
[226] Art 15(1) OLAF Regulation.
[227] ibid.
[228] Citing SC Opinion 2/2012 on the Dalli case, see M Luchtman and M Wasmeier, 'The political and judicial accountability of OLAF' in M Scholten and M Luchtman (eds) *Law Enforcement by EU Authorities: Implications for Political and Judicial Accountability* (Edward Elgar 2017) 221, 230–232.
[229] New Arts 9a and 9b OLAF Regulation.
[230] New Art 9a(2) OLAF Regulation.
[231] COM (2014) 340 final, Art 9a.
[232] ibid Art 9b.
[233] New Arts 9a(8) and 9b OLAF Regulation.
[234] New Art 9a(6) OLAF Regulation.
[235] New Art 9b(7) OLAF Regulation.
[236] ibid.

infringements of procedural requirements and fundamental rights'.[237] Subject to short time limits, the Controller shall examine the complaint in an adversarial procedure, in the course of which he may ask witnesses to provide written or oral explanations.[238] The complaints mechanism is without prejudice to the means of redress available under the Treaties, including actions relating to compensation for damage.[239]

In addition to the complaints mechanism, the Controller also takes over an advisory function on procedural guarantees. According to the new Article 9b(9), the Director-General may request the opinion of the Controller on any matter related to procedural guarantees or fundamental rights that falls within the Controller's mandate. In such cases, the Director-General may indicate the time limit within which the Controller shall respond.

IV. Remedies at the National Level

A. Judicial Review of Investigatory Actions

Given the fragmented legal framework, judicial protection in relation to the investigative acts of DG Competition, the ECB, ESMA and OLAF – or of their national counterparts – is necessary not only at EU level, but also at the national level. Review mechanisms at national level are particularly important when direct judicial review at EU level appears to be limited, for instance in the case of OLAF. The national systems studied here[240] reveal considerable differences regarding the extent to which investigatory measures can be directly challenged, whether launching such a challenge (where possible) requires prior exhaustion of internal administrative remedies or is only possible at the time of sanctioning proceedings, and whether such review has suspensive effect. Differences can also be observed as to the limitations of judicial review.

In Germany, Italy and the Netherlands, investigatory measures are not autonomously subject to judicial review. They may be challenged only by lodging an appeal against the decision on which the measure is based, or the necessary *ex ante* authorisation of the measure.[241]

[237] New Art 9b(1) OLAF Regulation.

[238] New Art 9b(2)–(6) OLAF Regulation.

[239] New Art 9b(8) OLAF Regulation.

[240] As mentioned in section I.B, this section is based on a comparative analysis of the domestic legal regimes of France, Germany, Hungary, Italy, Luxembourg, the Netherlands and Poland. See the Annex to this chapter for an overview of the domestic counterparts of DG Competition, the ECB, ESMA and OLAF in France, Germany, Hungary, Italy, Luxembourg, the Netherlands and Poland.

[241] In Germany, under competition law, investigative measures (request for information, production orders, inspection) have to be based on a formal decision (*Verwaltungsakt*). This formal decision is subject to judicial review by the Higher Regional Court (*Oberlandesgericht*) Düsseldorf. Concerning searches, it is the necessary *ex ante* authorisation that is subject to appeal at the competent district court (*Landgericht*): Report Germany (Study One, n 17) 84. In Italy, concerning actions of the Italian ECB and ESMA counterparts (*Banca d'Italia* and *Consob*), when the final decision is an administrative measure, the judicial review is carried out by the Regional Administrative Tribunal in Rome (*Tribunale amministrativo regionale – Lazio*). Actions for annulment must be brought within 60 days of the date of notification. Appeals are sent to the Council of the State (*Consiglio di Stato*). When the final decision is an administrative sanction, it will be subject to the authority of the civil courts: Report Italy (Study One, n 17) 150.

Germany, the Netherlands and Poland require that internal administrative remedies be exhausted before review by a court may be requested.[242] Time limits to file an internal remedy vary, ranging from two weeks in Poland to six in the Netherlands,[243] and so do time limits applying to judicial review.[244] Usually, the scope of internal remedies is wider than the scope of judicial remedies, with the former extending to all formal and substantive issues, and the latter being limited to reviewing the legality of the administrative decision.[245]

The Polish and French counterparts of DG Competition and OLAF respectively do not require the exhaustion of internal administrative remedies. Instead, investigative measures of these authorities can be directly challenged in court.[246]

In several countries, investigatory actions are subject to review only at the moment of sanctioning decisions.[247] In practice, operators subject to investigative measures are therefore deprived of the means to challenge the regularity of these measures and must wait until the sanctioning body is seized or an appeal can be filed against the decision of the latter.[248]

Remedies do not have any suspensive effect in Germany, Poland or France.[249] In the Netherlands too, neither the procedure for lodging an objection nor an appeal procedure before the administrative judge has suspensive effect, unless statutory regulation provides otherwise.[250]

The overview shows that there is almost no common thread between countries concerning judicial protection against investigatory measures taken by DG Competition, the ECB, ESMA or OLAF, or their domestic counterparts. Rules differ between states, and partly also depending on which EU authority's actions are concerned.

Judicial protection at national level follows the respective national logic of checks and balances that are rarely similar to those of other states and thus hardly comparable. It is therefore impossible to assess whether judicial protection against investigative measures of the examined EU authorities and/or their domestic counterparts is better or stronger in one country than in another. Instead, one can only assess whether judicial protection is adequate with regard to standards stipulated in Article 47 of the Charter *within* each individual country.[251]

[242] Decisions of the German ESMA counterpart (*Bundesanstalt für Finanzdienstleistungsaufsicht*, BaFin), for instance, are subject to the internal remedy available in administrative law (*Widerspruch*) and to the action of annulment before the administrative court (*Anfechtungsklage*). Also, German tax law provides for an internal remedy (*Einspruch*) and for judicial review before the fiscal court: Report Germany (Study One, n 17) 84.

[243] Report the Netherlands 125; Report Poland 186 (both Study One, n 17).

[244] In Germany, both time limits for internal and judicial review is one month: Report Germany (Study One, n 17) 85. In Poland, an appeal must be lodged within one month: Report Poland (Study One, n 17) 186.

[245] Report Germany, 85; Report the Netherlands, 125; Report Poland, 186–87 (all Study One, n 17).

[246] Report Poland, 185; Report France, 216 (both Study One, n 17).

[247] This is the case in France for the domestic counterpart of the ECB (*Autorité de contrôle prudentiel et de résolution*, ACPR) concerning the measures of interviewing of persons, access to premises (without search or seizure), monitoring of bank accounts and access to traffic data: Report France (Study One, n 17) 214–16. See also Report the Netherlands (Study One, n 17) 125–26.

[248] Report France (Study One, n 17) 214–16.

[249] Report Germany, 84; Report Poland, 186; Report France, 215 (all Study One, n 17).

[250] Report the Netherlands (Study One, n 17) 127; such an exception is foreseen in competition law: when the Dutch DG Competition counterpart (*Autoriteit Consument en Markt*, ACM) imposes an administrative fine by decision and an objection is lodged, the execution of this decision is suspended by 24 weeks: ibid.

[251] Even though, generally, in several countries, the possibilities to have investigatory measures reviewed by the examined European authorities or their domestic counterparts are rather limited. In Poland, for instance,

The plethora of different rules is, however, problematic when it comes to transnational cases. Indeed, judicial protection in purely domestic cases might be comprehensive and straightforward – and thus effective. However, as soon as the case has a transnational element, the rules on judicial protection become a patchwork. As a consequence, it is not only impossible to determine whether protection would be complete in a given transnational case, but it is also difficult to obtain protection in a concrete case because of the opacity of the patchwork of rules. It is therefore doubtul whether judicial protection at the national level regarding transnational cases is truly effective.[252]

B. Review of Decisions on Admissibility of Evidence

Alongside the possibilities to review the merits of a case and to challenge an investigative measure, the possibility to contest the admissibility of evidence is of the essence to ensure both adequate protection of the parties' rights and the lawful functioning of punitive systems.[253]

Admissibility of evidence is – just as judicial review of investigative measures – dealt with in a different way in each Member State. When it comes to the possible review of decisions on the admissibility of evidence, however, a certain degree of consistency seems to exist throughout the EU. In almost all Member States' criminal justice systems, there is reportedly no decision on admissibility as such that may be subject to judicial review. A review of evidence and its admissibility may nonetheless be triggered in two ways.

First, the admissibility of evidence can be contested by appealing the decision that criminal courts adopt at the end of the criminal proceedings. While this is a general principle, there are some specificities in each Member State. In Italy, for instance, only the non-admission of decisive counter-evidence can represent a ground for appeal before the Court of Cassation, whereas no such limitation applies to appeals lodged before the Courts of Appeal.[254] In Germany, defence counsel seeking to raise an objection that inadmissible evidence has been accepted and used must do so during the trial, otherwise the potential appeal of the court's decision cannot contest issues related to the admissibility of that evidence.[255]

Second, although there is often no explicit provision in national criminal procedural rules specifying a stage of the procedure when admissibility must be assessed,

there is a general rule that investigatory measures taken by domestic counterparts of DG Competition, ECB, ESMA or OLAF may only be challenged if such a possibility is clearly foreseen in the relevant statute. If the statute is silent the act may not be challenged: Report Poland (Study One, n 17) 185. In Italy, under competition law, a company can only appeal against decisions of the Italian Competition Authority that directly affect its rights: Report Italy (Study One, n 17) 150.

[252] On this topic see conclusions of ch 1 of this volume (Luchtman). See also, ch 2 (De Vries and Widdershoven).

[253] On this topic see ch 6 (Giuffrida and Theodorakakou) and ch 9 (Vervaele) of this volume.

[254] Report Italy (Study Three, n 17) 174.

[255] Report Germany (Study Three, n 17) 135–36. The German rapporteurs note, however, that such a requirement has been highly criticised and does not apply, according to recent case law, to inadmissible evidence that has been collected by illegally searching private premises.

in most Member States it is usually possible to challenge, already during the pre-trial phase, an investigative measure carried out by public authorities (eg public prosecutors or judicial police). If this action is successful, the evidence collected through that investigative measure shall not be included in the case file.[256] This scheme is known in many countries as the 'nullity' (or 'invalidity') of investigative acts.[257] The French system is a case in point. Acts or documents of the procedure – a notion that covers not only the procedural acts of the investigative judge and his or her delegates, but also acts carried out in the course of investigations and prosecutions – can be annulled by the investigating chamber (and not by the investigative judge), in principle upon request of the interested parties. The nullity of an act can be provided for by the law, such as when given measures comply with a given requirement 'under penalty of nullity', but can also depend on the failure to abide by a substantive formality enshrined in a rule of criminal procedure, when such a failure adversely affected the interests of the party concerned.[258]

Similarly, in Luxembourg, nullities can be 'formal', that is provided for by the law, or 'substantial/virtual'. Substantial/virtual nullities have been introduced via case law, when serious irregularities, including irregularities affecting the rights of defence, occur.[259] Luxembourgish public prosecutors, as well as any interested party having a legitimate interest, can ask the pre-trial chamber of the district court, within strict deadlines, to decide on the invalidity of acts (*requête en nullité*) of pre-trial investigations. The legislator aims to ensure that objections to the admissibility of evidence are confined to the pre-trial phase, since the *requête en nullité* cannot – save for in exceptional circumstances – be lodged before the trial court. If no review of illegally or improperly obtained evidence is triggered in time (or at all), such evidence becomes valid (*purge des nullités*).[260] Similar possibilities to challenge the legality of investigative acts such as searches and seizures or surveillance measures are mentioned in the German report, which clarifies:

> If the court quashes the seizure, the public prosecutor must return the seized documents to the appellant. Upon request, the public prosecutor must delete corresponding data … and the applicant may bring the matter before court if the public prosecutor's office does not comply with its obligation.[261]

Finally, as in criminal proceedings, in administrative proceedings there is reportedly no decision on admissibility as such that may be subject to judicial review. Again, issues

[256] By way of exception, for instance, in the Netherlands, at least in non-criminal procedures, even if unlawfulness is found, materials will remain in the case file as long as that is in the interest of the procedure ('*belang van de strafvordering*').

[257] See ch 9 of this volume (Vervaele).

[258] Report France (Study Three, n 17) 99–100. The notion of 'acts or documents of the procedure' is contested in French doctrine and does not cover mere means or proof of information, which cannot be annulled but are subject to adversarial debate during the trial and to the unfettered evaluation of the judge.

[259] Report Luxembourg (Study Three, n 17) 187–89. In line with the Luxembourgish courts' monist approach, alleged violations of the ECHR rights, especially the rights of defence, could determine the nullity of a given procedural act.

[260] Report Luxembourg (Study Three, n 17) 189.

[261] Report Germany (Study Three, n 17) 135–36.

concerning the admissibility of evidence can be contested when challenging the decision adopted by administrative authorities at the end of the administrative proceedings.[262]

Administrative courts are usually competent for this review, but in some cases a review is first carried out within the administrative authorities.[263]

C. Limitations on the Transfer of Information

Judicial protection against measures of the EU authorities studied and/or their domestic counterparts in the wider sense of the term also includes protection against the transfer of information from the national level to these EU authorities. National laws stipulate several principles that limit such a transfer of information. Their applicability depends not only on the recipient of the information, but also on what kind of institution would be the sender – the national counterpart of the EU authority in question, another administrative authority or a judicial authority.[264]

Under Regulation 1/2003 on the implementation of the rules on competition laid down in Articles 81 and 82 of the Treaty, information transferred for the purposes of applying Articles 101 and 102 may only be used in respect of the subject matter for which it was collected by the transmitting authority. This rule is called the 'specialty principle' and is applicable in the Netherlands,[265] Germany,[266] Luxembourg[267] and Italy[268] with regard to transfers of information between DG Competition and its respective counterparts.

Regarding transfers to the ECB, most national rules (with the exception of Luxembourg[269]) do not prescribe any limitation based on the specialty principle, as there is a general obligation under EU law to transfer information to the ECB.[270]

[262] The above-mentioned criminal law rules on the judicial review of investigative measures apply as well, as long as a given investigative measure is available in punitive administrative proceedings: Report Germany (Study Three, n 17) 136.

[263] In Luxembourg, for instance, VAT Administration decisions that impose financial penalties are first subject to the so-called 'reclamation', by which the individual requires the Administration to reconsider its decision. This further decision of the Administration can then be challenged before the civil chamber of the district court of Luxembourg: Report Luxembourg (Study Three, n 17) 192.

[264] On this topic see also ch 5 of this volume (Bovend'Eerdt and Karagianni).

[265] Under Dutch national law, the domestic DG Competition counterpart (*Autoriteit Consument en Markt*, ACM) may only transfer information to foreign institutions if the non-disclosure of the information by DG Competition is sufficiently guaranteed and there is a sufficient guarantee that the information will not be used for a purpose other than that for which it is supplied: Report the Netherlands (Study Two, n 17) 142.

[266] In Germany, the specialty principle is, however, not an absolute bar to the exchange of information but is subject to exceptions provided by the law. Since the wording of the applicable domestic law allows for the transfer of information that has been collected for a purpose other than the application of Arts 101 and 102 TFEU, the *Bundeskartellamt* (BKartA) has to balance the interests of the Commission (and the principle of loyal cooperation) on the one hand, and the interests of the undertaking concerned, on the other, when taking its decision on whether or not to submit the information requested by the Commission: Report Germany (Study Two, n 17) 61.

[267] Report Luxembourg (Study Two, n 17) 115.

[268] Report Italy (Study Two, n 17) 98.

[269] According to Luxembourg law, the domestic ECB counterpart (*Commission de surveillance du secteur financier*, CSSF) can exchange information to the extent that such information is needed for the performance of the ECB's supervisory tasks: Report Luxembourg (Study Two, n 17) 43.

[270] See for instance Report Germany (Study Two, n 17) 64.

By virtue of Recital 78 of Regulation 648/2012 and Recital 33 of Regulation 1060/2009, ESMA is in any case bound by the principle of purpose limitation. Therefore, and in view of the obligation to transfer information to ESMA, again, national law generally does not limit the transfer of information – even if it has been collected for other purposes.[271] Only Dutch law does so.[272]

As for OLAF, the Netherlands and Germany require that information transferred by their domestic administrative counterparts be used by OLAF only for the purpose for which it was requested or transferred.[273] Limitations are less strict when it comes to transfers by a judicial authority.[274]

Other principles limiting the transfer of information are the principle of secrecy of investigations, banking secrecy, professional secrecy or the principle of business secrecy.

The principle of secrecy of investigations only limits the transfer of information from domestic authorities to OLAF.[275] Banking secrecy is no longer a limitation in any of the countries examined here.[276] In Luxembourg, whilst information covered by banking secrecy may not be transferred, this is so not by virtue of banking secrecy laws but because of the fact that once such information is collected, it becomes part of the criminal case file and is thus covered by the secrecy of criminal investigations.[277] The same applies to information covered by business secrecy and stemming from judicial authorities in Luxembourg,[278] while in none of the other countries is it an impediment to the transfer of information.[279]

Professional secrecy is, compared to the aforementioned principles, a more important impediment to the transfer of information to DG Competition and OLAF in Germany, the Netherlands and Italy.[280]

[271] Report Germany (Study Two, n 17) 65.

[272] Report the Netherlands (Study Two, n 17) 146–48.

[273] Report the Netherlands, 126; Report Germany, 54 (both Study Two, n 17).

[274] Report the Netherlands (Study Two, n 17) 136.

[275] On the applicability of the principle regarding DG Competition, see Report the Netherlands, 142; Report Germany, 61; Report Luxembourg, 115 (all Study Two, n 17). On the applicability of the principle regarding the ECB, Report Germany, 64; Report the Netherlands, 146; Report Luxembourg, 118 (all Study Two, n 17). And regarding ESMA, Report Germany, 66; Report the Netherlands, 152 (both Study Two, n 17). German customs authority may still refuse to transfer information to OLAF, because although the legal basis for the exchange of information does impose an obligation, it leaves it to the discretion of the competent authority to decide whether or not to transfer information to OLAF: Report Germany (Study Two, n 17) 54. In the Netherlands, on the other hand, a public prosecutor can request that the Dutch OLAF counterpart does not transfer information to OLAF if this is in the best interests of an ongoing criminal investigation. In practice, however, due to the nature of the information transferred on the basis of Regulation 515/97 (ie control information), the secrecy of investigations does not easily act as a limitation: Report the Netherlands (Study Two, n 17) 126.

[276] Report the Netherlands, 126, 137, 142, 146, 152; Report Luxembourg, 115, 118; Report Italy, 92, 97, 98; Report Germany, 55, 61, 64, 66; Report Hungary, 72, 84 (all Study Two, n 17).

[277] Report Luxembourg (Study Two, n 17) 113.

[278] ibid 113 and 115.

[279] Report Germany, 56, 61–62, 64, 66; Report the Netherlands, 127, 137, 143, 152; Report Italy, 97, 98; Report Hungary, 72 (all Study Two, n 17).

[280] Regarding DG Competition, in Germany, professional secrecy may give rise to limitations where the evidence has been obtained illegally because the German DG Competition counterpart (BKartA) has violated the law on the protection of professional secrecy: Report Germany (Study Two, n 17) 61. In Italy, confidentiality is strongly protected in competition cases. Any information or data regarding undertakings being investigated by the Italian DG Competition counterpart is completely confidential. In the exercise of their

Professional secrecy grants the right to certain categories of people to withhold information in criminal investigations. Whilst these rights should usually be respected by the authorities when gathering information, any failure to do so can bar the transmission to OLAF of the relevant information. Protection of professional secrecy is often accorded to members of the clergy in order to protect citizens' freedom and liberty of religion, to legal counsel and notaries in order to protect citizens' defence rights, to doctors and medical staff in order to protect access to health experts and facilities,[281] as well as to members of parliament, tax consultants or representatives, or auditors and accountants.[282] Judges can overcome a situation where a witness refuses to provide information, when they believe that the alleged privilege is unfounded.[283]

On the other hand, transfer to ESMA or the ECB is allowed.[284] Regarding the ECB, according to Article 10(1) of the SSM Regulation, the ECB may require legal and natural persons mentioned therein 'to provide all information that is necessary in order to carry out the tasks conferred on it' by the Regulation. Article 10(2) adds that 'the persons referred to in paragraph 1 shall supply the information requested' and clarifies that even 'professional secrecy provisions do not exempt those persons from the duty to supply that information' and that 'supplying that information shall not be deemed to be in breach of professional secrecy'. These general rules apply to Italy, Germany and Luxembourg. As a consequence, when it comes to the exchange of information between the domestic counterparts and the ECB, the ordinary professional secrecy privilege does not apply.[285]

In fact, while the rules differ considerably from country to country, it appears that limitations on the transfer of information are kept to the level of protection required by the human rights framework and do not constitute an inroad to efficient enforcement. There is no difference here between domestic and transnational cases.

V. Comparative Conclusions

The principal differences between the routes to EU-level judicial review of investigative acts and/or sanctions carried out or imposed by the four analysed authorities are set out in comparative Tables 3.1–3.4.

functions, officials of the Italian Competition Authority shall be considered 'public officials'. As a consequence, they are sworn to secrecy and any information acquired in the process of enforcing Italian competition law shall only be used for the purposes for which it has been requested, and it is to be treated as confidential and may not be divulged even to government departments and authorities, notwithstanding the obligation to cooperate with the institutions of the EU: Report Italy (Study Two, n 17) 98. For the Netherlands, see Report the Netherlands (Study Two, n 17) 142.

[281] A special rule applies to journalists. They can only withhold information concerning the identity of their sources, and a judge can compel them to reveal their sources when he or she believes that certain information is essential in proving an alleged crime and that the reliability of information can only be checked by identifying the journalist's source: Report Italy (Study Two, n 17) 92.

[282] Report Germany (Study Two, n 17) 55–56.

[283] Report Italy (Study Two, n 17) 92.

[284] Regarding ESMA, Report Germany, 66; Report Italy, 104–05 (both Study Two, n 17).

[285] Report Germany, 64; Report Italy, 101; Report Luxembourg, 118 (all Study Two, n 17).

Table 3.1 Direct Review – Requests for Information

DG Competition	**ECB**	**ESMA**	**OLAF transfer of final report to NAs**
Commission must: - state legal basis; - state purpose of request; - specify information required.	Obligations on ECB as to precision of request unclear. But requests used rarely due to strong information position of ECB.	(As DG Competition) ESMA must: - state legal basis; - state purpose of request; - specify information required.	Action for annulment of decision to transfer to national authorities is inadmissible (*Tillack*)
Fishing expeditions are prohibited.	Review only if: - request is taken in form of decision; - non-compliance leads to fine (?)	Review only if: - request taken in form of decision that sanctions non-compliance; - no resolution at Board of Appeal stage.	

Table 3.2 Direct Review – Inspections

DG Competition	**ECB**	**ESMA**	**OLAF**
Commission must clearly indicate presumed facts it intends to investigate.	ECB decision must indicate legal basis and purpose of inspection.	ESMA must have written authorisation, state purpose and penalties for non-compliance.	Action for annulment is inadmissible. (*Tillack*)
Need to safeguard rights of defence!	Need to safeguard rights of defence?		
No separate action against individual investigative measures!	No separate action against individual investigative measures?		
		(No *enforcement* inspections yet; cf many supervisory inspections.)	

Table 3.3 Direct Review – Review of Fines

DG Competition	ECB	ESMA	OLAF
EU Courts may quash, reduce or increase a fine on basis of all factual evidence presented before them.	Penalties imposed by ECB are open to review by EU Courts.	Penalties imposed by ESMA are open to review by EU Courts.	No power to impose fines.
But EU Courts are not entitled to carry out a complete *de novo* review of facts and evidence.	But EU Courts may not review an ECB request to NCA to open proceedings. (*Tillack*?)		
	Relevance of 'complex economic and technical assessments' (as in competition law case law)?	Relevance of 'complex economic and technical assessments' (as in competition law case law)?	

Table 3.4 Direct Review – Actions for Damages

DG Competition	ECB	ESMA	OLAF
The rule of law infringed must be intended to confer rights on individuals.	Test as in left column.	Test as in left column.	Test as in left column.
The breach must be sufficiently serious.	May be difficult to assign responsibility for specific investigative act to either ECB or NCA.		Handful of successful actions, but only internal investigations.
And a direct causal link between such a breach and the allegedly sustained damage must be established. (*Bergaderm and Goupil*)			Length of process at EU level undermines reparation; file used regardless by national authorities.

Not all points of comparison can be represented in such a form due to the manifold differences between the authorities, with the ECB and ESMA being more supervision-oriented entities than DG Competition, whilst OLAF lacks – for now – the capacity to oblige national authorities to open investigations. The absence of this power has, indeed, been the single biggest cause of the extreme paucity of successful challenges to OLAF investigative acts before the EU Courts. Should it be envisaged to increase the autonomous powers of OLAF in future (eg should OLAF be able to address binding requests for information to national authorities), a commensurate level of review before the EU Courts will be an essential corollary in order to ensure the effective judicial protection of implicated persons.

Finally, due to the dearth of information provided on this aspect by the national reports, the complex relationship between judicial control at the national level and the EU level has not here received the attention that it merits.[286] With the benefit of more years of practice and more developed jurisprudence, this interplay ought to provide fertile ground for comprehensive comparative analysis in future.[287]

Annex

	DG Competition	ECB	ESMA	OLAF
F	Competition Authority (*Autorité de la concurrence*, ADLC)	Prudential Supervision Authority (*Autorité de contrôle prudentiel et de résolution*, ACPR)	Financial Market Authority (*Autorité des marchés financiers*, AMF)	French Anti-fraud coordination service is the DLNF (National Anti-Fraud Unit); Operational cooperation with OLAF: Customs Administration (administrative investigation services); Judicial police services acting under the authority and direction of the public prosecutor (in particular, Financial Prosecutor's Office (*Parquet National Financier*)) (judicial investigation services); National Judicial Customs Service (*Service National de la Douane Judiciaire*) (hybrid investigative services)
GER	Federal Cartel Office (*Bundeskartellamt*, BKatA)	Federal Financial Supervisory Authority (*Bundesanstalt für Finanzdienstleistungsaufsicht*, BaFin) and German Federal Bank (*Deutsche Bundesbank*)	Federal Financial Supervisory Authority (*Bundesanstalt für Finanzdienstleistungsaufsicht*, BaFin) and German Federal Bank (*Deutsche Bundesbank*)	Federal Ministry of Finance (*Bundesministerium der Finanzen*, BMF), supported by national authorities competent for implementing EU funds and by customs authorities

(continued)

[286] Report the Netherlands (Study One, n 17) does address this issue, at 126–127, citing the observations of Wissink et al in relation to mixed administration mentioned in section III.C.i.b of this chapter.
[287] On this topic, see also ch 1 of this volume (Luchtman), sections II.V and following.

(Continued)

	DG Competition	ECB	ESMA	OLAF
HU	Hungarian Competition Authority (*Gazdasági Versenyhivatal*, HCA)	Hungarian National Bank (*Magyar Nemzeti Bank*, HNB)	Hungarian National Bank (*Magyar Nemzeti Bank*, HNB)	OLAF Coordination Office (OLAF *Koordinációs Iroda*) (= unit within the National Tax and Customs Administration (*Nemzeti Adóés Vámhivatal*, NTCA), which is part of the Ministry for National Economy (*Nemzetgazdasági Minisztérium*)
IT	Italian Competition Authority (*Autorità Gerante della Concorrenza e del Mercato*, AGCM)	Bank of Italy (*Banca d'Italia*)	Italian Companies and Exchange Commission (*Commissione Nazionale per le Società e la Borsa*, *Consob*)	Italian Anti-fraud Committee (*Comitato per la lotta contro le drodi nei confronti dell'Unione europea*, COLAF)
LU	Competition Council (*Conseil de la concurrence*)	*Commission de surveillance du secteur financier* (CSSF)	*Commission de surveillance du secteur financier* (CSSF)	Directorate of International Financial Relations, Development Aid and Compliance (*Affaires multilatérales, développement et compliance*), within the Ministry of Finance
NL	Authority for Consumers and Markets (*Autoriteit Consument en Markt*, ACM)	Dutch Central Bank (*De Nederlandsche Bank*, DCB)	Netherlands Authority for the Financial Markets (*Autoriteit Financiële Markten*, AFM)	Minister of Finance supported by the Dutch Customs Information Centre (*Douane informatiecentrum*, DIC)
POL	President of the Office of Competition and Consumer Protection (*Urząd Ochrony Konkurencji i Konsumentów*, UOKiK)	(Financial Supervision Authority (*Komisja Nadzoru Finansowego*, KNF))	Financial Supervision Authority (*Komisja Nadzoru Finansowego*, KNF)	Ministry of Finance (*Ministerstwo Finansów*), more specifically the Department for the Protection of the EU Financial Interests (*Departament Ochrony Interesów Finansowych Unii Europejskiej*)

PART II

Models for Punitive Enforcement in Composite Procedures

4

The Investigative Stage

MARTIN BÖSE AND ANNE SCHNEIDER

I. Introduction

Law enforcement, and the imposition of sanctions in particular, cannot be done without investigations. The collection of information and evidence not only serves public interests in effective law enforcement and the proper administration of justice, but also ensures that a sanction is not imposed upon natural or legal persons unless the illegal conduct has been established. In criminal proceedings, this is expressly guaranteed by the presumption of innocence under Article 48(1) of the Charter of Fundamental Right of the European Union ('the Charter') and Article 6(2) of the European Convention on Human Rights (ECHR). So, the investigative stage is crucial for the effective enforcement of EU law in the areas of competition, financial markets and fraud affecting the financial interests of the Union.

This chapter will begin in section II with an overview of the architecture of law enforcement by the competent EU law enforcement authorities (Directorate-General for Competition ('DG Competition'), the European Central Bank (ECB), the European Securities and Markets Authority (ESMA) and the European Anti-Fraud Office (OLAF)) and of their legal and institutional framework. In section III, a comparative analysis of the EU authorities' counterparts at the national level will identify commonalities and differences in the institutional framework of law enforcement in the Member States, and vertical cooperation between the national competent authorities and their European counterparts. Section IV will discuss investigative powers and procedural safeguards in the four policy areas and will analyse the different modes of vertical cooperation. The interaction between EU institutions and their national counterparts raises several questions about the applicable law (including procedural safeguards), the distribution of tasks and responsibilities between EU institutions and national authorities, and the consequences for the scope of judicial review on both the European and the national level. Special attention will be paid to potential gaps in judicial protection with regard to procedural rights and safeguards in criminal proceedings (eg the privilege against self-incrimination) triggered by vertical cooperation.

II. Overview of Tasks and Powers of EU Law Enforcement Authorities

The architecture of EU law enforcement varies significantly among the different sectors. First and foremost, these differences arise from the mandate of the competent authority and its sanctioning and investigative powers, but the scope and limits of these powers have repercussions on the relationship with their national counterparts and the rules on vertical cooperation too. The following overview will outline the institutional setting of EU law enforcement in the areas of competition law (Commission – DG Competition), financial markets (the ECB, ESMA) and the fight against fraud (OLAF).

A. Commission (DG Competition)

Within the European Commission, DG Competition is responsible for the enforcement of EU competition law, in particular the prohibition of agreements restricting competition (Article 101 of the Treaty on the Functioning of the European Union (TFEU)) and of abuse of a dominant position within the internal market (Article 102 TFEU). The enforcement of EU competition law is mainly based on Regulation 1/2003,[1] which provides the Commission (DG Competition) with investigative and sanctioning powers under Articles 17 et seq, but also empowers the national competition authorities to apply and enforce EU competition law (decentralised enforcement) under Article 5.

Within its mandate under Regulation 1/2003, the Commission (DG Competition) may conduct an investigation into an alleged breach of EU competition law,[2] or into a particular type of agreement or of a particular sector of the economy.[3] To that end, the Commission is vested with autonomous investigative powers, that is, information requests,[4] taking voluntary statements[5] and making on-site inspections of business premises[6] or any other premises, including private homes.[7] According to the Court of Justice of the European Union ('the Court of Justice' or CJEU), the inspection powers imply a right to search for documents that are not yet identified, because otherwise it would be impossible for the Commission to carry out an investigation if the undertakings refused to cooperate.[8] The Commission has no coercive powers, however, and may enforce its investigative measures only indirectly by fines and penalty payments.[9]

[1] Council Regulation (EC) No 1/2003 of 16 December 2002 on the implementation of the rules on competition laid down in Articles 81 and 82 TEC [2003] OJ L1/1; see also Commission Regulation (EC) 773/2004 of 7 April 2004 relating to the conduct of proceedings by the Commission pursuant to Articles 81 and 82 TEC [2004] OJ L123/18.
[2] Arts 18 et seq Regulation 1/2003.
[3] Art 17 Regulation 1/2003 (sector inquiries).
[4] Art 18 Regulation 1/2003.
[5] Art 19 Regulation 1/2003.
[6] Art 20 Regulation 1/2003.
[7] Art 21 Regulation 1/2003.
[8] Joined Cases 46/87 and 227/88 *Hoechst AG v Commission* ECLI:EU:C:1989:337, para 27.
[9] Arts 23 and 24 Regulation 1/2003.

In so far as on-site inspections require force or coercion, the Commission must rely on the assistance of the national competent authorities.[10] Such assistance by national authorities is governed by domestic law and may be subject to the requirement of judicial authorisation (eg, with regard to the search of business premises).[11] In any case, such authorisation is required for the inspection (and search) of private homes.[12] However, according to the Court of Justice, the jurisdiction of national courts is limited by the principle of effectiveness: it is not a matter for the national court to review the necessity for and lawfulness of the inspection ordered by the Commission, because such review falls within the exclusive competence of the Court of Justice; the national court may only examine whether the Commission is authentic and the coercive measures to be applied are neither excessive nor arbitrary.[13] As a consequence, judicial protection *ex ante* will be less effective, in particular as the national court may request the Commission for information, but may not demand to be provided with the Commission's file on the alleged infringement.[14]

The EU legislator did not expressly subject the Commission's investigative powers to limitations derived from procedural rights and safeguards. However, according to the case law of the Court of Justice, the Commission must respect the confidentiality of written communications between the undertaking and its lawyer if such communications are made for the purpose of the client's right of defence and emanate from an independent lawyer (legal professional privilege).[15] As far as the privilege against self-incrimination is concerned, the Court of Justice has taken a rather restrictive view and ruled that the undertaking has no right to remain silent and not to give evidence against itself but may only refuse to provide the Commission with answers that are tantamount to an admission of guilt.[16]

Where the Commission establishes an infringement of EU competition law, under Article 7 of Regulation 1/2003 it may by decision require the undertaking concerned to bring such infringement to an end. Furthermore, the Commission may impose a fine upon the undertaking[17] and/or compel the undertaking by periodic penalty payments to terminate the infringement.[18]

The system of parallel (centralised and decentralised) enforcement of EU competition law requires close cooperation between the Commission and the national competition authorities. To that end, the Council and Commission have established the

[10] Art 20(6) and Art 21(4) Regulation 1/2003.

[11] Art 20(7) Regulation 1/2003.

[12] Art 21(3) Regulation 1/2003.

[13] Art 20(8) and Art 21(3) Regulation 1/2003. See in this regard Case C-94/00 *Roquette Frères* ECLI:EU:C:2002:603, paras 36 et seq.

[14] Art 20(8) and Art 21(3) Regulation 1/2003. M Böse, 'The System of Vertical and Horizontal Cooperation in Administrative Investigations in EU Competition Cases' in K Ligeti (ed), *Towards a Prosecutor for the European Union* (Hart Publishing 2013) 838, 848.

[15] Case 155/79 *AM & S* ECLI:EU:C:1982:157, paras 21 et seq; Case C-550/07 P *Akzo Nobel Chemicals* ECLI:EU:C:2010:512, paras 40 et seq.

[16] Case 374/87 *Orkem* ECLI:EU:C:1989:387, paras 33–34; Case C-301/04 P *SGL Carbon* ECLI:EU:C:2006:432, paras 40 et seq. See also Regulation 1/2003, Recital 23.

[17] Art 23 Regulation 1/2003.

[18] Art 24 Regulation 1/2003.

European Competition Network (ECN).[19] If a national competition authority decides to investigate a case, the Commission must be informed, and under Article 11(5) of Regulation 1/2003 it may take over the case and thereby relieve the national authority of its competence to apply and enforce EU competition law. Otherwise, the national competition authority continues the investigation according to the applicable domestic law. However, the institutional and procedural framework for the decentralised enforcement of EU competition law has been harmonised by Directive (EU) 2019/1.

If the Commission initiates an investigation, under Article 20(5) of Regulation 1/2003 the national competition authorities are obliged to assist the Commission in exercising their investigative powers. As far as their officials afford such assistance and actively participate in inspections, they enjoy the same investigative powers as the Commission.[20] However, where recourse to coercive powers is necessary to enforce the Commission's investigative powers, the national authority may (and must) take the necessary measures according to national law (Article 20(6)).

Instead of carrying out inspections by itself, the Commission may request the national competition authority to undertake inspections of business premises.[21] Commission officials may assist the national authority and participate in the inspection[22] As the national competition authority has no investigative powers under EU law, it conducts the requested inspection in accordance with its national law.[23] Due to the harmonisation of the investigative powers in competition cases, the national competition authority's power to inspect business premises corresponds to the Commission's power under Article 20 of Regulation 1/2003.[24]

B. The ECB

In the framework of the Single Supervisory Mechanism (SSM), the ECB is exclusively competent for the financial supervision of 'significant' credit institutions; this supervision entails granting and withdrawing authorisations to credit institutions, and conducting the daily supervision of and ensuring compliance with the relevant EU law.[25] The ECB classifies credit institutions according to their size, importance and cross-border activities as 'significant' or 'less significant', and thereby determines those

[19] Regulation 1/2003, Recitals 15 and 18. See Commission, 'Joint Statement no 15435/02 of the Council and the Commission of 10 December 2002 on the functioning of the network of competition authorities'; Commission, 'Commission notice on cooperation within the network of competition authorities' [2004] OJ C101/43; see also, with regard to horizontal cooperation, Directive (EU) 2019/1 of the European Parliament and of the Council of 11 December 2018 to empower the competition authorities of the Member States to be more effective enforcers and to ensure the proper functioning of the internal market [2019] OJ L11/3.

[20] Böse (n 14) 846.

[21] Art 22(2), 1st sentence, Regulation 1/2003.

[22] Art 22(2), 3rd sentence Regulation 1/2003.

[23] Art 22(2), 2nd sentence Regulation 1/2003. See further Böse (n 14) 849.

[24] Art 6 Directive (EU) 2019/1.

[25] Council Regulation (EU) No 1024/2013 of 15 October 2013 conferring specific tasks on the European Central Bank concerning policies relating to the prudential supervision of credit institutions [2013] OJ L287/63 ('SSM Regulation'), Art 4(1).

credit institutions subject to supervision at the European level.[26] In addition, under Article 6(5)(b) of the SSM Regulation, the ECB may decide to exercise its supervisory powers for one or more less significant credit institutions.

The supervision by the ECB entails daily monitoring by Joint Supervisory Teams (JSTs), which, under Article 4 of the SSM Framework Regulation, are composed of staff members of the ECB and from the national competent authorities. By its JSTs, the ECB may issue information requests[27] and require the submission of documents, examine books and records and take statements,[28] and order an on-site inspection.[29] Inspections are conducted by On-site Inspection Teams that are composed of staff members of the ECB and the national competent authorities.[30] The officials of the national authority where the inspection is carried out shall assist the ECB in accordance with domestic law, in particular where the exercise of coercive powers is necessary.[31] If such assistance or the on-site inspection itself requires judicial authorisation under national law, such authorisation shall be applied for; however, judicial protection by national courts is subject to the same limitations as in EU competition law (see section II.A).[32]

The ECB must respect the procedural rights of the supervised entity and its right to be assisted by lawyers,[33] but the ECB's investigative powers are not expressly limited by legal professional privilege. That privilege, however, is a fundamental principle of EU law, so that the case law of the Court of Justice on the protection of the confidentiality of communications between undertakings and its lawyers in EU competition law applies accordingly (see section II.A).[34] In contrast, as the SSM Regulation is silent on the privilege against self-incrimination, the EU legislator seems to indicate that the supervised entity has no right to refuse to give evidence against itself, but has to 'provide all information that is necessary',[35] except for statements involving an admission of guilt (section II.A).

The investigation of alleged breaches of EU law that may be sanctioned by administrative penalties under Article 18 of the SSM Regulation is assigned to the ECB's investigating unit, an internal and independent division of the ECB[36] vested with the investigative powers previously mentioned.[37] At the end of the investigation, the investigating unit may submit a proposal for a sanctioning decision to the supervisory board,[38]

[26] ibid Art 6(4); Regulation (EU) No 468/2014 of the European Central Bank of 16 April 2014 establishing the framework for cooperation within the Single Supervisory Mechanism between the European Central Bank and national competent authorities and with national designated authorities (SSM Framework Regulation) [2014] OJ L141/1, Arts 39 et seq.

[27] Art 10 SSM Regulation.

[28] Art 11 SSM Regulation; Arts 139 and 141 SSM Framework Regulation ('general investigations').

[29] Art 12 SSM Regulation; Art 143 SSM Framework Regulation.

[30] Art 144 SSM Framework Regulation.

[31] Art 12(4) and (5) SSM Regulation.

[32] Art 13 SSM Regulation.

[33] Art 126 SSM Framework Regulation.

[34] SSM Regulation, Recital 48. See JE Windthorst and W Bussian, 'Europäische Bankenaufsicht und Legal Privilege' [2015] *Wertpapiermitteilungen – Zeitschrift für Wirtschafts- und Bankrecht* 2265, 2267 ff.

[35] Art 10(1) SSM Regulation.

[36] Art 123 SSM Framework Regulation.

[37] Art 125 SSM Framework Regulation; Arts 10 et seq SSM Regulation.

[38] Art 26 SSM Regulation.

which will prepare a complete draft decision; the final decision on the imposition of an administrative penalty is taken by the ECB's Governing Council.[39]

The SSM has established a system of financial supervision composed by the ECB and national competent authorities.[40] The national authorities are subject to a duty of cooperation in good faith; they have to assist the ECB in carrying out its tasks.[41] This duty entails an obligation to exercise coercive powers against persons obstructing the investigation[42] and an obligation to actively assist the ECB in on-site inspections,[43] and thereby corresponds to the cooperation duties in EU competition law (section II.A).

The SSM goes one step further, however, imposing an obligation on the national authority to follow the ECB's instructions.[44] The ECB may require the national competent authority, by way of instructions, to make use of its powers, under and in accordance with the conditions set out in national law, where EU law does not confer such powers on the ECB.[45] Unlike the ECN, the SSM does not provide for the traditional request-based cooperation mechanism (section II.A).[46]

C. ESMA

ESMA forms part of the European System of Financial Supervision (ESFS) and must contribute to a sound, effective and consistent level of regulation and supervision of financial market participants.[47] In particular, ESMA is responsible for the registration and supervision of credit-rating agencies[48] and trade repositories.[49]

ESMA supervises credit-rating agencies and trade repositories by monitoring their daily operations. If ESMA's supervisors find serious indications of a violation of the relevant EU law, ESMA will assign the case to an independent investigation officer.[50] Supervisors and investigation officers have the same investigative powers: they may request information,[51] examine documents, records and data, take and obtain copies, summon and interview natural persons, representatives and staff in particular (general

[39] Art 127 SSM Framework Regulation.
[40] Arts 2(9) and 6(1) SSM Regulation.
[41] Art 6(2) and (3) SSM Regulation.
[42] Arts 11(2) and 12(5) SSM Regulation.
[43] Art 12(4) SSM Regulation.
[44] Art 6(3) SSM Regulation.
[45] Art 9(1) SSM Regulation; Art 22 SSM Framework Regulation.
[46] Art 22(2) Regulation 1/2003.
[47] Regulation (EU) No 1095/2010 of the European Parliament and of the Council of 24 November 2010 establishing a European Supervisory Authority (European Securities and Markets Authority) [2010] OJ L331/84 ('ESMA Regulation'), Arts 1(5) and 2.
[48] Regulation (EC) No 1060/2009 of the European Parliament and of the Council of 16 September 2009 on credit rating agencies [2009] OJ L302/1, [2011] OJ L145/30, [2011] OJ L174/1, [2013] OJ L146/1, [2014] OJ L153/1 and [2017] OJ L347/35 ('CRA Regulation') Arts 14 et seq.
[49] Regulation (EU) No 648/2012 of the European Parliament and of the Council of 4 July 2012 on OTC derivatives, central counterparties and trade repositories [2012] OJ L201/1 and [2021] OJ L49/6 (last amendment) ('European Market Infrastructure Regulation' or EMIR), Arts 55 et seq.
[50] Art 23e(1) CRA Regulation; Art 64(1) EMIR.
[51] Art 23b CRA Regulation; Art 61 EMIR.

investigations).[52] In the framework of its general investigations, ESMA may even request records of telephone or data traffic.[53] ESMA's power to inspect business premises[54] corresponds to the inspection powers of the ECB (section II.B). National authorities shall assist ESMA in conducting the inspection and, where necessary, enforce cooperation obligations by their coercive powers.[55] If the inspection or the assistance by the national authority requires judicial authorisation under national law, such authorisation shall be applied for;[56] the jurisdiction of the national court, however, is limited to the review of whether the decision is authentic and that the coercive measures are neither arbitrary nor excessive.[57] The same rules apply if the production of telephone or data traffic requires judicial authorisation.[58]

ESMA must not use its investigative powers in order to require the disclosure of information or documents subject to legal professional privilege;[59] in this respect, the case law of the Court of Justice applies accordingly (see section II.A).[60] The investigation officer must respect the rights of the defence;[61] the rules of procedure, however, do not provide for a right of the supervised entity to remain silent (see section II.B).

The investigation officer submits the file and the findings of the investigation to ESMA's Board of Supervisors,[62] which takes the final decision on whether or not to take supervisory measures or impose a fine.[63]

Under Article 26 of the CRA Regulation, ESMA and the national competent authorities are obliged to cooperate with each other in good faith. This general duty is specified in the national authorities' obligation to assist ESMA in its general investigations[64] and on-site inspections,[65] which corresponds to the cooperation duties in EU competition law (section II.A; see also section II.B).

Instead of directly exercising its investigative powers, ESMA may delegate its investigatory tasks to the national authorities[66] and require them to carry out specific investigatory tasks (general investigations) and on-site inspections on its behalf.[67] The delegation of investigatory tasks can be an option where the measures to be taken require knowledge and experience with respect to local conditions.[68] When carrying out the investigation, the national authority shall enjoy the same powers as ESMA,[69]

[52] Art 23c CRA Regulation; Art 62 EMIR.
[53] Art 23c(1)(e) CRA Regulation; Art 62(1)(e) EMIR.
[54] Art 23d CRA Regulation; Article 63 EMIR.
[55] Art 23d(5) and (7) CRA Regulation; and Art 63(5) and (7) EMIR.
[56] Art 23d(8) CRA Regulation; Art 63(8) EMIR.
[57] Art 23d(9) CRA Regulation; Art 63(9) EMIR.
[58] Art 23c(5) and (6) CRA Regulation; Art 62(5) and (6) EMIR.
[59] Art 23a CRA Regulation; Art 60 EMIR.
[60] W Spoerr, 'Article 64 EMIR' in HD Assmann, UH Schneider and PO Mülbert (eds), *Wertpapierhandelsrecht*, 7th edn (Otto Schmidt 2019) para 17.
[61] Art 23e(3) CRA Regulation; Art 64(3) EMIR.
[62] Arts 40 et seq ESMA Regulation.
[63] Arts 23e(5), 24 and 36a CRA Regulation; Arts 64(5), 65 and 73 EMIR.
[64] Art 23c(4) CRA Regulation; Art 62(4) EMIR.
[65] Art 23d(5) and (7) CRA Regulation; Art 63(5) and (7) EMIR.
[66] Art 30 CRA Regulation; Art 74 EMIR.
[67] Art 23d(6) CRA Regulation; Art 63(6) EMIR.
[68] Recital 80 EMIR.
[69] Art 23d(6) CRA Regulation; Art 63(6) EMIR.

whereas the request-based cooperation mechanism in the ECN (section II.A) and investigations following an instruction by the ECB (section II.B) are governed by national law. Furthermore, the delegation of tasks and powers shall not affect the responsibility of ESMA.[70] The delegation widely corresponds to the vertical mutual assistance upon request; however, it is not entirely clear whether the national authority is obliged to comply with ESMA's request ('may require') or whether the national authority enjoys a margin of discretion in this respect.[71]

D. OLAF

The European Anti-Fraud Office (*Office de Lutte Antifraude* – OLAF) is an independent office established with the European Commission that exercises the Commission's powers to combat fraud, corruption and any other illegal activity adversely affecting the Union's financial interests.[72] Thus, the mandate of OLAF covers any activity that allegedly affects the EU budget (revenues and expenditures) or the budget of its agencies.

In contrast to the other authorities (DG Competition, the ECB and ESMA), OLAF has no sanctioning powers. Its investigations conclude with a report that is sent to the national competent authorities and that, where appropriate, indicates the disciplinary, administrative, financial or judicial action to be taken by those authorities.[73] Even though OLAF's investigations may trigger different kind of proceedings (disciplinary, administrative and judicial) in the Member State concerned, they are qualified as administrative investigations that do not affect the Member States' competence to initiate and conduct criminal proceedings.[74]

Within its mandate, OLAF conducts internal investigations within the Union's institutions, bodies, offices and agencies,[75] and external investigations against economic operators.[76] The rules on external investigations have recently been amended in order to enhance the effectiveness of OLAF's investigations.[77]

[70] Art 30(4) CRA Regulation; Art 74(4) EMIR.

[71] See Döhmel, 'Article 63 EMIR' in Assmann, Schneider and Mülbert (eds) (n 60) para 18, arguing that the German wording ('*bitten*') and the interest in smooth cooperation support the view that the delegation of investigatory tasks requires the consent of the national authority.

[72] Commission Decision of 28 April 1999 establishing the European Anti-fraud Office (OLAF) [1999] OJ L136/20, [2013] OJ L257/19, [2015] OJ L81/4 and [2015] OJ L333/148 ('OLAF Decision'), Arts 1–3.

[73] Regulation (EU, Euratom) No 883/2013 of the European Parliament and of the Council of 11 September 2013 concerning investigations conducted by the European Anti-Fraud Office (OLAF) [2013] OJ L248/1, [2016] OJ L317/1 and [2020] L437/49 ('OLAF Regulation'), Art 11.

[74] Art 2(4) OLAF Regulation.

[75] Art 4 OLAF Regulation.

[76] Art 3 OLAF Regulation.

[77] Regulation (EU, Euratom) 2020/2223 of the European Parliament and of the Council of 23 December 2020 amending Regulation (EU, Euratom) No 883/2013, as regards cooperation with the European Public Prosecutor's Office and the effectiveness of the European Anti-Fraud Office investigations [2020] OJ L437/49, Recital 15; see also the Commission's legislative proposal: Commission, 'Proposal for a Regulation Of The European Parliament And Of The Council amending Regulation (EU, Euratom) No 883/2013 concerning investigations conducted by the European Anti-Fraud Office (OLAF) as regards cooperation with the European Public Prosecutor's Office and the effectiveness of OLAF investigations' COM (2018) 338 final, 9.

In the framework of external investigations, OLAF may carry out on-the-spot checks and inspections.[78] Economic operators are obliged to cooperate with OLAF in the course of its investigations; at OLAF's request, they shall provide written and oral information.[79] Where the economic operator complies with its cooperation obligation and submits to an on-the-spot check and inspection, the investigation is governed by EU law alone, so that national law capable of restricting access to information no longer applies.[80] This provision originates from the case law of the General Court, according to which there is no obligation for national requirements to be met unless the economic operator opposes and resists the inspection.[81] If the economic operator resists an on-the-spot check or inspection and refuses to grant OLAF access to its premises, or prevents the conduct of the investigation, the national competent authorities shall afford the necessary assistance; such assistance, and the exercise of coercive powers in particular, is provided in accordance with national law.[82] Where the necessary measures require judicial authorisation under national law (eg a search warrant), such authorisation shall be applied for (see section II.A).[83]

The Member State concerned and its competent authorities are obliged to assist OLAF in its investigations[84] and to ensure that OLAF has access to all information, documents and data relating to the subject matter under investigation.[85] Privately-owned devices used for work purposes are subject to inspection only under the same conditions and to the same extent that national authorities may access the data stored on those devices, and where OLAF has reasonable grounds for suspecting that their content may be relevant to the investigation.[86]

In the exercise of its investigative powers, OLAF has to comply with the procedural guarantees established by EU law.[87] In particular, the economic operator concerned has the right not to make self-incriminating statements, to be assisted by a lawyer or any other person of his or her choice, and to make statements in any of the official languages of the Member State where that economic operator is located.[88] These procedural guarantees also apply to other persons suspected of having committed fraud, corruption or any other illegal activity affecting the Union's financial interests ('person concerned'[89]) that is interviewed by OLAF.[90] A witness has the right to avoid self-incrimination too; if, in the course of interview, evidence emerges that the witness may be a person concerned, the interview must be ended and the interviewed person must be informed of his or her rights.[91]

[78] Art 3(1) OLAF Regulation.
[79] Art 3(3) OLAF Regulation.
[80] Art 3(4) OLAF Regulation.
[81] Case T-478/16 *Sigma Orionis SA* ECLI:EU:T:2018:245, paras 80–82.
[82] Art 3(6) OLAF Regulation.
[83] Art 3(6), 2nd sentence OLAF Regulation.
[84] Art 7(3) OLAF Regulation.
[85] Art 3(5) OLAF Regulation.
[86] Art 3(5), 2nd sentence OLAF Regulation.
[87] Art 3(8) OLAF Regulation; see also ibid Art 9.
[88] Art 3(8) OLAF Regulation.
[89] Art 2(5) OLAF Regulation.
[90] Arts 9(2), 1st and 4th sentences, and 9(5) OLAF Regulation.
[91] Arts 9(2), 1st and 5th sentences OLAF Regulation.

Despite the commitment to the privilege against self-incrimination, there is still a tension to the economic operator's obligation to cooperate and to provide information.[92] According to Recital 25 of Regulation 2020/2223,[93] OLAF

> should be able to require economic operators to supply relevant information where they may have been involved in the matter under investigation or may hold such information. When complying with such requests, economic operators should not be obliged to make self-incriminating statements, but they should be obliged to answer factual questions and provide documents, even if that information may be used to establish against them or against another economic operator the existence of illegal activity.

This reasoning refers to the case law in EU competition law, where the Court ruled that the privilege against self-incrimination provides only limited protection to corporations (section II.A). The Court, however, stated in a more recent ruling that the right to a fair trial and the defence rights (under Articles 47 and 48 of the Charter) include a right to silence of natural persons that cannot reasonably be confined to statements of admissions of wrongdoing or directly incriminating remarks, but also covers information that may subsequently be used in evidence against the defendant.[94] Thus, the Court distinguished between the protection of legal and natural persons, and argued that, with regard to the latter, the privilege against self-incrimination must have a wider scope.[95] Given the fact that a 'person concerned' is defined as a person suspected of illegal activities,[96] such a (natural) person should per se have the right to avoid self-incrimination and to refuse to provide any information on the subject matter of the investigation against him or her. If information obtained from the suspect will be used in criminal proceedings, the suspect must not be compelled to disclose such information; a duty to cooperate would imply a corresponding enforcement obligation of the Member States (eg by sanctions) and thereby violate the privilege against self-incrimination.

In order to enhance and facilitate cooperation between OLAF and the national competent authorities, each Member State shall establish an anti-fraud coordination service (AFCOS) that provides or coordinates the necessary assistance for OLAF.[97] Furthermore, the AFCOS shall assist OLAF in its coordination activities,[98] in particular with regard to horizontal cooperation between Member States, but also with third states and international organisations.[99] In this context, OLAF may also participate in joint investigation teams (JITs) and exchange operational information acquired by its investigations.[100]

The new framework of OLAF's autonomous investigations does not affect the cooperation regime of mutual assistance between administrative authorities under

[92] Art 3(3) OLAF Regulation.
[93] Regulation (EU, Euratom) 2020/2223.
[94] Case C-481/19 *DB v Consob* ECLI:EU:C:2021:84, paras 40 and 45.
[95] ibid para 48.
[96] Art 2(5) OLAF Regulation.
[97] Art 12a(1) and (2) OLAF Regulation; see nn 70, 72, 73 with regard to Art 3(5) and (6) and Art 7(3) OLAF Regulation.
[98] Art 12a(3) OLAF Regulation.
[99] Art 12b(1) OLAF Regulation.
[100] Art 12b OLAF Regulation.

Regulation 515/97.[101] If there are indications that irregularities have taken place in one or more Member States, OLAF shall inform the Member State concerned, and that State shall carry out an investigation; OLAF officials may participate in that investigation ('mixed inspections') and have access to the same business premises and documents as the national authority, but may not, on its own initiative, assume investigative powers of inspection under national law.[102] Similar mechanisms are established by sectoral regulations that also provide for on-the-spot checks conducted by OLAF, while officials of the national competent authority may take part in such checks.[103]

III. Cooperation by EU Enforcement Authorities with National Authorities

As has been shown, all EU authorities analysed here depend to varying extent on cooperation with national authorities. Even the Commission, which arguably has the strongest investigative powers, requires assistance by national enforcement authorities. This section will focus on this vertical cooperation from a comparative perspective and point out similarities and differences between the Member States. Other types of investigation, that is autonomous investigations by national competent authorities that exist in competition law, will not be covered.

The following discussion will focus on those states that were analysed in the project *Investigatory Powers and Procedural Safeguards: Improving OLAF's Legislative Framework through a Comparison with Other EU Law Enforcement Authorities (ECN/ESMA/ECB)*.[104] Those were Germany, France, Italy, the Netherlands, Poland and the United Kingdom (UK). Because the parameters for vertical cooperation depend to a large extent on the applicable EU law and the legal powers of the EU authority concerned, this section is structured by referring to the EU authorities too.

A. National Authorities Cooperating with the Commission (DG Competition)

According to Article 22 of Regulation 1/2003, it is the task of the national competition authorities to support the Commission in its investigations. Usually, there is a

[101] Council Regulation (EC) No 515/97 of 13 March 1997 on mutual assistance between the administrative authorities of the Member States and cooperation between the latter and the Commission to ensure the correct application of the law on customs and agricultural matters [1997] OJ L82/1, [2003] OJ L122/36, [2008] OJ L218/48, [2015] OJ L243/1 and [2021] OJ L172/110.

[102] Arts 18(4) and 9(2) Regulation 515/97.

[103] Regulation (EU) No 1306/2013 of the European Parliament and of the Council of 17 December 2013 on the financing, management and monitoring of the common agricultural policy [2013] OJ L347/549 and [2020] OJ L437/1 (last amendment), Art 47(2).

[104] See the final report M Luchtman and J Vervaele (eds), *Investigatory Powers and Procedural Safeguards: Improving OLAF's Legislative Framework through a Comparison with Other EU Law Enforcement Authorities (ECN/ESMA/ECB)* (Utrecht University 2017) available at http://dspace.library.uu.nl/handle/1874/352061 (accessed 7 October 2021).

central national competition authority responsible for coordinating competition law investigations (eg the German *Bundeskartellamt*, the Polish *Urząd Ochrony Konkurencji i Konsumentów*, the Italian *Autorità Garante della Concorrenza e del Mercato* and so on). While most national competition authorities are independent from the government,[105] the Polish Office of Competition and Consumer Protection has recently lost its independence due to the Polish Government's policy to strengthen the Government's influence on law enforcement.[106]

The national competition authorities have different functions, one of which is to give assistance to the Commission as prescribed by Regulation 1/2003. As has been explained already, the Commission has autonomous investigative powers, but notably lacks the competence to use force or other forms of coercion (section II.A). Moreover, Article 21(3) of the Regulation requires judicial authorisation for the inspection and search of private homes. When the national competition authorities provide assistance to the Commission, they apply the investigative powers granted to the Commission by EU law.[107] National law becomes relevant when the authorities undertake measures that are not foreseen in EU law, such as the use of coercion,[108] and when the courts need to grant judicial authorisation. In theory, national law also applies when the Commission requests assistance under Article 22(2) of Regulation 1/2003, but in practice the Commission favours undertaking investigations itself over such a request.[109]

The proceedings by the national competition authorities are administrative in nature. This means that the threshold for opening investigations is low. In contrast to criminal proceedings, suspicion of wrongdoing is not necessary.[110] Only the most general rules of administrative law, such as non-arbitrary use of the margin of appreciation and the proportionality principle, which is a general principle of EU law, apply.[111] Polish law requires a formal opening of administrative proceedings.[112]

The relationship between proceedings in competition law cases and criminal proceedings differs from state to state. In Germany, proceedings by the national competition authorities for violation of competition law that may lead to an administrative sanction follow the rules for criminal proceedings. This means that purely administrative investigations are practically non-existent.[113] Parallel criminal and administrative proceedings are possible in some Member States (eg, UK, Poland and France). However, the criminal and administrative authorities in the UK cooperate in order to prevent the prejudicing of criminal proceedings.[114] In Dutch law, parallel proceedings may only lead to one (usually criminal) sanction (*una via* principle).[115] In France, parallel proceedings

[105] See, eg, S Allegrezza, 'Report Italy', ibid 129, 131; J Tricot, 'Report France' ibid 189, 191 ff.

[106] C Nowak and M Błachucki, 'Report Poland' ibid 165, 166 ff.

[107] Art 20(5), 2nd sentence Regulation 1/2003. See further Böse (n 14) 846.

[108] Art 20(6) Regulation 1/2003.

[109] See M Böse and A Schneider, 'Report Germany' in Luchtman and Vervaele (eds) (n 104) 57, 63; J Graat, 'Report the Netherlands' ibid 87, 89.

[110] Graat, 'Report the Netherlands' (n 109) 87, 95; Allegrezza, 'Report Italy' (n 105) 129, 131.

[111] Böse and Schneider, 'Report Germany' (n 109) 57, 60.

[112] Nowak and Błachucki, 'Report Poland' (n 106) 165, 168.

[113] Böse and Schneider, 'Report Germany' (n 109) 57, 63.

[114] P Alldridge, 'Report the United Kingdom' in Luchtman and Vervaele (eds) (n 104) 153, 163.

[115] Graat, 'Report the Netherlands' (n 109) 87, 95.

and double sanctions were traditionally allowed, but have now been discarded due to the finding of a violation of *ne bis in idem* in the jurisprudence of the European Court of Human Rights.[116]

B. National Authorities Cooperating with ECB and ESMA

The framework for vertical cooperation in the financial market area is similar to competition law. All Member States analysed here have a national central bank that cooperates with the ECB. However, the powers of the ECB and the national bank do not completely overlap. In some Member States, banking supervision is a shared task between the national central bank and the authorities cooperating with ESMA;[117] while in others, the power shifts either towards the central bank or towards the national counterpart of ESMA.[118] These counterparts are independent central authorities, such as the Italian *Commissione Nazionale per le Società e la Borsa* (Consob) or the English Financial Conduct Authority.

The tasks of the national authorities in the banking and financial sector are like those of the authorities cooperating with DG Competition. The national competent authorities are obliged to assist ECB and ESMA in their general investigations, particularly by providing coercion when necessary[119] and on-site inspections.[120]

Because supervision plays a more important role in the banking and financial sector, the threshold for opening an investigation is even lower than in competition law. Investigations may be opened without any reason. Clear rules on the applicable threshold are often lacking.[121] In contrast to competition law, the status of the proceedings as administrative seems to be undisputed. Accordingly, the proceedings are sometimes conducted parallel to criminal proceedings, if applicable. Those Member States that do not allow parallel sanctions apply the mechanisms set out in section III.A in order to reach a feasible solution.

C. National Authorities Cooperating with OLAF

The institutional framework for cooperation with OLAF is fundamentally different. As has been explained already, the OLAF Regulation requires the Member States to name an anti-fraud coordination service (AFCOS), whose task it is to cooperate with OLAF and coordinate proceedings in the Member State.[122] In many Member States, this AFCOS is associated with or part of the Ministry of Finance (eg, Germany, the

[116] Tricot, 'Report France' (n 105) 189, 200 and 202 ff; see section III.C.

[117] Böse and Schneider, 'Report Germany' (n 109) 57, 58; Allegrezza, 'Report Italy' (n 105) 129, 132 ff.

[118] See the Netherlands, where there are neither credit-rating agencies nor trade repositories: Graat, 'Report the Netherlands' (n 109) 87, 95; or Poland, which does not have the Euro currency: Nowak and Błachucki, 'Report Poland' (n 106) 165, 167.

[119] Art 23c(4) CRA Regulation; Art 62(4) EMIR; Arts 11(2) and 12(5) SSM Regulation.

[120] Art 23d(5) and (7) CRA Regulation; Art 63(5) and (7) EMIR; Art 12(4) SSM Regulation.

[121] Tricot, 'Report France' (n 105) 189, 196.

[122] Art 12a(1) and (2) OLAF Regulation; see section II.D.

Netherlands, Poland). In Italy, the AFCOS is a special committee including people from different national agencies (*Comitato per la lotta contro le frodi nei confronti dell'Unione europea – COLAF*) and the Ministry.[123] In contrast, the UK had chosen a police authority as the AFCOS (National Police Coordinators Office for Economic Crime).[124]

The AFCOSs do not have operative powers and are not entitled to investigate themselves, at least not under the OLAF Regulation. When OLAF requires assistance, the AFCOS refers the Office to the national competent authorities for investigating a potential violation of the financial interests of the EU. Which authorities these are depends on several factors: whether the potential violation concerns revenue or expenditure; whether the national proceedings are administrative or criminal; and, in case of Germany, which federal State (*Land*) has jurisdiction.[125]

In the matter of expenditure, there are a huge number of national authorities that could potentially be asked to investigate expenditure fraud. In practice, the grant agreements include clauses that allow the authorities to withdraw the grant if certain investigative measures, such as on-the-spot checks, are not allowed.[126] Therefore, administrative investigative proceedings do not play a significant role in this respect. In the matter of revenue, the competent authorities for cooperating with OLAF are mostly the national customs or tax authorities.[127] However, Italy has set up a special branch of the financial police for investigating crime against the financial interests of the EU.[128]

OLAF is an administrative body and its investigations are administrative in nature. Criminal investigations affecting the financial interests of the EU are the mandate of the European Public Prosecutor's Office (EPPO),[129] whose criminal investigations take precedence over OLAF's administrative investigations.[130] On the part of the Member States, the situation is slightly different. This is because OLAF investigations concern the fight against fraud and, subsequently, areas in which criminal offences have likely been committed too. Parallel criminal investigations therefore occur more often than in case of financial supervision law.

Because OLAF's mandate is limited to administrative law, most Member States do not allow national authorities to support OLAF on the basis of administrative law when criminal investigations have been initiated by the national prosecuting authorities.[131] The reason for this is that criminal procedure law generally offers better protection of defence rights and more procedural safeguards than administrative law.[132] These standards would be undermined if OLAF were able to continue

[123] Allegrezza, 'Report Italy' (n 105) 129 ff.

[124] See Alldridge, 'Report the United Kingdom' (n 114) 153, 156 ff.

[125] See Böse and Schneider, 'Report Germany' (n 109) 57, 71.

[126] ibid 71.

[127] See, eg, Tricot, 'Report France' (n 105) 189, 191 ff.

[128] Allegrezza, 'Report Italy' (n 105) 129, 129–30.

[129] Council Regulation (EU) 2017/1939 of 12 October 2017 implementing enhanced cooperation on the establishment of the European Public Prosecutor's Office ('the EPPO') [2017] OJ L283/1, Art 3. See also Art 12d OLAF Regulation, as amended in 2020.

[130] Art 101(2) EPPO Regulation.

[131] Böse and Schneider, 'Report Germany' (n 109) 57, 62; Graat, 'Report the Netherlands' (n 109) 87, 96ff; Allegrezza, 'Report Italy' (n 105) 129–30.

[132] Böse and Schneider, 'Report Germany' (n 109) 57, 62.

its administrative investigation and later on offer its report as evidence (see, on the use of evidence, chapter 6). In this context, it should be noted that cooperation with OLAF by the national authorities strictly follows an administrative law regime in some Member States (eg Germany and the Netherlands),[133] while others grant the powers of the judicial police to the national authorities cooperating with OLAF (eg Italy)[134] or have entities entitled to do both and blurred boundaries.[135] The threshold for administrative investigations, especially in tax and customs proceedings, is, again, lower than that for criminal investigations.

Polish law allows parallel proceedings, although evidence gathered in administrative proceedings that lacked certain procedural safeguards might be inadmissible.[136] In France, parallel proceedings and parallel sanctions had been the rule in tax proceedings.[137] In the light of the European Court of Human Right's judgment in *Grande Stevens v Italy*,[138] in which a cumulation of Consob and criminal sanctions was ruled to be in breach of the *ne bis in idem* principle, the French Constitutional Court reassessed the criteria for complementary sanctions. It came to the conclusion that parallel proceedings were still possible in certain circumstances.[139] This argument was backed by the European Court of Human Rights[140] and confirmed by the CJEU in *Menci*.[141] Accordingly, parallel proceedings remain possible in France.

The different approaches for dealing with concurrent administrative and criminal proceedings show that the plurality of investigations is one of the key challenges in composite legal orders. This is most strongly apparent in OLAF investigations because, here, there is the biggest tension between OLAF's administrative approach and national criminal proceedings. However, other EU law enforcement authorities, such as the Commission in competition law cases, encounter the same difficulties.

IV. Investigative Measures and Procedural Safeguards

The difference between administrative investigations and criminal investigations can also be seen when looking at the investigative measures. As has been explained previously, the EU law enforcement authorities most particularly need the assistance of the national competent authorities when the addressee of an investigative measure needs to be coerced to comply with it.

The most important investigative measures are interviews and production orders, and to a lesser extent inspections and access to documents. All Member States acknowledge these investigative measures and allow the national competent authorities to

[133] H Gemmel, *Kontrollen des OLAF in Deutschland* (Mendel 2002) 134; S Strobel, *Die Untersuchungen des Europäischen Amtes für Betrugsbekämpfung (OLAF)* (CH Beck 2012) 138 ff.
[134] Allegrezza, 'Report Italy' (n 105) 129, 130.
[135] Alldridge, 'Report the United Kingdom' (n 114) 153, 154.
[136] Nowak and Błachucki, 'Report Poland' (n 106) 165, 169 ff.
[137] Tricot, 'Report France' (n 105) 189, 191 ff.
[138] *Grande Stevens v Italy* App no 18640/10 (ECtHR, 14 March 2014).
[139] Conseil Constitutionnel no 2016-545 QPC.
[140] *A and B v Norway* App nos 24130/11 and 29758/11 (ECtHR, 15 November 2016).
[141] Case C-524/15 *Menci* ECLI:EU:C:2018:197, para 63.

assist the EU law enforcement authorities in this context. Nonetheless, the legal bases for providing assistance in national law are very diverse. Not only are the cooperating authorities different depending on which EU authority needs assistance, but each of these authorities has its own set of rules for operational purposes. It is therefore neither feasible nor desirable to give detailed information on investigative measures in administrative law.[142]

However, it should be noted that the applicable law is even less clear in the case of OLAF. While the other authorities have a single cooperating partner, each with investigatory powers provided by EU law too, OLAF has to deal with a variety of legal partners. The AFCOS is mostly a non-operative body with a purely coordinative function (see section III.C). Explicit rules referring to OLAF are missing. This leads to uncertainty for the parties concerned.[143] Although the rules on external investigations have recently been clarified by an amendment to the OLAF Regulation[144] in order to provide an explicit obligation for cooperation, the lack of a strong partner still handicaps OLAF when it needs assistance from the national competent authorities.

Considering that investigative measures such as interviews, production orders, and search and seizure are in principle allowed in all Member States, the question of procedural safeguards is of the utmost importance. While some safeguards, such as access to a lawyer, are universally recognised without any problems, the privilege against self-incrimination and legal professional privilege and other forms of professional secrecy are more problematic.

A. The Relationship between EU and National Procedural Safeguards

When looking at procedural safeguards in composite proceedings, the first thing to note is that those exist in EU law and in national law. Accordingly, it must be asked which safeguards apply in cases of vertical cooperation (see also chapter 2). There are four theoretically possible solutions:

1. only procedural safeguards in EU law apply;
2. only procedural safeguards in national law apply;
3. both types of safeguards apply; or
4. none of the safeguards applies.

Options 2 and 4 could only be convincing if EU law did not apply in cases of vertical cooperation. However, when the national competent authorities assist EU authorities in their administrative investigations, the national authorities are implementing EU law. This means that vertical cooperation falls within the field of application of the Charter

[142] For more details, see Luchtman and Vervaele (eds) (n 104).

[143] M Luchtman and J Vervaele, 'Comparison of the Legal Frameworks' ibid 247, 268.

[144] Regulation (EU, Euratom) 2020/2223 of the European Parliament and of the Council of 23 December 2020 amending Regulation (EU, Euratom) No 883/2013, as regards cooperation with the European Public Prosecutor's Office and the effectiveness of the European Anti-Fraud Office investigations [2020] OJ L437/49.

of Fundamental Rights (Article 51(1)). Accordingly, the EU procedural safeguards as laid down in the Charter apply.[145]

The next question is whether EU law replaces national law (option 1), or whether both EU and national standards need to be met (option 3). One could argue that only EU law applies because the national authorities are implementing EU law.[146] However, in cases of vertical cooperation, EU law specifically refers to national law in order to fill in blanks in its legislation. This means that the matter in question is not completely determined by EU law. If national acts of sovereignty such as intrusive measures or judicial authorisation are required, they should be judged by national fundamental rights standards too.[147] Accordingly, both EU and national procedural safeguards apply (option 3). Following this line of argument, national procedural safeguards only become relevant when they go beyond the protection granted by EU law.[148] If national law offers lower protection, EU law will take precedence.[149]

B. Privilege against Self-Incrimination

The privilege against self-incrimination has been recognised in EU law.[150] Although it is not explicitly expressed in the Charter of Fundamental Rights, it is included in Articles 47(2) and 48(2) of the Charter, which are understood to correspond to Article 6(1) and (2) ECHR.[151] It has also been accepted by the Court of Justice (see sections II.A and II.C).[152] The privilege is also part of the directives on the protection of the defendant in criminal proceedings.[153] The myriad sources of the privilege in supranational law do not mean that there are several different privileges in EU law for, for example, competition law and market abuse law.[154] Rather, these elements highlight different facets of the one principle that forms a fundamental right in EU law.[155]

[145] See Böse and Schneider, 'Report Germany' (n 109) 57, 76; Graat, 'Report the Netherlands' (n 109) 87, 102.

[146] See Graat, 'Report the Netherlands' (n 109) 87, 102.

[147] See also K Gärditz, 'Kap. 6: Verfassungsrechtliche Grenzen der Strafrechtsanwendung' in M Böse (ed), *Europäisches Strafrecht* (Nomos 2021) margin no 50.

[148] See Böse and Schneider, 'Report Germany' (n 109) 57, 76.

[149] See Nowak and Błachucki, 'Report Poland' (n 106) 165, 181; Böse (n 14) 849 ff; A zur Nieden, '§ 59' in W Jaeger and others (eds), *Frankfurter Kommentar zum Kartellrecht*, 80th inst (Otto Schmidt 2014) margin no 30; differently: District Court (Landgericht) Bonn [2007] *Neue Zeitschrift für Strafrecht* 605, 607.

[150] See ch 2 of this volume (de Vries and Widdershoven), section IV.

[151] S Reinel, *Der "nemo tenetur"-Grundsatz als Grenze steuerlicher Informationshilfe in der Europäischen Union* (Mohr Siebeck 2015) 375 ff; BC Kizil, *Strafrechtliche Verfahrensgarantien im europäischen und deutschen Wettbewerbsrecht* (Nomos 2015) 248.

[152] *Orkem* (n 16); *DB v Consob* (n 94).

[153] Directive (EU) 2016/343 of the European Parliament and of the Council of 9 March 2016 on the strengthening of certain aspects of the presumption of innocence and of the right to be present at the trial in criminal proceedings [2016] OJ L65/1, Art 7.

[154] Cf *Orkem* (n 16); *DB v Consob* (n 94).

[155] See A Schneider, *Strafprozessuale Ermittlungsmaßnahmen und Zeugnisverweigerungsrechte* (Mohr Siebeck 2020) 424 ff; A Schneider, 'Collection and Evaluation of Evidence in the Constitutional Multi-level System: The Hidden Effects of EU Law' in A Farkas, G Dannecker and J Jacsó (eds), *Criminal Law Aspects of the Protection of the Financial Interests of the European Union* (Wolters Kluwer 2019) 495, 499 ff; A Schneider, 'Search and Seizure of Documents generated in Internal Investigations: Lessons to Learn from European Law' (2018) 89 *Revue Internationale de Droit Pénal* 311, 317ff, all for legal professional privilege.

This is also true for Article 7 of Directive (EU) 2016/343. By proclaiming minimum standards for defence rights, this Directive also shapes the guarantee in Article 48(2) of the Charter.[156] In consequence, a violation of these minimum standards is also a violation of Article 48(2).

The practical consequence for the composite proceedings discussed in this book is that the rights in the Directives could thus become applicable to administrative proceedings, although the Directives only refer to defence rights in criminal proceedings. Whether the shaping effect of the Directives on defence rights goes so far that it establishes – via Article 48(2) of the Charter – 'defence rights' for administrative proceedings remains to be seen. In *DB v Consob*, the CJEU pointed out that some of the administrative sanctions of Consob, the national authority responsible for cooperation with ESMA in Italy, were punitive in nature and could trigger the privilege against self-incrimination.[157]

Not all Member States unconditionally recognise the privilege against self-incrimination in administrative proceedings. Most Member States accept it for oral interrogations. However, in German and Dutch tax proceedings, the person concerned is not exempt from providing information documents, even though their use as evidence in criminal proceedings is limited.[158] The privilege against self-incrimination does not apply to production orders in administrative law in Germany, the Netherlands, France and Poland. Nor does it hinder search and seizure, although it applies to oral interrogations during the search. Altogether, the privilege does not seem to offer much protection beyond the right to remain silent.

Whether EU law has higher standards for production orders is unclear. In *Orkem*, the CJEU developed a narrow understanding of the privilege against self-incrimination (see section II.A). Although this approach has been broadened in *DB v Consob*, that case was about oral interrogations, not production orders. Article 7(3) of Directive (EU) 2016/343 allows the authorities to gather 'evidence which may be lawfully obtained through the use of legal powers of compulsion and which has an existence independent of the will of the suspects or accused persons'. This includes 'material acquired pursuant to a warrant, material in respect of which there is a legal obligation of retention and production upon request, breath, blood or urine samples and bodily tissue for the purpose of DNA testing'.[159] Therefore, the privilege apparently does not apply to production orders in EU law.

C. Legal Professional Privilege

The protection of legal professional privilege follows the same rules (see section IV.A). This means that procedural safeguards in EU law and national law apply. The CJEU early on recognised the importance of legal professional privilege in competition law cases

[156] A Schneider, 'In Absentia Trials and Transborder Criminal Procedures: The Perspective of EU Law' in S Quattrocolo and S Ruggeri (eds), *Personal Participation in Criminal Proceedings* (Springer 2019) 605, 623 ff.
[157] *DB v Consob* (n 94) para 41.
[158] Graat, 'Report the Netherlands' (n 109) 87, 103.
[159] Recital 29 Directive (EU) 2016/343.

(see section II.A).[160] Confidentiality of lawyer-client communication is also guaranteed by Article 4 of Directive (EU) 2013/48.[161] Apart from this, there is some indication that EU law respects other types of professional secrecy.[162] For example, the execution of a European Investigation Order (EIO) may be refused if there is an immunity or a privilege under the law of the executing State preventing execution, or if the freedom of the press would be endangered.[163] However, the extent of this respect is largely unclear. Recital 20 of the EIO Directive provides:

> There is no common definition of what constitutes an immunity or privilege in Union law; the precise definition of these terms is therefore left to national law, which may include protections which apply to medical and legal professions …

This is another reason why national procedural safeguards should also apply in composite proceedings (section IV.A); otherwise, there might be no protection of professional secrecy beyond legal professional privilege.

The Member States naturally have more rules on professional secrecy. Again, the law is diverse and very much dependent on the institutional framework.[164] Persons sworn to professional secrecy are generally not obliged to answer questions in competition law and tax law and customs proceedings (Germany, Poland), though they lack protection in other Member States (Italy).[165] If granted, this right usually does not apply to administrative proceedings in the area of financial supervision and SSM proceedings.

In cases of search and seizure, the protection offered, if any, basically focuses on legal professional privilege. In France, until recently, global seizure of a whole email account had been allowed, although French law protects legal professional privilege.[166] Moreover, it should be noted that the understanding of whose professional secrecy is protected differs very much among the Member States. For example, France has a narrow understanding of the professions that are protected (lawyers only),[167] while Germany protects a large number of professional actors, including certified accountants and tax consultants. In many Member States, searches require prior judicial authorisation, at least if a private home is to be entered.[168]

In Poland, legal professional privilege as accepted in EU competition law is recognised by the national competition law authorities, but not in the financial sector.[169] Taking into account what has been said in section IV.B, this reasoning seems to be in breach of EU fundamental rights. The interpretation of legal professional privilege

[160] *AM & S* (n 15); *Akzo Nobel Chemicals* (n 15) .

[161] Directive (EU) 2013/48 of the European Parliament and of the Council of 22 October 2013 on the right of access to a lawyer in criminal proceedings and in European arrest warrant proceedings, and on the right to have a third party informed upon deprivation of liberty and to communicate with third persons and with consular authorities while deprived of liberty [2013] OJ L294/1.

[162] See Schneider, *Strafprozessuale Ermittlungsmaßnahmen* (n 155) 393 ff.

[163] Directive 2014/41/EU of the European Parliament and of the Council of 3 April 2014 regarding the European Investigation Order in criminal matters [2014] OJ L130/1 ('EIO Directive'), Art 11(1)(a).

[164] For details, see Luchtman and Vervaele (eds) (n 104).

[165] Allegrezza, 'Report Italy' (n 105) 129, 145.

[166] Tricot, 'Report France' (n 105) 189, 212 ff.

[167] ibid 189, 206 ff.

[168] Allegrezza, 'Report Italy' (n 105) 129, 144.

[169] Nowak and Błachucki, 'Report Poland' (n 106) 165, 181.

in competition law cases is not specific to this area of law but concerns the fundamental right that applies in EU law. Accordingly, EU legal professional privilege should be accepted not only in competition law, but also in other areas of law.

V. Judicial Review

Composite proceedings also provide challenges for judicial review (see further chapter 3). The main concern in this respect is the question of which legal order is responsible for providing judicial review. Again, there are four theoretically possible solutions:

1. only EU Courts provide judicial review;
2. only national courts provide judicial review;
3. both provide judicial review; or
4. no one provides judicial review.

The last option is obviously in breach of Article 47(1) of the Charter, considering that vertical cooperation means that the national authorities implement EU law by their actions, and can therefore be disregarded. Options 1 and 2 would require the EU Courts to rule on the validity of measures adopted by national authorities and vice versa. So far, the prevailing opinion is that neither is allowed to do so due to their limited competence.[170] Accordingly, the current system of judicial review at the investigative stage is a shared system of judicial review (option 3).

Such a shared system avoids the problematic consequences that would be attached to having national courts decide on the legality of EU law and vice versa. However, it is also prone to – unwillingly – creating gaps in judicial review. At EU level, the most problematic point is that judicial review against actions by OLAF is notoriously complicated to achieve and does not cover all situations.[171] In the case of *ex ante* judicial authorisation, the national court may only assess whether the EU authorities' decision is authentic and that the coercive measures envisaged are neither arbitrary nor excessive (eg under Article 20(8) of Regulation 1/2003).

At national level, judicial review is dependent on the acting authority and the applicable legal framework, which makes the applicable rules hard to find in some Member States. Moreover, not all Member States allow administrative investigative measures to be reviewed individually. In some cases, only the final sanction or a fine for non-compliance with an order to provide information or produce documents can be challenged in court.[172] Moreover, the legality under national law might depend on the reasons that made the EU authorities ask for assistance. This would be hard to assess without having a closer look at the decision by the EU authority in question. Finally,

[170] See, eg, Case 314/85 *Foto-Frost v Hauptzollamt Lübeck-Ost* ECLI:EU:C:1987:452; JFH Inghelram, *Legal and Institutional Aspects of the European Anti-Fraud Office (OLAF)* (EuropaLaw Publishing 2011) 226 ff; C Silberzahn, 'Rechtsschutz gegen OLAF' [2016] *Juristische Arbeitsblätter* 205, 208.

[171] See Joined Cases F-5/05 and F-7/05 *Violetti and Schmit v Commission* ECLI:EU:F:2009:39 (Judgment of the Civil Service Tribunal); Case T-261/09 P *Commission v Violetti and Others* ECLI:EU:T:2010:215; Inghelram (n 170) 227 ff.

[172] See, eg, Graat, 'Report the Netherlands' (n 109) 87, 125 ff.

this shared competence for judicial review is problematic in view of the principles of equivalence, because national law cannot by itself offer the protection it affords in purely national cases.

For the persons concerned, shared judicial review means that they have to use more time and money in order to achieve the same results they would achieve if the investigative measure (eg search and seizure) did not occur in the context of vertical cooperation. None of the frameworks take this disadvantage into account. This issue is more often discussed in cases of horizontal cooperation between the Member States, in which the person concerned must usually file complaints in the issuing and the executing states.[173] But it is at least as problematic in cases of vertical cooperation: because vertical cooperation proceedings are considered to form a unity, fragmentation of and gaps in judicial review should not occur.

VI. Conclusion

The analysis in this chapter has shown that a comprehensive legal framework for composite investigations is lacking. Each EU authority operates under its own framework. Combined with the legal framework of the national partners in the Member States, the cases can be considerably different. However, some common features have been found.

First, there is a clear difference between OLAF on the one hand and DG Competition, the ECB and ESMA on the other hand. This is because the last three bodies have a centralised partner with operative powers. In contrast, OLAF mostly cooperates with an AFCOS that has only a coordinating function.

Second, it has become clear that the relationship between punitive administrative proceedings and criminal proceedings is problematic. Whether administrative proceedings go on when criminal investigations have started or not is dependent on general rules in national law that have often not been explicitly written down. The reason seems to be that the nature of the administrative proceedings undertaken by DG Competition, the ECB, ESMA and particularly OLAF is unclear.

Third, most Member States do provide adequate investigative measures for the purpose of composite proceedings. Again, the applicable law is not easy to determine because many different actors are involved. In case of procedural safeguards, it has been argued here that both EU safeguards and national safeguards offering better protection apply. However, the scope of the EU procedural safeguards does not seem to be completely clear. National procedural safeguards in administrative law tend to provide less protection than the equivalent safeguards in criminal proceedings. This might cause problems when the results are to be used as evidence in criminal proceedings (see chapter 6).

[173] There are only special rules for the European Arrest Warrant, eg Directive 2013/48/EU, Art 10; see, on horizontal cooperation, M Böse, M Bröcker and A Schneider (eds), *Judicial Protection in Transnational Criminal Proceedings* (Springer 2020).

Finally, judicial review is challenging because of the shared competence of the EU Courts and national courts. Because the national systems regarding judicial review differ considerably, but the EU system is fixed, it is possible that full judicial review cannot be granted. Moreover, the person concerned might be burdened by having recourse to two different systems of judicial review.

Overall, although composite proceedings are not new per se, they have proved to be problematic when used for enforcement. The investigatory phase of these proceedings is especially challenging. In particular, the questions of which procedural safeguards apply and how the interests of the person concerned can best be protected remain open. These questions become even more crucial when evidence gathered in the investigative phase is transferred (chapter 5) or used as evidence in criminal proceedings (chapter 6).

5

The Exchange of Operational Information between EU and National Authorities

KOEN BOVEND'EERDT AND IRO KARAGIANNI

I. Introduction

Exchange of information is a difficult concept to define in the abstract.[1] In terms of scope it is seemingly boundless. 'Information', after all, encompasses any type of communicated knowledge that reduces uncertainty concerning some type of fact, subject or event.[2] The conjoined term 'exchange' does very little to shrink the terrain that 'information' covers. To speak about an exchange presupposes the existence of at least two parties that are bound together by some kind of reciprocal relationship. Contrary to transfer, exchange is a two-way street. Exchange is at least as much about giving as it is about receiving.[3] There are many reasons to exchange information, or something else for that matter, but if we reduce all these reasons to their bare bones, they are all essentially expressions of supply and demand: you have something that I need. While exchange of information is premised on a relationship between sender and receiver,[4]

[1] While the etymology of the respective terms does not raise too many questions, its meaning in relation to law enforcement, of interest in this chapter, in particular by European Union (EU) authorities, is unclear. A search for definitions in the existing body of literature leaves the authors unsatisfied. See F Boehm, *Information Sharing and Data Protection in the Area of Freedom, Security and Justice: Towards Harmonised Data Protection Principles for Information Exchange at EU-level* (Springer 2012) 12–15; Á Gutiérrez Zarza, *Exchange of Information and Data Protection in Cross-Border Criminal Proceedings in Europe* (Springer 2015) 3–7. In specific contexts, such as horizontal judicial cooperation, authors do, but also can, define the meaning of 'exchange of information'. See M Simonato, 'The "Spontaneous Exchange of Information" between European Judicial Authorities from the Italian Perspective' (2011) 2 *New Journal of European Criminal Law* 221, 222–23.

[2] Cf R Losee, 'A Discipline Independent Definition of Information' (1997) 48 *Journal of the American Society for Information Science* 254, 255–56.

[3] The reciprocal nature of the relationship expresses itself through contingency and equivalence. With respect to the first, reciprocity implies that an action is conditional on a rewarding action. With respect to the second, there needs to be a rough equivalence between the respective actions. On these dimensions of reciprocity as a general concept, see R Keohane, 'Reciprocity in International Relations' (1986) 40 *International Organization* 1, 5–6. In the exchange of information, reciprocity, in both its dimensions, is ensured through legal obligation.

[4] Both positions that, due to the reciprocal nature of exchange, all parties to the transaction take.

as a generic term, it specifies little in terms of the content of this relationship. It does not define who the parties involved are, when they exchange information, what information they may exchange, and for what purpose, or how they do so. The net cast by the term 'exchange of information' consequently is wide.

The net we cast – or, depending on your perspective, the pond we fish in – is smaller. In this chapter we are concerned solely with the exchange of information in law enforcement. Law enforcement is the process through which violations of substantive norms are monitored, investigated and sanctioned.[5] The parts of the process with which most are familiar are the direct gathering of information by authorities (see chapter 4) and the later use thereof in punitive proceedings against those to which the substantive norm in question is addressed (see chapter 6). The exchange of information is considered the juncture or hinge between the gathering of information by one authority and the use thereof by another. Whenever one authority is in need of information not directly available to it,[6] the exchange of information is the necessary link through which authorities can connect to chains or channels (i) in different policy areas (eg, exchange between the tax authority and the public prosecution service), (ii) in different Member States (eg, exchange between public prosecution services of two Member States), and (iii) in the EU legal order (eg, the exchange between national competition authorities and the Directorate-General for Competition ('DG Competition')).[7] Information sharing between authorities allows law enforcement to better respond to threats: it allows for 'intelligence-led policing' and makes it possible for authorities to build up information positions.[8]

This chapter focuses on the third strand: the exchange of information between EU law enforcement authorities (hereinafter ELEAs) – in particular the European Anti-Fraud Office (OLAF), DG Competition and the European Central Bank (ECB) – and the competent national authorities.[9] The need for legal frameworks that regulate the

[5] J Vervaele, 'Shared Governance and Enforcement of European Law: From Comitology to a Multi-Level Agency Structure?' in C Joerges and E Vos (eds), *EU Committees: Social Regulation, Law and Politics* (Hart Publishing 1999) 131.

[6] The reasons for this can be various, but can roughly be grouped into one of the following categories: no competence in a particular policy area; no power; or no jurisdiction to obtain the information in question.

[7] This list is in no way meant to be exhaustive. The exchange of information could also link up different chains. Think, for instance, of transversal exchanges at the EU-level between, eg, Eurojust and Europol, or between the EU and international organisations (eg, between Eurojust and Interpol). On the former, see Regulation (EU) 2018/1727 on the European Union Agency for Criminal Justice Cooperation (Eurojust) [2018] OJ L295/138, Art 49; Regulation (EU) 2016/794 on the European Agency for Law Enforcement Cooperation (Europol) [2016] OJ L135/53, Art 21. On the latter, see, eg, Regulation (EU) 2018/1727, Arts 52, 56–59; more specifically, we refer the reader to the 'Memorandum of understanding on cooperation between Eurojust and the International Criminal Police Organisation (ICPO-Interpol)', Arts 3 and 4. What is more, multiple 'channels' can coincide. Think, for instance, of the exchange of information between national members through Eurojust. See Regulation (EU) 2018/1727, Arts 7(8), 8(1)(b) and 21(3). On the exchange of information in the EU between administrative and judicial authorities in a horizontal setting, see M Luchtman, *European Cooperation between Financial Supervisory Authorities, Tax Authorities and Judicial Authorities* (Intersentia 2008).

[8] Intelligence-led policing is 'the application of criminal intelligence analysis as an objective decision-making tool in order to facilitate crime reduction and prevention through effective policing strategies and external partnership projects drawn from an evidential base'. See J Ratcliffe, 'Intelligence-led Policing in Crime and Criminal Justice' [2003] *Trends and Issues in Crime and Criminal Justice* 1, 3.

[9] To be clear – if it was not already – this chapter deals only with the vertical exchange of information between EU authorities and their national counterparts. We do not consider the exchange of information within Member States, between Member States (horizontal) or between EU authorities (transversal).

exchange of information is evident. Due to the composite system of enforcement in the respective fields in which these authorities operate, as a result of which tasks and mandates are spread across legal orders, the relevant actors in these respective orders depend, in some way, on each other for the provision of information to ensure effective enforcement.[10] How do the legal frameworks of the four authorities address and regulate this informational dependence and, particularly, how do they compare? From a top-down perspective, how are exchange of information frameworks of EU authorities integrated into national legal systems? In turn, how do these national legal systems accommodate EU systems on the exchange of information? And, in line with the overarching topic of this book, do the EU authorities' frameworks recognise the needs of criminal justice *sensu stricto*, which is also the topic of ch 8 of this volume, where Allegrezza et al discuss the specifics of the relationships between EU enforcement authorities and national criminal justice authorities?

As stated above, while the concept of 'exchange of information' is premised on the existence of a relationship, it leaves, without further definition, the content of this relationship wide open. To try to fill in this relationship, we make a distinction between an inner circle of authorities (EU authorities' institutional partners) and an outer circle (which consists of other administrative authorities and judicial authorities that are not institutionally linked to an EU authority).[11] To answer the questions posed above we propose, in line with what was mentioned before, the following four objects of comparison: the authorities involved in the exchange of information; when exchange takes place (ie the enforcement phase); the type and purpose of the information exchanged; and the modalities of exchange.

The above also informs the structure of this chapter, which proceeds in the following fashion. Having discussed the tasks and mandates of the examined ELEAs (section II), we proceed with a comparative analysis of the four ELEAs along the lines of the above-mentioned objects of comparison both from a top-down (ELEA-Member State) (section III) and bottom-up (Member State-ELEA) point of view (section IV).[12] Whereas the former (top-down) section solely concerns the transfer of information from ELEAs to national authorities, the latter (bottom-up) section deals only with the transfer of information from national authorities to ELEAs. To avoid confusion, we wish to make clear that, irrespective of the direction of transfer (ie top-down or bottom-up), we discuss how the ELEA legal frameworks regulate the exchange between the ELEA and national authorities in question (the 'EU-perspective'), and how this is accommodated by national law and authorities (the 'Member State-perspective'). In short, to answer the questions posed in the previous paragraph we analyse the transfer to and from ELEAs from the point of view of EU and national law.

[10] For the definition, see ch 1 of this volume (Luchtman).

[11] M Luchtman, M Simonato and J Vervaele, 'Comparative Analysis' in M Simonato, M Luchtman and J Vervaele (eds), *Exchange of Information with EU and National Enforcement Authorities. Improving OLAF legislative framework through a comparison with other EU authorities (ECN/ESMA/ECB)* (Utrecht University 2018) 166.

[12] The national systems considered in this chapter coincide with those of the study by Simonato, Luchtman and Vervaele: Germany, Hungary, Italy, Luxembourg, the Netherlands, and the United Kingdom (UK). See Simonato, Luchtman and Vervaele (n 11).

In both sections III and IV we distinguish further between inner-circle national partners (section III.A and section IV.A respectively) and outer-circle authorities that can either be administrative and/or judicial authorities (section III.B and section IV.B respectively). This means that we examine top-down and bottom-up information flows between ELEAs and a variety of authorities by looking at EU law and corresponding national law provisions. We make this distinction between inner- and outer-circles to try and establish whether ELEA legal frameworks on the exchange of information recognise the (potential) punitive dimension of ELEAs' work and, if so, how they, individually, deal with this recognition. In the penultimate section (section V), prior to some concluding remarks (section VI), we consider the regimes on the exchange of information, their differences and their similarities, and – where possible – try to explain how and why they are different, especially in light of the ELEAs' linkages with criminal justice and the needs that sprout therefrom.

Note that our analysis is limited to legal problems: we do not assess, as such, practical problems related to information exchange (although, of course, the latter can be the result of the former).[13] Furthermore, we do not touch upon issues of data protection, which nevertheless is hugely important.[14] Legal protection and the exchange of information are dealt with in chapter 3 by Ligeti and Robinson.

Before dealing with the EU authorities, it is appropriate to issue a caveat here. The way in which we, somewhat rigidly (and even arbitrarily), position the exchange of information in this chapter likens law enforcement to a linear and successive process. Information is gathered; where necessary this information is transmitted or received, in order to put it in the hands of the authority that can make use of it in punitive proceedings against the person suspected of violating the substantive norm in question. The exchange of information is so much more than that and is better conceived of not as merely the link between the gathering and use of information, but as a continuous process that transcends or overarches the triptych put forward here ('gather', 'exchange', 'use'). We are aware that, so to speak, the map is not the territory.[15] That does not mean that maps are useless. Instead, just like our analytical grid here, they promote an understanding, albeit a partial one, of a very complex reality. Having said that, to try and nestle the exchange of information in between the gathering and use of information as best as we possibly can, this chapter only considers what we call, 'operational information': case-specific information that can be of (potential) use in ongoing punitive proceedings. Operational information, in this sense, should be distinguished from, amongst others, strategic information or information exchanged for policy-making purposes.[16] Strategic

[13] On practical problems with respect to the exchange of information between OLAF and, amongst others, national authorities, see Ecorys, 'Study on impact of strengthening of administrative and criminal law procedural rules for the protection of the EU financial interests' JUST/A4/2011/EVAL/01, 14–19.

[14] EU authorities also take measures to ensure that exchanges of information are in line with data protection regulations. See, for instance, OLAF's appointment of its own data protection officer, which is to ensure that OLAF correctly applies the rules protecting individuals' personal data. See Decision of the Director General of OLAF adopting implementing rules concerning the Data Protection Officer for OLAF and the Secretariat of the Supervisory Committee. The decision is based on Regulation (EU, Euratom) 883/2013 concerning investigations conducted by the European Anti-Fraud Office (OLAF) [2013] OJ L248/1 ('OLAF Regulation'), Art 10(4).

[15] A phrase used by A Korzybski, *Science and Sanity: An Introduction to non-Aristotelean Systems and General Semantics* (The International Non-Aristotelian Library Publishing Company 1933) 747–61.

[16] See, eg, Art 1(2) OLAF Regulation.

information is information not associated with a specific case but used for identifying often large-scale and/or long-term trends. Policy information is, as the name suggests, information exchanged with the purpose of developing, making or evaluating policies.

For a good understanding of what this chapter does and does not do, we must make some important distinctions. While some, rightfully, distinguish between 'information' and 'intelligence',[17] the latter being the product of raw information that has been evaluated and given purpose (for instance, providing knowledge about a particular criminal threat through analysis), we conflate the two because this distinction is not recognised in the frameworks of the four authorities studied.[18] When the authors refer to 'information', we mean to include the subset of 'intelligence', unless specifically stated.

With an eye on chapter 6, on the admissibility of evidence, there is a further distinction that should be made between 'information'/'intelligence' on the one hand and 'evidence' on the other. Evidence is data on the basis of which proof can be established in punitive proceedings. While there is certainly some overlap between the notions – information can function as evidence or as a prelude to evidence gathering – the primary purpose is different. The purpose of information and intelligence is first and foremost to help law enforcement, particularly investigators, take decisions by identifying information gaps and bring focus to supervision or an investigation; it is not, or at least not initially, to establish proof.[19] Whether information or intelligence, as such, constitutes or can be used as evidence in punitive proceedings is a separate question altogether.[20]

[17] MAP Willmer, *Crime and Information Theory* (Edinburgh University Press 1970) 24–34; J Sheptycki, 'Organisational Pathologies in Police Intelligence Systems: Some Contributions to the Lexicon of Intelligence-led Policing' (2004) 1 *European Journal of Criminology* 307, 310; UNODC, *Criminal Intelligence: Manual for Front-Line Law Enforcement* (United Nations 2010) 1. That does not mean, of course, that information is not turned into intelligence by the four authorities (or their national counterparts), or that they do not exchange intelligence.

[18] According to Cocq, 'the EU has not yet provided any clear and distinct definition of either "information" or "intelligence"'. See C Cocq, '"Information" and "Intelligence": The Current Divergences between National Legal Systems and the Need for Common (European) Notions' (2017) 8 *New Journal of European Criminal Law* 352, 359.

[19] D Plecas et al, 'Evidence-Based Solution to Information Sharing between Law Enforcement Agencies' (2010) 34 *Policing: an International Journal of Police Strategies & Management* 120, 121.

[20] J Spencer, 'The Green Paper on Obtaining Evidence from one Member State to another and Securing its Admissibility: The Reaction of one British Lawyer' (2010) 5 *Zeitschrift für Internationale Strafrechtsdogmatik* 602, 604–05. While some EU authorities, like OLAF and the European Public Prosecutor's Office (EPPO), contain rules on the admissibility of evidence, they do not dictate what is (or in any case ought to be) evidence under national law. Art 11(2) OLAF Regulation, for example, states that OLAF investigation reports 'constitute admissible evidence in administrative or judicial proceedings of the Member State in which their use proves necessary, in the same way and under the same conditions as administrative reports drawn up by national administrative inspectors'. While the provision forces national authorities to treat OLAF reports as if they were national (administrative) reports with respect to their admissibility, it says nothing about the possibilities of the latter's use. If, hypothetically, national law would not allow for the use of administrative reports as evidence in punitive proceedings, an OLAF report would, in like manner, not be admissible. Its European origins do not affect what materials are to be considered evidence under national law. The EPPO rules on the admissibility of evidence are different and reflect the body's (relatively) decentralised architecture and the (subsequent) transnational nature of its investigations. Council Regulation (EU) 2017/1939 implementing enhanced cooperation on the establishment of the EPPO [2017] OJ L283/1, Art 37, which deals with the issue of the admissibility of evidence, is essentially a rule of non-discrimination. It holds that evidence shall not be denied admission on the mere ground that the evidence was gathered in another Member State or in accordance with the law of another Member State. Here too, EU law does not state what materials can serve as evidence under national law. This is left to the discretion of each respective legal system.

The principal functions of rules that govern the exchange of information and (admissibility of) evidence, understandably, also differ. Rules on the exchange of information seek to facilitate decision-making of law enforcement 'elsewhere' (in our case at the EU or the national level). Rules on information exchange establish formalised channels that bring into contact authorities in different policy areas, Member States, or EU legal order so that – through these channels – information can be transported to where it is necessary. The rules on evidence serve to establish whether the accused has committed the offence for which he has been indicted. Both sets of rules do (at the EU and the national levels), in different ways, also fulfil an important fundamental rights function, in that they allow for the exercise of control on the exchange of information and the (subsequent) use thereof as evidence in punitive procedures.[21]

Now, without further ado, let us press forward to section II on ELEAs' tasks and mandates.

II. ELEAs' Tasks and Mandates

A. OLAF

OLAF is a Commission service whose mandate is to fight fraud, corruption and any other illegal activity that affects the financial interests of the Union (hereinafter 'PIF'), that is, all expenditure, revenues, assets, and the budgets managed and monitored by the EU.[22] OLAF thereby operates on the basis of a broad mandate that encompasses all areas of Union activity in so far as PIF are affected.

To carry out its mandate, OLAF primarily conducts administrative investigations that consist of measures undertaken by OLAF with the purpose of gathering evidence to establish whether illegal activities affecting PIF have occurred.[23] OLAF conducts internal and external investigations.[24] This chapter focuses solely on the exchange of operational information in OLAF's external investigations, that is, those carried out in the Member States.[25] OLAF's investigative task is by no means exclusive; national (punitive) investigations can run in parallel with or consecutive to OLAF investigations.[26]

While OLAF's investigations are administrative in nature, they often concern acts that are punishable by punitive administrative penalties or, as the case may be, criminal law penalties. OLAF's tasks however, are limited strictly to carrying out investigations:

[21] F Giuffrida, 'Comparative Analysis' in F Giuffrida and K Ligeti, *Admissibility of OLAF Final Reports as Evidence in Criminal Proceedings* (University of Luxembourg 2019) 227.

[22] Art 1 OLAF Regulation.

[23] Decision 1999/352 establishing the European Anti-fraud Office [1999] OJ L 136/20, Art 2(1); OLAF Regulation, Art 1(1) and 2(4); Guidelines on investigations procedures for OLAF staff (Ref Ares(2013)3077837) (hereinafter GIP 2013), Art 8(1).

[24] Arts 3 and 4 OLAF Regulation.

[25] In practice the distinction between internal and external investigations is at times artificial, as the presence of evidence concerning a particular illegal activity prejudicing the Union's financial interests may necessitate investigations in both the Member States and the Union's institutions, bodies, offices and agencies.

[26] Art 2(4) OLAF Regulation.

OLAF does not fulfil monitoring, prosecutorial or sanctioning functions. For (punitive) follow-up to its investigations, OLAF relies on national authorities (or, increasingly, the EPPO).[27] Evidence gathered by OLAF, where this is to result in punitive sanctions, is therefore to end up as evidence before national courts (for more on this see chapter 6).[28] So, while OLAF is, without a doubt, an administrative authority that conducts administrative investigations, it can – and does – operate at the interface of administrative and punitive law. OLAF's legal framework clearly recognises, as we demonstrate later, the possible (national) criminal law dimension of its work.

An important consequence of OLAF's circumscribed set of tasks is that, as we show in section IV, OLAF depends largely on national authorities to supply it with the information necessary to counter acts that prejudice the Union's budget.[29] This applies not only prior to, but also during and after an investigation.[30] After all, OLAF needs information for it to detect behaviour worth investigating and to decide whether or not to open an investigation (pre-investigation). Because of OLAF's limited operational capacity and strong integration in national legal orders, it also requires information during its investigations (investigation). Last, to see whether OLAF's investigations have had any impact (or further action needs to be taken), OLAF also needs input from national authorities (post-investigation).[31] The Member States, on the other hand, will depend on information in the hands of OLAF, especially in transnational cases, to take effective action against EU fraud. This chapter concerns only the exchange of information between OLAF and national authorities in OLAF's investigations, excluding the pre- and post-investigative exchanges of information on the basis of OLAF's horizontal legal framework.[32] It also excludes the exchange of information with the EPPO. Whereas the limited tasks allocated to OLAF require it to cooperate with national authorities, its broad mandate requires the Office to cooperate *with an array of different national authorities* depending on the policy area affected. For example, while in the area of structural funds, the European Regional Development Fund (ERDF) in particular, OLAF needs to cooperate and exchange information with management, certifying, and audit authorities, in the area of customs OLAF needs to cooperate with national customs authorities.

[27] Art 11(2) OLAF Regulation.

[28] ibid.

[29] Other important sources of information are whistle-blowers and EU institutions, bodies, offices and agencies. Whistle-blowers can directly report to OLAF via its website at https://fns.olaf.europa.eu/. The EU's institutions, bodies, offices, and agencies are under an EU duty to transfer information to OLAF. For the extent of this duty, see Regulation (EU, Euratom) 2020/2223 as regards cooperation with the European Public Prosecutor's Office and the effectiveness of the European Anti-Fraud Office investigations [2020] OJ L437/49 ('New OLAF Regulation'), Art 8.

[30] This is reflected in Art 8(2) and (3) OLAF Regulation.

[31] M Simonato, 'Introduction' in Simonato, Luchtman and Vervaele (eds) (n 11) 1–2.

[32] OLAF's horizontal legal framework ought to be distinguished from its sectoral legal framework. Whereas the first applies generally, irrespective of the policy area affected, the latter offers – more specific – rules on the exchange of information in a particular policy area, for instance customs of structural funds. Given that the structure and set-up of this chapter is already dense and complex, we avoid even further complication and do not deal with OLAF's sectoral legislation on the exchange of information, regardless of how interesting this is.

B. DG Competition

The Directorate-General for Competition is a European Commission Directorate-General responsible for the application of EU competition law, that is, Articles 101 to 109 TFEU. In this chapter, however, we limit ourselves to discussing the exchange of information between DG Competition and national competition authorities for the purposes of the enforcement of Articles 101 and 102 TFEU, which prohibit – respectively – agreements that restrict competition and abuses of dominance in a given market.[33]

To carry out its mandate, DG Competition primarily conducts administrative investigations, which consist of measures undertaken by the Directorate with the purpose of gathering evidence to establish whether violations of the aforementioned provisions have occurred. To this end, DG Competition has been entrusted with direct investigating[34] and sanctioning powers.[35]

The fact that such extensive powers are vested in DG Competition does not, however, mean that national authorities do not play a role in the application of antitrust rules. In 2003, the enforcement of EU antitrust rules underwent decentralisation. From that time, DG Competition has enforced the substantive EU provisions in parallel with the national competition authorities of the EU Member States, which together form the European Competition Network (ECN), a '*de facto* organization, devoid of legal personality'.[36] Indeed, the ECN as such does not have enforcement powers at its disposal; rather, it constitutes a forum for coordination of EU antitrust enforcement. Given that a system of parallel competence requires clear rules as to the allocation of tasks, the ECN Notice[37] provides certain criteria governing which authority or authorities can be considered to be well placed to deal with a particular case.[38]

Concerning the system of (punitive) administrative law enforcement of EU antitrust rules and its relation to national systems of criminal justice *sensu stricto*, the following can be said. Various national laws foresee the imposition of criminal law sanctions for the violation of Articles 101 and 102 TFEU.[39] As a result, there are strong links between administrative enforcement and criminal law enforcement, and it is not inconceivable that information initially obtained for purposes of administrative law enforcement may at a certain stage also reach criminal justice authorities.

[33] Council Regulation (EC) No 1/2003 of 16 December 2002 on the implementation of the rules on competition laid down in Articles 81 and 82 of the Treaty [2003] OJ L1/1 ('Regulation 1/2003'), Art 12(1).

[34] Arts 17–21 Regulation 1/2003.

[35] Arts 23 and 24 Regulation 1/2003.

[36] D Gerard, 'Public Enforcement: The ECN – Network Antitrust Enforcement in the European Union' in I Lianos and D Gerardin (eds), *Handbook on European Competition Law – Enforcement and Procedure* (Edward Elgar 2013) 194.

[37] Commission, 'Commission Notice on cooperation within the Network of Competition Authorities' [2004] OJ C 101/043 ('ECN Notice').

[38] ECN Notice, paras 8 et seq.

[39] See P Whelan, 'Legal Certainty and Cartel Criminalisation within the EU Member States' (2012) 71 *Cambridge Law Journal* 677; W Wils, 'Is Criminalization of EU Competition Law the Answer?' (2005) 28 *World Competition* 117.

C. The ECB

The ECB is an EU institution that has a dual mandate: to ensure price stability, a monetary policy objective; and to contribute to the stability of the financial system, by carrying out prudential supervision over the credit institutions operating in the euro area.[40] In essence, the latter mandate consists of overseeing banks' compliance with the applicable banking regulation. In this chapter, we focus only on the ECB's supervisory mandate.

The ECB does not exercise its supervisory mandate completely autonomously. The ECB directly supervises significant banks, while national competent authorities (NCAs) carry out the day-to-day supervision of less significant ones. However, it should be kept in mind that even though enforcement largely takes place through composite procedures, the overall responsibility for the functioning of the Single Supervisory Mechanism (SSM) rests with the ECB. Indeed, according to the CJEU, the SSM system can be seen as a mechanism that allows the exclusive *competences* given to the ECB to be implemented within a decentralised framework.[41]

Concerning the system of (punitive) administrative law enforcement of banking supervision law and its relation to national systems of criminal justice *sensu stricto*, the following links may be identified. In many Member States, violations of prudential requirements are sanctioned (also) through criminal law.[42] As a result, it may often be the case that national judicial authorities responsible for the investigation and prosecution of these types of offences have an interest in receiving information initially obtained by an SSM authority for purposes of ongoing supervision.

III. Transfer of Information from ELEAs to National Authorities

A. Transfer of Information from ELEAs to their Inner-Circle National Partners

i. ELEAs' Inner-Circle National Partners

OLAF's inner-circle partner in the Member States is the anti-fraud coordination service (AFCOS). The function of the AFCOS is, amongst other things, to facilitate effective cooperation and exchange of information, including information of an operational

[40] Council Regulation (EU) No 1024/2013 of 15 October 2013 conferring specific tasks on the European Central Bank concerning policies relating to the prudential supervision of credit institutions [2013] OJ L287/63 ('SSM Regulation'), Art 1.

[41] Case C-450/17 P *Landeskreditbank Baden-Württemberg v European Central Bank* ECLI:EU:C:2019:372, para 49.

[42] See A Karagianni, *The Protection of Fundamental Rights in Composite Banking Supervision Proceedings* (Europa Law Publishing 2022); S Allegrezza (ed), *The Enforcement Dimension of the Single Supervisory Mechanism* (Wolter Kluwer 2020).

nature, with OLAF.[43] The AFCOS was created because it was often very difficult for OLAF to address the competent authority in a given Member State for two interrelated reasons. The first is that, because of the vast range of illegal activities that could potentially detriment the Union's financial interests – and, as a result, the large number of policy areas OLAF must protect – there is a wide array of national authorities with which OLAF must cooperate. The situation is exacerbated, and this is the second reason, by the fact that each and every Member State appoints different authorities in these policy areas, each of which operates under its own set of rules and under a different structure. At the most basic level, the AFCOS, resolves this by serving as a first point of contact for OLAF in each Member State, and in that sense facilitates effective cooperation and exchange of information with OLAF.[44]

OLAF's legal framework regulates only the exchange of information between OLAF and 'national competent authorities'.[45] The legal framework does not have a regime in place tailored specifically to institutional partners (the inner circle) or other administrative or judicial authorities (the outer circle).[46] OLAF therefore only transfers information to national authorities that are considered competent. Whether these national authorities are in fact competent is largely left for the Member States to decide, and in practice is often unclear.[47] More on that in section IV.

The inner-circle partner of DG Competition in the EU Member States is the national competition authority. According to Recital 35 of Regulation 1/2003, Member States should designate and empower authorities to apply Articles 101 and 102 TFEU as public enforcers. Unlike the OLAF legal framework, DG Competition has 27 institutional national counterparts.[48] In that respect, wherever the EU legal framework makes reference to information transmissions or exchanges between the European Commission and national competition authorities, it is clear that DG Competition can only transmit to or receive information from its 27 national counterparts. The EU legal framework foresees the exchange of information between DG Competition and the 27 national competition authorities. According to the relevant legal provision,[49] DG Competition and national competition authorities retain the power to provide one another with, and use in evidence, any matter of fact or law, including confidential information.

The ECB's inner-circle partners in the euro area Member States are the 19 national competent authorities.[50] Besides being responsible for the supervision of less significant

[43] Art 12a(1) New OLAF Regulation.

[44] V Covolo, 'Regulation 883/2013 Concerning Investigations Conducted by OLAF: A Missed Opportunity for Substantial Reforms' (2017) 2 *European Criminal Law Review* 151, 157. See also ch 8 of this volume (Allegrezza et al), section II.A.

[45] Art 12 OLAF Regulation.

[46] In section V we clarify why that is the case. I can already divulge here that it has to do with OLAF's broad mandate.

[47] ICF, 'Evaluation of the application of Regulation No 883/2013 concerning investigations conducted by the European Anti-Fraud Office (OLAF)' 90 available at https://op.europa.eu/nl/publication-detail/-/publication/d6926554-b2e6-11e7-837e-01aa75ed71a1/language-en/format-PDF/source-65845507 (accessed 29 September 2020).

[48] See at https://ec.europa.eu/competition-policy/antitrust/national-competition-authorities_en (accessed 17 April 2022).

[49] Art 12(1) Regulation 1/2003. See also ch 8 of this volume (Allegrezza et al), section II.B.

[50] Most of the NCAs, albeit not all, are the national central bank of the respective Member State. For an overview of the specific NCAs, see www.bankingsupervision.europa.eu/organisation/nationalsupervisors/html/index.en.html (accessed 17 April 2022).

credit institutions, NCAs' pivotal function in relation to the supervision of significant credit institutions is to assist the ECB in the preparation and implementation of any acts relating to the exercise of the ECB's supervisory tasks. This includes, in particular, the ongoing day-to-day assessment of a credit institution's situation and on-site verification activities.[51] Unlike the OLAF legal framework and similarly to the legal framework of DG Competition, it is quite clear who are the ECB's 19 institutional partners (inner circle). In that respect, wherever the EU legal framework makes reference to information transmissions or exchanges between the ECB and NCAs, it is unambiguous that the ECB can only transmit to or receive information from the 19 national counterparts. The ECB legal framework foresees specifically the exchange of information between the ECB and NCAs. According to the relevant legal provision, the ECB and NCAs are subject to a duty of cooperation in good faith and an obligation to exchange information.[52]

ii. The Types and Purposes of Information Transfers

The types of information that OLAF can transfer to the AFCOS, or more generally the Member States' competent authorities, and the purposes for which transfer is allowed, are regulated in OLAF's EU-level legal framework. OLAF can transmit information obtained 'in the course' of an investigation to the AFCOS.

The goal or purpose of an OLAF investigation is, from the outset, not always clear. OLAF's investigation can be the lead-up to civil recovery, administrative action or punitive (administrative criminal) follow-up at the national level. While the purpose for which information transferred by OLAF may serve therefore differs, OLAF's legal framework does not, at least not on paper, distinguish between the transfer for any of these punitive or non-punitive purposes.[53]

OLAF's legal framework imposes only a few limits on the transfer of information obtained in the course of an external investigation, particularly information gathered by OLAF in the context of an on-the-spot check.[54] Professional secrecy is one such limit. Information covered by professional secrecy falls under the heading of either (i) business secrets or (ii) other confidential information, which includes material the

[51] Regulation (EU) 468/2014 establishing the framework for cooperation within the Single Supervisory Mechanism between the European Central Bank and national competent authorities and with national designated authorities (SSM Framework Regulation), Recital 37.

[52] Art 6(2) SSM Regulation. See also ch 8 of this volume (Allegrezza et al), section II.B.

[53] The original Council Proposal was not much clearer in this respect. See Commission, 'Proposal for a Council Regulation concerning on-the-spot checks and inspections by the Commission for the detection of frauds and irregularities detrimental to the financial interests of the European Communities' COM (95) 690 final, Art 6(1). This provision holds that all information collected in connection with on-the-spot inspections and checks shall be covered by the rule of confidentiality and by the Community's provisions on data protection. It may not be communicated to anyone except those persons within the institutions of the Community or the Member States who are, by the nature of their duties, required to be acquainted with it, nor may it be used for any purpose other than to ensure that the relevant rules are applied uniformly and effectively, to forestall or detect irregularities, to recover or collect the sums involved and to ensure that penalties are applied. This provision did however, include a purpose limitation – albeit a broad one – on the exchange of information.

[54] Arts 12(1) and 10(1) OLAF Regulation. We refer here to purposes other than for AFCOS to take appropriate action in accordance with their national law.

disclosure of which would significantly harm a person.[55] In practice this limit does not seem to pose a real obstacle to OLAF's work. The reason for this is that, while information transmitted to OLAF or obtained in the course of investigations, in whatever form, must be treated as confidential and is subject to professional secrecy, this information may still be communicated to persons in the Member States whose functions 'require them to know it'.[56] OLAF's legal framework does not define – and probably could not, even if it wanted to – what this term means. Because of OLAF's broad mandate (see section II.A), which extends to all areas of EU activity whenever the Union's financial interests are prejudiced, OLAF must operate in a large number of policy areas and must cooperate with an even larger number of national actors active in those policy areas. In turn, all these actors, including the AFCOS, fulfil – more often than not – multiple functions, each of which may 'require them to know' a piece of information in OLAF's possession for the execution of their own tasks, which in all likelihood, but not necessarily, have to be in line with those of OLAF. We argue, therefore, that it is not for OLAF to decide whether a national authority is required to know certain information. If anything, the national authority in question is in a better position to decide on this. As a result, OLAF's legal framework thereby allows for the transfer of information gathered by OLAF during an on-the-spot check to, theoretically, just about any national authority, as long as it is plausible that this national authority 'requires to know it' (or the national authority makes a plausible case why it needs the information in question for the fulfilment of its tasks).

That there are no real limitations on the *transfer of information* by OLAF in OLAF's legal framework, does not mean, however, that there are no limits imposed on national authorities. The first of these is that OLAF's legal framework requires that information received by national authorities from OLAF is 'protected in the same way as similar information is protected by the national legislation'.[57] It is it not entirely clear what is meant by this assimilation obligation. We assume it refers, in particular, to the application of national rules with respect to data protection to the further transfer or dissemination of the information received from OLAF. The second limit is that OLAF's legal framework imposes some kind of purpose limitation, not on OLAF but on the Member State that wishes to use the information for purposes other than for which it was obtained. The scope of the purpose limitation is relatively confined, however. It applies only to those situations in which OLAF conducts an on-the-spot check in one Member State and observers from another Member State are present at that check, and these observers, in that guise, have received information from OLAF. In such, rather exceptional, circumstances, the Member State wishing to use the information for 'other purposes' must seek the agreement of the Member State in which the information was

[55] Case T-353/94 *Postbank v Commission* ECLI:EU:T:1996:119, para 86.

[56] Art 12(1) OLAF Regulation in combination with Council Regulation (Euratom, EC) 2185/96 concerning on-the-spot checks and inspections carried out by the Commission in order to protect the European Communities' financial interests against fraud and other irregularities [1996] OJ L292/2, Art 8(1). The OLAF investigator's duty of confidentiality stems from Regulation 31 (EEC), 11 (EAEC) laying down the Staff Regulations of officials and the conditions of employment of other servants of the European Economic Community and the European Atomic Energy Community [1962] OJ 45/1385, Art 17, and Art 339 TFEU.

[57] Art 8(1) Regulation (Euratom, EC) 2185/96.

obtained.[58] It is obvious that this is not an outright ban on the use of information for purposes other than for which they were obtained; it merely imposes a (horizontal) obligation to obtain the approval of the Member State in which the information in question was obtained.

The types of information and the purposes for which DG Competition can transfer to the national competition authorities are regulated in the EU-level legal framework. In Regulation 1/2003 we find the broadly-formulated articulation that ECN authorities may exchange with each other 'any matter of fact or of law',[59] which may include documents, statements and digital information.[60] In the second place, we also find a number of more specific legal provisions that further elaborate upon the types of information that may be transferred to national competition authorities. For instance, DG Competition shall transfer copies of the most important documents it has gathered[61] that concern the finding of an infringement, the adoption of interim measures, the adoption of commitment decisions, the finding of inapplicability of Articles 101 and 102 TFEU and the fact that given conduct benefits from an exemption. In addition to that, whenever DG Competition addresses a request for information to an economic undertaking, it shall also forward a copy of that request to the relevant national competition authorities.[62]

As far as the purpose of information transfers is concerned, DG Competition transfers to the national competition authorities information for the purpose of applying Articles 101 and 102 TFEU.[63] In that respect there is one, overarching purpose, namely, the enforcement of EU antitrust law; and within that context information can be transferred at different points in time. The EU legal framework does not impose any noteworthy limits on top-down information transfers. Even though professional secrecy is mentioned in Regulation 1/2003,[64] it does not concern the relationship between the national competition authorities and DG Competition, since no limit is imposed on the exchange of information within the ECN; professional secrecy thus only imposes limits on information transfers outside the ECN.

As far as the ECB is concerned, the EU-level legal framework fails to distinguish between different purposes for which information can be transferred from the EU to the national level; information can be transferred for virtually any purpose, ranging from monitoring the compliance of all credit institutions with the applicable laws, to carrying out investigations and opening sanctioning proceedings.

For instance, the ECB must transfer to the NCAs any information that is necessary for NCAs to carry out their role in assisting the ECB.[65] Furthermore, the ECB must transfer to NCAs any information that is necessary for NCAs to carry out their tasks related to prudential supervision.[66] When a significant bank is later classified as being

[58] Art 8(1) Regulation (Euratom, EC) 2185/96.

[59] Art 12(1) Regulation 1/2003.

[60] Commission, 'Antitrust Manual of Procedure – Internal DG Competition working documents on procedures for the application of Articles 101 and 102 TFEU' (November 2019) 4.2.2 available at https://ec.europa.eu/competition/antitrust/antitrust_manproc_11_2019_en.pdf (accessed 24 February 2022).

[61] Art 11(2) Regulation 1/2003.

[62] Art 18(5) Regulation 1/2003.

[63] Art 12(1) Regulation 1/2003.

[64] Art 28(2) Regulation 1/2003. See also ch 8 of this volume (Allegrezza et al), section III.

[65] Art 21(1) SSM Framework Regulation.

[66] Art 21(3) SSM Framework Regulation.

less significant, there is an additional obligation on the part of the ECB to provide the NCA concerned with all necessary information in respect of the particular bank.[67]

Finally, the ECB may transmit information to NCAs so that the latter may open sanctioning proceedings vis-à-vis natural persons and/or the opening of sanctioning proceedings against legal or natural persons for breaches of national law transposing Union directives.[68]

The EU legal framework does not impose any limits on the transfer of information from the ECB to the national level.[69] All persons working for NCAs or acting on behalf of NCAs are under an obligation to retain professional secrecy, but that obligation exists only in relation to third parties and not within the SSM inner circle.[70]

iii. The Enforcement Phase in Which Information Transfers Take Place

OLAF transmits information obtained 'in the course' of an investigation to the AFCOS. The reference to information obtained 'in the course' of an investigation does not limit the time of transfer but puts in place a limit on the information eligible for transfer (ie information obtained during an investigation). OLAF can therefore transfer information to the AFCOS not only during an investigation, but also prior or after such an investigation. Keep in mind, however, that the timing of transfer does not affect the type of information that can be transferred: the type of information remains that obtained by OLAF in the course of an investigation.

With respect to DG Competition, the European Commission Directorate and the national competition authorities have a shared database, and the opening of a new case, the intention to adopt a decision and the fact that a case has been closed shall be registered on that database.[71] It may thus be deduced that information is shared on a continuous basis and not only in the course of investigations.

In similar vein, with respect to the ECB, the EU legal framework does not set any limits as to the timing of a potential transfer. It is immaterial whether an NCA has launched an investigation or a sanctioning procedure. The ECB can transfer information to the national level before, during and after the conclusion of an investigation, for any purpose, as long as that relates to prudential banking supervision.

iv. The Modalities of Information Transfers

OLAF has a discretionary competence to transmit information obtained in the course of external investigations to the AFCOS. It is therefore for OLAF to decide how – and also

[67] Art 48(1) SSM Framework Regulation.

[68] Art 18(5) SSM Regulation; Art 134(1)(b) SSM Framework Regulation.

[69] EU law does, however, impose limits on the use of transferred confidential information. NCAs receiving confidential information may only use it in the course of their duties and only for supervisory purposes, for the imposition of penalties and in court proceedings. See Directive 2013/36/EU of the European Parliament and of the Council of 26 June 2013 on access to the activity of credit institutions and the prudential supervision of credit institutions and investment firms, amending Directive 2002/87/EC and repealing Directives 2006/48/EC and 2006/49/EC [2013] OJ L176/338 ('Directive CRD IV'), Art 54.

[70] Art 53(1) Directive CRD IV. See also ch 8 of this volume (Allegrezza et al), section III.

[71] Antitrust Manual (n 60), 2.3.1.

when – to transfer information to the AFCOS. In practice, OLAF can transfer information through shared databases, at the request of the AFCOS, and spontaneously. With respect to the first, OLAF can make use of the Union's Anti-Fraud Information System (AFIS) – an umbrella system clustering a set of applications in particular policy areas, facilitating the exchange of anti-fraud information between OLAF and national competent authorities, not only the AFCOS. Under this umbrella, there are various layers of sectoral legislation that put in place different modalities of transfer, each reflecting the various sectoral needs of the actors operating therein. The OLAF Regulation recognises this by saying little with respect to the modalities of information transfer: OLAF 'may' transfer information, thereby keeping open all doors for sectoral legislation to fill in exactly how OLAF is to transfer information in each policy area in particular.

As far as DG Competition is concerned, the Commission has designated an Authorised Disclosure Officer (ADO). That person retains the key to the secure e-mail system, and is therefore responsible for receiving from and sending messages to the national competition authorities, whenever the use of that encrypted system is necessary.[72] In other words, whenever DG Competition wishes to transfer sensitive information to a national competition authority, such as business secrets or other confidential information, that information is transferred with encryption, through the ADO.[73]

With respect to the ECB, it is for the EU authority to decide when and how to transfer information to the NCAs. In practice, supervisory information is shared through a database, DARWIN, which is the ECB's IT tool for the management of documents and records.[74] The EU legal framework requires that information is transferred 'in a timely and accurate manner'[75] and that the ECB shall provide to the NCAs regular access to the necessary information so that they can carry out their supervisory tasks.[76] From these provisions, it can be deduced that the ECB may upload such information on the shared database either ad hoc or at recurring intervals.

B. Transfer of Information from ELEAs to the Outer-Circle National Authorities

As stated previously, OLAF's legal framework regulates only the exchange of information between OLAF and 'national competent authorities'. As such, the qualification of an authority as inner-circle (AFCOS) or outer-circle (other administrative or judicial authority) is therefore immaterial for the transfer of information from OLAF to the national level. What does matter is when these outer-circle authorities become relevant in the context of an OLAF investigation and when OLAF may want to transfer information to them. This depends, first of all, on the policy area affected. If an OLAF investigation

[72] ibid 4.1.
[73] ibid.
[74] European Central Bank, 'Audit and user content creation functionalities of the ECB Document and Records Web-based Interface (DARWIN)' (February 2020) available at www.ecb.europa.eu/ecb/access_to_documents/data_protection/shared/pdf/ecb.dpr.dgse_management_DARWIN_user_data20200224.en.pdf (accessed 24 February 2022).
[75] Art 21(2) SSM Framework Regulation.
[76] Art 21(3) SSM Framework Regulation.

concerns customs irregularities, the national customs authority is, in all likelihood, the authority to which OLAF will want to transfer information. In case of an irregularity in the area of structural funds, this will be the affected Member State's management, certifying or audit authority (whichever that may be). It depends, second of all, on the Member State(s) affected. Each Member State appoints different authorities in each policy area. For instance in the ERDF (one of the structural funds), the Netherlands has appointed four geographically dispersed management authorities. In Germany, because ERDF subsidies are implemented at the *Länder*-level, OLAF has to deal with 16 management authorities. In North Rhine Westphalia, for instance, the management authority is *Referat V 1* of the state's Ministry of Economic Affairs, Innovation, Digitalisation and Energy. Which outer-circle authority is relevant depends, third and last, on the purpose of an OLAF investigation. Where OLAF investigates customs or subsidy fraud, it may be necessary for OLAF to transfer information to national judicial authorities, most likely the national competent public prosecutor, rather than any of the above-mentioned administrative outer-circle authorities, because of the ultimate punitive purpose OLAF's investigation may serve. All in all, however, there are no hard rules in OLAF's EU-level legal framework that dictate to which authority it is to transfer information (ie, which authority is 'competent') or how such an authority is to be identified.

Regardless of authority relevance, because of OLAF's 'one size fits all' regime on the transfer of information, what is said in section III.A.i with respect to the AFCOS (ie, on the types of information that may be transferred, on the enforcement phase in which transfer may take place, and on the modalities of information transfer) applies mutatis mutandis to OLAF's outer circle of authorities, irrespective of the administrative or judicial nature of these national authorities.

With respect to DG Competition, as stated in section III.A.i, the EU-level legal framework regulates only the exchange of information between DG Competition and the national competition authorities. Information transfers directly from DG Competition to other administrative authorities do not take place, at least not formally, but may not be excluded either, especially in view of the principle of sincere cooperation. As we have noted elsewhere,[77] if such transfers were to take place, that would likely happen via the relevant national competition authority.

On the other hand, transfers to national judicial authorities do take place, especially in view of the fact that national courts have the power to apply EU antitrust law.[78] In that respect, the judicial authorities mentioned in Regulation 1/2003 are not criminal courts or public prosecutors, but rather those courts or tribunals within each Member State that are competent to enforce EU antitrust law.[79] Observations may be submitted to national courts by DG Competition on its own initiative,[80] or at the request of the competent national court.[81] Such observations are limited to an economic and legal

[77] A Karagianni, M Scholten and M Simonato, 'EU Report' in Simonato, Luchtman and Vervaele (eds) (n 11) 7.

[78] Art 6 Regulation 1/2003.

[79] Commission Notice on the cooperation between the Commission and the courts of the EU Member States in the application of Articles 81 and 82 EC [2004] OJ C101/54 ('Cooperation Notice'), para 1.

[80] Art 15(3) Regulation 1/2003; Case C-429/07 *Inspecteur van de Belastingdienst v X BV* ECLI:EU:C:2009:359, para 27.

[81] Art 15(1) Regulation 1/2003.

analysis of the facts surrounding the case before the national court.[82] Lastly, observations are provided in accordance with national procedural rules.[83] On the other hand, the EU legal framework does not foresee interactions with criminal justice authorities. We are of the opinion, that – similarly to other administrative authorities – should that be necessary, information transfers would take place via the national competition authorities and in accordance with their national law, within the limits set by the general principles of EU law, such as the principles of effectiveness and of sincere cooperation.

As far as the ECB is concerned, the EU-level legal framework states that, where necessary, the ECB should conclude memoranda of understanding (MoUs) with national competent authorities responsible for markets in financial instruments.[84] For instance, the ECB and the Netherlands authority for the financial markets (AFM) have entered into such an MoU, which, inter alia, lays down the modalities pertaining to exchange of information.[85]

With respect to outer-circle judicial authorities, due to the fact that several Member States utilise both administrative and criminal law enforcement to punish violations of prudential legislation,[86] the ECB may often need to interact with national judicial authorities whose tasks revolve around the enforcement of prudential regulation. The EU legal framework recognises these likely interactions and provides for the following two modalities.

First, information transfers from the ECB to national judicial authorities – via the NCAs – may take place at the latter's request. The modalities applicable to information requests addressed to SSM authorities by national criminal investigating authorities, and the circumstances in which such information can be transferred to them, are laid down in ECB Decision 2016/1162.[87] It is worth noting that national judicial authorities requesting information from the ECB do not liaise directly with the ECB. Any request by, for instance, a public prosecutor should first be addressed to the local NCA. The NCA in turn 'commits to acting on behalf of the ECB in responding to such a request'.[88] Transmission of requested information takes place only if the following conditions are met: either (i) there is an express obligation to disclose such information to a national criminal investigation authority under Union or national law;[89] or (ii) the relevant legal framework permits the disclosure of such confidential information. However, in this case, if the ECB considers that transmission may jeopardise the accomplishment of its tasks or its independence, or may undermine the public interest, transmission can be refused.[90] In any case, the NCA in question must commit itself to asking the requesting

[82] Cooperation Notice (n 79), para 32.
[83] Cooperation Notice (n 79), para 34.
[84] Art 3(1) SSM Regulation.
[85] Memorandum of Understanding on cooperation between the European Central Bank and the Netherlands Authority for the Financial Markets (2017) available at www.bankingsupervision.europa.eu/legalframework/mous/html/ssm.mou_2017_afm~9aa14b7f26.en.pdf (accessed 24 February 2022).
[86] S Allegrezza (ed), *The Enforcement Dimension of the Single Supervisory Mechanism* (Wolter Kluwer 2020).
[87] Decision (EU) 2016/1162 of the European Central Bank of 30 June 2016 on disclosure of confidential information in the context of criminal investigations (ECB/2016/19) [2016] OJ L192/73, Arts 2 and 3.
[88] Art 2(1)(a) Decision (EU) 2016/1162.
[89] Art 2(1)(b)(i) Decision (EU) 2016/1162.
[90] Art 2(1)(b)(ii) Decision (EU) 2016/1162.

outer-circle authority to guarantee that the confidential information provided will be protected from public disclosure.[91]

Second, the ECB may transfer information to national judicial authorities – through the NCAs – spontaneously. According to Article 136 of the SSM Framework Regulation, if the ECB – while carrying out its supervisory powers – comes across facts that could potentially give rise to a criminal offence, it must transfer that information to the *relevant* NCA and request it to refer the matter to the appropriate authorities for investigation and possible criminal prosecution, in accordance with national law.[92] The EU legal framework does not specify whether that obligation exists only with respect to 'prudential offences', or more generally with respect to any criminal offence.[93]

IV. Transfer of Information from National Authorities to ELEAs

A. Transfer of Information from the Inner-Circle National Partners to ELEAs

There is no specific legal regime governing the transfer of information from Member States' AFCOSs to OLAF. OLAF's legal framework states that the competent authorities of the Member States shall, at OLAF's request or at their own initiative, transmit to OLAF any document or information they hold that relates to an ongoing investigation.[94] In other words, also with respect to bottom-up transfers of information, OLAF's legal framework regulates only the exchanges between OLAF and national competent authorities. Obligations with respect to the transfer of information from the national level to the EU level apply, therefore, only with respect to these authorities.

According to OLAF's legal framework, the AFCOS *may*, not must, be regarded as a competent authority.[95] If the AFCOS is not designated as competent authority, it does not fall within the ambit of the rules. If, however, the AFCOS is considered a competent authority, EU rules click into place and the AFCOS must, at the request of OLAF or on its own initiative, transmit to OLAF any document or information it holds that relates to an ongoing OLAF investigation. The possibilities to transfer information therefore depend on whether or not the AFCOS is designated a 'competent authority'. It is left to national law to decide on this matter.

[91] Art 2(1)(c) Decision (EU) 2016/1162.

[92] Art 136 SSM Framework Regulation.

[93] See in that respect Allegrezza, who distinguishes between 'financial crime', under which she groups market abuse, money laundering, terrorism financing and insider dealing, and 'crimes that protect fair banking as Rechtsgut', which coincides with what we term here 'prudential offences', examples of which are false supervisory disclosure, carrying out banking activities without an authorisation, etc. S Allegrezza, 'Information Exchange Between Administrative and Criminal Enforcement: The Case of the ECB and National Investigative Agencies' *eucrim* 4/2020, 302.

[94] Art 8(2) OLAF Regulation.

[95] Art 12a(1) New OLAF Regulation.

It is a devil of a job to ascertain whether Member States' AFCOSs are considered competent. As a rule, 'competent' is a qualifier that is not the result of any such designation by national authorities; rather, it must be deduced from practice and/or the regulation of the transfer of information to and from these authorities. For example, there is no national law that appoints the Dutch AFCOS as the competent authority under OLAF's legal framework. Nevertheless, one can conclude that it is competent in the area of customs, because there is a legal framework in place that allows it to transfer information to OLAF. The situation in Italy is slightly different. There are no provisions in Italian law that regulate transfers from the *Guardia di Finanza* and OLAF. There is, however, an MoU between OLAF and the *Guardia di Finanza*, not available to the public, that sets out obligations with respect to information exchange. An AFCOS is not necessarily competent in all policy areas. The Dutch AFCOS, because it is part of the customs authority, is only competent with respect to this area of law. In the area of structural funds, the Dutch AFCOS refers OLAF to the national authorities in charge of implementing and enforcing structural funds law. Wholly contrary to the Dutch and Italian position, the German and Luxembourgish AFCOSs, to give just two examples, have not been the subject of any regulation whatsoever. Their AFCOSs function as nothing more than letterboxes to help OLAF connect to the authorities that are competent in the respective policy areas in which an OLAF investigation takes place.

But even where an AFCOS is considered competent, the obligation to transfer information – and the types of information to be transferred, the modalities and the timing thereof – exists only in so far as national law allows for such a transfer (at least until the 2020 revision of OLAF's legal framework discussed below).[96] If and, if so, how an AFCOS exchanges information with OLAF is thereby subject entirely to national law. This gives rise to the often-mentioned *géométrie variable*. While Member States are under an EU obligation to establish an AFCOS, the status and competence to exchange information with OLAF differs from Member State to Member State. In section III.A.i we stated that the AFCOS, at the most basic level, is OLAF's first point of contact in each and every Member State.[97] What the AFCOS does beyond that depends on what role Member States have allocated to it. Thus EU law leaves it to national law to decide whether to dub an existing authority an AFCOS or to create an AFCOS anew, to decide in which administrative structures the AFCOS is embedded, and to rule on the competences and powers of the AFCOS. This results in considerable diversity in the roles, profiles, and effectiveness of cooperation and exchange of information between OLAF and the Member States' AFCOSs.[98]

[96] Art 8(2) and (3) OLAF Regulation.

[97] Covolo (n 44) 157; ICF (n 47) 161.

[98] OLAF, *The OLAF Report 2015* (Publications Office of the European Union 2016) 22; Commission, 'Evaluation of the application of Regulation (EU, Euratom) No 883/2013 of the European Parliament and of the Council of 11 September 2013 concerning investigations conducted by the European Anti-Fraud Office (OLAF) and repealing Regulation (EC) No 1073/1999 of the European Parliament and of the Council and Council Regulation (Euratom) No 1074/1999' (Commission Staff Working Document) SWD (2017) 332 final, 23–24; Commission, 'Assessment: Accompanying the document Proposal for a Regulation amending Regulation (EU, EURATOM) No 883/2013 of the European Parliament and of the Council of 11 September 2013 concerning investigations conducted by the European Anti-Fraud Office (OLAF) as regards cooperation with the European Public Prosecutor's Office and the effectiveness of OLAF investigations' (Commission Staff Working Document) SWD (2018) 251 final, 10; K Bovend'Eerdt, 'The Commission Proposal Amending the OLAF Regulation' *eucrim* 1/2018, 73, 73; Simonato (n 31) 2; ICF (n 47) 14, 161.

How the level of support changes from Member State to Member State, and even from policy area to policy area (or sometimes both), may be illustrated through two examples. In Germany, for instance, the AFCOS is embedded in the Federal Ministry of Finance, and its function is limited to that of a point of contact to help OLAF to find the national authority with which it wishes to establish cooperation.[99] In the Netherlands, the AFCOS is placed under the customs authority's wing and functions as the competent authority in the area of customs, but not in the area of structural funds. As a result, in customs cases, OLAF cooperates directly with the AFCOS; in cases involving structural funds, the AFCOS refers OLAF to the competent national authority that is charged with the implementation or supervision of the fund in question.[100]

We expected that where an AFCOS is indeed competent, there would be a (specific) basis in national law that would connect to this EU law provision. Nothing is further from the truth. National law is often lacking. The transfer of information from the AFCOS to OLAF is not regulated by Italy, nor was it regulated by the UK. While a legal basis is missing altogether in Italy, the transfer of information in the UK was based on a general statutory gateway provision that applied to all public bodies engaged in the fight against fraud. That does not mean that transfer of information does not take place – it does – but it obscures when and what information may be transferred, under what conditions, the limitations to which such transfer is subject or the modalities of transfer. A notable exception in this regard is the Netherlands. The Dutch AFCOS, which is competent only in the area of customs, deems a national basis for the transfer of information unnecessary when an EU legal basis is at its disposal. The Dutch AFCOS transfers information directly on the basis of EU law,[101] irrespective of national law to the contrary.

In short, the AFCOS offers little in terms of strong institutional embedment or a regulated regime for the transfer of information. Both are delegated largely to the national level. In the 2020 Regulation amending OLAF's legal framework, the AFCOS's organisation and powers remain the competence of each Member State, and there has been no specification of minimum standards in terms of the role and powers of an AFCOS.[102] What did change, however, was the phrasing of the provisions that regulate the bottom-up transfer of information from the AFCOS, or more generally the 'national competent authorities', to OLAF. Whereas the old provision states that the AFCOS, and other competent authorities, must transfer information 'in so far as their national law allows', the new Regulation amends it by providing that transfer must take place 'unless prevented by national law'.[103] This seemingly semantic adjustment can have considerable consequences for the flow of information from the national to the EU level. As demonstrated, most Member States have no legislation in place to regulate the transfer of information to OLAF. In the worst situation, the absence of such bottom-up legislation means that there is no legal basis in national law and, as a result, transfer is not

[99] M Böse and A Schneider, 'Germany' in Simonato, Luchtman and Vervaele (eds) (n 11) 47.
[100] K Bovend'Eerdt, 'The Netherlands' in Simonato, Luchtman and Vervaele (eds) (n 11) 123, 123–24.
[101] Regulation 515/97 to be precise.
[102] ICF (n 47) 14; Commission, 'Proposal for a Regulation of The European Parliament and of The Council amending Regulation (EU, Euratom) No 883/2013 concerning investigations conducted by the European Anti-Fraud Office (OLAF) as regards cooperation with the European Public Prosecutor's Office and the effectiveness of OLAF investigations' COM (2018) 338 final, 11.
[103] Art 8(2) and (3) New OLAF Regulation.

allowed. The Regulation flips the situation: unless there is a national law or provision that explicitly forbids transfer, the AFCOS – if it is a competent authority – must transfer information to OLAF.

With respect to EU antitrust law enforcement, the EU legal framework regulates the transfer of information from the 27 national competition authorities to DG Competition. According to Article 12 of Regulation 1/2003, ECN authorities are under an obligation to exchange information for the purpose of applying Articles 101 and 102 TFEU. In light of the fact that this provision is laid down in an EU Regulation, in our view, it comprises a sufficient legal basis for bottom-up information transfers. Notwithstanding that view of ours, it is worth noting that various Member States, such as Germany and Luxembourg, Hungary and the Netherlands, 'implement' Article 12(1) of Regulation 1/2003 by designating and authorising the national competition authorities to transfer information to the EU level.[104]

As far as limits imposed by national laws to bottom-up information transfers are concerned, due to the strong institutional embedment of national competition authorities, the only potential limit is that of purpose limitation, as is the case, for instance, with German law.[105] But even where national laws, like the law of Luxembourg, do provide for a purpose limitation, such a purpose limitation may only apply as a limit to the future *use* of information by DG Competition, rather than as a limit on the transfer itself.

In short, we observe that, unlike the OLAF situation, the enforcement of EU antitrust law is premised upon a regulated regime for information transfers and a strong institutional embedment of the 27 national counterparts in the EU legal framework. The national competition authorities and DG Competition form a closed network, without any noteworthy limits being imposed by EU or national laws on bottom-up information transfers.

Concerning the ECB, as already explained (section III.A.i), the ECB's inner-circle national counterparts are the NCAs of the 19 euro area Member States. Similar to the DG Competition situation discussed above, ascertaining the national competent authority of each SSM participating Member State is no hard task. One can see, in the case of the SSM as well, a strong institutional embedment of NCAs, similar to the ECN.

With respect to limits on the transfer of information from NCAs to the ECB, EU law imposes a duty of cooperation in good faith and an obligation of mutual exchanges of information between the ECB and the NCAs, without any specific limits as regards the types of information to be transferred, modalities and timing.[106] Given that this provision is contained in an EU Regulation, it is – in our view – by and of itself a sufficient legal basis for bottom-up information transfers, without a need for further implementation in national law. While certain national legal orders, including the German[107] and the Greek, have indeed not introduced additional national provisions to regulate information transfers from the national to the EU level, other Member States, such as the Netherlands[108] and Luxembourg,[109] have introduced specific national legal bases to

[104] Simonato, Luchtman and Vervaele (n 11) 184.

[105] Böse and Schneider (n 99) 60.

[106] Art 6(2) SSM Regulation.

[107] Simonato, Luchtman and Vervaele (n 11) 190–91.

[108] Dutch Financial Supervision Act (*Wet van 28 september 2006, houdende regels met betrekking tot de financiële markten en het toezicht daarop, Stb* 2006, 475), Art 1:90(8) in combination with Art 1:90(1–3).

[109] V Covolo, 'Luxembourg' in Simonato, Luchtman and Vervaele (eds) (n 11) 117.

facilitate information transfers to the ECB in particular. The Netherlands is quite unique in that it imposes limits on bottom-up transfers.[110] These limits range from a specialty rule[111] to a prohibition on transmissions that are incompatible with Dutch law or public order.[112] We can see that even though the SSM Regulation implies an unconditional obligation on the part of NCAs, to transmit information to the ECB that is relevant for the performance of the latter's supervisory tasks,[113] Dutch law does not embrace such unconditional transfers, which goes as far as to question the compatibility of these national provisions with EU law.[114]

Concerning the point in time at which NCAs transmit information to the EU level, as well as the type of information to be transmitted, neither EU law nor any of the national legal orders covered in earlier studies by Luchtman et al shed additional light.[115] It may thus be concluded that there is no requirement that NCAs may only – for instance – transfer information to the ECB after the latter has launched an investigation. The fact that, from a temporal point of view, information can be transferred at any time ties in with the prudential supervisory mandate of the ECB, which consists mostly of monitoring banks' compliance with the applicable laws. We can also conclude that EU law, that is, the SSM Regulation and Directive CRD IV, have created a closed system consisting of the ECB and the 19 NCAs, characterised by a constant flow of information relevant for prudential supervision. In the second place, all these authorities are bound by a purpose limitation as regards the use of transferred information.[116]

B. Transfer of Information from the Outer-Circle National Authorities to ELEAs

The EU rules on the transfer of information from 'competent authorities' to OLAF also apply to the transfer from other administrative authorities and judicial authorities (ie, the outer circle) to OLAF. These authorities must, like the AFCOS, at OLAF's request or on their own initiative, transmit to OLAF any document or information they hold that relates to an ongoing OLAF investigation. Again, under OLAF's old legal framework, this obligation to transfer information existed only in so far as national law allowed for such a transfer.[117]

First, the role of other administrative authorities is contingent on the role played by the AFCOS and the positioning of the latter in a particular Member State's legal

[110] Bovend'Eerdt (n 100) 147.

[111] Art 1:90(1)(f) Dutch Financial Supervision Act.

[112] Art 1:90(1)(c) Dutch Financial Supervision Act.

[113] Art 6(2) SSM Regulation.

[114] Simonato, Luchtman and Vervaele (n 11) 191.

[115] See, in order: MJJP Luchtman et al, *Investigatory Powers and Procedural Safeguards: Improving OLAF's legislative framework through a comparison with other EU law enforcement authorities (ECN/ESMA/ECB)* (Utrecht University 2017); M Simonato, M Luchtman and J Vervaele (eds), *Exchange of Information with EU and National Enforcement Authorities: Improving OLAF legislative framework through a comparison with other EU authorities (ECN/ESMA/ECB)* (Utrecht University 2018); F Giuffrida and K Ligeti (eds), *Admissibility of OLAF Final Reports as Evidence in Criminal Proceedings* (Luxembourg University 2019).

[116] Art 54 Directive CRD IV.

[117] Art 8(2) and (3) OLAF Regulation.

system. In certain Member States, such as Hungary, the AFCOS operates as a central unit, charged with the exchange of all information between national administrative authorities and OLAF. In those instances, other administrative authorities, regardless of their competence in a specific policy area, do not transfer information to OLAF. In other Member States, the Netherlands for instance, the AFCOS is also competent in additional policy areas, such as customs. In those cases, the AFCOS is competent in one policy area but not another, and transfers information to OLAF only with respect to the substantive fields for which it is competent. In yet even other Member States, Germany for instance, the AFCOS is nothing more than a letterbox. In these Member States, it is only the administrative authorities competent in a particular policy area that transfer information to OLAF.[118]

Second, regardless of this contingency, the rules on the transfer of information are the same, irrespective of the authority's qualification as an AFCOS or other administrative authority: information must be transferred only in so far as national law allows. As may be expected by now, the problems we encounter here are similar to those of OLAF's inner-circle authorities. The most pressing problem is that there is often no national law linking the competent administrative authority to OLAF. As a result, there are no legal grounds on the basis of which information can be transferred to OLAF. Again this does not mean that no information is exchanged, but that it may be done on an informal basis, as is the case in Italy, for instance. In other Member States, such as the Netherlands, the transfer of information, in the areas of customs and structural funds, takes place directly on the basis of Union law. In Luxembourg, the fact that Union law refers back to national law results, in the absence of that national law, in loopholes that can hinder the transfer of information to OLAF. In Germany, in the field of customs, it is clear that transfers require a basis in national law, but it is unclear which law could serve as a legal basis.

With respect to judicial authorities, the question of competence, particularly difficult to answer with respect to the AFCOS (and at times also for the other administrative authorities), is of only minor importance. In a criminal investigation it is generally clear-cut which authorities are competent. Nevertheless, the reference to national law requires that, to get a full picture of information flows from judicial authorities to OLAF, we also need to examine connecting national provisions, if any. Here again, the Member States' legal systems are a mixed bag and it is difficult to discern a common thread.

The Hungarian Criminal Code, for example, provides for a national provision that neatly links up to OLAF's legal framework. Article 71/B(2) BE states that 'upon the request of a body established by … Union law,' such as OLAF, 'the court, the prosecutor, the investigating authority or the national member of Eurojust shall provide the respective body with information, access to files and with authentic copies of criminal records to the extent necessary for the performance of its tasks'. Information is transferred to OLAF on request or spontaneously, and is limited to the specific purposes of such requests. It matters not at what point OLAF requires information (pre-, during or post-investigation). In principle all information gathered in criminal proceedings can be transferred to OLAF, and there are no limits imposed by national law that ban the

[118] Simonato, Luchtman and Vervaele (n 11) 174.

transfer from judicial authorities to OLAF or that put in place limitations with respect to the use of the transferred information.

In Luxembourg and Germany, on the other hand, national law does not provide for the requisite legal basis to transfer information to OLAF. In Luxembourg there is no legal basis whatsoever and transfers cannot take place. In German law there is a guideline on the cooperation between judicial authorities and OLAF, but this guideline is not matched by the necessary statutory law. A basis in statute is deemed necessary, because of the interference with fundamental rights – in particular the right to respect for private life – a transfer of (private) information from judicial authorities to OLAF would entail.

Does Regulation 2020/2223 amending OLAF's legal framework address this *géométrie variable*? Again, the new provision states that Member States' competent authorities must transfer information to OLAF 'unless prevented by national law'. While this amendment circumvents situations in which the absence of a legal basis as such prevented the transfer of information – as is the case in structural funds in Germany – it does not render national law obsolete. Where there are limits in national law, it is still within the realm of possibilities that transfer will not take place. This is the case in Luxembourg, for example, in which the secrecy of criminal investigations prohibits national law enforcement and judicial authorities from disclosing information relating to ongoing investigations to persons who are not parties to the criminal proceedings. The variable geometry OLAF faces in its investigations therefore remains, at least partly, intact.

Neither EU nor national legal provisions[119] regulating bottom-up information transfers to DG Competition by administrative authorities other than competition authorities exist. Such transfers do not seem to be taking place informally either. If deemed necessary, DG Competition's national counterparts would likely be the ones transferring information to the EU level.[120]

Concerning outer-circle administrative and civil judicial authorities applying Articles 101 and 102 TFEU, which transfer information to the EU level, we may discern two main trends. First, judicial authorities like the ones in Luxembourg,[121] relying solely on the EU legal provision (Article 15 of Regulation 1/2003). Second, judicial authorities like the ones in Germany and the Netherlands, which rely on national legal bases restating the EU provisions and enabling national courts to transmit to the EU level a copy of judgments deciding on the application of Articles 101 and 102 TFEU.

Rules concerning bottom-up transfers to the ECB by administrative authorities other than the ECB's institutional counterparts, such as financial markets and tax authorities, are not foreseen in the EU legal framework. If we take a look at national laws, we will see that the Netherlands Authority for Financial Markets (AFM) and the Italian Authority for Financial Markets (Consob) may (but not must) transfer information to the ECB;[122] while in Luxembourg, the Central Bank can transfer information to the NCA (*Commission de Surveillance du Secteur Financier*), which may in turn

[119] To be more precise, this statement concerns the jurisdictions that were included in the Hercule II study, ie, the Netherlands, UK, Italy, Hungary, Luxembourg and Germany.

[120] Simonato, Luchtman and Vervaele (n 11) 186.

[121] Covolo (n 109) 116.

[122] Simonato, Luchtman and Vervaele (n 11) 193.

further transmit it to the ECB.[123] In short, the extent to which bottom-up transfers by outer-circle administrative authorities are allowed is an issue that depends solely on national law.

Regarding the issue of information transfers to the ECB by national judicial authorities, even though EU law does recognise the potential links of the SSM with national systems of criminal law enforcement,[124] the general trend that may be discerned is that national laws are generally silent on that issue and not generally aware of the relationship between national criminal law enforcement and SSM prudential supervision. Certain Member States, like the Netherlands and Italy, do not a priori exclude the possibility. However, any potential transfers would need to take place in accordance with ordinary rules of national criminal procedure. And even if transfers from judicial authorities to the ECB were to take place, an overarching observation is that national judicial authorities do not liaise directly with the ECB. Should it be necessary, the transfer of information would take place only indirectly, via the relevant NCA, that is, the institutional partner of the ECB.

V. Synthesis

In this section we consider the ELEA regimes on the exchange of information, their differences and their similarities, and – where possible – try to explain how and why they are different, especially in light of the ELEAs' linkages with criminal justice and the needs that sprout therefrom.

On the basis of our top-down and bottom-up analysis of the rules regulating information transfers in sections III and IV respectively, it is, at this point, clear that – in the enforcement of PIF, EU competition law and EU banking supervision – there exists informational dependence between the ELEAs and the national authorities involved: all authorities, in one way or another, depend on each other for the provision of information. The reason for this informational dependence (ie, why they need to transfer information back and forth) lies in the fact that enforcement in each of these individual areas is composite. The exact composite nature of enforcement in a particular policy area, in turn, is a product of the (circumscribed) mandate and tasks of the EU enforcement authority in question. Therefore, we contend that the differences between the legal frameworks that regulate the transfers to and from OLAF, DG Competition and the ECB can be explained, at least in part, with reference to their (different) individual mandates and tasks. The ELEAs' mandates and tasks, in turn, can also help explain the linkages between the ELEAs and (national) criminal justice, and the way in which information exchange takes – or does not take – place between ELEAs and criminal justice actors.

The subsections following adopt the same approach we have taken thus far in this chapter. In section V.A we explain the differences between the regimes for the transfer of information from ELEAs to national authorities in light of the different tasks and mandates – and thereby their composite nature – of the respective ELEAs.

[123] ibid.
[124] Decision (EU) 2016/1162.

We conduct the same exercise in section V.B, which deals with the transfer of information from national authorities to ELEAs. Both of these sections are divided into further subsections, each of which deal with the exchange of information between ELEAs and inner-circle and outer-circle authorities respectively.

A. Transfer of Information from ELEAs to National Authorities

i. Transfer of Information from ELEAs to the Inner Circle

The need to transfer information to national authorities stems from OLAF's limited set of tasks. OLAF is only an investigatory body. When it wishes to see things done outside the confines of investigation (eg, prosecution, fining, etc) it needs to cooperate with, and transfer information to, national authorities.

OLAF's EU-level legal framework regulates the transfer of information from OLAF to the 'national competent authorities'. This implies first of all that, for the purpose of top-down information transfer, OLAF's legal framework neither distinguishes between OLAF's inner circle (ie, AFCOS) or its outer circle (ie, other administrative and judicial authorities), nor confines itself to a closed circuit of authorities: the OLAF Regulation only refers to 'national competent authorities'. What is said here, therefore, also applies to section V.A.ii on the transfer of information from ELEAs to the administrative and judicial outer circle. This is not a normative judgement, but merely a statement based on our distinction between ELEAs' inner and outer circles drawn up for analytical purposes. Second of all, it is EU law, rather than national law, that determines the timing of transfers, the modalities of transfer, and what information may be transferred to OLAF's inner- and outer-circle/national competent authorities. There is no room for national law in regulating top-down transfers of information; rather, OLAF transfers information on the basis of a uniform EU-based set of rules.

With respect to *which authorities* OLAF transfers information to, the most plausible explanation for OLAF's one-size-fits-all EU approach to top-down information transfer lies in the sheer breadth of its mandate. OLAF's investigations can theoretically concern any area of Union activity, as long as the Union's finances are at stake. Moreover, unlike the ECB, the subject of its investigations can be any natural or legal person on which national law has conferred legal capacity.[125] The activities OLAF investigates can be criminal and/or administrative in nature. As a result, OLAF's mandate explains why OLAF's legal framework does not have in a place a specific network of institutional partners but relies on the more open-ended term 'competent authorities of the Member States'.

With respect to *what* information OLAF can transfer (ie, the scope *ratione materiae*), OLAF's legal framework poses no real obstacles: OLAF can transfer almost all information as long as it is obtained 'in the course of external investigations'.[126]

[125] Regulation (EC, Euratom) 2988/95 on the protection of the European Communities financial interests [1995] OJ L312/1, Art 7.

[126] Art 12(1) OLAF Regulation.

The motive for this no-holds-barred approach lies in the many purposes an OLAF investigation may serve, none of which is necessarily known at the onset of an investigation. It is possible that an investigation will result in the recovery of irregularly spent money out of the Union's ERDF; it is equally possible that in that same case – or another – OLAF transfers information for the purpose of a criminal prosecution in relation to fraudulently tinkering with time sheets. In short, the punitive (administrative or criminal) or non-punitive purpose that the information obtained by OLAF may serve is not always a known variable, while it always remains a possibility. OLAF, since it is only an investigatory body, exercises little control over what happens with its information once transferred. The avenues for follow-up to OLAF's work are plenty. The needs of all these avenues – be they punitive or non-punitive – differ wildly. Hence, the scope of information OLAF must be able to transfer is very broad and subject to no real substantive legal limits. It is clear that, also and especially here, the criminal law dimension of OLAF's work is evident.

All in all, from the 'transfer' side, OLAF's legal framework imposes no substantial limits. As established, OLAF may transfer information gathered during its on-the-spot checks and that falls within the ambit of professional secrecy to Member State authorities whose functions 'require them to know it'.[127] Because of the eventual purpose of OLAF investigations, which Member State authorities are 'required to know' is not confining in the least. OLAF's legal framework seems to recognise the risks inherent in such a system and imposes restrictions not on OLAF's regime of *information transfer*, but on the Member States that wish to *use this information* for a purpose other than for which it was obtained. Not only are they bound to treat the information received from OLAF in the same way as similar information protected by the national legislation, but, more importantly, when a Member State – whose officials took part in an OLAF check – wish to use information received from OLAF for a purpose other than that for which it was obtained, it must get permission from the Member State where the check took place. As said, this EU-imposed purpose limitation is not an outright ban and applies only in very exceptional cases. With respect to information that is not gathered by OLAF in the context of on-the-spot checks, OLAF's legal framework poses no limits on the use thereof by national authorities whatsoever. Again, we wish to state, at the risk of repeating ourselves, that this is understandable in light of the open-ended purpose that OLAF investigations, and the information obtained and transferred therein, can potentially serve. Having said that, it is problematic that once information is in the hands of OLAF, the origins of this information and the means and purpose by and for which it has been obtained are concealed. OLAF's legal framework in a way, then, can operate as a 'clearing house' in the sense that it imposes few to no limits on how, for instance, information gathered and transferred to OLAF by one Member State for a particular (non-punitive) purpose can be used in another Member State for a different (punitive) purpose, thereby circumventing – often national – safeguards that aim to prevent such abuse.

With respect to *when* OLAF can transfer information (ie, the scope *ratione temporis*), OLAF's top-down regime of information transfer equally imposes few to no limitations.

[127] ibid, in combination with Art 8(1) Council Regulation (Euratom, EC) 2185/96. The OLAF investigator's duty of confidentiality stems from Art 17 Regulation 31 (EEC), 11 (EAEC), and Art 339 TFEU.

OLAF can transfer information prior to, during or after its investigation, as long as the information in question was obtained 'in the course of external investigations' (without specifying any investigation in particular). The absence of any temporal limits lies in the non-exclusive task OLAF fulfils. National investigations (again, punitive or non-punitive in nature) and prosecutions can run prior to, in parallel with or consecutive to an OLAF investigation. Considering that these investigations are not always connected, in the sense that they are aware of each other, let alone that they are coordinated, for OLAF's fight against fraud to pack any punch at all in this loose-knit constellation of PIF-protectors, it is indispensable that OLAF can transfer information without any limits regarding the time.

With respect to *how* OLAF transfers information, OLAF enjoys a great deal of discretion. Its horizontal legal framework merely states that OLAF 'may' (not must!) transfer information, without thereby specifying precisely how this is to be done. In theory OLAF can therefore transfer information through shared databases, spontaneously or on request. In reality, how OLAF transfers information is often dictated in sectoral legislation (not discussed in this chapter). Without going into detail, we can say that each policy area has in place its own modalities reflecting the various sectoral needs of the actors operating therein. OLAF's horizontal legal framework seems to recognise this and captures all possible modalities through refrainment: it says very little, aside from the fact that OLAF 'may' transfer information, thereby keeping open all doors for sectoral legislation to fill in exactly how OLAF is to transfer information in each policy area in particular. Again, our explanation for this is the scope of OLAF's mandate. There are many fields in which OLAF is to act, and (at least) an equal number of authorities with which it must cooperate and to which it must transfer information. It would be unworkable to pour all of this into one and the same mould of transfer modalities.

With respect to the system of EU antitrust law enforcement, the need for information transfers from DG Competition to national competition authorities stems from the fact that enforcement of EU antitrust law is based on a system of parallel competences: both DG Competition and national competition authorities are competent to enforce EU antitrust rules.[128] When a case has been allocated to a single national competition authority or to several national competition authorities acting in parallel,[129] DG Competition may need to cooperate and transfer information to those national competition authorities.

The EU-level legal framework regulates the transfer of information from DG Competition to the national competition authorities. It explicitly foresees that the Directorate and national competition authorities have the power to provide one another 'with any matter of fact or of law, including confidential information'.[130] Therefore, the EU-level legal framework clearly foresees a closed circle of authorities within which information can be exchanged. Furthermore, EU law dictates the modalities of transfer and what information may be transferred between the ECN authorities. There is no room for national law in the regulation of top-down information transfers.

[128] Arts 4 and 5 Regulation 1/2003.
[129] ECN Notice (n 38), para 5.
[130] Art 12(1) Regulation 1/2003.

With respect to *which authorities* DG Competition transfers information to, the EU-level legal framework foresees almost unconditional transfers to the national competition authorities. The most plausible explanation lies in the fact that the national authorities potentially able to enforce EU antitrust rules are the 27 national competition authorities.[131] Furthermore, the activities DG Competition investigates are clear at the outset: anticompetitive agreements and abuses of a dominant position. As a result, DG Competition's mandate explains why the EU-level legal framework lays down a specific network of institutional partners. This is in sharp contrast with OLAF, whose investigations can theoretically concern a broad range of Union activities and therefore whose potential national counterparts can vary.

With respect to *what information* DG Competition can transfer, again, the EU-level legal framework poses no real obstacles: DG Competition can transfer all information, namely documents, statements and digital information,[132] the only limit being that information should be transferred for the purpose of applying Articles 101 and 102 TFEU.[133] However, the latter limit ties in well with the fact that ECN investigations serve a very specific purpose, that is, the enforcement of EU antitrust rules.

With respect to *when* DG Competition transfers information, the EU-level legal framework poses no limitations. The absence of temporal limits can be justified by the fact that ECN authorities have at their disposal all enforcement powers, that is, monitoring, investigating and sanctioning. The transferred information may thus be utilised – by the national competition authorities – at any time in the enforcement process.

Concerning the system of banking supervision, the fact that the ECB may need to transfer information to NCAs stems from the fact that enforcement of prudential banking supervision law is shared between the ECB and the NCAs. For instance, often the ECB does not have direct sanctioning powers and may thus need to request the opening of sanctioning proceedings from the competent NCA.[134] Logically, that also presupposes transfers of evidence.

The EU-level legal framework regulates the transfer of information from the ECB to the NCAs. It is explicitly foreseen that the ECB and the NCAs are under an obligation to exchange information.[135] Similarly to DG Competition and unlike the OLAF legal framework, the ECB EU-level legal framework clearly foresees a closed circle of authorities within which information can be exchanged. Furthermore, EU law dictates the modalities of transfer and what information may be transferred between the SSM authorities. There is no room for national law in the regulation of top-down transfers information transfers.

That the ECB often needs to transfer information to the NCAs can be justified by the fact that the NCAs actively assist the ECB in that day-to-day implementation of the latter's exclusive tasks under the SSM Regulation.[136] In other words, while an exclusive

[131] Commission, 'National Competition Authorities' available at https://ec.europa.eu/competition-policy/antitrust/national-competition-authorities_en (accessed 24 February 2022).
[132] ECN Notice, para 26.
[133] ibid para 25.
[134] Art 18(5) SSM Regulation.
[135] Art 6(2) SSM Regulation; Art 21 SSM Framework Regulation.
[136] *Landeskreditbank Baden-Württemberg* (n 41) para 49.

competence has been vested in the ECB, at the same time the EU legislator also took into account the long-lasting experience of national supervisory authorities in supervising the credit institutions established within their jurisdiction. That explains why the SSM Regulation has in place a specific network of institutional partners, consisting of the ECB and the NCAs of the euro area Member States, and why the ECB, even though it does have extensive information-gathering powers, often needs the assistance of NCAs for the execution of its mandate.

With respect to what information the ECB can transfer, the EU-level legal framework poses no notable obstacles. The ECB can transfer any information. Limitations apply only to the use of the information transferred.[137]

With respect to when and how the ECB transfers information, given that the EU-level legal framework does not pose any limitations, the ECB can transfer information at any time during the enforcement process. The absence of any temporal limits lies in that NCAs' assistance to the ECB is not limited to a particular enforcement stage. To the contrary, the NCAs assist the ECB in the monitoring, in the investigating and in the sanctioning stages of law enforcement, hence information can be transferred at any point in time. The ECB mostly transfers information through shared databases, but it may also be the case that the ECB transfers information spontaneously[138] or at the NCAs' request.[139]

ii. Transfer of Information from ELEAs to the Outer Circle

As follows from the foregoing analysis, only the EU-level legal frameworks of DG Competition and of the ECB foresee the transfer of information from the EU authority to 'outer-circle' administrative and judicial authorities.

With respect to the system of antitrust law enforcement, the need for information transfers from DG Competition to national judicial authorities stems from the fact that national courts have the power to apply Articles 101 and 102 TFEU.[140] A logical corollary of that is that DG Competition may often need to transfer relevant information that is in its possession.[141]

As to the type of information that may be transferred to national courts, this mostly relates to written and oral observations. While written observation may also be submitted on the Commission's initiative,[142] oral observations may only be submitted if the national court so permits or requires.[143] The Cooperation Notice explains that national courts may request from the EU Commission documents or information of a procedural nature, which may help them determine whether a case is already pending

[137] See, for instance, Art 54 Directive CRD IV.

[138] See, for instance, Arts 92 and 139(3) SSM Framework Regulation.

[139] See, for instance, Art 134(2) SSM Framework Regulation.

[140] Art 6 Regulation 1/2003; see also, Directive (EU) 2019/1 of the European Parliament and of the Council of 11 December 2018 to empower the competition authorities of the Member States to be more effective enforcers and to ensure the proper functioning of the internal market [2019] OJ L11/3 ('Directive ECN+'), Art 30(1).

[141] Art 15(1) Regulation 1/2003.

[142] Art 15(3) Regulation 1/2003; Cooperation Notice (n 79) para 31.

[143] Art 15(3) Regulation 1/2003; Cooperation Notice (n 79) para 31.

before the Commission. Furthermore, the Commission may – at the national court's request – give its non-binding opinion on economic, factual and legal matters.[144]

The EU-level legal framework does not specify when DG Competition can transfer information to national courts. However, from the foregoing it may be deduced that – from a temporal point of view – the Commission/DG Competition would transfer necessary information to national courts at the point in time in which a case is pending before a national court. Of course, that is a rather broad timeline; it covers any moment, ranging from the investigative stage to the sanctioning stage.

All in all, we can see that DG Competition can transfer a wide range of information to national courts, while it may also participate as *amicus curiae* in national court proceedings for the enforcement of EU antitrust law. The only limit set by EU law is that national courts must use the transferred information for the purpose for which it was acquired (purpose limitation).[145] The fact that EU law does not set any significant limits on the transfer of information from DG Competition to national courts is certainly justifiable; national courts have a clear role to play in the enforcement of EU law. In turn, this necessitates unconstrained access to any information at the Commission's disposal and that can serve the purpose of effective EU competition law enforcement by the national courts.

Concerning the system of banking supervision, the need for information transfers from the ECB to national judicial authorities stems from the fact that certain Member States impose criminal law sanctions for violations of prudential requirements.[146] Given that the ECB oversees credit institutions' compliance with the same rules, it is not inconceivable that often, national judicial authorities may receive information obtained by the ECB in the course of its supervisory mandate.

The EU-level legal framework does not specify which national judicial authorities may receive information in the ECB's possession. Article 136 of the SSM Regulation merely refers to 'appropriate' authorities. At the same time, ECB Decision 2016/1162 explains that confidential information may be transferred to 'national criminal investigation authorities', meaning national authorities with competence in criminal law matters.[147] As can be seen, the EU-level legal framework leaves the determination of the receiving authority to national law.

Concerning the question of what information may be transferred by the ECB to the aforementioned national judicial authorities, the SSM Regulation refers to 'evidence of facts potentially giving rise to a criminal offence'. Decision 2016/1162 refers to 'confidential information', meaning information covered by data protection and professional secrecy rules, and to documents that, under the ECB's confidentiality regime, have been classified as 'ECB-CONFIDENTIAL' or 'ECB-SECRET'.[148] The EU-level legal framework does not set any temporal limits on when the ECB may transfer such information to national judicial authorities. We may therefore conclude that the ECB has discretion in determining when it will proceed with such information transfers. Lastly, it is worth

[144] Cooperation Notice (n 79) paras 28 and 29.
[145] Art 28(1) Regulation 1/2003.
[146] Art 65 Directive CRD IV.
[147] Art 1(b) Decision EU/2016/1162.
[148] Art 1(a) Decision EU/2016/1162.

noting that the EU-level legal framework does not specify any modalities regarding how the aforementioned information is to be transferred. However, given that information transfers from the ECB to national judicial authorities always take place via the NCAs,[149] we are of the opinion that the ECB's IT tool for the management of documents and records, to which both the ECB and the NCAs have access, is most likely the platform through which such information transfers take place.

Finally, it is worth noting that, as already mentioned in section III.B, EU law, and more specifically Decision 2016/1162, does impose certain conditions on the transfer of information by the ECB to national judicial authorities. For example, information may be transferred as long as there is no other overriding reason for refusing to disclose such information 'relating to the need to safeguard the interests of the Union'.[150] In our view, that EU law imposes such limits can be attributed to the fact that the national judicial authorities are not institutionally embedded in the SSM. Unlike the system of EU competition law enforcement and Regulation 1/2003, which explicitly specifies the role of national courts in the enforcement of EU competition law (Articles 6 and 15), in the case of banking supervision, national judicial authorities are not institutionally linked to the ECB. As a corollary, unlike the field of EU competition law enforcement, in the field of banking supervision, EU law does not foresee unconditional information transfers to national judicial authorities.

B. Transfer of Information from National Authorities to ELEAs

We have already stated a number of times throughout this chapter that OLAF's tasks are limited: it is only an investigatory body. This statutory restriction explains why OLAF needs information from national authorities prior to, during and after its investigations. OLAF's broad mandate then explains why its legal framework, unlike those of the ECB or DG Competition, which operate within regulated, tight-knit and relatively uniform networks of single national authorities (ie, the national supervisors and the national competition authorities respectively), only regulates the bottom-up transfer from 'national competent authorities' to OLAF. This reasoning applies not only to the top-down transfer of information, but also, here, to the bottom-up transfer of information. Precisely because OLAF can investigate in areas ranging from structural funds to customs and from the common agricultural policy to VAT, OLAF's legal framework needs to apply to different administrative and judicial authorities in every policy area where PIF is at stake. Given that, furthermore, there are different authorities in each and every one of the 27 Member States, the sheer number of authorities with which OLAF must cooperate increases exponentially. To try to capture all the authorities, fragmented across both policy and Member State lines, on which OLAF can possibly depend for the provision of information, its legal framework must resort – almost by necessity it seems – to the rather hollow or empty-sounding term 'national competent authority'.

[149] Art 2 Decision EU/2016/1162; Art 136 SSM Framework Regulation.
[150] Art 2(1) Decision EU/2016/1162.

Considering the above, it may come as no surprise that OLAF's legal framework on the bottom-up transfer of information does not distinguish between an inner or an outer circle: it refers only to 'national competent authorities'. Hence what is said here, in this section on the transfer of information from the inner circle to ELEAs, also applies mutatis mutandis to bottom-up transfers originating from the outer circle. OLAF's legal framework brought the AFCOS into existence to help deal with the plethora of national authorities in and across policy areas and Member States: EU law obliges Member States to establish an AFCOS. However, to say that, as a result of this obligation, Union law created an OLAF inner circle in the same way as DG Competition or the ECB would be a gross misrepresentation. OLAF's legal framework states that the AFCOS is 'to facilitate effective cooperation and exchange information with the office', but it says nothing with respect to the AFCOS's architecture, powers or general functioning.[151] This is left entirely to national law. For the purpose of the transfer of information to OLAF, the AFCOS 'may' be considered a national competent authority, thereby demonstrating that, exactly, OLAF's legal framework does not differentiate between inner-circle or outer-circle authorities. In many instances, the institution of the AFCOS, though noble in its intentions, added just another layer of authorities of which OLAF must take cognisance when exchanging information. This is different in those Member States in which the AFCOS was installed as a central unit through which all information coming from national (administrative) authorities must pass before being transmitted to OLAF.

OLAF's legal framework (i) neither determines whether a Member State' s AFCOS must be considered a 'national competent authority', (ii) nor does it determine when a national authority is to be qualified as 'competent' for the purpose of bottom-up information transfers. One would expect that, in the absence of an EU qualifier of sorts, national law would step in and offer designations of 'competence' under national law and would (clearly) appoint the state's AFCOS as the competent authority. This, as demonstrated in section III.A.i, is hardly ever the case. National law does not reach upwards to connect to OLAF's legal framework by appointing particular authorities. We think part of the issue lies in the fact that the use of the 'competent authority' runs the risk of conflating two different but interrelated terms. Whether an authority is competent to act in and enforce a particular policy area is usually determined by national law.[152] However, that designation of competence does not also automatically render that authority competent to transfer information to OLAF. The general competence to enforce ought not to be confused with the more specific competence to transfer information, which national law often fails to confer on national authorities competent to act in a particular policy area. Based on our analysis, it seems that national law is not cognisant of or fails to recognise the EU/OLAF dimension that many of its authorities have or can have. As a result, it is extremely difficult, especially for an outsider, to establish which national authorities transfer information to OLAF. The new Regulation (EU, Euratom) 2020/2223 does little

[151] Art 12a(1) New OLAF Regulation.

[152] For example, Dutch legislation appoints the *Autoriteit Consument en Markt* as competent competition authority for the purpose of EU competition law enforcement. See Art 88 *Mededingingswet*. Likewise, the 'inspector' (*inspecteur*) is the competent authority for the purpose of the application of EU customs law in the Netherlands. See *Algemene douanewet*, art 1:3(c).

to clarify matters with respect to the question 'which authorities transfer information to OLAF'. Under the new Regulation, the designation of national authorities, including the AFCOS, as 'competent' remains within Member States' procedural autonomy. All the while, from the national level, we have thus far not witnessed any significant change.

Consequently, similar difficulties – that can also be traced back to OLAF's mandate – arise when considering the types of information and the purpose for which they may be transferred; the enforcement phase in which transfer to OLAF takes place; and the modalities national authorities use when transferring information. Under OLAF's old legal framework, EU law offered little clarification with respect to the above-mentioned three factors. Instead, national competent authorities had to transfer information to OLAF, at OLAF's request or on their own initiative, in so far as national law allowed. Prior to OLAF's new legal framework, which we get back to in a bit, the 'what, when, and how' of bottom-up information transfers was entirely subject to national law; national law that, in turn, often did not reach up and connect to OLAF's legal framework, resulting in, amongst other things, transfers of information without a legal basis in national law.[153]

Are these issues resolved by the amendments made by Regulation (EU, Euratom) 2020/2223? We think the answer is yes, but with a number of important caveats. Under the new Regulation, national competent authorities must transfer 'unless prevented by national law'. This turns the rules on the transfer of information upside-down and reduces the role allocated to national law, from allowing information transfers when such allowance is given by national law to only preventing information transfers where national law poses an obstacle. Surely the amendment allows for bottom-up transfers of information considered impossible before – for reasons of a lack of a legal basis or otherwise – but the legislative adjustment side-steps the real issue, which is that national law does not reach up and connect to OLAF's legal framework. Regulation (EU, Euratom) 2020/2223 thereby brushes over the fact that, in terms of scoping, bottom-up transfers of information need national law for guidance and direction.

Unlike OLAF, DG Competition and the ECB operate within uniform networks of single national authorities (the ECN and the SSM respectively). That is why, in our opinion, the EU-level legal frameworks make reference to the different authorities' 'obligation to exchange information', rather than one-way information transfers. In other words, the EU-level legal framework not only regulates top-down information transfers, but – by introducing mutual obligations to exchange information – essentially also regulates bottom-up information transfers. Unlike the OLAF legal framework, Regulation 1/2003 and the SSM Regulation capture all the inner-circle national authorities that can potentially transfer information to DG Competition and the ECB respectively.

Considering the above, one would expect that, owing to the fact that – in the case of DG Competition and ECB – EU Regulations lay down a mutual obligation for exchanges of information, there would no longer be room for national law to regulate bottom-up transfers. While this generally holds true and the majority of the national legal orders studied in the second Hercule project do not provide for additional legal

[153] Though, it should be said, some Member States circumvented this pitfall by simply transferring information on the basis of European law. See for instance Bovend'Eerdt (n 100) 124–25.

bases in national law, it is worth referring to the Netherlands as an example of a Member State that – notwithstanding the explicit provision in the SSM Regulation – imposes certain limits on unconditional information transfers. According to the Dutch Financial Supervision Act (*Wet op het financieel toezicht*),[154] the Dutch Central Bank – the national supervisory authority – may only transfer confidential information to other supervisory authorities – thus to the ECB too – if, amongst other things, the provision of such confidential data or information is not incompatible with Dutch law or public order.[155] The compatibility of that provision with EU law is, in our view, debatable.

To sum up, unlike OLAF's legal framework, which – as already discussed – obliges the AFCOS to transfer information to the EU level 'unless prevented by national law', the EU-level legal frameworks of DG Competition and the ECB make it clear that national competition authorities and NCAs respectively are obliged to transfer information to their EU partners, and there is, at least in principle, no room for contradicting national law.

VI. Conclusion

To conclude, due to the composite system of enforcement in the respective fields in which OLAF, DG Competition and the ECB operate, EU and national authorities depend, in some way, on one another for the provision of information to ensure effective enforcement.

Our first overarching conclusion is that the ECB and DG Competition operate in a closed-circuit type of network, meaning that they cooperate with specific national counterparts, with whom they exchange information almost unconditionally: as long as the information is exchanged and used for the purposes that fall under the relevant authorities' mandates, there are no noticeable limits. On the other hand, OLAF, because of its broad mandate, cannot depend on a tight-knit network of national authorities with which to exchange information. While top-down there are no substantial limits that restrict OLAF's transfer of information, bottom-up, national law can prevent transfers – or in any case certain transfers – from taking place.

From a bottom-up perspective, we may conclude that when it comes to DG Competition and to the ECB, the respective EU Regulations seem – in principle – to form a sufficient legal basis for bottom-up transfers. On the other hand, OLAF's legal framework struggles in making EU law a basis for information transfer: national competent authorities must transfer information to OLAF 'unless prevented by national law'. While the phrasing under OLAF's legal framework circumvents earlier problems, in which the absence of a legal basis in national law prevented transfers from taking place, bottom-up transfers of information still need national law for guidance and direction.

Lastly, in line with the overarching topic of this book, and the question of whether the EU authorities' frameworks recognise the needs of criminal justice *sensu strictu*, we arrive at the following conclusions. OLAF's legal framework definitely recognises this

[154] Art 1:90(1) Dutch Financial Supervision Act.
[155] Art 1:90(1)(c) Dutch Financial Supervision Act.

dimension of its work. This features prominently in its mandate, which encompasses both criminal and non-criminal activity that affects the Union's financial interests. With respect to the exchange of information, this is reflected in the undifferentiated use of the term 'national competent authorities', which is to include authorities active in both the punitive field (administrative authorities that impose punitive administrative penalties and judicial authorities) and the non-punitive field. Besides Article 12(3) of Regulation 1/2003, which stipulates that the receiving authority may not use the received information for the imposition of custodial sanctions, the legal framework of DG Competition does not clearly foresee the links that exist with criminal justice *sensu stricto*. On the other hand, the ECB EU-level legal framework does foresee such interactions, in the sense that the need for information *transfers* from the ECB to national judicial authorities is recognised and regulated. To what extent the ECB EU-level legal framework sufficiently deals with the *use* of ECB information as evidence for the imposition of *sensu stricto* criminal sanctions at the national level is, however, questionable at the moment.[156]

[156] Karagianni (n 42).

6

The Use of Investigative Results as Evidence in National Punitive Proceedings: The Case of OLAF

FABIO GIUFFRIDA* AND GEORGIA THEODORAKAKOU

I. Introduction

The European Anti-Fraud Office (OLAF) is a central actor in the domain of the protection of the Union's financial interests (PIF – '*protection des intérêts financiers*'). OLAF carries out administrative investigations into conduct affecting the Union budget and its findings may trigger the initiation of (criminal) proceedings in the Member States. Therefore, the admissibility of evidence collected during OLAF investigations in national proceedings is crucial for the effective protection of the Union's financial interests. This chapter analyses the admissibility of OLAF-collected evidence in national punitive proceedings, with a focus on criminal proceedings. For the purpose of this chapter, 'punitive administrative proceedings' refers to national proceedings leading to the issuing of administrative sanctions, and more precisely fines, which would qualify as having a criminal nature in accordance with the so-called *Engel* criteria laid down by the European Court of Human Rights (ECtHR)[1] and endorsed by the Court of Justice of the European Union (CJEU).[2] References to 'punitive proceedings' should therefore be understood as referring to both punitive administrative and criminal proceedings.

This chapter takes a comparative approach, looking at six national legal orders (France, Germany, Italy, Luxembourg, the Netherlands and Hungary). While this chapter cannot delve into the details of each of the six systems, it aims to point out at least some common trends and significant differences that have emerged in the study of national case law and legislation concerning the admissibility of evidence in punitive proceedings, with the aim of drawing conclusions about the admissibility of OLAF-collected evidence. To

* The opinions expressed in the chapter by Fabio Giuffrida are personal opinions of the author and do not reflect those of the European Commission.

[1] See *Engel and Others v The Netherlands* Apps nos 5100/71; 5101/71; 5102/71; 5354/72; 5370/72 (ECtHR, 8 June 1976).

[2] See, for instance, Case C-489/10 *Bonda* ECLI:EU:C:2012:319.

this end, section II examines the main provision of Regulation 883/2013,[3] as recently amended by Regulation 2020/2223 ('OLAF Regulation'),[4] which lays down, inter alia, the rule on the admissibility of evidence collected by OLAF. Section III sets the scene for the main analysis by presenting the main features of national systems as regards the use of evidence. Sections IV and V focus on the admissibility of OLAF-collected evidence in national punitive administrative proceedings and criminal proceedings respectively. In light of the partially similar mandate of the European Public Prosecutor's Office (EPPO) and OLAF to ensure effective protection of the Union's financial interests, section VI looks at the relation between the two offices and its implication for the admissibility of evidence. Section VII draws some conclusions.

II. Admissibility of OLAF-Collected Evidence in National Proceedings: The OLAF Regulation

OLAF is an investigative body set up in 1999 within the Commission by Commission Decision 1999/352/EC,[5] with the aim of strengthening the fight against illegal activities affecting the financial interests of the European Union (EU).[6] To this end, OLAF is competent to carry out *administrative* investigations into conduct detrimental to the Union budget either within EU institutions, bodies, offices and agencies, where suspected illegal activity concerns EU officials and members of the institutions ('internal investigations'),[7] or in the Member States, in cases where economic operators may be involved ('external investigations').[8] As was discussed in the previous two chapters of this volume, OLAF is entrusted with the exercise of the powers laid down mainly – but not exhaustively[9] – in the OLAF Regulation, as amended by Regulation 2020/2223 ('OLAF Regulation'). For instance, OLAF may conduct on-the-spot checks and inspections on the premises of economic operators,[10] take statements from any person able to provide relevant information[11] ('person concerned' by the investigation or a witness)

[3] Regulation (EU, Euratom) No 883/2013 of the European Parliament and of the Council of 11 September 2013 concerning investigations conducted by the European Anti-Fraud Office (OLAF) [2013] OJ L248/1.

[4] Regulation (EU, Euratom) 2020/2223 of the European Parliament and of the Council of 23 December 2020 amending Regulation (EU, Euratom) No 883/2013, as regards cooperation with the European Public Prosecutor's Office and the effectiveness of the European Anti-Fraud Office investigations [2020] OJ L437/49.

[5] Commission Decision 1999/352/EC of 28 April 1999 establishing the European Anti-fraud Office (OLAF) [1999] OJ L136/20.

[6] V Covolo, 'Regulation 883/2013. Concerning Investigations Conducted by OLAF: A Missed Opportunity for Substantial Reforms' (2017) 2 *European Criminal Law Review* 151, 152.

[7] Art 4 OLAF Regulation.

[8] Art 3 OLAF Regulation.

[9] OLAF activities are governed by a complex legal framework composed of several instruments. Although the OLAF Regulation has laid down the general framework concerning OLAF powers in the context of its internal and external investigations, it is complemented by other EU instruments, such as Regulation 2988/96 on the protection of the European Communities financial interests and Regulation 2185/96 concerning on-the-spot checks and inspections carried out by the Commission (C Brière, 'La modernisation des règles régissant les activités de l'OLAF' [2021] *Journal de Droit Européen* 1, 4).

[10] Art 3(1) OLAF Regulation.

[11] Arts 3(3) and 9(2) OLAF Regulation.

and so on. However, the OLAF Regulation has not set out a self-standing set of rules, as it often refers back to the applicable national law of the Member State concerned; hence, the standards for gathering evidence within OLAF vary according to the Member States in which OLAF acts.[12]

At the end of its investigations, OLAF draws up a report in accordance with the rules set out in Article 11 of the OLAF Regulation. OLAF reports are complex legal products that contain the findings of investigations conducted by OLAF,[13] and may be accompanied by other relevant documents, such as records of the interviews and reports of the on-the-spot checks or of digital forensic operations. While OLAF cannot itself establish the liability of the person concerned by its investigations, and it has no sanctioning powers, it may address – non-binding – recommendations to national authorities of the Member State concerned on the follow-up actions that should be taken.[14] Therefore, after OLAF reports and accompanying documents are transmitted to the national competent authorities,[15] the latter may decide to initiate national proceedings, including criminal ones in cases where the conduct under investigation amounts to a criminal offence. The admissibility of evidence gathered by OLAF in national proceedings, especially criminal ones, may therefore prove essential to ensuring the effective protection of the Union's financial interests.[16] Article 11(2) of the OLAF Regulation sets out the admissibility rule of evidence collected by OLAF; in accordance with the original text, that is, before the text was amended by Regulation 2020/2223:

> OLAF reports shall constitute admissible evidence in *administrative or judicial proceedings* of the Member State in which their use proves necessary, in the *same way* and under the *same conditions* as administrative reports drawn up by national administrative inspectors. They shall be subject to the *same evaluation rules* as those applicable to administrative reports drawn up by national administrative inspectors and shall have the *same evidentiary value* as such reports.[17]

[12] See, for instance, Art 3(6) OLAF Regulation. Nevertheless, Regulation 2020/2223 has further harmonised OLAF powers when conducting external investigations, thus limiting the degree of reliance on national law. Brière (n 9) 4 ff. See also Recital 21 of the OLAF Regulation, which provides that 'The conduct by the Office of on-the-spot checks and inspections in situations where the economic operator concerned submits to the on-the-spot check and inspection should be *subject to Union law alone*. This would allow the Office to exercise its investigative powers in an effective and coherent manner in all Member States with a view to contributing to a high level of protection of the financial interests of the Union throughout the Union in accordance with Article 325 of the Treaty on the Functioning of the European Union' (emphasis added).

[13] The first subparagraph of Art 11(1) OLAF Regulation reads as follows: 'That report shall give an account of the legal basis for the investigation, the procedural steps followed, the facts established and their preliminary classification in law, the estimated financial impact of the facts established, the respect of the procedural guarantees in accordance with Article 9 and the conclusions of the investigation.'

[14] In accordance with Art 11(1) OLAF Regulation, the recommendations may indicate any disciplinary, administrative, financial or judicial action to be taken by the institutions, bodies, offices and agencies – in the case of internal investigations – and by the competent authorities of the Member States concerned, in the case of external investigations.

[15] Unless an internal investigation reveals the existence of criminal conduct in respect of which the EPPO could exercise its competence; in this case, OLAF should submit a report to the EPPO (Art 12(c) OLAF Regulation).

[16] M Simonato, 'OLAF Investigations in a Multi-Level System. Legal Obstacles to Effective Enfoncement' *eucrim* 3/2016, 136, 137.

[17] Art 11(2) Regulation 883/2013, in the version before amendment by Regulation 2020/2223 (emphasis added).

Article 11(2) of the OLAF Regulation therefore included – in its original version – an assimilation rule for both *administrative punitive* and *criminal* proceedings, according to which OLAF final reports had to be treated in the same way as national reports in terms of their admissibility, evaluation and evidentiary value. As a consequence, the previous version of Article 11(2) left it to the discretion of the Member State to decide whether or not OLAF-collected evidence should constitute admissible evidence in national proceedings, provided that the equivalence with administrative reports by national authorities was ensured.[18]

However, such an assimilation rule raised some questions and was thus subject to criticism, as it could hamper the use of OLAF-collected evidence and therefore the effectiveness of OLAF activities.[19] First, this rule could apply only if there was, at the national level, an administrative authority with a mandate and powers that could be considered 'equivalent' to those of OLAF; however, finding such an 'equivalent' authority might not always be a straightforward task. Second, national rules and practices on the admissibility of administrative reports in criminal proceedings vary across Member States, in this way hampering a consistent judicial follow-up to OLAF investigations across the Union. Third, national judicial authorities, once they received OLAF reports, sometimes ended up repeating the investigative activities already performed by the Office in order to obtain admissible evidence. Such duplication of investigative activities is nonetheless contentious from different perspectives: it violates the principle of procedural economy, as human and technical resources are deployed twice to obtain the same result; it prolongs the time that has elapsed since the commission of the alleged crimes, with the consequence that there are higher risks of their becoming statute-barred before any decision on the merits can be taken; at the same time, persons under OLAF investigations would undergo the ordeal of an investigation for a second time; and, finally, the element of surprise that is needed for some investigative activities – such as inspections and searches – is lost when suspects are already aware of investigations concerning them.[20]

In May 2018, the Commission tabled a proposal for an amendment of Regulation 883/2013 – in order, inter alia, to strengthen the admissibility of OLAF-collected evidence and improve follow-up at the national level – which was finally adopted by the Parliament and the Council in 2020. Article 1(11) of the above-mentioned

[18] M Luchtman, A Karagianni and K Bovend'Eerdt, 'EU administrative investigations and the use of their results as evidence in national punitive proceedings' in F Giuffrida and K Ligeti (eds), *Admissibility of OLAF Final Reports as Evidence in Criminal Proceedings* (University of Luxembourg 2019) 7, 46.

[19] Already in 2011, the Commission noted that the 'results of EU administrative investigations frequently remain unused by national criminal courts' (Commission, 'On the protection of the financial interests of the European Union by criminal law and by administrative investigations. An integrated policy to safeguard taxpayers' money' COM(2011) 293 final 8). See also OLAF, 'Analysis on Member States Follow-Up to OLAF's Judicial Recommendations Issued between 1 January 2008 and 31 December 2015' Ref Ares(2017)461597 – 27/01/2017 (2017) 1–2, where OLAF reported that Member States' authorities repeatedly take the view that Art 11(2) Regulation 883/2013 'is not always a sufficient legal basis to allow Member States' judicial authorities to use OLAF reports as evidence in trial', so that national authorities often 'perform investigation activities again in order to acquire admissible evidence'.

[20] K Ligeti, 'The Protection of the Procedural Rights of Persons Concerned by OLAF Administrative Investigations and the Admissibility of OLAF Final Reports as Criminal Evidence' *Study for the Committee on Budgetary Control of the European Parliament* (July 2017) 27–28.

Regulation 2020/2223 introduced two main changes in Article 11(2) of Regulation 883/2013, which now reads as follows:

> 2. In drawing up the reports and recommendations referred to in paragraph 1, account shall be taken of the relevant provisions of Union law and, in so far as it is applicable, of the national law of the Member State concerned.
>
> Reports drawn up on the basis of the first subparagraph, together with all evidence in support and annexed thereto, shall constitute admissible evidence:
>
> (a) in judicial proceedings of a non-criminal nature before national courts and in administrative proceedings in the Member States;
>
> (b) in criminal proceedings of the Member State in which their use proves necessary in the same way and under the same conditions as administrative reports drawn up by national administrative inspectors and shall be subject to the same evaluation rules as those applicable to administrative reports drawn up by national administrative inspectors and shall have the same evidentiary value as such reports;
>
> (c) in judicial proceedings before the CJEU and in administrative proceedings in the institutions, bodies, offices and agencies. …

Compared to the previous version, the new Article 11(2) has, first, extended the admissibility rule – in addition to the OLAF reports – to *all evidence* supporting and attached to them. As mentioned above, OLAF reports contain the findings of the investigation carried out by OLAF and may be accompanied by other relevant documents. National practice showed that national authorities were likely to assess the admissibility of the various elements supporting OLAF reports rather than the reports as such. However, in the absence of EU legislation on the matter, the use of the information included in such additional documents in national proceedings fell within the scope of Member States' procedural autonomy.[21] Therefore, the extension of the rule envisaged in Article 11(2) to these additional pieces of evidence was welcomed, as it could bring clarity regarding their admissibility, thus strengthening the admissibility of OLAF-collected evidence.

Second, the version of Article 11(2)(a) currently in force replicates the Commission's proposal and abolishes the assimilation clause for judicial proceedings of a non-criminal nature before national courts and *national administrative proceedings*. On the other hand, nothing has changed for *criminal proceedings*, as the assimilation principle continues to apply pursuant to Article 11(2)(b) of the OLAF Regulation.[22] Therefore, OLAF-collected evidence should still be treated in the same way as the administrative reports drawn up by national inspectors; it follows that where national criminal proceedings allow the use

[21] Luchtman, Karagianni and Bovend'Eerdt (n 18) 7, 42.

[22] The European Parliament had proposed to subject both administrative and criminal proceedings to the same regime and suggested the following amendment: 'Upon simple verification of their authenticity, reports drawn up on that basis including all evidence supporting and annexed to these reports shall constitute admissible evidence in judicial proceedings before national courts and in administrative proceedings in the Member States. The power of the national courts to freely assess the evidence shall not be affected by this Regulation' (European Parliament, 'Legislative resolution of 16 April 2019 on the proposal for a regulation of the European Parliament and of the Council amending Regulation (EU, Euratom) No 883/2013 concerning investigations conducted by the European Anti-Fraud Office (OLAF) as regards cooperation with the European Public Prosecutor's Office and the effectiveness of OLAF investigations (COM(2018)0338 – C8-0214/2018 – 2018/0170(COD)', amendment 85).

of evidence gathered by means of administrative law in domestic cases, they should also allow the use of OLAF-collected evidence on equal terms.[23]

As far as punitive administrative proceedings are concerned, they seem prima facie to fall within the remit of Article 11(2)(a) of the OLAF Regulation, while Article 11(2)(b) applies only to *criminal proceedings*, which could not be interpreted as referring to proceedings before administrative authorities or courts even in cases where the latter apply administrative sanctions that would qualify as having a criminal nature in accordance with the *Engel* criteria. Nevertheless, it is worth noting that Recital 36 of the OLAF Regulation is worded more broadly, as it does not refer to 'criminal proceedings' but it rather states that 'the rule providing for equivalence with the reports of national administrative inspectors should continue to apply in the case of national judicial proceedings *of a criminal nature*' (emphasis added). This broader wording has led some commentators to interpret Article 11(2)(b) of the OLAF Regulation as covering punitive proceedings in general, that is, criminal proceedings *sensu stricto*, but also proceedings before administrative courts whenever the *Engel* criteria are met.[24] Further clarity could be achieved in this regard if the CJEU is given the opportunity to interpret this provision.

With regard to Article 11(2)(a), it should also be noted that this provision seems to introduce a mandatory inclusion rule,[25] which requires national authorities to consider OLAF-collected evidence as admissible in punitive administrative proceedings irrespective of what national evidentiary rules set out.[26] However, this *de iure* admissibility of OLAF-collected evidence that Regulation 2020/2223 seems to lay down has not affected the power of national authorities to freely assess this evidence – that is, to evaluate whether this has any probative value and, if so, what probative value – as one can glean from the last sentence of the revised Article 11(2).[27] As a consequence, national authorities remain free to consider this evidence unreliable or insufficient, and could thus adopt further measures or require further investigations. Therefore, the *de iure* admissibility of OLAF-collected evidence introduced by Regulation 2020/2223 does not entail its automatic use in punitive administrative proceedings.

[23] Luchtman, Karagianni and Bovend'Eerdt (n 18) 7, 46. It is worth noting that the new version of Art 11(2) requires OLAF, when drawing up its reports, to take into account – apart from the national law of the Member State concerned – the relevant provisions of Union law. Even though the requirement of compliance with EU law is unquestionable, this clarification may strengthen the reliability of OLAF reports and thus their admission by national courts. Nevertheless, as Brière notes, such a provision cannot prevent the duplication of investigative acts by national authorities, in particular in cases where national safeguards in criminal law are higher than those of EU law (Brière (n 9) 1, 9–10).

[24] See, for instance, K Bovend'Eerdt, 'The Commission Proposal Amending the OLAF Regulation' *eucrim* 1/2018, 73, 75, who states that 'the equivalence rule will remain applicable to OLAF reports and recommendations in cases of national criminal proceedings *(including punitive administrative proceedings)*' (emphasis added).

[25] See also ch 9 of this volume (Vervaele); and J Vervaele, 'Lawful and Fair Use of Evidence from a European Human Rights Perspective' in Giuffrida and Ligeti (eds) (n 18) 56, 94.

[26] See more in section IV.

[27] 'The power of the CJEU and national courts and competent bodies in administrative and criminal proceedings to *freely assess* the evidential value of the reports drawn up by the Office shall *not* be affected by this Regulation' (last sentence of Art 11(2) OLAF Regulation, emphasis added).

This interpretative approach is indirectly confirmed by comparing the OLAF Regulation with Directive (EU) 2019/1, which concerns the field of competition.[28] Article 32 of the Directive concerns 'Admissibility of evidence before national competition authorities' and obliges Member States to ensure that

> the types of proof that are admissible as evidence before a national competition authority include documents, oral statements, electronic messages, recordings and all other objects containing information, irrespective of the form it takes and the medium on which information is stored.

Although this provision concerns the 'horizontal' relationship between national competition authorities while the OLAF Regulation addresses the 'vertical' admissibility in national proceedings of evidence collected by an EU body, the Preamble to Directive 2019/1 nonetheless clarifies the notion of 'admissibility' as such, which may help in understanding the meaning of the new provisions of Article 11(2) of the OLAF Regulation. In accordance with Recital 73 of the Directive, when a given type of proof is 'admissible', national authorities 'should be able to consider' it in taking their decision. The same goes for OLAF-collected evidence in accordance with the revised rule on admissibility: national courts and national authorities will be in a position to consider this evidence when taking a decision, but would not be automatically bound by it. Therefore, admissibility does not mean or imply 'use' of the evidence, even when it comes from an EU entity, but can be considered equivalent to 'availability'.

III. Rules on Evidence in National Law: An Overview

A. Admissibility Rules in National Law

Since the admissibility of evidence has so far not been harmonised at EU level, nor has Regulation 2020/2223 introduced specific evidentiary rules on OLAF-collected evidence, the use of evidence collected by OLAF in national punitive proceedings is regulated by national rules on evidence.[29] While the rules on the admissibility of evidence vary considerably from country to country,[30] some broad categorisations are possible as regards both the rationale behind such rules and the rules as such.[31] As Vervaele points out:

> [T]he conceptual framework of evidence is related to the finality of the punitive process, based on the formal and substantive *truth* sustained by evidence/proof that does respect

[28] Directive (EU) 2019/1 of the European Parliament and of the Council of 11 December 2018 to empower the competition authorities of the Member States to be more effective enforcers and to ensure the proper functioning of the internal market [2019] OJ L11/3.

[29] The CJEU has constantly held that as EU law currently stands, it is, in principle, for national law alone, in accordance with the principle of procedural autonomy, to determine the rules relating to the admissibility and assessment of evidence in criminal proceedings. In this regard see, for instance, Case C-746/18 *Prokuratuur* ECLI:EU:C:2021:152, paras 41–44.

[30] See more in Vervaele 'Lawful and Fair Use of Evidence' (n 25) 56, 59 ff.

[31] Vervaele makes a distinction among countries adopting: the 'vindication of rights approach' (evidence is excluded because its admissibility would infringe fundamental rights); the 'deterrence approach' (rules

> due process. This therefore includes the *legality of the proceedings* from the start of the pre-trial investigations and respect for *fundamental rights* and procedural guarantees during the proceedings.[32]

That said, one could argue that the rationale behind the rules on the admissibility of evidence is linked with the need to seek the truth and ensure adequate protection of both the rights of persons involved – either as such or as part of the fairness of the proceedings[33] – and the rule of law principle.[34]

In a CJEU judgment on the admissibility of evidence in criminal proceedings (*Dzivev*),[35] the Court stressed both the human rights and the rule of law dimensions behind the rules on admissibility. In the frame of Bulgarian investigations on serious value-added-tax-related (VAT-related) crimes, the recording of some conversations involving the defendant had been ordered by a court that was not competent to do so and, apparently, without sufficient reasons to justify it. The Specialised Criminal Court of Bulgaria thus required the CJEU to rule on whether the national rule providing for the inadmissibility at trial of such a recording was at variance with Article 325(1) of the Treaty on the Functioning of the European Union (TFEU), that is, with the obligation of Member States to adopt effective and dissuasive measures to counter illegal activities affecting the Union budget. It was clear that, without the recording, the defendant would be acquitted of the serious crimes with which he had been indicted in Bulgaria.[36]

Sharing in essence the Advocate General's view,[37] the Court of Justice argued that the Bulgarian court was not required to disapply national legislation on the admissibility of evidence, as the protection of the Union's financial interests could not trump respect for fundamental rights and general principles of the EU. As for the former, in particular, the CJEU emphasised the importance of the principles of legality and of the rule of law, which forbid national courts from acting beyond the legal limits set out by national legislation.[38] Furthermore, the Court reiterated that the interception of telecommunication entailed a violation of the right to private life enshrined in Article 7 of the Charter of Fundamental Rights of the European Union ('the Charter'). Hence, as the interception was authorised by a court lacking the necessary jurisdiction, it amounted

on evidence aim to ensure that law enforcement authorities do not collect evidence in an illegal way); and the 'judicial integrity (or balancing) approach' (evidence is declared inadmissible after a balancing exercise between the violation of individual rights and the Member State's interest in convicting the alleged offenders) (ibid 56, 60–61).

[32] ibid 56, 60 (emphasis added). See also P Alldridge, 'The United Kingdom' in Giuffrida and Ligeti (eds) (n 18) 216, 216, who notes that 'in criminal procedure, the exclusion of an item of evidence may be for one or more of the following reasons: (a) to prevent irrelevant information going into the proceedings; (b) to ensure the fairness of the proceedings; (c) to exercise control over the enforcement authorities; or (d) to provide more widely acceptable decisions'.

[33] With regard to the human rights dimension of the rules on the admissibility of evidence, see, eg, J Tricot, 'France' in Giuffrida and Ligeti (eds) (n 18) 95, 96 ff.

[34] See, eg, M Böse and A Schneider, 'Germany' in Giuffrida and Ligeti (eds) (n 18) 132, 132–33, who point out that in Germany, the main aim of admissibility rules is to maintain the rule of law and – according to some authors – to deter law enforcement authorities from illegally collecting evidence.

[35] Case C-310/16 *Dzivev and Others* ECLI:EU:C:2019:30.

[36] Reference for a preliminary ruling from the *Spetsializiran nakazatelen sad* (Bulgaria) lodged on 31 May 2016 – *Criminal proceedings against Petar Dzivev* (Case C-310/16).

[37] Case C-310/16 *Dzivev and Others*, Opinion of AG Bobek, ECLI:EU:C:2018:623.

[38] *Dzivev* (n 35) paras 33–35.

to a limitation of the right to private life that was not in accordance with the law and thus violated Article 52(1) of the Charter.[39] In other words, 'Article 325 TFEU cannot be used as the legal base for introducing a balancing test between EU effectiveness and applicable legal safeguards in case of unlawful evidence'.[40]

Against this background, it is now appropriate to look more closely at the rules on admissibility as such, in order to understand how they (can) impact on OLAF-collected evidence. More specifically, two systems of proof may be found across the Member States: the system of 'free proof' and the system of 'controlled proof'. When national law provides for a system of free proof, any kind of evidence is in principle admissible, and can be accepted and taken into account by courts when deciding a case. However, 'free' does not mean 'unconditional'. Even if there is no *numerus clausus* of means of proof, evidence collected should meet some requirements in order to be admissible. In general, such requirements are justified by the need to protect the fundamental rights of persons subject to criminal investigations and, more broadly, the legality and fairness of the proceedings. By contrast, in countries where the controlled proof system applies, there is an exhaustive list of means of proof. For instance, according to Dutch law, admissible means of evidence comprise only: (i) the court's own observations; (ii) the statements of the defendant; (iii) the statements of a witness, including experts; and (iv) written materials.[41] By the same token, there is an exhaustive list of means of proof in Germany (examination of witnesses, expert opinion, inspection, documentary evidence and defendant statements)[42] and in Italy.[43]

As further discussed in Section V, both systems of free proof and systems of controlled proof in principle consider OLAF-collected evidence admissible. In the former, this conclusion is straightforward, as freedom of proof implies that evidence collected by OLAF – as long as the other requirements are met – is admissible. In controlled systems, OLAF-collected evidence usually falls within the notion of 'written materials'/'documents', the admissibility of which is not contentious. Therefore, the nature of the criminal justice system – that is whether it is a controlled system or one of free proof – does not seem to have a bearing on the *de iure* admissibility of OLAF-collected evidence in national proceedings.

B. Review of the Decisions on Admissibility of Evidence

Unlike the rules on admissibility of evidence, which differ extensively from one Member State to another, when it comes to the possible review of the decisions on the (in)admissibility of evidence, a certain degree of consistency seems to exist throughout the EU.

[39] 'Any limitation on the exercise of the rights and freedoms recognised by this Charter must be *provided for by law* and respect the essence of those rights and freedoms …' (Art 52(1) of the Charter, emphasis added).

[40] Vervaele, 'Lawful and Fair Use of Evidence' (n 25) 56, 66–67. For further remarks on *Dzivev*, see also Luchtman, Karagianni and Bovend'Eerdt (n 18) 7, 25 ff.

[41] APW Duijkersloot, AJ de Vries and RJGM Widdershoven, 'The Netherlands' in Giuffrida and Ligeti (eds) (n 18) 197, 200–01.

[42] Böse and Schneider (n 34) 132, 135.

[43] M Caianiello and G Lasagni, 'Italy' in Giuffrida and Ligeti (eds) (n 18) 170, 174.

In the criminal justice systems of the six Member States under analysis there is no decision on admissibility as such that may be subject to judicial review. A control on evidence and its admissibility may nonetheless be triggered in two different ways. First, the admissibility of evidence can be contested by appealing the decision that criminal courts adopt at the end of the criminal proceedings. Second, in most Member States it is usually possible to challenge, already during the pre-trial phase, an investigative measure carried out by public authorities (eg, public prosecutors or judicial police). If this action is successful, the evidence collected through that investigative measure should not be included in the case file. This scheme is known in most countries as '*nullity*' (or 'invalidity') of investigative acts.[44]

As in the criminal law domain, there is no decision on admissibility as such in administrative proceedings that may be subject to judicial review. Again, issues concerning the admissibility of evidence can be contested when challenging the decision adopted by administrative authorities at the end of the administrative proceedings. Administrative courts are usually competent for this review, but in some cases a first review is carried out within the administrative authorities themselves.[45]

The possibility to challenge the admissibility of evidence – even if not as such but together with the merits of the case or by indirectly challenging an investigative measure – is of the essence to ensure both adequate protection of the parties' rights and the lawful functioning of punitive systems. This becomes all the more important vis-à-vis OLAF-collected evidence, which are acts of an EU body that, albeit often adopted at the end of investigations that build on a blend of national and supranational law, enter national punitive proceedings. Precisely because of the nature of OLAF as an EU body, the right to challenge its reports should take into account the well-established CJEU case law according to which national courts cannot invalidate EU acts and decisions, as further discussed in sections IV and V.

C. Use of Evidence Declared Inadmissible in Different Sets of Proceedings

As discussed in section II, OLAF carries out administrative investigations, yet the results of its activities can (or at times should) be used in another set of proceedings, that is, in criminal or punitive administrative proceedings in the Member States. Therefore, it is appropriate to examine whether evidence declared inadmissible in administrative proceedings can be used in criminal ones, with the aim of drawing lessons for the transfer and use of OLAF-collected evidence in national proceedings.

[44] Vervaele, 'Lawful and Fair Use of Evidence' (n 25) 56, 59 ff. See also M Kusak, *Mutual Admissibility of Evidence in Criminal Matters in the EU. A Study of Telephone Tapping and House Search* (Maklu 2016) 169 ff.

[45] In Luxembourg, for instance, VAT Administration decisions that impose financial penalties are first subject to the so-called '*reclamation*', by which the individual requires the Administration to reconsider its decision. This further decision of the Administration can then be challenged before the civil chamber of the district court of Luxembourg. In this respect, see K Ligeti and F Giuffrida, 'Luxembourg' in Giuffrida and Ligeti (eds) (n 18) 184, 192.

The question has not often come to the attention of the Court of Justice, and when it has, the solution has not always been clear-cut. In one of the few cases where the CJEU addressed the issue of the 'migration' of evidence from one set of proceedings to another, *WebMindLicenses*,[46] the Court in essence ruled that the transfer of evidence obtained in the frame of criminal proceedings to parallel administrative procedures concerning violations of VAT rules does not breach EU law, and especially the fundamental rights enshrined in the Charter, as long as some requirements are complied with. However, if they are not respected, national courts *must* disregard the evidence so collected. This case thus seems to suggest that

> the Luxembourg approach towards the appreciation of unlawfully obtained evidence in criminal proceedings is different from that of 'Strasbourg' … The latter court has held that violations of the right to privacy do not necessarily render a trial unfair, not even when these violations concern the use of intrusive techniques, such as covert listening devices without a legal basis … After all, a violation of Article 8 ECHR does not necessarily amount to a violation of Article 6 ECHR. Yet for 'Luxembourg', serious violations of procedural safeguards do seem to have an impact on, particularly, Articles 41 [Charter] (good administration) and 47 [Charter] (fair trial). If correct, the argument is, presumably, that proceedings in which the investigative or prosecutorial bodies can afford not to follow the 'rules of the game' cannot be considered 'fair', nor can one maintain that such a situation is in line with the principles of a good administration.[47]

At the national level, Member States have adopted different approaches with regards to the use of evidence in criminal proceedings if declared inadmissible in administrative ones, and therefore there seem to be loopholes and gaps, leaving the fate of OLAF-collected evidence unpredictable. For instance, in Germany, this would not be in principle possible, as the same rules on the admissibility of evidence apply to criminal and punitive administrative procedures;[48] hence, if evidence is declared inadmissible in administrative proceedings, it should be also denied admission in the criminal ones, and vice versa. On the other hand, in other countries where the principle of autonomy of criminal and administrative proceedings applies, pursuant to which criminal courts are not obliged to align themselves with administrative authorities' decisions, evidence declared inadmissible in administrative proceedings is in principle admissible in criminal proceedings. However, it is still possible that, on a case-by-case basis, evidence that has been declared inadmissible in administrative proceedings is not admitted in criminal proceedings either.[49]

It is difficult to draw lessons for OLAF from this multifaceted state of affairs. One might expect, for instance, that – although clear and conclusive data are not available – the more national systems have an open attitude towards the 'migration' of evidence from criminal to administrative proceedings (and vice versa), the fewer problems the admissibility of OLAF-collected evidence would encounter when passing from the EU

[46] Case C-419/14 *WebMindLicenses* ECLI:EU:C:2015:832.
[47] Luchtman, Karagianni and Bovend'Eerdt (n 18) 7, 18–22.
[48] Böse and Schneider (n 34) 132, 136.
[49] For instance, this is the case in Italy and Luxembourg; see more in Caianiello and Lasagni (n 43) 170, 175 and Ligeti and Giuffrida (n 45) 184, 192, respectively.

to the national level. In addition, the more the issues dealt with in this section are left to the decision of national courts rather than being regulated by the legislator, the less foreseeable is the eventual admissibility of OLAF reports in domestic proceedings. At the same time, however, fundamental rights of individuals concerned by these proceedings may be better protected thanks to the involvement of national courts and their assessment of the admissibility of evidence on a case-by-case basis. In a way, as mentioned, this also seems required by the *WebMindLicenses* decision by the CJEU.

IV. Admissibility of OLAF-Collected Evidence in National Punitive Administrative Proceedings

As mentioned in section I, the notion of 'punitive administrative proceedings' is used in this chapter to refer to national proceedings at the end of which administrative sanctions that would qualify as having a criminal nature according to the *Engel* criteria could be issued. Pursuant to these criteria, national courts – or rarely the legislation itself[50] – consider some administrative proceedings 'punitive', with the consequence that the typical criminal law guarantees – presumption of innocence, *ne bis in idem*, *nemo tenetur*, etc – (should) apply in the context of these procedures as well.[51]

In most countries, the application of the *Engel* criteria by national courts goes hand in hand with a highly fragmented legislative scenario, as there is no single code on 'punitive administrative proceedings' – considering that these are not an independent category – and therefore different pieces of legislation apply and lay down the relevant provisions concerning administrative proceedings in the fields of, for instance, competition, tax, financial supervision, customs, etc.[52] It follows that the application of the assimilation clause laid down in the previous provision of Article 11(2) of the OLAF Regulation – in light of the lack of clear rules at national level on evidence admissibility in punitive administrative proceedings – made the fate of OLAF-collected evidence uncertain, when such evidence was transmitted to national authorities. The amendment of Regulation 883/2013 and the suppression of the assimilation principle for administrative proceedings may thus create a level playing field among Member States as regards the admissibility of OLAF-collected evidence in punitive administrative proceedings.

[50] In Germany, for instance, rules on administrative fines and punitive administrative proceedings are to be found in the Act on Regulatory Offences (*Ordnungswidrigkeitengesetz*), which applies to all 'regulatory offences' – ie offences that may be punished with a fine – under federal and state law.

[51] For instance, in Luxembourg, administrative courts have sometimes considered administrative proceedings before the Financial Sector Supervisory Commission (*Commission de Surveillance du Secteur Financier*) – which supervises the financial sector in Luxembourg and is the competent authority for the purpose of the Market Abuse Regulation and the European Market Infrastructure Regulation – as having a penal nature when a sanction is issued at the end of these proceedings. See more in Ligeti and Giuffrida (n 45) 184, 185.

[52] More in general, administrative punitive proceedings seem to have an unclear identity within the EU, as in some countries, such as in Germany, they are closer to criminal than civil proceedings, and then criminal law rules on evidence admissibility apply accordingly, while in others they are based on civil procedure rules. See more in F Giuffrida, 'Comparative Analysis' in Giuffrida and Ligeti (eds) (n 18) 222, 230–31.

In accordance with Article 11(2)(a) of the OLAF Regulation, as revised in 2020, OLAF-collected evidence should be considered admissible in national administrative proceedings. The laconic wording of Article 11(2)(a), which only provides that '[r]eports drawn up on the basis of the first subparagraph, together with all evidence in support and annexed thereto, *shall constitute admissible evidence*',[53] raises some questions as regards the power of national authorities to admit OLAF-collected evidence, and in particular whether national rules on the admissibility of evidence continue to regulate punitive administrative proceedings.

As long as the OLAF Regulation has only partially harmonised the rules on evidence gathering, while it has not set any relevant admissibility standards on the use of unlawfully gathered evidence, the obligation of national authorities to automatically consider OLAF-collected evidence admissible might be problematic. As Vervaele notes, such provision may indeed raise questions regarding the power of national authorities to declare this evidence inadmissible because of unlawfulness or unfairness.[54] It is indeed unclear how national authorities should deal with evidence in cases where they find that OLAF has violated EU safeguards. Article 11(2)(a) has not provided for any clarification in this respect; hence, one cannot but conclude that national rules on the use of unlawfully gathered evidence in punitive administrative proceedings still apply.[55] Likewise, in so far as the OLAF Regulation refers to national law,[56] OLAF investigations should be carried out in accordance with both the OLAF Regulation and the national law of the Member State concerned. Hence, the violation of the latter could also lead to evidence being unlawful.[57]

The revised version of Article 11(2)(a) of the OLAF Regulation triggers even more questions when national law provides for higher standards of protection of fundamental rights than EU law, and in particular questions as to whether it still allows national authorities to apply these standards. Such a question may arise notably when evidence lawfully collected in a Member State in the frame of OLAF's investigations results in the initiation of punitive administrative proceedings in another Member State whose applicable standards are higher. The guiding principle is the one singled out by the CJEU in *Melloni*, namely, that higher national standards are allowed as long as 'the level of protection provided for by the Charter, as interpreted by the Court, and the primacy, unity and effectiveness of EU law are not thereby compromised'.[58] Therefore, one could argue

[53] Art 11(2)(a) OLAF Regulation (emphasis added).

[54] Vervaele, 'Lawful and Fair Use of Evidence' (n 25) 56, 94.

[55] For instance, some Member States provide for rules rendering evidence unlawfully gathered automatically inadmissible, while others lay down more flexible rules on the admissibility of evidence by which the nullity/exclusion of evidence depends on the impact of the violation upon the fairness of the procedure, or which prescribe that the unlawfulness of the evidence reduces the reliability of evidence. In this regard, see G Vermeulen, W De Bondt and Y Van Damme (eds), *EU Cross-Border Gathering and Use of Evidence in Criminal Matters. Towards Mutual Recognition of Investigative Measures and Free Movement of Evidence?* (Maklu 2010) 129–30.

[56] See more in section II.

[57] Vervaele, 'Lawful and Fair Use of Evidence' (n 25) 56, 92. In addition, Art 11(2) OLAF Regulation provides that the OLAF reports constitute admissible evidence when drawn up on the basis of the first subparagraph, that is, in accordance with the relevant provisions of EU law and of the *national law* of the Member State concerned.

[58] Case C-399/11 *Melloni* ECLI:EU:C:2013:107, para 60. See more in ch 2 of this volume (De Vries and Widdershoven) and in Luchtman, Karagianni and Bovend'Eerdt (n 18) 7, 14–16.

that higher standards in relation to procedural safeguards cannot apply, as these may in principle hinder the admissibility of OLAF-collected evidence in domestic punitive administrative proceedings, and in turn jeopardise the effectiveness of OLAF's activities in the fight against illegal activities affecting the Union's financial interests. However, it should be borne in mind that the *Melloni* case concerned a different legal framework, as the CJEU was asked to interpret a ground for non-execution of the European Arrest Warrant (EAW), that is, an instrument of mutual recognition regulated entirely by EU law.

In this context, it is worth recalling the reasoning of the Court of Justice in the so-called *Taricco II* judgment. The CJEU held that the national courts are allowed to apply national standards of protection of fundamental rights even if these compromise the principle of primacy, unity and effectiveness of EU law, in cases where their disapplication entails a breach of the principle of legality.[59] One of the main arguments on which the CJEU based its decision was the fact that the rules on the limitation period applicable to VAT fraud had not been harmonised by the EU legislature.[60] In light of the foregoing, one might wonder whether the provisions of the OLAF Regulation that have partially harmonised OLAF's investigatory powers and evidence admissibility rules could set higher national standards of protection of fundamental rights aside in administrative punitive proceedings.

It should be noted that this discussion may have overall limited practical consequences, as the safeguards provided for in the OLAF Regulation are 'generally *higher* than the guarantees established in national administrative proceedings, and more similar to the safeguards required under criminal procedural law'.[61] It is not surprising that, in the six Member States under analysis, no issues of inadmissibility of OLAF-collected evidence in punitive administrative proceedings flowing from the differences between EU and national standards have been raised before national courts.

Nevertheless, there may be cases where national administrative law provides for higher standards than EU law. Such a situation could arise, for instance, with regard to legal professional privilege (LPP). According to the case law of the Court of Justice, in-house lawyers are not covered by this privilege;[62] however, in some countries, such

[59] Case C-42/17 *MAS and MB* ECLI:EU:C:2017:936, para 62.

[60] ibid para 44.

[61] Caianiello and Lasagni (n 43) 170, 176 (emphasis added). See also Böse and Schneider (n 34) 132, 142, who note that the privilege against self-incrimination could perhaps be problematic in this context, since it enjoys absolute protection under German constitutional law as an expression of inviolable human dignity, so that when individuals are obliged to disclose self-incriminating information in tax or insolvency proceedings, this information cannot be used in criminal proceedings. Yet – they point out – as long as Art 9(2) OLAF Regulation recognises the right to avoid self-incrimination, in principle there should be no issues concerning the violation of the privilege at hand in OLAF interviews. It should also be noted that, further to the revision of the OLAF Regulation in 2020, the procedural safeguards of persons involved in OLAF investigations have been reinforced. Pursuant to Art 3(7) and (8) OLAF Regulation, the persons concerned by on-the-spot checks and inspections are now explicitly – and no longer through referring to other legal instruments – granted the right to be informed of the procedure applicable to such checks and inspections, including the applicable procedural safeguards, the right not to make self-incriminating statements and to be assisted by a person of their choice, and the right to use any of the official languages of the Member State where they are located when making statements. In addition, Art 10(3b) OLAF Regulation has recognised the (limited) right of access to the file of the persons concerned by OLAF investigations.

[62] See more in M Scholten and M Simonato, 'EU Report' in M Luchtman and JAE Vervaele (eds), *Investigatory Powers and Procedural Safeguards: Improving OLAF's Legislative Framework through a Comparison with Other*

as the Netherlands, all lawyers who are members of the Bar Association, including in-house lawyers, enjoy LPP. In the literature, it has been argued that OLAF-collected evidence could not be excluded if gathered with the different (and lower) EU standards, but would have to be excluded if it was obtained in a way that runs so excessively counter to what may be expected of an administrative authority that its use should be considered inadmissible in all circumstances (the so-called 'manifestly improper criterion').[63] However, this is a rather high threshold; hence, one might expect that Dutch courts would declare OLAF-collected evidence admissible, because the violation of LPP is not likely to qualify as a breach of the right to fair trial, nor to affect the essence of the right to privacy.[64]

In Germany, the LPP does not cover in-house lawyers, but it applies to other categories of professionals who are not taken into account by EU law, such as tax accountants. Nevertheless, Böse and Schneider note that it is unlikely that evidence collected by OLAF in violation of the accountants' LPP would lead to its inadmissibility, as previous national case law suggests that – in the balancing exercise that characterises the German system of evidence[65] – the interest in effective law enforcement would trump the safeguarding of the privilege at hand.[66]

One last question relates to whether and how – in punitive administrative proceedings – the person concerned by an OLAF investigation can challenge evidence that was allegedly obtained in violation of EU rules, including rules on procedural safeguards provided for in the OLAF Regulation. However, in this respect, national case law offers very limited, if any, input. As mentioned in section III.B, there is usually no judicial review of the admissibility decision as such in national punitive administrative proceedings, so violations of EU rules in OLAF's gathering of evidence could be brought to the attention of the competent courts when the interested party challenges the legality of the sanction issued at the end of punitive proceedings. Apart from that, challenging OLAF-collected evidence is even more complicated due to the CJEU case law pursuant to which national courts cannot invalidate acts and decisions of EU bodies, as is also discussed in chapter 3 of this volume by Ligeti and Robinson.

Nevertheless, in a recent case decided by the Court of Appeal of Paris, the interested parties challenged OLAF activities because they had allegedly been initiated in breach of the principle of confidentiality enshrined in Council Regulation 384/96.[67] This decision shows that, 'while some judges stress that they are not "judges of the European investigation", they agree to review "the nullity of OLAF's investigation" in the light of EU texts (in this case Regulation 1073/1999), since *OLAF's investigation is likely to lead to the irregularity of the French procedure*'.[68]

EU Law Enforcement Authorities (ECN/ESMA/ECB) (Utrecht University 2017) 9, 38 and 51. For further remarks on competition proceedings, see Luchtman, Karagianni and Bovend'Eerdt (n 18) 7, 28 ff.

[63] Duijkersloot, de Vries and Widdershoven (n 41) 197, 207.

[64] ibid.

[65] See more in section V.

[66] Böse and Schneider (n 34) 132, 140 ff.

[67] Council Regulation (EC) No 384/96 of 22 December 1995 on protection against dumped imports from countries not members of the European Community [1996] OJ L56/1.

[68] Tricot (n 33) 95, 115 (emphasis added).

The clarification that national judges are not judges of the European investigations follows from the status of OLAF as an EU entity, which thus implies that – unlike the EPPO – its acts and decisions are subject to the jurisdiction of the CJEU. Although OLAF and the EPPO share the common key feature of extensively relying on national law,[69] different rules apply to their acts. Article 42 of Regulation 2017/1939 bestows the competence to review EPPO procedural acts and decisions having legal effects vis-à-vis third parties upon *national* courts, with limited exceptions.[70] As we can read in the Preamble to the EPPO Regulation, the 'specific nature of the tasks and structure of the EPPO, which is different from that of all other bodies and agencies of the Union … requires special rules regarding judicial review'.[71] Providing that an EU office is subject to the judicial control of national courts is indeed quite exceptional in EU law.

The OLAF Regulation, on the other hand, includes no provision on the judicial review of OLAF-collected evidence. The ordinary EU principles thus apply, especially that according to which '*EU courts* alone have jurisdiction to determine that *an act of the European Union is invalid* … OLAF's report continues to be lawful in the EU legal order in so far as it has not been invalidated by the EU judicature'.[72] It is known, however, that the CJEU is reluctant to invalidate OLAF reports. According to established case law, as these reports do not bring about a distinct change in the individuals' legal position, requests to annul them are inadmissible.[73] Hence, in practice, OLAF reports cannot be subject to the CJEU's judicial review in accordance with Article 263 TFEU.[74] At the most, the EU shall make good any damage caused by OLAF misconduct.[75] As for national courts, since they cannot assess the legality of OLAF measures and declare them null and void, even if they violate EU law,[76] they can (or should) refer a request for a preliminary ruling, if they have doubt about the validity of OLAF reports,[77] or decide

[69] See Vervaele, 'Lawful and Fair Use of Evidence' (n 25) 56, 58.

[70] Council Regulation (EU) 2017/1939 of 12 October 2017 implementing enhanced cooperation on the establishment of the European Public Prosecutor's Office ('the EPPO') [2017] OJ L283/1 ('EPPO Regulation').

[71] Recital 86 EPPO Regulation.

[72] Case T-48/16 *Sigma Orionis SA v Commission* ECLI :EU:T:2018:245, paras 62–63 (emphasis added). This principle dates back to Case 314/85 *Foto-Frost v Hauptzollamt Lübeck-Ost* ECLI:EU:C:1987:452. See more in ch 3 of this volume (Ligeti and Robinson); K Ligeti and G Robinson, 'Transversal Report on Judicial Protection' in Luchtman and Vervaele (eds) (n 62) 219 ff; Luchtman, Karagianni and Bovend'Eerdt (n 18) 7, 22–23; Vervaele, 'Lawful and Fair Use of Evidence' (n 25) 56, 88–89.

[73] The leading case is Case T-193/04 *Tillack* ECLI:EU:T:2006:292. See more in, eg, X Groussot and Z Popov, 'What's Wrong with OLAF? Accountability, Due Process and Criminal Justice in European Anti-Fraud Policy' (2010) 47(3) *CML Rev* 605, 609–15; JFH Inghelram, *Legal and Institutional Aspects of the European Anti-Fraud Office (OLAF). An Analysis with a Look Forward to a European Public Prosecutor's Office* (Europa Law Publishing 2011) 203 ff; Ligeti and Robinson, 'Transversal Report' (n 71) 219, 238–39; Vervaele, 'Lawful and Fair Use of Evidence' (n 25) 56, 81, who highlights that the principle at stake has been upheld in, among others, Case T-289/16 *Inox Mare Srl v Commission* ECLI:EU:T:2017:414, para 20.

[74] See also the recent judgment of the CJEU in Case C-351/20 P *Dragnea v Commission* ECLI:EU:C:2022:8, where the Court of Justice makes a short reference to the issue of judicial review of OLAF reports yet refrains from elaborating on it ('the letter issue constitutes, in any event, a measure which merely confirms the final reports drawn up following those investigations, with the result that, *without it even being necessary to examine*, in the present case, *the question whether those reports constitute acts open to challenge for the purposes of Article 263 TFEU* … the appellant's action cannot, in the present case, in any event, be declared admissible': para 51 (emphasis added).

[75] Böse and Schneider (n 34) 132, 143–45.

[76] ibid.

[77] See more in Inghelram (n 73) 226–29; Ligeti and Robinson, 'Transversal Report' (n 72) 219, 242–43. For further critical remarks on whether the request lodged in accordance with Art 267 TFEU is likely to fulfil

not to use that piece of evidence altogether if it is considered unreliable or unlawful and national law so allows.

V. Admissibility and Use of OLAF-Collected Evidence in Criminal Proceedings

While the previous section focused on punitive administrative proceedings, the present section deals with criminal procedures, in which the admissibility of OLAF-collected evidence becomes crucial. After all, one of the reasons that justified the establishment of the EPPO was precisely the allegedly ineffective follow-up to OLAF investigations, which is due, among other causes, to issues connected with the admissibility of evidence gathered by this body. In accordance with the assimilation principle – and considering that none of the six Member States under analysis provides for special rules on admissibility of evidence collected by OLAF in criminal proceedings – the applicable rules on admissibility of evidence gathered by national administrative authorities in criminal proceedings apply also to evidence collected by OLAF.

In Germany, which builds on the principle of controlled proof (*numerus clausus* of types of evidence), information gathered by administrative authorities – and therefore evidence collected by OLAF as well – can be used as evidence in criminal proceedings, in accordance with the general admissibility rules.[78] Hence, objects may be subject to inspections and the official who carried out the investigative act can be examined as a witness, as the reading out of administrative documents cannot replace the hearing of witnesses. Likewise, if a report includes questioning of witnesses or suspects, or opinions of experts, it will be necessary to hear them again before the court. In addition, in cases of an alleged violation of procedural rules, OLAF-collected evidence would not be automatically excluded, as German admissibility rules in criminal proceedings are based on what could be called a 'balancing approach'.[79] Hence, the exclusion of evidence should follow an overall balancing exercise between the gravity of individual rights violations and the impact of admitting that evidence on the fairness of the proceedings, as well as on the public interest in enforcing criminal law.[80]

Furthermore, in Italy and in the Netherlands, whose law also provides for a system of controlled proof,[81] OLAF-collected evidence falls within the remit of the provisions

the requirements of admissibility, see V Covolo, *L'Émergence d'un Droit Pénal en Réseau. Analyse Critique du Système Européen de Lutte Antifraude* (Nomos 2015) 578–80.

[78] Böse and Schneider (n 34) 132, 150–52.

[79] Vervaele, 'Lawful and Fair Use of Evidence' (n 25) 56, 61.

[80] For instance, the failure to inform the defendant of the right to free legal assistance would not lead to the exclusion of evidence collected by interrogating him or her, if the defendant was properly informed of the right to consult with a defence counsel and has sufficient means to afford a defence lawyer. See more in Böse and Schneider (n 34) 132, 133.

[81] However, Art 189 of the Italian code of criminal procedure also allows for 'atypical' means, in so far as they contribute to proving the *thema probandum* and do not breach the moral freedom of subjects potentially involved. The provision mentioned is used, for instance, in case of online searches, which the Italian code of criminal procedure does not explicitly regulate. Hence, the Italian system can be defined as one of controlled proof with a rather broad opening clause. See more in Caianiello and Lasagni (n 43) 170, 174.

of the code of criminal procedure on documentary evidence.[82] Nevertheless, in Italy – as in Germany – it is also common to hear the administrative official who carried out the investigative measure as a witness in criminal trials. In addition, in Italy the admissibility of evidence also extends to digital documents and data stored abroad (if the owner gives his or her consent). Evidence is instead inadmissible when documents concern anonymous information or information about the morality of the parties to the proceedings.[83] It is currently debated whether documents containing administrative authorities' evaluations are admissible.

On the other hand, in countries that provide for a free proof system, such as France and Luxembourg, the admissibility of OLAF-collected evidence follows from the principle of freedom of proof and, as explained in section III, requires compliance with the rules on evidence set out in national criminal procedural laws. In Luxembourg, to be admitted at trial, evidence – and therefore also OLAF-collected evidence – should be 'loyally' obtained, useful and subject to the adversarial principle ('*contradictoire*').[84] Likewise in France, the principle of freedom of evidence is tempered by those of lawfulness and fairness. As stated in French literature, 'evidence may be obtained *beyond* legal provisions, but not *against* legal provisions'.[85] If the law is violated in the collection of evidence, such evidence – including evidence gathered by OLAF – is inadmissible (principle of lawfulness). In addition, even when the procedure of gathering evidence is lawful, the principle of fairness may still come into consideration and lead to the exclusion of evidence.[86]

French case law has also addressed an issue that is relevant for all Member States, namely, whether and to what extent national authorities can scrutinise OLAF acts. In particular, such scrutiny may focus on the differences in procedural safeguards between administrative (OLAF) proceedings and national criminal proceedings. Since the 1980s, the Court of Justice has ruled that national authorities cannot declare a Union act invalid.[87] In *Sigma Orionis*, the Court of Justice dealt with a case where a French court posited that some documents used by national authorities in French criminal proceedings, including OLAF reports, were invalid due to the fact that French judicial police

[82] See, respectively, Caianiello and Lasagni (n 43) 170, 179–81; and Duijkersloot, de Vries and Widdershoven (n 41) 197, 211–13.

[83] Caianiello and Lasagni (n 43) 170, 180.

[84] Ligeti and Giuffrida (n 45) 184, 191 and 194. See also Court of Cassation, 22 November 2007, No 2474, where the Luxembourgish Court of Cassation ruled that criminal courts cannot base a conviction on evidence that has been unlawfully obtained if: (i) respect for given formal requirements is imposed by law under penalty of nullity; (ii) the irregularity committed has tainted the credibility of evidence; or (iii) the use of evidence is contrary to the defendant's right to a fair trial. The wording of this judgment would imply that, in principle, evidence that has been unlawfully obtained could be admitted at trial even if none of these conditions were met. However, the Court of Cassation clarifies that the defendant's right to a fair trial can only be ensured if legality in the administration of evidence is respected. Hence, in practice, illegally or improperly obtained evidence cannot be used at trial.

[85] E Vergès, G Vial and O Leclerc, *Droit de la Preuve* (Presses Universitaires de France 2015) no 272 (translation by Juliette Tricot in Tricot (n 33) 98).

[86] See more in Tricot (n 33) 95, 97–100 and 124 ff.

[87] See also section IV. See more in Luchtman, Karagianni and Bovend'Eerdt (n 18) 7, 22–23.

did not assist OLAF investigators.[88] The Court of Justice was rather clear in restating its traditional stance:

> [T]he EU courts alone have jurisdiction to determine that an act of the European Union is invalid … Therefore, irrespective of the findings made by the Indictment Division in its judgment, OLAF's report *continues to be lawful in the EU legal order* in so far as it has not been invalidated by the EU judicature.[89]

The Court thus makes a distinction between the *validity* of the OLAF reports in the EU legal order and the *use* that national courts may make of them in national procedures:

> OLAF's report continues to be *lawful* in the EU legal order in so far as it has not been invalidated by the EU judicature, without prejudice to any decisions that might be taken by the national authorities or courts concerning the *use* that can be made of such a report in proceedings under national law. It follows from … Article 11(2) of Regulation No 883/2013, that reports drawn up by OLAF may be used in national proceedings to the extent that they were drawn up in accordance with the rules and procedures laid down by national law. If national law was infringed … the result is that it will not be possible to use the report drawn up by OLAF in national proceedings, but that does not affect the possibility for the Commission to base its decisions on that document.[90]

The French Court of Cassation seems to endorse this distinction as well. In a case decided in December 2015, the French Court noted that the lower court (Indictment Chamber of the Court of Appeal of Colmar) was wrong in declaring itself incompetent to decide on the regularity of OLAF investigative acts that were included ('*versé*') in French criminal proceedings, since those acts *can be annulled to ensure effective judicial review* if they have been carried out in violation of fundamental rights.[91] This approach has been adopted in other judgments of the Court of Cassation as well,[92] so one could say that in the French case law there is a clear distinction between the nullity of the OLAF-collected evidence as such – not a matter for criminal courts – and the nullity of the OLAF evidence when used in criminal proceedings. As Tricot notes, OLAF evidence, when the procedure that leads to its adoption violates French law,

> is obviously not annulled as such, but insofar as it constitutes an act of the (French) criminal procedure, which implies its exclusion from the file. It cannot be used as a basis for decisions by judges or national (investigative or prosecutorial) authorities. The annulment also has the effect of depriving all subsequent acts of any merit.[93]

The Paris Court of Appeal had also noted that, in carrying out interviews,

> OLAF investigators … complied with procedural guarantees and proceeded to notifications of rights, which are not contrary to the invoked provisions of the Convention [ie Articles 6, 8 and 13 ECHR], and are in conformity with the Community texts governing that body and compatible with the provisions of domestic criminal procedure.[94]

[88] Vervaele, 'Lawful and Fair Use of Evidence' (n 25) 56, 88–89.

[89] Case T-48/16 *Sigma Orionis SA v Commission* ECLI :EU :T :2018 :245, paras 62–63 (emphasis added).

[90] ibid paras 76–77 (emphasis added).

[91] Court of Cassation, Criminal Division, 9 December 2015, no 15-82300. See more in Tricot (n 33) 95, 129–30; and Vervaele, 'Lawful and Fair Use of Evidence' (n 25) 56, 86.

[92] Court of Cassation, Criminal Division, 16 January 2013, no 12-84.221; Court of Cassation, Criminal Division, 9 November 2016, no 16-83.602. See more in Giuffrida (n 52) 222, 259–60; and Tricot (n 33) 95, 129.

[93] Tricot (n 33) 95, 129–30.

[94] Court of Cassation, 9 December 2015 (n 90).

This conclusion may thus lead one to think that it is unlikely that issues of inadmissibility of OLAF-collected evidence can be related to the insufficient guarantees ensured by OLAF, as long as the Office's investigative activities comply with Article 9 of the OLAF Regulation.

In this respect, in Italy, according to the literature, if evidence collected by OLAF is documentary in nature, no issues concerning its admissibility arise. When a different kind of evidence is at stake, the lower safeguards surrounding its gathering may instead impair its admissibility in criminal proceedings. However, it should be pointed out that no problem has so far come to the fore as to the admissibility of OLAF-collected evidence, possibly because – as Caianiello and Lasagni note – the OLAF Regulation provides for very high procedural standards (especially with regard to the privilege against self-incrimination enshrined in Article 9(2) of the OLAF Regulation).[95] Likewise in Germany, there is no case law on the inadmissibility of OLAF-collected evidence in national criminal proceedings, yet evidence could in principle be excluded if it has been gathered in a way that is incompatible with the standards of German criminal procedural law (eg, protection of professional privacy or *nemo tenetur*).[96] Nonetheless, in a way confirming that OLAF standards are rather high and thus unlikely to lead to the inadmissibility of OLAF-collected evidence because of differences with criminal law standards, Böse and Schneider have noted that 'national standards will only be relevant where EU law does not provide for a corresponding protection, [eg] by a right to remain silent and to consult with counsel (Article 9(2)(2) and (6) of Regulation No 883/2013)'.[97]

The admissibility of evidence collected by OLAF has not so far been denied by Dutch criminal courts either. In a case decided in 2013, a Dutch criminal court of first instance stated that OLAF-collected evidence should be set aside only in exceptional circumstances.[98] In that case, the Fiscal Intelligence and Investigation Service (FIOD), the specialised judicial tax enforcement authority, used reports of an OLAF inspection mission as evidence, which the legal person accused challenged because, among other things, it was not informed of their existence. However:

> The Dutch Court of First Instance emphasised that the Dutch Public Prosecutor's office is '*dominus litis*' and that the sanction of the inadmissibility of the prosecution under Dutch criminal procedure can only be used in the case of *very serious infringements* of the essence of the procedure or other fundamental rights which result in the right of the accused to a fair trial being violated, either intentionally or as a result of serious negligence. This was not the case as far as the court was concerned.[99]

It follows, therefore, that the differences in procedural safeguards between OLAF proceedings and national criminal proceedings could lead to the exclusion of OLAF-collected evidence only where the breach of national safeguards is of such a nature that it makes the procedure as a whole unfair. Nevertheless, for instance in case of LPP, where Dutch law does provide for higher standards of protection than EU law as explained in

[95] Caianiello and Lasagni (n 43) 170, 181.
[96] Böse and Schneider (n 34) 132, 153.
[97] ibid.
[98] Court of Noord-Holland (*Rechtbank Noord-Holland*), 23 July 2013, case no 15/993018-06. See more in Vervaele, 'Lawful and Fair Use of Evidence' (n 25) 56, 90.
[99] Vervaele, 'Lawful and Fair Use of Evidence' (n 25) 56, 90 (emphasis added).

section IV, it is unlikely that Dutch criminal courts would exclude evidence coming from a country where the LPP principle is less protected than in the Netherlands, as this breach would not meet the manifestly improper criterion.[100]

To summarise, it is clear that the above-mentioned legal systems accept that evidence gathered by national administrative authorities – and therefore OLAF-collected evidence – is admissible in criminal proceedings. On the other hand, it is worth noting that Hungary is the only country among those under analysis where information lawfully gathered in administrative proceedings, albeit being admissible as documentary evidence in criminal proceedings, has *de iure* a weaker probative value than evidence collected in accordance with criminal law rules.[101] Thus, usually, investigative measures of both national administrative authorities and OLAF will be repeated (eg witnesses will be heard again) and the administrative official who carried out the investigative act can be examined as a witness.[102] There seems to be an established practice of repeating OLAF activities in Hungary, which is arguably a problem flowing from the assimilation principle, as acts carried out by national criminal law authorities have higher probative value than evidence collected by other (non-criminal) authorities; and this applies to both EU and national administrative authorities.[103]

Unlike Hungary, in the rest of the countries under analysis, even if some duplications take place,[104] these are not required by law. They are rather due either to the inadequate knowledge of the probative value of OLAF-collected evidence,[105] or to the different aims and natures of OLAF investigations and criminal investigations. OLAF's ultimate aim is to ensure the Union's financial interests are adequately protected, while the national competent authority's aim is to establish the criminal liability of an individual.[106] Therefore, criminal courts and public prosecutors can be interested in delving further into elements and circumstances that OLAF could have neglected, and vice versa; national authorities, for instance, may be interested in asking witnesses

[100] Duijkersloot, de Vries and Widdershoven (n 41) 197, 213. See section IV.

[101] A Csúri, 'Hungary' in Giuffrida and Ligeti (eds) (n 18) 157, 167–68.

[102] ibid.

[103] In addition, some Hungarian criminal law rules make the admissibility of OLAF-collected evidence more difficult than in other countries. When it comes to the authenticity of documents, for instance, handwriting experts can only work with original documents, while OLAF usually provides copies of the documents received from the persons under investigation. See more in Csúri (n 101) 157, 168–69. In this respect, Covolo notes that if national law – such as the Hungarian one – requires the originals for the purpose of national procedures while OLAF can only provide copies of documents, this may further impair the admissibility of OLAF-collected evidence and require national authorities to repeat OLAF activities (Covolo (n 77) 311).

[104] See, for instance, Caianiello and Lasagni (n 43) 170, 183, who note that Italy has witnessed such duplications. In Germany, even though the OLAF investigative act (inspection, on-the-spot check, etc) is not repeated as such, its findings are presented in a different manner, as the OLAF report's author is usually called as a witness before the court. However, this is due to the general principle applying in Germany that the reading out of administrative documents cannot replace the hearing of witnesses and would not qualify as a 'repetition' as such.

[105] This is certainly a 'pathological' duplication, which can arguably be repaired only by increasing national authorities' awareness of EU instruments and bodies (eg, by means of more training at the national level). In a somewhat similar vein, OLAF noted that '[t]here are also cases where dismissals appear to be motivated by limited knowledge of the rules governing EU funding' (in OLAF, 'Analysis on Member States Follow-Up to OLAF's Judicial Recommendations' (n 19), para 100).

[106] ICF, Evaluation of the Application of Regulation No 883/2013 Concerning Investigations Conducted by the European Anti-Fraud Office (OLAF) (Publications Office 2017) 126.

or suspects questions different from those that OLAF posed during its investigations. However, in such a case, duplications are physiological and seem to be unavoidable, as long as OLAF remains an administrative authority carrying out activities with effects that touch upon (or even end up in) criminal proceedings.[107]

VI. The EPPO-OLAF Relationship and its Implication for the Admissibility of Evidence

The principle guiding the EPPO-OLAF relationship is that OLAF should not conduct investigations when the EPPO is already dealing with the same facts.[108] Under Article 101(3)(c) of the EPPO Regulation, however, the EPPO may '*request* OLAF, in accordance with OLAF's mandate, to *support* or *complement* the EPPO's activity'[109] by, among other actions, 'conducting administrative investigations'.[110] Bearing in mind that they may be requested 'in the course of an investigation by the EPPO',[111] it is not entirely clear what would be the nature of these OLAF investigations, especially those 'in support' of EPPO investigations.[112] Both Article 101(3) of the EPPO Regulation and Article 12(e) of the OLAF Regulation point out that the requested action by the EPPO should be *within the mandate* of OLAF; hence, it should be related only to administrative investigations or the other tasks conferred upon OLAF by the OLAF regulatory framework.[113] The EPPO cannot delegate to OLAF tasks that go beyond its mandate and can be carried out only by national law enforcement authorities.

Even so, the relation between the OLAF investigations and the EPPO's investigation that they support is still unclear. As Weyembergh and Brière note, the Regulation 'entertains some sort of "constructive ambiguity" around the notion of OLAF's supporting and complementing the work of the EPPO'.[114] It might even be argued that the way the above-mentioned provision is couched seems to imply that OLAF may become – at least

[107] See Caianiello and Lasagni (n 43) 170, 183, who note that, in Italy, when OLAF has interviewed a person who then becomes subject to criminal investigations, Italian criminal law authorities examine him or her again; while when it comes to witnesses, public prosecutors decide on a case-by-case basis whether there is a need to replicate the interview.

[108] Recital 103 and Art 101(2) EPPO Regulation. See also Art 12(d) OLAF Regulation ('non-duplication of investigations').

[109] Art 101(3) of the EPPO Regulation (emphasis added). See also Art 12(e) OLAF Regulation, which regulates in more detail the OLAF's investigations in support of the EPPO.

[110] Art 101(3)(c) EPPO Regulation.

[111] Art 101(3) EPPO Regulation.

[112] The working arrangement concluded between the EPPO and OLAF in July 2021 has shed light on the nature of the support provided by OLAF to the EPPO in the course of its investigation by providing for a list of cases where OLAF may support the EPPO by means of operational, forensic and analytical expertise and tools (para 6.1.1). Nevertheless, this is only a non-exhaustive list, and therefore the EPPO is entitled to request OLAF to perform any other act in accordance with its mandate. In this regard, see N Kolloczek and J Echanove Gonzalez de Anleo, 'The European Anti-Fraud Office and the European Public Prosecutor's Office' *eucrim* 3/2021, 187, 189.

[113] D Brodowski, 'Article 101 – Relations with OLAF' in H-H Herrnfeld, D Brodowski and C Burchard, *European Public Prosecutor's Office. Article-by-Article Commentary* (Hart Publishing 2020) 596, 606.

[114] A Weyembergh and C Brière, 'The Future Cooperation Between OLAF and the European Public Prosecutor's Office', *Study for the CONT Committee of the European Parliament* (December 2017) 20.

on an *ad hoc* basis and for the Member States participating in the EPPO – a sort of *police judiciaire* of the EPPO,[115] although the negotiators had clearly ruled out such transformation of OLAF's role. The working arrangement concluded between the EPPO and OLAF does not endorse this possible role of OLAF as the EPPO's *police judiciaire* either. Paragraph 6.1.4 of the arrangement (concerning OLAF's support of the EPPO) provides that 'OLAF will *decide* promptly on the EPPO's *requests* under this point [ie requests for support], taking into account the complexity of the support activity requested, the timeline envisaged for its completion and the availability of resources'.[116] Therefore, the requests addressed to OLAF are not binding orders but instead leave OLAF room for manoeuvre, allowing it not to execute the EPPO's request in the circumstances mentioned therein.[117]

At any rate, the European Parliament noted that the risk looming in this unclear scenario is that the EPPO may delegate tasks to OLAF with the 'aim of circumventing'[118] the applicable framework on criminal investigations – including cross-border investigations and the specific rules laid down in Articles 31 and 32 of the EPPO Regulation – and on the involvement of national authorities, as well as the procedural safeguards applicable to criminal proceedings.[119] As explained above, the safeguards provided for by the OLAF Regulation are high but not entirely aligned with the more protective safeguards to be found in national criminal legislation (or even in national constitutions). In other words, it has been argued that the EPPO may be tempted to 'outsource' some of its investigative activities to OLAF, which will conduct administrative investigations – with lower safeguards – to gather evidence that the EPPO itself can use at a later stage. It is thus to be welcomed that Article 12(e)(3) of the OLAF Regulation clarifies that the EPPO and OLAF should ensure that the applicable procedural safeguards of Chapter VI of the EPPO Regulation are observed, where OLAF performs *supporting* measures at the request of the EPPO.[120]

Apart from the investigations in *support* of the EPPO's activities, the OLAF Regulation sets out in Article 12f one further exception from the principle of non-duplication of investigations, which has not been included in the text of the EPPO Regulation. Article 12f of the OLAF Regulation confers on OLAF the power to initiate *on its own initiative*[121] complementary administrative investigations in parallel to an

[115] Thanks to its expertise, OLAF could, for instance, be in an ideal position to offer its support to the EPPO in cross-border cases, in cases involving third countries or EU officials.

[116] Working Arrangement between the European Anti-Fraud Office ('OLAF') and the European Public Prosecutor's Office ('EPPO'), concluded on 5 July 2021. This arrangement lays down, among other things, the details about the modalities by which the EPPO and OLAF will exchange information, report and transfer cases, and support each other in their respective investigations. See more in Kolloczek and Echanove Gonzalez de Anleo (n 112) 187, 188.

[117] As Weyembergh and Brière note, a more systemic reading of the EPPO Regulation seems to exclude any possible role for OLAF as the EPPO's *police judiciaire*, as the Regulation endorses an approach according to which 'the EPPO's main support would come from the national authorities; and the relation between the EPPO and OLAF is envisaged as a relation between two autonomous bodies. In this context, OLAF is still supporting the EPPO's work, but in a more "subsidiary manner", and OLAF keeps its own margin of manoeuvre' (Weyembergh and Brière (n 114) 21).

[118] European Parliament, 'Legislative resolution of 16 April 2019' (n 22), amendment 110.

[119] See also Brodowski (n 113) 596, 606.

[120] Art 12(e)(3) OLAF Regulation.

[121] Unlike Art 101(3) EPPO Regulation and Art 12(e) OLAF Regulation, which both regulate the possibility for OLAF to complement the EPPO's activity *at the request of the EPPO*.

ongoing criminal investigation by the EPPO, with a view to facilitating the adoption of precautionary measures or of financial, disciplinary or administrative action.[122] One might question the compatibility of such a provision with Article 101(2) of the EPPO Regulation, which expressly prevents OLAF from initiating any parallel administrative investigation.[123] However, Recital 103 of the EPPO Regulation provides:

> [O]LAF should in principle not open any administrative investigations parallel to an investigation conducted by the EPPO into the same facts. This should, however, be *without prejudice* to the power of OLAF to start an administrative investigation *on its own initiative*, in close consultation with the EPPO.[124]

When OLAF decides to carry out a parallel administrative investigation for the purposes mentioned in Article 12(f) of the OLAF Regulation, it should always coordinate its actions with the EPPO.[125] Otherwise, parallel investigations would risk undermining the *ne bis in idem* principle in cases where an OLAF external investigation leads to the initiation of national punitive proceedings that end up imposing a sanction of a criminal nature on the person under an investigation conducted by the EPPO.[126]

A further connected issue concerns the status of the evidence gathered by OLAF while conducting administrative investigations at the request of EPPO, or complementary investigations on its own initiative. OLAF- and EPPO-collected evidence have different statuses.

When cases have a *purely national dimension*, EPPO-collected evidence will be admitted in national proceedings pursuant to the 'ordinary' rules of criminal procedure, that is, the same rules that apply to national non-PIF criminal investigations.[127] After all, the European Delegated Prosecutors – who will form the linchpin of EPPO investigations – are national prosecutors carrying out their activities on the basis (mostly) of national law, under the direction of the EPPO's Central Office (Permanent Chamber and supervising European Prosecutor). With regard to OLAF, the rule on the admissibility of the evidence collected by it is mostly thought to apply in national cases. In accordance with the text of Article 11(2) of the OLAF Regulation, OLAF conducts administrative investigations in a given Member State, taking into account to some extent its national law, and the evidence gathered through this investigation should be considered equivalent to that collected by comparable national administrative authorities.

[122] Brodowski (n 113) 596, 605.

[123] ibid.

[124] Recital 103 of the EPPO Regulation (emphasis added).

[125] Paragraph 6.2.7. of the EPPO-OLAF working arrangement provides that OLAF and the EPPO should coordinate and consult regularly during the course of the complementary investigations conducted by OLAF. Furthermore, para 6.2.1. of the same arrangement provides for a non-exhaustive list of cases where OLAF may conduct complementary investigations either on its own initiative or at the request of the EPPO.

[126] Brodowski (n 113) 596, 605. The recent case law of the CJEU clarifies under what conditions a combination of administrative and criminal proceedings can constitute a justified limitation of the right to *ne bis in idem* under Art 50 of the Charter. According to that case law, a duplication of criminal proceedings and penalties may be justified where those proceedings and penalties pursue complementary aims relating to different aspects of the same unlawful conduct. There must be also clear rules allowing individuals to predict such a duplication, and rules ensuring coordination that limits the disadvantage resulting from such duplications and the overall punishment to what is strictly necessary (Case C-524/15 *Menci* ECLI:EU:C:2018:197, paras 44 et seq; Case C-537/16 *Garlsson Real Estate SA, et al* ECLI:EU:C:2018:193, paras 46 et seq).

[127] In the EPPO Regulation, there is no rule on the admissibility of evidence collected by the EPPO in cases that do not involve a cross-border element. Therefore, in accordance with Art5(3) EPPO Regulation ('National

When the case has a *cross-border dimension*, the EPPO Regulation lays down a rule of, so to speak, 'non-inadmissibility',[128] in so far as it merely provides that evidence collected abroad *cannot* be denied admission only because of its foreign origin.[129] As for OLAF, it is not entirely clear whether Article 11(2) of the OLAF Regulation also applies when OLAF-collected evidence is to be used in Member States other than the one(s) where OLAF conducted its investigations. If OLAF carries out its activities in Member State A, taking into account the legislation of this country, it is unclear whether the assimilation principle also applies when authorities from Member State B wish to rely on that piece of OLAF-collected evidence. Article 11(2)(b) of the OLAF Regulation provides that OLAF reports 'shall constitute admissible evidence … in criminal proceedings of the Member State *in which their use proves necessary*',[130] which could therefore be a Member State different from the one where OLAF conducted its investigations.

In the light of the above, it remains to be seen to which of the two sets of rules OLAF-collected evidence will be subjected in cases when OLAF conducts investigations at the request of EPPO.[131] One might think that evidence gathered by OLAF could not be considered, or be equated to, EPPO-collected evidence. The EPPO can require OLAF to support or complement ongoing investigations by conducting *administrative* investigations 'in accordance with OLAF's mandate',[132] but cannot 'delegate' to OLAF tasks that should be carried out (usually by national police) in accordance with the code of criminal procedure. Should this be deemed possible instead, OLAF-collected evidence would be eventually subject to the rules on EPPO-collected evidence; hence, respect for criminal procedural safeguards by OLAF would be all the more necessary in order to ensure its admissibility. Although respect for the procedural safeguards of the EPPO Regulation by OLAF when performing *supporting* measures requested by the EPPO is to be welcomed, such a rule cannot ensure by itself the admissibility of evidence gathered by OLAF, as national safeguards in the field of criminal law may be higher than those laid down in the EPPO Regulation. And since the EPPO Regulation seems to allow the trial court to consider the national standards of protection of procedural safeguards when assessing the admissibility of evidence,[133] the risk of denial of admission of OLAF-collected evidence is evident.

law shall apply to the extent that a matter is not regulated by this Regulation …'), the ordinary rules of national criminal procedure apply.

[128] See also S Allegrezza and A Mosna, 'Cross-Border Criminal Evidence and the Future European Public Prosecutor. One Step Back on Mutual Recognition' in L Bachmaier Winter (ed), *The European Public Prosecutor's Office. The Challenges Ahead* (Springer 2018) 141, 159, who note that Art 37 EPPO Regulation introduced a simple *non-discrimination clause*.

[129] Art 37 EPPO Regulation.

[130] Art 11(2)(b) OLAF Regulation (emphasis added).

[131] See also Vervaele, 'Lawful and Fair Use of Evidence' (n 25) 56, 82, who underlines that 'it is unclear whether OLAF evidence … will have the same status as evidence gathered by the delegated EPPO prosecutor, as OLAF is not a judicial but an administrative authority'.

[132] Art 101(3) EPPO Regulation and Art12(e) OLAF Regulation.

[133] See Recital 80 of the EPPO Regulation, which reads as follows (emphasis added): '… This Regulation respects the fundamental rights and observes the *principles* recognised by Article 6 TEU and in the Charter, in particular Title VI thereof, by international law and by international agreements to which the Union or all the Member States are party, including the European Convention for the Protection of Human Rights and Fundamental Freedoms, and *by Member States' constitutions* in their respective fields of application. In line with those principles, and in respecting the different legal systems and traditions of the Member States as provided for in Article 67(1) TFEU, *nothing in this Regulation may be interpreted as prohibiting the courts*

Less ambiguous is the case of the admissibility of evidence gathered in the course of OLAF's *complementary* investigations launched on its own initiative.[134] In so far as OLAF's complementary investigations will be conducted in parallel to an ongoing EPPO's investigation and will pursue different aims from the latter, the evidence gathered in the course of such an investigation should arguably be subject to OLAF admissibility rules. Article 12(e)(3) of the OLAF Regulation, which does not make the measures carried out by OLAF in the course of a complementary investigation subject to the procedural safeguards of Chapter VI of the EPPO Regulation – unlike the investigations carried out by OLAF in *support* of EPPO's activities – endorses this approach, that is, that evidence collected in the course of complementary investigations should constitute OLAF-collected evidence and be subject to the rules thereof.

VII. Conclusion

By ensuring the *de iure* admissibility of OLAF-collected evidence in punitive administrative proceedings, the revised version of Article 11(2)(a) of the OLAF Regulation certainly constitutes a step forward in the architecture of EU law and in the legal framework of OLAF. This provision manages to create, to some extent, a level playing field among Member States, leaving behind the fragmentation created by the assimilation rule. Nevertheless, as explained in section IV, its added value remains limited, as the Regulation has not harmonised the rules on evidence gathering or those on the use of unlawful evidence, nor it has touched upon the power of national authorities to freely assess this evidence, thus allowing Member States to apply their own procedural rules. Therefore, divergences in the follow-up actions to OLAF investigations will continue to arise among Member States.

Regulation 2020/2223 has not changed anything vis-à-vis criminal proceedings. The use of OLAF-collected evidence in such proceedings is still governed by the assimilation principle. Despite the differences in the admissibility rules across the Member States, OLAF-collected evidence is in principle admissible in criminal proceedings in each of the Member States under analysis. Furthermore, in all those Member States – except for Hungary – duplications of OLAF activities sometimes occur, but they are mostly due to the different aims and applicable safeguards between OLAF and criminal investigations rather than being required by law. National authorities, for instance, may be interested in asking witnesses or suspects different questions than those asked by OLAF during its investigations. Risks of such 'physiological' duplications are inherently related to the

from applying the fundamental principles of national law on fairness of the procedure that they apply in their national systems, including in common law systems.' In this respect, see also T Wahl, 'The European Public Prosecutor's Office and the Fragmentation of Defence Rights' in K Ligeti, MJ Antunes and F Giuffrida (eds), *The European Public Prosecutor's Office at Launch. Adapting National Systems, Transforming EU Criminal Law* (Wolters Kluwer – CEDAM 2020) 85, 93–94.

[134] In accordance with para 6.2.8 of the working arrangement between OLAF and the EPPO, 'once OLAF has concluded the complementary investigation, it will *forward to the EPPO* its final report … as well as any additional information or evidence collected in the course of the complementary investigation' (emphasis added).

nature of OLAF as an administrative authority carrying out activities with effects that extend to criminal proceedings.

In order to enhance the admissibility of OLAF-collected evidence in national punitive proceedings, one solution could arguably be to strengthen the safeguards and guarantees for individuals concerned by OLAF investigations. As illustrated in the previous sections, the procedural safeguards provided for in the OLAF Regulation are overall rather robust – and Regulation 2020/2223 has further strengthened them – when compared with the usual safeguards for administrative investigations in the Member States, yet there are still some shortcomings from a criminal law perspective.[135] Some harmonisation of the procedural safeguards of persons involved in criminal proceedings is already provided for by EU law, yet these safeguards do not apply to OLAF investigations, as the latter do not qualify as criminal investigations. Therefore, the European legislator could extend the application of the Directives at hand to OLAF investigations or/and introduce a general ground for refusal of OLAF-collected evidence when such evidence has been gathered in a way that would undermine the obligation to respect the safeguards laid down in those Directives. In spite of the obvious added value such a solution might have, one could argue that this is not itself sufficient to enhance the admissibility of OLAF-collected evidence – notably in cross-border cases – and to ensure consistency throughout the EU, as these Directives set out only the minimum protection that should be granted to persons involved in criminal proceedings.

Furthermore, such an approach has often been met with some resistance by practitioners at the national and EU levels, who consider subjecting OLAF investigations to criminal law standards disproportionate, since the Office does not have criminal law powers. Against this backdrop, the establishment of the EPPO, which is competent to carry out *criminal* investigations for offences affecting the Union's financial interests, may contribute to limiting the problems arising from the interference between administrative – OLAF – investigations and national criminal investigations, and in particular from the transfer and use of OLAF-collected evidence in national criminal proceedings, as OLAF should no longer conduct investigations when the EPPO is already dealing with the same facts.

Nevertheless, considering the competence of OLAF to support or complement the EPPO's activities by conducting administrative investigations, OLAF still plays an important role in the fight against offences affecting the Union's financial interests. On the one hand, OLAF is independent from the EPPO and it should conduct *administrative* investigations in accordance with its mandate. On the other hand, however, Article 101(3)(c) of the EPPO Regulation seems to hint at a situation where the EPPO

[135] For instance, even though Regulation 2020/2223 has recognised the right of access to the file, its scope is rather limited, as it seems to grant the person concerned by the OLAF investigations only the right to *request* access to the OLAF report. Besides, the reference to 'report' instead of 'any relevant documents' – as initially suggested by the European Parliament – raises some doubts about whether the right of access covers, apart from the report itself, all evidence accompanying an OLAF report ('the person concerned may request the Office to provide the *report* drawn up under Article 11 to the extent that it relates to the person concerned' (emphasis added)). Furthermore, as Ligeti argues, several aspects of the rights listed in Art 9 OLAF Regulation should be further detailed, such as the threshold to invoke the privilege against self-incrimination, the minimum information to be provided to the interviewee and the regime for carrying out digital forensic operations (Ligeti (n 20) 7).

could somehow end up delegating to OLAF investigative activities aimed at collecting evidence that the EPPO intends to use in national proceedings. If this is the right understanding of the provision at hand, the full respect of criminal law rules and guarantees by OLAF would be imperative. This would however require, in the long run, further thought regarding OLAF's future nature and identity, which would arguably exceed the purely administrative law domain.

PART III

Capita Selecta: Topical Issues of EU Enforcement Authorities and their Relations with the National Legal Orders

7

Where *Engel* Fears to Tread?

Applicable Law, Choice of Forum and Ne Bis in Idem *in a Composite Administrative Punitive Legal Order*

GAVIN ROBINSON

I. Introduction

A half-century up, and still not out. It is now almost 50 years since the adoption of the *Engel* criteria by the European Court of Human Rights (ECtHR),[1] and the relevance of the autonomous notion of 'criminal charge' those criteria together compose shows no sign of abating. Viewed in the light of the rapid growth of the composite administrative punitive (read: *Engel*-criminal) legal order studied in this volume, they may never have found such a broad potential scope of application.

By its very nature, composite administrative punitive enforcement involves choices: the choice of when, where and how an inquiry is opened, investigative powers are used, proceedings are brought (or transferred, split, shared or dropped) and sanctions are applied. This discretion is regularly exercised, in fields such as those studied in this volume, by competent authorities at European Union (EU) and national level with greater or lesser degrees of consultation, cohesion and collegiality. Composite administrative punitive enforcement in the EU also inherently takes place within the scope of EU law, engaging the protections set out in the Charter of Fundamental Rights of the European Union,[2] which include the legality principle enshrined in Article 49, in both its procedural and substantive dimensions.[3] Closely connected to the principle of the equality of arms, in the criminal law register procedural legality exists in order to

[1] *Engel and Others v The Netherlands* App Nos 5100/71; 5101/71; 5102/71; 5354/72; 5370/72 (ECtHR, 8 June 1976); adopted by the CJEU in Case C-489/10, *Bonda* ECLI:EU:C:2012:319, para 37.

[2] Charter of Fundamental Rights of the European Union [2012] OJ C326/391 ('the Charter'), Art 51(1).

[3] In the criminal law context, see M Panzavolta, 'Choice of Forum and the Lawful Judge Concept' in M Luchtman (ed), *Choice of Forum in Cooperation Against EU Financial Crime* (Eleven International Publishing 2013) 143.

protect the defendant against any abuse of public authority, in order to guarantee the fairness of the procedure with which the accused is confronted.

Departing from the premise that '[t]here appears to be no good reason not to apply this maxim also in punitive (administrative) procedures that have not yet reached the stage of judicial review',[4] this chapter aims to discern the potential risks to procedural legality generated by the largely discretionary nature of decisions relating to case allocation, forum choice and the applicable law in the EU composite administrative punitive legal order.

To that end, section II explores those rules that are in place at EU level on case allocation, forum choice and applicable law in three areas of EU composite enforcement (competition law, banking law,[5] and the protection of the financial interests of the Union or 'PIF' law).[6] A general paucity of (hard) rules often goes hand-in-hand with high levels of discretion for authorities, combined with varying degrees of vertical and horizontal integration and cooperation. Especially in light of the persistent discrepancies between national laws, is there a risk of forum shopping by enforcers in these fields, how significant is that risk and where does it leave the targeted (natural or legal) person?

The existence of a suite of options open for enforcement in a composite legal order furthermore necessarily raises the prospect of a multiplication of sanctions or proceedings in relation to the same (natural or legal) person. Where multiple instances of enforcement respond to the same unlawful conduct, a related risk may arise – that of violations of the *ne bis in idem* (or double jeopardy) principle enshrined in Article 50 of the Charter. Until recently, the guidance of the Court of Justice of the European Union (CJEU) on the contours of proportionate limitations of that right through reasonably foreseeable, coordinated and non-excessive 'duplication' of proceedings and penalties has focused on the national setting, in particular the interplay between administrative and criminal law. However, the latest case law may have changed this picture – with potentially far-reaching ramifications for composite administrative punitive enforcement. The significance of that case law is discussed in section III, before some closing remarks in section IV.

II. Rules and Reality: Case Allocation, Forum Choice and Applicable Law in Three Areas of Composite Enforcement

A. Competition Law

i. The Legal Framework: Decentralisation and Discretion

Regulation 1/2003 sets out in detail the enforcement powers of the Commission,[7] which co-exist with those of the national competition authorities. In terms of applicable

[4] See ch 10 of this volume (Luchtman), section III.A.

[5] The European Securities and Markets Authority (ESMA) is not included in the chapter.

[6] *Protection des intérêts financiers de l'Union* ('PIF').

[7] Council Regulation 1/2003 on the implementation of the rules on competition laid down in Articles 81 and 82 of the Treaty [2003] OJ L1/1 ('Regulation 1/2003'), Art 4.

law, the situation regarding the Commission is cut-and-dried: the Regulation applies to the Directorate-General for Competition (DG Competition). As concerns the national competition authorities, according to Article 3(1) of the Regulation, where they (or national courts) apply national competition law to agreements, decisions by associations of undertakings or concerted practices that may affect trade between Member States, or to any abuse of a dominant position, they shall also apply the corresponding Treaty provisions: respectively Article 101 of the Treaty on the Functioning of the European Union (TFEU) (formerly Article 81 TEC) and Article 102 TFEU (formerly Article 82 TEC).

The decentralised architecture of EU competition law enshrined in the Regulation is thus founded on a system of parallel competences or 'concurrent jurisdiction'.[8] Indeed, nothing in the instrument precludes all 27 national competition authorities as well as the Commission having competence in relation to the same prohibited conduct – so long as it qualifies under Article 101 or Article 102 TFEU – wherever that conduct took place, wherever the parties are located and wherever the anticompetitive impact obtains.[9] Although national law greatly limits this possibility through the effects doctrine (most systems circumscribe local national competition authority competence to only cover conduct affecting competition in the domestic territory), as Brammer has noted, even the effects doctrine will not reduce the number of competent authorities to one in the context of Regulation 1/2003 – which, after all, only targets anticompetitive conduct that may affect trade between Member States.[10]

In very many cases, therefore, the Commission as well as multiple national competition authorities are in a position to claim competence to enforce under Regulation 1/2003, raising the twin issues of vertical (COM-national competition authority) and horizontal (national competition authority-national competition authority) division of labour.

In the vertical setting, the Regulation clearly gives the Commission enforcement priority: most notably, Article 11(6) provides that the initiation by the Commission of proceedings for the adoption of a decision shall relieve the national competition authorities of their competence – subject to prior consultation of national competition authorities that are already acting on a case.[11] To this end, Article 11(3) binds national competition authorities to inform the Commission in writing before or without delay after commencing the first formal investigative measure in their own cases.[12] Yet unlike, for instance, the Single Supervisory Mechanism (SSM) ('significant supervised entities')

[8] S Brammer, 'Concurrent jurisdiction under Regulation 1/2003 and the issue of case allocation' (2005) 42 *CML Rev* 1383.

[9] J Basedow, 'Who Will Protect Competition in Europe? From central enforcement to authority networks and private litigation' (2001) 2 *European Business Organization Law Review* 443, 449 et seq.

[10] Brammer (n 8), 1385–86. In his recent Opinion in *Nordzucker*, AG Bobek reflected at length on the contested degree of extraterritoriality that may be implied by the condition 'may affect trade between Member States' in Regulation 1/2003. The original Commission proposal, Mr Bobek noted, provided that in the event of effect on trade between Member States 'Community competition law shall apply to the exclusion of national competition laws'. *Nordzucker* and *bpost*, two cases decided on the same day, are discussed in sections III.A et seq.

[11] *A contrario*, the Commission may also decide to reject a complaint on the ground that an national competition authority is dealing with the case; Art 13(1) Regulation 1/2003.

[12] Fellow national competition authorities may be thus alerted, but this is not mandatory; Art 11(3) Regulation 1/2003.

and in keeping with the fact that DG Competition operates in an 'open environment' – unlike the European Central Bank (ECB), which both supervises and enforces[13] – the Regulation defines no exclusive EU competence for any kind of (particularly significant) cases of restriction of competition in the internal market.[14] The vertical division of labour is thus intentionally left open by Regulation 1/2003.

Nor does the Regulation contain any provision tackling the question of which national competition authority is to enforce in the horizontal setting. It limits itself rather to rules of cooperation: Article 12 governs exchange of information (both horizontally and vertically, with the Commission), whilst Article 13(1) provides that where national competition authorities of two or more Member States have received a complaint or are acting on their own initiative against the same anticompetitive conduct, the fact that one national competition authority is dealing with the case shall be sufficient grounds for the others to suspend the proceedings before them or to reject the complaint. The objective, as signalled in Recital 18, is that cases are dealt with by a single authority, which is the 'most appropriate'. As also recalled by Recital 18, however, this is an optional ground.

Another Recital of the Regulation (Recital 15) provides that the Commission and the national competition authorities 'should form together a network of public authorities applying the Community competition rules in close cooperation' – the European Competition Network (ECN),[15] a forum for discussion and cooperation in the application and enforcement of EU competition policy, which is now approaching its third decade of operations.

ii. Justiciability and the ECN

Guidelines for the division of enforcement work amongst the Commission and the national competition authorities were set out in 2004, in a Commission Notice on cooperation within the Network of Competition Authorities, (the 'Network Notice').[16] According to the Network Notice, the authority that receives a complaint or starts an *ex officio* procedure (intended to mean investigations and/or formal proceedings) will in most cases remain in charge of the case.[17] This is reflected in the fact that the term 're-allocation' appears just as often as the term '(initial) allocation' in the text of the Notice. Where re-allocation is 'found to be necessary for an effective protection

[13] See ch 1 of this volume (Luchtman), section I.

[14] Elsewhere, 'sector inquiries' have been identified as Commission tasks in the competition field, which to a degree resemble the market supervision proper routinely carried out by the ECB. The threshold to open such an inquiry is low: DG Competition requires only a 'suggestion' that competition may be restricted or distorted in a market or sector of the economy. The formal decision to initiate an inquiry is normally announced, and whilst an investigation may thereafter be opened, the line between pre-investigative and investigative phases is blurred; see M Scholten and M Simonato, 'EU Report' in M Luchtman and J Vervaele (eds), *Investigatory Powers and procedural safeguards: Improving OLAF's legislative framework through a comparison with other EU law enforcement authorities (ECN/ESMA/ECB)* (Utrecht University, 2017) 9, 23.

[15] See also the Joint Statement of the Council and the Commission on the functioning of the network of competition authorities, issued on the day of adoption of Regulation 1/2003 (10 December 2002); Council of the EU 15435/02 ADD 1, available at https://ec.europa.eu/competition/ecn/joint_statement_en.pdf.

[16] Commission Notice on cooperation within the Network of Competition Authorities (2004/C 101/03) [2004] OJ C101/34 ('Network Notice').

[17] Network Notice, para 6.

of competition and of the Community interest, network members will endeavour to re-allocate cases to a single well placed competition authority as often as possible'.[18] Such matters should be resolved swiftly, normally within a period of two months, starting from the date of the first information sent to the network pursuant to Article 11 of Regulation 1/2003, mentioned in section II.A.i.[19]

For present purposes, the key development in the Network Notice lies in its guidance on when an authority can be considered 'well-placed to deal with a case' and – more to the point – how situations wherein multiple authorities are 'well-placed' ought to be handled.[20] A national competition authority is considered 'well-placed' where:

(a) the impugned conduct has substantial direct actual or foreseeable effects on competition within its territory, is implemented within or originates from its territory;
(b) the authority is able to effectively bring to an end the entire infringement (cease-and-desist order is available and effective; where appropriate, sanctioning is adequate); and
(c) the authority can gather, acting alone or with the assistance of other authorities, the evidence required to prove the infringement.[21]

The above are cumulative criteria. In most cases where the first (territorial) criterion is fulfilled, the Notice provides, the local Member State's national competition authority will be well-placed to take the case.[22] However, parallel action by 'two or three' national competition authorities may be appropriate where the respective territories are impacted and action taken by one national competition authority would not bring to and end the entire infringement and/or sanction it adequately;[23] in such circumstances national competition authorities are to coordinate as far as possible and may designate one national competent authority (NCA) as lead authority.[24] Alternatively, the Commission will be particularly well-placed where competition is affected in more than three Member States,[25] where a case is closely linked to other Community provisions that may be exclusively or more effectively applied by the Commission, if the Community interest requires the adoption of a Commission decision to develop competition policy, when a new competition issue arises or to ensure effective enforcement.[26]

Where, on the one hand, certainty in terms of vertical division of labour is provided by the 'three plus' rule,[27] it is then rather taken away again by the malleability of the 'EU interest' test. Brammer labels the penultimate ground (that a new competition issue has arisen) a 'fallback provision' and a necessary complement to Article 11(6) of

[18] Network Notice, para 7.
[19] Network Notice, para 18.
[20] Compare the Joint Statement (n 15), which had previously announced 'Where an agreement or practice substantially affects competition in more than one Member State, the Network members will seek to agree between them who is *best placed* to deal with the case successfully' (para 17, emphasis added).
[21] Network Notice, para 8.
[22] Network Notice, paras 9 and 10.
[23] Network Notice, para 12.
[24] Network Notice, para 13.
[25] Network Notice, para 14.
[26] Network Notice, para 15.
[27] Assuming that some impact on competition in more than three Member States can be unequivocally established.

Regulation 1/2003, which empowers the Commission to lift a case out of the hands of any national competition authority.[28] Yet this tool may also be relied upon to trammel the Commission's discretion: indeed CJEU case law is clear that in adopting rules of conduct, such as guidelines, and in announcing by their publication that it will thereafter apply such rules in relevant cases, the Commission restricts the exercise of its own powers. Any deviation from those rules is liable to result in a violation of the general principles of law, such as equal treatment or the protection of legitimate interests.[29]

Reading a Commission notice as a merely organisational (arguably, 'soft law') document, which is not legally binding, thus requires a degree of nuance as far as the Commission is concerned. In the case of the Network Notice, notwithstanding its insistence that 'the allocation of cases … does not create individual rights for the companies involved in or affected by an infringement to have the case dealt with by a particular authority', undertakings are free to attempt to turn the guidelines around on the Commission in proceedings before the EU judicature – although the hurdle is likely to be a high one, particularly where one Member State is in the box seat (typically due to territorial impact).[30] The Commission has to a limited extent bound its own hands through the Network Notice, allowing us to place case allocation as currently calibrated in EU competition law somewhere between the two poles of (fixed) 'regulatory allocation' and (ad hoc) 'allocation in specific cases' distinguished by Widdershoven and Craig.[31]

In contrast, no such nuance is called for as regards horizontal division of labour: the Network Notice places no obligation upon the Member States or their national competition authorities. In addition to its non-binding nature, the steering of case allocation set down in its terms is light, diminishing the predictability of allocation, whilst complainants and undertakings are excluded from deliberations, greatly reducing transparency.[32] Nor is there competence, where conflicts of jurisdiction arise between national competition authorities, for the Commission (or the ECN's Advisory Committee, which in any event lacks legal personality, for that matter) to settle the conflict.[33] This cluster of limitations makes it easy to agree with Schwab and Steinle that the Notice 'clearly misses the goal of recital 18 of Regulation 1/2003 that a case should preferably be pursued by one authority'.[34] Yet as the same authors also affirm, the 'miss' was intentional on the part

[28] Brammer (n 8), 1391.

[29] As recognised in Judgment of the Court of Justice (Fifth Chamber) of 16 February 2017, Case C-95/15 P *H&R ChemPharm GmbH v European Commission* ECLI:EU:C:2017:125, para 57.

[30] For a recent example, see the Judgment of the General Court (Tenth Chamber, Extended Composition) of 9 February 2022, Case T-791/19 *Sped-Pro SA v European Commission* ECLI:EU:T:2022:67. In the General Court's view, the applicant company (a complainant) had failed to demonstrate that a new question of competition law had arisen, thereby necessitating allocation to the Commission (paras 61–64). The applicant did, however, successfully challenge the Commission's rejection of its complaint on other grounds – discussed in section II.A.ii.a.

[31] R Widdershoven and P Craig, 'Pertinent issues of judicial accountability in EU shared enforcement' in M Scholten and MJJP Luchtman (eds), *Law Enforcement by EU Authorities – Implications for Political and Judicial Accountability* (Edward Elgar Publishing, 2017) 334.

[32] Brammer (n 8), 1424.

[33] ibid.

[34] A Schwab and C Steinle, 'Pitfalls of the European Competition Network – why better protection of leniency applicants and legal regulation of case allocation is needed' (2008) 29(2) *European Competition Law Review* 523, 524.

of the Commission, whose preference was for a flexible allocation mechanism – against the wish of some Member States for stronger allocation principles.[35]

To recapitulate the limitations of the system established under Regulation 1/2003 and the Network Notice: the latter document is non-binding, its guidelines aim only at identifying 'well-placed' national competition authorities (as opposed to the single best-placed national competition authority) without providing a mechanism to select from amongst them, and its focus on *re*-allocation entails that the first authority to take control of a case benefits from a kind of rebuttable presumption that it will remain in control. What, then, are the possibilities for interested firms – whether subject to investigation or a complainant[36] – to seek to rebut that presumption when a case is (re-)allocated vertically (national competition authority-Commission or Commission-national competition authority) or horizontally (national competition authority-national competition authority)?

a. Vertical Transfers of Proceedings

In neither scenario is a discrete referral decision or act adopted within the ECN[37] – either by its Advisory Committee (which lacks legal personality), or by the Commission or by national competition authorities.[38] In the vertical scenario, when the Commission activates the 'ouster rule' in Article 11(6) in order to remove a case from a national competition authority, the switch of forum is corollary to the initiation of proceedings by DG Competition.[39] Whereas the mere initiation of proceedings is assumed to be impervious to a challenge under Article 263 TFEU, since it produces no direct legal effects on the third parties concerned (the targeted firm or group),[40] might this change where initiation of proceedings by the Commission brings with it a vertical switch of forum?

In the *IBM* case,[41] the applicant attempted to rely on the 'consequence in law' of the Commission's ousting of a national competition authority[42] – 'that the authorities of the

[35] ibid.

[36] Natural persons may also lodge complaints. Applications for leniency are briefly discussed in section II.A.iii.

[37] M De Visser, *Network-based Governance in EC Law: The Example of EC Competition and EC Communications Law* (Hart Publishing 2009) 226.

[38] National law may, however, afford the right to a formal allocation decision.

[39] The Commission may initiate proceedings at any point in time, but no later than the date on which it issues a preliminary assessment as referred to in Art 9(1) Regulation 1/2003, or a statement of objections or the date on which a notice pursuant to Art 27(4) Regulation 1/2003, whichever is the earlier: Commission Regulation (EC) No 773/2004 of 7 April 2004 relating to the conduct of proceedings by the Commission pursuant to Articles 81 and 82 of the EC Treaty [2004] OJ L123/18, Art 2(1). As Scholten and Simonato (n 14) have observed, the line between the pre-investigative and investigative phases is somewhat blurred, in particular since the Commission may exercise its powers of investigation pursuant to Chapter V of Regulation 1/2003 *before* initiating proceedings; see Art 2(3) Commission Regulation 773/2004. As such, challengeable investigative acts may occur before a 'vertical' case allocation implicit in the initiation of proceedings by the Commission.

[40] For discussion of judicial protection routes available to undertakings against DG Competition (action for annulment of Commission decisions to issue a request for information, to carry out an inspection, or to fine an undertaking, as well as actions for damages and interim relief), as well as possibilities for *ex post* non-judicial review by the hearing officer, see ch 3 of this volume (Ligeti and Robinson), section III.A.

[41] Case 60/81 *International Business Machines Corporation v Commission of the European Communities* ECLI:EU:C:1981:264 ('*IBM*').

[42] Under Art 9(3) Regulation No 17, the predecessor of Art 11(6) Regulation 1/2003.

Member States cease to be competent' – as an argument in support of its view that 'legal consequences' are indeed produced by that act, and that judicial review thereof 'prior to the stage at which a final decision is made ensures observance of the principles of good administration and the right to be heard and reduces the possibility of the final decision's being annulled for procedural irregularity'.[43] The Court summarily dispatched the argument, concluding that a switch from national to European control did not adversely affect the interests of IBM, and adding the view that such an act 'essentially results in protecting the undertaking concerned from parallel proceedings brought by the authorities of the Member States'.[44]

This outcome has attracted some criticism on the part of practitioners and academics. According to Geradin and Petit,[45] notwithstanding the Court's categorical tone in *IBM* (a case where, as the Court itself observed, no national proceedings were in fact underway),[46] such forum changes entail both a 'preparatory decision' (Commission proceedings are opened) which is unreviewable[47] and a 'final decision' (national proceedings are closed) capable of qualifying as 'the culmination of a special procedure' – and thus reviewable[48] so long as a distinct change in legal position obtains.

The same authors put forward three arguments in support of their view that it does. One of those arguments, concerning the coherence of EU competition law, turns on an analogous application of case law on merger control and falls outwith the scope of this chapter. The other two arguments fall squarely within its scope: the prospect of a new procedure governed by different rules, and the related extra costs incurred by undertakings when a forum is switched.[49] Whilst De Visser takes the view that such costs should be manageable in light of the two-month window advised in the Network Notice,[50] this would seem to depend greatly on the circumstances. The matter of the degree and nature of differences between the national competition authority's local rules and those applicable to the Commission will likely also vary from Member State to Member State.[51]

Before turning to horizontal (re-)allocations, it is necessary to address another role in which undertakings (as well as natural persons) find themselves in EU competition law: that of complainant. In the vertical setting, the rejection of a complaint may entail the transfer of proceedings 'upstream' (national competition authority-Commission) or 'downstream' (Commission-national competition authority). In the former case, as seen

[43] *IBM* (n 41), Facts and Issues, para III.1.

[44] *IBM* (n 41), Decision, para 18.

[45] GD Geradin and N Petit, 'Judicial Remedies under EC Competition Law: Complex Issues arising from the "Modernisation" Process' (2005) 32 *Annual Proceedings of the Fordham Corporate Law Institute* 393. Text cited at II.2.2.a) in version available at https://papers.ssrn.com/sol3/papers.cfm?abstract_id=877967

[46] ibid.

[47] *IBM* (n 41) Decision, para 10.

[48] 'It would be otherwise only if acts or decisions adopted in the course of the preparatory proceedings not only bore all the legal characteristics referred to above but in addition were themselves the culmination of a special procedure distinct from that intended to permit the Commission or the Council to take a decision on the substance of the case': ibid para 11.

[49] Geradin and Petit (n 45) II.2.2.a.

[50] Network Notice, para 18. See De Visser (n 37) 295.

[51] The reforms ushered in by the ECN+ Directive – which aims to close both vertical and horizontal discrepancies by aligning national competition authorities with the Commission – are discussed in more detail in section II.A.iii.

in section II.A.i, Regulation 1/2003 permits a national competition authority to reject a complaint on the mere basis that another authority is dealing with the case; no facility to challenge such a rejection is provided.[52] The matter thus falls to be determined by national courts under national procedural law.[53]

For rejections carrying a transfer of proceedings from the Commission to a national competition authority, there is the right to launch an appeal before the General Court.[54] The copious case law confirms that the Commission has broad discretion in each of the three main categories of reasons that can justify the rejection of a complaint: lack of Union interest, substantive grounds where the evidence does not support the finding of an infringement, and where national competition authorities are dealing or have dealt with the same case.[55] As lack of space prohibits an exploration of connections between all three categories and the 'downstream' transfer of proceedings, the analysis here will be limited to highlighting the hint of a shift in the General Court's approach in recent case law.

In *Si.mobil*, the General Court reiterated that neither Regulation 1/2003 nor the Network Notice creates individual rights or expectations for an undertaking to have its case dealt with by a specific competition authority; thus, even on the assumption that the Commission had been particularly well placed to deal with the case at hand and the national competition authority had not been well placed to do so, the applicant did not have a right to have the case dealt with by the Commission.[56] Indeed, reading Article 13 of the Regulation together with Recital 18 shows that the Council intended to introduce a new ground for rejecting a complaint that is different from the ground based on lack of EU interest; the Commission was not therefore required to carry out such a balancing test.[57] Nor could the requirement to ensure the effective application of EU competition rules have the effect of imposing an obligation on the Commission to verify, in implementing Article 13, whether the national competition authority concerned has the institutional, financial and technical means available to it to enable it to accomplish the task entrusted to it by that Regulation.[58]

The Commission is, however, bound to provide its reasons for rejecting a complaint.[59] Should those reasons convey the view that a national competition authority is in a better position to initiate proceedings than another national competition authority or the Commission, the recent judgment in *Sped-Pro*[60] seems to call for careful

[52] Art 13(1) Regulation 1/2003.

[53] See De Visser (n 37), 292–93 and the sources cited there.

[54] 'Settled case-law since Case 210/81 *Oswald Schmidt, trading as Demo-Studio Schmidt v Commission of the European Communities* [1983] ECR 3045', per para 77, Commission Notice on the handling of complaints by the Commission under Articles 81 and 82 of the EC Treaty (2004/C 101/05) [2004] OJ C101/65. For there to be a rejection decision against which it may appeal, a complainant must make known its views within the time-limit set by the Commission in its initial communication indicating that it sees insufficient grounds for acting on the complaint: Art 7 Commission Regulation No 773/2004 (n 39) and Network Notice, para 35.

[55] See in detail A Dawes and E Rousseva, 'Handling and Rejecting Complaints' in E Rousseva (ed), *EU Antitrust Procedure* (Oxford University Press 2020).

[56] Case T-201/11 *Si.mobil telekomunikacijske storitve d.d. v European Commission* ECLI:EU:T:2014:1096, paras 39–40 and the CJEU case law cited there.

[57] ibid para 41.

[58] ibid para 57.

[59] As recalled, inter alia, in Art 7 Commission Regulation No 773/2004 (n 39).

[60] *Sped-Pro SA* (n 30).

consideration. The case emerged from a complaint lodged by a Polish undertaking and rejected by the Commission on the grounds, 'in substance, that the Polish competition authority was better placed to examine it'.[61] The General Court dismissed two of the petitioner's arguments (violation of the Article 41 of the Charter right to good administration, under the 'within a reasonable time' head; manifest errors in appreciation of the Union interest in pursuing the complaint by the Commission), before turning to the claim that the Commission had violated the petitioner's right to effective judicial protection owing to the systemic or generalised failures of the rule of law in Poland, in particular the lack of independence of the Polish competition authority and of the national courts competent in the matter.[62]

Intriguingly, in its rejection decision the Commission had applied by analogy[63] the decision of the CJEU in *LM*, the well-known European Arrest Warrant (EAW) case.[64] Before the General Court in *Sped-Pro*, Poland sought to distinguish *LM* along those very lines: it concerned judicial cooperation in criminal matters, in particular the EAW framework, and the right to a fair trial under Article 47 of the Charter – none of which ought to apply to administrative authorities such as the Polish national competition authority.[65]

The General Court disagreed, holding that the rules on cooperation between national competition authorities and the Commission pursuant to Articles 101 and 102 TFEU – just as in the setting of the Area of Freedom, Security and Justice (AFSJ) of the EAW system – establish a system of close cooperation between competent authorities based on the principles of mutual recognition, mutual trust and loyal cooperation.[66] The General Court supported this assimilation by reference not only to pertinent aspects of Regulation 1/2003 and of the Network Notice, but also the ECN+ Directive,[67] in particular its emphasis on the independence and impartiality of national competition authorities – notwithstanding the fact that the implementation deadline for that Directive had not yet passed.[68] Respect for the requirements of the rule of law is, the General Court confirmed, a relevant factor that the Commission must take into account in order to determine the 'best placed authority'.[69]

Had it done so in this instance? The General Court, having inventoried the wealth of arguments put forward by the petitioner, concluded that the Commission had not

[61] '[S]ince, on the one hand, the alleged infringement was limited, essentially, to the Polish market and, on the other, that the said authority had acquired detailed knowledge of the (relevant market) and the practices of (the denounced firm) through the handling of several investigations and adoption of decisions in the sector since 2004': ibid para 42 (author's own translation).

[62] Guaranteed by Art 2 read in conjunction with Art 19(1) of the Treaty on European Union (TEU) and Art 47 of the Charter; *Sped-Pro* (n 30) para 71.

[63] *Sped-Pro* (n 30) para 74.

[64] Case C-216/18 PPU *LM/Minister for Justice and Equality* ECLI:EU:C:2018:586. In essence, the case involved the refusal in Ireland to execute an EAW received from Poland amid concerns that a fair trial would not take place in the latter Member State. T Konstadinides, 'Judicial independence and the Rule of Law in the context of non-execution of a European Arrest Warrant: *LM*' (2019) 56 *CML Rev* 743.

[65] *Sped-Pro* (n 30) para 75.

[66] Ibid para 85.

[67] Discussed below in section II.A.iii.

[68] *Sped-Pro* (n 30) paras 84–86.

[69] ibid para 92.

examined the complaint in sufficiently concrete and precise fashion to allow the petitioner to know the reasons why the points (*indices*) it had raised were set aside,[70] or for the Court to perform an effective review of the legality of the decision in order to gauge whether there were serious and proven (*avérés*) grounds for believing that there existed a real risk of the petitioner's rights being violated.[71]

The decision of the General Court is striking in its own right for the manner in which rule-of-law protections set out in the AFSJ are read across to EU competition law by the General Court, placing it in some tension with the jurisprudential and doctrinal position emphasising the particular nature of competition law.[72] Whilst the cross-application of *LM* can likely be sorted into the folder marked 'certain Member States' (at least for the time being), the Court's reliance on the goals of the ECN+ Directive's standards is sure to add further weight to the drive toward full implementation of that instrument. We return to the ECN+ Directive in section II.A.iii of this chapter.

b. Horizontal Transfers of Proceedings

As with vertical transfers of proceedings, there is no requirement, at least under EU law,[73] for horizontal allocation (ie national competition authority – national competition authority transfer) to be taken on the basis of a formal decision. When a case is transferred from one national competition authority to another, the transferring authority closes its proceedings or rejects the complaint that prompted an investigation,[74] and its counterpart commences proceedings (possibly armed with information received from the transferring authority pursuant to Article 12 of Regulation 1/2003).

Much of the discussion set out in section II.A.ii.a in the context of vertical transfers is also valid here, albeit from a different perspective. For undertakings that may be involved in enforcement action in more than one national system either as subject or as complainant, the non-binding and fluid nature of allocation pursuant to Regulation 1/2003 and the Network Notice matters above all due to the discrepancies between those national systems. Chiefly, these are institutional aspects of national competition authorities, their investigatory and sanctioning powers, safeguards and remedies – and the attendant risk of forum shopping amongst national competition authorities. The EU legislature has recently taken steps to align national competition authorities with the Commission in several respects, with the so-called 'ECN+ Directive'.

[70] ibid para 104.

[71] ibid.

[72] cf WPJ Wils, 'Fundamental Procedural Rights and Effective Enforcement of Articles 101 and 102 TFEU in the European Competition Network' (2020) 43(1) *World Competition* 5, at III.C.2. See further in detail, also taking in purely national competition law proceedings, M Veenbrink, 'The Impact of Criminal Law Concepts on the Enforcement of National and European Competition Law: A Silent Take-over?', PhD thesis (Radboud University Nijmegen 2019) esp ch 8. The author of this chapter thanks Dr Małgorzata Kozak for bringing the *Sped-Pro* case to his attention.

[73] A comprehensive view of which Member States do or do not provide the right to a formal decision on horizontal (re-)allocation falls outwith the scope of this chapter.

[74] As seen in section II.A.i, grounds for doing so are set out in Art 13 Regulation 1/2003.

iii. Convergence and Discretion: The ECN+ Directive

In 2014, a Commission Communication on 10 years of antitrust enforcement under Regulation 1/2003 came and went without any direct mention of case allocation, although the varying abilities of national competition authorities to choose cases ('set their enforcement priorities') was identified as a brake on convergence of procedures.[75] Case allocation was discussed in the accompanying Staff Working Document (SWD), but exclusively within the context of leniency programmes,[76] with the Commission highlighting the steps (such as the introduction of a Model Leniency Programme[77]) taken to redress the imbalance and impracticalities identified in the early years following the introduction of Regulation 1/2003: whilst several national systems for a time did not run leniency programmes at all, any careful firm vulnerable to enforcement action in multiple Member States (typically, one involved in a cross-border cartel) would ultimately be obliged to apply to each and every national competition authority in order to shore up its legal position. The intertwining of the leniency application problem – the very opposite of a 'one-stop shop' – with that of insufficiently foreseeable case allocation is self-evident.[78]

Closing divergences in leniency programmes across the Union was thus a core pillar of the Commission's ensuing efforts to boost the enforcement of the EU competition rules, alongside institutional weaknesses of national competition authorities (chiefly independence and resources), and deficiencies in investigative powers, effective fines and mutual assistance.[79] When a draft Directive emerged in 2017, however, it too declined to engage with the possibility of formalised case allocation,[80] preferring to maintain the flexible system under the ECN whilst pursuing convergence across those aspects just mentioned.[81]

[75] European Commission, Communication from the Commission to the European Parliament and the Council, 'Ten Years of Antitrust Enforcement under Regulation 1/2003: Achievements and Future Perspectives', Brussels, COM(2014) 453, point 32.

[76] European Commission, Commission Staff Working Document, 'Enhancing competition enforcement by the Member States' competition authorities: institutional and procedural issues', Brussels, 9.7.2014 SWD(2014) 231 final, at 23–25.

[77] See European Competition Network, *ECN Model Leniency Programme* (as revised in November 2012) available at https://ec.europa.eu/competition/ecn/mlp_revised_2012_en.pdf.

[78] Schwab and Steinle (n 34) 523.

[79] European Commission, Proposal for a Directive of the European Parliament and of the Council to empower the competition authorities of the Member States to be more effective enforcers and to ensure the proper functioning of the internal market, Brussels, 22.3.2017 COM(2017) 142 final, 2–3.

[80] ibid. Compare the Commission's Impact Assessment, which recognised the following: 'The allocation of cases is done on a flexible basis within the ECN and means that enforcement is not hampered, eg because one authority lacks resources to investigate a particular case at a given moment in time. The system presupposes that for companies it does not matter which authority acts. However this is not the case when companies can have very different fines imposed on them depending on which authority takes up the case or when cases are time barred before some authorities but not others because of differences in rules on when NCAs can act': European Commission, Impact Assessment accompanying the (draft ECN+ Directive), Brussels, 22.3.2017, SWD(2017) 114 final, PART 1/2 at 29.

[81] For Temple Lang, 'the proposal does little to strengthen the procedural rights of companies in national authorities' procedures'; see J Temple Lang, 'Fundamental Rights and the Proposed Directive' (2017) 3(3) *Competition Law & Policy Debate* 48, 48.

The text of the adopted instrument, the overall aim of which is to align national competition authorities both institutionally and procedurally with the Commission,[82] is also silent on the matter.[83] Notably, whilst the Directive calls for appropriate safeguards in respect of undertakings' rights of defence, in the main articles only the right to be heard and the right to an effective remedy before a tribunal are briefly mentioned.[84] Although one of the express aims of the reform was to provide a legal basis for cooperation within the ECN,[85] the Network itself remains without legal personality, and ultimately the Directive does little to channel cooperation under its aegis in ways that are visible to parties.[86] Mutual (cross-border) assistance between national competition authorities is boosted,[87] but piercing the veil of information exchange between national competition authorities remains a challenge for parties seeking, inter alia, to anticipate the destination of a (re-)allocated case. Kozak has argued that the lack of a mechanism for contesting the transmission of information within the ECN fails to adequately ensure the equality of arms between national competition authorities and undertakings.[88]

B. Banking Law

i. *The SSM, Case Allocation and Forum Choice*

Mutual assistance between authorities offers a bridge between EU competition law and EU banking law, and an immediate riposte to the contention that case allocation or forum choice either do not exist or do not matter in the latter context.

That impression is prima facie tempting, in light of the neat dichotomy between exclusive supranational competence (for 'significant supervised entities') and residual national competence (for 'less significant supervised entities'). The significance of the entity thus settles vertical distribution, whilst the 'home rule' principle settles things horizontally: a 'less significant' financial institution (FI) is supervised in its home state.

[82] Arts 6 to 12 replicate to a great extent the investigative powers conferred on the Commission by Regulation 1/2003. See F Rizzuto, 'The ECN Plus Directive: the harmonisation of national procedural rules governing the parallel enforcement of EU competition law in the internal market' (2019) 40(12) *European Competition Law Review* 574, 579.

[83] Directive (EU) 2019/1 of the European Parliament and of the Council of 11 December 2018 to empower the competition authorities of the Member States to be more effective enforcers and to ensure the proper functioning of the internal market [2019] OJ L11/3 ('ECN+ Directive').

[84] Art 3(2) ECN+ Directive. Recital 14 includes further safeguards that *should* apply (including access to the case file), but these largely reflect CJEU case law and/or Commission Regulation No 773/2004 on the conduct of proceedings.

[85] Hence the twin legal bases on which the Directive was adopted: Arts 114 and 103 TFEU.

[86] I Maher, 'Competition Law Networks and the Challenge of Transparency', *UCD Working Papers in Law, Criminology and Socio-Legal Studies*, Research Paper 1/2019, available at https://papers.ssrn.com/sol3/papers.cfm?abstract_id=3339884.

[87] In particular by Art 24(2) ECN+ Directive.

[88] M Kozak, 'ECN+ Directive: a missed opportunity for strengthening the rights of parties?' in CS Rusu, et al (eds), *New Directions in Competition Law Enforcement* (Wolf Legal Publishers 2020) 49. For a discussion of information exchange within and beyond the ECN (drawing also on interviews with practitioners) shortly before the introduction of the ECN+ Directive, see A Karagianni, M Scholten and M Simonato, 'EU Vertical Report' in M Simonato, M Luchtman and J Vervaele (eds), *Exchange of Information with EU and National Enforcement Authorities: Improving OLAF legislative framework through a comparison with other EU authorities (ECN/ESMA/ECB)* (Utrecht University 2018), 14–21.

Indeed, it might be said that the very notion of *case* allocation sits rather awkwardly within the 'closed environment' in which FIs operate, where supervisor is also enforcer – in contrast with the 'open environment' in which firms and competition law authorities operate.[89] Under the SSM, there are no parallel competences: an FI is supervised either by the ECB or by its home national authority, and enforcement competence ascribes to that same authority. Nor does it fully make sense to refer to vertical or horizontal 'transfers' of cases or proceedings, in particular given the mixed composition of On-Site Inspection Teams (OSITs) and day-to-day Joint Supervisory Teams (JSTs).[90]

There are no (re-)allocation decisions within the SSM's investigation and sanctioning processes. When a JST 'considers that there is reason to suspect one or more breaches' of relevant EU rules, the ECB shall refer the matter to the independent[91] investigating unit,[92] which may exercise the powers granted to the ECB under the SSM Regulation.[93] Even if there were such a decision (taken by the ECB since the SSM – like the ECN in competition law – lacks legal personality), it seems highly unlikely, in light of the competition law jurisprudence already expounded upon and that one assumes to apply *mutatis mutandis* in the banking law field, to avoid the label of mere 'preparatory acts' that escape judicial review.[94]

ii. Discretion and Applicable Law as Kompetenz-kompetenz*?*

The foregoing matters, first and foremost for the following reason: national systems still differ in important ways. It has been seen that the area of EU competition law is undergoing a process of convergence designed to 'align up' institutional and operational aspects of national competition authorities to match the Commission; a dedicated analysis of national implementations of the ECN+ Directive will be necessary in order to detect and appreciate what discrepancies remain. But even in the highly-harmonised area of banking law, there may be national safeguards to respect or additional powers at the national level to deploy.[95] And although a 'significant FI' may be supervised day-to-day

[89] As noted in section II.A.i.

[90] Categorised as *Organleihe* (national authorities 'become part of the EU structure in legal terms; participating states lose control over their authorities, which act as functional part of the EU authority') in ch 1 of this volume (Luchtman), section IV; on OSITs and JSTs, see further ch 3 of this volume (Ligeti and Robinson), section III.B.

[91] Independent of the Supervisory Board and Governing Council; Regulation (EU) No 468/2014 of the European Central Bank of 16 April 2014 establishing the framework for cooperation within the Single Supervisory Mechanism between the European Central Bank and national competent authorities and with national designated authorities (SSM Framework Regulation) (ECB/2014/17) [2014] OJ L141/1 ('SSM Framework Regulation'), Art 123(3).

[92] Art 124 SSM Framework Regulation. Based on informal exchanges with a member of a JST (in October 2016), Scholten and Simonato (n 14) 23–24, fn 40, have reported that 'the threshold for sending the file to the investigating unit would be a very significant breach of the law or if the supervised entity would not follow the JST's (remedial) recommendations'.

[93] Art 125(1) SSM Framework Regulation; Council Regulation (EU) No 1024/2013 of 15 October 2013 conferring specific tasks on the European Central Bank concerning policies relating to the prudential supervision of credit institutions [2013] OJ L287/63 ('SSM Regulation').

[94] A Türk and N Xanthoulis, 'Legal accountability of European Central Bank in bank supervision: A case study in conceptualizing the legal effects of Union acts' (2019) 26(1) *Maastricht Journal of European and Comparative Law* 151, 160–61.

[95] See ch 10 of this volume (Luchtman), section III.A.

by a JST, and, being familiar with its national banking law, well able to anticipate the ramifications of 'instructions' from the ECB to its home state under Article 9(1) of the SSM Regulation,[96] if it has any footprint in other Member States it may still face the consequences of weak spots in legal protection across national systems should that 'instruction' be issued to another state.

Additionally, Article 4(3) of the SSM Regulation provides that in carrying out its tasks, 'the ECB shall apply all relevant Union law, and where this Union law is composed of Directives, the national legislation transposing those Directives'. An investigative act performed in Member State A, in accordance with standards there, is clearly ascribable to the ECB and in principle reviewable. But what if the fruits of the investigation carried out in Member State A then find their way to administrative punitive proceedings in Member State B, where standards are higher?[97]

In composite settings like the SSM, the classic problem of forum shopping is inflected in new, still-understudied ways. As Luchtman observes, in the concluding chapter in this volume:

> If the same information is … accessible via the laws of different legal orders, and if that information can be obtained either by the EU authority itself or by that authority's 'asking', 'requiring' or 'instructing' a national partner to do so, the requirement of a lawful basis inevitably loses part of its function. Within composite enforcement systems, the applicable law is seldom precisely defined in such horizontal relations; a number of national laws are potentially applicable, at the investigative stage and/or at the sanctioning stage. That means a new type of discretion comes to the fore in these systems; the discretion to determine which set of legal rules is applicable to any given case.
>
> The question is whether this type of discretion must also be subject to the rule of law. …[98]

C. PIF Law

The European Anti-Fraud Office (OLAF) and the European Public Prosecutor's Office (EPPO) are key players in the protection of the financial interests of the EU. OLAF is an administrative office, with administrative powers, that combats fraud and related activities. As is well known, it is not competent to commence procedures for fraud or recovery. For that, it relies on partners at both EU (including EPPO) and national levels. The long-standing problems experienced by OLAF in having its recommendations taken up at the national level are widely recognised.[99]

[96] For discussion of the reviewability (and forum for review) of ECB instructions, see Türk and Xanthoulis (n 94) 159.

[97] See ch 9 of this volume (Vervaele).

[98] See ch 10 of this volume (Luchtman), section III.A.

[99] After receiving an OLAF report, competent authorities of the Member States 'shall take such action as the results of the external investigation warrant' and report back to the Office: Art 11(3) Regulation No 883/2013 of 11 September 2013 concerning investigations conducted by the European Anti-Fraud Office (OLAF) [2013] OJ L248/1 ('OLAF Regulation'), as amended by Regulation 2020/2223 of 23 December 2020 amending Regulation No 883/2013, as regards cooperation with the European Public Prosecutor's Office and the effectiveness of the European Anti-Fraud Office investigations [2020] OJ L 437/49.

Notwithstanding the contingent nature of follow-up at national level, transmission of the final report by OLAF to a national partner is as close as the OLAF framework comes to case allocation in a strict sense. All the same, the Court of Justice has consistently rejected challenges under Article 263 TFEU, essentially on the grounds that the forwarding of OLAF's findings, in the shape of a final report, to NCAs does not lead automatically to the opening of judicial or disciplinary proceedings: recipient authorities remain entirely free to decide whether or not to act upon the report – and thus whether or not to alter the legal position of the person(s) concerned by OLAF's investigations.[100]

The same logic applies to investigative acts carried out by OLAF prior to the delivery of final reports. Unlike the powers of coercion enjoyed by Commission in the competition law field, when, for instance, an undertaking denies OLAF access to premises, OLAF's only option is to request the aid of the NCAs. Should an NCA decide to give it, this triggers reviewability. Notably, the 2020 reform clarified (in conformity with the General Court's 2018 ruling in *Sigma Orionis*[101]) that the applicable law in the context of inspections and on-the-spot checks hinges on the cooperation afforded by the economic operator under investigation: if it acquiesces, Union law (including procedural safeguards) applies; if it resists, national law does.[102]

It is well beyond the scope of this chapter to delve into the diversity of national powers, safeguards and remedies that may be triggered by OLAF-originating enforcement action.[103] Likewise, the complex matter of ('horizontal' yet supranational, administrative-criminal) cooperation between OLAF and the EPPO cannot be dealt with in any detail here, except to note that discretion – unequivocally, that of the EPPO – also governs the treatment of cases touching the remits of the two Offices.[104]

The point is rather to emphasise, notwithstanding the great number of discrepancies between the three authorities seen heretofore and their respective fields, their remits and competences, powers and constraints, the dominant model that seems to structure their interactions with heterogeneous national jurisdictions: the 'star pattern' model. In this formation, it is through the EU authority that interactions between national legal orders essentially run. Yet '[t]he resulting focus of these models on the vertical axis of coherence seems to conceal that important decisions on case allocation, the applicable law, etc are made within the confines of the EU authorities, but often without a clear framework'.[105]

[100] See ch 3 of this volume (Ligeti and Robinson), section III.D.i, with further references.

[101] Case T-48/16 *Sigma Orionis SA v European Commission* ECLI:EU:T:2018:245, paras 81–82.

[102] Arts 3(6) and 7(3) OLAF Regulation as amended. See ch 3 of this volume (Ligeti and Robinson), section III.D.i.b, with further references.

[103] This applies *a fortiori* to the great diversity of national partners (not limited to EU Member States) OLAF may interact with; see especially Arts 12a and 12b OLAF Regulation as amended.

[104] See Arts 12c-12g OLAF Regulation as amended, in particular Art 12d on 'Non-duplication of investigations'. Possible *ne bis in idem* risks are touched upon in section III.C. For analysis of the case allocation system operated by the newly-launched EPPO, see in detail M Panzavolta, 'Choosing the National Forum in Proceedings Conducted by EPPO: Who Is to Decide?' in L Bachmaier Winter (ed), *The European Public Prosecutor's Office: The Challenges Ahead* (Springer Publishing 2018) 59; P Caeiro and JA Rodrigues, 'A European Contraption: The Relationship between the Competence of the EPPO and the Scope of Member States' Jurisdiction over Criminal Matters' in K Ligeti, MJ Antunes and F Giuffrida (eds), *The European Public Prosecutor's Office at Launch: Adapting National Systems, Transforming EU Criminal Law* (Wolters Kluwer CEDAM 2020) 57.

[105] See ch 1 of this volume (Luchtman), section IV.

Section II has explored those lacunae and the 'foreseeability gaps' they may present to EU citizens who find themselves involved (as the case may be, as either passive objects or active participants) in the composite administrative punitive legal order. In section III, which deals with the tensions between *ne bis in idem* protections and composite enforcement settings, foreseeability – *in concreto* of dual-track proceedings and cumulative sanctions – remains a central theme.

III. *Ne Bis in Idem* and Foreseeable Composite Enforcement in the EU

The *ne bis in idem* principle, often referred to as the 'double jeopardy' rule, is enshrined in varying forms in national legal systems, in the set-up of the European Convention on Human Rights (ECHR),[106] and in both secondary[107] and primary[108] EU law. It forbids (*ne*) the repeated prosecution or punishment (*bis*) of individuals in relation to the same unlawful conduct (*idem*) in so far as that conduct qualifies as 'criminal' under the *Engel* doctrine.

The oscillations of *ne bis in idem* protection before the ECtHR and the CJEU over the past few decades has attracted a vast wealth of commentary and criticism from EU lawyers.[109] Criminal lawyers – at least, those of a European ilk – are naturally most familiar with those scenarios that engage the criminal law proper: on the one hand, where two sets of proceedings in different national jurisdictions are 'true' criminal proceedings, raising the question of whether and how transnational protection ought to be configured (as in *van Esbroeck*),[110] and on other hand where 'true' criminal enforcement is coupled within one country with administrative measures (so-called 'dual-track' enforcement), often pertaining to tax offences, and leading to the making by both Courts of contested accommodations for national enforcement priorities (in *A and B v Norway* at the ECtHR, and the '*Menci* case law' from the CJEU).[111]

[106] Art 4, Protocol no 7 to the ECHR.

[107] Convention implementing the Schengen Agreement of 14 June 1985 [2000] OJ L239/19 ('CISA'), Art 54; Framework Decision 2002/584/JHA on the European arrest warrant and the surrender procedures between Member States [2002] OJ L190/1 ('EAW Framework Decision'), Art 3(2).

[108] Art 50 of the Charter via Art 4(2) TEU. The principle is also notably found in Art 14(7) of the International Covenant on Civil and Political Rights (Concluded 16 December 1966, Registration Number I-14668, UNTS 999, 171), and features as a standard clause in multilateral and bilateral extradition treaties. For a historical view see Dissenting Opinion of Judge Pinto de Albuquerque in *A and B v Norway* Apps nos 24130/11 and 29758/11 (ECtHR GC, 15 December 2016) paras 3–15.

[109] See, eg, X Groussot and A Ericsson, '*Ne Bis in Idem* in the EU and ECHR Legal Orders: A Matter of Uniform Interpretation? in B van Bockel (ed), *Ne Bis in Idem in EU Law* (Cambridge University Press, 2016) 53.

[110] Case C-436/04 *Van Esbroeck* ECLI:EU:C:2006:165.

[111] Case C-524/15 *Menci* ECLI:EU:C:2018:197; Case C-537/16 *Garlsson Real Estate SA* ECLI:EU:C:2018:193; Joined Cases C-596/16 and C-597/16 *Di Puma and Zecca* ECLI:EU:C:2018:192. See, eg, M Luchtman, 'The ECJ's recent case law on *ne bis in idem*: implications for law enforcement in a shared legal order' (2018) 55 *CML Rev* 1717; K Ligeti, 'Fundamental rights protection between Strasbourg and Luxembourg: Extending Transnational ne bis in idem across administrative and criminal procedures' in K Ligeti, G Robinson and European Law Institute (eds), *Preventing and Resolving Conflicts of Jurisdiction in EU Criminal Law* (Oxford University Press 2018) 160; S Mirandola and G Lasagni, 'The European *ne bis in idem* at the Crossroads of Administrative and Criminal Law' *eucrim* 2/2019, 126.

A. '*Idem*' at the CJEU: Bifurcation Since 1969

Criminal lawyers may be less familiar with scenarios (whether 'domestic' or cross-border) where both sets of proceedings are formally administrative but can be deemed *Engel*-criminal for the purposes of fundamental rights protection. In this connection, the CJEU has until very recently followed something of its own 'dual track' in applying different tests for '*idem*' in respect of EU competition law and any other administrative punitive field. Within the realm of EU competition law, settled case law stemming from *Wilhelm and others*[112] in 1969 sets a more demanding 'triple-identity' test of '*idem*' (same offence or '*idem crimen*'), unlike the case law developed much later under CISA, which sets a less demanding 'double-identity' test according to which the qualification of the legal act as 'criminal' is irrelevant: sameness or identity of the underlying conduct ('*idem factum*') will suffice, assuming identity of the putative offender.

The rationale for operating a less demanding '*idem*' test in CISA and EAW 'hard cases' has been clearly established by the CJEU: the need to avoid encumbering – through the threat of repeated prosecutions – free movement within an EU AFSJ bearing no (or very little) harmonisation of national criminal laws.[113] In contrast, the more demanding '*idem*' test in competition law, ultimately driven by the imperative of effective enforcement, has lived a long and rather chequered life, surviving overhauls of the legal framework. Indeed, it began life under the old Regulation No 17 before the parallel application of national and EU law ushered in by Regulation 1/2003, but continued after that modernisation to be seen as neutralising *ne bis in idem* in the competition law setting: a Commission fine could follow a national competition authority fine, or vice versa, without triggering its protection: each instance of enforcement pursued a 'different legal interest'.

Successive Advocates General criticised this special treatment of EU competition law. In 2011, Advocate General Kokott invited the Court to abandon it in *Toshiba*,[114] seeing no reason to single out competition law amongst all areas of EU law. More recently, in *Marine Harvest*, Advocate General Tanchev deemed it to be 'at odds with the increasing convergence of EU and national competition rules and with the decentralisation for the application of EU competition rules brought about' by Regulation 1/2003.[115] Still, the triple identity test had recently been re-affirmed in *Slovak Telecom*[116] – despite its third limb ('protected legal interest') never having been applied in practice[117] – when the *bpost* and *Nordzucker*[118] cases came before the Court.

[112] Case 14-68 *Walt Wilhelm and others v Bundeskartellamt* ECLI:EU:C:1969:4.

[113] See further S Coutts, *Citizenship, Crime and Community in the European Union* (Hart Publishing 2019) 155–75.

[114] Opinion of AG Kokott in Case C-17/10 *Toshiba Corporation and Others* ECLI:EU:C:2011:552.

[115] Opinion of AG Tanchev in Case C-10/18 P, *Marine Harvest ASA v European Commission* ECLI:EU:C:2019:795, para 95, fn 34. Critical voices in the literature include, eg, R Nazzini, 'Parallel Proceedings in EU Competition Law: *Ne Bis in Idem* as a Limiting Principle' in van Bockel (ed) (n 109) 131, 141–45; JM Veenbrink, 'Bringing Back Unity. Modernizing the Application of the Non Bis In Idem Principle (2019) 42(1) *World Competition* 67.

[116] Case C-857/19 *Slovak Telekom* ECLI:EU:C:2021:139, para 43.

[117] 'The intra-Union competition law cases that the Court has so far dealt with have involved, in the Court's view, different acts' – obviating assessment of the third limb of the triple identity test; Opinion of AG Bobek in Case C-117/20 *bpost SA v Autorité belge de la concurrence*, delivered on 2 September 2021, para 51.

[118] Case C-151/20 *Bundeswettbewerbsbehörde v Nordzucker AG and Others* ECLI:EU:C:2022:203 ('*Nordzucker*').

In *bpost*, the Court was faced for the first time with a duplication in one Member State of administrative proceedings (deemed *Engel*-criminal) spanning both tests of '*idem*': on the one hand, proceedings under postal sector regulations that would ordinarily follow the *idem factum* test only, and on the other hand competition proceedings (a parallel application of national and EU law) that would ordinarily trigger the *idem crimen* test. The opportunity thus arose for the Court to answer the following question: in such a scenario, which *idem* test is to apply?

Whereas *bpost* featured a domestic yet 'trans-procedural' (competition and regulatory) set of proceedings, *Nordzucker* concerned the transnational application of *ne bis in idem* within one area of EU law: competition law (sugar markets in Austria and Germany). Whichever '*idem*' test settled on by the Court in *bpost* would thus find immediate application in *Nordzucker*. The broader potential ramifications of the Court's landmark rulings are discussed in section III.C, building upon a presentation of both cases in section III.B following.

B. Unity under the Charter: Article 50 Giveth …

In *bpost*, the Court decided that the double-identity *idem factum* test is to apply in future across all areas of EU law. The triple-identity *idem crimen* test for competition law, which had stood for over 50 years, is thus consigned to history. The Court did so in order to settle a dispute emerging from the market in postal services in Belgium. *bpost*, the historical service provider, had been fined €2.3 million by the national sectoral regulator (*Institut belge des services postaux et des télécommunications* – IBPT) in 2011 for operating a discriminatory tariff system. That fine was overturned by the CJEU in 2015, which found no discrimination; the Belgian Court of Appeal thereafter annulled the IBPT's decision. In the time after the IBPT fine had been levied but before the CJEU finding of no discrimination, the Belgian competition authority (*Autorité belge de la concurrence*) found that the difference in treatment amounted to an abuse of a dominant position purusant to Article 102 TFEU and the corresponding national law. The Belgian national competition authority fined *bpost* over €37 million.

Domestic proceedings eventually resulted in the Brussels Court of Appeal issuing a reference for a preliminary ruling to the CJEU based on two incompatible readings of the scope of *ne bis in idem* protection in EU law. The Belgian national competition authority contended that the concluded regulatory proceedings and the competition proceedings responded to different legal interests; no *idem crimen* thus obtained and the principle did not apply. *bpost* relied on *idem factum* – as both sets of proceedings concerned the same tariff system – in order to argue that the principle did apply.

In its judgment, the Court recalls the scope of '*idem*' in its *Menci* case law:

> [T]he relevant criterion for the purposes of assessing the existence of the same offence is identity of the material facts, understood as the existence of a set of concrete circumstances which are inextricably linked together and which have resulted in the final acquittal or conviction of the person concerned.[119]

[119] Case C-117/20 *bpost SA v Autorité belge de la concurrence* ECLI:EU:C:2022:202, para 33.

The rationale for eschewing *idem crimen* as expressed in *Menci* is also recited ('the scope of the protection conferred by Article 50 of the Charter cannot vary from one Member State to another'[120]) before the Court makes a clean incision:

> The same is true of the application of the non bis in idem principle laid down in Article 50 of the Charter in the field of EU competition law, inasmuch as … the scope of protection conferred by that provision cannot, unless otherwise provided by EU law, vary from one field of EU law to another.[121]

The material facts must be identical (not merely similar, following the *Zolotukhin*[122] line of case law at the ECtHR) – a determination to be made by the referring national court. This could be safely assumed in *bpost*, allowing the heart of the analysis to shift to permissible limitations to *ne bis in idem* under Article 52(1) of the Charter, as will be discussed in section III.C.

The factual picture underlying *Nordzucker*, which unlike *bpost* involved the enforcement efforts of two Member States (Germany and Austria) in one area of EU law (competition law), was rather less crisp. The case took root in parallel investigations opened by the German and Austrian national competition authorities after the German company Nordzucker filed leniency applications with both authorities. Those applications revealed a cartel between Nordzucker and two other German firms, one of which was Südzucker, essentially aiming to resist the impact of competition on prices from new sugar market entrants from those Member States that joined the EU in the 2004 enlargement.

In 2010, the Austrian national competition authority brought cartel proceedings pursuant to Article 101 TFEU and the corresponding provisions of Austrian law before a Vienna court against Nordzucker and Südzucker (both German firms) and Agrana, an Austrian subsidiary of Südzucker. The material evidence relied upon by the Austrian national competition authority in order to establish the existence of a cartel on the Austrian sugar market included a telephone conversation between directors of the two German firms in the course of which the Austrian market was discussed.

Whilst court proceedings in Austria were still underway, in 2014 the German national competition authority found that Nordzucker, Südzucker and a third German producer had infringed Article 101 TFEU and the corresponding provisions of national law. Südzucker received a fine of €195.5 million. The German national competition authority's decision, which subsequently became final, reproduced the content of the same telephone conversation during which representatives of the two German firms had discussed the Austrian market. Of all the matters of fact established by the German national competition authority, that conversation was the only one pertaining to the Austrian market.

Back in Austria, the Supreme Court faced a *ne bis in idem* challenge and stayed proceedings in order to ask the CJEU, inter alia, whether it ought to apply the traditional '*idem*' test, including a third limb of 'protected legal interest', even where both national

[120] ibid para 34.
[121] ibid para 35.
[122] *Sergey Zolotukhin v Russia*, App no.14939/03 (ECtHR GC, 10 February 2009).

competition authorities had applied the same provisions of EU law (Article 101 TFEU) in parallel with the corresponding provisions of national law. In a series of paragraphs perfectly mirroring those in *bpost* discussed previously,[123] the CJEU held that a unified *idem factum* test was now to apply to EU competition law – and then drew on *Toshiba* and *Slovak Telecom* to advise that the identity of the facts 'cannot be assessed in the abstract, but must be examined by reference to the territory and the product market in which the conduct in question had such an object or effect'.[124]

Concretely, in the case at hand this implied a duty on a national court (in Austria) to verify whether the prior decision of a national competition authority in another Member State (Germany) had had extraterritorial reach. Arrangements such as the ECN, discussed in some detail in section II, of course ought to reduce or eliminate the risk of such enforcement overlaps in practice; in this light, *Nordzucker* emerges as a fine example of flexible, soft law-based cooperation gone awry. Ultimately, the CJEU left the referring court with the unenviable task of gauging precisely how much extraterritoriality can be tolerated before a *ne bis in idem* violation is found: a final decision that merely *refers* to conduct that has had an anticompetitive object or effect in Austrian territory does not preclude consecutive proceedings in Austria, but the latter will be precluded should that decision be *based on* a finding of an anticompetitive object or effect in the territory of the first Member State.[125]

C. … and Article 52(1) Taketh Away?

The preceding section set out how the double-identity test has been erected in *bpost* and *Nordzucker* as the uniform test of '*idem*' across all areas of EU law, triggering the protection enshrined in Article 50 of the Charter. The envelopment within a broad factual '*idem*' test of ever more concurrent (or perhaps co-existing) sets of proceedings necessarily shifts the focus of analysis toward the calibration of permissible limitations of that right under Article 52 of the Charter.

In *bpost*, the Court held that public authorities can 'legitimately choose complementary legal responses to certain conduct that is harmful to society' if the relevant procedures form 'a coherent whole so as to address different aspects of the social problem involved [and] provided that the accumulated legal responses do not represent an excessive burden for the individual concerned'.[126]

Even without the reference to the ECtHR's decision in *A and B v Norway*, from the language alone (which is near-identical to the Strasbourg Court's decision) it would be clear that the CJEU is closely aligned thereto – even if the technique of modulation is different. The ECtHR's reasoning effectively short-circuits double-jeopardy protection by refuting the existence of a *bis* in the first place (two procedures labelled 'separate' are *considered* as one procedure for the purposes of Protocol 7, Article 4), resulting in

[123] ibid paras 31–35; *Nordzucker* (n 118) paras 36–40.
[124] *Nordzucker* (n 118) para 41.
[125] *Nordzucker* (n 118) para 58.
[126] *bpost* (n 119) para 49.

a partial roll-back of the *Engel* criteria (which allows sanctions labelled 'administrative' to be *considered* criminal for the purposes of Article 6 ECHR). In contrast, the CJEU, in making *Menci* the standard, embraces the notion of duplication subject to the 'escape hatch'[127] in Article 52(1) of the Charter.

According to that article, limitations of Charter rights may be made only if they are necessary and genuinely meet objectives of genuine interest recognised by the EU, or the need to protect the rights and freedoms of others. It is here especially that *bpost* tasks national courts with a potentially daunting mission: further to establishing that two sets of proceedings pursue complementary aims relating to different aspects of the same unlawful conduct, determining the strict necessity of a duplication of penalties requires an assessment of

> whether there are clear and precise rules making it possible to predict which acts or omissions are liable to be subject to a duplication of proceedings and penalties, and also to predict that there will be coordination between the different authorities, whether the two sets of proceedings have been conducted in a manner that is sufficiently coordinated and within a proximate timeframe and whether any penalty that may have been imposed in the proceedings that were first in time was taken into account in the assessment of the second penalty, meaning that the resulting burden, for the persons concerned, of such duplication is limited to what is strictly necessary and the overall penalties imposed correspond to the seriousness of the offences committed.[128]

D. Ramifications in Composite Settings

The shape and contents of that multifaceted assessment are familiar from the *Menci* case law, and indeed very soon after *bpost* and *Nordzucker* the Court added a further decision to its growing line of dual-track value added tax (VAT) cases, providing further detailed guidance on both the 'foreseeability' in national law of potential duplication and the total proportionality of combined penalties (financial penalties and a custodial sentence) in *BV/Direction départementale de la Haute-Savoie.*[129] The pertinent question for present purposes remains: how far might the *bpost* and *Nordzucker* rulings extend in both trans-procedural and trans-jurisdictional dimensions?

In competition law, for example, the co-existence of national antitrust enforcement *au sens propre* and the parallel enforcement of EU and national competition law (where trade between Member States may be affected under Regulation 1/2003) will soon welcome a new constellation in the shape of the Digital Markets Act (DMA).

It seems entirely possible that an undertaking could face one set of proceedings brought by the Commission under the DMA and another set of proceedings under EU and national competition law.[130] Provided that the material facts clear the hurdle

[127] Opinion of AG Bobek in Case C-151/20 *Bundeswettbewerbsbehörde v Nordzucker AG and Others*, delivered on 2 September 2021, para 38.

[128] *bpost* (n 119) para 51.

[129] Case C-570/20 *Criminal proceedings against BV/Direction départementale des finances publiques de la Haute-Savoie* ECLI:EU:C:2022:348 ('*BV*').

[130] For an analysis see D Katsifis, 'Ne bis in idem and the DMA: the CJEU's judgments in bpost and Nordzucker – Part II', *The Platform Law Blog* (29 March 2022), available at https://theplatformlaw.blog/2022/03/29/ne-bis-in-idem-and-the-dma-the-cjeus-judgments-in-bpost-and-nordzucker-part-ii/.

of 'identity' and trigger Article 50 protection, the limitation framework inspired by *Menci* and *A and B v Norway*, as previously discussed, kicks in. Assuming, too, that both frameworks may be said to target 'conduct that is harmful to society', will enforcement measures under the DMA and EU (and national) competition law constitute 'complementary legal responses' forming 'a coherent whole so as to address different aspects of the social problem involved'?

Faced with 'double-*Engel*' enforcement[131] by authorities in different jurisdictions (one national and the other supranational), it may prove difficult to cleanly parse two complementary aims in the fashion of either the *Menci* case law (administrative sanctions for any VAT infringement; criminal penalties for serious violations) or *bpost* (which ascribed the aim of liberalising the postal market to enforcement by the national regulator, and the fostering of open competition to the Belgian national competition authority). Of such matter is 'fertile ground for litigation'[132] indeed made.

In the event that the identified aims are deemed more than complementary, to the extent that they converge to pursue the same objective of general interest, the Court has been clear: such duplication 'cannot in all events be justified under Article 52(1) of the Charter'.[133] In this regard, *Nordzucker* was straightforward: since the application by national competition authorities of national and EU competition law in parallel per se[134] seeks to avoid distortions of competition in the internal market, if the national court determines that the double-identity test of '*idem*' has been met, a violation of *ne bis in idem* is imminent.

Within that 'if' resides a telling difference between the Court's rulings in *bpost* and *Nordzucker* and the elaborate Opinions of Advocate General Bobek, also issued together in September 2021. Whilst the Court and Mr Bobek were both of the view that the '*idem*' test was in need of unification,[135] the Court opted to unify on the basis of *idem factum* (ie extending the 'residual' test to also cover competition law) against the advice of its Advocate General, who had proposed unifying on the basis of *idem crimen* (ie extending a version of the test hitherto applicable only to competition law to all other areas of EU law). In Mr Bobek's view, *Menci* is a 'paradox'[136] and a 'problematic decision',[137] and its adoption as the uniform standard, by pushing the centre of analysis toward the limitation clause in Article 52(1) of the Charter, would result in an *ex post* correction

[131] Where both sets of proceedings are formally administrative; in the absence of any true criminal proceedings.

[132] Katsifis (n 130).

[133] The wording in the original German ('*jedenfalls nicht nach Art. 52 Abs. 1 der Charta gerechtfertigt werden kann*') is perhaps more immune to ambiguity; *Nordzucker* (n 118) para 57, referring to *Menci* (n 111) para 44.

[134] Since, as seen, Art 101 TFEU only applies (and must apply) when trade between Member States may be affected.

[135] In his Opinion in *bpost* (n 117), AG Bobek referred (in para 122, fn 98) to AG Kokott's position in *Toshiba* (n 114) (at para 117 of that Opinion) that 'the crucial importance of the *ne bis in idem* principle as a founding principle of EU law which enjoys the status of a fundamental right means that its content must not be substantially different depending on which area of law is concerned', and found the notion of the content of Article 50 of the Charter differing between areas of EU law to which it is applied 'rather difficult to maintain in conceptual terms'; *bpost* (n 119) para 95.

[136] Opinion of AG Bobek in *bpost* (n 117), para 101.

[137] ibid para 100.

(which is bound to be 'circumstantial'), rather than the *ex ante* protection warranted by Article 50 of the Charter.[138]

The question of whether a unified triple-identity '*idem*' in the jurisprudence may have delivered greater – *qua* earlier – protection against the initiation of proceedings, fully protecting the essence of the right enshrined Article 50, than the 'one *Menci* to rule them all'[139] (capable only of later protection, per Mr Bobek, against a disproportionate whole of punishment)[140] ultimately endorsed by the Court, would require a deeper analysis than it is possible to perform here.[141]

In any event, the *bpost* and *Nordzucker* rulings appear to demand greater coordination between national and EU enforcers across a multitude of fields of law in order to exclude the possibility of *ex post* 'correction' under the expanded *Menci* test.[142] This goes even for the SSM, which although 'owing to the allocation of sanctioning competences between the ECB and the NCAs … is generally *ne bis in idem* foolproof',[143] may still leave some scope for potential violations depending on the interpretation of certain provisions of the SSM Regulation on competence division between the ECB and national authorities.[144] To return momentarily to the PIF area briefly visited in section II.C, the recent reform of the OLAF framework in 2020, itself largely driven by the need to regulate the relationship between OLAF and the EPPO, incorporates several provisions dealing carefully with investigations by the two Offices into the 'same facts'. In particular, OLAF must inform the EPPO of any criminal conduct in respect of which the latter Office could exercise its competence; if that conduct comes to light during an OLAF investigation, in principle that investigation is discontinued,[145] although dual-track 'complementary investigations' can still be pursued, following consultations, at the EPPO's discretion.[146]

[138] ibid para 111. The converse of a 'circumstantial' or even 'accidental' *ex post* correction is neatly captured by Katsifis (n 124), who refers to the ability of the *ne bis in idem* principle to act 'prophylactically'.

[139] Opinion of AG Bobek in *bpost* (n 117, section heading B.2.

[140] ibid para 109.

[141] For another solution put forward in the time between delivery of the Opinions and of the judgments, see P Rossi-Maccanico, 'A Reasoned Approach to Prohibiting the *Bis in Idem*' *eucrim* 4/2021, 266.

[142] For Luchtman, *bpost* and *Nordzucker* demonstrate that 'the *ne bis in idem* principle is not only responsive to a larger trend in law enforcement – that towards integrated or hybrid enforcement models – but is also actively promoting it'. See M Luchtman, 'The CJEU judgments in C-117/20 bpost and C-151/20 Nordzucker: Fundamental rights as a vehicle for hybrid enforcement mechanisms?', *RENFORCE Blog*, Utrecht University (12 May 2022) available at http://blog.renforce.eu/index.php/en/2022/05/12/the-cjeu-judgments-in-c-117-20-bpost-and-c-151-20-nordzucker-fundamental-rights-as-a-vehicle-for-hybrid-enforcement-mechanisms/

[143] A Karagianni, 'A roadmap toward protecting fundamental rights in composite banking enforcement', *EU Law Enforcement* (30 June 2022) available at https://eulawenforcement.com/?p=8305. See further AM Karagianni, *The Protection of Fundamental Rights in Composite Banking Supervision Procedures* (Europa Law Publishing 2022).

[144] A Witte, 'The application of national banking supervision law by the ECB: Three parallel modes of executing EU law' (2014) 21(1) *Maastricht Journal of European and Comparative Law* 89, 97; and in detail B van Bockel, 'The Single Supervisory Mechanism Regulation: Questions of *ne bis in idem* and implications for the further integration of the system of fundamental rights protection in the EU' (2017) 24(2) *Maastricht Journal of European and Comparative Law* 194.

[145] Arts 12c(1)–(5) and Art 12d OLAF Regulation as amended.

[146] Art 12f OLAF Regulation as amended.

The broader question, as noted at the outset of this section, is how far the *Menci*-based test can and ought to now expand. *Nordzucker* confirmed its application to transnational duplications of administrative punitive enforcement within one area of law (competition law) – what of other such areas? *bpost*, meanwhile, confirmed its application to 'domestic' duplications of administrative punitive enforcement across two different areas of law. What then of administrative punitive enforcement – within the scope of EU law – that crosses both jurisdictional and procedural borders? To cite only one possible field of application, as regards financial institutions, van Bockel has noted that national regulators remain in charge of supervisory tasks falling outwith the scope of the SSM Regulation, such as consumer protection, the prevention of money laundering, payment services and 'conduct of business' regulations.[147]

Assuming the facts pass the '*idem*' test, will the bar for coordination be set lower in such cases – and can this be credibly squared with the legitimate expectations of EU citizens to move, work and face reasonably foreseeable enforcement action within a single AFSJ? And lastly, is there anything to stop the test finding application where one set of proceedings is within the scope of EU law but the other is not – for example, in the field of direct taxation?[148]

IV. Conclusion: To be Continued

The need for answers to the host of questions just raised in section III of this chapter will doubtless gradually draw further indications from the CJEU and warrant further (comparative) research efforts.

As the chapter was being completed, the Court issued its judgment in *BV*, which – although a 'domestic' case confined to the interpretation of national law in light of the Charter[149] – can be used, by way of conclusion, to demonstrate some key aspects of the core challenge at hand: how to scale the requirements of the legality principle from the national 'dual-track' setting to a composite administrative punitive one – that is, to uphold 'composite legality'.

The *BV* case concerned the subsequent criminal prosecution and sanction by custodial sentence (of an accountant, for serious tax fraud) in relation to the same conduct that had already attracted administrative sanction (tax penalties amounting to 40 per cent of the VAT evaded). The CJEU was asked for guidance on the compliance of French law with what I term the 'before, during and after' of the Court's strict necessity test in *Menci*: as seen, for such a duplication not to violate the *ne bis in idem* principle, there must be clear and precise rules that:

(i) Allow the individual to predict which acts and omissions are liable to be subject to such a duplication of proceedings and penalties (*before* enforcement);
(ii) Ensure the procedures are coordinated so as to reduce to what is strictly necessary the additional disadvantage associated with the duplication of proceedings of a criminal nature conducted independently (*during* enforcement); and

[147] van Bockel (n 144) 196.
[148] Luchtman 'The CJEU judgments' (n 142).
[149] *BV* (n 129).

(iii) Make it possible to guarantee that the severity of all penalties imposed corresponds with the seriousness of the offence concerned (*after* enforcement).[150]

Before enforcement, French 'duplication law' in this specific area was found to be solidly in place: the Tax Code provided guidance as to the seriousness of (fraudulent) conduct liable to attract a 'true' criminal fine or a custodial sentence in addition to administrative penalties, the constitutionality of such duplications had already been tested and trammelled by the French Constitutional Council, and the 'interpretative reservations' of the latter had in turn been applied on several occasions in proceedings before the *Cour de Cassation*. Against that (domestic) background, the CJEU stressed that the existence of 'clear and precise rules' on possible duplication is for the national court to determine and 'depends to a considerable degree on the content of the text in question, the field it covers and the number and status of those to whom it is addressed'.[151]

Extrapolating to the composite setting of punitive enforcement in the EU, it was seen in this chapter that clear and precise rules are generally lacking at the stage before any such duplication occurs – at the moment cases are allocated and applicable laws are determined. It was shown that EU competition law places the emphasis on discretion and flexibility, hindering predictability, foreseeability and agency for the subject. In the ECB setting, whilst there is no case allocation *sensu stricto*, the very discretion to determine the applicable law runs the risk of draining away a principal intended function of a legal basis: to enable ascertainment of one's legal position before acting.[152]

During enforcement, in *BV* the French system was also found to be well-integrated, with the opening of criminal proceedings requiring, inter alia, that a complaint first be lodged by the tax authorities with the public prosecutor's office.

Pivoting once more to the focus area of this chapter, whilst an express aim of the reforms of the ECN+ Directive in EU competition law was to provide a legal basis for cooperation within the ECN, and although that cooperation should be further tightened internally, the ECN remains without legal personality and still offers little visibility to parties affected by the decisions taken therein. And as Mr Bobek observed in his Opinion in *bpost*, having noted the 'teething problems' experienced in competence attribution under both the ECN as well as the General Data Protection Regulation,[153]

> if that is the current state of affairs within dedicated and expressly regulated networks across the European Union, it is not immediately obvious how the necessary level of coordination could reasonably be expected and achieved in various areas of law, within various bodies, and across various Member States.[154]

[150] *BV* (n 129) para 36, citing *Menci* (n 111) paras 49, 53 and 55.

[151] *BV* (n 129) para 43.

[152] In *BV*, the Court also indicated that legal precedent can play an important role, that individuals may be expected to consult it in order to ascertain their exposure to duplicate sanctions – and indeed that a higher standard may be expected of professionals (including accountants, as was the case): ibid para 48. How might these extra-legislative indications translate to the transnational (composite) setting?

[153] Regulation (EU) 2016/679 of the European Parliament and of the Council of 27 April 2016 on the protection of natural persons with regard to the processing of personal data and on the free movement of such data, and repealing Directive 95/46/EC (General Data Protection Regulation) OJ L119/1 ('GDPR').

[154] Opinion of AG Bobek in *bpost* (n 117) para 116.

Lastly, the question of punishment meted out *after* enforcement presented the thorniest question in *BV*, seeing as the proportionality test applied in French law to the relevant duplicate tax sanctions only considered financial penalties: the total amount cannot exceed the maximum amount for either sanction. This, it had been contended, was at odds with the requirement in the *Menci* case law that the severity of *all* penalties imposed (ie a fine *and* a prison sentence) does not exceed the seriousness of the offence identified. The CJEU again returned the matter to the national court, which was tasked with reconciling seemingly incompatible readings by the CJEU and the French Constitutional Council.

Turning to (composite) administrative punitive proceedings, whilst custodial sanctions are out of the question, taken to its logical conclusion, might this line of reasoning require national courts to assess the severity of accumulations of fines or other administrative sanctions (such as licence revocations) across jurisdictions and procedures, and is this a realistic scenario?

To close, it is worth recalling that whilst the *ne bis in idem* case law provides a crucial window onto examples – both positive and negative – of national and transnational combinations of enforcement action, for the reasons set out in this chapter (and especially in section II), no duplication of proceedings or sanctions is required for there to be justifiable concerns around the risks of forum shopping and foreseeability of punishment in composite administrative punitive settings. Coming full circle to the starting point of the analysis, and whilst the two fundamental rights are interrelated, the scope of protection against *bis in idem* enshrined in Article 50 of the Charter exists alongside the legality required by Article 49 of the Charter in relation to the definition of penalties.[155]

This chapter has sought to contribute to deepening the discussion on the need for a greater honouring of the principle of legality in both its substantive and procedural dimensions whenever citizens are confronted with composite administrative punitive enforcement in the EU. In so doing, its aim has been to add to growing calls for legislators at the EU and national levels to accept the challenge of engineering, through binding rules on forum choice, applicable law and coordination, more foreseeability (and thereby, ultimately, greater equality of arms) in the composite administrative punitive legal order – even in the absence of any 'true' criminal proceedings, where *Engel* fears to tread.

[155] Opinion of AG Sánchez-Bordona in Case C-570/20 *BV v Direction départementale des finances publiques de la Haute-Savoie*, delivered on 9 December 2021, para 56.

8

Information Sharing between the EU Administrative Enforcement Agencies and the Criminal Authorities *Sensu Stricto*

SILVIA ALLEGREZZA, ANNA MORAITI, LEONARDO ROMANÒ AND ANDREA SALEMI

I. Introduction: Mapping the Interaction between Administrative and Criminal Enforcement – Focus on Information Exchange

In the last two decades, the European Union (EU) has increased its administrative enforcement system enormously in several fields, all of them interacting with criminal law.[1] From the establishment of the Anti-Fraud Office (OLAF) to protect European financial interests[2] to the most recent proposal on the creation of an Anti-Money Laundering Agency (AMLA),[3] the EU has constantly enriched the plethora of agencies in charge of

[1] S Allegrezza (ed), *The Enforcement Dimension of the Single Supervisory Mechanism* (X, Wolters Kluwer/CEDAM 2022); M Luchtman and J Vervaele, 'Enforcing the Market Abuse Regime: Towards an Integrated Model of Criminal and Administrative Law Enforcement in the European Union?' (2014) 5 *New Journal of European Criminal Law* 192; V Franssen and C Harding (eds), *Criminal and Quasi-criminal Enforcement Mechanisms in Europe, Origins, Concepts, Future* (Hart Publishing 2022); F Galli and A Weyembergh, *Do Labels Still Matter?: Blurring boundaries between administrative and criminal law. The influence of the EU* (Université Libre de Bruxelles 2014); A Weyembergh and N Joncheray, 'Punitive Administrative Sanctions and Procedural Safeguards: A Blurred Picture That Needs to Be Addressed' (2016) 7 *New Journal of Criminal Law* 190.

[2] Regulation (EU, Euratom) No 883/2013 of 11 September 2013 concerning investigations conducted by the European Anti-Fraud Office (OLAF) and repealing Regulation (EC) No 1073/1999 of the European Parliament and of the Council and Council Regulation (Euratom) No 1074/1999 as amended by Regulation (EU, Euratom) 2020/2223 of the European Parliament and of the Council of 23 December 2020 [2013] OJ L248/1.

[3] Proposal for a Regulation of the European Parliament and of the Council establishing the Authority for Anti-Money Laundering and Countering the Financing of Terrorism and amending Regulations (EU) No 1093/2010, (EU) 1094/2010, (EU) 1095/2010 COM(2021) 421 final. See S Allegrezza, 'The proposed Anti-Money Laundering Authority, FIU cooperation, powers and exchanges of information A Critical Assessment', Research Paper for the EU Parliament, June 2022 (forthcoming).

investigating and sanctioning via administrative fines potential breaches of the EU legal framework in the field of competition, fraud, finance, securities, banking and, more recently, money laundering. Only in recent years was the European arsenal completed by a fully-fledged criminal investigative body, the European Public Prosecutor's Office (EPPO), introduced in 2017 and operative since June 2021.[4]

The proliferation of EU enforcement bodies conferred with punitive powers (EU Commission, the European Central Bank (ECB), the European Securities and Markets Authority (ESMA), OLAF) has several reasons. The lack of a legal basis in the Treaties for the EU to use criminal law as an enforcement tool resulted in administrative enforcement as the only way for the EU to centralise control over vital fields of the Union.[5] However, the various financial crises – and the many scandals – that unfolded over the past few years laid bare the weaknesses of such enforcement bodies when deprived of strong sanctioning powers. This led to the unprecedented centralisation of EU administrative investigation and sanctions with frequent overlaps with national criminal enforcement. The double-track system, which combines both administrative and criminal enforcement, is not new at the national level, where the growth of administrative enforcement and the associated contraction of criminal law enforcement have different rationales. Not the lack of a legal basis but rather the inefficiency of the latter, dominated by strict rules of evidence, suggested departure from traditional criminal justice enforcement and a move towards smoother administrative sanctioning. The coexistence of the two systems caused some clashes when administrative fines targeted the same conduct covered by traditional criminal offences. When transposed to the European level, this complex system of interactions triggered unprecedented issues.

The current picture sees several EU enforcement bodies endowed with sanctioning powers for certain breaches that are also targeted by national administrative fines, as well as by national criminal offences. Therefore, the traditional horizontal interaction between the two enforcement systems has to face an additional layer of complexity, represented by the vertical relationship between the EU and the national levels.

In order to develop a map of the different types of interaction, we can identify three main areas: (i) the transfer of information between administrative bodies; (ii) the transfer of information between administrative bodies and the criminal law agencies; and (iii) the impact of the sanctioning decision adopted by an EU or a national body on the other actors, be they of an administrative or a criminal nature.

This chapter focuses on the exchange of information between administrative and criminal law authorities at both the European and the national levels, with no distinction based on the potential use of that information as evidence nor on the impact of the potential for *bis in idem*.[6] With this aim in mind, we have selected four fields in which EU enforcement bodies cooperate with national administrative and criminal agencies: we consider OLAF and the national investigative agencies concerned with the so-called Euro-Frauds; the field of competition law that served as a blueprint for the development of more recent policies of the EU; the ECB and the flow of information to

[4] Council Regulation (EU) No 2017/1939 of 12 October 2017 implementing enhanced cooperation on the establishment of the European Public Prosecutor's Office ('the EPPO') [2017] OJ L283/1.

[5] O Jansen (ed), *Administrative Sanctions in the European Union* (Intersentia 2013).

[6] On these topics, see ch 6 (Giuffrida and Theodorakakou) and ch 7 (Robinson) of this volume respectively.

national administrative and criminal agencies; and ESMA and the network of financial supervisors.

This study will reveal how direct and indirect channels are used, and their efficiency in building the crucial network so much needed in such pivotal fields of EU action. For the sake of clarity, we have divided the analysis into two sections according to the dynamic of the flow of information: section II will deal with the top-down movement, when the information is transferred from the EU level to the national one; while section III concerns the opposite bottom-up movement, describing how national authorities, in particular of a criminal nature, are communicating with the EU actors. Within those sections, another division is made according to the way EU agencies and national criminal enforcement are communicating. The first group will include those cases in which the EU legal framework provides for a direct channel of communication between the EU body and criminal investigative agencies; while a second group will consider cases in which national administrative authorities are called on to fulfil a role of intermediation between the EU agency and national criminal enforcement.

II. The Vertical Dimension of Information Flow: From EU Enforcement Agencies to National Authorities

A. Direct Contact between EU Enforcement Agencies and National Criminal Enforcement Authorities

i. The Case of OLAF

OLAF is the European administrative agency in charge of conducting administrative investigations into fraud, corruption and any other illegal activity affecting the financial interests of the Union.[7]

Since the early 1990s, the Court of Justice has clarified that the principle of 'sincere cooperation' operates not only at the horizontal level but also at the vertical level, for example from the Commission to the national authorities that are responsible for ensuring that EU law is applied and respected in the national legal systems.[8] Recent amendments to OLAF's legal framework[9] have codified this obligation, but OLAF maintains some discretion in handling information (not evidence per se)[10] on illegal activities

[7] Art 1 Regulation 883/2013.

[8] Case C-2/88 Imm, *Zwartveld and Others* ECLI:EU:C:1990:440. The case was a referral from a Dutch court hearing a criminal case involving financial embezzlement in the common market in fisheries.

[9] Regulation (EU, Euratom) 2016/2030 of 26 October 2016 amending Regulation (EU, Euratom) No 883/2013, as regards the secretariat of the Supervisory Committee of the European Anti-Fraud Office (OLAF) [2016] OJ L317/1; Regulation (EU, Euratom) No 2020/2223 of the European Parliament and of the Council of 23 December 2020 amending Regulation (EU, Euratom) No 883/2013, as regards cooperation with the European Public Prosecutor's Office and the effectiveness of the European Anti-Fraud Office investigations [2020] OJ L437/49.

[10] M Luchtman, A Karagianni and K Bovend'Eerdt, 'EU Administrative Investigations and the Use of Their Results as Evidence in National Punitive Proceedings' in F Giuffrida and K Ligeti (eds), *Admissibility of OLAF Final Reports as Evidence in Criminal Proceedings* (Luxembourg University 2019) 42.

that affect EU financial interests. Rules on information exchange vary according to the phase (prior to and during an investigation) or the type of investigation (internal or external),[11] but also primarily according to the means of transmission of information.

Article 3(12) of Regulation 883/2013 provides that OLAF, even before it has decided to open an external investigation, 'may' liaise with the competent authorities of the Member States concerned and share with them 'information which suggests that there has been a fraud, corruption or any other illegal activity affecting the financial interests of the Union.'[12] This exchange of information must be done without prejudice to Article 12(c)(1), which covers the reporting of criminal conduct to the EPPO.[13] A similar rule with regard to internal investigations is provided by Article 4(8) of Regulation 883/2013: before deciding on the opening of such an investigation, OLAF 'may' provide the institution, body, office or agency concerned with information that suggests that there has been a fraud, corruption or any other illegal activity affecting the Union budget; in this case, OLAF 'shall' also inform, 'where necessary', the competent authorities of the Member State concerned.[14]

The decision to open an investigation shall be taken by the Director-General when there is sufficient suspicion that there has been fraud, corruption or any other illegal activity affecting the financial interests of the Union.[15] According to Article 5(5) of Regulation 883/2013, if the Director-General decides not to open an investigation, OLAF may inform without delay the competent authorities of the Member States concerned (whichever these might be) and send any relevant information, as appropriate, for action to be taken in accordance with Union and their respective national laws.[16] This option becomes a duty when the decision not to open an investigation is taken

[11] For a comprehensive approach on the matter, see V Covolo, 'Regulation 833/2013 Concerning Investigation Conducted by OLAF: A Missed Opportunity for Substantial Reforms?' (2017) 7 *European Criminal Law Review* 151; G De Amicis and RE Kostoris, 'Vertical Cooperation' in RE Kostoris (ed), *Handbook of European Criminal Procedure* (Springer 2018) 206.

[12] Art 3(12) Regulation 883/2013: 'Without prejudice to Article 12(c)(1), where, before a decision has been taken whether or not to open an external investigation, the Office handles information which suggests that there has been fraud, corruption or any other illegal activity affecting the financial interests of the Union, it may inform the competent authorities of the Member States concerned and, where necessary, the institutions, bodies, offices and agencies concerned.'

[13] Art 12(c)(1) Regulation 883/2013: 'The Office shall submit a report to the EPPO without undue delay on any criminal conduct in respect of which the EPPO could exercise its competence in accordance with Chapter IV of Regulation (EU) 2017/1939. The report shall be sent without undue delay before or during an investigation of the Office.'

[14] Art 4(8) Regulation 883/2013:

> Without prejudice to Article 12(c)(1), where, before a decision has been taken whether or not to open an internal investigation, the Office handles information which suggests that there has been fraud, corruption or any other illegal activity affecting the financial interests of the Union, it may inform the institution, body, office or agency concerned. Upon request, the institution, body, office or agency concerned shall inform the Office of any action taken and of its findings on the basis of such information.
>
> Where necessary, the Office shall also inform the competent authorities of the Member State concerned. In this case, the procedural requirements laid down in the second and third subparagraphs of Article 9(4) shall apply. If the competent authorities decide to take any action on the basis of the information transmitted to them, in accordance with national law, they shall, upon request, inform the Office thereof.

[15] De Amicis and Kostoris (n 11) 207.

[16] Art 5(5) Regulation 883/2013.

despite there being sufficient suspicion that a crime of fraud, corruption or any other illegal activity affecting the EU financial interests has taken place.[17] The difference is easily explained: in the latter case, national authorities can use this information for their autonomous investigations, despite OLAF's refusal to act.

Article 12(1) of Regulation 883/2013 also provides that OLAF 'may transmit to the competent authorities of the concerned Member States information obtained in the course of external investigation'. No duty exists, but the transmission has to be made 'in due time' to enable national authorities 'to take appropriate action in accordance with their national law'.[18] However, an exception to the general rule of discretion is to be found in Regulation 2185/96,[19] according to which OLAF 'shall report as soon as possible to the competent authority of the State within whose territory an on-the-spot check or inspection has been performed any fact or suspicion relating to an irregularity which has come to its notice in the course of the on-the-spot check or inspection'.[20] A real obligation exists for OLAF to transmit information obtained in the course of internal investigations to national judicial authorities (which may be either administrative or judicial) if such information concerns facts that fall within their jurisdiction.[21]

Special rules apply when information collected by OLAF in an internal investigation reveals the existence of a crime. Article 11(5) of Regulation 883/2013 requires OLAF's report, together with the recommendations, to be transmitted without delay to prosecutorial authorities of the Member State concerned.[22]

The European Court of Auditors (ECA) raised some doubts about the effectiveness of the coordination between OLAF and national authorities, as the latter in most cases have no contact with OLAF before receiving its final report.[23] National prosecutors also indicated that they would prefer to be informed of any suspected criminal offence much earlier than at the end of OLAF's investigation, in order to better assist OLAF and, where appropriate, start their own criminal investigation: delays in such complex cases increase the risk of having their criminal cases time-barred.[24] When suspicions of crimes arise, early contact between national authorities and OLAF would definitely benefit OLAF investigations and their follow-up at the national level.

In conclusion, OLAF does not have an obligation to promptly inform national competent authorities (NCAs) about conduct of a criminal nature before the conclusion of its investigations, since its investigations are administrative and it may not be clear from the outset whether they will end up revealing or dealing with criminal offences.

[17] Art 5(6) Regulation 883/2013.

[18] Covolo (n 11) 158.

[19] Council Regulation (Euratom, EC) No 2185/96 of 11 November 1996 concerning on-the-spot checks and inspections carried out by the Commission in order to protect the European Communities' financial interests against fraud and other irregularities [1996] OJ L292/2.

[20] Art 8(2) Regulation 2185/96.

[21] Art 12(2) Regulation 883/2013: 'Without prejudice to Articles 10 and 11, the Director-General shall transmit to the judicial authorities of the Member State concerned information obtained by the Office, in the course of internal investigations, concerning facts which fall within the jurisdiction of a national judicial authority.'

[22] De Amicis and Kostoris (n 11) 209.

[23] F Giuffrida, 'Comparative Analysis' in F Giuffrida and K Ligeti (eds) *Admissibility of OLAF Final Reports as Evidence in Criminal Proceedings* (University of Luxembourg 2019) 264.

[24] European Court of Auditors, *Fighting Fraud in EU Spending: Action Needed*, Special Report No 1 (2019) 40–41.

Nonetheless, an OLAF duty to report any potential *notitia criminis* to NCAs may better serve the general scope of an integrated system offering the opportunity to reach a common agreement on how to proceed with the case.[25]

ii. The Case of ESMA

An exchange of information with a national judicial authority can only occur when ESMA has to refer matters to the relevant national authorities for the purposes of criminal prosecution. So, on the one hand, when the request comes from judicial or prosecutorial authorities, there is an obligation in this respect. On the other hand, for the exchange of information with other national administrative authorities, there is no obligation nor an official channel for communication. It is likely that the exchange of information with those entities will take place via NCAs.[26]

According to Article 23(e)(8) of Regulation 1060/2009 (Credit-rating Agencies Regulation – CRAR)[27] and Article 64(8) of Regulation 648/2012[28] (European Markets Infrastructure Regulation – EMIR), ESMA

> shall refer matters for criminal prosecution to the relevant national authorities where, in carrying out its duties under this Regulation, it finds that there are serious indications of the possible existence of facts liable to constitute criminal offences. In addition, ESMA shall refrain from imposing fines or periodic penalty payments where a prior acquittal or conviction arising from identical facts, or from facts which are substantially the same, has acquired the force of res judicata as the result of criminal proceedings under national law.

The 'relevant national authorities' to which ESMA shall refer matters for criminal prosecution are most likely criminal law authorities.

B. Indirect Contact between EU Enforcement Agencies and National Criminal Enforcement Authorities via National Administrative Competent Authorities

The most successful model of vertical information sharing between the EU administrative agencies and national criminal enforcement authorities sees the involvement of national administrative authorities. No direct contact is foreseen between the European administrative level and the national criminal agencies. The information flow is channelled from the EU level via the national administrative counterparts. The reasons for this choice are many: the need to protect administrative discretionary powers; the

[25] Giuffrida (n 23) 266.

[26] M Scholten and M Simonato, 'EU Report' in M Luchtman and J Vervaele (eds), *Report Investigatory Powers And Procedural Safeguards: Improving OLAF's legislative framework through a comparison with other EU law enforcement authorities (ECN/ESMA/ECB)* (Utrecht University 2017) 32.

[27] Regulation (EC) No 1060/2009 of the European Parliament and of the Council of 16 September 2009 on credit rating agencies [2009] OJ L302/1.

[28] Regulation (EU) No 648/2012 of the European Parliament and of the Council of 4 July 2012 on OTC derivatives, central counterparties and trade repositories [2012] OJ L201/1.

need to avoid delays linked to criminal investigations; and a certain sceptical approach towards a direct flow of information when confidential information is at stake. This model is adopted in the field of competition, banking and finance.

i. DG Competition: Obligations to Transfer Information to National Judicial Authorities

The EU Commission's Directorate-General for Competition (DG Competition) is responsible for the enforcement of EU competition law, in particular for the enforcement of Article 101 of the Treaty on the Functioning of the European Union (TFEU), which prohibits agreements between competitors having as their object or effect the distortion of EU competition law (cartel prohibition), and Article 102 TFEU, which bans abuses of a dominant position. Articles 101 and 102 TFEU are enforced by DG Competition together with its national counterparts. According to Recital 34 of Regulation 1/2003,[29] Member States should designate and empower authorities to apply Articles 101 and 102 TFEU as public enforcers. These authorities are referred to throughout Regulation 1/2003 as 'national competition authorities'. The legal nature of the 'competent authority' will depend on the national system in a given Member State. In most Member States competition authorities have been granted more or less independent status from the political sphere. By delegating competition law powers to an independent body, the legislature tries to guarantee that the application and interpretation of competition rules are mainly based on economic and legal arguments alone, and are not shaped by political pressure.[30]

The national competition authorities and DG Competition have formed a network, the European Competition Network (ECN). The cornerstone of the system of EU competition law enforcement is Regulation 1/2003, which, *inter alia*, lays down rules for the exchange of information within the Network.

Pursuant to Article 12(1) of Regulation 1/2003, the EU Commission and the national competition authorities shall have the power to provide one another with any matter of fact or law including confidential information and use it in evidence for the purpose of applying Articles 101 and 102 TFEU.[31] The range of information is very wide, from documents and statements to digital information. These documents include the Commission's decisions on the finding and termination of an infringement, decisions on interim measures, and commitment decisions finding that Articles 101 and 102 TFEU are not applicable to a specific agreement (the finding of inapplicability). In addition, if a national competition authority so requests, DG Competition must

[29] Council Regulation (EC) No 1/2003 of 16 December 2002 on the implementation of the rules on competition laid down in Articles 81 and 82 of the Treaty [2003] OJ L1/1.

[30] See generally JW van de Gronden and SA de Vries, 'Independent Competition Authorities in the EU' (2006) 2(1) *Utrecht Law Review* 32.

[31] Luchtman, Karagianni and Bovend'Eerdt (n 10) 31: 'Presumably, the rationale underpinning this provision is the need to overcome potential hurdles that could be posed by diverging national procedural standards. In this respect, Article 12(1) of Regulation 1/2003 must be read in conjunction with Recital 16, which states that the exchange of information between the ECN members and its use in evidence should be allowed "notwithstanding any national provision to the contrary".'

provide it with a copy of other existing documents that are important for assessing a certain case.

The most relevant duty is the one in Article 11(2) of Regulation 1/2003, according to which the EU Commission must transmit to national competition authorities copies of the most important documents that it has in its possession. The official opening of a DG Competition investigation does not have any consequence for the transfer of information.

While DG Competition does not have many obligations to transfer information to national competition authorities, the national authorities have many. No special regime exists with regard to the obligation of national competition authorities to transfer information to DG Competition. Nevertheless, as a general rule, Regulation 1/2003 seems to allow the flow of information between national competition authorities and DG Competition, and its use in evidence is allowed even if such information is confidential and notwithstanding any national provisions to the contrary. Moreover, according to Article 11(4) of Regulation 1/2003, 'at the request of the Commission, the acting competition authority shall make available to the Commission other documents it holds which are necessary for the assessment of the case'. Thus, the transmission of information at DG Competition's request is indeed possible.[32] Moreover, information gathered by a national competition authority on the basis of Article 22(2) of Regulation 1/2003, at the request of DG Competition, shall be transmitted to the Directorate-General.

There are also important obligations on DG Competition to transfer specific categories of information to national judicial authorities.[33] The relationship between DG Competition and national courts is regulated by Article 15 of Regulation 1/2003, which states, inter alia, that national courts can request the Commission to transmit to them certain information it has in its possession or its opinion on questions concerning the application of EU competition rules.[34] In this respect, it is important to clarify which authorities qualify as 'judicial authorities' according to EU law. The judicial authorities envisaged by Regulation 1/2003 are *not* criminal law courts or prosecutors. As explained by the Commission Notice on cooperation between the Commission and the courts of the EU Member States,[35] judicial authorities are 'those courts and tribunals within an EU Member State that can apply Articles 101 and 102 TFEU and that are authorised to ask a preliminary question'.[36]

[32] A Karagianni, M Scholten and M Simonato, 'EU "vertical" report. The exchange of information between national and EU authorities' in M Simonato, M Luchtman and J Vervaele (eds), *Exchange of Information with EU and National Enforcement Authorities – Improving OLAF legislative framework through a comparison with other EU authorities (ECN/ESMA/ECB)* (University of Utrecht 2018) 16.

[33] ibid 20.

[34] Art 15(1) Regulation 1/2003: 'In proceedings for the application of Article 81 or Article 82 of the Treaty, courts of the Member States may ask the Commission to transmit to them information in its possession or its opinion on questions concerning the application of the Community competition rules.' Secondary sources may also apply.

[35] Commission Notice on cooperation between the Commission and the courts of the EU Member States in the application of Articles 81 and 82 EC, 2004/C 101/4 [2004] OJ C101/54 ('Cooperation Notice').

[36] Cooperation Notice para 1.

ii. The Case of the ECB: The Single Supervisory Mechanism and Criminal Enforcement

a. The Transmission of Notitiae Criminis

As a response to the enormity of the 2008 financial crisis, the ECB has been vested with direct monitoring, investigating and sanctioning powers for breaches of prudential regulation committed by significant credit institutions of the Eurozone.

Given that irregularities in banking activities often give rise to criminal responses, the information gathered by the Single Supervisory Mechanism (SSM) within the scope of prudential regulation may be relevant for criminal law enforcement agencies located at the national level.[37] Therefore, a situation of parallel proceedings, involving the ECB conducting prudential supervision, on the one hand, and national criminal law enforcement authorities conducting a criminal investigation, on the other hand, is not purely theoretical.[38]

According to Article 136 of Regulation 468/2014 (SSM Framework Regulation – SSMFR),[39] where,

> in carrying out its tasks under the SSM Regulation, the ECB has reason to suspect that a criminal offence may have been committed, it shall request the relevant NCA to refer the matter to the appropriate authorities for investigation and possible criminal prosecution, in accordance with national law.

This means that the ECB informs NCAs, which may – or shall – pass the information on to national prosecutors, the extent of the duty depending on national law.

Several issues arise from this apparently straightforward provision. First, the wording of Article 136 SSMFR seems to suggest that the duty to report criminal offences is only related to the facts discovered during the ECB's supervisory activities and related to significant banks over which the ECB has direct supervisory powers. It would nevertheless be hardly arguable to exclude the ECB's duty to report potential crimes committed by less significant credit institutions if they were to catch the attention of the ECB. The need for sincere cooperation requires this communication to take place even in the absence of a duty on the part of the ECB. A second remark concerns the type of crimes that trigger the ECB's duty to report. Article 136 SSMFR lacks any indication of this sort, clearly suggesting the will to leave the field open to any potential misconduct. These criminal offences are not necessarily strictly related to banking supervision. And the need for an administrative breach of prudential requirements is nowhere mentioned. Evidence of a potential crime might emerge as a purely accidental event. This would allow the supposition that even money laundering or terrorist financing – formally excluded from the competence of the SSM[40] – is covered by this duty.

[37] S Allegrezza, 'The Single Supervisory Mechanism: Institutional Design, Punitive Powers and the Interplay with Criminal Law' in Allegrezza (ed) (n 1) 33.

[38] Luchtman, Karagianni and Bovend'Eerdt (n 10) 37.

[39] Regulation (EU) No 468/2014 of the European Central Bank of 16 April 2014 establishing the framework for cooperation within the Single Supervisory Mechanism between the European Central Bank and national competent authorities and with national designated authorities [2014] OJ L141/1.

[40] See Recitals 28–29 Council Regulation (EU) No 1024/2013 of 15 October 2013 conferring specific tasks on the European Central Bank concerning policies relating to the prudential supervision of credit institutions [2013] OJ L287/66 (SSM Regulation – SSMR).

As for the legal basis upon which the ECB should determine the existence of a potential crime, the existing European legal framework on financial crimes could serve as such: in particular, money laundering, terrorist financing, market abuse and insider trading, as well as the crimes related to the protection of EU financial interests. For these criminal offences partial harmonisation has already been achieved, and national legislatures are at least forced to criminalise certain misconduct. On the other hand, for those crimes that have not yet been harmonised, the ECB cannot draw on any common European reference. In those cases, the above-mentioned incongruences between national systems might have a negative impact on the correct exercise of reporting duties. In the absence of a European reference, the criminal nature of the potential offence (detected during the course of supervisory tasks) is determined by national law. This can be deduced from the wording of the SSMFR, which indicates that reporting duties shall be exercised 'in accordance with national law'.[41]

Once the ECB reports to the NCAs, national rules on the transfer of information from the administrative to the criminal authorities apply.[42] However, the picture at the national level is highly fragmented.[43] In the majority of countries, the NCAs are under an obligation to report any suspicion of a crime that has emerged during their supervisory activity to the competent judicial authorities. In this case, the same duty applies to the facts reported by the ECB. Some other NCAs retain a margin of discretion as to whether to inform the judicial authorities. The consequences of such reporting might, however, differ according to the applicable national legislation. National law determines the extent of and level of constraint on reporting duties from the NCAs to the criminal enforcement agencies. Considering how transnational financial crime has spread in the last few decades, a multi-level reporting duty could be regarded as good practice by the ECB, involving the transfer of information about a transnational criminal offence to all the NCAs of the countries potentially involved. It would then be for the national authorities to coordinate the investigation and cooperation among themselves, at both the administrative and criminal levels.

In conclusion, we should note that no direct contact with criminal agencies is provided for by the European Regulation. While, on the one hand, it is true that direct contact with national prosecutors would have made the exchange of information easier, and perhaps enabled better coordination among the different enforcement tracks, on the other hand we should consider that the lack of previous harmonisation of criminal offences in this field implies that national law has become the main and only normative reference by which to define the potential criminal offence.

b. The ECB's Duty to Disclose Information to Criminal Enforcement Agencies

The reluctance of the European supervisor to cooperate with criminal law enforcement appears even clearer in the opposite case, that is, when the national authorities

[41] Art 136 SSMFR.

[42] For a wider analysis of this issue, see Simonato, Luchtman and Vervaele (eds) (n 32).

[43] See G Lasagni and I Rodopoulos, 'A Comparative Study on Administrative and Criminal Enforcement of Banking Supervision at National Level' in Allegrezza (ed) (n 1) 621.

require the ECB to disclose information relating to its prudential supervisory tasks in the context of an ongoing criminal investigation.

The relationship between the ECB and authorities in the area of criminal justice is unclear. It is defined in very vague terms in Article 53(1) of the Capital Requirements Directive (CRD) IV,[44] which seems to permit supervisors to provide information to judicial bodies, either on request or spontaneously, thus directly facilitating the tasks of the police and/or public prosecutors.

Meanwhile, the ECB has issued Decision 2016/1162 on the disclosure of confidential information in the context of criminal proceedings.[45] The Decision adopts very strict rules regulating the conditions for cooperation between the ECB and the national criminal investigation authorities. Information may be disclosed under the following conditions: (i) if it is due to an express obligation under EU or national law; or (ii) if it is admissible under the relevant legal framework and 'there are no overriding reasons for refusing' to disclose it, such as 'the need to safeguard the interests of the Union or to avoid any interference with the functioning and independence of the ECB, in particular by jeopardising the accomplishment of its tasks'.[46] In these cases, the NCA 'commits to acting on behalf of the ECB in responding to such a request' and 'commits to asking the requesting national criminal investigation authority to guarantee the protection from public disclosure of the confidential information provided'.[47] Therefore, the current legal framework does not provide for any form of direct communication from the ECB to national criminal enforcement.

Some attempts to improve the network of the information channels, in particular between banking supervisors and the agencies in charge of anti-money laundering/countering the financing of terrorism (AML/CFT), have taken place in the last few years. And many more will be made in the next few months, should the reform package presented by the EU Commission in July 2021 be approved.[48] Thanks to the amendments to the AML Directive that entered into force in 2018,[49] a Multilateral Agreement

[44] Directive No 2013/36/EU of the European Parliament and of the Council of 26 June 2013 on access to the activity of credit institutions and the prudential supervision of credit institutions and investment firms, amending Directive 2002/87/EC and repealing Directives 2006/48/EC and 2006/49/EC [2013] OJ L176/338.

[45] Decision 2016/1162 of the European Central Bank of 30 June 2016 on disclosure of confidential information in the context of criminal investigations (ECB/2016/19) [2016] OJ L192/73.

[46] ibid Art 1(a).

[47] ibid Art 2(1).

[48] The reform package is composed of three Draft Regulations and one Draft Directive: Draft Regulation establishing an EU AML/CFT Authority in the form of a decentralised EU regulatory agency (COM(2021) 421); Draft Regulation, containing directly applicable AML/CFT rules, including a revised EU list of entities subject to AML/CFT rules and a revised policy on third countries whose AML/CFT approach pose a threat to the EU's financial system (COM(2021) 420); Proposal for a Regulation of the European Parliament and of the Council on information accompanying transfers of funds and certain crypto-assets (recast); Sixth AML Directive, replacing the existing EU AML/CFT Directive (Directive 2015/849 as amended) and containing provisions which are not appropriate for a Regulation, and requiring national transposition, eg, rules concerning national supervisors and Financial Intelligence Units in Member States (COM(2021) 423); S Allegrezza, 'European Strategies Against Money Laundering' in J Crijns, M Haentjiens and R Haentjiens (eds), *The Enforcement of EU Financial Law* (Hart Publishing 2022) 197.

[49] Directive (EU) 2018/843 of the European Parliament and of the Council of 30 May 2018 amending Directive (EU) 2015/849 on the prevention of the use of the financial system for the purposes of money laundering or terrorist financing, and amending Directives 2009/138/EC and 2013/36/EU [2018] OJ L156/69, Art 57a(2) requires the ECB and the competent authorities to conclude, with the support of the European Supervisory Authorities, an agreement on the practical modalities for the exchange of information.

('the Agreement') between the ECB and the AML competent authorities (CAs) was signed in January 2019, indicating the practical modalities for the exchange of information in the area of prevention of misuse of financial systems for the purpose of money laundering and terrorist financing.[50]

As a first remarkable step towards more effective cooperation, the Agreement refers to a dialogue between the ECB and the AML CAs: 'The exchange of information shall take place between the CAs and the ECB, on request or on their own initiative.' The exchange is, however, not limited to the duty to answer specific requests; still, it does include autonomous input from one agency to the other. The AML CAs are in principle obliged to transmit that information to the ECB when the latter requests them to do so. They can also act on their own initiative, providing 'any other information, which they deem to be relevant and necessary for the exercise of the ECB's tasks'.[51] As for transmission in the opposite direction, CAs 'may submit a request to the ECB for information gathered or created by the ECB in the exercise of its direct supervisory tasks under the SSM Regulation that is relevant and necessary for the performance of their tasks in the area of AML/CFT supervision'.[52] The ECB should in principle transmit this information upon request or on its own initiative. The only limitation on this duty to cooperate is the respect of national and supranational legality. Both the ECB and the AML CAs can decline a request for information where (i) the request does not conform with the Agreement or the applicable laws; or (ii) fulfilling the request would require the requested participant 'to act in a manner that would violate any applicable laws'.[53]

The mechanism described represents the most advanced model of information exchange between the ECB and national authorities in relation to a criminal offence. The possibility for both participants to act on their own initiative has to be welcomed as a positive improvement in the field of inter-agency enforcement mechanisms.[54] Nevertheless, the information flow as described in the Agreement does not necessarily imply direct contact between the banking regulator and criminal enforcement: the Agreement is intended to channel the flow to the AML CAs, that is, 'the authority or authorities designated as the competent authorities for supervising and ensuring supervised entities' compliance with the requirements of AMLD [Anti-Money Laundering Directive]'.[55]

This Agreement coexists with the already mentioned duty of the ECB to request the relevant NCAs to 'refer the matter to the appropriate authorities for investigation and possible criminal prosecution, in accordance with national law'.[56] As anticipated, this provision justifies the exclusion of any direct contact between the European regulator and national criminal agencies based on the lack of harmonisation of criminal offences. However, this is not the case with AML/CTF, where a certain degree of harmonisation has been attained. Furthermore, the NCAs mentioned in Article 136 SSMR are not the

[50] Allegrezza (n 48) 205–07.
[51] European Central Bank, 'Multilateral Agreement on the practical modalities for exchange of information pursuant to Article 57a(2) of Directive (EU) 2015/849', Art 3(3).
[52] ibid Art 3(4).
[53] ibid Art 6(3).
[54] Allegrezza (n 48) 205–07.
[55] Art 2(f) Multilateral Agreement.
[56] See Art 136 SSMFR.

ones in charge of AML/CTF but rather the national regulators that comprise the SSM. In the case of money laundering, once the ECB reports to the NCAs, national rules on the transfer of information from the administrative to the criminal authorities apply, with no necessary involvement of the local Financial Intelligence Unit (FIU). The ECB no longer has any duty, and it is up to the NCAs to transmit the information to criminal agencies and ensure follow up of the case.[57]

C. Limitations on the Exchange of Information: Purpose Limitations and Professional Secrecy

The transmission of information from the EU enforcement agencies to the national authorities encounters some restrictions.[58] They can be grouped into two general clusters: purpose limitations and confidentiality obligations.

First and foremost, when the information exchange is instrumental to obtaining judicial authorisation from a national court, EU law may impose restrictions on the transfer and use of the information received from EU administrative agencies. These restrictions mostly apply to specific investigative measures where prior judicial authorisation is required. Prior judicial authorisation might be necessary, for instance, in the case of inspections by DG Competition of 'other premises',[59] and when an undertaking opposes the inspection (only if judicial authorisation is necessary according to national rules).[60] In this respect, according to Article 12(1) of Regulation 1/2003, notwithstanding any national provision to the contrary, the exchange of information and the use of such information in evidence is strictly limited to the application of Articles 101 and 102 TFEU.[61] This is a codification of the *Dow Benelux case*,[62] where the Court of Justice crystallised the principle of purpose limitation by explaining that information obtained during investigations by DG Competition must not be used for purposes other than those indicated in the order or decision of the EU Commission under which the investigation is carried out. According to the Court, the *raison d'être* of a purpose limitation is to safeguard the rights of the defence of the undertakings, as those rights would be seriously endangered if the CA could rely on evidence against undertakings that was obtained during an investigation but was not related to the subject matter or purpose thereof.

[57] Allegrezza (n 48) 205–07.

[58] Beyond the general need to respect data protection. An analysis of this issue falls outside the scope of this chapter. However, it is important to signal how EU administrative enforcement generally applies the General Data Protection Regulation, whereas criminal enforcement falls within the scope of the Law enforcement Directive. This problem is particularly acute in the case of information collected by Financial Intelligence Units in the field of AML/CFT. Regulation (EU) 2016/679 of the European Parliament and of the Council of 27 April 2016 on the protection of natural persons with regard to the processing of personal data and on the free movement of such data, and repealing Directive 95/46/EC ('GDPR') [2016] OJ L119/1.

[59] Art 21(3) Regulation 1/2003.

[60] Art 20(7) Regulation 1/2003.

[61] Recital 16 and Art 12(1) Regulation 1/2003.

[62] Case 85/87 *Dow Benelux v Commission* ECLI:EU:C:1989:379, paras 17–18.

A symmetrical power exists in the field of banking supervision. According to Article 10(1)[63] of Regulation 1024/2013,[64] for the purposes of on-site inspections of the business premises of legal persons and in cases where a person obstructs the inspection, the ECB/SSM is required, if national rules so oblige, to obtain authorisation by a judicial authority according to national rules.[65] In this case,

> the national judicial authority shall control that the decision of the ECB is authentic and that the coercive measures envisaged are neither arbitrary nor excessive having regard to the subject matter of the inspection. In its control of the proportionality of the coercive measures, the national judicial authority may ask the ECB for detailed explanations, in particular relating to the grounds the ECB has for suspecting that an infringement of the acts referred to in the first subparagraph of Article 4(3) [SSMR] has taken place and the seriousness of the suspected infringement and the nature of the involvement of the person who is subject to the coercive measures. However, the national judicial authority shall not review the necessity for the inspection or demand to be provided with the information on the ECB's file. The lawfulness of the ECB's decision shall be subject to review only by the CJEU.[66]

Should national judicial authorities, required to authorise the aforementioned on-site inspections, detect any criminal activity from the information they have received, a potential clash between the two levels is possible. On the one hand, the national authorities need to refer the matter back to the EU enforcement agency and leave it with the initiative to share that information with criminal law enforcement, according to the different models previously analysed. On the other hand, they may find themselves forced to share that information when national law does require them to be proactive in denouncing criminal activities. However, no sufficient data or literature are available to investigate this sensitive issue further.

The second cluster of limitations refers to confidentiality and professional secrecy obligations. Many provisions deal with the need to combine information exchange with the need to respect professional secrecy.

According to Article 28 of Regulation 1/2003, the Commission and the national competition authorities 'shall not disclose information acquired or exchanged by them pursuant to this Regulation and of the kind covered by the obligation of professional secrecy'. However, the same Regulation does provide for exceptions to such a duty of secrecy. Indeed, EU law clearly states that for the purpose of applying Articles 101 and 102 TFEU, DG Competition and the national competition authorities 'have the power to provide one another with and use in evidence any matter of fact or of law, including confidential information'.[67] Before transmitting information covered by

[63] '(a) credit institutions established in the participating Member States; (b) financial holding companies established in the participating Member States; (c) mixed financial holding companies established in the participating Member States; (d) mixed-activity holding companies established in the participating Member States; (e) persons belonging to the entities referred to in points (a) to (d); (f) third parties to whom the entities referred to in points (a) to (d) have outsourced functions or activities.'

[64] Council Regulation (EU) No 1024/2013 of 15 October 2013 conferring specific tasks on the European Central Bank concerning policies relating to the prudential supervision of credit institutions [2013] OJ L287/63.

[65] Scholten and Simonato (n 26) 25.

[66] Art 13 Regulation 1024/2013.

[67] Art 12(1) Regulation 1/2003.

professional secrecy to a national authority, DG Competition must ask the national court whether it will guarantee the protection of confidential information and business secrets. If the national court cannot give such a guarantee, DG Competition will not transmit this information.[68] Furthermore, the Directorate can refuse to transmit information if it believes that there are overriding reasons in relation to the need to safeguard the interests of the EU, or to avoid any interference with the EU Commission's independence.[69]

Similarly, the flow of information between the ECB and NCAs under the SSM is subject to a limitation, particularly if the transmission is prohibited by a specific provision under Union or national law relating to the disclosure of confidential information. According to Article 2 of ECB Decision 2016/1162,[70] confidential information may be disclosed, provided that

> the relevant legal framework permits the disclosure of such confidential information and there are no overriding reasons for refusing to disclose such information relating to the need to safeguard the interests of the Union or to avoid any interference with the functioning and independence of the ECB, in particular by jeopardising the accomplishment of its tasks.

The equivalent position of the SSM and the NCAs, ensured by Article 9(1) SSMR, according to which the SSM shall have all the powers and obligations that the competent and designated authorities shall have under the relevant Union law, is contradicted by Decision 2016/1162, which leaves questionable discretion to the ECB.[71] This latter consideration shows how unavoidable the clash seems between European confidentiality and national rules imposing the duty on national supervisors to cooperate with criminal investigative authorities. In several Member States, regulators must cooperate with national prosecutors and disclose information. A breach of this duty – refusal to cooperate or incomplete disclosure of relevant information – constitutes a criminal offence.[72] This clash between conflicting duties is even more problematic if the request by the investigative authorities concerns confidential information that is at the disposal of the NCAs. In these cases, Decision 2016/1162 strongly suggests that the NCAs 'consult' – to use a euphemism[73] – 'the ECB, where possible, on how to respond to the request', in order for the latter 'to advise as to whether the information in question may be disclosed'.[74]

Furthermore, both the ECB staff and NCA staff are bound by the provisions of CRD IV.[75] Pursuant to Article 53(1) CRD IV, persons working or who have worked

[68] Case T-353/94, *Postbank NV v European Commission* ECLI:EU:T:1996:119, para 93.

[69] Karagianni, Sholten and Simonato (n 32) 21.

[70] See n 45.

[71] G Lasagni, *Banking Supervision and Criminal Investigation. Comparing the EU and US Experience* (X, Springer 2019) 221.

[72] See Lasagni and Rodopoulos (n 43) 632.

[73] The wording is 'the ECB shall request the NCAs and NCBs to agree to consult' or 'to inform the ECB' of the national request; Art 3(1)(2) ECB Decision 2016/1162.

[74] Art 3(1) ECB Decision 2016/1162.

[75] Directive 2013/36/EU Of the European Parliament and of the Council of 26 June 2013 on access to the activity of credit institutions and the prudential supervision of credit institutions and investment firms, amending Directive 2002/87/EC and repealing Directives 2006/48/EC and 2006/49/EC (Text with EEA relevance) [2013] OJ L176/338.

for competent authorities are bound by the obligation of professional secrecy.[76] At the same time, Article 53(2) CRD IV provides that professional secrecy obligations prevent competent authorities from exchanging information with each other. Thus, professional secrecy provisions only limit the circulation of information outside this closed circle of authorities and do not impose any limits on the circulation of information within the SSM.[77]

Concerning OLAF, the information transferred prior to opening an investigation does not concern facts established as a result of investigative activities (eg interviews and/or inspections) as the latter can only take place after the opening of an investigation.[78] Likewise, the information transmitted cannot concern data retrieved from EU agencies or databases, as OLAF only has access to such information during an investigation.[79] Similarly, Article 7(2) of the Second Protocol to the PIF Convention,[80] as well as the PIF Directive 2017/1371[81] provides that 'The Commission and the NCAs shall take account, in each specific case, of the requirements of investigation secrecy and data protection.' Another limitation on the exchange of information is represented by Article 10 ('Confidentiality and data protection') of Regulation 883/2013. In particular, information transmitted or obtained in the course of internal investigations, in whatever form, shall be subject to professional secrecy.[82] Furthermore, according to Article 4(6), paragraph 2, 'in cases where the confidentiality of the internal investigation cannot be ensured using the usual channels of communication, the Office shall use appropriate alternative channels for transmitting information.'

A weaker restriction applies to financial law. The EMIR framework regulates the limitations on the exchange of confidential information. According to Recital 78,

> without prejudice to cases covered by criminal or tax law, the competent authorities, ESMA, bodies or natural or legal persons other than the competent authorities, which receive confidential information should use it only in the performance of their duties and for the exercise

[76] ibid Art 53(1): 'Member States shall provide that all persons working for or who have worked for the competent authorities and auditors or experts acting on behalf of the competent authorities shall be bound by the obligation of professional secrecy. Confidential information which such persons, auditors or experts receive in the course of their duties may be disclosed only in summary or aggregate form, such that individual credit institutions cannot be identified, without prejudice to cases covered by criminal law.'

[77] ibid Art 53(2) (footnote omitted): 'Paragraph 1 shall not prevent the competent authorities from exchanging information with each other or transmitting information to the ESRB, EBA, or the European Supervisory Authority (European Securities and Markets Authority) ("ESMA") established by Regulation (EU) No 1095/2010 of the European Parliament and of the Council in accordance with this Directive, with Regulation (EU) No 575/2013, with other Directives applicable to credit institutions, with Article 15 of Regulation (EU) No 1092/2010, with Articles 31, 35 and 36 of Regulation (EU) No 1093/2010 and with Articles 31 and 36 of Regulation (EU) No 1095/2010. That information shall be subject to paragraph 1.'

[78] Art 3(11) Regulation 883/2013: 'During an external investigation, the Office may have access to any relevant information and data, irrespective of the medium on which it is stored, held by the institutions, bodies, offices and agencies, connected with the matter under investigation, where necessary in order to establish whether there has been fraud, corruption or any other illegal activity affecting the financial interests of the Union. For that purpose Article 4(2) and (4) shall apply.'

[79] Art 4(2) Regulation 883/2013.

[80] Convention drawn up on the basis of Article K.3 of the Treaty on European Union, on the protection of the European Communities' financial interests [1995] OJ C316/49.

[81] Directive (EU) 2017/1371 of the European Parliament and of the Council of 5 July 2017 on the fight against fraud to the Union's financial interests by means of criminal law [2017] OJ L198/29.

[82] Art 10(2) Regulation 883/2013.

> of their functions. However, this should not prevent the exercise, in accordance with national law, of the functions of national bodies responsible for the prevention, investigation or correction of cases of maladministration.

Finally, Article 83 EMIR regulates professional secrecy. Interestingly, Article 83(5) states that 'paragraphs 1, 2 and 3 shall not prevent the competent authorities from exchanging or transmitting confidential information, in accordance with national law, that has not been received from a competent authority of another Member State'. Concerning the CRAR framework, Article 23(a) states that 'the powers conferred on ESMA or any official of or other person authorised by ESMA by Articles 23(b) to 23(d) shall not be used to require the disclosure of information or documents which are subject to legal privilege'.

A fragmented and partially incoherent picture emerges from this short overview. In reality, further research is needed on the very concept of 'professional secrecy' within administrative and criminal investigation in order to detect the level of harmonisation existing among Member States and how to promote a shared concept among different branches of enforcement at EU level.

III. Information from National Criminal Authorities to EU Administrative Enforcement Agencies

The second movement of information flow concerns communication from national criminal authorities to the EU enforcement system. In symmetry with the first movement, the bottom-up flow may occur directly – national criminal authorities may choose to share information directly with EU administrative enforcement agencies – or indirectly – when national criminal authorities transmit information via national administrative authorities that form part of the EU enforcement system (indirect contact). Both EU law and national legislation are often fragmented with respect to the regulation of these types of contacts. Information sharing related to criminal offences is only a part of the larger problem regarding rules governing the transfer of law enforcement information from criminal judicial authorities to EU or national administrative authorities. The secrecy of criminal investigations represents a major obstacle, as the Court of Justice pointed out in a case back in 1979.[83] Despite its importance for a better integration process, the duty of loyalty to the Union does not offer a sufficient degree of precision to overcome the need to preserve criminal investigations.[84]

A number of subsequent EU legal acts contributed to a more solid legal basis. For instance, the preamble to Regulation 595/91[85] stated that the Commission should be systematically informed of judicial and administrative procedures against persons

[83] Case C-267/78, *Commission v Italy* ECLI:EU:C:1980:6, para 22.

[84] In the *Zwartveld* rulings, the Court of Justice stressed the duty of reciprocity and joint obligations when it comes to the enforcement of EU law and the protection of the Union's financial interests. Case C-2/88, *Imm, JJ Zwartveld and others* [1990] ECR I-365.

[85] The Regulation has been replaced by Commission Regulation (EC) 1848/2006 of 14 December 2006 concerning irregularities and the recovery of sums wrongly paid in connection with the financing of the common agricultural policy and the organization of an information system in this field [2006] OJ L355/56.

who have committed irregularities. Similarly, the Second Protocol to the Convention on the protection of the European Communities' financial interests of 1997[86] establishes a general cooperation duty and empowers the Commission to offer technical and operational assistance in order to facilitate the coordination of national investigations.[87] Article 7(2) deals specifically with the exchange of information between Member States and the Commission, and provides for the respecting of investigative secrecy and data protection, where necessary.[88] Finally, Article 15 of PIF Directive 2017/1371 brings some clarity in this specific field. According to Article 15, the national competent authorities 'may, within their competences, exchange information with the Commission'. Information exchange is not a duty, though, but it needs to be decided, taking into account 'in each specific case the requirements of confidentiality and the rules on data protection'. Should the national authorities decide to share this information, they can set 'specific conditions' covering its use.

However, the EU picture remains unclear and incomplete, even in respect of information related to PIF crimes for which no common regime of secrecy exists. The EU provisions seem to refer to national law, with the consequent fragmented puzzle of different provisions.

A. Indirect Contact by National Criminal Authorities with National Administrative Authorities that Form Part of the EU Enforcement System

i. Obligations for National Judicial Authorities to Transfer Information to DG Competition

European Union law provides for some obligations on national judicial authorities to transfer information to DG Competition. Most importantly, there are two main obligations. First, according to Article 15(2) of Regulation 1/2003, Member States must transmit to DG Competition a copy of any written judgment of a national court deciding on the application of Articles 101 and 102 TFEU.[89] Second, the Commission may submit written observations to the national courts. In applying Articles 101 and 102 TFEU, the national courts can request DG Competition to submit *amicus curiae* observations on

[86] Second Protocol to the Convention on the protection of the European Communities' financial interests [1997] OJ C221/12.

[87] ibid Art 7.

[88] Art 7(2) reads as follows: 'The competent authorities in the Member States may exchange information with the Commission so as to make it easier to establish the facts and to ensure effective action against fraud, active and passive corruption and money laundering. The Commission and the competent national authorities shall take account, in each specific case, of the requirements of investigation secrecy and data protection. To that end, a Member State, when supplying information to the Commission, may set specific conditions covering the use of information, whether by the Commission or by another Member State to which that information may be passed'.

[89] Art 15(2) Regulation 1/2003: 'Member States shall forward to the Commission a copy of any written judgment of national courts deciding on the application of Article 81 or Article 82 of the Treaty. Such copy shall be forwarded without delay after the full written judgment is notified to the parties.'

the application of EU competition rules. For this purpose, they can either send a request in writing to the postal address of DG Competition or make a request electronically by sending an e-mail.[90] By requesting the Commission's observations, national courts must – in accordance with Article 15(3) of Regulation 1/2003 – transmit documents that are necessary for the Commission to assess the case and submit its views.[91]

On the other hand, there are no specific rules on the transfer of information from public prosecutors to DG Competition, not even at the national level. This is explained by the fact that, in most Member States (such as Hungary, Italy and Germany), infringements of EU competition law are not considered to be criminal offences but constitute administrative offences, and for this reason there is no exchange of information with criminal judicial authorities.[92]

However, for the sake of our analysis, it might be considered that the concept of 'national judicial authority' might include criminal judicial authorities as long as the infringement of competition rules represents a criminal offence. In the rare cases where there is a criminal investigation and prosecution of individual offenders for cartel offences within some Member States,[93] public prosecutors act in close cooperation with the national competition authority, and the latter mediates in the transfer of information.

Finally, it has been accurately observed that 'the absence of a national legal basis in most Member States makes it impossible to assess whether new limits to the transfer of information are created by national law'.[94] At the same time – as is the case in Luxembourg, where there is similarly no pertinent national legal basis at all[95] – the secrecy of investigations could in principle be an obstacle if the Commission were to decide to request information from judicial authorities in criminal proceedings. In any case, the rarity of interactions between competition and criminal law within national jurisdictions renders the extraction of generalised conclusions fairly difficult.

ii. The Case of the ECB

As for the field of banking prudential supervision, the relevant EU rules do not cover the transfer of information from criminal law authorities to the ECB. In general terms, as there is no direct channel of communication between criminal enforcement and the European regulator, the main role is conferred on NCAs. Where direct venues for transferring information do not exist, that transfer of information could be made indirectly via the NCAs. Despite the general obligation of professional secrecy, the ECB and the NCAs, both vertically and horizontally, are enabled to exchange information with each

[90] Cooperation Notice para 18.

[91] Art 15(3) Regulation 1/2003.

[92] M Böse and A Schneider, 'Germany' in Simonato, Luchtman and Vervaele (eds) (n 32) 63.

[93] In France, Greece and Romania, it is possible for cartel behaviour to be prosecuted under provisions covering fraud offences. In Germany, Austria, Italy, Poland and Hungary, criminal sanctions only apply to bid rigging. See generally K Cseres, M Schinkel and F Vogelaar (eds), *Criminalization of Competition Law Enforcement: Economic and Legal Implications for the EU Member States* (Edward Elgar 2006).

[94] Luchtman, Simonato and Vervaele, 'Comparative Analysis' in Luchtman, Simonato and Vervaele (eds) (n 32) 163, 187.

[95] V Covolo, 'Luxembourg' in Simonato, Luchtman and Vervaele (eds) (n 32) 116.

other. Such information may only be used for specific purposes – inter alia, to impose penalties.

A composite framework of national provisions regulates whether the transfer is mandatory or non-mandatory. The majority of national jurisdictions indicate that the transfer of information from national judicial authorities to the ECB is at any rate not an obligation. With the obvious exception of the Federal Financial Supervisory Authority (BaFin) and the German Federal Bank (Bundesbank), other administrative authorities, as well as judicial authorities, are not obliged by German legislation to transfer information to the ECB.[96] As already mentioned, Decision 2016/1162 only regulates communications by which national criminal authorities make a request to the ECB. Likewise, under both Dutch and Italian law, there are no express obligations for judicial authorities to transfer information to the ECB.[97] Luxembourg law does not impose any such obligation either with regard to the ECB, as far as the transfer of information is concerned. When it comes to provisions protecting the secrecy of investigations or establishing a duty of professional secrecy, the available data are very limited indeed. As mentioned previously, it is to be anticipated that when an on-site inspection leads to the requirement for prior judicial authorisation, some form of information exchange will have to take place. Admittedly, in Luxembourg, the secrecy of criminal investigations constitutes an obstacle to the exchange of information as far as ongoing criminal proceedings are concerned; such provisions are therefore largely determinative in similar situations.[98]

iii. The Case of ESMA

As for information in the field of financial supervision, an exchange of information with a national judicial authority can only occur when ESMA has to refer matters to the relevant national authorities for the purposes of criminal prosecution.[99] So, if these authorities are judicial, there is a relevant obligation.[100] It is unlikely that information held by national judicial authorities will be transferred to ESMA. In addition, the secrecy of criminal investigations constitutes an obstacle to the exchange of information relating to ongoing criminal proceedings.

Cooperation with judicial bodies in cases covered by criminal law is 'taken outside the scope of directly applicable EU rules regarding secrecy and purpose limitation'.[101] That information may, however, be obtained indirectly from other NCAs or relevant partners. If ESMA has received unsolicited information, it may use that information solely for the purposes stated in the transmission letter, or for the purposes of criminal

[96] Böse and Schneider (n 92) 64.

[97] K Bovend'Eerdt, 'The Netherlands' in Simonato, Luchtman and Vervaele (eds) (n 32) 150; Allegrezza, 'Italy', ibid 104.

[98] Covolo (n 95) 119. See also ch 5 of this volume (Bovend'Eerdt and Karagianni), section IV.B.

[99] Art 64(8) EMIR; Art 23e CRAR: 'ESMA shall refer matters for criminal prosecution to the relevant national authorities where, in carrying out its duties under this Regulation, it finds that there are serious indications of the possible existence of facts liable to constitute criminal offences.'

[100] Karagianni, Scholten and Simonato (n 32) 32.

[101] Luchtman, Simonato and Vervaele (n 94) 196.

or administrative proceedings resulting from a breach of the laws and regulations or for discharging the obligation to report to judicial authorities.[102]

B. Direct Information Flow from National Criminal Authorities to EU Administrative Enforcement Agencies: The Case of OLAF

In its sectoral instruments,[103] the EU legal framework also provides for a general obligation for the NCAs to share information with OLAF. However, such an obligation is formulated in such a way that it often refers back to national law. Therefore, in order to assist OLAF in accessing information held by national authorities (and to seek their cooperation), Regulation 883/2013 obliges Member States to designate an anti-fraud coordination service (AFCOS) to facilitate effective cooperation and exchange of information 'of an operational nature' between OLAF and the 'competent authorities'.[104] In other words, the national partners of OLAF that are designated as being 'competent' by national law are the 'competent authorities' for the purposes of the applicable instrument (either horizontal or sectoral). An AFCOS is just a service to facilitate cooperation between OLAF and the 'competent authorities'; nevertheless, an AFCOS might occasionally be regarded by national law, 'where appropriate', as the competent authority for the purposes of Regulation 883/2013 (but not necessarily so).

However, after the amendment of Regulation 883/2013 by means of Regulation 2020/2223, the duty of national authorities to transfer information to OLAF has been further detached from national law.

Former Article 8(3) of Regulation 883/2013 stated that the NCAs were obliged to transfer information only 'in so far as their national law allows'. Article 8 was replaced as a whole and now provides in Article 8(1):

> In the areas referred to in Article 1, the institutions, bodies, offices and agencies shall transmit to the Office without delay any information relating to possible cases of fraud, corruption or any other illegal activity affecting the financial interests of the Union. Where the institutions, bodies, offices and agencies report to the EPPO in accordance with Article 24 of Regulation (EU) 2017/1939, they may comply with the obligation set out in the first subparagraph of this paragraph by transmitting to the Office a copy of the report sent to the EPPO.

Article 8(2) on the transmission of information related to an ongoing investigation and Article 8(3) on the transmission of information relating to the fight against fraud, corruption and any other illegal activity affecting the financial interests of the Union state that the NCAs shall transmit the pertinent data without delay, 'unless prevented by national law'.

[102] ibid.

[103] See, eg, Regulation (EU) 2015/1525 of 9 September 2015 amending Council Regulation (EC) No 515/97 on mutual assistance between the administrative authorities of the Member States and cooperation between the latter and the Commission to ensure the correct application of the law on customs and agricultural matters [2015] OJ L243/1.

[104] Art 3(4) Regulation 883/2013.

Article 3(5) of Regulation 883/2013 as it stands provides that 'the competent authority of the Member State shall, without undue delay, provide the staff of the Office with the assistance needed in order to carry out their tasks effectively' and that the Member State concerned shall ensure that 'the staff of the Office are allowed access to *all* information, documents and data relating to the matter under investigation … and that the staff are able to assume custody of documents or data to ensure that there is no danger of their disappearance'.[105]

References to national law can also be found in sectoral legislation. As to structural funds, Article 3(5) of Regulation 2015/1970 clarifies that 'where national provisions provide for the confidentiality of investigations, communication of the information shall be subject to the authorisation of the competent tribunal, court or other body in accordance with national rules'.[106] In a similar vein, Article 3 of Regulation 515/97 with regard to customs and agricultural matters provides that any communication relevant to the national authorities' decisions 'must have the prior authorization of the judicial authority if the necessity of such authorization derives from national law'.[107]

The following overview of different national provisions should help to identify both common practices and divergences in the field of information sharing with OLAF within the Union.

First, with regard to Germany, it should be noted that according to Article 151b of the Directive on Cooperation in Criminal Matters,[108] judicial authorities may render assistance to OLAF, but they cannot be obliged to transfer information that is part of criminal investigative proceedings.

In Hungary, the key provision on the exchange of information between judicial authorities and OLAF is laid down in Article 71/B(2) BE of the Hungarian Code of Criminal Procedure. The exchange of information is based on a request and is limited to the specific purposes of such requests.[109] OLAF has the right to receive any information that has become part of the criminal files, irrespective of whether the information is considered to be confidential under other statutes (professional, business, banking secrecy, etc).[110]

In Italy, COLAF (*Comitato per la lotta contro le frodi*), the national AFCOS, has no – or very limited – access to operational information relating to ongoing investigations that are being conducted by the competent law enforcement authorities. However, thanks to an Administrative Cooperation Agreement (ACA) of 2013 between OLAF and the Prosecutor General of the Italian Court of Auditors in Brussels,[111] ongoing

105 Emphasis added.

106 Commission Delegated Regulation (EU) 2015/1970 of 8 July 2015 supplementing Regulation (EU) No 1303/2013 of the European Parliament and of the Council with specific provisions on the reporting of irregularities concerning the European Regional Development Fund, the European Social Fund, the Cohesion Fund, and the European Maritime and Fisheries Fund [2015] OJ L293/2.

107 Council Regulation (EC) No 515/97 of 13 March 1997 on mutual assistance between the administrative authorities of the Member States and cooperation between the latter and the Commission to ensure the correct application of the law on customs and agricultural matters [1997] OJ L82/2.

108 Böse and Schneider (n 92) 57.

109 ibid.

110 ibid.

111 ibid.

collaboration and investigative reporting are now also possible in the enforcement of convictions. With reference to the secrecy of investigations, Article 329 of the Italian Code of Criminal Procedure lays down the principle of the secrecy of every investigative activity carried out by the prosecutor or by the police until the end of the investigation, but this does not apply to OLAF because the secrecy of investigations does not apply to those agencies that are required to provide information to the police and/or prosecutors.

As for Luxembourg, national law does not provide for specific rules governing an obligation for the national judicial authorities to inform OLAF.[112] In other words, the duty to report to or inform the Office stems from directly applicable rules under sectoral regulations and Regulation 883/2013, and it is noteworthy that no specific implementing measures have been adopted in Luxembourg, even where Union law refers to domestic law. Moreover, the lack of specific legal provisions under Luxembourg law that explicitly lift the duty of secrecy vis-à-vis OLAF prevents the exchange of information and documents recorded in the criminal case file. In other words, in so far as OLAF has no specific legal status in national criminal proceedings, it does not have access to the materials in the case file.

Finally, under Dutch law, there are no obligations on judicial authorities to transfer information to OLAF. However, such a transfer is possible under the Judicial Data and Criminal Records Act.[113] Thus, the transfer of data is possible if deemed necessary for the purposes defined therein. More specifically, criminal and judicial data may be transferred by the Board of Procurators General (*College van procureurs-generaal*, 'the College'). While the College can transfer information, such a transfer is not an obligation. General duties regarding secrecy are laid down in the Act on the Organisation of the Judiciary, which states that judicial officers (ie judges and public prosecutors) are under a duty of secrecy with regard to information that has come to their knowledge in the exercise of their official duties and of which the confidentiality should be known or should reasonably be inferred. Whether information is to be considered confidential is left to the discretion of the judge or public prosecutor.

In conclusion, it stems from the foregoing that national law does not always prescribe clear obligations for national judicial authorities when it comes to information exchange with OLAF; and certainly, no distinction is made as to the stages of an investigation process during which information exchange may become necessary.[114]

IV. Conclusions: Towards Better Multilevel Enforcement via Strengthening Information Channels

The analysis of the contact and potential conflicts between the different enforcement systems at both EU and national levels revealed how direct and indirect information

[112] Covolo (n 95) 111.
[113] Bovend'Eerdt (n 97) 134.
[114] Luchtman Simonato and Vervaele (n 94) 181. See also ch 5 of this volume (Bovend'Eerdt and Karagianni), section IV.B.

channels are used and their efficiency in building the crucial network so much needed in such pivotal fields of EU action.

The endeavour to investigate and sanction potential breaches of the European legal framework in the field of competition, fraud, finance, securities, banking and money laundering implies an innovative regulatory framework in which administrative and criminal enforcement actors are called on to cooperate at different levels.

The analysis of the vertical dimension of the information flow between the EU and the national levels revealed an EU multilevel enforcement system *à geometrie variable*. Within this system, the exchange of information between administrative and criminal law authorities at both European and national levels is complicated by a number of factors. Time, geography and the nature of the power are the three factors to be considered when describing the different forms of interaction, the vertical one – between the EU and the national level – as well as the more traditional horizontal interaction between administrative and criminal enforcement.

First and foremost, the EU enforcement bodies do not represent a consistent group in terms of institutional design or division of power. They are instead very different as regards their status, and their empowerment follows different models. Nor does consistency exist among the different substantive fields in which enforcement bodies do operate: some of them have been strongly harmonised and have been at the heart of the EU for many years. Consequently, the different maturity of EU law – and EU courts – in dealing with certain fields influences the vertical interaction with national administrative and criminal systems. Where EU law is more advanced – that is, competition law – the different levels of enforcement act coherently, information channels are effective, and conflicts are resolved according to a clear-cut division of competence between the EU and the national levels. However, the fragmented picture in terms of criminalisation of the related breaches does increase the complexity as to the very existence of a contact with criminal law enforcement.

When the field of intervention is more recent and practice less developed at the EU level – that is, administrative sanctions within the SMM – interaction is scarce and the flow of information struggles to reach the relevant offices. This is particularly true in the field of money laundering, where the inefficiencies of the network, involving EU regulators with scarce powers, multiple financial intelligence units and a plethora of national actors, all having different status and powers, led to the many scandals of the last decade.

Moreover, the expanding notion of 'punitive sanctions' within 'criminal-administrative law', elaborated by the ECtHR with the famous *Engel* criteria[115] and progressively adopted by the CJEU in its case law, contributed to increasing the potential clash between administrative and criminal law enforcement, first at the national and later at the EU level. It cannot be doubted that many of the sanctions imposed by EU enforcement bodies are in fact '*sanction à la coloration pénale*', implying the adoption of specific guarantees during the procedure that leads to their adoption.[116] The expansion

[115] *Engel and Others v the Netherlands* App no 5100/71 (ECtHR, 8 June 1976).

[116] M Luchtman, 'Trans-National Multi-disciplinary Investigations and the Quest for the Compatible Procedural Safeguards' in K Ligeti and V Franssen (eds), *Challenges in the Filed of Economic and Financial Crime* (Bloomsbury 2019)191; Lasagni (n 71)197 ff.

of procedural rights originally dedicated to criminal procedure added an additional layer to the complex matrix, reducing the distance between the two fields but triggering the inevitable clash with the principle *ne bis in idem*.[117]

Additional complexity is due to the fragmentation of territorial competence and powers within the EU, also linked to the different levels of harmonisation. If the EU represents one single legal area for competition law, when it comes to banking activities, only some of the EU Member States adopted the euro as their currency and are therefore subject to the ECB as a common regulator within the SSM. And when it comes to crimes affecting EU financial interests, only 22 of the Member States adhered to the EPPO initiative, whereas all of them are subject to the OLAF power to investigate. The territorial puzzle designs an EU system of enforcement that is '*à géographie variable*', where solutions adopted in one field cannot always be transferred to a different one because of the limits on territorial competence.

Time also has an impact on the function of information exchange. When the exchange of information occurs at the very beginning of an investigation – be it administrative or criminal – it not only serves a need to share knowledge, but also prevents potential conflicts and *bis in idem*.[118] When it occurs at a later stage, it might avoid duplication of evidence, allowing the different agencies to share evidentiary materials. However, time has an impact on the efficiency of cooperation as well. Generally, there is no reference throughout the fields concerned to an obligation to inform judicial authorities as regards information obtained during the course of investigations, so that discretion is the general rule. Although some exceptions to discretion are provided for in certain cases, there is little doubt that when suspicions of crime arise, early contact between EU enforcement and national judicial authorities would definitely benefit investigations and their follow up at the national level. For instance, national prosecutors indicated that they would prefer to be informed of any suspected criminal offence much earlier than at the end of the OLAF investigation; and that if they were so informed, they would assist OLAF and, where appropriate, start their own criminal investigation in order to avoid cases becoming time-barred.

Some attempts to improve the top-down dimension of the information channels and overcome barriers have taken place in the last few years, in particular between banking supervisors and the agencies in charge of AML/CFT. However, EU agencies and supervisors are still clearly reluctant to set up a direct channel of communication with criminal enforcement agencies. This is particularly apparent with reference to the transmission of *notitiae criminis*. As anticipated, when it has a suspicion that a crime has been committed, the ECB's only obligation is to ask NCAs to refer the matter to the appropriate authorities for investigation and possible criminal prosecution. Similarly, OLAF does not have an obligation to promptly inform NCAs before the ending of its investigations when it becomes aware of conduct that may have a criminal nature.

Essentially, the limits on information exchange are the same across different fields and authorities. This study showed that both EU law and national legislation can often

[117] G Lasagni and S Mirandola, 'The European ne bis in idem at the Crossroads of Administrative and Criminal Law' *Eucrim* 2/2019; and the essays in B Van Bockel (ed), *Ne Bis in Idem in EU Law* (Cambridge University Press 2016).

[118] Allegrezza (n 48) 207.

be found to be fragmented with respect to the regulation of the bottom-up dimension of information exchange; the limitations are strongly dependent on national law – with an exception made for OLAF – thus giving rise to a composite framework of national provisions liable to impair the efficiency of information sharing.

What can be done to improve the information exchange among the different authorities?

The clear reluctance to set up a direct channel of communication should be transformed into a more efficient communicating-vessels system between the EU level and criminal enforcement agencies.[119] For instance, a direct channel of communication between the ECB or ESMA and criminal law enforcement needs to be introduced in order to strengthen the chances of criminal enforcement to sanction the most serious financial crimes and avoid impunity. National criminal agencies might identify a contact point entitled to receive information and requests for information and transmit them to the law enforcement agency in charge at the EU level. This centralisation would be extremely beneficial, offering better coordination while protecting the necessary needs of confidentiality and secrecy. This network of NCAs already exists in the field of AML/CTF, and it will be further strengthened with the approval of the reform package presented in July 2021 and the introduction of the AMLA. For trans-border cases, an additional possibility would be to increase the role of pre-existing coordination agencies in the field of criminal justice, such as Eurojust, whose core mission is to build up synergies to fight supranational crime. This would not mean the exclusion of the NCAs in their function of filtering the data flow in the light of relevant national provisions, but rather the inclusion of the prosecutors or other investigative agencies among those with whom the European enforcement agencies may directly communicate.

A particularly strong need concerns the duty to report *notitiae criminis* directly to the competent authorities. As regulators are better placed to detect suspicious operations – especially when it comes to banking and financial supervision – a direct channel for the mandatory communication of the most serious financial crimes would be extremely beneficial for crime prevention and repression.

An integrated enforcement strategy in which a concerted effort is made by the different actors to counter serious crime seems to be the only answer. This is the challenge of the coming years for the Union.

[119] S Allegrezza, 'Information Exchange Between Administrative and Criminal Enforcement: The Case of the ECB and National Investigative Agencies' *Eucrim* 4/2020, 302.

9

Lawful and Fair Use of Criminal Evidence in the EU: The Unwritten Script for European Enforcement Agencies

JOHN VERVAELE

I. Introduction

European enforcement agencies vested with real investigative powers, be they of an administrative nature, like the European Anti-Fraud Office (OLAF), or of a judicial nature, like the European Public Prosecutor's Office (EPPO), do of course collect evidence, and this evidence is used in punitive proceedings[1] against suspects of financial crimes. What makes this evidence illegal or unlawful? What makes the use of this evidence unfair, meaning that it would lead to a violation of due process and a fair trial under human rights standards? In case of unlawfulness or unfairness, can the evidence still be used or must it be excluded? The answers to these questions are not at all elaborated in European Union (EU) legislation. Their investigative powers are not harmonised at the EU level and are defined to a large extent by cross-references to national law. So when it comes to the assessment of the admissibility and potential evidentiary value of OLAF- or EPPO-related evidence, the applicable law is largely domestic.

The EU has recognised the necessity for common standards regarding evidence and its unlawfulness in the Member States and has taken steps towards harmonisation (section II), but without success for the time being. This is the reason why in this chapter we need a conceptual approach starting from the domestic level. We have to understand, first, the rationale behind the national legal traditions concerning unlawful evidence and nullity/exclusion, and their very different approaches (section III). Given the lack of common standards, we have to assess to what extent the European Convention on Human Rights (ECHR) and the related Charter of Fundamental Rights of the European Union ('the Charter') (section V) offer standards to assess when breaches of fundamental

[1] Due to the autonomous definition of 'criminal charge' in Art 6 ECHR, they include all punitive proceedings, as laid down in the *Engel* doctrine of the European Court of Human Rights (ECtHR). *Engel and Others v The Netherlands* App Nos 5100/71; 5101/71; 5102/71; 5354/72; 5370/72 (ECtHR, 8 June 1976).

rights can or must lead to the nullity of evidence as such, or to the exclusion of evidence because of a violation of the fairness of the proceedings (section IV). Once we have all of these elements on the table, we can then apply them to the gathering and use of evidence by European enforcement agencies, for which we will use the OLAF setting (see section V), as many parameters do correspond with the future EPPO setting.

II. Admissibility of (Cross-Border) Criminal Evidence in the EU: Legislative Initiatives

The differences between the legal regimes in the Member States when it comes to the legal parameters for the gathering of evidence, the use of this evidence, and the related admissibility and nullity or exclusion of evidence do lead, in the cross-border gathering and cross-border use of evidence, to divergent and even unpredictable outcomes. This is a problem both for law enforcement in the Area of Freedom, Security and Justice (AFSJ), including OLAF and the EPPO, and for the due process of citizens, and puts at risk the quality and fairness of criminal justice in the EU.

Unlawful evidence and the unfair use of evidence seem to be two of the great taboos in European criminal justice. They have been greatly neglected by all cooperation instruments, be they instruments of mutual legal assistance or mutual recognition. Outside the framework of the EPPO,[2] the European Commission did attempt to pave the way for a legislative initiative by issuing the Green Paper of 2009 on obtaining evidence in criminal matters and transferring it from one Member State to another with the aim of *securing its admissibility*.[3] The Commission was very aware of the fact that the rules on cross-border evidence gathering, as laid down in the European Evidence Warrant of 2005, 'only approach the issue of admissibility of evidence in an indirect manner as they do not set any common standards for gathering evidence'. There is therefore a risk that the existing rules on obtaining evidence in criminal matters will only function effectively between Member States with similar national standards for gathering evidence. As set out in the 2009 Communication entitled 'An area of freedom, security and justice serving the citizen', the best solution to this problem would seem to lie in the adoption of common standards for gathering evidence in criminal matters.[4] The Commission is therefore advocating additional rules on the admissibility of evidence. However, the Green Paper was so poorly elaborated that it did not lead to any added value or substantial support from the Member States and resulted in no further action from the Commission.

The 2009 Lisbon Treaty[5] does, however, offer new perspectives for legislative action, as Article 82(2)(a) TFEU provides for an explicit legal basis for approximation in the

[2] See ch 11 of this volume (Vervaele).

[3] Commission, 'Green Paper on obtaining evidence in criminal matters from one Member State to another and securing its admissibility' COM (2009) 624 final (emphasis added).

[4] Commission, 'An area of freedom, security and justice serving the citizen' (Communication) COM (2009) 262.

[5] Treaty on the Functioning of the European Union of 13 December 2007 – consolidated version [2016] OJ C202/47 (TFEU or 'Lisbon Treaty').

field by referring to the mutual admissibility of evidence between Member States. Although the approximation is in theory limited to minimum rules in order to facilitate the mutual recognition of judicial decisions,[6] it has become clear from the use of Article 82(2)(b)–(c) by the legislator that this approximation is in fact the harmonisation of domestic criminal procedure (so not limited to mutual recognition instruments) in order to facilitate potential mutual recognition. The harmonisation is not strictly limited to minimum harmonisation but to minimum rules, meaning those that are necessary for facilitating and enhancing mutual recognition between the Member States. The new and interesting potential of Article 82(2)(a), for the harmonisation both of obtaining evidence and of criminal investigative tools with a view to the admissibility of evidence, has not been used at all however. Neither the Commission, nor the Member States have triggered any legislative proposal, leaving Article 82(2)(a) dormant; a legislative failure thus remains in place. So, due to the lack of standards for the type of evidence, the admissibility of evidence or the exclusion of unlawful or unfair evidence, we fall back on the domestic dimension and have to discover how convergent or divergent the approaches are under national law.

III. Rationale of the Admissibility and the Nullity/Exclusion of Evidence

Investigations into illegal conduct can suffer from failures or errors in law or in fact. This can lead in one single jurisdiction to problems with the admissibility of the evidence gathered. The rules on the gathering and use of evidence in criminal matters do differ extensively from one Member State to another, and this difference is not limited to the common law-civil law divide.[7] Some Member States have closed prescribed systems of admissible evidence, while others have open systems based on the discretion of the judiciary. The rules differ not only on the legal ways to obtain evidence, but also as to the consequences of unlawfully obtained evidence for its eventual use in criminal proceedings. The common law, for instance, was traditionally indifferent as to how evidence was gathered, as long as it was reliable and probative. Some Member States, though, have very strict rules on the nullity of unlawful evidence, even for minor legal errors that do not harm the interests of the defence. In some of these Member States, the exclusion of evidence as the fruit of the poisonous tree is even a constitutional norm, although the case law of their constitutional courts has softened this concept by bringing in links with the rights of the defence (the so-called *Schutznorm*). Other Member States have very

[6] According to the prevailing opinion in doctrine, Art 82(2)(a) TFEU only constitutes a legal basis for partial harmonisation of criminal procedure laws (or in this case the law of evidence) by means of minimum standards. The admissibility of evidence facilitates only indirectly the mutual recognition of judicial decisions by establishing common standards for the admission of evidence and so facilitating the recognition of decisions taken on that basis by foreign judicial authorities. See, for instance, H Satzger, *Internationales und Europäisches Strafrecht* (Nomos 2018) § 10 Rn. 81.

[7] The British Law Society, *Study of the Laws of Evidence in Criminal Proceedings throughout the European Union* (European Commission, DG Justice and Home Affairs 2004).

flexible rules on the admissibility of evidence, even in cases involving violations of due process rules. The moment at which evidence is assessed also varies from one Member State to another. Some countries provide for specific pre-trial procedures to check and assess the legality of evidence; others do not. The former, mostly civil-law countries exclude evidence on the basis of 'invalid acts', also called '*purge des nullités*'.[8] The latter, mostly common-law countries, use exclusionary rules.

Already from the terminology, we see that the rationale behind the assessment of unlawful evidence and the related consequences might differ from country to country. In all legal systems the conceptual framework of evidence is related to the finality of the punitive process, based on the formal and substantive truth sustained by evidence/proof that respects due process. This therefore includes the legality of the proceedings from the start of the pre-trial investigations, and respect for fundamental rights and procedural guarantees during the proceedings. However, in the case of unlawful evidence, the approach and the consequences are very different from one legal order to another, depending on what and whom they want to protect by the exclusion or nullity of the evidence, as well as why they should be protected.

From comparative studies[9] on the topic we can define groups of countries, depending on the rationale of the protection. Countries like the USA, which is the champion of the doctrine of the fruit of the poisonous tree (although this has been strongly reduced by case law),[10] mainly aim at deterring unlawful police conduct (a deterrence approach). The exclusion of evidence is a tool to guide law enforcement on the right path. Countries like France,[11] Italy,[12] Spain,[13] Colombia, etc aim to protect the rights of suspects. So this exclusion or nullity is strictly related to the infringement of fundamental or substantial rights (the vindication of rights approach). Within that group some countries, like Spain, also directly relate it to the presumption of innocence.[14] Many

[8] C Benoît and S Pierre-Olivier, 'Le Point en Matière de Nullités de Procédure Pénale au fil des Cent Dernières Décisions de la Chambre d'Accusation de Paris' [1997] *Gazette du Palais* 1473.

[9] C Slobogin, 'A Comparative Perspective on the Exclusionary Rule in Search and Seizure Cases' [2013] *Vanderbilt Public Law Research Paper* 13, available at https://ssrn.com/abstract=2247746 or at http://dx.doi.org/10.2139/ssrn.2247746; SC Thaman, 'Fruits of the Poisonous Tree in Comparative Law' (2010) 16 *Southwestern Journal of International Law* 333; S Ruggeri, *Transnational Evidence and Multicultural Inquiries in Europe Stefano Ruggeri, Developments in EU Legislation and New Challenges for Human Rights-Oriented Criminal Investigations in Cross-border Cases* (Springer 2014).

[10] See already in 1968: RM Pitler, 'The Fruit of the Poisonous Tree Revisited and Shepardized' (1968) 56 *California Law Review* 579; JG Casaccio, 'Illegally Acquired Information, Consent Searches, and Tainted Fruit' (1987) 87 *Columbia Law Review* 842.

[11] M Delmas-Marty, *Procès Pénal et Droits de l'Homme* (PUF 1992); E Vergès, G Vial and O Leclerc, *Droit de la Preuve* (Presses Universitaires de France 2015); P Bolze, *Le Droit à la Preuve contraire en Procédure Pénale* (Droit. Université Nancy 2010) available at https://hal.univ-lorraine.fr/tel-01752930/document; J Pradel, *Procédure Pénale*, 19th edn (Cujas 2017).

[12] P Tonini, *Manuale di Procedura Penale*, 16th edn (Giuffrè 2015).

[13] V Moreno Catena and V Cortés Domínguez, *Derecho Procesal Penal*, 4th edn (Tirant lo Blanch 2010); VC Guzmán Fluja, *Anticipación y Preconstitución de la Prueba en el Proceso Penal* (Tirant Monografias 2006); JL Gomez Colomer, *Prueba y Proceso Penal* (Tirant lo Blanch 2008); I González Cano, *La Prueba en el Proceso Penal* (Tirant Tratados 2017).

[14] T Armanta Deu, *La Prueba Ilícita* (Pons 2011); A Planchadell Gargallo, *La Prueba Prohibida: Evolución Jurisprudencial* (Thomson Reuters-Aranzadi 2014).

countries, like Canada, the United Kingdom[15] and Germany,[16] use a so-called systemic integrity model with a balancing approach (the judicial integrity approach). This means that they apply the exclusion of evidence only for significant violations of important rights, and only in cases where the dismissal of the charges will not significantly undermine the state's interest in convicting those who have committed serious crimes. For instance, in Germany the Constitutional Court does limit the exclusion of evidence (*Fernwirking des Beweisverbots*)[17] by relating it to protected persons (*Rechtskreistheorie*) and the aim of the protection (*Schutzzwecklehre*).

The determining factors for exclusion or nullity are – depending on the group – the deterrent effect, the impact of the exclusion or admission for the reputation of the punitive justice system, the seriousness of the offence and the importance of the evidence for successful prosecution, the investigator's potential awareness of the illegality and of alternative methods for obtaining the evidence, and the nature of the right that has been violated.

Finally, the doctrine of the exclusion or nullity of evidence is also related to the architecture of the punitive justice system. In an adversarial system such as that in England and Wales, each party collects its evidence and the evidence is presented at the oral trial only. The exclusion of evidence is mainly aimed at making sure that the judges – who have a passive role when assessing the merits of the case – do not know about this evidence at all. In a semi-inquisitorial system, like in France, Germany, the Netherlands or Belgium, the judiciary is actively involved in the pre-trial investigation and prosecution and has an active role. A great deal of the evidence produced during the pre-trial setting will also be presented in a written form at the trial, without further cross-examination. Assessing the legality of the pre-trial investigative acts, before forwarding the file to the trial court, must avoid the situation where decisive elements of the evidence at trial would be based on unlawful pre-trial judicial decisions (like, for instance, a search warrant or an order to intercept telecommunications). Under the nullity approach, when investigative action violates certain specified statutory rules, and when it prejudices the interests of the accused, the action is declared void and its evidentiary result may not be used. So the nullity approach aims at sound legal acts at any stage of the procedure, while exclusion of evidence mainly has consequences for the trial setting.

In all systems, exclusion or nullity has become less absolute over the years. Nullities have been divided into absolute nullities and relative nullities, or into nullities and irregularities. Relative nullities are not sufficiently serious to exclude the evidence from the file. Irregularities are those acts that can still be repaired in due time, for instance by providing the right authorisation or calling in the defence for a pre-trial hearing, etc. Also, the fruit of the poisonous tree has been softened by requiring a causal link with the suspect, good faith of the agent, inevitable discovery, a link with the legal aim protected by the offence, etc.[18] Just to give an example: on the basis of the illegal interception

[15] A Keane and P McKeown, *The Modern Law of Evidence* (Oxford University Press 2012) 58–81; R May and S Powles, *Criminal Evidence (Criminal Practice)* (Sweet & Maxwell 2004).

[16] K Ambos, *Beweisverwertungsverbote, Grundlagen und Kasuistik – internationale Bezüge – ausgewählte Probleme* (Duncker & Humblot 2010).

[17] S Gless, 'Beweisverbote und Fernwirkung' (2010) 128 *ZStrR* 146.

[18] See Thaman (n 9).

of communications, law enforcement officers obtain a legal search warrant against a person who was already a suspect and under surveillance. The search results in the discovery of quantities of hard drugs. In the softened version of the fruit of the poisonous tree, the illegal interception is a neutral act that no longer prejudices the legality of the search.

From this overview, it is easy to see that the approaches under national law to standards of evidence and exclusion of evidence are so divergent that this can undermine not only the effectiveness of proceedings in the EU, but also due process and mutual trust between the enforcement authorities. So the question remains whether the ECHR and the Charter can provide for common standards under the concept of a fair trial.

IV. Human Rights Case Law on Evidence and its Exclusion in Punitive Proceedings: Common Standards?

A. The ECtHR's Approach

Evidence or proof is not mentioned as a topic in the ECHR, not even under the concept of 'fairness' in Article 6 ECHR. The point of departure is that the admissibility of evidence in criminal matters (including the exclusion of unlawful evidence) is a matter that is dealt with by domestic jurisdictions.[19] Evidentiary issues do, however, play an essential role in assessing the fairness of proceedings under Article 6 ECHR. Although the point of departure is that all evidence must be presented at a public hearing that allows for an adversarial procedure in which the evidence submitted can be challenged by the parties,[20] the ECtHR assesses the fairness of the proceedings as a whole, meaning from the opening of the judicial investigation until the final sentencing. As this adversarial character can manifest itself at different stages in these proceedings, it is perfectly compatible with the ECHR to have an adversarial hearing on evidentiary issues in the pre-trial setting and a written presentation thereof at the trial setting. Indirect evidence and hearsay evidence at trial are therefore not by definition violations of the fair trial concept.[21] By this approach the ECtHR has been able to develop osmosis between the common law procedure (focusing on an oral defence by the parties in the trial setting) and the civil law procedure (focusing on truth finding by the judicial authorities).

The ECHR and the case law of the Strasbourg Court do not contain specific rules on unlawfully obtained evidence either, as the ECHR does not prescribe legal means for the gathering of evidence. The way in which criminal evidence is gathered is also the exclusive domain of domestic jurisdictions. This means that the use of unlawfully obtained

[19] *Van Mechelen and Others v the Netherlands* App nos 21363/93; 21364/93; 21427/93; and 22056/93 (ECtHR, 23 April 1997), para 50; *Hümmer v Germany* App no 29881/07 (ECtHR, 19 July 2012).

[20] See, eg, *Kostovski v The Netherlands* App no 11454/85 (ECtHR, 20 November 1989).

[21] See, eg, *Bricmont v Belgium* App no 10857/84 (ECtHR, 7 July 1989).

evidence is not a violation of the ECHR as such.[22] Even if the way in which evidence has been obtained constitutes a breach of respect for private and family life and a person's home under Article 8 ECHR, due to, for instance, the lack of a clear and foreseeable legal basis or its disproportionality with regard to the aim protected in a democratic society, this does not automatically mean that this unlawful evidence has to be excluded from the criminal proceedings.[23] Neither does the ECHR prescribe any sanctions for the use of unlawful evidence, such as, for instance, exclusion (the fruit of the poisonous tree doctrine), the inadmissibility of the prosecution or mitigation of the criminal sanction imposed. Nevertheless, evidence obtained in breach of absolute human rights has to be excluded on that ground. Typical examples are evidence obtained by means of torture or inhuman treatment. This evidence has to be excluded to protect the integrity of the trial process and, ultimately, the rule of law itself.[24] In certain cases, however, the Court will only impose an exclusion if the evidence obtained in breach of Article 3 ECHR had an impact on the defendant's conviction or sentence.[25]

Besides evidence gathered by way of torture and inhuman treatment (absolute human rights), there are other violations of relative human rights that are so serious that the ECtHR considers that they will lead to a flagrant denial of justice, which means to a trial that is manifestly contrary to the provisions of Article 6 ECHR or the principles embodied therein.[26] Which forms of unfairness can amount to a flagrant denial of justice? Typical examples are evidence obtained by entrapment and incitement, and in which there is no indication that the offence would have been committed without the intervention;[27] evidence based on confessions that have been made without the assistance of a lawyer and that are used as key evidence without further legal assistance being given to the accused;[28] and serious violations of the right to remain silent[29] or of the right to cross-examination.[30] In these cases the violation leads automatically, just as in the fruit of the poisonous tree doctrine, to a violation of Article 6 ECHR and therefore to the exclusion of the evidence. The consequences of the exclusion of evidence in punitive proceedings depend on the availability of other forms of key evidence.

[22] *Popescu v Romania* App nos 49234/99 and 71525/01 (ECtHR, 26 April 2007), para 106.

[23] See, eg, *Khan v UK* App no 35394/97 (ECtHR, 12 May 2000).

[24] *Gäfgen v Germany* App no 22978/05 (ECtHR, 1 June 2010), paras 98–99; *Othman (Abu Qatada) v the United Kingdom* App no 8139/09 (ECtHR, 17 January 2012); *El Haski v Belgium* App no 649/08 (ECtHR, 25 September 2012); *Al Nashiri v Poland* App no 28761/11 (ECtHR, 24 July 2014), paras 565–569; *Husayn (Abu Zubaydah) v Poland* App no 7511/13 (ECtHR, 24 July 2014), paras 555–561.

[25] *Khan v the United Kingdom* App no 35394/97 (ECtHR, 12 May 2000), paras 35 and 37; *Gäfgen v Germany* App no 22978/05 (ECtHR, 1 June 2010), para 104. In this case the evidence in dispute had not been necessary for determining the sentence for the accused, therefore his trial as a whole was considered to have been fair.

[26] *Sejdovic v Italy* App no 56581/00 (ECtHR, GC, 1 March 2006), para 84; *Stoichkov v Bulgaria* App no 9808/02 (ECtHR, 24 March 2005), para 56; *Drozd and Janousek v France and Spain* App no 12747/87 (ECtHR, 26 June 1992), para 110.

[27] *Teixeira de Castro v Portugal* App no 44/1997/828/1034 (ECtHR, 9 June 1998), paras 38–39.

[28] *Salduz v Turkey* App no 36391/02 (ECtHR, 27 November 2008).

[29] *Allan v the United Kingdom* App no 48539/99 (ECtHR, 5 November 2002).

[30] *Vidgen v the Netherlands* App no 29353/06 (ECtHR, 10 July 2012).

B. EU Courts and the Admissibility of Evidence

Unless EU law contains specific provisions on the law of evidence, like Article 12 of Regulation 1/2003 (competition law),[31] it falls under the general rule of national procedural autonomy. Unlike the ECtHR, the EU Courts do not have a general approach to standards of evidence, the admissibility of evidence or its exclusion. Under the *Rewe* requirements,[32] Member States must provide for equivalent and effective protection. So Member States must have remedies available to be able to give effect to EU law just as effect is given to national law, and must ensure that these remedies for breaches of EU law can be obtained at national level without undue burden. Moreover through Article 52(3) of the Charter, the EU authorities and the EU Courts do have to apply the minimum standards of the ECtHR when evidentiary issues are at stake in cases where EU law does apply.

In this subsection I have selected emblematic cases to show how the EU Courts deal with evidentiary issues.

i. *Case T-54/14,* Goldfish BV v European Commission

In this case,[33] the company Goldfish contested a decision by the Directorate-General for Competition (DG Competition)/European Commission,[34] based on a variety of sources of evidence, but also including a number of audio recordings of telephone conversations and related handwritten notes of telephone conversations made by a private person (in this case one of the applicant's competitors), in which two competitors had exchanged sensitive commercial information, including on price setting.

The General Court commenced its reasoning by recalling a couple of principles. First, lawfully obtained evidence cannot be contested before the Court and the only relevant criterion for the purpose of assessing the probative value of evidence lawfully obtained relates to its credibility.[35] Second, given that there is no legislation at the EU level governing the concept of proof, any type of evidence that is admissible under the procedural law of the Member States in similar proceedings is in principle admissible.[36] However, there might be reasons to exclude some evidence from the file, for instance if there are serious doubts about the credibility of the piece of evidence, related to the nature of the evidence or the way in which it has been obtained.

Third, the General Court underlined in *Goldfish* that:

> Whether the use of unlawfully obtained evidence does deprive the applicant of a fair trial and the related defence rights depends on the ability of the defence to challenge the authenticity

[31] Council Regulation (EC) No 1/2003 of 16 December 2002 on the implementation of the rules on competition laid down in Articles 81 and 82 of the Treaty [2003] OJ L1/1.

[32] Case 33/76 *Rewe* ECLI:EU:C:1976:188.

[33] Case T-54/14 *Goldfish BV v European Commission* ECLI:EU:T:2016:455.

[34] For a general overview of evidentiary issues in EU competition law, see F Castillo de la Torre and E Gippini Fournier, *Evidence, Proof and Judicial Review in the EU Competition Law* (Edward Elgar Publishing 2017).

[35] *Goldfish* (n 32) para 42; with reference to Joined Cases C-239/11 P, C-489/11 P and C-498/11 P *Siemens v Commission* ECLI:EU:C:2013:866, para 128.

[36] *Goldfish* (n 32) para 43; with reference to Joined Cases C-310/98 and C-406/98 *Met-Trans and Sagpol* ECLI:EU:C:2000:154, para 29.

and use of the evidence and whether the evidence was the only and decisive item of evidence in support of liability.[37]

In this case the applicant had had an ample opportunity to check the source and content of the evidence and this evidence was not the sole piece of evidence either. The Court was also not impressed by the references to national law, and it underlined the fact that the Commission's assessment of the evidence in competition disputes is governed by EU law.[38] Otherwise, the use of rules or legal concepts in national law and deriving from the legislation of a Member State would adversely affect the unity of EU law.[39] The Commission had not committed any illegality by using the disputed telephone recordings to establish an infringement of Article 101 TFEU. As we can see from the reasoning, the General Court was using the ECtHR standards to assess the fairness of the EU proceedings in these punitive competition proceedings.

ii. Case C-419/14, WebMindLicenses Kft v Nemzeti Adó- és Vámhivatal Kiemelt Adó- és Vám Főigazgatóság

In this case,[40] the question was whether, in the case of parallel proceedings, the use of evidence obtained by judicial authorities through the tapping of telecommunications and the seizure of e-mails by tax authorities was consistent with fundamental rights, in particular with Article 8(2) ECHR, Articles 7, 8, 41, 47, 48, 51(1) and 52(2) of the Charter, the rights of the defence and the right to good administration. In this case EU law did apply, as it concerned a value added tax (VAT) debt procedure.

For the Court of Justice the starting point was the lawfulness under national law. Second, the fundamental rights guaranteed in the legal order of the EU are applicable in all situations governed by EU law.[41] Fundamental rights can only be limited if this is provided for by law and if, when observing the principle of proportionality, this is necessary and genuinely meets the objectives of the general interest recognised by the EU. As for examining the necessity of the investigative measures, in the absence of prior judicial authorisation, a strict legal framework for and strict limits on such seizure are required if individuals are to be protected from arbitrary interference with the rights guaranteed under Article 7 of the Charter by the authorities.[42] Thus, such a seizure can only be compatible with Article 7 of the Charter if domestic legislation and practice afford adequate and effective safeguards against any abuse and arbitrariness.[43] The Court stated in paragraph 78 that it is incumbent upon the referring court to examine

[37] *Schenk v Switzerland* App no 00010862/84 (ECtHR, 12 July 1988), para 48.

[38] *Goldfish* (n 32) para 77.

[39] Case C-550/07 P *Akzo Nobel Chemicals and Akcros Chemicals v Commission* ECLI:EU:C:2010:512, paras 69–76.

[40] Case C-419/14 *WebMindLicenses Kft v Nemzeti Adó- és Vámhivatal Kiemelt Adó- és Vám Főigazgatóság* ECLI:EU:C:2015:832.

[41] Case C-617/10 *Åkerberg Fransson* ECLI:EU:C:2013:280, para 19.

[42] *Camenzind v Switzerland* App no 136/1996/755/954 (ECtHR, 16 December 1997), para 45.

[43] *Funke v France* App no 10828/84 (ECtHR, 25 February 1993), paras 56–57; *Miailhe v France* App no 12661/87 (ECtHR, 25 February 1993), paras 37–38; *Société Colas Est and Others v France* App no 37971/97 (ECHR, 16 April 2002), paras 48 and 49.

whether the absence of a prior judicial warrant was, to a certain extent, counterbalanced by the availability to the person concerned by the seizure of an *ex post factum* judicial review relating to both the legality and necessity of the seizure, a review which must be effective in the particular circumstances of the case in question.[44]

It must also be examined whether that use of the evidence satisfies the requirements set out in Article 52(1) of the Charter. Besides legality, the legitimate aim and proportionality, the Court of Justice strongly insisted on the right to an effective judicial remedy, guaranteed by Article 47 of the Charter. In order for the judicial review to be effective, the court reviewing the legality of a decision implementing EU law must be able to verify whether the evidence on which that decision is founded has been obtained and used in breach of the rights guaranteed by EU law and especially by the Charter. The Court came to the conclusion that the transfer of the evidence was not precluded as such under EU law, provided that obtaining that evidence in the context of the criminal procedure and its use in the context of the administrative procedure do not infringe the rights guaranteed by EU law. The Court thus concluded in paragraph 91 (emphasis added) that

> by virtue of Articles 7, 47 and 52(1) of the Charter it is incumbent upon the national court which reviews the legality of the decision founded on such evidence adjusting VAT to verify, first, whether the interception of telecommunications and seizure of e-mails were means of investigation provided for by law and were necessary in the context of the criminal procedure and, secondly, whether the use by the tax authorities of the evidence obtained by those means was also authorised by law and necessary. It is incumbent upon that court, furthermore, to verify whether, in accordance with the general principle of observance of the rights of the defence, the taxable person had the opportunity, in the context of the administrative procedure, of gaining access to that evidence and of being heard concerning it. If the national court finds that the taxable person did not have that opportunity or that that evidence was obtained in the context of the criminal procedure, or used in the context of the administrative procedure, in breach of Article 7 of the Charter, *it must disregard that evidence and annul that decision* if, as a result, the latter has no basis. *That evidence must also be disregarded if* the national court is not empowered to check that it was obtained in the context of the criminal procedure in accordance with EU law or cannot at least satisfy itself, on the basis of a review already carried out by a criminal court in an inter partes procedure, that it was obtained in accordance with EU law.

This conclusion contains very clear instructions on the exclusion of evidence if the necessary standards of the rights of defence and an effective judicial remedy are not complied with.

iii. *Case C-746/18 (Grand Chamber),* HK v Prokuratuur

In this case,[45] dealing with the access by judicial authorities in Estonia to data that are retained by service providers as gatekeepers, the Court of Justice had to deal, inter

[44] With reference to *Smirnov v Russia* App no 71362/01 (ECtHR, 7 June 2007), para 45.
[45] Case C-746/18 *HK v Prokuratuur* ECLI:EU:C:2021:152.

alia, with the question of the admissibility of evidence of these data, when not legally obtained, in criminal proceedings. The reasoning of the Grand Chamber in this case is fully in line with its reasoning in the *La Quadrature du Net and Others* case.[46] As EU law currently stands, it is in principle for national law alone to determine the rules relating to admissibility and assessment.[47] However, in the absence of EU rules, it is for the national legal order, in accordance with the principle of procedural autonomy, to guarantee the effective and equivalent protection of procedural individual safeguards.[48] The effectiveness can include exclusion of this evidence under national law, but can also be achieved by rules and practices governing the assessment and weighting of such material, or by taking it into account when determining sentencing.[49] If eventual admissibility would lead to a risk of breach of the right to fair trial, the evidence must be declared inadmissible. This could be the case if the suspects were, for instance, not in a position to comment effectively on that information and evidence (lack of adversariality), and the information and evidence pertain to a field of which the judges have no knowledge and are likely to have a preponderant influence on the findings of fact.[50]

C. Interim Conclusion

From this analysis of the case law of the ECtHR and the EU Courts, it is obvious that they have not developed common standards as to the gathering of evidence (the type of evidence), the admissibility of the evidence, or the exclusion or nullity of evidence. Nevertheless, certain forms of evidence gathering do infringe upon human rights and the essence of justice to such a serious extent that they automatically lead to the exclusion of evidence or the invalidity of the act. In other cases both the unlawfulness and the unfairness of the gathering and use of evidence (the lack of rights of the defence or effective judicial remedies) can lead to a situation in which the use of that evidence infringes upon the 'fairness of the proceedings as a whole'. This means that in certain situations, unlawful evidence can be admissible evidence in punitive proceedings, even if that evidence is inculpatory for the suspect or the person concerned.

Looking back at the rationale of the concept of the admissibility of evidence, we can state that the ECtHR and the EU Courts mostly use a systemic integrity model with a balancing approach (the judicial integrity approach). This means that they only resort to the exclusion of evidence for serious violations of important rights, and only in cases where the dismissal of the charges will not significantly undermine the justice interest in convicting those who have committed serious crimes. There are nevertheless exceptions based on a nullity approach for evidence based on violations of Articles 2 and 3 ECHR, some serious unlawful acts under EU law or flagrant violations of the fair trial.

[46] Joined Cases C-511/18; C-512/18; and C-520/18 *La Quadrature du Net and Others* ECLI:EU:C:2020:791, paras 223–227.

[47] Case C-746/18 *HK v Prokuratuur* [2021] ECLI:EU:C:2021:152, para 41.

[48] ibid para 42.

[49] ibid para 43.

[50] ibid para 44.

What does all this mean for the European enforcement agencies, when they collect evidence and when this evidence is used in criminal (or punitive) proceedings?

V. European Enforcement Agencies and the Admissibility or Exclusion of Evidence

A. The OLAF Experience as a Telling Narrative

The choice of OLAF is deliberate, as it is an investigative agency that is mainly collecting evidence in the field of the so-called PIF offences, meaning illicit acts that affect the EU budget, like subsidy fraud, customs fraud and VAT fraud, and related corruption and money laundering.[51] Although its investigative powers are of an administrative nature, its evidence can be used in a punitive follow up by national enforcement agencies, including proceedings of a judicial, criminal nature. So for any questions relating to lawful evidence and the exclusion of evidence, we do have to start from the complex setting in which OLAF is exchanging information,[52] investigating[53] and forwarding final reports of this investigation to be followed up by the competent national and European authorities, and what the status of this OLAF evidence is at the time of assessing its admissibility and evidentiary value. It is also important that OLAF proceedings cannot be qualified as punitive proceedings in the sense of the 'criminal charge' concept of Article 6 ECHR, as OLAF has no sanctioning powers at all. In the report *Investigatory Powers and Procedural Safeguards*,[54] Michiel Luchtman, the present author and other contributors elaborated different models for interaction between the EU and the national level: autonomous investigations by OLAF inspectors (internal and/or external); mixed investigations (in cooperation with the national authorities); mandated investigations (execution by national authorities); and mutual administrative assistance. The way in which evidence is gathered and transferred depends to a great extent on which investigative model is used. Nevertheless, all OLAF models resulting in external investigative acts do involve interaction with the national legal order. Even for external autonomous investigations, the EU legal OLAF framework regularly refers to the applicable national law.

If we then ask what makes OLAF evidence illegal as such, based on the invalidity of the act producing it, or when OLAF evidence is not apt for use as evidence in punitive

[51] See also ch 6 of this volume (Giuffrida and Theodorakakou).

[52] M Simonato, M Luchtman and J Vervaele (eds), *Report Exchange of Information with EU and National Enforcement Authorities Improving OLAF Legislative Framework through a Comparison with Other EU Authorities (ECN/ESMA/ECB)* (Utrecht University 2018) available at https://orbilu.uni.lu/bitstream/10993/35503/1/Utrecht_University_Hercule_III_Exchange_of_information_with_EU_and_national_enforcement_authorities.pdf (accessed 16 April 2022).

[53] M Luchtman and J Vervaele (eds), Report, *Investigatory Powers and Procedural Safeguards: Improving OLAF's Legislative Framework through a Comparison with Other EU Law Enforcement Authorities (ECN/ESMA/ECB)* (Utrecht University 2017) available at https://eulawenforcement.com/wp-content/uploads/2019/03/Report_Investigatory_powers_and_procedural_safeguards_Utrecht_University_1_.pdf(accessed 16 April 2022).

[54] ibid; see also ch 1 of this volume (Luchtman).

proceedings, leading to exclusion; and if we ask who and what the nullity of the act or the exclusion of the evidence aims to protect, the answers will not to a large extent be provided by EU law but by the applicable national law. This does not mean that the EU legal framework has no legal impact. It certainly does have an impact when it comes to the procedural safeguards contained in Article 9 of Regulation 883/2013,[55] which apply to all OLAF investigations and thus to the fairness of OLAF evidence.

When OLAF evidence is presented as admissible evidence in punitive proceedings, assessing the lawfulness and fairness of this OLAF evidence will depend on:

(a) the applicable law for the competent authority and investigative act;
(b) the applicable procedural safeguards;
(c) purpose limitations on its transfer and use; and
(d) the applicable fundamental rights (constitutional, ECHR and the Charter).

It is also important that the admissibility assessment of OLAF evidence, although reviewed internally by OLAF before including it an OLAF report, will always be made by national authorities/courts. This is of course very different from proceedings by the European Central Bank (ECB), the European Securities and Markets Authority (ESMA) or DG Competition, as the results of their investigations will generally be used in EU punitive proceedings, meaning that these results will be used as evidence at the EU level and will be subject to the remedies/control of the EU Courts. This is very different in the OLAF setting, as Regulation 883/2013 governs the link between OLAF investigations and any (judicial) follow-up action at the national level. The purpose relation is thus explicitly regulated by EU law. The OLAF report is a document that contains statements and recommendations based on evidence gathered by OLAF investigations. If OLAF forwards evidence to the national competent authorities, it must assess the lawful status of its own investigation and the outcome in the form of potential evidence for national procedural follow-up actions. In Article 11(1) of Regulation 883/2013[56] it is clearly stated that that report shall give an account of the legal basis for the investigation, the procedural steps followed, the facts established and their preliminary classification in law, the estimated financial impact of the facts established, the respect given to the procedural guarantees in accordance with Article 9 and the conclusions of the investigation. This therefore means that OLAF has to assess the legality, quality and reliability of its investigations and the related evidence, also in the light of the applicable safeguards and fundamental rights when this evidence is included in the report and elaborating recommendations for (judicial) follow-up action. Depending upon the type of investigation (autonomous, mixed, mandated, MLA-based), the assessment will contain a different mix of European and national applicable law. This also means that the potential causes of and the reasons for the unlawful acts and the related nullity/exclusion of

[55] Regulation (EU, Euratom) No 883/2013 of the European Parliament and of the Council of 11 September 2013 concerning investigations conducted by the European Anti-Fraud Office (OLAF) and repealing Regulation (EC) No 1073/1999 of the European Parliament and of the Council and Council Regulation (Euratom) No 1074/1999 [2013] OJ L248/1.

[56] As amended by Regulation 2020/2223 of 23 December 2020 amending Regulation (EU, Euratom) No 883/2013 of 11 September 2013 concerning investigations conducted by the European Anti-Fraud Office (OLAF), as regards cooperation with the European Public Prosecutor's Office and the effectiveness of the European Anti-Fraud Office investigations [2020] OJ L437/49.

evidence can have their background at the EU level, the national level or a combination thereof. OLAF's assessment based on Article 11(1) can also be considered as a first filter ('*purge des nullités*') before forwarding the report to the national competent authorities. The use of the reports as evidence in punitive proceedings by the national authorities will and must lead to a second filter when they have to assess the admissibility of OLAF evidence in the light of national law and in the light of mandatory EU law (based on the primacy of the OLAF Regulation). Thanks to the case law of the Court of Justice, we do know that the transfer of the report to the national competent authorities does not change the legal situation of the person concerned and cannot for this reason be challenged as such before the Court.[57] In the more recent order in *Inox Mare Srl*,[58] the EU General Court clearly reaffirmed its position.

The EU and OLAF are and must be very conscious of the consequences of the Office's reports, as the evidence contained therein can be not only admissible evidence but also key evidence for punitive enforcement in the Member States. This is the reason why former Article 11(2) of Regulation 883/2013 contained instructions not only on the way in which the reports and recommendations should be elaborated upon, but also on the admissibility of the evidence and its evidentiary value (emphasis added):

> In drawing up such reports and recommendations, account shall be taken of the national law of the Member State concerned. Reports drawn up on that basis *shall constitute admissible evidence in administrative or judicial proceedings* of the Member State in which their use proves necessary, in the same way and under the same conditions as administrative reports drawn up by national administrative inspectors. They shall be subject to the *same evaluation rules* as those applicable to administrative reports drawn up by national administrative inspectors and shall have *the same evidentiary value* as such reports.

Former Article 11(2) was based on an assimilation rule between equivalent authorities under the EU and national legal orders and the legal consequences of their acts as evidence in the domestic setting. In reality there are very substantial differences between the legal orders of the Member States. Some of them refuse to recognise that OLAF evidence has any evidentiary value. Some of them simply apply the national rules that are applicable to national administrative agencies, while a minority have introduced special features for OLAF evidence and also accept that OLAF can provide evidence or be heard as a victim in criminal trials.

In December 2020, the OLAF Regulation 883/2013 was amended by Regulation 2020/2223, with the aim, inter alia, of enhancing the effectiveness of OLAF investigations. Article 11(2) has been replaced with the following (emphasis added):

> 2. In drawing up the reports and recommendations referred to in paragraph 1, account shall be taken of the relevant provisions of Union law and, in so far as it is applicable, of the national law of the Member State concerned.
>
> Reports drawn up on the basis of the first subparagraph, together with all evidence in support and annexed thereto, shall constitute admissible evidence:

[57] Case T-261/09 P *Violetti v Commission* ECLI:EU:T:2010:215, para 47.

[58] Case T-289/16 *Inox Mare Srl v Commission* ECLI:EU:T:2017:414.

(a) in judicial proceedings *of a non-criminal nature* before national courts and in administrative proceedings in the Member States;
(b) *in criminal proceedings* of the Member State in which their use proves necessary in the same way and under the same conditions as administrative reports drawn up by national administrative inspectors and shall be subject to the same evaluation rules as those applicable to administrative reports drawn up by national administrative inspectors and shall have the same evidentiary value as such reports …

So, the assimilation rule for OLAF evidence has been cancelled as far as use in administrative proceedings is concerned: OLAF evidence would always have to be admissible evidence. As to use in judicial proceedings, the assimilation rule is upheld and the admissibility thus depends on the status of equivalent administrative evidence under national proceedings in judicial criminal cases.

B. OLAF-Related Cases

I have selected some OLAF-related cases to show the complexity of evidence issues at the national criminal courts.

i. Tendering Fraud and Related Active and Passive Corruption in France and Belgium

The French Supreme Court[59] has had to deal with the nullity of an OLAF final report (and annexes) that had been determined by the Indictment Chamber at the Court of Appeal in Versailles.[60] Based upon information from OLAF, the French judicial authorities started a judicial investigation, headed by an investigating magistrate, into an EU fraud case. The investigating magistrate requested OLAF inspectors to join the judicial investigations as experts. The judicial investigations included searches and seizures at the premises of several suspects in France. OLAF inspectors were also requested by the French judicial authorities to assist in the analysis of the seized digital data. The legal basis for the participation of the OLAF inspectors was based on Article 77-1-1 of the French Penal Code of Procedure. Unfortunately, this was a legal error and their participation should have been based on Article 77-1, as the OLAF inspectors had participated in a judicial investigation. This resulted in a violation of Article 166 of the French Code of Criminal Procedure, which regulates the status of judicial experts. For that reason, the pre-trial chamber determined that the report and all the related annexes had to be nullified because of a violation of the fairness of the proceedings.

At the Supreme Court, the European Commission, as a civil party, contended that national courts do not have jurisdiction to annul an OLAF report, being a European act, and that the jurisdiction to do so is exclusively reserved for the Court of Justice and that the primacy of EU law sets aside the national provisions. The Supreme Court did

[59] Cour de Cassation, Paris, Chambre Criminelle, ECLI:FR:CCASS:2016:CR05486, Audience publique du mercredi 9 novembre 2016, N° de pourvoi: 16-83602.

[60] Dated 3 May 2016, unpublished.

not follow this reasoning at all and concluded in 2016 that the report and its annexes were the result of annulled acts under French criminal procedure and thus also had to be annulled in order to guarantee a fair criminal procedure. The French Supreme Court had already reached such a decision in a Judgment in 2015,[61] in which it also made a very clear distinction between the nullity of the OLAF reports as such – not a matter of criminal jurisdiction – and the nullity of the OLAF evidence when used in criminal proceedings.

It is interesting that the former file that led to the Supreme Court decision in 2016 also had a transnational dimension, as elements of this OLAF report were also used in parallel judicial procedures against the same suspects in Belgium. However, a specific Belgian statute regulates the transnational use of illegal evidence, and this explicitly[62] applies to Europol, Eurojust and OLAF:

> CHAPITRE V. – De l'utilisation d'éléments de preuve recueillis à l'étranger.
>
> Art 13. Ne peuvent être utilisés dans le cadre d'une procédure menée en Belgique, les éléments de preuve: 1° recueillis irrégulièrement à l'étranger, lorsque l'irrégularité: – découle, selon le droit de l'Etat dans lequel l'élément de preuve a été recueilli, de la violation d'une règle de forme prescrite à peine de nullité; – entache la fiabilité de la preuve; 2° ou dont l'utilisation viole le droit à un procès équitable.[63]

In a contradictory procedure between the Commission (as a civil party) and the suspects before the Brussels first instance court,[64] this court decided that the French decisions were final decisions with a *res judicata* status on the admissibility of OLAF evidence, based on nullified acts. Their use in Belgium would undermine the essence of the fairness of the proceedings in Belgium, which was the reason why the evidence was also inadmissible under Belgian law.

In a second decision on the same date,[65] the Court of First Instance had to deal with the legality of the analysis of digital data obtained during searches and seizures at Belgian premises in the Belgian investigation, which involved the same OLAF inspectors as were also involved in the analysis of the French digital data. In the opinion of the Indictment Chamber at the Brussels Court of Appeal, these experts were not involved as judicial experts but did provide technical assistance under OLAF Regulation 1073/1999. An extraordinary appeal at the Supreme Court was rejected.[66] However, the Court of First Instance also determined that this evidence was inadmissible, as it was impossible to make a distinction between evidence that was directly affected by the annulled acts in France and the parallel evidence obtained in Belgium.

[61] Cour de Cassation, Chambre criminelle, 9 December 2015, nr 15-82300.

[62] Art 2.

[63] Loi sur la transmission policière internationale de données à caractère personnel et d'informations à finalité judiciaire, l'entraide judiciaire internationale en matière pénale et modifiant l'article 90ter du Code d'instruction criminelle, 9th December 2004, Article 13.

[64] Judgment of 5 October 2017, file no 04605, unpublished.

[65] Judgment of 5 October 2017, file no 0606, unpublished.

[66] Judgment of 14 September 2016.

ii. Case T-48/16 Sigma Orionis v Commission, *Judgment of 3 May 2018*

On the basis of Article 3 of Regulation 883/2013, OLAF initiated an investigation in 2014 into claims that time sheets had been manipulated and excessively high hourly wages had been paid in FP7 projects; and accordingly a production order was submitted and witness statements were taken from former employees. That evidence persuaded OLAF that it was necessary to conduct an on-site check under Article 5 of Council Regulation 2185/96.[67] OLAF thereby informed the local public prosecutor and requested all necessary assistance from the French authorities, including the adoption of precautionary measures under national law in order to safeguard the evidence. OLAF's final report was sent to the Commission. OLAF also forwarded the report to the French authorities, with the recommendation that they initiate criminal proceedings at the national level, based on French law, in respect of the conduct found to have occurred, in so far as such conduct was covered by French law. The persons concerned were prosecuted for fraud in respect of acts to the detriment of the EU. However, in 2015 the Indictment Chamber of the Court of Appeal of Aix-en-Provence determined[68] that the documents used by the French authorities in the criminal proceedings brought against the accused in France were invalid. According to the court, those documents had been obtained in breach of a number of procedural safeguards designed to protect the rights of the defence. The documents held to be invalid included the final report sent by OLAF to the French authorities. In 2017, the Commercial Court rejected the claims entered by the Commission in the inventory of the applicants' liabilities, on the ground that the investigation conducted by OLAF, as a result of which the Commission found that the applicants should not have received payment for some services, had been 'invalidated' by the judgment of the Indictment Chamber of 17 December 2015. In a procedure before the EU General Court, the applicants claimed the amounts owed by the Commission in the context of the implementation of the grant contracts and non-contractual liability.

At the EU General Court, the applicants maintained that the *res judicata* effect barred the use of those reports in EU proceedings. The EU Court did not follow that reasoning and stated that, irrespective of the findings by the French Indictment Chamber in its judgment, OLAF's report continued to be lawful in the EU legal order in so far as it had not been invalidated by the EU judicature. As long as this report and evidence had not been invalidated by the EU judicature, it could be used in administrative proceedings under EU law, as those related to breaches of contractual grant provisions under FP7.

It is interesting that in this case the applicants also claimed that the use of this report and the evidence therein was in breach of Article 47 of the Charter, in so far as the on-site checks and inspections had been carried out by OLAF without its investigators being accompanied by national police officers, and without the applicants having been informed of their right to resist those operations and without the operations having

[67] Council Regulation (Euratom, EC) No 2185/96 of 11 November 1996 concerning on-the-spot checks and inspections carried out by the Commission in order to protect the European Communities' financial interests against fraud and other irregularities [1996] OJ L292/2.

[68] Chambre de l'Instruction (Indictment Division) of the Cour d'appel (Appeal Court) of Aix-en-Provence, which delivered its judgment on 17 December 2015.

been authorised beforehand by a national court. The EU Court rejected these arguments, as the first two were not covered by the EU legislation in question, and did not fall under Article 47 of the Charter, and as the last one could be compensated by an effective national remedy.

The EU Court also rejected the reasoning of the applicants that Article 53 of the Charter contains a 'minimum safeguards' clause, under which OLAF, in its investigations, is required to comply with national rules where they afford individuals more extensive safeguards than those provided for in EU law, by stating that Article 53 of the Charter cannot be construed as allowing a Member State to disapply EU legal rules that are fully in compliance with the Charter on the ground that they infringe the fundamental rights guaranteed by that state's constitution.[69]

iii. Court of Appeal, Amsterdam, Customs Chamber, Judgment 4 October 2012

In this case,[70] due to indications of fraud at the place of origin, OLAF carried out an inspection of a company in Malaysia that specialised in exporting bicycles. The OLAF report contained evidence of the fact that a large number of the bicycles imported into the Community that were stated to be of Malaysian origin had not been produced in Malaysia but in China. These bicycles were transhipped via the Malaysian Free Zones to the Community with false or incorrectly obtained Malaysian preferential origin certificates. In the Dutch customs debt proceedings, the company challenged the use of OLAF's reports as evidence. The Appeal Court adopted a clear stance on this in point 4.4:

> Setting aside the findings of a fact-finding mission by OLAF is such a far-reaching act that in general this will only be justified if the plaintiff's allegations against the findings of OLAF's fact-finding mission are so serious that any credibility can no longer be attached to the findings of OLAF.[71]

The allegations of the person concerned did not convince the Court of the lack of credibility of the findings in the OLAF report.

iv. Rechtbank Noord-Holland, Judgment 23 July 2013

In this criminal case against a firm accused of falsifying certificates of origin from Cambodia and Thailand,[72] the criminal investigation had been commenced on the basis of an OLAF inspection mission in these third countries. The reports of these investigations were used by the FIOD (the specialised judicial tax enforcement authority) as

[69] With reference to Case C-399/11 *Melloni v Ministerio Fiscal* ECLI:EU:C:2013:107, para 58.

[70] Rb Haarlem 26 September 2011, ECLI:NL:RBHAA:2011:BV1238.

[71] ibid point 4.4 (translation by the author): 'Het terzijde stellen van de bevindingen van een onderzoeksmissie door het OLAF is een dusdanig ingrijpende handeling, dat dit in het algemeen slechts gerechtvaardigd zal zijn, indien de door eiseres onderzoeksmissie van het OLAF zodanig ernstig zijn, dat geen geloofwaardigheid aan de bevindingen van het OLAF (meer) kan worden toegekend.'

[72] Rb Noord-Holland 23 juli 2013, ECLI:NL:RBNHO:2013:9668.

preliminary information for the Dutch criminal investigation and as criminal evidence. The legal person accused challenged these reports, because the firm was not informed about their existence and because of the fact that a conceptual report had been used by the FIOD and not the final report.

The Dutch Court of First Instance emphasised that the Dutch Public Prosecutor's Office was '*dominus litis*' and that the sanction of the inadmissibility of the prosecution under Dutch criminal procedure could only be used in the case of very serious infringements of the essence of the procedure or other fundamental rights that resulted in violation of the right of the accused to a fair trial, either intentionally or as a result of serious negligence. The Court stated that no specific defence interests had been infringed. As for the report of the OLAF mission, the Criminal Court of First Instance literally reproduced verbatim paragraph 4.4 of the decision of the Customs Chamber of the Court of Appeal quoted in section V.B.iii. By doing so the Court transferred the reasoning on the admissibility and validity of evidence from an administrative non-punitive customs procedure to a criminal procedure. The Court was also not convinced of the reasoning of the defence as to the lack of credibility that could be attached to the OLAF report.

The approach of the Dutch courts contrasts with the French approach, being mainly based on comity and trust, unless there are very serious allegations that undermine the credibility of the evidence. Moreover, it is for the accused or the defence to come up with convincing arguments to rebut this presumption of credibility. If the rationale of the concept of unlawful evidence is also aimed at the protection of the defence rights and the fundamental rights of the person concerned, then this presumption of lawfulness and credibility is a doubtful approach, as it does not take into account that even lawful evidence used in this way can lead to the unfair use of evidence and thus to unfair proceedings.

VI. Concluding Observations

Although the European Commission has openly recognised that in the AFSJ there is a need for harmonised common standards on evidence and the admissibility thereof, Article 82(2)(a) TFEU has not been used to instigate a legislative proposal in that respect. Even within the framework of the European Investigation Order or the establishment of the European Public Prosecutor, no common standards have been elaborated. The result is that the treatment of evidence and of unlawful evidence differs greatly from one Member State to another, to such an extent that we cannot even speak of a presumption of equivalent standards across the EU. This is of course a problem, I would say both for the enforcement side and for the persons concerned or for the defendants (be they suspects or accused).

The only potential protection offered at this stage could come from the ECtHR. However, the ECtHR does not offer common standards when it comes to evidence gathering, the admissibility of evidence or the exclusion thereof. Besides serious violations of absolute human rights or very serious violations that undermine the essence of justice, the ECtHR uses the doctrine of the fairness of the proceedings in order to test the admissibility and use of unlawful evidence. The main weakness of this approach is not only that the balancing exercise is not always very predictable, as it depends on the concrete facts and circumstances of the case, but also that this approach, as in many cases, is meaningless in a transnational setting of a horizontal nature (between Member States) and/or in a vertical setting (with EU actors). The test of fairness in these cases is extremely unpredictable, unless it leads to a flagrant denial of justice,[73] but this standard has a very high threshold.

Finally, the EU legislator should accept its responsibility and submit a proposal for a directive under Article 82(2)(b)–(c), with the aim of harmonising the standards for the admissibility of evidence and unlawful evidence. This would strengthen the setting for the use of mutual recognition instruments and also the future work of the European enforcement agencies, and would give the European Court of Justice a basis for further developing standards for lawful and fair criminal evidence in a transnational setting.

[73] See M Luchtman, *Transnationale Rechtshandhaving – Over Fundamentele Rechten in de Europese Strafrechtelijke Samenwerking* (oration, Boom Juridische uitgevers 2017); M Luchtman, 'Transnational Multi-Disciplinary Investigations and the Quest for Compatible Procedural Safeguards' in K Ligeti and V Franssen (eds), *Challenges in the Field of Economic and Financial Crime in Europe and the US* (Hart Publishing 2017) 191.

PART IV

Outlook and Perspectives

10

Pertinent Issues of Punitive Enforcement in a Composite Legal Order

MICHIEL LUCHTMAN

I. Introduction

The enforcement reality in which European Union (EU) enforcement authorities and their national partners operate does not square easily with traditional notions of enforcement sovereignty or cooperation on the basis of international mutual (administrative or judicial) assistance agreements. Yet to a large extent these authorities have taken the place of these structures. The typical elements of international enforcement cooperation have been removed from their legal frameworks to address the specific needs of the EU and its Member States. These authorities were entrusted with the task of reducing significant enforcement deficits, particularly in transnational cases where individual states cannot always live up to this task. They function in an environment in which transnational citizenship or agency is strongly advocated.[1] The need for effective enforcement, as well as effective legal protection, relates directly to the legitimacy of the composite European legal order, that is, not only the EU but also its Member States. Yet the need for both may also come into conflict with notions of state sovereignty. National legal orders not only need to open up, but also require a common narrative that guides these processes of enforcement integration.[2]

In this chapter I aim to bring together the main findings of the previous chapters, in search of what could be the principal elements of such a narrative. I have structured my findings around the two distinct yet related perspectives: the perspective of the *effective enforcement* of EU laws and policies (section II); and that of *effective legal protection* in this complicated composite setting (section III). I will conclude with a series of what I have called 'benchmarks' for enforcement in a composite legal order (section IV).

[1] J Graat, *The European Arrest Warrant and EU Citizenship. EU citizenship in relation to foreseeability problems in the surrender procedure* (Springer 2022).

[2] See ch 1 of this volume (Luchtman), section III.

A particular feature of all EU enforcement authorities is their EU-wide[3] mandate. The notion of territorial borders, that is so distinctive for the international law framework, has been removed from the institutional design of the EU authorities, or at least has been given a different function within it. In some instances, such as in competition law, EU officials have operational powers that bring to mind the concept of European territoriality, to the extent that these officials may perform their operations *anywhere* in the territories of the participating states, regardless of their own nationality and of national borders. Yet in other areas, such as the European Public Prosecutor's Office (EPPO), national enforcement jurisdiction has been transformed into a European system of territorial competences (*örtliche Zuständigkeit*), connected via informal methods for transnational cooperation.[4]

In all composite models, it is not the European states that are working together but their authorities. These authorities do not act in their capacity as national representatives or state agents but as part of an EU enforcement structure. Cooperation within the framework of EU enforcement authorities is not guided by such concepts as diplomacy, reciprocity or sovereignty but by commonly defined goals, enforcement policies and strategies. These policies and strategies are, by their very definition, not developed within the confines of a single legal order. They are the product of institutionalised forms of mutual consultation and the coordination of enforcement efforts, within the frameworks of the EU authorities studied. It should be noted, however, that there are significant differences in each policy field. Clearly, the influence of the EU is much stronger in the field of competition law than in the area of the protection of the EU's financial interests, wherein the European Anti-Fraud Office (OLAF) lacked (and still lacks) powers to coordinate punitive follow up at national level, although this will change, for criminal cases, with the arrival of the EPPO.

At the same time, however, all of the regimes studied in this book point back to the national legal orders on numerous occasions. Composite enforcement frameworks therefore inherently lead to questions on the vertical relationships between the standards of national and EU law, particularly where EU standards are absent, vague or refer back to national law (with respect to investigative powers or safeguards, for instance). Decentralised enforcement structures also raise puzzling questions that relate to their many horizontal or transnational elements. The transnational scope of their investigations – to a certain extent the raison d'être of their existence – inherently means that a number of national laws may be applied during those investigations.

Despite their advantages compared to international cooperation, decentralised enforcement frameworks may thus constitute a risk for effective law enforcement. Lack of clarity with respect to the applicable legal rules – vertically, but also horizontally – can have a negative effect on law enforcement operations. Uncoordinated action, for instance, not only carries the risk of enforcement competition and violations of *ne bis in*

[3] That is to say, covering the territories of the Member States that are participating in the legal arrangements establishing those authorities.

[4] cf CMJ Ryngaert and JAE Vervaele, 'Core Values Beyond Territories and Borders: The Internal and External Dimension of EU Regulation and Enforcement' in T van den Brink, M Luchtman and M Scholten (eds), *Sovereignty in the Shared Legal Order of the EU: Core Values of Regulation and Enforcement* (Intersentia 2015) 299.

idem, but may also result in efficiency losses. No doubt these problems get bigger if one also takes into account the relationships between the EU authorities and national criminal justice actors. Indeed, a strict separation of European and national procedures can imply, as is demonstrated in a number of OLAF cases,[5] that shared materials may not be used as evidence in criminal proceedings. These issues are a problem not only for the EU legal order, which must think up a strategy to stimulate the admissibility of evidence obtained by EU authorities in criminal proceedings, but also for national legal systems, which ought to consider how such materials can indeed be used in national proceedings of an administrative, but occasionally also a criminal, nature.

Another concern of fundamental importance is the legal position of individuals who get involved in investigations that are conducted by the EU authorities and their partners. The EU is, as was noted before, a polity that houses not only its Member States but also its citizens.[6] These individuals have been given transnational economic or even citizens' rights of free movement. Where free movement is encouraged, those individuals will establish connections to multiple legal orders, and will in fact be stimulated to do so by EU law and policies. Consequently, individuals may become the victims of crime, become charged persons in composite administrative investigations or be approached as third parties that have relevant information.[7] Yet the scope of their rights and duties vis-à-vis the EU authorities and their national partners will inevitably vary, depending on the applicable set of rules, even though this composite system itself is operated by a single EU authority. The composite enforcement structures and their complicated relationships with criminal justice systems thus raise many pertinent questions of fundamental rights protection, including effective judicial protection.

As said, concerns for the effective enforcement of laws and EU policies on the one hand (section II) and the protection of the individual vis-à-vis EU enforcement authorities and their national partners on the other (section III) are interrelated. They are also related to other risks, particularly the undermining of public confidence in state authority (in a composite sense) and in the legitimacy and added value of the EU as such. It will not be enough to remove or reshape the role of national borders within the composite enforcement frameworks. In a composite legal order that is bound by the rule of law, there is also a need for a common narrative and subsequent action, at both the EU level and at the national level. Benchmarks for it are developed in section IV.

II. Effective Composite Enforcement of EU Laws and Policies

What is needed when it comes to the effective enforcement of EU rules and policies in the setting of EU authorities and their relationships with their national partners? Is the notion of an EU-wide operational competence reconcilable with an often decentralised

[5] See ch 6 of this volume (Giuffrida and Theodorakakou); and F Giuffrida, 'Comparative Analysis' in F Giuffrida and K Ligeti (eds), *Admissibility of OLAF Final Reports as Evidence in Criminal Proceedings* (Luxembourg University 2019) 222.

[6] See ch 1 of this volume (Luchtman), section III.

[7] cf the Resolution of the Council of 30 November 2009 on a Roadmap for strengthening procedural rights of suspected or accused persons in criminal proceedings [2009] OJ C295/1, 3 (the 'Stockholm roadmap').

enforcement framework? What is needed to ensure a level enforcement playing field? Is coordination with national criminal justice also necessary for this? Who is to act in these matters – the EU level and/or the national level? All of these questions have a vertical dimension, but also a horizontal or transnational dimension. In many cases, a strict distinction between the two dimensions may not even be possible. Information that was obtained under the auspices of a national authority may end up in a report of findings, drawn up by an EU authority, and introduced as evidence in a court in yet another jurisdiction.[8]

As has been highlighted in the previous chapters, there are many ways in which the tension between European operational competence and national diversity can be resolved. Yet even fully autonomous investigations still need coordination with national law. As this author and John Vervaele have written previously:

> [T]he examples of ECB, ESMA and also DG Comp show how important a strong national framework is for the EU authorities. The relevant rules and regulations ensure a) that there is a national counterpart for cooperation with the EU authority in each sector, b) that these authorities cooperate with the EU authority by sharing operational information, c) possess a certain set of investigative powers for that purpose (interviews, productions orders, site visits), including – particularly – the assistance of the police or equivalent forces, and d) – in cases of concurrent jurisdiction, such as in competition law with respect to Arts 101 and 102 TFEU – coordination with ongoing national cases, as well as e) provisions with respect to admissibility as evidence (including the need for equivalent standards of legal protection).[9]

A. Organisational Issues

Even the most autonomous systems of EU enforcement need to reconnect at some stage with the national legal orders. Composite enforcement is a joint enterprise of the executive, legislative and judicial branches at EU and national levels. In this regard, it is useful to differentiate between problems relating to the tasks and organisation of law enforcement at the national level, the ways in which national legal orders are capable of 'feeding' the EU authorities with information or assisting during their investigations, and the subsequent use of the results as evidence in punitive procedures at the national level.

Without doubt, organisational problems are most significant in the area of OLAF's competences. This is, first of all, because it has proved very difficult to raise a sufficiently strong level of awareness at the national level that cooperation with OLAF is part and parcel of the mandate of the national partners. The so-called Anti-Fraud Coordination Services (AFCOSs) have only to a limited extent been capable of resolving this problem. It turns out that, partly because the area of crimes against the financial interests of the EU ('PIF area') is so wide in scope and covers so many sectoral regulations, it is virtually impossible to establish a clearly defined circle of national partners for OLAF,

[8] See also the observations in ch 2 of this volume (De Vries and Widdershoven).

[9] M Luchtman and J Vervaele, 'Summary of Main Findings and Overall Conclusions' in MJJP Luchtman et al, *Investigatory Powers and Procedural Safeguards: Improving OLAF's Legislative Framework through a Comparison with Other EU Law Enforcement Authorities (ECN/ESMA/ECB)* (Utrecht University 2017) 324.

that is, authorities that are aware of their duty to share information with OLAF and are provided with the legal tools to do so by their legal orders.[10] Sometimes its national partners are not even known to OLAF, and vice versa.[11] While OLAF regulations refer back to national law on numerous occasions, national laws often remain silent. A legal limbo is the result. Quite strikingly, the EU sectoral PIF arrangements also lag behind in the creation of such a level playing field; tasks and powers of national partners are often far from harmonised, particularly on the expenditure side of the EU budget. The EPPO may run into the same problem, as its creation has not changed the relevant legal rules.

B. The Applicable Law: Investigatory Powers, Safeguards and Admissibility of Evidence

OLAF's institutional design is also most problematic, in terms of effective enforcement, when it comes to the legal design of the stage of the investigation, as well as the possibility to use the acquired materials as evidence in national punitive procedures. In other areas of study, we notice stronger forms of supervisory and enforcement convergence on the side of the executive, that is, the EU authorities and their national partners. Indeed, the development of common policies and strategies is strongly encouraged by the institutional frameworks in banking law, competition law and other areas of EU (financial) regulation, like the proposed establishment of the Anti-Money Laundering Authority.[12]

When it comes to the investigative stage of composite enforcement procedures, four issues may affect the effective enforcement of EU rules and policies. First of all, there are still policy areas, quite astonishingly, where EU authorities lack a clear set of powers. Again, OLAF is the most prominent case in point. Even after its revision in 2020, the relevant legal instruments do not attribute investigative powers to OLAF but describe what materials OLAF should be able to retrieve. In cases of non-cooperation, OLAF must rely on its national partners to ensure cooperation. Only its national partners are able to impose sanctions for non-cooperation, or use physical coercion to obtain materials, if necessary.[13]

Powers of enforcement do exist in other domains. The Directorate-General for Competition (DG Competition) and the European Central Bank (ECB), as well as their national partners, have powers of compulsion. They are able to impose financial punitive and non-punitive sanctions for non-cooperation. As a general rule, real powers of coercion are not available to EU administrative authorities. For that, cooperation and coordination with criminal justice bodies, including the EPPO, may be necessary.

[10] See ch 4 (Böse and Schneider) and ch 5 (Bovend'Eerdt and Karagianni) of this volume.

[11] MJJP Luchtman, M Simonato and JAE Vervaele, 'Comparative Analysis' in M Simonato, M Luchtman and J Vervaele (eds), *Exchange of Information with EU and National Enforcement Authorities: Improving OLAF Legislative Framework through a Comparison with Other EU Authorities (ECN/ESMA/ECB)* (Utrecht University 2018) 172.

[12] Commission, 'Proposal for a Regulation establishing the Authority for Anti-Money Laundering and Countering the Financing of Terrorism and amending Regulations (EU) No 1093/2010, (EU) 1094/2010, (EU) 1095/2010' COM (2021) 421 final.

[13] See ch 4 of this volume (Böse and Schneider).

There are no real indications, however, that this lack of coercive powers (as opposed to powers of compulsion) is perceived as a real problem for the relevant EU authorities.

A third issue is the surplus of safeguards that appears to be applicable for OLAF investigations. Though OLAF does not perform criminal investigations and has no powers of compulsion, it nonetheless needs to take account of a series of safeguards that are normally part of criminal procedures. In terms of the effectiveness of its operations, this can be considered as yet another flaw in its institutional design. Arguably, there may be some added value to this, because the inclusion of such safeguards may facilitate the later use of materials as evidence in punitive procedures.[14] However, this added value is limited, because of the restrictions that apply for its use in evidence in criminal procedures *sensu stricto*.[15]

Finally, the preceding chapters draw attention to almost the opposite of the problem just discussed. There is also a clear lack of attention to the safeguards that apply within the context of administrative investigations by the EU authorities or their partners. Issues with respect to, for instance, legal professional privilege, access to counsel or the privilege against self-incrimination (relevant in punitive administrative proceedings or in cases where later use in those procedures cannot be excluded) have received little to no attention in the applicable frameworks.[16] Consequently, there are a number of questions that are currently unanswered. First of all, even assuming that the EU courts will apply the well-known EU competition law standards to the actions of other EU authorities, such as ECB (which is not yet clear), the question is how the competent authorities and courts should deal with the diverging national and EU standards during the gathering of information and judicial review of investigative acts. After all, EU standards fall below national standards in some instances. Which of those standards should prevail?[17] The same issue may arise once materials are introduced as evidence in another legal order (EU or national). Do higher national standards, for instance, preclude the use of such materials as evidence? What laws are to be applied? Clearly, there is a vertical and horizontal dimension to each of these questions, depending on the institutional architecture of the relevant EU authority.

The issue of diverging standards also needs attention in light of judicial review of the relevant investigative acts, to which I will return in section II.C, and with a view to the smooth transfer of materials from one legal order to another so that they may be used as evidence. Otherwise, there is a risk that materials that have been collected under EU law or foreign law may not be used as evidence in punitive procedures. The latter would certainly be a problem in light of the principle of effectiveness of EU law. Yet, quite surprisingly, highly harmonised areas such as banking law also lack provisions on the admissibility of evidence. Moreover, the rules on admissibility of materials

[14] See, *in extenso*, Bovend'Eerdt in his forthcoming dissertation.

[15] Art 11(2) Regulation 2013/883 concerning investigations conducted by the European Anti-Fraud Office (OLAF) [2013] OJ L248/1 as revised by Regulation 2020/2223 amending Regulation No 883/2013, as regards cooperation with the European Public Prosecutor's Office and the effectiveness of the European Anti-Fraud Office investigations, [2020] OJ L437/49, and discussed by Giuffrida and Theodorakakou in ch 6 of this volume.

[16] On the specifics of those rights, see ch 2 of this volume (De Vries and Widdershoven).

[17] See also the analysis and recommendations in ch 2 of this volume (De Vries and Widdershoven).

as evidence in cases of competition law seem to be limited to evidence that has been obtained *lawfully*.[18]

Rules on the admissibility of evidence can be said to have two core functions that are related to the principle of mutual trust: they are an expression of the recognition of equivalence; which in turn implies that diverging standards with respect to, for instance, fundamental rights can no longer hamper the admissibility of materials as evidence, save in exceptional circumstances.[19] Arguably, such rules build upon the principle of mutual trust and would then constitute hard-and-fast rules of non-inquiry of the legality of acts that are alien to the legal order of the forum. In principle, those materials cannot and should not be tested by any authority, or measured against any kind of standard of the forum state. The precise scope of such a rule, however, has yet to be determined, particularly for situations in which there are claims of unlawful investigative acts that interfere with the rights of individuals.

C. Judicial Protection and Unlawfully Obtained Evidence

Case law on the relationships between the admissibility of evidence, procedural safeguards and defence rights, as well as judicial protection, is still scarce and barely touches upon these relationships in the specific setting of composite procedures.[20] One of the first relevant cases is *WebMindLicenses*,[21] which deals with the conditions under which materials, obtained through the interception of telecommunications and seizure of e-mails in the context of ongoing parallel criminal procedures, can be used as evidence in value added tax (VAT) procedures. The Court, quite firmly, introduced a responsibility for tax courts to offer redress for possible violations of the right to respect for private life that occurred in the parallel criminal procedure. It held that tax courts must verify whether the taxable person had the opportunity, in the context of the administrative procedure, to gain access to the disputed evidence and to be heard concerning it. If a breach of Article 7 of the Charter of Fundamental Rights of the EU[22] were to be established, the court would be obliged to disregard that evidence. The same would apply if the tax court was not empowered to check that the evidence was obtained in the context of the criminal procedure in accordance with EU law, or was not able to satisfy itself, on the basis of a review already carried out by a criminal court in an inter partes procedure, that it was obtained in accordance with EU law.

The judgment is interesting, because it introduces a division of labour between different courts that may also be relevant for composite procedures. Moreover, it takes a very firm stance on the exclusion of unlawfully obtained evidence. Regarding the latter, the question is whether this judgment still stands. In recent cases on the ePrivacy

[18] MJJP Luchtman, AM Karagianni and KHP Bovend'Eerdt, 'EU Administrative Investigations and the Use of Their Results as Evidence in National Punitive Proceedings' in Giuffrida and Ligeti (eds) (n 5) 7, 18, 34.

[19] ibid 52; ch 2 of this volume (De Vries and Widdershoven).

[20] For an overview, see ch 9 of this volume (Vervaele).

[21] Case C-419/14 *WebMindLicenses* ECLI:EU:C:2015:832.

[22] Charter of Fundamental Rights of the European Union [2012] OJ C326/391 ('the Charter').

Directive,[23] the Grand Chamber of the Court held that in those situations where EU law is silent on the law of evidence, it is for the national legal order of each Member State to establish procedural rules for actions intended to safeguard the rights that individuals derive from EU law. Therefore, it is for national law to determine the appropriate reaction to unlawfully obtained or transferred evidence. Those rules must, however, be no less favourable than the rules governing similar situations subject to domestic law (the principle of equivalence) and may not render impossible in practice or excessively difficult the exercise of rights conferred by EU law (the principle of effectiveness).[24]

Yet despite the leeway that it now offers to the national legal orders, the Court also confirms in *Prokuratuur*, and that is still in line with *WebMindLicenses*, the need to remedy breaches of EU rights of defendants in criminal procedures. Legal orders must have in place, in the words of the Grand Chamber, 'procedural rules for actions intended to safeguard the rights that individuals derive from EU law', subject to the conditions of equivalence and effectiveness.[25] The Court continued that

> regard must be had, in particular, to the risk of breach of the adversarial principle and, therefore, of the right to a fair trial entailed by the admissibility of … information and evidence [obtained in contravention of the requirements of EU law]. If a court takes the view that a party is not in a position to comment effectively on evidence pertaining to a field of which the judges have no knowledge and that is likely to have a preponderant influence on the findings of fact, it must find an infringement of the right to a fair trial and exclude that evidence in order to avoid such an infringement.[26]

Therefore, remedies for violations of EU rights, as required and provided for by Article 47 of the Charter, should be in place not only for persons with a view to the prevention, reparation or compensation of those breaches,[27] but also, specifically, for defendants in punitive procedures, in light of their right to a fair trial. There appears to be no good reason not to require the same in administrative punitive procedures.

It is puzzling, however, what the Court means precisely when it refers to the requirement to be able to 'comment effectively on evidence pertaining to a field of which the judges have no knowledge', and how this case law relates, if at all, to composite procedures. *Prokuratuur*, after all, dealt with the covert collection and retention of personal data for national security and law enforcement purposes. I submit that the same line of reasoning can be used, however, when individuals have no opportunity to question the lawfulness of investigations for other reasons. One of those reasons could be that the information has been gathered in another jurisdiction. The case law of the Court suggests that courts in punitive procedures either ascertain that the remedies have already been provided for by another court, or they offer the possibility to comment

[23] Directive 2002/58/EC of the European Parliament and of the Council of 12 July 2002 concerning the processing of personal data and the protection of privacy in the electronic communications sector (Directive on privacy and electronic communications) [2002] OJ L201/37.

[24] Case C-746/18 *Prokuratuur* ECLI:EU:C:2021:152, para 42; also discussed in ch 2 (De Vries and Widdershoven) and ch 9 (Vervaele) of this volume.

[25] *Prokuratuur* (n 24) para 42.

[26] ibid para 44.

[27] cf Case C-852/19 *Gavanozov II* ECLI:EU:C:2021:902, para 33.

on the evidence themselves.[28] Yet to accept such an approach in composite procedures would surely be at odds with, for instance, the approach in international criminal law, where the so-called *Trennungsprinzip* organises legal protection along the lines of the legal orders involved. Under that principle, it is not for the trial state, for instance, to offer a remedy for violations of the right to respect for private life that took place in another state (unless those violations can affect the right to a fair trial). The consequence of that is that courts do not have to concern themselves with breaches of the right to respect for private life, as guaranteed by the Charter or the European Convention on Human Rights (ECHR),[29] in another jurisdiction, nor with the application of foreign laws.[30]

The *Trennungsprinzip* has even become a hard-and-fast legal rule under the mutual recognition schemes in the Area of Freedom, Security and Justice (AFSJ). Mutual recognition, too, starts from a strict separation of responsibilities between the involved judicial authorities of different EU Member States. The Court of Justice held in its *Opinion 2/13* that

> Member States may, under EU law, be required to presume that fundamental rights have been observed by the other Member States, so that not only may they not demand a higher level of national protection of fundamental rights from another Member State than that provided by EU law, but, save in exceptional cases, they may not check whether that other Member State has actually, in a specific case, observed the fundamental rights guaranteed by the EU.[31]

More recently, however, the Court added in *Gavanozov II* that issuing states must have remedies in place for that purpose under the framework of the European Investigation Order (EIO).[32] It held that 'the right of the person concerned to contest the need for, and lawfulness of, [investigative] measures means that that person must have available to him or her a legal remedy against the EIO ordering that they be carried out'.[33] The Court thus not only confirmed that legal remedies should be available for interferences with Charter rights, but it also created, specifically for mutual recognition regimes, a division of responsibilities along the lines of the legal orders involved. A similar development is discernible in surrender law, under the framework of the European Arrest Warrant.[34]

It remains to be seen what the precise scope of the rules implementing the principle of mutual recognition will be. Sooner or later, for instance, questions will come up that relate to the secrecy of investigations, in relation both to proceedings of the issuing authority and to those of the executing authority. Questions relating to effective judicial

[28] cf *WebMindLicences* (n 21).

[29] Convention for the Protection of Human Rights and Fundamental Freedoms, Rome, 4 November 1950, *ETS* 5.

[30] See M Böse, M Bröcker and A Schneider, 'Introduction' in M Böse, M Bröcker and A Schneider (eds), *Judicial Protection in Transnational Criminal Proceedings* (Springer 2021).

[31] *Opinion of the Court of 18 December 2014 [on the accession of the European Union to the European Convention for the Protection of Human Rights and Fundamental Freedoms] pursuant to Article 218(11) TFEU* ECLI:EU:C:2014:2454, para 192.

[32] *Gavanozov II* (n 27).

[33] ibid, paras 35 and 41.

[34] cf Joined Cases C-508/18 and C-82/19 PPU *OG & PI* ECLI:EU:C:2019:456, para 75; Joined Cases C-566/19 PPU and C-626/19 PPU *JR & YC* ECLI:EU:C:2019:1077, para 48.

protection may after all conflict with considerations of operational secrecy, and this can affect the legal position of the later accused, but also third parties. Ultimately, it will be the issuing authority that is best placed to make such assessments. Yet it may later have to compensate for a lack of legal protection in the executing state. Difficult issues relating to the access to the case file, the application of foreign law, etc lie ahead.

Moreover, the principle of mutual recognition does not (yet) cover the admissibility as evidence of the materials that were gathered. Trial courts may, despite the resulting limitations on the right to effective legal protection, still apply the *Trennungsprinzip* and refuse to hear arguments concerning violations of rights of respect for private life and foreign laws in that regard. In the present circumstances, it cannot be excluded, and it is in fact confirmed by legal practice in a number of countries,[35] that limitations to the principle of effective judicial protection will occur. That situation is not in line with the principles established by *WebMindLicenses* and, at least implicitly, *Prokuratuur*. It implies, after all, that we cannot exclude situations where the defendant is not in a position to comment effectively – not in the gathering/transferring jurisdiction (eg for reasons of secrecy), nor in the trial jurisdiction (due to the *Trennungsprinzip*) – on matters that allegedly amount to a violation of his or her (EU) rights. A violation of the right to a fair trial is then imminent, because in my understanding of both cases, the Court connected the right to an effective remedy to the right to a fair trial.

Under the rules of international law and, arguably, even in the horizontal AFSJ, this situation – that is, the limitation of the right to legal protection – is often accepted as a given. This is due to the complexities of these forms of cooperation, but also to the fact that transnational cooperation schemes essentially relate to situations where one authority assists another in the performance of the latter's duties. The former is not conducting the procedure itself and can consequently only be responsible for a small portion of it. That substantial grounds cannot be challenged in that legal order is understandable in that light, as it would also require access to the file and knowledge of foreign laws, for instance. The decision that certain acts are best kept secret is a decision that executing authorities cannot always make either.

At this point in time, it is unclear if the Court of Justice will apply Article 47 of the Charter to such transnational situations and is willing to accept limitations to Article 47 as a result of it, under the framework of Article 52(1) of the Charter.[36] But even if it were so willing, the question is whether the same should go for composite procedures. This is, first of all, because composite procedures intend to overcome, rather than emphasise the formal separations between, those legal orders; and, second, – most importantly – because those procedures are legally characterised, despite their reliance on a multitude of legal orders, by their internal coherence.[37] How, then, can one accept limitations to Article 47 of the Charter, similar to those just described, in that context? The arguments that may explain the situation in transnational cooperation have no value within structures that are meant to be composite. Being an intrinsic part of the composite procedure, authorities cannot turn a blind eye to what happened earlier in the same procedure, not even when it happened in another jurisdiction.

[35] See Böse, Bröcker and Schneider (eds) (n 30).
[36] See also ch 4 of this volume (Böse and Schneider).
[37] See ch 1 of this volume (Luchtman), section IV.

All of this does not change because sanctioning authorities or courts in a particular jurisdiction are under no obligation to actually impose a sanction, after being requested or instructed to do so. Even in situations where, for instance, a national supervisory authority imposes a sanction on an undertaking of its own volition, that decision followed upon the investigations and prosecutorial decisions that were made under the supervision and coordination of one and the same composite entity. Courts are, as a rule, consequently under a responsibility to offer remedies, either by making sure that remedies were de jure and de facto available in the gathering or transferring jurisdiction, or by offering the remedy themselves. If both options are not available, the consequence seems to be that those materials cannot be used as evidence, as that would infringe the right to a fair trial. It is a division of labour on the basis of on the basis of a chain approach, rather than on the basis of the *Trennungsprinzip*.

More specifically, the foregoing implies four rules of thumb:

1. Where investigative acts interfere with EU rights, particularly Charter rights, and the investigating authority is not itself an independent judicial body or the measure was not authorised by such an authority, the principle of effective judicial protection requires that a legal remedy is available to the person who is directly adversely affected by it. Depending on the policy field, including whether the measures involve third parties or only the later defendants, and/or whether the measures affect natural persons or legal persons, this legal order can be the order where the act is executed or the legal order where the measure was 'ordered' or 'requested'.[38] In both situations, there appears to be no solid reason why the substantial reasons cannot be challenged before any of those courts in principle, save, of course, for such considerations as operational secrecy in the investigative stage.
2. When there are no concerns raised as to the lawfulness of the ordering or execution of investigative acts or to their transmission, even if this would have been legally available to the party affected by the measure, materials obtained in or transferred by one legal order can as a rule be used as evidence in another.[39] In this situation, it is not for the authorities or courts of the sanctioning legal order to offer redress, should arguments be made by those same parties.
3. In situations where remedies were available for the affected parties and used in the transferring legal order, a finding of unlawfulness is not to be discussed again before the court of the sanctioning legal order, as that would be at variance with the principle of mutual trust. However, if the transferring legal order did establish irregularities and has not itself attached further consequences to them, it is for the forum court to decide on the procedural consequences, in light of the right to a fair trial and taking into account the principles of equivalence and effectiveness. A relevant yardstick could be, in light of the principle of equivalence, to determine what the procedural consequences of that or a similar unlawful act would have been, had it taken place in the legal order of the trial state.[40]

[38] The former situation, for instance, will usually do more justice to the situation of third parties who are natural persons and will offer them a one-stop-shop solution.

[39] cf ch 2 of this volume (De Vries and Widdershoven), discussing Case C-188/92 *Textilwerke Deggendorf* ECLI:EU:C:1994:90.

[40] cf M Luchtman, 'Het Europees Openbaar Ministerie in Nederland: Over Zijn Ondeelbaarheid en Verhouding tot de Nederlandse Strafrechter' [2021] *Delikt en Delinkwent* 63, 819–20.

4. Particularly in cases where no remedies were or could be offered by the gathering/transferring legal order to the (later) defendant, yet his or her EU rights were at stake, loopholes have been known to occur under a strict application of the *Trennungsprinzip*. In composite procedures, the authorities, as well as the courts that are competent to review the sanctioning decision, will then need to provide for the opportunity to 'comment effectively on evidence pertaining to a field of which the judges have no knowledge'. Such situations might occur, for instance, because EU law precludes the courts of the gathering legal order from performing such a test.[41] Other examples are cases in which the law of that legal order offers no specific remedy, contrary to Article 47 of the Charter, or where remedies against the acts of the transferring legal order were not available to the defendant, for instance because the investigative measures as such did not directly affect his or her interests or, in cases where his or her interests were directly affected, for reasons of operational secrecy.

The ways in which these principles are further implemented depends on the specifics of the legal regime that is applicable. Following the observations of De Vries and Widdershoven (chapter 2), as well as Ligeti and Robinson (chapter 3), it may be useful to make a further distinction between situations where the punitive sanction is ultimately imposed by the EU authority, subject to the jurisdiction of the EU judiciary, or by a national authority.[42] In the latter case, a further distinction may be necessary between the use of materials that were obtained and transferred by an EU authority, subject to the rules of *Foto-Frost*,[43] or by the national authority of another jurisdiction, under the auspices of an EU authority.

Obviously, to complete the circle, the foregoing observations will have an impact on the effectiveness of composite procedures. The ultimate consequence of having no remedy available is after all that certain materials – that is, those of preponderant importance – cannot be used as evidence in the procedure. To avoid problems, authorities and courts may decide not to use such materials in cases of unlawfulness,[44] yet that will hamper the effective enforcement of EU law and, moreover, may have as a consequence that alleged breaches of EU law remain undiscovered. My conclusion, therefore, is that there is ample reason for the EU and national legislator to overthink their system of legal remedies in light of the effectiveness of composite law enforcement.

[41] The latter may occur in situations where EU law attributes sanctioning powers to the EU level and the 'EU institution exercises, alone, the final decision-making power without being bound by the preparatory acts or the proposals of the national authorities': Case C-219/17 *Berlusconi* ECLI:EU:C:2018:1023, para 43. See the discussion in ch 2 of this volume (Widdershoven and De Vries), section III.

[42] See also L Arroyo Jiménez, 'Effective Judicial Protection and Mutual Recognition in the European Administrative Space' [2021] *German Law Journal* 22, 344.

[43] Case 314/85 *Foto-Frost* ECLI:EU:C:1987:452.

[44] As pointed out by RJGM Widdershoven and P Craig, 'Pertinent Issues of Judicial Accountability in EU Shared Enforcement' in M Scholten and M Luchtman (eds), *Law Enforcement by EU Authorities: Implications for Political and Judicial Accountability* (Edward Elgar Publishing 2017) 330; Giuffrida (n 5) 257–60.

D. Composite Enforcement Procedure and National Criminal Justice

The foregoing observations relate to enforcement procedures that are performed by or under the auspices of the EU authorities themselves. The following relates specifically to their relationships with criminal law enforcement at the national level. These relationships go in two directions. In some cases, they will be triggered 'bottom up', when criminal justice bodies ask for, or even order, information that is in the hands of EU authorities or their national partners. The top-down aspect covers the many implications that the work of the EU authorities may have for national criminal justice. As I have already highlighted the problematic relationships in terms of national follow up to OLAF investigations by criminal justice bodies, I will not deal with this issue here again.

To start with, questions of legal protection arise in situations where materials gathered by EU authorities are used in criminal procedures, or vice versa,[45] and there are issues with respect to their lawfulness. One of these issues is whether the national courts and European Courts will define the relationship between criminal justice and composite administrative procedures in the same way as they have defined the relationships between administrative authorities and criminal justice in the national setting of, for instance, *WebMindLicenses*. Do the EU Courts wish to uphold their firm position that administrative courts should fully assess the legality and proportionality of the actions of criminal justice bodies, if criminal courts have not done so already, and that they should otherwise exclude the materials as evidence in the administrative procedures?[46] There may be reason to mitigate this stance, also in light of *Prokuratuur*.[47] It could be argued that such a test – which is now performed outside the context of composite procedures – is to be limited to a test of fairness and to manifest, grave breaches of EU rights, such as the right to respect for private and family life or property. It is not always clear, after all, why defendants in administrative punitive procedures should be able to comment on violations of their right to to respect for private and family life that occurred in another (criminal) procedure and therefore should be remedied under that framework. Of course, that may change again in situations where EU authorities and national bodies of criminal justice do start to cooperate more intensively than they do now. The rest of this section highlights a number of scenarios regarding how this could evolve.

The scope of the investigations that are conducted by EU authorities can easily overlap with national substantive criminal law. Moreover, we see that in a large number of cases there may be multiple national criminal law systems competent to take up the case. The overlap, therefore, has vertical (EU-national), as well as horizontal dimensions. Nonetheless, the relationships between composite administrative enforcement at EU level and national criminal justice are often opaque or even deliberately cut off.

[45] cf Case C-469/15 P *FSL and Others v Commission* ECLI:EU:C:2017:308, discussed by Luchtman, Karagianni and Bovend'Eerdt (n 18) 18–21; and ch 2 of this volume (De Vries & Widdershoven).

[46] *WebMindLicences* (n 21).

[47] *Prokuratuur* (n 24).

The latter situation is omnipresent in competition law, where, in order to protect the rights of the defence in competition proceedings, the provision of information to criminal justice actors is severely restricted. Exchange of information from competition law authorities to criminal justice bodies is usually limited to providing information as a basis for the start of criminal investigations.[48] Moreover, there is no doubt that provisions, such as Article 12(3) of Regulation 1/2003,[49] facilitate the enforcement of competition law within the network, but they may simultaneously impede the administration of criminal justice. In the situations described in that provision, information may not be used by the receiving authority to impose custodial sanctions. This system, which in many aspects is more restrictive than the case law of the European Court of Human Rights (ECtHR) requires, clearly brings with it restrictions for effective criminal law enforcement. It creates a de facto rule of priority for administrative enforcement, which is not always warranted in light of the proper administration of justice.

In banking law too, the connections between administrative and criminal enforcement are not an intrinsic part of the design of the Single Supervisory Mechanism (SSM).[50] Both systems of enforcement are regarded as distinct areas of law. Though there are provisions that deal with exchanging information, and though those provisions do not carry the same restrictions as in competition law, exchanging information and coordination is not perceived as a task for the ECB but for its national partners (the national competent authorities) and national criminal justice bodies. In light of the division of competences within the SSM system, this is not always a logical choice. It blurs the clarity on the applicable legal rules, and it raises questions as to the scope of control that the ECB can exercise over its national partners, as well as what powers criminal justice actors can exercise, if necessary, to obtain relevant information from within the SSM framework.[51]

The strong information position of EU authorities will usually lead to a situation where their procedures are concluded first. A lack of coordination and exchange of information consequently raises questions in light of the *ne bis in idem* principle. Now that Article 50 of the Charter is applicable in cases where both the EU authority or its national partner and criminal justice bodies are competent to deal with the same set of facts, the question is whether the Court of Justice will accept a limitation on the scope of the principle under Article 52 of the Charter. Dual procedures as such are after all not – at least not in the absence of specific EU rules – prohibited, provided they serve complementary aims relating to different aspects of the same unlawful conduct. To ensure that the disadvantages resulting, for the persons concerned, from such a duplication are limited to what is strictly necessary, coordination between the procedures will be required.[52] A violation of Article 50 of the Charter then appears to be imminent

[48] See ch 8 (Allegrezza et al) and ch 5 (Bovend'Eerdt and Karagianni) of this volume; see also Luchtman, Karagianni and Bovend'Eerdt (n 18) 30–35, with further references.

[49] Council Regulation (EC) No 1/2003 of 16 December 2002 on the implementation of the rules on competition laid down in Articles 81 and 82 of the Treaty [2003] OJ L1/1.

[50] See ch 8 of this volume (Allegrezza et al).

[51] ibid.

[52] Case C-151/20 *Nordzucker* ECLI:EU:C:2022:203; Case C-524/15 *Luca Menci* ECLI:EU:C:2018:197; Case C-537/16 *Garlsson Real Estate and others* ECLI:EU:C:2018:193; Joined Cases C-596/16 and C-597/16 *Di Puma and Zecca* ECLI:EU:C:2018:192.

where such coordination does not take place. If that is true, it is wise for the EU and national legislators to ensure coordination between the procedures on a more structural basis, particularly in those policy areas where dual-track procedures are not uncommon.

It is currently not clear to what extent a violation is also imminent in cases where supplementary goals are indeed pursued and coordination did take place. Both criteria are inherently vague and imprecise.[53] Are complementary goals pursued if national provisions of criminal law, such as general fraud offences, serve to implement the relevant EU directives and regulations, and the criminal or administrative sanctions can each and of themselves be considered to be effective, dissuasive and proportionate?[54] Moreover, what is meant by a coordination of procedures? Is it the mere possibility of an information exchange, or does it involve a division of labour, consultation, etc?[55]

These questions are relevant because, according to the Strasbourg case law (if it were applicable),[56] coordination would mean that both types of procedures are de facto considered as part of one and the same procedure, thus preventing a breach.[57] Yet the Luxembourg Court seems to follow a different approach. Dual-track procedures are not forbidden as such, but they do interfere with Article 50 of the Charter. To prevent this interference from becoming a breach, the goals pursued in both procedures must be supplementary and not go beyond what is strictly necessary. The more the subject matter comes within the domain of EU law, the more stringent this necessity test presumably will be. The (open) question is to what extent this necessity is still there, where both types of punitive sanctions each and of themselves can be considered to be effective, dissuasive and proportionate, and – also depending on the content of the legal provisions at play – can be said to pursue objectives similar to or even the same as EU law. In those situations, dual-track procedures, and the double prosecutions or sanctions that follow from it, even if well coordinated, seem to go beyond what is needed to ensure the effective enforcement of EU law. Those situations could lead to a violation of Article 50 of the Charter.

The issue of coordination is also relevant for certain defence rights, including, but not limited to, situations in which the EU and national authorities investigate the same acts conducted by the same (legal) persons or their representatives.[58] Some have expressed concerns as to the adverse consequences the European Courts' case law on *ne bis in idem* – that is, the requirement of coordination to prevent a violation in dual-track systems – may have for the applicable defence rights in criminal procedures.[59] Will it lead to a circumvention of these rights? The problem may be actually the opposite. For instance, we know that there are instances in which the rights and safeguards of criminal justice, particularly the right to silence, but in its wake also the right to a lawyer, cast

[53] Case C-151/20 *Nordzucker and others* ECLI:EU:C:2021:681, Opinion of AG Bobek.

[54] As was the case in Case C-617/10 *Åkerberg Fransson* ECLI:EU:C:2013:105.

[55] The Court does seem to require actual coordination, see Case C-117/20 *bpost SA* ECLI:EU:C:2022:202, para 55.

[56] The territorial scope of Art 4 P7 ECHR is after all limited.

[57] *A and B v Norway* App nos 24130/11 and 29758/11 (ECtHR, 15 November 2016).

[58] On the relationships between the privilege against self-incrimination of legal persons and their representatives, see S Lamberigts, *The Privilege Against Self-Incrimination of Corporations* (Leuven 2018).

[59] *A and B v Norway* (n 57) Dissenting Opinion of Judge Pinto de Albuquerque, para 21.

their shadow forward over non-punitive procedures. Where it is reasonably foreseeable that information obtained under compulsion in non-punitive procedures can end up in punitive procedures by other authorities, this can lead to a violation of the right to a fair trial, at least if compulsion is indeed exercised. The relevant question in these cases is whether these procedures are '*sufficament liées*',[60] a criterion reminiscent of that regarding procedures being 'closely connected in substance and in time' in the *ne bis in idem* case law.

The impact of this case law on composite enforcement and its relation to criminal justice is unclear. Can national safeguards on criminal justice impact the composite operations of EU authorities? To what extent is it relevant that these safeguards implement EU law?[61] The ECtHR's case law implies that sufficiently strong connections between non-punitive and punitive procedures cover far more situations than an organisational union of both tasks within one and the same authority. In *Chambaz*, the Court concluded that Article 6 ECHR also applied to the tax procedure, because of the overlapping tasks and the mutual legal information and assistance obligations, which indeed led to a strong overlap between the investigations at hand. In those circumstance, the persons concerned will have to take account of the impact of their declarations, performed under compulsion, beyond the non-punitive procedure in which they were obtained. A duty to obtain the requested information under compulsion in those procedures may consequently violate the privilege against self-incrimination, particularly the right to remain silent.

Now, can we say that the situation is different for administrative composite procedures and their relation to national criminal justice? Usually, the territorial scope of the privilege is limited to a specific national jurisdiction.[62] But again, why would that be so now that the notion of territorial borders has largely been removed from or reshaped by the legal design of the relevant authorities? Do criminal investigations in the Netherlands have an impact on administrative acts of investigation in Germany, if these are conducted by or under the responsibility of the EU authorities?

It may come as no surprise that I am of the opinion that, with the reshaping of the role of nation-state borders within the institutional design of these enforcement modalities, there no longer appears to be a good reason to treat these mechanisms differently from comparable national enforcement mechanisms. National borders cannot be, as they would be under international law, a decisive factor, as they no longer serve as formal separations between administrative investigations in one legal order and criminal investigations in another.[63] Consequently, there appears to be no good reason to limit the scope of the relevant EU rules – particularly Directive 2016/343 on the presumption of innocence – and Articles 47 and 48 of the Charter to a specific national jurisdiction.

[60] *Chambaz v Switzerland* App no 11663/04 (ECtHR, 5 April 2012).

[61] For instance, Directive 2016/343 of 9 March 2016 on the strengthening of certain aspects of the presumption of innocence and of the right to be present at the trial in criminal proceedings [2016] OJ L65/1.

[62] S Lamberigts, *The Privilege Against Self-Incrimination of Corporations* (Leuven 2018) 250–52.

[63] On transnational types of cooperation between administrative and judicial bodies, see MJJP Luchtman, *European Cooperation Between Financial Supervisory Authorities, Tax Authorities and Judicial Authorities* (Intersentia 2008).

Where compulsion is used in composite administrative procedures and exchange of information and coordination with criminal procedures is necessary (if only to prevent a violation of the *ne bis in idem* principle), this may lead to a sufficiently strong connection between the procedures of the EU authorities, their partners and national actors of criminal justice.[64] Consequently, in situations where all are acting within the scope of EU law, to prevent Articles 47 and 48 of the Charter from being violated and to ensure the effectiveness of the composite non-punitive procedure, which will entail duties of cooperation, provisions are necessary that exclude a later or parallel use of the materials obtained (will-dependent) in punitive procedures. I regard this as a matter not only of fairness, but also of legal certainty and legality. To determine their legal position, individuals must be able to determine their legal position in this regard ex ante, before the requested information is to be provided.

Finally, as much as actors within composite administrative procedures need to become aware of the intrinsic links of their work with criminal justice, the opposite is also true. And again, there are signals that criminal courts perceive the work of EU authorities as being of an entirely different order than their own everyday work. Once more, this is capable of affecting the effective enforcement of EU law. There is an EU side to this, was well as a national side. At the EU level, the aforementioned lack of clarity on the applicable safeguards plays a role, without doubt. The most pertinent example, however, is the provisions in the OLAF framework on the admissibility of OLAF reports as evidence in national punitive and non-punitive procedures.[65] Even after the OLAF reforms of 2020, the rules on the admissibility of evidence are regarded as unduly strict. Yet, as has been repeatedly noted before, the smooth transition of its reports and their use as admissible evidence in criminal procedures are vital for the protection of the EU's financial interests.

At the national level, the question is whether national authorities, particularly criminal courts, are sufficiently aware of the European dimension of their tasks and are willing to adapt to it. Though it will surely be a bridge too far to introduce in, for instance, the SSM framework provisions on the admissibility of evidence in criminal proceedings, the question is also to what extent national courts and legislators themselves need to open up, even on their own motion, to the impact of composite administrative proceedings on criminal justice. I disagree, therefore, with authors who say that national laws on evidence are not the EU's business. Even where the EU legislator does not or cannot take adequate account of this, there is also a responsibility for national courts and legislators in this regard.

III. Effective Legal Protection in Composite Enforcement

In the previous section, the aim was to demonstrate that the institutional design of the authorities that were studied does not always correspond to what is needed for effective

[64] Arguably, but I come back to this in section III.C; there may also be a horizontal, transnational dimension to this.

[65] See ch 6 of this volume (Giuffrida and Theodorakakou); Giuffrida (n 5); and K Ligeti and F Giuffrida, 'Policy Recommendations' in Giuffrida and Ligeti (eds) (n 5) 293.

enforcement in a composite setting. Further actions are needed, at both EU and national levels, to ensure the effective enforcement of EU law. Now that the administrative enforcement authorities of the EU and the participating states by and large seem to have found each other within the composite enforcement structures of the EU authorities and their partners, this finding relates particularly to the other two branches of state (in a functional sense). The impact of composite enforcement on the responsibilities of the legislative and judicial branches is still far from clear. Clear arrangements for the protection of defence rights and procedural safeguards, as well as judicial protection, do not appear to be in place. Even more so than its implications for effective enforcement, the current situation raises concerns in light of the legal protection of individuals. Those are the topic of this section.

Concerns like these are not new. It is well documented in international criminal law doctrine that the opacity of transnational criminal investigations and the great diversity among national legal systems pose problems for individuals, national courts and politicians, which need to keep an eye on law enforcement operations. The concern is that the cooperating authorities – each of them accountable to the actors of their state of origin – are de facto put in a position where they are able to 'rule with law'[66] instead of being governed by it. Those authorities may agree, for instance, to obtain information in a jurisdiction where legal conditions are more lenient, and subsequently introduce the materials as evidence in another jurisdiction.[67] Yet in the international law context, this situation is also more or less presented as a given, precisely because the applicable rule-of-law safeguards are connected to the nation-state and the relevant enforcement procedures are considered as *national* procedures that, at best, coincide with procedures running in parallel in other states and for which other actors are responsible. Within that framework, national authorities are held to account by national courts or political organs in light of national interests and perspectives. Those courts are usually not concerned with the actions of foreign authorities. That implies that the often intensive processes of mutual coordination that take place between the cooperating authorities are not taken into account by the national accountability forums of other states.[68] Remedies for actions that are carried out by other authorities must consequently be offered in the other legal order. What is more, to the extent that such problems are recognised, it is often maintained that fundamental rights standards should be lowered

[66] B Bowling and J Sheptycki, 'Global Policing and Transnational Rule with Law' (2015) 6 *Transnational Legal Theory* 141, 146 write 'These agents act in conditions of low visibility, act with considerable discretion and are largely unregulated by any superordinate form of authority.' See also JP Brodeur, *The Policing Web* (Oxford University Press 2010); B Loftus, *Police Culture in a Changing World* (Oxford University Press 2012).

[67] See, for instance, the following remarks by a former lead investigator of the Dutch financial police (the FIOD) in 'De Fraudeur is ons Altijd Drie Stappen Voor' *NRC* (21 May 2016) (translated from Dutch): '"Fraudsters have ever smarter advisers. They are always three steps ahead of us. If the British Virgin Islands has new legislation next year, there is already a tax expert who knows about it, while we just know how it goes in the Cayman Islands." But where criminals look for the most comfortable legislation internationally, so does the FIOD. In an investigation with the Americans, they were able to infiltrate the country most easily, while the Netherlands was more lenient with telephone taps.'

[68] cf F Meyer, 'Protection of Fundamental Rights in a Multi-Jurisdictional Setting of the EU' in M Scholten and A Brenninkmeijer, *Controlling EU Agencies: The Rule of Law in a Multi-jurisdictional Legal Order* (Edward Elgar 2020) 134.

under international legal assistance instruments, because of the complexities of international legal assistance and for the sake of the greater good.[69]

There is good reason not to be so lenient in the composite setting of the EU, where economic actors and citizens have been granted enforceable rights of free movement in a transnational setting. The international law narrative fits poorly with the integrationalist, composite reality of the EU and enforcement practice by EU authorities. The EU is in need of a narrative that guides the removal of the traditional barriers of international law; a narrative that focuses not only on the need for swift and efficient cooperation, but also on the relevant rule of law standards, particularly the legality of the procedures and their fairness, as well as the legal protection for individuals. This is necessary not only because a lack of attention will ultimately hamper effective enforcement, as was discussed in the previous section, but mainly because this is what Articles 2 and 3 TEU call for.

A. The Applicable Law: Legality and Fairness in Composite Enforcement Procedures

Let us assume that a financial institution is operating under a European licence and active in multiple EU Member States on the basis of that licence. Such an institution may be subject to the supervision of an EU supervisory authority, for instance, the ECB or a national competent authority. That institution may have stored information on servers or in the Cloud that is relevant for supervision and enforcement purposes. Consequently, the information may be accessible from a number of its offices in different Member States. Requests for information may involve methods or contain information that fall within the scope of Article 7 or Article 8 of the Charter. The use of such investigatory powers then constitutes an interference with the right to respect for private life. In those circumstances, the applicable law is to define the conditions under which the competent authority is given access to that information. The same applies when personal data are transferred to other authorities. All of that follows directly from the aforementioned articles, in conjunction with Article 52 of the Charter.

In the case of an on-site inspection, the legal position of the institution and the powers of the investigative authority are defined by the law that attributes the investigative power to that authority. To that extent, there is no uncertainty about the applicable law.[70] It is that law – be it national or European – that provides the basis for interferences with the right to respect for private life. It grants those powers, yet also defines their scope and the conditions under which they are considered 'lawful'. It permits what otherwise would have been an illegal act, a breach of the right to respect for private life. If it is the ECB exercising that power, it will be the relevant EU provisions of, for instance,

[69] For discussion, see A Klip, *European Criminal Law: An Integrative Approach* (Intersentia 2021) 562; MJJP Luchtman and AAH van Hoek, 'Transnational Cooperation in Criminal Matters and the Safeguarding of Human Rights' (2005) 1 *Utrecht Law Review* 1.

[70] cf Case C-550/07 P *Akzo Akcros* ECLI:EU:C:2010:512, paras 100–108.

the SSM Regulation[71] that apply to the specific situation. Those who are confronted with these measures can assess their legal position with reference to the specific law that is applicable to the case; they are able to determine what their legal position is vis-à-vis the authorities, or to assess to what extent the law has been correctly applied by the authorities during review procedures, with reference to the applicable law.

In composite procedures, differences in investigative powers and the corresponding safeguards remain. Even where EU powers are almost fully harmonised, there may be national safeguards to respect or additional powers at the national level to deploy. Such differences continue to exist, even in the banking area. The legal arrangements that determine the applicable law have been discussed in chapter 1. It was noted that particularly the arrangements that regulate the horizontal dimensions of composite procedures often remain implied. If the same information is then accessible via the laws of different legal orders, and if that information can be obtained either by the EU authority itself or by that authority's 'asking', 'requiring' or 'instructing' a national partner to do so, the requirement of a lawful basis inevitably loses parts of its function. Within composite enforcement systems, the applicable law is seldom precisely defined in such horizontal relations; a number of national laws are often potentially applicable, at the investigative stage and/or at the sanctioning stage. That means that a new type of discretion comes to the fore in these systems; the discretion to determine which set of legal rules is applicable to any given case.[72]

The question is whether this type of discretion must also be subject to the rule of law. Sometimes, case allocation rules exist, as in banking law, with a system of home-state control. That system is particularly relevant for prosecutorial decisions and the sanctioning stage within the SSM system.[73] Yet even those rules do not necessarily prevent authorities from *gathering* information in jurisdictions other than the home state.[74] Issues of legality, particularly with regard to the legal basis of the interference and its proportionality, may still arise in light of the right to right to respect for private life, for instance. This reality is even an intrinsic part of the composite system of banking supervision, with its joint inspection teams or on-site inspection teams.

It would be naive to assume that such differences between legal systems are unknown or play no role in enforcement practice. Of course they do. They are a legal reality. The EPPO Regulation, for instance, stipulates that Member States must notify the EPPO when national law limits access to information via investigative powers in their jurisdiction.[75] In another area of law, ESMA guidelines on transnational cooperation between

[71] Council Regulation (EU) No 1024/2013 of 15 October 2013 conferring specific tasks on the European Central Bank concerning policies relating to the prudential supervision of credit institutions [2014] OJ L287/63.

[72] See ch 1 of this volume (Luchtman), section III.

[73] For legality and case allocation in competition law, see S Brammer, *Co-operation Between National Competition Agencies in the Enforcement of EC Competition Law* (Hart Publishing 2009) 212.

[74] As is put forward by A Karagianni, *The Protection of Fundamental Rights in Composite Banking Supervision Proceedings* (Europa Law Publishing 2022).

[75] Regulation (EU) 2017/1939 implementing enhanced cooperation on the establishment of the European Public Prosecutor's Office ('the EPPO') [2017] OJ L283/1 ('EPPO Regulation'), Art 30(3). The wording in itself is interesting: 'limitations', not 'safeguards' or 'conditions for lawful application'.

national authorities and/or ESMA urge cooperating authorities in the context of joint investigations to consider, inter alia,

> the identification and assessment of any legal limitations or constraints and any differences in procedures with respect to investigative or enforcement action or any other proceedings, including the rights of any Person subject to investigation ...[76]

Finally, mention should be made of the Eurojust Guidelines 2016, which also point specifically to the necessity to take account of differences between the legal systems of EU Member States. Those Guidelines hold:

> The existing legal framework, including obligations and requirements that are imposed in each jurisdiction, should be considered as well as all the possible effects of a decision to prosecute in one jurisdiction rather than in another and the potential outcome in each jurisdiction.[77]

They also warn, however, that 'judicial authorities should not decide to prosecute in one jurisdiction rather than another simply to avoid complying with the legal obligations that apply in one jurisdiction but not in another'.[78] However, it is totally unclear where the first situation ends and the second begins.

That these discretionary margins exist and that authorities must deal with them does not mean that the status quo is not problematic within the EU framework. Should such new types of discretion, inherent in all the legal frameworks of this study, be left untouched? Questions with respect to the role of national and EU law in regulating the discretion to apply a specific set of legal rules in composite procedures relate not only to the right to respect for private life. Depending on the specific framework at hand, the role of the legality principle also comes into play as a safeguard against breaches of other fundamental rights. Those rights concern the rights to liberty (in cases where custodial measures are available) and property, but also the right to a fair trial and the substantive legality principle. All of these rights are covered by the EU Charter, which as a general rule will be applicable in these procedures. By their very definition, composite procedures fall within the scope of EU law (Article 51(1) of the Charter).

A distinction between two types of norms may be helpful to identify the relevant areas of attention. On the one hand, 'primary norms' seek to guide the conduct of individuals in their daily affairs; and on the other hand, 'secondary norms' guide the actions of enforcement authorities, as well as the conduct of individuals in the setting of those enforcement actions (secondary or enforcement norms).[79] Regarding the first category of norms, the substantive legality principle requires that if violations of those norms are enforced with punitive penalties, the norms, as well as their punitive enforcement, be laid down, ex ante, by law in sufficiently clear provisions. The same goes for the applicable penalties. That is provided for by Article 49 of the Charter.

[76] See Article 6(3–5) of *Guidelines 2014/298 on cooperation arrangements and information exchange between competent authorities and between competent authorities and ESMA*.

[77] *Eurojust 2016 Guidelines for deciding 'Which jurisdiction should prosecute?'* (December 2016) 3.

[78] ibid 4.

[79] Inaction, incidentally, may also lead to actions by individuals, for instance procedures to force authorities to commence procedures.

With regard to the second category, the main purpose of procedural rules is to protect the defendant against any abuse of authority.[80] In that respect, when it comes to guaranteeing the fairness of the procedure, the requirement of procedural legality is closely connected to the principle of equality of arms. In presenting his or her case, the defendant should be afforded a reasonable opportunity to do so under conditions that do not place him or her at a substantial disadvantage vis-à-vis his or her opponent. The law protects 'the defence which is the most likely to suffer from omissions and lack of clarity in such rules' by introducing binding rules for all parties concerned. That is the core of the maxim '*nullum judicium sine lege*'. There appears to be no good reason not to apply this maxim also in punitive (administrative) procedures that have not yet reached the stage of judicial review.[81]

The requirement of procedural legality has a role different than that of the substantive legality principle. In connection to the right to a fair trial, its primary focus is to enable defendants, on whom I will focus in the following, to take part in or become part of the procedure in due time, to design an effective defence strategy and to present their case. Corresponding rights and duties of defendants – for instance the duty to produce documents or to appear during a hearing – should be sufficiently clear in that regard. Conversely, abuses of authority within these processes are to be prevented by the law. This brings with it the requirement that such rules need not necessarily be foreseeable at the time of the commission of an offence,[82] but they must be so once punitive proceedings have started. In light of the latter, the law should also preclude authorities from any possibility of influencing or even manipulating the commencement of such procedures, for instance by postponing any communication thereof to defendants.

The procedural focus of the legality principle is also inherent in another category of secondary norms, during the investigative stage in the regulation of investigatory powers, as well as in the applicable procedural safeguards. When it comes to such rights as the protection of privacy, liberty or property, the legality principle, as laid down in the said rights and Article 52 of the Charter, is only to a limited extent capable of guiding the actions of individuals. I would even argue that offering such guidance is not its primary goal. Third parties, for instance, may also be subject to such investigatory powers, but are in no position whatsoever to anticipate their application. At best, the law allows them to determine their position, including their procedural rights and duties, once they are confronted with these measures. Yet sometimes even that is not possible. Some interferences with privacy may by their very nature not be made known to individuals, in view of the risk of their absconding or of collusion regarding evidence.

Does that mean that the procedural legality principle is of no importance? Far from it. The requirement for lawful interference seeks to protect such individuals against abuses of authority, by subjecting the executive and the judiciary to the rule of law. The law determines the acceptable degree of discretion that is to be afforded to the

[80] *Coëme and others v Belgium* App nos 32492/96; 32547/96; and 32548/96 (ECtHR, 22 June 2000), para 102.

[81] ibid.

[82] On this, see also M Panzavolta, 'Choice of Forum and the Lawful Judge Concept' in M Luchtman (ed), *Choice of Forum in Cooperation Against EU Financial Crime – Freedom, Security and Justice and the Protection of Specific EU-Interests* (Boom/Eleven 2013) 143.

authorities. In that regard, the requirements regarding the legality of the interference and its proportionality coincide.[83] The law, after all, stipulates the criteria by which the proportionality of a measure must be assessed. The more these measures are concealed, the stricter the corresponding safeguards must be. The more intrusive the interference, the stricter the requirements for the application of a certain power. The requirements of foreseeability and accessibility consequently reveal the yardsticks by which the conduct of the authorities is to be assessed, ex ante or ex post, by individuals and by courts or other authorities.

The question for composite procedures is to what extent national laws are still capable of fulfilling these functions in cases where EU law makes way for the application of multiple national laws and provides no further guidance as to the applicable rules. In chapter 1, I argued that, despite its often fragmented or decentralised character, composite enforcement by EU authorities is characterised by its legal coherence, and that that should have consequences for the interpretation of, inter alia, fundamental right standards. Yet what precisely are those consequences? Depending on the specific right at hand and the fundamental right in play, I propose the following three hypotheses:

1. Regarding the substantive legality principle, as protected by Article 49 of the Charter, the principle requires that at the time when individuals undertake an action that may constitute a criminal offence,[84] they must be able to assess which criminal law or set of criminal laws will be applicable to their case.

   This hypothesis does justice to the concept of transnational agency or citizenship.[85] If the EU aims to promote the free movement of persons, that also means that the potential consequences of such movement under the criminal law must be foreseeable to those individuals (natural or legal persons). The principle of free movement means that, where free movement rights have been exercised, the law of the host state constitutes the default position and, hence, the primary point of orientation for individuals, as is reflected, for instance, in banking law and its system of home-state control. After all, the host state is the state where the financial institution chose to establish its undertakings. Where free movement rights have not been used by individuals, the laws of the home state will apply, by default.

   Of course, that does not mean that the punitive laws of other states may not be applicable either, for instance if part of the business is conducted in another state or if the legal harm of the offence is done there. Yet where punitive sanctioning in legal orders other than the 'default order' remains a possibility, composite enforcement procedures should exclude the possibility for EU authorities and national partners to determine the applicable legal regime or regimes and, hence, the applicable offences and sanctions in a way that could not be anticipated, at the time of

[83] As was more recently also emphasised in Case C-140/20 *GD* ECLI:EU:C:2022:258, paras 53 et seq.

[84] The same applies to negligence, of course.

[85] On the relationships between EU citizenship and criminal law, see, inter alia, S Coutts, *Citizenship, Crime and Community in the European Union* (Hart Publishing 2019); K Ligeti and A Marletta, 'EU Criminal Justice Actors: Accountability and Judicial Review vis-à-vis the EU Citizen' (2016) 7 *New Journal of European Criminal Law* 175; M Luchtman, 'Choice of Forum and the Prosecution of Cross-Border Crime in the European Union: What Role for the Legality Principle?' in Luchtman (ed) (n 82) 3.

action, by the individual or undertaking. Such 'foreseeability gaps' may be closed by secondary rules, for instance rules on forum choices, that in turn must meet the requirements of procedural legality.[86] The foregoing also means, by implication, that the potential application of offences and sanctions from those other jurisdictions (other than the default legal order) is as such not impermissible in light of the free movement of persons, but that it needs a clear, foreseeable basis in the law. To that extent, rules on jurisdiction are in my view also influenced by the substantive legality principle of Article 49 of the Charter.[87] Arguably, one could even raise the standard for Article 49 and point to the fact that diverging offences and sanctions, even if foreseeable, still pose a problem in light of the contradictory signals that are thus sent to persons.

The foregoing brings with it the fact that composite systems that lack a 'case allocation system' require our specific attention. OLAF's framework is again an exemplar here. The PIF area lacks a system that designates the competent forum in a manner that is foreseeable to individuals. For OLAF, the question is whether this system should be part of the OLAF framework, or that of the authorities that are required to provide for (punitive) follow up, including the criminal justice authorities.[88] Case allocation mechanisms are in place in the area of banking law and, in a more informal way, in EU competition law.[89] Particularly interesting in this regard is also, of course, the EPPO, which has a system of forum choices that closes foreseeability gaps at the secondary level, that is, in the determination of the competent forum state.

2. The procedural legality principle that is part of the right to a fair trial (Articles 47 and 48 of the Charter) implies that individuals, as soon as punitive procedures can reasonably be anticipated, must be able to determine their procedural position and to design an effective defence strategy in light of the punitive finality of the procedure. Abuses of authority are a particular risk where the competent forum remains undetermined after procedures have started, or where procedural acts in other legal orders, ordered or executed by or under the auspices of the competent EU authority, adversely affect the rights and duties of the defendant in that forum.

   For the procedural part of the legality principle, a key issue is to determine if and when abuses of authority are likely to take place in composite procedures. Composite enforcement procedures may end up with punitive sanctions at either the EU or the national level. The principle of legality requires (i) that it is not possible for enforcement authorities to postpone the opening of punitive procedures,[90] (ii) that the competent forum must preferably be known at this stage too,

[86] cf, in the national setting, *Camilleri v Malta* App no 42931/10 (ECtHR, 22 January 2013). For an example of how this could be done, see Luchtman (n 85); and K Ligeti et al (eds), *Preventing and Resolving Conflicts of Jurisdiction in EU Criminal Law* (Hart Publishing 2018).

[87] Luchtman (n 85).

[88] As will be explained and further elaborated in due course by Koen Bovend'Eerdt in his dissertation.

[89] Commission, 'Commission Notice on cooperation within the Network of Competition Authorities' [2004] OJ C101/43, discussed, inter alia, by Brammer (n 73).

[90] cf the ECtHR's case law on the notion of a criminal 'charge', eg, *Deweer v Belgium* App no 6903/75 (ECtHR, 27 February 1980); *Serves v France* App no 20225/92 (ECtHR, 20 October 1997), para 42; *Marttinen v Finland* App no 19235/03 (ECtHR, 21 April 2009), para 62.

and (iii) that procedural acts that are conducted in other legal orders cannot negatively affect or bypass the exercise and scope of defence rights as guaranteed by the forum, nor increase the (scope of) enforcement duties already applicable to the person concerned by the laws of that forum. Moreover, (iv) in those cases where non-punitive procedures can have an impact on parallel or consecutive punitive procedures, those consequences should be foreseeable to individuals as well.[91]

Though these propositions are still quite broad, they do offer a frame of reference for assessing procedural legality in a composite setting. These propositions do not in themselves prevent procedural acts from being performed in jurisdictions other than the jurisdiction of the forum (EU or national), not even after punitive procedures have officially commenced. Nor do they entail that it should always be the highest standards of defence rights that apply to a given case (provided the standards of the Charter are respected at all times), or that it should be the defendant who chooses under which applicable legal regime he or she wishes to proceed.

I do consider it problematic, however, that procedural acts that are relevant for the procedure in the forum jurisdiction may also be conducted under the legal regimes of other legal orders that fall below the level of protection of the forum. Such situations could occur, for instance, where the forum offers more extensive protection with regard to the privilege against self-incrimination. Another case in point is the protection of legal professional privilege, which varies in scope among different Member States and the EU level.[92] These are situations where risks for abuses are the greatest, even when the relevant Charter standards are met by those other legal orders. Such changes are problematic, if and when they are made unilaterally by the executive. This is so, first of all, because change affects legal certainty and hampers the development of a defence strategy. Moreover, it affects the principle of equality of arms and, in plain language, fair play, if no law prevents the authority – being a party to the procedure – from applying rules that have an impact on the procedural position of other parties to that same procedure. Such a degree of executive discretion must be prevented by the law. Perhaps we should go even further than that and tackle the possibility of changing the applicable procedural rules in and of themselves. It will not always be easy, after all, to determine when a standard falls short of another, or to isolate specific procedural acts and corresponding rights and duties from the proceedings as a whole. This aligns with the principle of *forum regit actum* that is, for instance, (partly) incorporated in Article 32 of the EPPO Regulation.

Though this finding does not per se lead to a uniform set of procedural rules at the EU and national levels, it does require clear rules on the choice of forum. Even the SSM framework, implementing a system of home-state control, allows for the possibility that procedural preparatory acts may be conducted outside the jurisdiction of the forum, for instance by means of instructions.

[91] cf *Chambaz* (n 60); *Marttinen v Finland* App no 19235/03 (ECtHR, 21 April 2009).

[92] See ch 2 (De Vries and Widdershoven) and ch 4 (Böse and Schneider) of this volume; Widdershoven and Craig (n 44) 338.

Moreover, the foregoing stresses the need to make a timely forum decision. This seems particularly relevant to OLAF. As long as it remains unclear where OLAF reports or materials collected and transferred by it will end up, it is difficult to design an effective defence strategy. Parallel punitive procedures are then not precluded, to the detriment of, mostly, the defendant. Again, the question is whether this is a problem deriving from the OLAF framework itself (which is after all not competent for punitive follow up) or whether it requires a broader sectoral approach, including the punitive follow up at national level. At the moment, OLAF does not make forum choices in the proper meaning of the term, nor can it formally commence punitive procedures.

3. Regarding the legality principle that aims to protect against arbitrary interferences with one's privacy, property or even liberty, the EU authority or its national partners should not be in the position, by determining the applicable set of investigatory powers, to exert influence on the applicable standards and procedures for the ex ante proportionality assessment of the required interference, as defined by law, nor on the possibility and scope of an ex post review thereof.

Though there may be good reasons for an authority to collect evidence in one legal order and not in another, concerns remain. Those concerns do not, in general, relate to the specific legal basis for the actual interference with one's right to respect for private life, as provided for by the legal order in play. The applicable legal rules of that order will after all be accessible to and foreseeable by the parties concerned. In fact, one could even maintain that it is incorrect to assume that private parties ought to know beforehand which set of rules will be applied to their affairs, in cases where multiple laws may be applied. Just as private parties should in principle not be in in the position to influence the choice of the investigative measure against them,[93] the same arguably applies to the decision as to in which jurisdiction these measures are deployed. Those decisions belong to the domain of the executive, which of course needs to be able to account for its decisions if necessary. In similar vein, one might wonder to what extent judicial control has been negatively affected in situations where the exercise of specific investigative measures was put to test against the yardsticks of the laws of a specific legal order and found to be in compliance with those laws? Can an interference with the right to respect for private life be unlawful, if it is in line with the laws of the legal order where the investigative actions were ultimately performed? Is there a right for individuals to have at their disposal the procedural rights, safeguards and remedies of the laws of other legal orders, which potentially could also have been applied?

The significance of these questions in my view varies, depending on the intrusiveness of the investigative measures at stake. In a purely national case, wherein a single authority applies a single set of rules, the law will force that authority to subject its case to the conditions of that law. It is the law itself, and not the authority bound by it, that structures the assessment of the necessity, feasibility and

[93] cf Case C-247/14 P *HeidelbergCement AG v European Commission* ECLI:EU:C:2015:694, Opinion of AG Wahl, para 56, discussed in ch 3 (Ligeti and Robinson) of this volume.

proportionality of the requested investigative measure at stake by including formal (for instance the intervention of an independent judicial body) or substantive conditions (such as the necessity of a degree of suspicion or purpose limitations) for its lawful application. The more intrusive or covert the investigative measures become, the stronger the need to have these laws in place, as the Strasbourg Court has consistently emphasised.

Enforcement reality, however, shows that a proper balancing of the privacy of the individual and the interests of the investigations can be achieved in many different ways. Composite enforcement is markedly different from a purely national situation. In such a reality, the applicable laws become a part of the decision-making process, as the aforementioned legal texts clearly demonstrate,[94] rather than structuring the decision-making process and subjecting it to the rule of law. Which executive authority would refrain from deploying an investigative measure that is allowed in legal order A but not in legal order B, if that measure were deemed important, if not essential, for the course of its investigations? Consequently, the necessary connection between the degree of precision of the law, the intrusiveness of the measure and the assessment of its proportionality gets lost. This problem appears to be most urgent for measures that are covert and not easily subjected to public scrutiny. Particularly intrusive are coercive measures that can be executed without the help of the persons involved, thus de facto reducing those persons or their affairs to mere objects of investigation (searches, for instance), instead of parties to a procedure. The collection of bulk data is a third category of measures that raise concerns.

Incidentally, these concerns are relevant not only in light of the interests of the persons concerned, but also in light of the legitimacy of the applicable laws themselves. What is the point, after all, of inserting certain conditions for the exercise of investigative powers if the same, single authority can also obtain the information elsewhere, where such additional conditions or restrictions on the access to information do not exist? If such a single authority can avail itself of powers that are available under a multitude of potentially applicable laws, all of them defining the scope of the right to respect for private life and the lawfulness of its interference differently, it will be relatively easy to find a legal regime that grants the authority what it seeks. Again, it appears to be vital not only that the EU offers more guidance, particularly for the more intrusive types of measures, but also that Member States open up and, if necessary, adjust their legal systems to the composite reality.

The question is to what extent the application of this third rule of thumb poses problems for composite enforcement. Existing research leads to the provisional conclusion that the problem does not appear to be a particularly pressing issue in composite administrative enforcement, for two reasons.[95] First of all, investigative measures usually take place 'out in the open', that is in public, and are subject to judicial review. Second, the conditions that apply for administrative investigative powers are usually subject to more or less comparable and usually broadly defined

[94] See the text to nn 76–78 above.
[95] See Karagianni (n 74) and Bovend'Eerdt in their forthcoming dissertations.

conditions. In some cases, however, there is room for improvement. Specifically with respect to administrative enforcement, the lack of harmonisation of ex ante judicial authorisations for on-site inspections and dawn raids are problematic.[96] I will come back on this in the next section. As regards OLAF, moreover, it is striking to note that the applicable legal rules do not define powers for OLAF but merely investigative techniques.

More issues are expected within the framework of criminal investigations. Powers of criminal investigation are usually subject to a number of stringent criteria, yet within national margins of appreciation. However, looking at the EPPO Regulation,[97] harmonisation of those conditions has hardly taken place, nor have national legal orders tackled this problem bottom-up.

The foregoing analysis illustrates that the legality principle in composite procedures is a topic that has many different facets. 'Composite legality' seeks to secure the position of individuals in a highly complicated, transnational legal reality, and to empower, yet also to regulate, the actions of the relevant authorities in punitive enforcement procedures. However, that finding does not inevitably point towards the full harmonisation or unification of the legal frameworks of the EU authorities studied. Rather, the different rights at stake seem to allow for different approaches.[98] The need for harmonisation is most urgent for the more intrusive powers of investigation. For other fundamental rights, clear rules on a timely choice of forum may be an equally suitable mechanism to deal with issues of legality and fairness. What should be kept in mind then is that rules for forum choices should allow persons not only to determine their position once involved in procedures, but also – depending on the applicable rules of jurisdiction – to assess the consequences of their actions at the time they commit the offences. Again, all of this means that there is more work to be done for both the EU legal order and those of its Member States. Despite their decentralised frameworks, composite procedures are in need of a minimum degree of coherence.

B. Judicial Protection and Unlawfully Obtained Evidence

In section II.C, I made an analysis of the potential impact of recent caselaw of the Court of Justice on unlawfully obtained or transferred evidence in composite procedures.[99] It remains to be seen whether that case law will be applied in that setting. From the perspective of legal protection, the most pertinent question is to what extent composite procedures show loopholes in legal protection, due to a lack of coordination of the work of the courts in different legal orders. In the previous section, I discussed a number of problems that relate to the legality principle in such procedures and to the identification

[96] As is already noted by many others, see ch 2 of this volume (De Vries and Widdershoven), with further references.

[97] Particularly Arts 30–32 EPPO Regulation.

[98] Sometimes the scope of these rights overlap, for instance with respect to legal professional privilege. I will disregard that situation here. It seems wise to cumulatively apply the requirements of all the relevant fundamental rights standards in those situations.

[99] See also ch 3 (Ligeti and Robinson) and ch 2 (De Vries and Widdershoven) of this volume.

of the applicable law. There are two other issues that also have a significant negative impact on legal protection, even in cases where the applicable law can be identified. These two issues are the potential adverse consequences of the application of the principle of mutual trust in composite procedures and the systemic flaws that may hamper effective remedies for interferences with fundamental rights. A third issue concerns the question of what the procedural consequences are in cases where unlawful action by the authorities in enforcement procedures is established.[100]

Regarding the first issue, it is striking how poorly developed the case law still is on points of composite law enforcement, particularly on the national side of it.[101] Questions that relate to the mutual division of responsibilities between courts in composite procedures have not yet reached the EU courts.[102] These questions relate not only to the division of labor between the EU and national courts, but also to the horizontal relations between national courts, in cases where materials were gathered by national authorities in jurisdiction X are introduced as evidence in jurisdiction Y. It may be that these issues have not yet been raised before national courts, or that national courts decided on their own motion that materials unlawfully obtained or transferred could not be used as evidence.[103] We cannot exclude, however, that such lawfulness was not tested because of arguments that rely on the principle of mutual trust.[104] Indeed, we have occasionally seen court rulings where that line of reasoning was apparently used. National courts sometimes appear to refrain from testing the lawfulness of investigative actions because they are of the opinion that they are not allowed to do so. In their view, the lawfulness is to be tested either at EU level (for which, however, a preliminary reference will often be needed) or in another national jurisdiction; it is, however, not considered to be the responsibility of the trial court.

Though this 'separationist' approach is, as said, not uncommon in international criminal law, a 'chain approach' appears to be more appropriate for composite procedures, at least in situations where legitimate doubt as to the lawfulness of the gathering or transfer of the materials has been raised. For materials to be used as evidence, a full judicial review of the materials must be guaranteed, either by the court itself or after confirmation that it has indeed been already guaranteed by another court. Existing rules on the admissibility of evidence do not contradict this approach. That materials that were obtained in one legal order should also be admissible in another does not automatically imply, after all, that materials unlawfully obtained should also be admissible evidence.

The chain approach that is advocated here, and which does not yet seem to be a common standard in composite procedures, does not in itself tackle the second issue

[100] See also ch 9 (Vervaele) of this volume.

[101] See also ch 3 of this volume (Ligeti and Robinson), section IV.

[102] A rare example is *FSL Holdings*, dealing with (allegedly) unlawfully obtained or transferred evidence by the Italian fiscal police to the European Commission, see Case C-469/15 P *FSL Holdings and others* ECLI:EU:C:2017:308.

[103] cf Widdershoven and Craig (n 44).

[104] cf T Duijkersloot, A Karagianni and R Kraaieveld, 'Political and Judicial Accountability in the EU Shared System of Banking Supervision and Enforcement' in Scholten and Luchtman (eds) (n 44) 28; and M Luchtman and M Wasmeier, 'The Political and Judicial Accountability of OLAF' in Scholten and Luchtman (eds) (n 44) 221.

that was identified, the existence of so-called systemic flaws. Systemic flaws occur where investigative powers are not harmonised and the respective conditions and safeguards for their application consequently diverge from legal order to legal order.[105] The result may be that the individual lacks the protection that each of the legal orders involved would have provided.[106] Interferences with the respect for private life of persons – an on-site inspection, for instance – may be allowed in one jurisdiction, because ex ante judicial authorisation is required, whereas in another jurisdiction such authorisation is not mandatory but ex post remedies are available. Both types of safeguards are accepted in the case law of the European Courts with respect to the inspection powers of competition authorities and, presumably, other comparable administrative bodies.[107] It can thus happen that investigative acts are performed in a legal order that does not require an ex ante authorisation and the results are subsequently used in another legal order where such authorisations are mandatory. The concept of ex ante judicial intervention, which is regarded as an important safeguard for the more intrusive investigative measures (dawn raids, inspection of premises, large-scale interceptions of data, etc), then literally falls between two stools. The fact that there has been no judicial authorisation cannot be part of any subsequent legality assessment, in any of the jurisdictions involved, because it is not a requirement in the gathering jurisdiction. Worse still, the defendant may also lack the protection that the legal order of the forum would normally have offered him or her. That is certainly so in cases where the forum court refuses to hear arguments with respect to the legality of the measure in the gathering jurisdiction, because of the principle of mutual trust. The present situation therefore raises concerns not only in light of the legality principle, but also in light of the principle of effective judicial protection. As said in section III.A, this problem is best prevented by harmonising the applicable safeguards, particularly for the more intrusive investigative measures.

Systemic flaws may also relate to vertical divisions of labour, that is, between the EU and national levels involved. For instance, the purpose of an ex ante judicial authorisation (eg for on-site inspections) is to have the proportionality of a measure tested by an independent body before the interference takes place, and thus to prevent arbitrary interferences with fundamental rights. Some national legal orders have such safeguards in place. Yet the well-known case law of the Court of Justice in competition law cases,[108] and its subsequent implementation in secondary law, is said to hinder the full application of those guarantees.

To be able to give an ex ante authorisation, the authorising judge or court will need a clear assessment frame, responsive to the intrusiveness of the measure at stake, and detailed information, perhaps even access to the file. If either of the two conditions is not fulfilled, the authorising judge or court will not be in a position to question the competent authority critically, to form its own informed opinion and to motivate it with sufficient authority.

[105] Luchtman (n 63) 162.

[106] The opposite may also be true, incidentally; the defendant then enjoys the cumulated safeguards of both legal orders, which may be seen as a problem for effective enforcement, as discussed in sections II.B and II.C.

[107] See Case C-583/13 P *Deutsche Bahn* ECLI:EU:C:2015:404; and *Delta Pekárny v the Czech Republic* App no 97/11 (ECtHR, 2 October 2014).

[108] Case C-94/00 *Roquette Frères* ECLI:EU:C:2002:603.

Are these conditions met? On the one hand, we should note that the lawfulness of the inspection decision (as well as the execution of it) always remains under the full jurisdiction of the EU Courts. Moreover, the applicable EU laws indeed indicate the relevant criteria for the assessment.[109] The Commission is to provide the relevant detailed information, if asked to do so by the courts. To that extent, one may say there are no gaps in the system of legal protection. On the other hand, in the relevant rules of competition law and banking supervision, the scope of the assessment that is performed by the national courts is limited to issues of proportionality in the strict sense of the word and of preventing arbitrariness. Access to the files is moreover explicitly prohibited,[110] whereas review by the European Courts of the inspection decision may take place only years later. The question is whether such an ex post review can ever be a substitute for ex ante authorisations.[111]

Clearly, the current model sends mixed signals. For some legal orders authorisations are an important safeguard against abuses, but for others – under the same composite framework – they are not. The question is also why the bar is not raised. Should not intrusive measures, such as dawn raids and on-site inspections decisions, always require an ex ante judicial test of proportionality and lawfulness?[112] Moreover, why is this test in the hands of a judge or court in the gathering jurisdiction, now that that choice brings with it significant limitations on the nature and degree of the test these judicial bodies have to perform. Similar concerns are known in international or European criminal law, where legal protection in the requested or executing state is severely limited by a combination of the rule of non-inquiry and the (practical or even legal) impossibility to enter into an assessment of 'the substantive reasons for issuing' a request or EIO in the requested or executing state.[113] Even more than in the area of composite administrative enforcement, this issue is pertinent in criminal law – in the setting of the EPPO for instance – where the investigative measures are particularly invasive.

Finally, some remarks on the procedural consequences of unlawfully obtained or transferred materials are in order. There are no EU rules for this yet. Case law that relates specifically to composite procedures is also absent. In *Prokuratuur*, the Court held

> that the objective of national rules on the admissibility and use of information and evidence is, in accordance with the choices made by national law, to prevent information and evidence obtained unlawfully from unduly prejudicing a person who is suspected of having committed criminal offences. That objective may be achieved under national law not only by prohibiting the use of such information and evidence, but also by means of national rules and practices governing the assessment and weighting of such material, or by factoring in whether that material is unlawful when determining the sentence …[114]

[109] See, eg, Arts 20(8) and 21(3) Regulation 1/2003.
[110] cf ch 4 of this volume (Böse and Schneider), section I.A.
[111] Brammer (n 73)103.
[112] Widdershoven and Craig (n 44).
[113] cf Directive 2014/41/EU of the European Parliament and of the Council of 3 April 2014 regarding the European Investigation Order in criminal matters [2014] OJ L130/1, Art 14; see also Art 31(2) EPPO Regulation, discussed by Luchtman (n 40) 806.
[114] *Prokuratuur* (n 24) para 43.

In the absence of EU law, the legal consequences are to be determined by the national legislators. Whereas the requirement that defendants must be able to comment effectively on 'evidence pertaining to a field of which the judges have no knowledge and that is likely to have a preponderant influence on the findings of fact' predominantly implements the principle of effectiveness, the procedural sanctions for a finding of unlawfulness seem to relate more to the principle of equivalence; they are to be determined in accordance with the applicable national rules.

It is not that easy, however, to find the relevant comparative yardstick for that in composite punitive procedures. In fact, there are multiple dividing lines, that is those between different jurisdictions, but also those between non-punitive and punitive administrative enforcement. As far as the interface between administrative and criminal enforcement is concerned, this adds a third dividing line.[115] It is not necessarily the case that the procedural consequences of a finding of unlawfulness in these three situations are all the same. Not only does the case law of each national court show significant differences in its approach;[116] the question is also what the relevant measure for comparison is in composite procedures? It appears to me that this measure cannot be the case law of national courts on the appreciation of unlawfully obtained or transferred evidence from other jurisdictions. In those cases, there usually is no responsibility to remedy, for instance, unlawful interferences with the right to respect for private life in other jurisdictions, as long as the right to a fair trial is not violated. Rather, it makes sense in composite procedures to follow the national case law that deals with the use of unlawfully obtained or transferred materials in punitive enforcement procedures and its use at the interface of administrative and criminal law enforcement. I discussed this in sections II.C and II.D.

C. Composite Enforcement Procedures and Criminal Justice

Many of the issues that have been touched upon in the preceding sections also play a role in relation to criminal justice. I have already mentioned, in section II.C, that a lack of attention to fundamental rights may backfire on the effectiveness of EU law enforcement, though this is far from certain. Where no specific legislative arrangements are made, the impact of criminal procedures in one jurisdiction may, for instance, affect the operations of composite enforcement and its possibility to exercise compulsion in another. A lack of coordination between the procedures may, moreover, have an impact on the scope of protection of the *ne bis in idem* guarantee of Article 50 of the Charter.

Whether these concerns will actually materialise is uncertain. In fact, it is not unrealistic to assume that the fragmented enforcement landscape is at present more likely to affect the legal position of the persons concerned than to constitute a threat to effective law enforcement. Double prosecutions for the same conduct, double punishments and a risk of excessive sanctioning are prime candidates in this respect. Fragmentation of

[115] See also Luchtman, Karagianni and Bovend'Eerdt (n 18).
[116] See ch 6 (Giuffrida and Theodorakakou) and ch 9 (Vervaele) of this volume.

legal protection at the interface of administrative and criminal law enforcement is also not unrealistic.[117]

To avoid repetition, I will limit myself to one additional point. Even though composite enforcement by its very definition involves the legal orders of multiple EU states, the interactions with the respective criminal justice systems remain under-regulated. For instance, while EU banking supervision rules do have a clear system of case allocation implementing the home-state control system, this does not apply to the criminal law implications of it.[118] The manner and ways in which the ECB reports a case to State X and not State Y, which may also have jurisdiction, can have a profound influence on the course of the subsequent criminal procedures. Reporting to X instead of Y may well be completely contrary to the interests and legitimate expectations of the EU citizen or economic actor concerned.

This also impacts on the effective exercise of defence rights. For instance, (how) can one – a natural[119] or, depending on the rules of the national jurisdiction, a legal person – anticipate the initiation of criminal proceedings during administrative investigations, if the competent forum is unclear and has yet to be determined? Does this affect the effectiveness of composite procedures procedures, or does it place the defendant in a disadvantageous position? I have already discussed the relevant case law of the Strasbourg Court and noted that where administrative and criminal enforcement become '*suffisamment liées*',[120] the criminal limb safeguards of Article 6 ECHR – and the same will apply for Articles 47 and 48 of the Charter – cast their shadow forward over the exercise of compulsion in administrative procedures. In cases where there is a clear link to only one national jurisdiction, this case law, as I have argued, is capable of being applied to the composite EU setting. It would mean that the exercise of compulsion is at odds with the right to a fair trial if criminal procedures are running in parallel or can reasonably be anticipated.

In horizontal, transnational situations, however, this is not always that evident. One essential difference from situations like that in *Chambaz*[121] is that, in such cases, it is not all that clear *where* criminal procedures will be initiated. The consequence of this will most likely be that the privilege against self-incrimination will play a role (only) when it is used as evidence in criminal proceedings. It does not preclude, as is the case in purely national investigations, that materials that have been obtained under compulsion are used for other purposes in criminal procedures, such as enhancing the information position of the criminal authorities involved. The result is a certain paradox, in which one might rhetorically ask oneself whether or not it is improper for an EU authority to exercise compulsion if criminal procedures clearly lurk on the horizon, in light of the

[117] See my remarks in section II.D.

[118] See also ch 8 of this volume (Allegrezza et al); and S Allegrezza, 'The Single Supervisory Mechanism' in S Allegrezza (ed), *The Enforcement Dimension of the Single Supervisory Mechanism* (CEDAM/Wolters Kluwer 2021) 36.

[119] I will disregard the issue of to what extent representatives of undertakings also enjoy the protection of the privilege of their undertaking; see *in extenso* S Lamberigts, *The Privilege Against Self-Incrimination of Corporations* (Leuven 2018).

[120] *Chambaz* (n 60) para 43.

[121] ibid.

information that was asked for, yet that possibility cannot be demonstrated, as it cannot be foreseen, and consequently neither concluded nor excluded, how and where such criminal procedures will eventually be initiated.

IV. Benchmarks for Enforcement in a Composite Legal Order

It is time to come to a conclusion. European integration has had a significant impact on law enforcement. It affects the enforcement structures at the national level, but also manifests itself in transnational and vertical relations. Law enforcement by EU authorities is characterised by its integrative goals and effects. Instead of dividing the tasks among the authorities of the EU states along territorial lines, EU enforcement authorities aim to overcome or redesign the role and significance of national borders all together. Whereas some of those models, such as in EU competition law, almost entirely do away with national borders for the competences of DG Competition, others retain elements of them. Under the latter type of models, like in the EPPO, a genuine concept of European territoriality does not exist; the operational powers of the European (delegated) prosecutors are limited to their own territories. It is fair to say, however, that the notion of enforcement jurisdiction has been transformed under those systems into a system of territorial 'enforcement competence' (*örtliche Zuständigkeit*)[122] that has done away with traditional international mechanisms of mutual administrative or legal assistance to the benefit of often very informal types of transnational evidence gathering and evidence sharing.

The foregoing analysis has made it clear that even in these EU structures, national law is never far away. Even the most autonomous models of composite enforcement need to reconnect to the national level at some point. That goes a fortiori for their relationships with national criminal justice. The composite enforcement structures that have emerged thus have strong integrative effects. This is particularly the case for the executive branches within those models. Under all of the models that we have studied, officials from national legal orders and EU officials work together in the pursuit of common goals. This is most visible under the SSM structure, but it also applies to competition law (particularly via the European Competition Network, which in itself would fall outside my definition of composite procedures) and to a lesser extent also to OLAF. It is very likely that prosecutors within the EPPO structure will also gradually point their noses towards these common goals, as defined within the confines of that EU authority.

There can be no doubt that the integration of these national elements in the EU enforcement structures will have consequences in terms of policy development, operational strategies and specific investigations. The mindset of the participating officials is likely to shift away from national perspectives towards a shared mission. In fact,

[122] cf Ryngaert and Vervaele (n 4).

I do not think it is an exaggeration to state that this is – in addition to their EU-wide mandates – one of the underlying goals for establishing such authorities.

For the legal analysis of the impact of these processes, the notion of composite enforcement procedures is important. All the models are characterised by a legal design in which EU authorities are clearly in the lead, and meant to be in the lead, as well as capable of guiding and steering the actions of their national partners. This guidance is, however, not always translated into a legal obligation to achieve a certain result; rather, it takes shape as a duty of diligence for national authorities, without the possibility of formally refusing a 'request', 'order' or 'instruction'.

The degree of coherence (vertically and horizontally) that is thus achieved has normative consequences, despite the remaining numerous references to national legal orders. What is meant to be a functional unity should also be approached as one. Watertight distinctions along the lines of the legal orders involved consequently no longer exist. That is a fundamental difference from, for instance, the operation of the principle of mutual recognition in the AFSJ, which rather emphasises the strict division of responsibilities along territorial lines.[123] In the foregoing analysis, I have explored the impact of this for fundamental rights, particularly issues of legality, fairness and legal protection.

Whereas executive powers have found each other within composite enforcement structures, the same does not appear to be true for the other traditional branches of government. That is particularly the case for the legislative branches. Yet the question is to what extent enforcement integration can be achieved by merely removing the building blocks or barriers of international law-types of cooperation. What appears to be missing at the EU level, in particular, is an accompanying narrative, implemented by legislation, that integrates transnational agency for individuals and fundamental rights in the enforcement design.

Moreover, the question is to what extent the national legal orders involved are sufficiently aware of the need to open their own legal orders to these new enforcement structures and are prepared to do so. This also affects the many relationships that exist with criminal law enforcement. It is as if both types of enforcement are considered as two distinct, separate domains, which is obviously not correct. Another strategy of curtailing the influence of EU authorities over, particularly, criminal justice is to deny those authorities direct enforcement powers, making them dependent on the national enforcement structures for their work. OLAF is a clear example of this. Even the EPPO is still presented by some as a mechanism for inter-state 'coordination', in which the real power remains with the national criminal justice authorities (including the courts). However, the need to open up – for instance by allowing 'composite evidence' in national enforcement procedures[124] – is essential not only for the protection of the individual, but also for effective law enforcement itself.

What, then, could this narrative be, that needs further thought and subsequent implementation in the enforcement designs? The preceding analysis has identified a

[123] *Gavanozov II* (n 27).

[124] Other obvious examples are to provide the national partners of EU authorities with clarity on their tasks in relation to the EU authorities, and with the possibility (legal bases) to share (confidential) information. Opening up also implies – more controversially – the willingness to accept lower standards than one's own constitutional standards if that is necessary for the effective enforcement of EU law.

number of benchmarks. They mainly, though not exclusively, relate to the enhancement of legal protection under composite enforcement structures and their relationships to criminal justice. I have identified the following benchmarks for composite enforcement:

1. It is necessary to develop an integrated enforcement policy that integrates different policy areas into a single policy, bridging the gaps between specific policy domains and the horizontal domain of criminal justice. Such a policy implies that the goals are set in common, for the common European areas (the internal market, the AFSJ).

   On the national side, legislators need to open up their national legal orders, by including clear tasks in the national statutes for the partners of the EU authorities. Moreover, where EU law so requires, national law must provide for clear provisions to share information, to guarantee sufficient investigatory powers, as well as sufficient possibilities, also for national courts, to use information as evidence in national punitive procedures.

   On the EU side, specific attention to levelling the playing field of powers and safeguards and coordination between the different legal orders are focal points. The latter relates to the need to have clear mechanisms for forum choices in place, but also to the division of responsibilities for the many courts that may get involved in composite procedures. In the absence of such procedures, a 'chain approach' is most likely to prevent gaps in legal protection.

   In relation to criminal justice, an unresolved issue is the impact that ongoing criminal procedures may have on administrative composite enforcement. These relationships are left untouched at present, but do have an impact on, for instance, the *ne bis in idem* principle and the exercise of defence rights in criminal procedures. Because of that, they are capable of affecting the effectiveness of punitive enforcement procedures.

   Specifically in relation to criminal justice, the question is also whether these measures should form part of the composite structures, or rather of horizontal measures within the AFSJ. I argue in favour of the latter. Prime candidates appear to be rules on choice of forum and on the admissibility of evidence.[125]
2. Composite enforcement structures should take better account of the consequences of the legality principle for their work. There is a clear tension between, on the one hand, the efforts that are put into making sure that EU authorities are capable of guiding and directing national authorities in an often decentralised structure, and the consequences that follow from this in terms of the legality principle, fairness and legal protection. Yet with the influence should also come the responsibility. Three specific requirements follow from this:
   (a) *Composite legality*. As stated before, legality as such is a multi-faceted concept. In the preceding sections, I have developed three requirements that follow from it. This interpretation is grounded in the fact that the European Union and its Member States have established a legal order in which transnational

[125] See also JJM Graat, *The European Arrest Warrant and EU Citizenship: EU Citizenship in Relation to Foreseeability Problems in the Surrender Procedure* (Springer 2022).

agency for individuals plays an important role. Within the specific context of composite administrative enforcement, the legality principle is the corollary of the coherence that is strived for in those frameworks. It brings with it three basic requirements:

(i) That natural and legal persons are in a position to assess the punitive consequences of their behaviour – that is, the norms, the fact that punitive enforcement is an option, as well as the applicable sanctions – by being able to determine the applicable law or applicable laws.

In the 'thin' version, this requirement means that individuals should be able to know that their conduct is capable of attracting the attention of a multitude of legal orders. Should we use a 'thicker' version, one could also argue that contradictory signals from those legal orders – such as conduct's being punishable in one legal order but not in another, without an indication of which laws apply or different sanctions – should be prevented by a statutory framework. That framework – thin or thick – is necessary to allow individuals to determine their position in a transnational setting.

(ii) That individuals are in the position to design their defence strategy autonomously once involved in punitive procedures, without the executive's being able to change the applicable procedures.

This requirement essentially requires two things. In the first place, a mechanism is needed that guarantees that the opening of punitive procedures cannot be exclusively determined or even manipulated by the executive, for instance by postponing that moment. Second, consistency – in terms of the foreseeability of the applicable rules – after procedures have commenced is vital.

This requirement points to a number of necessary actions, including a mechanism that defines the official commencement of procedures and the competent forum, and, second, a mechanism that ensures that procedural acts from then on follow the procedures of that forum.

In turn, this requires, as a minimum, that national legal orders accept that the legal procedures of the forum are applied on their territories, even if they are different from or even of a lower standard than their own. It need be said that such a rule would also greatly facilitate the admissibility of evidence by the forum.

(iii) That the intrusive categories of investigative powers (including coercive powers and covert investigatory powers) are subject to further harmonisation with respect to their conditions of and safeguards for application.

Particularly for interference with the right to respect for private life and property (as well as liberty), there is a need to harmonise the conditions under which these powers can be invoked. This requirement is particularly important in the domain of criminal justice, where those powers are usually available. In the fragmented, decentralised enforcement landscapes of most of the EU authorities, there is no other way of preventing abuses.

(b) *Composite fairness*. Composite fairness and composite legality are not easily separated. In addition to the need for clear rules on the applicable procedures and the impossibility for the executive to change the procedural rules after procedures have commenced, issues of fairness predominantly seem to relate to the intersections between the non-punitive and punitive stages of the enforcement procedure and to the interfaces with criminal justice.

The integrative elements of composite administrative enforcement procedures are capable of connecting specific investigative acts in one legal order to punitive procedures in another. This applies to acts that are conducted within the administrative procedures as well as their impact on criminal procedures. Where punitive procedures have commenced or can reasonably be anticipated, the use of coercion is only possible under the legal guarantee that the materials obtained cannot be used in punitive procedures if they would fall within the scope of the privilege against self-incrimination.

(c) *Composite legal protection*. Formal separations between legal orders are not part of composite administrative enforcement structures. That implies that these separations may not be suitable to allocate court responsibilities within composite legal protection, certainly not in the absence of legal rules that define the responsibilities of the respective courts.

In section II.C, I have set out four guiding principles:

(i) Where investigative acts interfere with EU rights, particularly Charter rights, and the investigating authority is not itself an independent judicial body, or the measure was not authorised by such an authority, the principle of effective judicial protection requires that a legal remedy is available to the person that is directly adversely affected by it.

(ii) When no concerns are raised as to the legality, proportionality or lawfulness of certain investigative acts or to their transmission, while this would have been legally possible for the party concerned, materials obtained in or transferred by one legal order can as a rule be used as evidence in another.

(iii) Where remedies were available for the parties concerned and used in the transferring legal order, a finding of unlawfulness is not to be discussed again by the court of the sanctioning legal order.

(iv) And where no remedies were or could be offered by the transferring legal order to the (later) defendant, but his EU rights were at stake,[126] the authorities, as well as the courts that are competent to review the sanctioning decision, need to provide for the opportunity to comment effectively on the 'evidence of which they have no knowledge'.

In all other situations, one could end up in a situation wherein the defendants could not 'comment effectively on evidence pertaining to a field of which the judges have no knowledge.' That would lead to a breach of the right to affair trial.

[126] A typical example would be the interception of the defendant's communications.

As was noted, most of the benchmarks relate to the legal protection dimension of enforcement. That, of course, cannot come as a surprise. In addition to these benchmarks, one might add (at least) two others that have not been (or only to a limited extent) the object of study of the Hercule projects.[127] Those benchmarks relate to the need to prevent double prosecutions and excessive sanctioning, both within composite enforcement procedures and in their relationship to criminal justice, and, last but not least, to the political accountability for those procedures. Again, it will be clear that these elements also require more work for the cooperating branches of government, at both the EU and the national levels.

[127] On the Hercule projects, see the Introduction to this book (Luchtman, Ligeti and Vervaele) and the references included there at n 2.

11

Outlook on the European Public Prosecutor's Office: A Giant with National Clay Feet?

JOHN VERVAELE

I. Introduction

This edited volume approaches the rise of enforcement agencies in the European Union (EU) from a double perspective within the composite legal order of the EU. Effective enforcement of the policy goals is determined by their institutional design, tasks and powers, and their interactions with national partners. The rule of law and related due process include the fact that they have to comply with fundamental rights standards when it comes to the use of investigative powers and the imposition of punitive sanctions.

The impressive rise of EU agencies, bodies and offices[1] was further extended in June 2021 with the commencement of operational activities by the European Public Prosecutor's Office (EPPO). After more than 30 years of political and academic discussions,[2] the legal basis for its establishment was laid down in Article III-274 of the non-ratified Treaty establishing a Constitution for Europe of 2004,[3] which was almost completely copy-pasted into Article 86 of the Treaty on the Functioning of the European Union (TFEU). Article 86 TFEU grants the EPPO responsibility for 'investigating,

[1] M Scholten and M Luchtman (eds), *Law Enforcement by EU Authorities: Implications for Political and Judicial Accountability* (Edward Elgar 2017); M Scholten and A Brenninkmeijer (eds), *Controlling EU Agencies: The Rule of Law in a Multi-Jurisdictional Legal Order* (Edward Elgar 2020).

[2] M Delmas-Marty (ed), *Corpus Juris Introducing Penal Provisions for the Purpose of the Financial Interests of the European Union* (Editions Economica 1997); M Delmas-Marty and JAE Vervaele (eds), *The Implementation of the Corpus Juris in the Member States: Penal Provisions for the Protection of European Finances*, vols 1–4 (Intersentia 2001); Commission, 'Green Paper on criminal-law protection of the financial interests of the Community and the establishment of a European Prosecutor' COM (2001) 715 final; K Ligeti (ed), *Toward an European Public Prosecutor for the European Union*, vol 1 (Hart Publishing 2012); Commission, 'Commission staff working document impact assessment: Accompanying the Proposal for a Council Regulation on the establishment of the European Public Prosecutor's Office' SWD (2013) 274 final.

[3] Treaty establishing a Constitution for Europe [2004] OJ C310/01.

prosecuting and bringing to judgment … the perpetrators of, and accomplices in, offences' and exercising 'the functions of prosecutor in the competent courts of the Member States in relation to such offences'.[4] The article clearly stipulates that the function of the EPPO is one of an EU investigative and prosecutorial office, meaning that it is responsible for opening and running judicial investigations, acts of criminal prosecution and exercising the functions of a prosecutor in the competent courts of the Member States. Article 86(3) TFEU also contains clear instructions on what the EU regulations should provide for, namely:

> The regulations … shall determine the general rules …, the conditions governing the performance of [the EPPO's] functions, the rules of procedure applicable to its activities, as well as those governing the admissibility of evidence, and the rules applicable to the judicial review of procedural measures taken by it in the performance of its functions.

After very intensive negotiations on the Commission proposal for a regulation in 2013,[5] the majority of the Member States,[6] based on enhanced cooperation, did adopt the EPPO Regulation in 2017[7] with the aim of enhancing effective criminal investigation of fraud against the budget of the EU, including in the field of intra-community VAT fraud,[8] and related money-laundering and corruption offences (PIF offences).[9] The EPPO is not the first EU actor in the Are of Freedom, Security and Justice (AFSJ). Europol, the European Judicial Network and Eurojust have been around for a couple of decades, but they have only supportive and coordination functions, meaning that they have not been entrusted with investigative police or judicial powers. The position of the EPPO is unique and unprecedented to the extent that, as an EU body, it is empowered to investigate and prosecute persons suspected of committing these offences. The suspects are, as a rule, natural persons, but they can also be legal persons in those Member States that provide for this type of criminal liability for these offences.

This obviously means that EU Member States have transferred part of their sovereignty to the EU when it comes to the exercise of *ius puniendi*, even if the EPPO has to prosecute before national criminal courts and the EPPO's material competence is very limited. In the future, and based on unanimity among the participating Member States, this competence that is limited to PIF offences may be extended to serious offences having a cross-border dimension.[10] Some Member States and the Commission have

[4] Consolidated version of the Treaty on the Functioning of the European Union [2012] OJ C326/47, Art 86(2).

[5] Commission, 'Proposal for a Council Regulation on the establishment of the European Public Prosecutor's Office' COM (2013) 534 final.

[6] Finally, 22 Member States did join. Denmark and Ireland opted out, and Sweden, Poland and Hungary decided not to join for the time being.

[7] Council Regulation (EU) 2017/1939 of 12 October 2017 implementing enhanced cooperation on the establishment of the European Public Prosecutor's Office ('the EPPO') [2017] OJ L283/1.

[8] In 2015, the European Court of Auditors (ECA) published a special report on 'Tackling intra-community VAT fraud: More action needed' (special report no 24) available at https://op.europa.eu/en/publication-detail/-/publication/38316bbe-e1d3-11e5-8a50-01aa75ed71a1 (accessed 14 April 2022).

[9] Directive (EU) 2017/1371 of 5 July 2017 on the fight against fraud to the Union's financial interests by means of criminal law [2017] OJ L198/29.

[10] Art 86(4) TFEU.

already voiced their opinion that terrorist offences or serious offences against the environment might be good candidates for a substantive extension.

In the field of administrative enforcement, in the past the Member States had already accepted shared competence with EU actors in different policy fields, and in this edited volume we have analysed the composite and hybrid character of this law enforcement regime in an integrated legal order. The aim of this outlook on the EPPO is to assess whether and to what extent the main findings of the comparative research on the Directorate-General for Competition (DG Competition), the European Central Bank (ECB), the European Securities and Markets Authority (ESMA) and the European Anti-Fraud Office (OLAF) are relevant for this new actor in the domain of criminal justice, and to flag what the EPPO, as an outcome of the common effort of the legislative, executive and judicial powers of the *trias politica* at the EU and national levels, can learn from the strengths and flaws, as well as the gaps in the past performance of other EU enforcement bodies.

In order to enable that assessment, I first have to share with you some additional analysis on the legislative genesis of the EPPO. In fact the Commission proposal from 2013 and the adopted Regulation of 2017 both deal with the EPPO, but differ substantially on the general principles, institutional design, functions, powers and related procedural safeguards, and thus on the modalities of its hybrid character and compositeness.

II. The EPPO under Legislative Construction

A. Commission Proposal of 2013

It took the European Commission from 2009 to 2013 to submit its proposal, after carefully consulting with the capitals of the Member States.[11] The Commission was fully convinced – rightly so in my opinion – that the EPPO could not be successful in combating the high level of impunity in the area of customs fraud, subsidy fraud, VAT fraud, etc, if it were a fully centralised EU office. In other words, the EPPO must have a two-tier structure, namely, a centralised part and a decentralised part. In the proposal, the centralised part would consist of the European Chief Prosecutor and his or her Deputies. The decentralised part would comprise European Delegated Prosecutors (EDPs) in the participating Member States, with the capacity to lead domestic enforcement authorities (mainly police and administrative agencies). The EDPs would constitute the operational level, but they would act under the instructions and on behalf of the European Chief Prosecutor and apply European law and subsidiary national law. The European Commission was also convinced that the EPPO should be an indivisible, supranational

[11] K Ligeti and M Simonato, 'The European Public Prosecutor's Office: Towards a Truly European Prosecution Service?' (2013) 4(1–2) *New Journal of European Criminal Law* 7; A Weyembergh and C Brière, *Towards a European Public Prosecutor's Office (EPPO): Study for LIBE* (European Parliament 2016) PE 571.399. For a detailed article-based commentary, see HH Herrnfeld, D Brodowski and C Burchard, *European Public Prosecutor's Office: Regulation (EU) 2017/1939 implementing enhanced cooperation on the establishment of the European Public Prosecutor's Office ('the EPPO')* (Beck-Hart-Nomos 2021) 798.

EU judicial office that would act in the AFSJ based on EU general principles. Of course the EPPO should be independent and impartial, and it must comply with the European Charter of Fundamental Rights ('the Charter'). Innovatory, however, was the fact that the common territory of the Member States would be considered to be a single legal area in which the EPPO might exercise its competence based on exclusive competence for these types of offences. Based on this European territoriality, the Commission proposed partially harmonised investigative measures, including, for instance, special investigation techniques such as real-time surveillance and undercover operations, and the procedural safeguards that had to be respected, including all the basic defence rights. The proposal also included the harmonisation of national criminal procedure when it comes to the EU-wide requirement for prior judicial authorisation of the EPPO's most coercive investigative measures.

For the purpose of prosecution, the proposal contained a definition of autonomous prosecutorial acts at the EU level, dealing with dismissals, transactions and the choice of forum for prosecution. Evidence presented by the EPPO in the national courts should be admissible if the courts considered that its admission would not adversely affect the fairness of the proceedings or the rights of the defence (Articles 47 and 48 of the Charter), even if the *lex loci* provided for different, more stringent rules on the collection or admission of such evidence.

As to judicial review, however, the Commission stipulated that the EPPO should be considered as a national authority for the purpose of judicial review, and that when national law applied (complementary to the Regulation) its provisions should not be considered as provisions of EU law for the purpose of preliminary rulings under Article 267 of the Treaty on European Union (TEU).

B. EPPO Regulation of 2017

The tripartite negotiations (Commission-Council-European Parliament) resulted in an EPPO that is still an indivisible Union body, operating as a single office, but with a completely different set of general principles, institutional design, and especially strong enhancement of the decentralised level and related national applicable law.[12] Here I will briefly flag the main changes in relation to its institutional design and the investigative phase. The organisational structure at the central level had become very complex and now consists of the European Chief Prosecutor (and his or her Deputies), a College of 22 European Prosecutors and the Permanent Chambers (consisting of two European Prosecutors and the Chief Prosecutor). The core of the operational and investigative work will be carried out by the EDPs at the decentralised level, whose competence is strictly limited to the territory of their jurisdiction and who will apply national law. The EDPs can also be national prosecutors and EDPs at the same time. They will have

[12] JAE Vervaele, 'The European Public Prosecutor's Office (EPPO): Introductory Remarks' in W Geelhoed, LH Erkelens and AWH Meij (eds), *Shifting Perspectives on the European Public Prosecutor's Office* (Asser Press 2018) 11.

the same powers as national prosecutors in respect of investigations, prosecutions and bringing cases to judgment. The EDPs no longer have exclusive competence, but the Regulation does contain rules on the right to evocation by the EPPO. The EPPO Regulation only prescribes which investigative powers should be available under national law for the most serious offences, and it refrains from a partial harmonisation of the measures. As the investigative measures are the ones that are available under the applicable national law, the harmonisation of procedural safeguards and defence rights has also disappeared from the Regulation. In relation to the rights of suspects and accused persons, the Regulation only refers to the Charter and the procedural rights directives based on Article 82 TFEU. For the rest, including the right to present evidence, to request the appointment of experts or an expert examination and the hearing of witnesses, the Regulation only states that in EPPO proceedings, the suspects, accused and other persons involved in the proceedings shall have the rights available under the applicable national law. It will not come as a surprise that the leading general principle of a single legal area or European territoriality in which the EPPO is operating has also disappeared from the Regulation.

In fact the operational arm of the EPPO consists of 140 EDPs acting under national jurisdiction, and they apply national criminal procedure and are thus confined to their respective national territories. The EDPs should have the same powers as national prosecutors in respect of investigations, prosecutions and bringing cases to judgment. Only exceptionally, under Article 28(4) of the Regulation, can the supervising European Prosecutor conduct the investigation personally and take it over from the handling EDP, but he or she also has to apply national law. On its website the EPPO refers with pride, for example, to the successes of the EPPO Venice office or the EPPO Palermo office, but in reality these are judicial actions taken by the Italian EDPs under Italian law, which have been approved and monitored by the Permanent Chamber and supervised by the Italian European Prosecutor.[13]

In cross-border cases the handling EDP, given his or her limited territorial mandate, will need to trigger transnational requests or orders for mutual legal assistance. If there is a need for a suspect to be surrendered, the European Arrest Warrant (EAW) will be used; in the case of investigative measures, a sui generis system is elaborated between the EDPs. In any case, in transnational cases the handling EPPO, the suspect and his or her defence lawyer, as well as the competent national court, will have to consider evidence that has been gathered in often diverging national legal systems when it comes to investigative powers, procedural safeguards, defence rights and rules of evidence.

As for evidence, Article 37 of the Regulation contains only a mandatory inclusion rule, namely, that the competent court cannot deny admission on the mere ground that the evidence was gathered in another Member State or in accordance with the law of another Member State. Whether this includes the position that the competent court cannot further inquire into potential infringements of human rights during the gathering of evidence remains unclear and debatable.

[13] European Public Prosecutor's Office, 'News' available at www.eppo.europa.eu/en/news (accessed 14 April 2022).

C. The EPPO Subsidiary Regulatory Framework

i. National 'Implementation Laws'

Strictly speaking, a regulation has direct application, but the EPPO Regulation not only has a substantive impact on the design of the administration of national criminal justice, but also refers back to national law on many important issues. This is why the Member States have been working on national provisions for embedding the EPPO in their domestic criminal justice systems since 2017. In 2022, the European Commission's DG Justice launched a compliance assessment of how the Member States have adapted their systems to the EPPO Regulation.[14] In the terms of reference, the Commission has selected a list of articles in the Regulation that merit specific attention. The list contains no fewer than 30 articles. The Commission has indicated in the instructions that the EPPO Regulation largely relies upon, and often refers back to, the national laws. The Commission is of course aware of the fact that the adaptation laws in the Member States are very different in their approach and content. The Commission states that:

> Member States have adopted pieces of legislation that usually regulate only certain aspects of the EPPO's functioning, while for the rest they still apply the existing national legislation without adapting it to the EPPO's needs and specificities. Therefore, such national legislation may not be compatible with the EPPO Regulation.[15]

Examples that are given are the existing powers of investigative magistrates that could preclude the EDP powers, or even the powers of the supervising European Prosecutor, and preliminary court hearings in which judges could decide on the termination of investigations and prosecutions instead of the Permanent Chambers of the central office of the EPPO. It is very clear that these types of national decisions could undermine the EPPO as the *dominus* of the investigations and prosecutions concerning offences falling within its competence. Other articles also relate to specific modalities that have been part of our research in this edited volume, namely, information exchange and reporting and the right of the evocation of cases from the national level to the EPPO level. The Commission is interested in limits or obstacles to the duty of the national enforcement community (the police, a special administrative body) and the national prosecutors to report to the EDP/EPPO, and in obstacles that could undermine the right to evocation by the EDPs in the national legal order.

It is too early to formulate any conclusions on the 'implementation laws', but EDPs are faced with operational and important challenges in their day-to-day work, partly due to the novelty of their construction, but also partly due to inventive national legislative and practical constructions to retain the judicial files under national control.

ii. EU Soft Law

Since its operational commencement the EPPO has adopted a voluminous set of rules, agreements and working arrangements. The last of these are related to cooperation with

[14] Commission, 'Call for proposals for action grants to promote judicial cooperation in civil and criminal matters' JUST/2022/PR/JCOO/CRIM/0004.

[15] ibid pt 3.2.

the European Commission and other EU institutions (such as the European Investment Bank or the EU Court of Auditors), as well as with the other EU enforcement agencies in the AFSJ (OLAF, Europol and Eurojust). Besides this dimension of horizontal cooperation, the EPPO has also started to conclude working arrangements with national enforcement partners. A first interesting example of this vertical relationship is a recent one with the Italian Antimafia and Counterterrorism Directorate (DNA).[16] Although Italy has 15 EDPs, this does not mean that they and the EPPO are automatically recognised as constituting a competent authority under the Italian Code of Criminal Procedure for all information exchange with the DNA. In the Italian implementation legislation, the EPPO (and its EDPs) has been excluded from the scope of application of Article 371-bis of the Italian Code of Criminal Procedure, which provides for the chain of information flow and command between the Italian Antimafia prosecutors and the other enforcement authorities.[17] The working arrangement therefore provides for proper provisions for consultation, coordination and mutual support, inter alia to prevent a conflict of jurisdiction and to allow for the exchange of information in relation to strategic, operational and case-related information.

The array of national enforcement authorities that are labelled in the Regulation as competent national authorities for information exchange and for cooperation with the EDPs concerning certain operations is, thanks to the referral in the Regulation, defined by national law. These authorities are not the same when it comes to VAT fraud, subsidy fraud or procurement fraud, for instance. The assignment under national law will determine to what extent the EDPs can rely on the relevant national law.

For its part, the College, being the main governing board of the EPPO, has also adopted an internal body of law, including, for instance, the internal rules of procedure of the EPPO, a decision on the functions and procedures of the Permanent Chambers and guidelines on whistleblowing. The internal rules of procedure also deal with important aspects of the relationship between the decentralised and the centralised levels. It also becomes very clear that the handling EDP is the real driving force behind the procedural acts, but he or she has further duties to upload case files into the Case Management System and to report regularly to the Permanent Chamber, which will have been randomly assigned to monitor the investigations. In Article 47 of the internal rules of procedure, the internal rules also contain provisions on the review of instructions by the Permanent Chambers, at the request of the EDP, by the Permanent Chamber itself or by the Chief Prosecutor. On the other hand, Article 48 contains interesting elements on the internal review of acts by the EDP, if the national law provides for an internal review of acts within the structure of its own prosecutor's office. In this case the review will be dealt with by the supervising European Prosecutor, who will also inform the competent Permanent Chamber. In other words, the internal review within the national

[16] EPPO, 'Working arrangement between the European Public Prosecutor's Office (EPPO) and the National Antimafia and Counter Terrorism Directorate (DNA)' available at www.eppo.europa.eu/sites/default/files/2021-12/WA%20%28EN%29%20EPPO%20-%20The%20National%20Antimafia%20and%20Counter%20Terrorism%20Directorate%20%28DNA%29.pdf (accessed 14 April 2022).

[17] Decreto Legislativo 2 febbraio 2021, n. 9. Disposizioni per l'adeguamento della normativa nazionale alle disposizioni del regolamento (UE) 2017/1939 del Consiglio, del 12 ottobre 2017, relativo all'attuazione di una cooperazione rafforzata sull'istituzione della Procura europea «EPPO». (21G00012), *GU n.30 del 5-2-2021.*

prosecution service is taken over by the central office of the EPPO. In the case of the investigation's exceptionally being taken over by the supervising European Prosecutor, he or she has to send a reasoned request to the Permanent Chamber for approval.

III. EPPO Assessment in the Light of the Comparative Analysis of the EU Enforcement Agencies

In this overview we cannot of course offer an in-depth assessment of the symmetries and asymmetries or, worse, the failures or dysfunctions by design. However, from the comparative analysis there are certainly relevant points for the EPPO and its legislative, executive and judicial actors at the EU and national levels, who all have duties to realise the added value of the EPPO in the AFSJ.

Before tackling some challenges of the EPPO reality, let us first set out some features that are common to and significantly different from those of the administrative enforcement agencies that have been the subject of study in this edited volume.

A. Mirroring the EPPO: Common Features and Significant Differences

In 2012, the Council of Ministers, the European Commission and the European Parliament adopted a joint statement and a comprehensive set of guiding principles (a common approach) in order to make the EU agencies more coherent, effective and accountable.[18] The EU felt the need to intervene in order to align the so-called agencification of EU executive governance, also called decentralised governance.[19] The fact that the EU law enforcement agencies deviate from this common approach concerning substantive issues does not come as a surprise. These agencies are not regulatory agencies but enforcement agencies, and we also see that OLAF, the ECB, ESMA and DG Competition have their particularities – as compared to regulatory agencies – because of their enforcement dimension, albeit of an administrative nature.[20] This common approach also does not take into account that most enforcement agencies have a fairly hybrid character and are operating in a composite legal order. Finally, enforcement agencies, and certainly judicial ones, are not part of the streamlining of EU executive governance but should be based on independence and impartiality.[21] The work on

[18] Commission, 'European agencies – The way forward' (Communication) COM (2008) 135 final.

[19] European Parliament, 'EU Agencies, Common Approach and Parliamentary Scrutiny: European Implementation Assessment' available at www.europarl.europa.eu/RegData/etudes/STUD/2018/627131/EPRS_STU(2018)627131_EN.pdf (accessed 14 April 2022).

[20] Scholten and Luchtman (eds) (n 1).

[21] JAE Vervaele, 'Judicial and Political Accountability for Criminal Investigations and Prosecutions by a European Public Prosecutor's Office in the EU: The Dissymmetry of Shared Enforcement' in Scholten and Luchtman (eds) (n 1) 247.

streamlining EU enforcement agencies with punitive powers still has to start. A part of the problem is that when it comes to the enforcement of EU policies in the internal market and/or in the AFSJ, the common space and the common goals and interests do not automatically result in an integrated legal order in the field of enforcement. They much more resemble a patchwork with conflicting interests rather than an integrated approach.

The lack of a common approach for the EU enforcement agencies does not mean, however, that there are no similarities that can be identified. Even if OLAF, the ECB, ESMA and DG Competition have mandates that are strictly limited to administrative enforcement and are operating in the internal market, they still have a great deal in common with the judicial EPPO in the AFSJ. All of them deal with, in one way or another, investigating alleged breaches of EU law, and they collect evidence of such breaches. All of them have operational investigative powers that are related to the concept of a single European space or European territoriality, although for the EPPO the essence of Article 86 TFEU has been transformed into a European system of domestic territorial jurisdictions. With the exception of OLAF, they all elaborate administrative or judicial indictments and impose sanctions or prosecute. So there are important similarities in their missions, mandates, tasks and the chain of their procedural acts. Due to the potential punitive character of their proceedings and sanctions, they all have to comply with important fundamental rights standards, procedural guarantees and defence rights. In other words, they work in the field of punitive enforcement, in which the balance between effective enforcement (the sword of justice) and due process (the shield of justice) is the outcome of their regulatory framework, their enforcement practice and their supervision by the (mainly supranational) courts.

Even though their missions and tasks may be quite similar, their legal shaping has important differences. The EPPO is first of all the only judicial supranational authority with executive tasks, meaning that it has investigative powers that are much more coercive – and thus intrusive as far as civil liberties and fundamental rights are concerned – than those of the other administrative enforcement agencies. Moreover, the EPPO can prosecute before national courts and request high deprivation penalties. The second main difference is that although the EPPO is a single European body, its operational arm is embedded in the national legal orders of the Member States. The applicable law for the EDPs' investigative powers is to a large extent national, and the same applies to the related procedural safeguards and judicial protection provisions. In their work the EDPs are also very dependent on the national enforcement community (the police, administrative agencies, etc). Third, the position of the suspect or defendant is quite different from the persons concerned within the administrative investigations. The rights of the suspect/defendant are almost exclusively regulated by national law that has been harmonised only to a limited extent. The suspect/defendant also has no direct access to the EU Courts.

The contrast between the ECB, ESMA and DG Competition, on the one hand, and the EPPO, on the other, is therefore fairly extensive, as the former are much less dependent upon national law for their powers, related safeguards, remedies, etc. But EU agencification or verticalisation does not mean that these agencies and their operations are completely isolated from the national legal orders; indeed, quite the opposite. Agencies like DG Competition, the ECB and ESMA have enforcement networks with their national counterparts, they exchange information, they allocate investigations, they realise joint investigations, and they rely on national law and national authorities in the case of resistance or when judicial authorisations are necessary for the use of certain coercive powers. So they operate in a composite setting, but EU law steers their operational work much more than is the case compared to the EPPO. In their respective areas the tasks and powers of national enforcement partners have been harmonised. They also have the advantage that they are operating in a specialised policy area, meaning that the persons who can potentially breach EU duties are a precise group and that the national law enforcement community is a closed, specialised circle that can easily establish a cooperation network. The case law of the Court of Justice in relation to their activities has been the source of very important general principles of EU law in the punitive enforcement field, dealing with topics such as *nemo tenetur*/the privilege against self-incrimination, *ne bis in idem*, the presumption of innocence, the rights of the defence, fair trial rights, etc. This *acquis* could of course also be of great value to the EPPO, although two caveats have to be added. First of all, the judicial character of its operations can of course include a higher level of procedural safeguards, mainly imposed by national law, compared to the punitive administrative setting. Second, as it currently stands, the *acquis* is still to a certain extent sectoral and policy-based; a general approach is lacking at both the legislative and the praetorian levels.

It seems that there are some interesting similarities between OLAF and the EPPO, at least at first glance. First of all, for the time being they have the same material competence, namely, the protection of financial interests. So both have to deal with VAT fraud, customs fraud, EU subsidy fraud, and related corruption and money-laundering issues. Both also face the difficulty of a great variety of policy fields and a related fragmented enforcement community, thereby creating substantive challenges when it comes to exchanging information and operational investigative cooperation. From the analysis of OLAF in this volume, we can also deduce that OLAF has been very much dependent upon national law, at least as far as the investigative activities of its inspectors are concerned, and the OLAF regulations refer back to national law on numerous occasions. Our study shows that national laws do not complement this referral, with instances of legal limbo as a result. However, the point of departure is that OLAF inspectors use EU regulations as the primary applicable law, and resort to subsidiary national law when they interview the persons concerned and carry out on-the-spot checks within their premises. The fact that EU law governs OLAF investigations has become even clearer following the *Sigma Orionis* ruling by the Court of Justice[22] and the latest reform of the OLAF Regulation.[23] Only in cases of resistance by a person concerned, where OLAF will need the assistance of national authorities to gain access to certain premises, business records, the storage of goods, etc, will national law still apply.

The OLAF Regulation not only contains provisions on investigative measures, but also includes a very important part on procedural safeguards that have to be applied

[22] Case T-48/16 *Sigma Orionis v Commission* ECLI:EU:T:2018:245.

[23] Regulation (EU, Euratom) 2020/2223 of the European Parliament and of the Council of 23 December 2020 amending Regulation (EU, Euratom) No 883/2013, as regards cooperation with the European Public Prosecutor's Office and the effectiveness of the European Anti-Fraud Office investigations (OLAF Regulation) [2020] OJ L437/49.

during inspections. This does not mean, however, that OLAF's investigations can be automatically challenged before the EU Courts. The main reasons for this are twofold. First, OLAF has no sanctioning powers and has to transfer its non-binding reports and recommendations on a follow-up to the competent national authorities. Second, the Court of Justice considers that this communication of the reports does not change the legal position of the person concerned and does not allow for direct access to the EU Courts, meaning that if the contents of the report are used in punitive proceedings, this can only be challenged at the national level, which means that the evidentiary value of the OLAF reports become an important issue.[24]

The contrast between OLAF and the EPPO is thus greater than perceived at first glance. The EPPO setting has of course the advantage that the central office of the EPPO has 140 EDPs in the Member States with real investigative powers, and that these investigations are concentrated, according to the evocation procedure and the case management system, in a single European office monitored by the Permanent Chambers and the European Prosecutors. This bottom-up procedure strongly contrasts with the OLAF top-down procedure. However, in reality both greatly depend on the flow of information from and the willingness of the national enforcement community to inform and to cooperate. Even if OLAF has a stronger EU design than the EPPO, in reality it still relies on the national enforcement community for information input and for running many joint investigative operations. Also the EDPs are not kings of their own castle. The position of the EDPs in relation to other judicial actors at the national level and in relation to the whole enforcement chain (police-judicial and administrative-judicial) has divergent modalities in the Member States. The enforcement chain with the police and the administrative agencies, but also with the investigating magistrates, does not form a part of the EPPO regulations, and this is completely left to national autonomy. Not forgetting the fact that in quite a few Member States, and certainly in the area of VAT and customs duties, the judicial investigation is de facto or de jure in the hands of the police and administrative bodies with judicial powers, which do have complete or extensive autonomy vis-à-vis the prosecutors.

B. Challenges for the EPPO

i. Information Flow

The transmission of information to the EPPO will be a key factor in its functioning, whether for opening EPPO cases, the evocation of cases to the EPPO and the exchange of information in the running of the investigation and even for the prosecutorial choices. This information flow is certainly not limited to the internal circle of national prosecutors and the EPPO (EDPs – central office) but extends to the larger communities of national enforcement authorities that are competent in the multiple policy fields. This varies from customs and tax enforcement authorities to authorities that have

[24] Access to the EU Courts is mostly limited to extra-contractual liability cases.

enforcement powers in policy areas where EU subsidies play a role. The latter can in fact concern agriculture, fisheries, the environment, transport, energy, etc. This wide circle of enforcement agencies is in many Member States not structurally linked to the work of the prosecutors, meaning that the information flow to the EPPO is certainly not automatic. There may also be important legal obstacles to the sharing of information due to the different legal status of these agencies (the police, administrative bodies, etc) or purpose limitations for exchanging information. Not all of them have judicial tasks either. Exchanging information within the inner circle will also create problems. Due to the fragmented body of offences, based on the implementation of a directive, the EPPO cannot rely on a body of substantive offences that is clear-cut for all actors. My first assessment of the implementation legislation and of EPPO practice already shows that the national legislator and the national prosecutors have built in a certain amount of leeway to circumvent the obligation to report and to keep files in national hands. In fact there are already signs that some national competent authorities qualify certain breaches in such a way that they do not have to report such cases to the EPPO, first by only using the extent of national VAT harm for the VAT harm threshold, or by labelling the avoidance of customs duties as smuggling. In reality both might be more dependent on the national dimension than one might perceive from their legal design.

This phenomenon is certainly not new, as a parallel can be drawn here with the transmission of information to Europol, Eurojust or OLAF in the past. It is astonishing that the EU legislator has not been able or has been unwilling to build in stronger and more precise duties concerning reporting and the exchange of information. The experience within DG Competition, the ECB and ESMA is of value here. Without regulating who has to report and exchange information and the means of this exchange, the risk is that the reporting duty results in discretionary power, which may undermine the input flow towards the EPPO and thus the functioning of the EPPO itself.

ii. Equivalent Investigative Powers in the Domestic Legal Order

Within their own jurisdiction, the EDPs, even if they are also national prosecutors, do not automatically have the same set of investigative powers as their national counterparts. In fact the EPPO Regulation only imposes certain investigative measures for the most serious offences, without harmonising the means thereof and leaving space for further restrictions in relation to some special investigative measures. What is certain is that national law does apply (the box of the toolkit), but less certain is what type of investigative measures can be applied and how this is done by the EDP (the contents of the toolkit). Procedural legality, including a clear and precise prescription of investigative powers, is an important asset, not only for the prosecutors but of course also for the suspects. Uncertainty as to the applicable law is the worst enemy for efficient and fair investigations and prosecutions. The experiences of DG Competition, the ECB and ESMA demonstrate how important it is to define this common toolkit. The advantage is also that the same toolkit can be used by the central investigators, or by delegation by the decentralised ones. Of course, this common toolkit also facilitates the elaboration of shared operational goals and policies.

In the EPPO Regulation a common toolkit is also absent, and it is not even clear whether the supervising European Prosecutor, if he or she were to take over a running investigation from the EDP, would have the same investigative powers at his or her disposal.

iii. Transnational Investigations in the AFSJ

Compared to DG Competition, the ECB, ESMA and OLAF, the EPPO is not operating in a single legal area or in a space of European territoriality. The model is based on judicial investigations in every single domestic jurisdiction, which of course triggers several challenges. First of all, the toolkit of investigative powers and their modalities will not be the same in every jurisdiction. Second, going national also means that for transnational investigations in the 22 participating Member States, a system of judicial cooperation has to be put in place. The point of departure is that the Permanent Chamber chooses a handling EDP for the case, based on jurisdictional criteria that are laid down in the Regulation. The handling EDP will trigger the necessary cooperation. For the detention and transfer of suspects, use will be made of the existing EAW regime; for the gathering of evidence, a sui generis system of cross-border investigations is put in place. The handling EDP will assign, in conformity with his or her national law, investigative acts to a colleague EDP in another jurisdiction. If judicial authorisation is required by the jurisdiction of the assisting EDP, he or she will obtain that authorisation. If this is not the case but authorisation is required by the jurisdiction of the handling EDP, he or she will obtain such authorisation. The investigative measure required must be available under domestic law, or in legal instruments of judicial cooperation or mutual recognition. This procedure is supervised by the Permanent Chamber.

The model of a single toolkit in a single legal space, the model used for DG Competition, the ECB and ESMA, and partially OLAF, was completely dispensed with during the negotiations on the Regulation. The EPPO cannot operate in a single legal area but has to turn to national law and cooperation instruments. The assignment of investigative actions among EDPs is of course more flexible than the classic mutual legal assistance instruments (rogatory commissions), or even mutual recognition instruments such as the European Investigation Order, but the types of measures and their modalities are strongly governed by national law. The result is that the transnational toolkit is not predictable and depends on the jurisdictions involved and the types of investigative act required. This is once again in strong contrast with the means of informal enforcement cooperation and networking that exist for the EU administrative enforcement agencies, thanks to their common core of investigative measures that can apply in the single legal area. Enforcement based on European territoriality is radically different from a European enforcement model based on domestic jurisdictions.

iv. Rights of the Suspect in the AFSJ

The persons concerned in investigations by DG Competition, the ECB, ESMA and even OLAF know to a large extent what type of procedural safeguards are available to them, and what type of remedies they can use and which courts will be competent. This toolkit contains not only a common set of investigative measures, but also related procedural safeguards. However, it must be said that the regulatory framework for the newcomers (the ECB and ESMA) has not learned the necessary lessons from DG Competition and OLAF, resulting in loopholes, unknowns and the lack of a horizontal approach.

The suspects in EPPO investigations have a far more difficult task, however.[25] Their rights and remedies completely depend on the applicable national law, which has only been partially harmonised as far as procedural guarantees are concerned. This means that suspects have to deal with very divergent standards of legal protection, depending on the national jurisdiction in which the EPPO is operating and depending on the investigative jurisdiction choices that are made by the Permanent Chambers, or even by the EDP who triggers the case and becomes the handling EDP.

In transnational cases this can of course lead to cumbersome situations for the suspect. During the investigation he or she has to deal with divergent standards of legal protection in one single case that will be prosecuted in one jurisdiction. That jurisdiction will use its national law for the trial setting (and thus also for the assessment of evidentiary value). Which jurisdiction will deal with the case, certainly in complex transnational cases, is not always predictable and will again depend on a decision by the Permanent Chamber.

If suspects are directly and individually concerned by the decisions of the EPPO, even by the central office, such as, for instance, the decision on the jurisdiction in which the trial is to take place, remedies are only available in the domestic legal order. This system of legal protection in the EPPO Regulation is unique in EU law, as the Regulation has built in a legal presumption that procedural acts of the EPPO that produce legal effects shall only be subject to review by the competent national courts. The exclusion of the EU Courts is a doubtful construction under EU law and has been criticised by leading experts.[26] The existence and modalities of the remedies are not harmonised and depend on national law alone. The fact that the path to the EU Courts is blocked, and is also quite limited for judges when it comes to requesting preliminary rulings, also results in significantly reduced possibilities for the EU Courts to provide for common principles and to check the applicability of fundamental rights. This, of course, greatly contrasts with the setting for DG Competition, the ECB and ESMA, and it remains to be seen if this legal presumption that EPPO decisions are national decisions as far as remedies are concerned will survive a potential assessment by the EU Courts and even the European Court of Human Rights.

IV. Conclusions

Compared to the other European enforcement agencies, the EPPO has had to make a start in an area in which there is not really a common policy shared by the Member States and the EU. The difficult negotiations on the PIF Directive, and thus also the

[25] L Bachmaier Winter (ed), *The European Public Prosecutor's Office: The Challenges Ahead* (Springer Press 2018).

[26] A Meij, 'Some Explorations into the EPPO's Administrative Structure and Judicial Review' in L Erkelens, A Meij and M Pawlik (eds), *The European Public Prosecutor's Office: An Extended Arm or a Two-Headed Dragon?* (TMC Asser Press 2014) 101; G Giudicelli-Delage and others (eds), *Le Contrôle Judiciaire du Parquet Européen: Nécessité, Modèles, Enjeux*, vol 37 (Société de Legislation Comparée 2015).

material competence of the EPPO, especially in the field of VAT and procurement fraud, reflects the lack of common goals and the strong national reflex actions of the Member States. This shows that the national legislators (governments/parliaments) do not perceive the enforcement of EU fraud as a common interest that needs to be tackled in a common area. Against this background, it is very doubtful whether the EPPO can rely on enforcement actors that are fully conscious of their European dimension and obligations. In certain Member States this will even be the case for EDPs when they are combining the task with their classic work as national prosecutors. It is certainly the case for the large and diverse community of law enforcement authorities in the Member States, but also for the criminal courts in which these cases will be prosecuted by the EDPs. The fact that the operational work is strongly encapsulated in a single jurisdiction (the one of the handling EDP) is not very helpful either. Different legal and cultural traditions will also have an impact on how the EPPO will proceed in the domestic legal orders, and on how the competent national authorities will cooperate with the EPPO.[27]

These doubts relating to the existence and strength of the European dimension of the national enforcement community means that the European spirit and drive will have to come mainly from the European Prosecutors and Permanent Chambers (for the operational part), or from the College (for the policy part).[28] A great deal will depend on how they give content to their functions in the years ahead, and how they will be able to shape their work in the AFSJ. At this point in time they could learn a great deal from DG Competition, the ECB, ESMA and OLAF, even taking into account important differences in their composite setting. The central office of the EPPO will have to search for ways in which to organise a network setting for the whole chain of the enforcement community. Essential parts of the network setting must be: specific rules on information exchange; specific rules on the allocation of cases; investigative cooperation; and cooperation at the level of prosecution and in the trial setting. Strengthening the European dimension of the national enforcement community can also pave the way for new forms of enforcement cooperation in the AFSJ.

Compared to DG Competition, the ECB, ESMA and even OLAF, the EPPO Regulation of 2017 does not provide the EPPO with investigative powers that can be used in a single legal area, and completely refers back to national law for the types and means of investigative powers and related procedural safeguards. One could say that the mandate formulated in Article 86 TFEU has not been fulfilled by the secondary legislator, as the Regulation does not contain clear rules on investigative powers, procedural safeguards and related evidence issues. Here the EPPO is placed in a difficult position in comparison to the administrative enforcement agencies. In fact they can operate in a setting of composite procedures that do provide for a certain degree of coherence when it comes to the foreseeability of the applicable substantive and procedural law and the judicial protection of the persons concerned. This uncertainty is a great handicap for

[27] M Luchtman, 'Het Europees Openbaar Ministerie in Nederland: Over zijn Prioritaire Bevoegdheid, Verhouding tot het OM en de Bestuursrechtelijke Handhavingskolom' (2021) 54 *Delikt en Delinkwent* 694.

[28] JAE Vervaele, 'The Europeanisation of Criminal Law and the Criminal Law Dimension of European Integration' in P Demaret, I Govaere and D Hanf (eds), *30 Years of European Legal Studies at the College of Europe: Liber Professorum* (PIE-Peter Lang 2005) 277.

the EPPO, and it includes the risk of discretion that is too wide with regard to certain procedural decisions. Attractive jurisdictions from a prosecutor's perspective could lead to biased decisions on choices of jurisdiction for the investigations and/or the trial, and thus run the risk of forum shopping. As these decisions can only be challenged before the national courts, they are put in a really difficult position, as they do not have the necessary tools to define the most appropriate jurisdiction in the AFSJ.

Theoretically, suspects are well protected in national criminal proceedings; and as national criminal proceedings will be used by the EDPs, the legal protection for suspects seems to be well covered. This does not take into account, however, that important decisions are taken by the central office of the EPPO (opening investigations, investigative jurisdiction, the termination of proceedings, prosecution and the choice of forum for the trial) and that suspects' rights and remedies still differ very much between Member States. Compared to those persons concerned in EU administrative enforcement proceedings, their rights and remedies are uncertain (depending on the applicable national law) or are barred at the EU level by the EPPO Regulation. Even worse is certainly that the EU Courts are also largely excluded and will have great difficulty in providing for common standards in this field.

My comparative assessment leads to the final conclusion that important challenges in the EPPO establishment can really be qualified as failure by design. Certain asymmetries between the vertical and national levels and transnationality between the jurisdictions of the Member States can lead to important dysfunctions for the EPPO, and risk undermining its added value and legitimacy based on combating impunity and enhancing effective enforcement in the AFSJ with due respect to EU values, in particular the fundamental rights of suspects. The EPPO is by definition a hybrid and composite agency, but its success can only be guaranteed if its legal arrangements for powers, safeguards, remedies and legal accountability are not so strongly embedded in the narrative of the nation state as they are in the EPPO Regulation. In order to avoid a situation where the EPPO rather resembles a Hydra than a single office, and where the central office (the giant) becomes stuck in the national clay,[29] future revisions of the Regulation will have to take into account that the criminal law enforcement of AFSJ-wide common interests will need harmonised offences at the EU level, the harmonisation of investigative powers and safeguards, and definitely more remedies before the EU Courts.[30]

An interesting comparison can be made here with the proposal for a new EU authority for anti-money laundering and countering the financing of terrorism (AMLA).[31] All obligations of private entities, including the administrative illicit acts for which the AMLA will become a competent administrative investigative and sanctioning authority,

[29] See also C Chevallier-Govers and A Weyembergh, *La création du parquet Européen: Simple évolution ou révolution au sein de l'espace judiciaire Européen?* (Bruylant 2021).

[30] See, for a inspiring example, the model rules for the procedure of the EPPO, the result of a transnational research project under the lead of Prof K Ligeti: K Ligeti, *Model Rules for the Procedure of the EPPO* (2013) available at https://orbilu.uni.lu/bitstream/10993/42085/1/Model%20Rules%20and%20explanatory%20notes%20EN.pdf (accessed 14 April 2022).

[31] Commission, 'Proposal for a Regulation of the European Parliament and of the Council establishing the Authority for Anti-Money Laundering and Countering the Financing of Terrorism and amending Regulations (EU) No 1093/2010, (EU) 1094/2010, (EU) 1095/2010' COM (2021) 421 final.

will be transferred from the fifth anti-money laundering directive[32] to a single EU Rulebook on anti-money laundering in a new regulation,[33] thus being harmonised and directly applicable. The new sixth anti-money laundering directive will only harmonise obligations for state authorities.[34] The investigative and sanctioning powers of the AMLA will also be stipulated in an AMLA regulation, meaning that the applicable law is European, even though the AMLA will operate with joint inspections, including inspectors from the national agencies. Remedies for the financial entities will be provided for in the regulation and the Court of Justice will be fully competent. It remains to be seen what the outcome will be of the negotiations on this new regulatory design, but the national enforcement deficits have been so serious in this policy area that a national coordination model is not really a legitimate option anymore. The proposed model is certainly also an interesting design for the assessment of the EPPO in the future.

In the meantime, the EPPO praxis in the years to come will indicate which gaps and flaws in the EPPO Regulation will be the most urgent to remedy. And further legal research will be necessary to assess whether and to what extent the participating EU Member States have adapted their domestic legislation and praxis in conformity with the aims of Article 86 TFEU and the EPPO Regulation, and to assess how non-participating EU Member States are dealing with the new actor under the EU obligation of sincere cooperation. Further legal research on the recognition of the EPPO as a competent authority under the Council of Europe instruments will also be of assistance concerning the added value of the EPPO in cases that reach out beyond the EU.

[32] Directive (EU) 2018/843 of the European Parliament and of the Council of 30 May 2018 amending Directive (EU) 2015/849 on the prevention of the use of the financial system for the purposes of money laundering or terrorist financing, and amending Directives 2009/138/EC and 2013/36/EU [2018] OJ L156/43.

[33] Commission, 'Proposal for a Regulation of the European Parliament and of the Council on the prevention of the use of the financial system for the purposes of money laundering or terrorist financing' COM (2021) 420; Commission, 'Proposal for a Regulation of the European Parliament and of the Council on information accompanying transfers of funds and certain crypto-assets (recast)' COM (2021) 422.

[34] Commission, 'Proposal for a Directive of the European Parliament and of the Council on the mechanisms to be put in place by the Member States for the prevention of the use of the financial system for the purposes of money laundering or terrorist financing and repealing Directive (EU) 2015/849' COM (2021) 423.

INDEX

Abbreviations used in the index
ADO (Authorised disclosure Officer)., 145
AFCOS (Anti-Fraud Coordination Services)
AFSJ (area of freedom, security and justice)
AML CAs (anti-money laundering competent authorities), 236
AMLA (Anti-Money Laundering Agency)
ASFJ (Area of Freedom, Security and Justice)
CFR (EU Charter of Fundamental Rights)
CISA (Convention implementing the Schengen Agreement (1985))
CJ (Court of Justice)
CJEU (Court of Justice of the European Union)
CN (Commission Notice on the cooperation between the Commission and the courts of the EU Member States)
CoE (Council of Europe)
College (EPPO College of European Prosecutors)
CR (Regulation 1/2003 on the implementation of the rules on competition laid down in TFEU 51/TFEU)
CRA (credit rating agency)
CRAR (CRA Regulation)
DMA (Digital Markets Act (2022))
DNA (Italian Antimafia and Counterterrorism Directorate)
EAW (European Arrest Warrant)
ECA (European Court of Auditors (ECA))
ECB (European Central Bank)
ECHR (European Convention on Human Rights)
ECHtR (European Court of Human Rights)
ECN (European Competition Network)
ECNN (Commission Notice on cooperation within the Network of Competition Authorities (2004))
EDP (European Delegated Prosecutor)
EEA (European enforcement agency (EEA))
EIA (European Implementation Assessment)
EIO (European Investigation Order)
EJN (European Judicial Network)
EMIR (European Market Infrastructure Regulation)
EPPO (European Public Prosecutor's Office)/EPPO Regulation
ESA BOA (European Supervisory Authorities Board of Authority)
ESMA (European Securities and Markets Authority)
ESMAR (ESMA Regulation 1095/2010)
EU (European Union)
FI ('less-significant' financial institution)
GDPR (General Data Protection Regulation)
IIO (independent investigation officer)
JIT (joint investigation team)

www.ingramcontent.com/pod-product-compliance
Ingram Content Group UK Ltd.
Pitfield, Milton Keynes, MK11 3LW, UK
UKHW020232290926
15470UKWH00002B/502

9 781509 94646